Look at the Evidence

ESSAYS AND REVIEWS

John Clute

Liverpool University Press · 1995

for Helen Nicholls

Copyright © 1987, 1988, 1989, 1990, 1991, 1992, 1995 by John Clute.

A British Library Cataloguing-in-Publication Record is available for this book.

Manufactured in the United States of America. First published in 1995 in the United States of America by Serconia Press. Published in Europe by Liverpool University Press, Senate House, Abercromby Square, Liverpool, L69 3BX.

Book design and composition by John D. Berry. Typeset in FF Quadraat. Printed by Braun-Brumfield, Ann Arbor, Michigan USA.

ISBN 0-85323-820-0 (cloth)
ISBN 0-85323-830-8 (paper)

FIRST EDITION

WA 1175809 0

LOOK AT THE EVIDENCE

ONE WEEK LOAN

Renew Books on PHONE-it: 01443 654456

Books are to be returned on or before the last date below

Contents

III. On Individual Writers 425

Preface

There are a lot of words in this book. I won't add many more here. *Look at the Evidence* is divided into three parts. Part One is short. It contains a piece on the nature of sf criticism, and a lecture on the nature of sf. Part One represents the Introduction I might have written had there been no Part One; the lecture in particular, a version of which was delivered in 1994, encapsulates what I think I think. Part Two takes up most of the rest of the book. It is broken into six sections, each of which contains reviews and essays covering a single year, from 1987 to 1992 inclusive, with exceptions. Most of the individual pieces I wrote during those years are reprinted here, with exceptions. Part Three is short. It contains essays on six individual authors. They were written around the same time, with exceptions.

Don Keller of Serconia Press has been calm, and tidal in his insistence that we could still do a book, even though the years continued to pass; and said Oh good, and said No problem, when I finally gave him a manuscript 50,000 words longer than his limit. There is a very loud amusement park right in front of my present lodgings.

For a while Don and I thought we might call this book *Scores*, for the same reason that my earlier book of reviews and essays for Serconia Press was called *Strokes*: because both terms contain multiple meanings. But we decided not to, somehow. Both books are, all the same, fairly similar in their construction, though the pieces assembled in *Look at the Evidence* follow chronological order more closely than do those in the earlier volume. As with *Strokes*, I've used original versions for my basic text, rather than edited copy. Some passages have been cleaned up, but no opinion, however stupid, has been edited in hindsight to look wiser. And I've inserted within square brackets [like this 1995] some comments, expansions, apologies, hindsights.

More acknowledgements need to be made. Helen Nicholls read most of these pieces as they were being written, and said Make sense, and said Only connect, and said I guess that's all right now. The dedication of *Look at the Evidence* to her is heartfelt. Judith Clute allowed me her cover. This has gone on for many years now. Robin Bloxsidge of Liverpool University Press gave me absolute sanction, in an astonishingly calm voice. David Pringle allowed me to say anything I wanted to say in *Interzone*. It was a rare thing to do, and an enormously generous thing to do, and I tried to grab the opportunity. Michael Dirda of the *Washington Post* continued to give me work, and to touch it like a surgeon. David Garnett, who edited the *Orbit Science*

Fiction Yearbook and the New Worlds anthologies before they were shafted, suffered hugely from my modest flirtations with deadlines, but played chicken and won; and James Morrow, who edited the Nebula anthology, also suffered. I edited myself (as Book Reviews Editor) on Foundation, but Edward James did let it go on. Rob Killheffer of Omni taught me how to write for Omni in my own voice: just write a bit better, John, he said. The mafia that run NYRSF were a pushover. I have to thank the various editors of other newspapers and journals for first publishing material which has come home here; these journals are The Correspondent, The Los Angeles Times, The Listener, The Nation, the New Scientist, the New Statesman, The New York Times, The Observer, the SFRA Review, the Times Literary Supplement, Vector. I have also to thank Jim Turner of Arkham House and Eric Lane of Dedalus Books.

The index was composed by Leigh Kennedy, with clarity and grace; and she had to work very fast. Christopher Priest sent it by E-mail to John Berry in Seattle, who designed the book. Micole Sudberg proofread it meticulously. It is now out of our hands.

John Clute
London
July 1995

1: OPENERS

Necessary Golems

[Here is a declaration of principle for reviewers. I've proposed it more than once. I called it the *Protocol of Candour* on its first appearance in *Interzone* 24 in 1988 (though I've always tended to think of it as the *Protocol of Excessive Candour*); and when (for a *Friends of Foundation Newsletter* in 1992) I revised a *Readercon* 4 piece on my own experience of being criticized, I grafted a modified version of the *Protocol* into my copy. In every case, I was addressing audiences made of men and women many of whom I quite likely knew personally, and who quite possibly knew me. Hence the interior tone of the thing. But it should be clear enough here in the open air. Here then – spatchcocked from three sources, and tinkered with yet again – is that *Protocol*, plus some thoughts on being the biter bit 1995.]

Most of us are writers and critics and readers of sf, and as such we inhabit a bee-hive-dense congregation of affinity groups, by virtue of which it is very difficult for anyone who has been involved in the genre for more than a few years *not* to have had contact with a significantly high proportion of those who've also been active in the field. The benefits of affinity are, in general, obvious enough. But there are reasons to think that this degree of personal contact is not the healthiest thing in the world for sf criticism. The club-like camaraderie of sf unsurprisingly tempts critics and reviewers (in particular) into any number of strategies designed to avoid internal friction: refusing to review books written by friends or acquaintances – which, for anybody who's been in the field for more than a decade or so, may well mean most of the writers going; muffling negative responses – after one has found oneself forced into a midnight spasm of honesty – in the dawn rewrite; dissimulating archly, in code. The end-result – that the sf beehive buzzes with "friends" who will not review the books of anyone they know, in case they might have to tell the truth – gives sf a sad face.

Reviewers who will not tell the truth are like cholesterol. They are lumps of fat. They starve the heart. I have myself certainly clogged a few arteries, have sometimes kept my mouth shut out of this "friendship" which is nothing in the end but self-interest. So perhaps it is time to call a halt. Perhaps we should establish a *Protocol of Excessive Candour*, a convention within the community that excesses of intramural harshness are less damaging than the hypocrisies of stroke therapy, that telling the truth is a way of expressing love: self-love; love of others; love for the genre, which claims to tell the truth about things that count; love for the inhabitants of the planet; love for the future. Because truth is all we've got. And if we don't talk to ourselves, and if we don't use every tool at our command in our time on Earth to tell the truth, nobody else will.

If that means we sometimes make errors, speak cruelly, carve caricature grimaces onto the raw flesh of books, so be it. Some golems are necessary.

I published a novel once, in 1977. As a long-time reviewer even then, I thought I was pretty well prepared to read whatever reviews this one garnered, good or bad or misprision. I thought the good reviews would be nectar, the bad ones gall, and the misprision irrelevant. I couldn't have been more wrong.

But let me define misprision, because what it means is central. Misprision, says the OED, can be defined as 1) "a wrong action of omission" in law, 2) "an offense or misdemeanour akin to treason or felony," 3) the same as 2, but transferred into popular use, 4) "wrongful capture," 5) "the mistaking of one thing, word, etc., for another; a misunderstanding; a mistake," 6) "a clerical error," 7) "a malformation," 8) "unjust suspicion." Misprision, in other words, is what happens when a critic talks about a book. What I would like to suggest is not only that misprision is inevitable, but that misprision is the right stuff.

[The paragraph immediately above, and the rest of this piece, is a version of a programme book filler I wrote for Readercon 4, as modified later for the *Friends of Foundation Newsletter*. The piece contained what turned out – as no one noticed it or called me on it – to be an utterly dumb piece of "humour": in going on and on about "misprision" without mentioning the famous American critic Harold Bloom, who had written several books, including *A Map of Misreading* (1975), on the very subject, I had – as it were – misprisioned misprision. Perhaps it was not entirely clear that this was supposed to be funny.... It's true I'd written the original piece pretty quickly, but that was my own fault. The joke was no joke (the sound of a joke falling flat in the wilderness is a proof of the nonexistence of God) but a petard. For the *Newsletter*, I tried to save face by mentioning Bloom, within square brackets very similar to the ones encasing these words, and therefore unmisprisioning the misprisioning of misprision. But the editor ran out of space, and cut everything within square brackets. So I was doubly hoist. 1995]

My novel came out. It was called *The Disinheriting Party*. It received some reviews in the UK and Canada, none that I recall in the USA, but I've lost most of them and can't check. Some of these reviews were positive; one at least was slashingly negative. I remember little of the praise or the accusations of perversity; but one review does stick in the mind. The author of this review [Paul Stuewe, in the Toronto *Globe* and Mail 1995] liked the novel well enough to think about it, though I don't remember if he thought it was exactly successful. The important thing is that his review got the book wrong. *The Disinheriting Party*, it said, clearly owed a great deal to Latin American models, and was specifically indebted to the magic realist mode. Every page, he said, demonstrated the extent of the debt.

This was pure misprision, unjust suspicion, mistake, wrongful capture. In the 1970s I was a lot more ignorant than I should have been (or would have admitted then); the only Latin American authors I could remember reading were Jorge Luis Borges, and Jorge Amado for a book review, and it was pretty clear that it wasn't Amado who was on the reviewer's mind. He was thinking of writers like Gabriel García Márquez, writers I'd known of but had never *encountered*. So it was misprision. The critic had seen something that looked like truth, and he had imposed this "truth" on a text, had "interpreted" my precious novel, had pummelled it into a shape of his own devising, had made a Necessary Golem of my Work. He had re-created the book. Was I glad?

I was. This reviewer's misprision is the only comment on the book I can recollect in any detail. It is the only review which represented a wrestling of the reader with the text, the only one which taught me anything about what I had written. By re-creating *The Disinheriting Party*, the reviewer had allowed me to look at it again, to see the thing as an autonomous text, no longer mine, no longer tied to me by the umbilicals and conceits and oneirisms of the creative heart. My book had become a Necessary Golem, smaller and colder perhaps than the first, but no parasitic *Pale Fire*, no Kinbote; my book was in the world now, and another maker had gone down into it; and in doing so had committed misprision. *The Disinheriting Party* had left home. Nothing (in other words) had happened that was any more alien to the workings of the world than a beloved son or daughter's first fuck, out in the workings.

I'm dodging a few issues here, certainly. The misprision in question was, not at all unsubtly, a flattering one. The book did not suffer any derogation through being compared with a great tradition. And the reviewer was, in any case, *literally* in error, because the provenance, as he phrased it, was false (though it was certainly the case that even a false provenance – by showing how a book *seems* – can teach an author much more than ample praise, which merely confirms a dream). So let me [the original title of this Readercon 4 piece was "On Being Criticized" 1995] go on to something less congenial. In 1988 I published a book of reviews and essays which I called *Strokes* and which, like the earlier novel, got reviewed in a few places. Some reviews were good, some were not; and one review, published by Robert Latham in *Journal of the Fantastic in the Arts* under the title "Snobbery, Seasoned with Bile,

Clute Is," was hilariously devastating. The review is very long, and rather hard to quote from, and although Latham makes the occasional tactical blunder (at one point, when he observes that "for a journalist commentator, [Clute's] repertory of shrewd barbs and liberal plaints is well above average," he sounds like a landgrant academic writing squibs for Kirkus Reviews in a doomed quest for tenure), the flow of his animus, as he assembles his argument, is refreshingly stinging: he mentions "wild rhetoric," he instances a good deal of "obfuscatory smoke blowing," he mocks "fumbles," he deplores "sentences that skitter and swerve like demented ostriches...in a critical void," he concludes that the "book is deeply disappointing as criticism." Most of this seems to be good honest fun, the sort of thing a reviewer does if s/he's on a roll: anybody who's reviewed a book knows what I mean, knows the feel of the thrum of the slap as you get your teeth into the bone. It is a feeling Latham – who eschews rant, mainly – may have felt, this flow of contumely, this conative/cognitive come, this masque-gavotte around the shape of the thing being put in its place: you throw mud, it sticks. It's a misprision, too.

But it's not the real-stuff misprision that makes a critic into a co-creator. Co-creation through epithet merely parodies the thing abused. The misprision I'm interested in – and that I hope to be capable of committing upon the next book I review – is not a parody of the thing misprisioned, but what Dr. Frankenstein thought he was doing; it is a form of redemption: because until a text is properly pronged – properly violated – it's dead meat. The words the author has given birth to are dead until they're read, until they're re-created by the critic (who is somebody writing a review, or somebody reading a book in bed, or somebody telling somebody else about something s/he's just finished: who is anybody, in other words, who is doing the job). So it wasn't until he began to screw me properly that Latham began to revitalize the meat. "Clute's arguments skip and/or limp along from review to review, and the reader is forced to piece them together. (Perhaps this is fixup at the level of criticism.)" (Right on.) Clute "ultimately naïvely seconds the hermeneutic strategies of classic bourgeois narration, its preemption of options, its suturing and cloture of the self." (Not, perhaps, uncomically put: but he's saying something here about the unthought-through conventions that arguably fuel the green shoot chez moi: and which might underlie some of the cognitive paucity of much sf criticism.) "The only broadly animating focus I could divine" in the entire book, he continues, "was...a vague sort of modernism...." But today "one requires a fairly comprehensive command of recent (postmodern) theory, the only framework capable of resolving all the paradoxes spawned by the binary logic of Clute's modernist humanism." [I now tend to think this particular assertion is a touch faddish 1995] But "hampered by an exhausted, martyrized modernism that demands a haughty, superior stance…," Clute's "critical practice has largely remained tied to the immediate, short-term concerns of generic production."

I began to understand what it meant to be *understood*. To be misprisioned in the daylight of another mind. To see what it meant to obey a *Protocol of Excessive Candour*. I could chuckle at Latham's inspired (though, one guesses, hardly conscious) imitations of the stylistic blunders I fell into in the more egregious flights of autodidactic BigThinking to which I was, and remain, so embarrassingly prone; but at the same time I felt that the strange scarecrow bumpkin of a book he saw in his mind's eye did indeed have its own objective reality. I might object to his trashing an assemblage of unconnected pieces because they failed to accomplish something they were not written to accomplish – these pieces had, after all, been written over a 20-year period, for particular occasions, for fees, and couched in a variety of registers designed to affront and chivvy and pleasure a wide variety of audiences; and it was unlikely that they would, on being brought together, "articulate an *immanent* locus for critique." On the other hand, it was clear that I *sounded* as though an agenda of that sort were being muffed. The very fact that a number of pieces by one writer was assembled in one place argued for agenda; and if no agenda was visible to analysis, then there was imposture afoot. The heart of Latham's misprision is that I was an impostor.

Old son, you're nicked.

As misprisions go, this seems fair enough. It is a sustainable reading of *Strokes*. In accomplishing this dismantling, Latham is performing the critic's task: that of unmasking the being of the book; re-creating that being; freeing the book from the author of the book, and from the beehive cloister of the affinity group; and, in the end, granting a privilege. The author's true privilege is to be misunderstood (how many of us, glaring into airless mirrors of unpublishable selfhood, ever get the chance?) and the critic's true function is to make misunderstanding into a door of perception. So with Latham's help, I open the door. I see how the book can be seen. There's some fucking going on in the workings, but that's life. And it all helps me see that when I, in turn, shape the books I review into what I understand them to mean, I shape them into monsters their parents might well weep to recognize: but at least, within sf, they are neighbourhood monsters. The blood kin monsters of sf wear, I do realize, my face. I give them my disease. Reviewing is raping the Golem. In the end, all we can do is beg forgiveness.

– Modified from: *Interzone* 24 (1988); *Readercon 4 Souvenir Book* (1991); *Friends of Foundation Newsletter* (1992)

Pilgrim Award Acceptance Speech

[In 1994 I got an Award – the Pilgrim Award, which is given annually by the Science Fiction Research Associaton – and went to Chicago in July of that year to receive it, and gave a short talk in thanks; a few sentences – not spoken in Chicago because of limited time – have been inserted 1995.]

Thanks must be my first word: thanks enormously for letting me in here. And in a few minutes, thanks will be my last word as well.

As a ringer in quite a few towers – as a non-English Englishman; as a writer of fiction who writes two stories a decade; as a non-academic who does bibliography with violent intensity; as a man of mature years who spends a good deal of his time writing with great passion book reviews for ephemeral journals; and as a solitary unsalaried freelance who spends the rest of his time, with a passel of colleagues, beavering away at encyclopedias – it is a most unusual experience for me to have a sense that I am coming home; but here I am, and I think I might well call it home.

The plane gives glimpses of Chicago as you land at O'Hare, but you never step into the same Chicago twice. The city I *remember* with supernatural clarity comes back to me now, over the steppes of the years, like sf or Oz, just as it came to me the first time. It was 1956. The airport that time was Midway. For a 16-year-old immigrant from Canada, who had spent the previous four years reading pulp magazines and Ace Books, the first sight of Chicago was like a vision of the Golden Age. Michigan Avenue – as far as the 16-year-old kid was concerned – gave off a Golden Age reek, raw and clean and real. Soldier Field was Nuremberg, without the camp smoke. And there was an iron web of subterranean roadways that underlaid the Loop like Caves of Steel. All in all, Chicago *looked* like what anyone who drew cities in *Astounding* thought a metropolis should look like. Chicago was where the Future Histories started.

A year later came the poison chalice of Sputnik, and although it took a long while to sink in, I suspect I was just the right age – like some vast baby duck – to find myself unconsciously bonded to disillusion, without yet knowing what it was I had lost. Certainly I'd lost the Golden Age of childhood, as we all do; but there was more than that. What I'd lost – and what sf had lost – after Sputnik had stitched its way back and forth across the new mundane sky, was the old sense that space was a magic portal, a sky-hook capable of *hiking us into the future*. What Sputnik did – what indeed the whole, archaic, doom-ridden space programme accomplished as it lunged into a future that did not work – was to drag traditional sf backwards into the real now. Space was no longer free space. Overnight, space became a sentence in the seamy contentious intricate story of humans upon the planet, a continuation of life on Earth by other means.

A child might not have noticed the change. An adult might have ridden it. A 17-year-old, on the other hand, might well have found himself stuck in midstream, only half aware that his dreamworld had been sign-changed into a continuation of homework. I don't want to erect a few tiny coincidences into bad theory, but I rather wonder if it might not be modestly relevant that I was born the same year as two sf writers with whom I feel a particularly strong cognitive rapport – Tom Disch and Norman Spinrad – and that we all impacted late adolescence, the end of the Eisenhower years, and Sputnik at the same time. Let us put fiction aside, as I've never written enough to sort it: but as critics, all three of us have seemed at times to evince a certain strange *pachydermatousness* about sf, like lovers who will not admit their wound. I (for one) *know* how truculently thinskinned I've been at times, how savage I've been about any sf text which seemed – through cynicism or fake camaraderie or apeing of the old – to mock our loss.

Here is the mountain which this molehill makes: I think certain kinds of loss, inflicted on the psyche at certain vulnerable moments, make for natural critics. I do not claim that a natural critic is necessarily a good one, nor that those who failed to have something to feel abandoned about when they were seventeen must necessarily produce flawed critical works; only that the obsessive acts of secondary re-creation which make up the work of the natural critic can be seen as a redemptive enterprise, and that what is being redeemed is the cracking of the Golden Age. I'd suggest, en passant, that the wounds which may spark a talent for creative writing almost certainly occur earlier in the life passage of the writer-to-be; and that the writer's search for those wounds can take forever. What in particular marks the critic's wound is that it *is* visible to the eye. What made me a critic was a loss I could read about in the newspapers.

But back to Sputnik. In all seriousness, I think it genuinely may be fitting – if we sidebar any cod theorizing about the wound that engenders the critic – to treat the beginning of the Space Age as a turning point, a point beyond which the quasi-organic conversation of American sf – for the moment let me call it First SF – began to ramble, and to lose the thread of the story; began to give off a sense that for all those years since 1926 it had been *telling the wrong story*, that we were now being shaped by futures which the sf story *had failed to notice*; began the long descent into the backward-looking, nostalgic, manic depressive, treasonous, faute-de-mieux blather of sharecrop. Before Sputnik, First SF had thrived in a native habitat, which included the moon and the stars as draws: speedlines pointing to the future and marshalling our dreams. Afterwards, new versions of sf, new conversations, began to collide with the dying gabfest of Future History, and First SF sporulated into a series of loose overlapping genres. As genre critics, it is right and proper for us to note that Sputnik changed – once and for all – the conversation of precedents that bathed First SF texts; that what followed was the teeming, immensely fruitful squabble we now inhabit, where old and new modes fight for lebensraum, Cyberpunk sagas cohabit with dinosaur senilities, sequels set in the worlds of dead authors share shelf space with with postmodernist pastiches set in nostalgia-choked alternate-history Toontowns, where fossil singletons technically occupy the same genre as works of genius written long after the wrong story of the future shriveled up like a salted snail [see also "Exogamy Dentata," p. 399].

Taking some few stabs at understanding this new world has filled up most of my working life.

It is also interesting, I think, to notice how markedly the new sf resounds to certain underlying continuities, base tonalities, that mark American literature as a whole. For me – speaking as an onlooker, as a ringer who lost his green card decades ago – it is remarkable how clearly the literature of the United States is marked by a sense of belatedness: a sense that the frontier is always beyond reach, or that when it is finally penetrated it will turn out already to have been abandoned; a sense that the Great Gatsby will never gain the garden or the city, no matter how hard he rows; a deep central disappointed knowing that the breast is shut. If this sense of things is at all accurate, then post-Sputnik sf has become all the more essentially American, now that its best authors tend to explore the recedingness of things, attempt to limn the uncapturable complexities of a world whose futures are profoundly various, profoundly pressing.

None of this alters the sense that First SF has become a bounded region, that its own, deeply unselfconscious belatedness is something we can – as it were – look back on as an object of study. Like the rockets at Cape Canaveral, First SF was tied to a version of history, and when that version passed it become part of a told story. A conviction of the usefulness of "belatedness" as a concept grew on me as I worked with Peter Nicholls, John Grant and Brian Stableford on the second edition of The Encyclopedia of Science Fiction (1993) – as careers and motifs continued to obsess my dreams, while the years passed. I don't think the Encyclopedia insists upon this thesis – it would be extremely inappropriate if it did argue, in an ex cathedra tone, a position which is both debatable and partial. But certainly, as I wrote, I felt, and I think my partners may have felt, that a large and significant and deeply loved part of what we were calling sf was, in 1993, a completed topic.

But if the old compact had told its tale by now, what on Earth was replacing it? If I was going to claim that the most significant American sf writers from 1960 on didn't really write First SF any more, what on Earth were they doing? While working on the *Encyclopedia*, I backed away from thinking too much about answering this question, partly because the *Encyclopedia* – as Peter Nicholls originally conceived it in 1975; and as we all continued to think of it in the 1990s – was intended to represent a broad-church, non-prescriptive sorting of anything we thought might possibly be describable as sf. But the question remained.

In twenty years, I may begin to believe some of the answers I come up with. For what it's worth, I tend at the moment to think that, over the last few decades, sf has begun to lose its profound attachment to the old set of Fables of the First World: tales whose protagonist, usually human, represents the dominant species in the venue being described, the species which knows how to get to the future. I think that sf stories today are more and more beginning to sound like Fables of the Third World: stories whose protagonists, often human, represent cultures which have been colonized by the future. The future may come in the form of aliens, or the catnip nirvana of cyberspace, or as AI's, or as bio-engineered transformations of our own species: but whatever it touches, it subverts. Sf stories of this sort can – depressingly – read rather like manuals designed to train Polynesians in the art of begging for Cargo; but they can also generate a sense of celebration of the worlds beyond worlds beyond our species' narrow path.

For me – to conclude – the *Encyclopedia* was not primarily designed to emphasize this change. In its sometimes manic comprehensiveness, it worked, in the end, for me, as an attempt to seal over the cracks in the Golden Age by surrounding the fissure. (Childless people – I am one – often tend to have large extended families.) For me, the *Encyclopedia* was an act of healing, on the part of a thin-skinned adolescent with a tendency to mourn.

In the end, standing here now in the late-century shadows of Chicago, I have to admit – it's an oddly difficult thing to say – that I do feel moderately healed. I do feel that we've not been wasting our time. I think we've all been having a good conversation these last few years, about the literature we bend our heads over. In the end, then, as it was in the beginning, the first and last thing for me to say is Thanks.

– *Science Fiction Research Association* 213, September/October 1994

II: COLUMNS AND REVIEWS: 1987–1992

ONE: 1987

1. Year Roundup

It may not be the worst thing that ever happened to sf that it died. Or became something sufficiently new that old books began to read like shed moult. There may have been a time, in the morning of the world, before Sputnik, when the empires of our sf dreams were governed according to rules neatly written out in the pages of *Astounding*, and we could all play the game of a future we all shared, readers, writers, fans; that we could steam in the dews of the dawn. But something happened. The future began to come true. It was no longer a game for the members of the club, no longer a secret handshake. The planet of our birth began to overheat from excessive spin, and that which was past or passing or to come began to merge into one fire, like spokes on the wheel of Juggernaut; sf writers began to have to run to stand still, like all of us, in the real world of the futures we now inhabit. Sf novels became larger, more worldly, more confused, more cynical, more like any other kind of novel (which also means that other kinds of novel began to resemble sf); for good and for ill, the indelible realities of our late twentieth century had begun to stain the white radiance of the old pulp. Which did nothing to stop the growth of sf, in a marketing sense.

Here are some damned statistics. Because they are extracted from *Locus*, an American trade journal which claims to serve every one of us as "The Newspaper of the Science Fiction Field," none of them deals with the UK. However, given the size of British publishers' sf lists (small), and the extent to which these lists are dominated by books originating in America (not quite total [a situation which has markedly improved since 1987 1995]), the omission of this material from the *Locus* calculations is only modestly unfortunate. The cautionary tale the statistics tell would change by only a few adjectives were British data to be included.

On the face of it, *Locus* tells a tale of relentless cheer, and there can be no doubt that, in a commercial sense, the news is good. In 1977, 445 new titles of all categories were released into the field of fantastic literature, which embraces fantasy and horror as well as sf; by 1982 there were 572, the next year 581, then 613, 715, 846, and in 1987 a total of 1026 new titles were published. Sounds triumphant. But put it another way and it may seem less boosterish: Even 20 years after Sputnik, in 1977, an omnivorous reader of independent means could have kept the field within his/her single grasp by mulching a mere 1.2 books per diem. By 1987 this omnivore's diet would have become bulimiacal, amounting to 2.8 books daily, or one book every 8.5 hours. What was once a field had become the Mississippi delta. If pre-Sputnik sf could be perceived as a *family of read books* which created (and inhabited) a knowable stage (or matrix) of possible worlds, by 1987 this perception had become deeply nostalgic. No longer could an ostensive definition of sf (sf is what smells like sf) even begin to match the corrosive intricacies of the exploded genre. By 1987, sf was no longer a family romance.

That total of 1026 new books of fantastic literature published in America (add a smidgen for the rest of the world) can, all the same, be broken down into more assimilable categories. Of the total only 650 – or 1.8 a day – are novels, a category which excludes the 74 novelizations published in 1987, and of the novels encompassed by Locus's remit only 298 are sf. The rest – 352 titles – are fantasy and horror novels, which increasingly dominate the field as a whole, much to its detriment. (For this writer, bad sf can be seen as a category of trash, and can be junked at sight. Bad fantasy is something else. Perhaps because it transforms archetypal material into sleaze, bad fantasy is junk-food, an addictive mockery of the true meal, which sticks to the stomach, and eats it.) Of those 352 fantasy and horror titles, only one or two need mentioning in any overview of fantastic literature in novel form published in 1987. And of the 298 books Locus designates as sf, 37 are Post-Holocaust Survivalist Adventures, and of the total 123 are series continuations. The task of gaining an overview may be less daunting than it first looked.

It is only polite to begin with dinosaurs. Writers so designated are relics of sf's long history as a relatively closed genre (until Sputnik blew the walls down). During that long period (1926–1957) within the closed walls of a genre whose members thought of themselves as beleaguered but elect, dominant writers tended to acquire a kind of siege significance, rather like the significance accorded bad singers of patriotic songs in times of war. Supercharged and overdetermined with all the signs of meaning that film stars famously bear, sf writers like Doc Smith or Robert A Heinlein became the Figures in the Carpet of sf, radiating the hot iconic glow of myths of origin, an effect supercharged by the fact they were still with us, in the flesh. They had the Royal Touch, like undead Davy Crocketts. None of this – need it be said – made them rich. Pre-Sputnik sf was too small to support more than a very few adult writers anything like full-time, no matter how deliriously s/he overproduced. After 1960, however, when sf began to think of its sacred history as a talisman against the heat-death of the new gigantism, it slowly became evident that the saturated iconicity of these oldsters or dinosaurs had become bankable.

It did not much matter that most of them never wrote very well in the first place, and now wrote worse, for they bore Cargo from the mists of time. Some had remained active, and did not now think of stopping; others, who had fallen silent, now returned to active work in the industrial parks of the modern. Sadly there were mishaps. A E Van Vogt decanted a slough of novels in the 1970s, but the oneiric odysseys of his prime had now flattened into stiff-kneed daydreaming, he sold poorly, and fell silent. Theodore Sturgeon remained prey, like Laocoön, to writer's block. Alfred Bester saw his *nous* appropriated by the snippy wee mammals of the new age, and his own talents peter out. Clifford D Simak, now dead, kept going until he was 80, but never seemed to cut a word after the age of 60. Unfortunately, he is now remembered for his unloosed stays, not *City* (1952).

On the other hand, Isaac Asimov (never silent as a writer) returned to fiction like Ozymandias to the desert, determined to salvage for eternity the ad-hoc works of his early primitive years; by continuing his Foundation and Robot series in the shape of great rigid retrospective novels, he clearly intended to bind almost every tale he had ever written, with ligaments of stone, into a vast megaseries, like death. [Those who attended the 1995 UK Eastercon – at a London Docklands hotel which could have been designed as a Monty Python pop-up of the inside of Mark Thatcher's skull – might have had a similar reaction to mine. It seemed to me that the tannoy system used by the management to demand of guests that they remove their cars from the turd-shaped porte-cochere – a system which penetrated all public rooms at a level so astonishingly loud that it was literally impossible to speak, or even *move* (lest one's ears break), while its diktats were being broadcast – was rather similar to the voice of the implied author in the 1980s novels of Isaac Asimov. His voice, too, was megaphonic, totalitarian, solitudinous: and whenever you tiptoed into a new instalment you felt like a rabbit daring spotlights to burgle a stalag. Most elderly people – including authors – tend to mix up the ruts of mind and the happening world outdoors; but it might be an idea (see comments below on Robert A Heinlein, too) to reflect upon the extremities of impoverishing strangeness that have so conspicuously entangled so many dinosaurs of classic sf as they aged. 1995] His 1987 novel, *Fantastic Voyage II: Destination Brain* (Doubleday), astonishingly rewrites a crapulous 1966 novelization, of which he was properly ashamed, into a long icy guided tour of the human body by miniaturized sub, all limned with numbing dispassion. After several years Jack Vance also returned to sf, and in *Araminta Station* (Underwood-Miller/Tor) began, once again, to landscape-garden a Big Planet. As always, his characters seemed less colourful than the arbours and grottos they adorned, and which constituted the genuine populace of his (a word this writer has used before) topiary terraforming vision. Arthur C Clarke continued to pump his indefatigable serenity into fictionalized travelogues of the mind, the latest being yet another episode in a series whose first instalment (novelized as *2001: A Space Odyssey*) was hilariously misprisioned into film by the dyspeptic Stanley Kubrick; by

1987 (though the book is copyright 1988 it was available before the end of the year) we had reached *2061: Odyssey Three* (Del Rey).

Of the dinosaurs still active in 1987, one of them, Robert A Heinlein, is already [1988] a late dinosaur. What now seems to be his last novel, and therefore the last instalment in an extraordinary series of valedictory summae, *To Sail Beyond the Sunset* (Putnam) gives off all the greenhouse foetor – all the tropical hypertrophies of narcissism – characteristic of its immediate predecessors. It smells of the inside of the head. By now there can be no novelty in describing Heinlein's late work as solipsistic – the author himself came close to doing so in more than one of the late books – but the distressed camp solipsism of novels like *Sunset* and *The Cat Who Walks Through Walls* (1985) and "*The Number of the Beast*" (1980) may well be their defining characteristic. Ostensibly peopled though they are by enormous casts (almost always made up of characters from the novels of Heinlein's glossy and insinuating prime), these novels are in fact nightmares of a most desperate solitude. At the most visible level of plotting, the elect members of these casts (after butchering the unelect) all turn out to be close relatives of one another, and engage in interminable bouts of gleeful incest on realizing the fact; at a deeper level, they are all aspects of one character, Lazarus Long (who is the author); they are shadows on his wall, and the worlds they inhabit dissolve at his touch. These worlds are skillful travesties of the sf worlds created by Heinlein (and others) before Sputnik, and their merciless disparagement in book after book bespeaks an enormity of disgust and rage on the author's part, seemingly directed at a genre grown monstrous. But in the end the disgust and the rage turn insatiably inwards, and in the end *To Sail Beyond the Sunset* is not a hecatomb but a mirror.

Of the dinosaurs who remain vigorously alive, Frederik Pohl is by far the most interesting case. The novels of his early career, with the possible exception of collaborations with C M Kornbluth like *The Space Merchants* (1953), were far less assured than his shorter fiction; he always seemed a writer too easily distracted from the task to stick to a novel without dithering, shifting his ground, backing off; and for several years he wrote very little in the longer form. But with the publication of *Man Plus* in 1976 he came at long last into his novel-writing prime. Gone was the cold dither and the demurring. Brilliant and vibrant, *Gateway* (1977) began the Heechee Saga, which concluded in 1987 (way downhill it must be granted) with *The Annals of the Heechee*. *JEM* (1979) was a narration of utopia – a task logically incompossible with the maintenance of utopia, but intriguingly assayed, and which pointed to *The Years of the City* (1984) and *Chernobyl* (Bantam), his second 1987 novel, which is not, however, sf. *The Annals of the Heechee* (Del Rey) is a baggy monster of a book, full of great lumbering logjams of resumé from the three previous volumes of the series, decked out with pages and pages of boiler-factory man-gal backchat à la Heinlein (perhaps designed as an homage), and featuring a first-person narrator whose glutinous coyness about his failures of Competence never manages to keep him from demonstrating supernormal street-wise powers of lateral thinking whenever the chips are down. The whole lazy farrago, which includes the saving of the universe, could have been told at half the length. It is a shambles which may, all the same, bear perverse testimony to Pohl's continuing savvy, because *The Annals of the Heechee* gives off ample signs of cynical deliberation in its catering to the taste-buds of series addicts. It was very well reviewed.

After the dinosaurs, and before we beard the alpha males of the veldt, an oddment or two might be mentioned. In *The Day of Creation* (Gollancz), J G Ballard continued to create work whose utter autonomy glows unscathed by his secondment to the British literary establishment after the success of *Empire of the Sun* (1984); this autonomy is only superficially belied by his use of the same animistic metaphorical substrate that fuels some of the worst fantasies ever written. Avram Davidson, too nocturnal and European to be conceived of as a dinosaur, resumed with *Vergil in Averno* (Doubleday) his sequence of tales set in a grievous, vulcanism-haunted alternate Naples. James Dickey's enormous *Alnilam* (Doubleday) explored an occult web of affinities linking father and dead son, but with an attention span that extends to mania. In *The Medusa Frequency* (Cape), Russell Hoban made short – indeed truncated – work of a confluence of the Orpheus Myth and Medusa, set in a curiously spastic here-and-now. William Kotzwinkle's *The Exile* (Dutton) dove (once again) into the occult tentacles of Nazi Germany in a tale of possession and paranoia. In *Fiasco* (Deutsch), Stanislaw Lem harshened into a series of cartoon disquisitions – though the final scene is stunning – much of the philosophical substance of *Solaris* (trans 1961), specifically the doctrine that the human armamentarium of praxis and perception must fail to comprehend the unsayable Otherness of any utter Thing Itself, which may be a sentient ocean, or an alien species (as in this novel), or the Boojum. In *The Child in Time* (Cape), Ian McEwan suggested that a further half decade of Thatcherism would transform England into a factory farm, squalid, eutrophicated, poison to the soul. Keith Roberts composed in *Gráinne* (Kerosina) an anguished submission to Woman as intoxicant and succubus, and as saviour of these Isles one day. And the rebarbative George Turner finally won something like his due (and more), gaining this year's Arthur C Clarke Award for *The Sea and Summer* (Faber & Faber), a dystopian vision of Melbourne (Australia) some decades hence, after a superflux of disasters has transformed the world into an overburdened slum. But the disasters are too pat, too bullyingly assumed as givens, to bear the burden he insists they must, and the complex structures of the tale tend to dry upon the reader. It is, all the same, his best book.

In one way or another, authors like Ballard or McEwan or Lem or Turner stand to one side of the ruined communal theatre of conventional sf (as ostensively defined by those who knew what they were pointing at). Their necessary presence in any survey of 1987 is another sign of the demands made by the spinning world upon any writer wishing to portray it, and for whom sf imagery may serve as a useful tool in that job of portrayal. It is still the case, all the same, that most of the novels yet to be mentioned come from authors whose origins lie deep in the original field, and whose commercial success must in part depend on the nostalgia value of their continuing loyalty to the pulp Umwelt of the old Future History. It is also the case that most of the hundreds of novels which will go unmentioned come from authors whose commercial success depends precisely upon nostalgia value, authors more or less adept at applying mascara to the known; like any entertainment genre, sf is predominantly a literature of nostalgia manipulation. Only the greatest novels, after all, ever *threaten* anyone.

Of the alpha males (there are relatively few women in this cohort) who began to dominate the field around 1965–75, only a handful, like Thomas M Disch and Samuel R Delany, fail to emit a nostalgic charm. But neither of these authors published significantly in 1987 (though if it weren't a collection of linked fantasy tales, and if it weren't set in Nevèrÿon, the land of Gongor the Tongue-Locked, Delany's *The Bridge of Lost Desire* might need mentioning). Deep into the nostalgia-realms of Future History with *Great Sky River* (Bantam), Gregory Benford continues to apply chilly intellection (in a style of greyish dignity) to material far too thin to merit such Thought. In this instalment of an ongoing saga, humans show their stuff on a planet dominated by several species of thick robots, and at the end of the day escape in a magic spaceship in the direction of some sort of cosmogonic Big Think at the heart of the galaxy (see next volume). *The Secret Ascension; or, Philip K. Dick Is Dead, Alas* (Tor), by Michael Bishop, gazes inward upon the memory and example of Philip K Dick, replicating both the man himself (who is a character in the novel) and his deepest literary concerns, in a parody with love, admirably executed. Joe Haldeman, who is far too decent a writer to mean a word of it, has a fine time in *Tool of the Trade* (Morrow) spoofing the Cold War and near-future thrillers and (perhaps) himself. His hero discovers an audio frequency which enforces absolute obedience on those he blows his whistle at, giving him (and Haldeman) every opportunity to run rings around a congeries of official spooks; and the climax of the book depends (if memory serves) on whether or not the Russian premier has cotton up his ears. And the allure of the known future is still potent in *The Smoke Ring* (Del Rey), Larry Niven's solo novel for 1987, full of gripping architectonics but muddily told. With Jerry Pournelle and Steven Barnes, Niven also published, in *The Legacy of Heorot* (Gollancz), quite incredibly, yet another novel in which private-enterprise Americans desolate a new planet and destroy its natives and call the solitude Dunroamin, just as though Vietnam had never happened – but then Vietnam never did happen to Starship Troopers.

Of this cohort, only Gene Wolfe released a novel of the first rank in 1987. But *The Urth of the New Sun* (Gollancz) is less a novel in its own right than a sustained coda to *The Book of the New Sun* (published in four volumes from 1980 through 1983), and all five volumes are best read as one single text, perhaps the finest single work the field has yet produced, though a text far removed from the usual concerns of sf. Grave, hermetic, daedal, *The Book* may magisterially sum up all the materials available to the modern sf writer (and reader), but at the same time the unremitting religious grasp of Wolfe's vision sea-changes these materials into something utterly strange, sui generis. *The Urth of the New Sun* is a fitting capstone to this vast and inspissate Theatre of Memory, and if Giordano Bruno were alive today he'd wander every niche of it. Severian, who is both Christ and Competent, tells his own story, reversing the usual poles of irony, for he knows much more than we ever can, which can be chilling and uncomfortable. A novella adjunct to *The Book*, and far less taxing, *Empires of Foliage and Flower* (Cheap Street) might give new readers some sense of Wolfe's tone and texture; but only the *Book* will really do.

To separate those writers first prominent in 1965–1975 from those who have only come to notice over the past decade or so may seem more convenient than analytic; but it can be argued, all the same, that some loosening of the bonds of genre can be detected in some of the newer writers, as well as a new parodic freedom in the handling of older material from the time before the stars were torn down. Iain M Banks's *Consider Phlebas* (Macmillan) may at first strike the reader as an almost excessively loyal homage to traditional space opera, for it is chock-full of galaxy-spanning star wars, nth-generation computers, "orbitals," decadent cults, space mercenaries, quests, ancient gods, pachydermatous aliens, nordic behaviour codes, espionage, sex, big bangs. But at its heart the book – despite an overwritten and desultory soft midriff – savagely deconstructs the essence of its ostensible form through a climax that resoundingly demonstrates the utter uselessness of all that space opera gear. It may seem unfair to include Neal Barrett Jr among the newcomers, but Through Darkest America (Congdon & Weed) has almost nothing in common with his Aldair of Albion fantasies of fifteen years ago, except perhaps for the travel. Through Darkest America may or may not have consciously repeated as apocalyptic farce the dawn-to-dark downriver hegira that makes The Adventures of Huckleberry Finn (1884) an archetype of the American experience, but the fable-like excesses of the journey it depicts with such monitory ferocity have a revisionary feel. In The Forge of God (Tor), Greg Bear had a go at sublimating his own anxiety of influence by radically subverting the kind of story hard-sf writers typically wax triumphalist over. Bevies of aliens bracket Earth, some bent on betraying us, others bent on giving us a hand. Yankee scientists soon work out that what is happening is the planned and irrevocable destruction of the planet, and that there is nothing anyone can do, however Competent he may be. Earth is therefore duly demolished, and a pathetic remnant of humanity hitchhikes (revenge-bound, it must be admitted) into interstellar vacancies (where sequels await). By itself – and may it remain a singleton [fat chance, as it turned out 1995] – it is a savage book.

James P Blaylock has also made some use of earlier material, and in Land of Dreams (Arbor House), taking a few lessons from Charles G Finney's The Circus of Dr Lao (1935), he transforms his alternate California into a land of steampunk bounty, opalescent and emollient, lush and lingering. In the dingy cacophonies of Michael Blumlein's Barea – a term which tellingly conflates San Fransisco Bay Area and barrio – a less consoling California comes into view, hierarchical but pastless. The Movement of Mountains (St Martin's Press), an austerely mannered first novel of very considerable stature, takes the obese doctor who narrates it from Barea to an alien planet, where he foments a revolution of the oppressed and becomes commensal, through a shared virus, with the rest of humanity. The last pages of the book may fail to sustain the Wolfe-like secret-passage intricacies of the confessional mode Blumlein crafts for his intriguing physician, but the body of the book burns remorselessly, like dry-ice. A sense of recessive elegy lightly embrocates Richard Bowker's Dover Beach (Bantam), whose title derives from Matthew Arnold; mixing together private-eye and post-catastrophe modes, he tells a tale by definition evocative of a demolished past, but the aptness of this particular marriage of modes generates a wry élan; nostalgia is kept in check. From David Brin came another fairy tale in wolf's clothing; The Uplift War (Phantasia), an exercise in space-operatic wish-fulfilment, bares its biceps like the strictest of hard-sf, but the magic machines, the magic FTL, the magic neo-chimps and magic Progenitors whose magic secret lore unlocks the magic secret of the magic universe all give the game away: That in hard-sf country the triumphs of the good guys come as easy as Alice. In the stricter world of Octavia E Butler, xenophilia and exogamy govern the behaviour of the aliens who dominate *Dawn* (Warner), which is the first of a potentially impressive series about the enlisting of post-catastrophe humanity into a brave new marriage; the style is cumulatively gripping, and the tale hardly begun.

In *Mindplayers* (Bantam), which is her first novel, Pat Cadigan bashes together a railroad flat of linked stories about a young gal on mind drugs cornered into going legit; as a trained therapist (or tinker) specializing in pathos, she enters sick minds for pay, setting off redemptive psychomachies in the theatres of their conveniently addressable souls. In the world of this novel, anguish is a *glitch*. But because Cadigan has found no tale to hang her beads on, there can be no real testing of this strange presumption, and the book soon trails into doodle. Orson Scott Card's *Wyrms* (Arbor House) – an exceedingly ramshackle premise couched with all the glitzy skill its author has at beck – was given an unduly civil reception from the sf press; but *Seventh Son* (Tor) deserved its praise. Set in an alternate version of America's past in which magic works, and the first of several planned titles, *Seventh Son* does occasionally suffer from Card's shiny swift slippery way with words, but the tale of Alvin the Maker, and of the Earth he knits within his hands, may grow and grow. (Or not. [It did, for a while, but stalled 1995]) On the other hand, John Crowley's *Ægypt* (Bantam) must either grow or dissolve utterly. As a sequence of doors opening into doors in the Theatre of Memory, it is a text of unparalleled and superb complexity. But just as the mouth of narrative opens to say the first words of the Story hidden within the stories told and told again in this first of four integral volumes, *Ægypt* snaps shut, like an amphitheatre echoing with laughter not yet laughed. It is an intensely frustrating moment; we can only await the outcome, a great novel, it may be.

Take Sam Spade, who digs the past. Or take Marlowe, whose name is buried under centuries. Or take the archaic Archer. They are haunted archaeologists of the century, curators of the western slope of latterday America: deciphering the past that calls the tune for the mayfly offspring of the dead father; delving through the catacombs of the mean streets of LA for hieroglyphs and papyrus that will reveal the crimes that fix the meaning of the world. The essence of the American thriller genre is contained in one title by Ross MacDonald: *The Underground Man* (1971). But Spade and Marlowe and Archer have something else in common, beyond the smell of Egyptian Incas in their clothing: by the end of the book they will have unpacked the scroll that reveals the name that propitiates the risen ancestor, and the scales will balance, and they will survive to scour again the Aztec middens of the West. As will the hero in any book by William Gibson, who did not publish a novel in 1987. Cyberpunk (as he – and others – have written it) shares with the thriller genre not only superficies of style and plot and cast and pacing, but more tellingly an obsession with brandnaming the governors of the world, the voodoo ancestors who call the tune of LA, or cyberspace. The tactile modernity of cyberpunk tends to conceal its deep structure, which is one of propitiation, so that its profound consanguinity with the literatures of nostalgia (that is, with all genre literatures) has been obscured.

Two cyberpunk novels of interest were published in 1987, or three, if one wishes to include William Burroughs's *The Western Lands* (Viking) for its conflation of America with the Egyptian land of the dead; but that might be lèse majesté. George Alec Effinger's *When Gravity Fails* (Arbor House) dumps its mean-streets hero into an almost indecipherable Middle East, sometime in the distant near future, where for much of the book he refuses the technology of plug-ins that will open the secrets of the world to him. It may be the case that Effinger loses control of the book when he finally manages to plug his hero into it, but neither author nor his shadow really had much choice. An archaeologist has got to do what an archaeologist has got to do. Michael Swanwick's *Vacuum Flowers* (Arbor House) carries its heroine down the gravity well from the asteroids to Earth in a constant buzz of information codes, the most important of which, and the secret of the past which shapes her, being the genetic "integrity" her mother (buried off-stage) has implanted into her; and it is this Integrity she must decipher or lose the game. By applying cyberpunk riffs and overloads to his material, Swanwick manages, in this deftly crammed novel, to give to the dervish masquerade of his solar system a lived-in tarnish, a potent sense of the governing interweaves of the past.

Of novels published in 1987 by writers recently prominent, only a few remain. Mary Gentle's *Ancient Light* (Gollancz), which is a sequel to *Golden Witchbreed* (1983), and which is designed to terminate the series, dots every i for innumerable pages, finally to come somewhat phosphorescently to life in its final hundreds, when the author gets properly aroused by her task of demolition, about which she is very thorough. No more Witches, no more books. Richard Grant's *Rumors of Spring* (Bantam) must be read as fantasy, which is also true of Jonathan Carroll's *Bones of the Moon* (Century), and Colin Greenland's *The Hour of the Thin Ox* (Unwin), and K W Jeter's *Infernal Devices* (St Martin's Press), and Tim Powers's *On Stranger Tides* (Ace), and Terry Pratchett's *Mort* (Gollancz), and William P Vollmann's *You Bright and Risen Angels*

(Deutsch). But that was also arguably the case with several books already fêted, and these strong cousins should be at least mentioned; most readers of sf could take any of them on without bends. Perhaps fatally to any poll success, Lisa Goldstein's *A Mask for the General* (Bantam) gives short shrift to nostalgia in her rendering of post-catastrophe California; it is a world which has no secrets to tell Goldstein's protagonist about any magical Integrity within her that will unlock the secrets of the past and make her super, and in that sense the novel must be seen as Humanist. Alan Moore's graphic novel, *Watchmen* (Warner), as illustrated by Dave Gibbon, depicts a film-noir alternate America distinguished from our own dear Land of Dreams mainly by a passel of 1930s and 1950s vigilantes who were allowed to prosper and to become costumed heroes; it is a Matter drenched in iconicity, and in crafting an adult comic from this rich mulch Moore has generated a superb tale of apocalypse at midnight. There is a Dying Earth in Paul Park's *Soldiers of Paradise* (Arbor House), with Helliconian seasons and a gnarled permafrost of Wolfean theology substrating the whole, whose narrative vigour belies the fin-de-siècle cod-swallop its protagonists spout; the erotic melancholia that infuses this brilliant first novel has a welcome adult tone. Finally, Lucius Shepard's *Life During Wartime* (Bantam) may have disappointed those readers who forgot that *Green Eyes* (1984) was very clumsy in the joints, despite the brilliance of its scene-setting; so with this book, which is, all the same, a far more ambitious text, and in its phantasmagorical portrait of the new Vietnams south of Texas (or America below the belt) manages something of an imperial conquest (of the pen).

Of 300 or so novels on show from 1987, it has been possible to mention fewer than 50 samples of a genre in the throes of change. Most of the unmentioned titles may ply strict genre routes to conclusions carved in stone by the ancestors, but still we have come a far piece from the old family of read books, as shown by the work of many of the younger writers, far more of them women than the texts of 1987 permitted one to demonstrate. The dinosaurs of the genre may continue to lay their giant pellets, and the alpha males to hatch them, but the future must lie in the delicate mad paws of the changeling creatures who roam the last years of the century, which is beginning to shut. May their bright eyes continue to reflect the omens of the dark.

– The Orbit Science Fiction Yearbook 1 (Futura, 1988), ed. David Garnett

2. Interzone Columns

Marching Initials

I.

THE DIFFERENCE between Iain Banks and Iain M Banks is more than having a publisher to gnash between your syllables. Both guises of the man, it is true, glare at one from within the bondage of the same skin. Both display a glittery extroverted bruising familiarity with material of penal-colony extremity, the sort of material most writers utter in very solemn terms out of a kind of dour awe at their having such darknesses within them to emit. And both versions of Banks seem chary of blotting a line. But Iain's tales of psychosis paradigms dance out of range of genre fixatives, and Iain M has begun his career with a space opera. (It was, by the way, his publishers, once known as Macmillan and Co, Limited, but now as merely M, who requested the insertion of the middle initial – which could signalize the beginning of a trend.) Despite the quotation from T S Eliot's *The Waste Land* (1921) which provides its title, *Consider Phlebas* (M, 1987; a limited edition of 176 copies is also available and will cost more than a week's dole) does look very much, for at least some of its excessive length, to be a full-hearted attempt at contributing to the subcategory of sf whose conventions are least easily breached.

Certainly, for a while, *Phlebas* does seem to obey most of the rules to which space opera – like any romance form – demands such unsmiling adherence. The setting is galactic, as it must be, but the vast expanses of the *Phlebas* "known" space are traversable within the characters' life-spans, as necessary, via FTL drives banged into shape in the enginerooms of space by the descendants of Scotsmen. The *Phlebas* universe is properly huger than we in the nursery can guess, but is not *unimaginable* (unlike any Stanislaw Lem universe), and the war which charges the entire canvas *seems* to be apprehensible as a form of conflict in which identifiable Good will fight identifiable Evil to a kinetically resounding close. Very properly, galaxy-wide strife obtains between the Nivenesque non-human Idirans (they seem to be the good guys) and the hi-tech but pacific and community-minded human Culture (who sure sound like your normal comsymp hive of baddies), while an ancient omnipotent race to whom we are as mayflies gazes on indifferently, so that God seems in his heaven and the main action can take place, as it should, in a baroque cacophony of interregnum reaching from the Golden Age of the Deep Past into a future of universal milk and honey, like it was when we were very young. And the protagonist of the book, a humanoid killer and mercenary named Borza Horza Gobuchul, does seem properly to combine two of the vectors whose junction generally proclaims a hero with a thousand faces: he's good at killing other beings; and his origin is a mystery. So far so good.

Horza's faces are indeed many. As one of a dwindling diaspora of Changers, most of whom inhabit Idiran territory as homeless hirelings, and all of whom are distrusted by other humans, he can take on the appearance of other humans at will. But here something oddly subversive in Iain M's larger strategy may begin to nag at the reader, like a premonition of adulthood. Other human societies distrust and shun Changers, who are sly, untrustworthy, mercenary and rootless, and who are clearly modeled upon the Phoenicians evoked by the title. Phlebas – no matter how many faces he may wear in *The Waste Land* – is so damningly the merchant, the haggling money-changer, that water in the end can only drown him; for there is no miracle of the Grail for Semites, according to Mr Eliot. So with the protagonist of this novel. Though no hint of racism even begins to touch *Consider Phlebas*, the title *does* inescapably invoke an exile that is unredeemable, a death without point. The hero of Banks's book – let us make this absolutely clear – is Phlebas. And he is as utterly doomed as Phlebas to a useless death, sans Grail.

Where the book stumbles is in the shenanigans that nearly trample its message into invisibility. A super-computer of Culture origins has crashlanded on a planet quarantined by the geezers to whom we are as mayflies, and Horza's Idiran commanders rescue him from certain death somewhere else so he can hightail it to Schar's World (which as a Changer – which does sound awfully like moneylender – he has previously visited) and gain control of the terribly powerful artificial Mind. But before he can get there, a battle in hyperspace dumps him into a series of picaresque detours which last most of the book, neatly herniating it. Picked up after the battle by a ragtag crew of freelancers whose captain could be played by Harrison Ford, Horza helps raid a temple (unsuccessfully) on one totally irrelevant planet, and then visits a ringworld-like Culture artifact called Vavatch Orbital (but as a visual writer Banks is foggy to the extreme, though loud, and I for one could never work out just what Vavatch actually *orbited*). On this Orbital Iain M twiddles his dials like Jack Vance at his most ditheringly picturesque, spending far too long on a corrupt religious sect's attempts to eat the Changer, and on a stunningly dim spectator-sport board game whose name I cannot remember, whose description would stupefy the paraphrast, and whose only plot function is to return Horza to the ship he only left because Iain M wanted to dally with his palette of gouache. Finally, deep into the night, everyone who has survived does manage motivelessly to reach Schar's World, where a denouement is played out whose decibel level and plot pattern strongly remind one of the last half of *Aliens*, without the laughs, and the novel ends in shambles.

Shambles is what Banks has been preparing for, though he almost loses us on Vavatch, which is merely doodle. What began as seemingly orthodox space opera turns – after the doodle is wiped – into a subversion of all that's holy to the form. The War Mind turns out to be a papier-mâché McGuffin which causes the destruction, in the end, of almost the entire cast, rendering both their hegira and their deaths entirely futile. As peripheral in the Grail Quest as ever Phlebas was (and ultimately as dead), Horza has also (in any case) been fighting for the wrong side (and never learns better). The Idirans are not only losers in the war, they are in fact the bad guys, great blundering insufferable Rambos, their claims to chivalric dignity a sadistic xenophobic mockery, even if they do talk Poul-Andersonese. It is the collegial pinko socialists of the Culture who win the day. In its rubbishing of any idea that kinetic drive and virtue are identical, in its treatment of the deeds of the hero as contaminatingly entropic, *Consider Phlebas* punishes the reader's every expectation of exposure to the blissful dream momentum – the healing retrogression into childhood – of true and terrible space opera. If only Iain M had turned the volume down, if only someone had the gumption to excise the odd half acre of fallow Vance, a phoenix of art might have burned into our vision out of the chaos and the splat. Maybe next time.

II.

We come into the quietude and melancholy periods of Richard "K" Cowper's most recent novel, *Shades of Darkness* (Kerosina, 1987; a limited edition at £25 includes a 37-page pamphlet of neat elegiac fables, *The Magic Spectacles and Other Tales*). About *Shades of Darkness* little need be said, except to praise the book for what it very precisely is. Richard Cowper is far too experienced a craftsman to go philandering – and if there is some marginal sense that his tale of a haunting in East Anglia rests too comfortably within its limits, undue chastity may be the cause. At the same time, he invests the nicely caught 1930s domesticity of the seaside cottage with a deft surrealist glow, so that the moments of genuine terror seem illuminated from within. The terror, in other words, seems strangely natural.

Jim Fuller, a journalist newly expelled from Uganda for truth-telling, needs solitude in which to write a novel about the haunting Matter of Africa. With his lover Karen he comes across the former home in East Anglia of some old Africa hands.

Before long, as though excited by his subject matter, haunting urgencies of African import begin to insert, into the upper world, clues about an old tragedy of miscegenation, murder, spoiled lives. Jim finally understands this excitation of distress to be longing for resolution, and compassionately exorcises the ghost, after being half frightened to death by it. Several subsidiary characters are sketched in Cowper's best manner – delicate, slightly waspish, stoic in its dealings with the large obdurate *passage* of the world – and a swift knowing portrait of *Peter Grimes* country is awarded us. Jim's novel is finished. He and Karen marry. They are alive. What more could such a book give us?

III.

There is something almost magical about the suave savvy ease of Leigh "Cape" Kennedy's first novel. *The Journal of Nicholas the American* (Cape, 1987) is about as rough-edged as a Fabergé egg, and about as easy to pick the heart out of. One must edge inside the thing, like a ghost, because Nicholas Dal lets his cats out of the bag with almost supernatural reluctance. I think the word "empath" is never mentioned, but it is his alienating curse – the journals impart a Dostoyevskyan savagery of estrangement – to have been born of a family of Russian empaths. After an earlier Dal has gone murderously insane from the stress of a paranormal sensitivity to the emotional content of others' minds, the family has fled to America, where Nicholas is born. Speaking Russian before he speaks Coloradan, and ravaged by every contact with the raw blood inside everyone else's head, he is by the time the novel opens an almost extinguished creature. He is in his late twenties, but remains a perpetual student in Boulder Colorado so he can stay out of sight, being terrified of discovery. To dull his empathy, he drinks almost constantly. He is unprepossessing, rude, tortured, gnarled and skinny. (Sartre could have conceived him.) He falls in love.

The girl is also a student. Her mother Susanne is dying of cancer. The emotions concerned with this turn the knife in Nicholas's psyche. Meanwhile a research psychologist seems to have tracked him down. Events darken and twist, but at the heart of the book the two anguishes – Dal's flayed openness to others, and Susanne's slow dying – dovetail slowly and plangently into a single exercise in the topos of reconciliation. To decipher this movement of the heart through Kennedy's impeccably crafted impersonation of Nicholas is rather like doing a crossword in Cyrillic, but something very much like hope begins eventually to dawn. To be sure the book then snaps shut. But something rich has been glimpsed. It is a novel to unpack more than once.

– *Interzone* 20, Summer 1987

Big Brothers Watch Avalon

[When I glanced at this review just now, it came back to me in a rush what had happened. Because I was playing Russian roulette with deadlines (as usual), but because I miscalculated pretty seriously on this occasion, I sort of shot myself in the head with this review of *The Legacy of Heorot* for *Interzone* 21. Not because I'd retract its negative conclusions; but because, although I had drafted everything, I'd not had the time to do any recasting-for-clarity, and some of that original review seems now too lacking in the joie de vivre of the finished product. So, without updating any of my 1987 opinions, I've attempted to turn this into a proper second-draft presentation of the material 1995.]

LET US kill three birds with one stone. Let us review a single novel by three massive simultaneous authors. Because we have had the strength to read *The Legacy of Heorot* (Gollancz, 1987), which is by Larry Niven, and by Jerry Pournelle, and by Steven Barnes, let us therefore sip marvelling from the fount of wisdom of the squad. Let us travel with them – as though ushered by Cerberus – to humanity's first colony beyond the solar system, which has been established on an island called Avalon in the middle of an ocean on the fourth planet of Tau Ceti. While the human colonists (almost all of them Americans) jerrybuild their appalling quonset slums, and finish laying out "a square kilometer of plastic-coated solar cells" upon the virgin land in a foredoomed attempt to sate their triumphalist energy-lust, and plunge headlong into the factory farming regimes that worked so well on Earth and should tame Avalon pretty damn quick, let us rejoice with them in the conviction that things couldn't be better. And let us rejoice also that the private organization behind the colony – with exquisite Yankee sagacity our threesome have put forward *The National Geographic Society* as the financial heavyweights behind humanity's first interstellar trip, presumably because all the actual governments of Earth have been *feminized* by infestations of Comsymp liberals and have shirked the Real Man's Job of funding space travel – is sending messages from Earth that indicate how thrilled it is with the snapshots the Avaloners are sending back for its magazine: as a big thank you, one presumes, for the ten trillion dollars already sunk.

But not everyone is fooled by this seemingly blissful infestation of yet another world. Enter (one might be forgiven for thinking) tough-minded Cook Jerry. Clearly, out of all the members of the squad, Jerry Pournelle is best qualified to undertake the task of creating a stern stiff-necked bromide-choked military man with doubts about matters of security. Who in any case but Jerry would muddy this gob of the broth by giving his dreadful ex-colonel a name like Cadmann Wayland? In case anyone misses the sentimentalizing bathos of this reference to Poul Anderson country, Cadmann Wayland actually has a limp. He also sings. He is also despised of man, until he pounds the shit out of them.

Enough jollity. The Singing Smith has noted several weird gaps in the island's ecosystem, and is aware of significant blank pages in humanity's damaged computer's knowledge of the new planet, so the reader will be inclined to agree with him that page 10 of The Legacy of Heorot is very early days for colonists to assume that there are no stray autochthones about in need of extermination, nor would there be any story to tell if Avalon were truly benign. If this conclusion seems not only likely but desperately obvious, and if The Legacy of Heorot begins to remind readers of old Idiot Plots he/she might have thought obsolete about the time Planet Stories bit the dust, it may be reassuring to discover that the entire cast of The Legacy of Heorot suffers from brain damage: a phenomenon of interstellar travel called Hibernation Instability has afflicted every manjack and womanpail of them, and not one person in the entire novel is actually very bright. It is good to know this.

But now it's Cook Larry's turn (probably). It's time to create a monster whose continued presence on Avalon will first threaten the colonists, then drive them into a patriotic feeding frenzy (for they're only human). And there's no doubt that the ravening hot-wired ruthless brand of beast Niven gives us, like an updated Coeurl from the earlier pages of A E Van Vogt, does generate an agreeable frisson or two; and because the colonists are extremely thick (see above, under brain damage) the Coeurl Upgrades do almost manage to eat everyone up. In its immature form, the beast is a fish-like animal called a samlon (because it tastes something like a salmon, and because this is the kind of joke that pleases the kind of people who need keepers [see above, under brain damage]); in its mature form, it is terribly strong and swift and female, and is therefore called a grendel (hence Heorot). These grendels attack in three waves. The second wave is similar to the first, though second time round there are a lot more of the beasts involved, but Caedmon the Lame soon manages to organize an extermination campaign. Unfortunately, not one of the highly trained colonists has given a thought (not too many to spare, perhaps [see above, under brain damage]) to problems of ecology, and no one asks any pertinent questions about the grendel's weird biology or about the relationship of grendels to the yummy samlon, the grendel young which humans eat with relish). So they fail to realize that their destruction of the parents will create a population explosion in the children – as grendels eat samlon whenever there are too many of them – and the last part of the novel sees a great wave of samlon metamorphose into ravening grendels, who duly gobble up everyone in reach. The grendel is (by the way) an amphibian creature, with a brain as large as a dolphin's, and in the water is capable of registering the traces of potential prey with extraordinary sensitivity. This pregnant depiction (by Cook Larry) of the grendel as ferociously intelligent and preternaturally sensitive to water-borne spoor cuts little ice, however, with Cook Jerry, who arranges for his beloved ex-colonel to react to the grendel onslaught by building himself a rural fortress, right through the middle of which he arranges – as though he were inhabiting some sort of Marriott atrium – for a brook to run, a brook which babbles (I guess), a brook which escapes blithely downwards into a river (see above, under *brain damage*) full of the famished autochthones who have already munched up most of the island, tartare, and who *have not lost their sense of smell*. The surviving members of the cast, having been driven out of their homes, now take refuge with the bleak Songster. Whew! they ejaculate, what a long day! I need a bath! They then bathe in the stream (see above, under *have not lost their sense of smell*, see above, under *brain damage*), and the final wave of grendels, nostrils flaring in disbelief at the cornucopia of good luck odours drifting down the river, charges upstream and eats them. *Wha' happen?* says Cook Jerry's mouthpiece, a little later (see above, under *brain damage*) to the few who didn't wash.

In the meantime, a few gobs of human interest have been inserted to keep the broth lumpy; these bits were probably assigned to Mr Barnes (scullery person). In these human interest pages, everyone (except for Wayland and a paralyzed sub-plot adversary in the camp) square dances cute, grabs ass cute, fucks cute, and jollifies cute about fucking cute. Like cheerleaders, or scouts, or youth counsellors, they hug each other a lot while grinning at the camera, or into mirrors. They think they are loveable, but they are not even likeable. They think they are friends of the earth, but they are not even neighbours. The trio who created Avalon may think they crafted a paradise whose only blemish – a few dolphin-brained native beasts who almost avoid being exterminated – is ultimately disposed of in a final solution, all clap hands. What they have in fact created is a prison camp. A few xenobiological flights may occasionally perk *The Legacy of Heorot* up for a page or two, and lighten the doldrums of this sour dystopian broth, but the taste remains. It is the taste bosses leave, the taste of bosses and owners. A boot taste.

– Interzone 21, Autumn 1987

Plug your Ears, it's Paxwax!

1.

[I preface the full column for Interzone 22 with part of a column I wrote for Interzone 17 in 1986, which constitutes a short notice of Phillip Mann's Master of Paxwax, volume one of the sequence reviewed at greater length below 1995.]

THE JACKET illustration for Phillip Mann's Master of Paxwax (Gollancz, 1986) depicts a scene which does not appear in the book, though it will assuredly loom large in the second volume of The Story of Pawl Paxwax, the Gardener. As Pawl Paxwax also does almost everything imaginable in this novel except actually garden, one feels mildly drawn to the conclusion that it might be the fairest course all round to proclaim Mr Mann as an author of continuing interest (his first novel, The Eye of the Queen [1982], had exceptional moments), and to serve him best by awaiting the full Paxwax. I shall do this.

It is, all the same, possible to make a few, remarkably provisional comments. There is a space-opera fundament to Mann's galaxy-spanning tale, which tells the story of the Eleven Families who rule known space on behalf of humanity, and oppress aliens everywhere. Provisionally, Mann should concentrate on this fundament – his descriptions of aliens are deft and melancholy and estranged; he does a good little space war; some of his planets could be returned to with profit; and the arabesque body-sculpting his bioengineered humans put themselves through gives off a rank, beguiling frisson. When he's cavorting with this fundament, Mann remains very impressively geared in to his task. But when he transcribes the excruciatingly prosaic poetry of his moody young Paxwax, and when he waxes (or should one say wanes) dithyrambic over adolescent love hots, which he does rather a lot of early on, then he gives us dead wood. Most of it is in the first half of this first volume. Provisionally, and with real high hopes, persevere.

[End of excerpt from Interzone 17]

THERE is really no way to be kind to Ernest Hill by mentioning him, but the deed must be done. To make a certain point about space operas, we must disinter and mention an old book of his, an Ace Double called Pity About Earth (1968). It was a tale whose impact (though it was, at most, minimal) on first publication seems, in retrospect, excessive. But this dreadful novel – unless the reviewer is in fact thinking of Frederick L Shaw's *Envoy to the Dog Star* (1967) – does offer the student of space opera one sharp small lesson in the rhetoric of scale, and for that alone it should be remembered. Unless memory serves the reviewer wrong, the cognitive and imaginative climax of the *Pity About Earth* comes when the protagonist discovers that the speed of light is considerably *slower* than anyone had guessed, and consequently learns that the universe itself is very much less immense than previously estimated, very much less mysterious, less dangerous, less visited. For the protagonist of *Pity About Earth*, space travel therefore becomes about as exciting as commuting to Basildon, and the novel ends in a state of such nerveless desuetude that it (or *Envoy to the Dog Star*) has always retained for itself a wee niche in the reviewer's mind.

That Mr Hill, like so many other authors of failed space operas, was indeed British should have surprised none of the original readers (there have been no subsequent ones) of *Pity About Earth*. The lesson the book provides – that one must not think of solar systems and council estates as topological twins – is not one that the American founders of space opera ever needed learning. This may not be entirely to the credit of the sons of the conquerors of the West, which is beside the point; of present interest is the fact that almost every non-American space opera *does* mismanage the rhetoric of scale, just as Mr Hill did, though less hilariously. Even when a subversive intention is obvious (as with Iain M Banks's *Consider Phlebas*), the risks of energy loss are very considerable. And when a story depends upon (and boasts of) a sense that the cataclysm it depicts is of galaxy-shaking immensity, then there can be no excuse for the dozy chuntering decline of *The Fall of the Families*, the second volume of Phillip Mann's The Story of Pawl Paxwax, the Gardener sequence, into unkempt paralysis.

After a few pages of resumé of *Master of Paxwax* matters, *Families* (Gollancz, 1987) continues the story without intermission. The Eleven Families of human descent who rule an entire galaxy continue to intrigue and squabble. The aliens they implausibly dominate continue to plot their downfall. Pawl Paxwax continues to write execrable poetry to his beloved bride, who stays with him all the same. Odin, a nice telepathic alien with a root, deepens his friendship with the poetaster (Pawl) who rules a million worlds or so, but is commanded by a wise machiavellian Tree to murder the bride, and does so. Convinced that she has been done in by one or more of the Families, Pawl goes over to the aliens, which apostacy spells the end of human hegemony over the one hundred billion stars of the galaxy. As before, Mr Mann's aliens are far more intriguing than his humans, and those of his humans who are so radically bio-engineered that they seem alien are far more intriguing than Pawl himself. Pawl, whose insane grief at the loss of his wife is presented without irony (or for that matter much interest) primarily as a cause of rapid balding, is not exactly the kind of protagonist even the silliest American writer would be much inclined to end an entire hegemony over the one hundred billion stars of the galaxy with. What Mr Mann has forgotten – just as Mr Hill forgot it long ago – is precisely scale. *The Fall of the Families* fails utterly to inhabit the grandiose domains of space opera it lays claim to; and it is only when Mr Mann can jigger himself into some xenobiological riff – as in the very moving pages that end the book – that *Paxwax* comes to life at all, too late.

II.

[There seems to be no end to prefacing. I now preface to the *continuation* of the full column for *Interzone* 22 a review of Gwyneth Jones's *King Death's Garden* from *Interzone* 18 1995.]

IN HER second novel this year, Gwyneth Jones becomes her old alter ego Ann Halam for a bit and gives us in *King Death's Garden* (Orchard, 1986) a ghost story in traditional English vein. Jones has used Halam for all her children's books after *Dear Hill* (1980) as by Gwyneth A Jones, but though the protagonist here is a young boy just entering adolescence, there is a chaste chill gravity to the tale, and a melancholy of hauntedness, that very much reminds one of the adult stories of Walter de la Mare, whose *Henry Brocken* (1904) is (not at all inadvertently, one suspects) quoted in the epigraph.

Maurice is an asthmatic, clever, lonely prig who feels that his parents – off in the Middle East trying to earn a Thatcher Era living – have abandoned him. Stuck with an otherworldly great-aunt in Brighton, he soon becomes fascinated by the eponymous cemetery next door, and by the girl Moth who seems to live there. He begins to have dreams in which the Brighton of previous centuries comes through. Moth is of course a ghost – an indentured manifestation of the genius loci – and Maurice comes closer and closer to a similar immurement. At the last moment he pulls free of the prison, and seems to be on the road to growing up. It is a classic theme, and Jones treats it with all the respect it merits. Her Brighton has been lived in. Nor is de la Mare, whose most haunting moments were almost always suburban, a dead hand on her page.

[End of excerpt from *Interzone* 18]

Once again as Ann Halam, Gwyneth Jones gives us another story for older children. Where her previous title (*King Death's Garden*) gave off a pellucid traditional glow, *The Daymaker* (Orchard, 1987) strikes a note of real defiance. The effect is grumpy, against the grain, daring, stubborn, abstract. Like so many other books in this age-group category of high fantasy, it is a menarche/quest tale whose goal is transformative; but most unusually the quest undertaken by wilful young Zanne will, if she succeeds in awakening the Daymaker, destroy her world of Inland. Long after an unmentioned (but subtextually pointed) catastrophe, Inland survives as an oasis of magically sustained ecological rapport. There are no machines. Men are loving but supernumerary; women rule, weave magically the fibres of the world together to sustain the haven of Inland. Even as a small child, Zanne is powerful and disruptive, and when she takes her choice journey she goes in search of the fabled Daymaker, a machine which gives life to other machines (subtextually it sounds rather like a nuclear power plant). Accompanied by a wise friend, she becomes more and more stubbornly attached to her dream of the shining Daymaker as they travel further and further into the desert terrains that surround the haven. Only in the nick of time does Zanne – after the death of her friend – begin to wise up. As the novel ends, it is clear she is destined to spend many years searching out and destroying other Daymakers.

It is almost totally impossible to spend more than a few pages with Zanne without wishing to kill the twerp. She is snarky, arrogant, wilful, and the wrongness of her course is totally and convincingly evident from the very beginning – for nothing is allowed to cloud for an instance Ms Jones's enraptured limning of the feminist paradise of Inland, which her protagonist would destroy. The only wisdom Zanne can acquire is that wisdom which Ms Jones has unequivocally told the reader is the only wisdom possible for Inland. There is nothing Zanne can learn that we, and the Inlanders, and Ms Jones, do not already know. A strange book.

[As this seems destined to be an omnium gatherum column, I thought it might be an idea to insert here a notice, from the *Interzone* 30 column, of the continuation of Zanne's story 1995.]

AS ANN HALAM, Gwyneth Jones continues in *Transformations* (Orchard, 1988) the series of books about Inland that began, quite auspiciously, with *The Daymaker* (1987). Zanne, the pig-headed heroine of that book, is now four years older, but continues to lack the ability to listen, and once again comes very close to disaster through her stiff-necked deafness to those around her. As she is now a covener – a woman charged with the task of maintaining through "magic" the harmonies of the living world – this refusal to listen may begin to seem a less than plausible device, given one's sense that in Inland coveners are, in essence, *listeners*. But Zanne also remains fascinated by the old Makers, the machines and forces of the old defunct male-dominated civilization whose relics Inland has inherited, and her deafness is clearly linked to that fascination. She remains at the moment a necessary cripple, and in any case Jones clearly intends her Inland books to depict the growth and transformation of a soul. In Zanne she has created a protagonist with much to learn.

She arrives at the mining community of Minith with a task to perform: an ancient Maker, reportedly sited somewhere in the dour mountains that surround the hardscrabble valley farms, must be dismantled or put to death. She is not made welcome, except by a young girl. Failing to detect the complexities of the lives she has encountered, she erects an injurious hypothesis to explain the rigid inturned puritanism of the Minithers; and only at the last moment does her psychic static cease to block her from the truths that lie before her. Her perceptions transformed, she sees the valley and its inhabitants in an entirely new light; she puts the Maker to sleep at last; and Minith is sea-changed into a state of harmony. The only real problem readers of *Transformations* may encounter is a certain impatience awaiting Zanne's comprehension of matters Halam/Jones has taken great pains to make clear – from very early on – to the rest of us.

[End of excerpt from *Interzone 30*]

III.

For the relative newcomer to a genre which he reportedly dominates, James Herbert's *Sepulchre* (Hodder & Stoughton, 1987) comes as a something of a shock. It might be called the shock of the un-new. Somewhere in a vast country house in the south of England, the heart of a Sumerian deity still beats. Devotees of this heart eat living flesh to keep their peckers up. Chief devotee is Kline, who runs a huge mining conglomerate in the City. Icy Halloran is seconded to protect Kline, who fears an unknown assailant. Icy Halloran falls in love with compromised PA of chief devotee. There is toing and froing. There is no unknown assailant, just some IRA thugs after Halloran. Jackals – Mr Herbert characterizes them as "loathsome" – prowl the estate. So does the entire cast, sooner or later. Eventually the heart is stomped on, Halloran gets the girl, Kline ages dramatically and frizzles up. In all this pomp and bombast, not one new thing. In 316 pages, not an excuse.

IV.

Karen Joy Fowler's brilliant collection of stories with the deeply inept title has been widely reviewed already, and we mention *Artificial Things* (Bantam, 1986) only to echo the praise – and to mention Ms Fowler's gaining of the John W Campbell Award for Best New Writer at the Worldcon recently held in Brighton. At first glance, her work seems reticent, held almost incommunicado in the steely dynaflow embrace of a dauntingly *forewarned* craftsperson. But gradually one becomes aware of a performative glamour investing each tale with an urgency that seems increasingly, as one finishes reading the book, humane. This is only enhanced by the seamless continuity of a craft which shifts without visible effort from sf to fantasy to fabulation and back in the telling of single tales. Once in a while she sounds rather like Barry Malzberg; occasionally there is a European corrosiveness to her handling of iconic material, chillingly: but in the end the dangerous shapeliness of the stories collected in *Artificial Things* reminds the reader of no one but Ms Fowler.

– Interzone 22, Winter 1987

Mimesis Chills Out

I.

THERE IS no cutting edge to the present, nowadays. Like acid rain, unnumbered futures eat into the darkling blade of now, serrating and pocking the moments of our time here; and – not at all surprisingly – it becomes less and less easy to designate the genre of a large number of the books published without tags to guide us. It is, one supposes, a kind of mimesis. Again and again, mainstream novels echo the cavities and lesions in the face of the millennium to come and prove, on examination, to be unfixed in time and place – alternate histories in a sense far more telling than the theoretical sense by which any fiction must be read as an alternative history. The last two novels of MacDonald Harris come to mind, as does Garry Kilworth's *Spiral Winds* (The Bodley Head, 1987). The mimetic presumptions that seem to underlie Ian McEwan's *The Child in Time* (Cape, 1987) are deeply compromised and corroded by chill fingers of a world to come. In *Tales of Natural and Unnatural Catastrophes* (Bloomsbury, 1987), Patricia Highsmith hovers, perhaps a little precariously, between the ahistorical freedoms of the exemplary fable and the prison cells of reportage.

11.

Somewhere lost in the draft of *Spiral Winds* there is a good book which has not yet quite been written, or for that matter edited (turn from page 185 to 186 for an example of proofing more negligent than one would normally tolerate in an amateur production). By intention, it seems to be a tale of predetermined fixation, though the action of the book is far too loose to convey any sense of foredoomed impulsion. It is the story of two men obsessed by their role in the death of a British desert hero. In an Author's Note, Mr Kilworth acknowledges that in some sense his novel takes off from the death of T E Lawrence in a 1935 motorcycle accident, but makes clear that he has in no sense attempted to portray the actual subsequent lives of the teenagers who were involved in the fatal crash, and whose lives it must have affected. Clearly (though in a highly limited sense) the teenagers of *Spiral Winds* inhabit an different world from the one in which Lawrence died; Lawrence is himself never mentioned in the body of the book, which is set mainly in South West Arabia, far from Lawrence's field of action; and clearly Jim and Alan, as they enter middle age in the 1960s, are meant to bear a burden of signification no author could impose on any real persons. But it is somewhere here – perhaps because his sense of decorum prevents Mr Kilworth from any intensity of re-creation of any Lawrentian figure, either literally or in the imaginations of his protagonists – that *Spiral Winds* loses focus. Very simply, though the reader might expect the tragedy of 1935 to shape the story of its survivors, what begins to happen in the 1960s has only an arbitrary connection with that event.

Mr Kilworth has been gifted with two protagonists, and studiously rises to the challenge of creating a spiralling plot to tell their story. Newsman Alan has been sent to witness the painful British withdrawal from Aden. Before disappearing inland with his guide, he meets Sarah, a young woman whose own obsession with the desert is the actual motor of the plot. She gets banker Jim's name from Alan, returns to England, meets him and beds him and alienates him, readying him in some extremely obscure fashion to meet his destiny, which is to go himself to Arabia to find Alan, and to confront whatever it is in the desert whose urgencies all three characters think they are obeying. Sarah then utterly disappears from the book to which she has thus vicariously given the kiss of life. Jim goes to Arabia. He and Alan meet, after tribulations. Each seems dubious of the other's sense that there is something animate about the desert. At a central spot, they meet a Lawrentian figure who attacks them with a rifle; they kill him; but before he can be identified the sands have covered his remains. Jim returns to England. Stiff-necked Alan stays in Arabia.

The desert is vivid. Aden is portrayed brilliantly. Sarah is briefly vital, though too soon dismissed. But in a novel necessarily dependent upon a sustained mimetic presentation of the interior life of its protagonists, both Jim and Alan seem cardboardy, passive, blank-countenanced, and both drift through their stories in odd discontinuous fragmented jerks, pulled by strings to which it is difficult to give credence. Because Mr Kilworth has refused the generic solace of telling us a ghost story, he is bound to the mere verities of the world, in which the Lawrentian figment has – literally – nothing to say. And no matter how intelligently reticent Mr Kilworth has been about forbidding them any cheap resolutions, neither Jim nor Alan can make us believe a word they utter. So we are left with stabs in the dark at telling the sand.

III.

There is something ponderous and skittish about the less satisfactory fables in Patricia Highsmith's new book, as though a very large lepidopterologist were trying not to stamp. Oh dear. About the better stories, those that refrain from balderdash unction in the author's own sad pious voice, there is a wise cold sureness of anger so far from the pachydermatous that one wonders how one book could contain both the unspeakable "Rent-A-Womb Vs. the Mighty Right" and the brilliant "Operation Balsam; or Touch-Me-Not." The one moralizes and pummels and cheats and editorializes; the other, like a stiletto, stitches nightmares. But they are clearly from the same author. There is the same underlying tone of lonely pessimism about the fate of the planet, the same unrelenting fixity of gaze upon the suicidal progression of the human cancer through the body of the mother; there is the same final desolate calm, as though these disasters were being told from a long way away and a long time from now. The stories are what the title claims – Tales of Natural and Unnatural Catastrophes. In "The Mysterious Cemetery," as in "Operation Balsam," the disaster is pollution, whether medical or nuclear. In "President Buck Jones Rallies and Waves the Flag" it is an underpowered American President unable to distinguish lies from truth and capable of ending the world in a pet. In "Trouble at the Jade Towers," cockroaches eat the poisons intended to exterminate them so that, in a world increasingly poisoned, they are bound to thrive. And always in these stories, these fables told from another world of the collapse of our own, it is too late to mend.

IV.

In Ian McEwan's The Child in Time, the focus on the irreparable narrows and sharpens into one overriding image of the near future in Britain. Spending little time on attempting a political characterization of a land further transformed by another five or so years of the rule of Margaret Thatcher, who (though unnamed) is clearly the Prime Minister who appears in the text, he restricts himself to a single image of extraordinary desolation: the countryside of England has become a factory farm, great stretches of monoculture desert alternating with huge stands of identical conifers in rows. As no more than five years can have passed from 1987 [and in 1995 there is a tree left 1995], this transformation drives a fable-like apocalyptic ground-bass through the chaste and recessive mimetic harmonies of his ostensible tale, which deals with individual traumata and their survival.

Stephen takes his small daughter to a supermarket and loses her – in a moment of inattention – to an unseen abductor. She is never recovered. Stephen is paralyzed at an early stage of mourning, a stage many men (the text implies) never transcend. He cannot keep himself from a litany of actions designed superficially to recover his daughter, but shaped secretly into a shield that will keep him from having to face the real living grief of her permanent loss. He stops writing the children's books which, in any case, only reflected an undue immurement in his own childhood, which they mined avidly. His wife Julie leaves him. Through his friendship with an editor turned politician he joins an appalling government committee whose task is to create a new Childcare Handbook in the spirit of the terrible new time. Years pass. Too much in the wind of the world, his friend literally reverts to childhood, at which point Stephen very slowly begins to come alive, though the world around him continues to die of the cancer of the state. He and Julie come together again. There has been some mystical flummery – beautifully written but somewhat discordant in a text otherwise wisely restrained – and a child is born in hope. But any sense of affirmation the text espouses must inch through the bars of that desolate bass, that recurring image of the desert into which any child will, this time, be born.

– *Interzone* 23, Spring 1988 [written late 1987]

3. Various Reviews

1.

Half a century and 360 books have passed since Isaac Asimov first began to publish sf, and the daunting flood continues. But even a machine for writing must eventually sense the coming of night, and in recent books Dr Asimov has consciously begun to put his vision of the world into final form. The four huge novels he has published since 1982 – with more in the pipeline – are determined attempts to link the Elijah Bailey robot novels of his middle career to the Foundation stories of his early years; as these series were written over a span of decades, and in their original form had nothing to do with one another, this project may seem both grandiose and foredoomed, but the rage for order scoffs at petty decorum. Similarly, there can be no other reason for the writing of *Fantastic Voyage II: Destination Brain* (Doubleday, 1987) than an overpowering hunger to make retroactive sense of – and to redeem – one of the few creative botches of his long career.

The first *Fantastic Voyage* (1966), which novelizes the film of the same name and leaves intact most of the pseudo-scientific absurdities of the original, was an embarrassingly silly book for a scientist to write. Asimov's redemptive strategy in *Destination Brain* is straightforward. He simply tells the story again, but in his own words. In *Fantastic Voyage*, a miniaturized crew of doctors inside a wee submarine struggles through the bloodstream of a defecting Soviet scientist and cures him of a blood clot by zapping it; they then escape through a tear duct before slamming back to normal size. In *Destination Brain*, an American scientist, who understands all about the "skeptic nodes" in the brain which engender thought at a molecular level, is kidnapped by benign Russians who understand all about how miniaturization can be accomplished without violating quantum physics. A Russian genius lies in an irreversible coma, but may retain the secret of faster-than-light space travel in his nodes. Duly miniaturized, the crew of scientists penetrate the molecular level of Shapirov's brain, only to find echoes of their own thoughts somersaulting down his skeptic axons. Slowly the American scientist comes to realize that he has discovered telepathy.

If even this sounds pretty silly – and it does – an actual reading of the book gives a somewhat different impression. Like so many nineteenth-century tales of miniaturization, *Destination Brain* is in reality an educational guided tour of the human innards, and is recounted with all the elated clarity for which, as an expounder of popular science, Asimov is justly famous. If nothing much actually happens in the 100,000 words of this illuminated lecture, for the Russian dies without imparting any of his secrets, and telepathy remains no more than a gleam in the eye of an American talking head, the text still closes with the sense of a task well done, of a gaffe redeemed, a lesson taught, another fruitful shudder of the writing machine.

II.

It is a good thing that Orson Scott Card gives interviews. In a recent one, on being asked about the simultaneous publication of *Wyrms* (Arbor House, 1987) and *Seventh Son* (Tor, 1987), he made it clear that the former title had languished for some time in publishers' vaults before being released, and that *Seventh Son* (with sequels in tow) more fully represented the current state of his art. It is good to know this. *Wyrms* is a humdrum quest novel with pretensions its author was clearly incapable of fulfilling, while *Seventh Son* begins what may be a significant recasting in fantasy terms of the tall tale of America.

But at least *Wyrms* has more sevens. On the planet Imakulata (readers of the famed French comic strip *Asteryx the Gaul* may have some idea where Card gets his weird taste in monikers), 343 generations after a human colony has been founded by a Greek Orthodox Space Captain, things have come to a pretty pass. Murderous young Patience, daughter of the deposed Heptarch and herself the rightful seventh seventh seventh Heptarch, plays Cinderella to the usurper's daughters while biding her time. When her father dies (ultimately at her hands) and the usurper orders her own assassination, she is at last given the chance to start killing people with her noose and poison darts, rather like Modesty Blaise.

Escaping the usurper's realm with her mysterious tutor Angel, she begins the long trek to Skyfoot, where Unwyrm, a classical bug-eyed monster with an ominous appendage, has been awaiting his bride since the Space Captain first gave him a taste for human folk. It is anticipated that the result of his mating with the seventh seventh seventh daughter of the Space Captain will be the birth of the Christos, who will redemptively unite in his one flesh the humans and the natives of Imakulata. The *reason* for this anticipation is given us by neither Mr Card nor Mr Unwyrm. On the road Patience picks up a brace of deposed native sibling rulers (Reck and Ruin are their deft soubriquets), a huge indomitable human male named Will, and some odds and ends. In the dizzy mayhem which concludes *Wyrms*, the bad perish and the good get married. Patience is rewarded with the entire world. She deserves no better.

A very simple premise fires *Seventh Son*, set at the end of the eighteenth century in an America which never experienced a Revolution because Oliver Cromwell lived to a great old age consolidating his Commonwealth. It is that some forms of magic actually work. Because Cromwell's heirs are the sort of Christians who find magic threatening to their rigid pieties, the American colonies have become populated, or in their view infested, with refugees from the Old World who boast various innate or acquired knacks. Young Alvin Miller, who in later volumes will be known as Alvin Maker, is the seventh son of a seventh son, and therefore comes burdened with magic potential far beyond the norm. As with Patience in *Wyrms*, there are even hints that he may represent a Second Coming. Future volumes, of which there will be several, may confirm this [but only three have yet appeared 1995].

In *Seventh Son* it is clear only that in a world of seers and dowsers and torches (who read "heart-fires"), Alvin is a healer of people and things. He is a maker, and may become the Maker. Water, allied to the eroding nothingness of his primordial adversary the Unmaker, is his enemy. His childhood in the small community of Vigor Church, which is located in Wobbish Territory (ie Indiana), has moments of Edenic joy when he and his family seem saturated with light, as in a John Ford film. But the adversary continues to loosen the knots of the world, a Christian minister identifies Alvin with the Devil, and political strife looms on the horizon. Alvin acquires an ally in the wandering Taleswapper, whose true name is William Blake, an impertinent suggestion on Card's part, but an effective one. Though Taleswapper quotes only a few of the simpler early poems, and though he resembles Daniel Boone to an uneasy degree, future volumes may see his portrait grow in maturity, and some of the complexity of the later Blakean vision may grace this alternate America. In the meantime, he and Alvin manage to survive the first years of the saga.

There are dangers of chauvinism and easy nostalgia in creating an America so clearly woven by the hands of the living God. Not to speak of the dangers of creating the God Himself. But there is also something deeply heart-wrenching about an America come true, even if it is only a dream, a fantasy novel. So far so good. The first volume of *The Tales of Alvin Maker* is sharp and clean and bracing. May its Maker grow.

III.

In *The Movement of Mountains* (St Martin's Press, 1987), which is his first novel, Michael Blumlein has managed two significant accomplishments. He has written one of the best books of the year. He has also managed to be influenced by Gene Wolfe, and live to tell his tale. The author of *The Book of the New Sun* (1980–1983), himself a very considerable parodist of earlier writers, has a knack of autonomy; his work seems self-contained, aloof, serene, and every passage seems intended down to the last detail. There would seem to be very little to extract from a Wolfe novel, except devotion to craft and to the job at hand. All the same, *The Movement of Mountains*, perhaps partly through being so much an accomplishment in its own right, is a recognizably Wolfean text.

Jules Ebert's story, which he tells himself as a form of confession to an unseen brother, begins at some point in the distant near future on Earth, in a cyberpunk vision of Greater San Francisco here called Barea (that is, Bay Area). Dr Ebert is one of the elite, and lives like the rest of the privileged in an armored enclave; the poor run

wild in the streets, chased by mutated dogs, and haunted by the first signs of an
AIDS-like viral disease which seems to ravage their psyches as well as their bodies.
He is a medical doctor, and a victim of bulimia, governed by insatiable gorging and
desperate fasts. He is very fat. He is in love with Jessica, who is attracted by fat men.
In most books their relationship would be doomed by its apparent grotesqueness; it
is a measure of Blumlein's stern and original mind that in The Movement of Mountains
their relationship only grows deeper.

Battered by poverty and the world, Jessica contracts with the huge drug firm
Mannus to do research on the planet of Eridis, where a race of biologically engineered slaves has been crafted to mine an invaluable drug. Ebert follows her. As
doctor to the huge entrapped Domers, who resemble him physically, Ebert becomes
politically radicalized by their plight, just as Jessica has been. Indeed, during his absence, she has been sleeping with one of them. Soon, however, she begins to show
the symptoms of the viral infection, now known as Herpes Amnesiac Syndrome or
HAS, and dies in a fall. Ebert dissects her, his hands dispassionate, his heart full.
He discovers HAS to be less a disease than an agent of transformation. Victims
share one another's thoughts; they live one another. The Domer she has slept with
becomes a revolutionary thanks to this process, and Ebert assists in a successful
revolt.

Back on Earth, he finds that a panicked government has made it illegal to contact HAS without taking treatment. His response is radical, and moves the final
pages of the novel into transcendental realms. In hiding, he starts to tell his story.
Some Wolfean elements are obvious – certain tricks of narrative; the confessional
form itself; the adult rightness of the love affair; the unflustered confrontation of
the text with its darkest implications – and some are less so. At the heart of both
writers there is something implacable, as though nothing could budge either of
them from saying exactly what he intended to say. That they both survive in a world
of commercial fiction speaks well for that world, and for its readership. Michael
Blumlein speaks well for us.

– The Washington Post Book World, 30 August 1987

IN HER introduction to Imaginary Lands (Julia MacRae, 1987), managing to sound
simultaneously fey and brazen, Robin McKinley first tells us how two New York editors vied to purchase her proposed anthology of original fantasy stories to be composed with "a particularly strong sense of location," then second goes on to boast
that "not many of the stories" in the finished volume actually fit her original specifi-
cations. It is not difficult to confirm this. Only one of the contributions to Imaginary

Lands – not, incidentally, the author's own effort – is about an imaginary land.

Peter Dickinson [he and Robin McKinley are now married 1995] should therefore be given credit for understanding his brief. "Flight," moreover, is the finest tale in the book (which was published last year in America) and has already merited reprinting elsewhere. Detailing the relationship over centuries between the Empire of Obanah and the White Rock Tribe which resists its sway, "Flight" seamlessly meshes history and geography into a densely hilarious and melancholy parable, whose implications say a great deal about our own devastating century. It is a tale to grace any anthology.

Any fantasy, of course, will be set in something like an imaginary land, if only as backdrop, and the remaining stories in the volume do at least fit this trivial reading of their remit. James P Blaylock's "Paper Dragons" limns a gauzy fog-choked magic-realist California; Michael de Larrabeiti's "The Curse of Igamor" might be set in an alternate Provence; Robert Westall's glowing Oz-like England, in "The Big Rock Candy Mountain," has some of the through-composed populousness of Joan Aiken's visions of a truer, brighter, histrionic Britain. But "The Stone Fey," McKinley's drab entry, "Tam Lin" by Joan D Vinge, "Evian Steel" by Jane Yolen, which dips rather gingerly into Arthurian legend, "Stranger Blood" by P C Hodgell, which is not remarkably readable, and "The Old Woman and the Storm" by Patricia A McKillip all give off a vague stale Celtic aroma terribly familiar to readers of contemporary American fantasy, whether written for teenagers or adults. Menarche bulks large in stories of this sort, and euphemized sex. The landscapes come readymade: hills, streams, mist, gnarled trees, runes, sacred groves, sheep. But there is really nothing, in these imaginary lands, to remark upon.

Joan Aiken seems lit from within. Her stories are like windows through which lanterns glow. Even a minor collection like *A Goose on Your Grave* (Cape, 1987), mostly made up of exemplary fables about children sidling into the minefields of adolescence, seems to set the darkness alight. Perhaps it is because her stories are not only wise, not only compassionate, but are also deeply gay, in the old sense. Nothing in this volume may generate the sustained exuberance of the Dido novels, but even the most casual of its eleven tales seems charged with potential joy. For the loneliest child in *A Goose on your Grave*, windows may at any point open onto the theatre of a populous and magic world.

This crowded world is full of flamboyant and at times unremitting melodrama, as undoubtedly befits Aiken's theatrical vision. In "Your Mind is a Mirror," two children begin to learn how to navigate the treacherous shoals of their father's desper-

ate depression, and may have found the key to unlock him from his prison of redundancy, longing, grief. In "Wing Quack Flap" and "Snow Horse" and "Potter's
Grey," the young learn magically how to sidestep their elders' life-denying iron control over the workings of the world. In "Lob's Girl," a faithful dog returns from the
dead to rouse its mistress from an otherwise fatal coma, in scenes that seem resur-
rected from the Victorian stage. In "Homer's Whistle," which is the darkest and
possibly the finest story here collected, an adolescent boy contrives a deathly return
through time to an idyllic cottage in Devon long drowned under the waters of a res-
ervoir; but his escape is precisely into death, and the narrator of the tale sometimes
thinks he "can hear the brown wall of water rolling down the valley...coming to
overwhelm the little house." But it is against this brown wall of water that the joy
seems sharpest; for the joy of even this minor Aiken book is wise, and sturdy, and
most welcome.

– Published as two separate reviews in *Times Literary Supplement*, 7 August 1987 and 10 July 1987

IT IS 1939. Eleven-year-old Vivian Smith has been sent away from London to avoid
the bombing, which has now begun after the months of phoney war which followed the outbreak of hostilities at Christmas 1938. She gets off the train and is met
by a boy whom she takes to be her cousin. But he is not her cousin. He bundles her
into a kind of silvery booth, which translates them to an utterly strange glowing
place. She has been abducted to Time City.

A Tale of Time City (Methuen, 1987), Diana Wynne Jones's nineteenth novel and
one of her more exuberant, has begun. The title is well-chosen. In the style of her
first rather helterskelter books, and in contrast to more sombre recent releases like
Fire and Hemlock (1984), the 285 pages of *A Tale* are all story. As the home of the Time
Patrol, responsible for monitoring the huge horseshoe of centuries which make up
the cycle of human history, Time City is in a state of crisis. Jostling the date of World
War Two earlier and earlier, an invasive presence has begun to shake reality loose in
the twentieth century, one of the Unstable Eras which provide generating energy to
fuel calmer eras. Catastrophe looms as Time City approaches – backwards, as it
must do in a kind of balancing act against the "real" direction of time – the end of
all things.

Mistaking Vivian for the disruptive invader, Jonathan and his younger companion Sam have taken matters into their own hands. When they discover the truth –
that she is only Vivian Smith – they must attempt to keep her identity secret from
their parents, who run Time City while its semi-mythical founder Faber John sleeps
like Arthur under a rock, while at the same time continuing to search for the villain

49

or villains responsible for the destabilization of the eras. An adroit android enters the picture, and a too-plausible older youth, and two Guardians who have lost their caskets containing the elements necessary to reconstitute reality when time ends, and a congeries of deeply confused adults who understand all too little of what is happening. Prominent among them is Jonathan's father, a portrait both hilarious and sympathetic of a man who only uneasily wears the robes of state.

And so forth. At times it all rather resembles an enormously extended episode of Dr Who, with grotesque dangers almost flippantly survived, and time-travel paradoxes knocking everyone for loops. Now and then the piled-up complexities of Ms Jones's story interact negatively with the streamlined thinness of texture her swift and reckless pacing necessarily entails, so that occasional moments of confusion are inevitable. Younger readers, all the same, being perhaps rather less likely than adults to question the patchwork quilt of sf and fantasy premises that underpin the tale, may find its dazzling speed genuinely exhilarating, its grotesqueries unshocking. At story's close, they will also find a lesson or two.

Present from the first as a burly bad-tempered tutor, Faber John recovers his memory in the nick – or more accurately the end – of time, and confounds the ambitions of the power-seeking family responsible for all the tumult. Selfishness is laid bare and punished, but with compassion; and Vivian brings the attention of the assembled adults of Time City sharply to bear on the subject of their collective guardianship. After the hilarity and the confusion – time travel stories, especially those built on paradoxes, are inherently difficult to narrate with any clarity – a mellow and familial glow suffuses the final pages of A Tale. It is a mark of Ms Jones's highly deliberate craft that this washed and humane glow of closing seems perfectly in order, and thoroughly welcome.

– Times Literary Supplement, 20 November 1987

BEGINNING Ægypt (Bantam, 1987) is not half the battle; it is very nearly the whole war. John Crowley's fifth book, the first part of a projected quartet, is much less a novel than a series of portals. Full of beginnings, plot spirals that return us to beginnings, and sudden vistas that signal even bigger beginnings to come, it does in fact literally begin several times – with an Author's Note that becomes part of the text, a Prologue in Heaven after Goethe's Faust, a Prologue on Earth to balance the first prologue, and more than one chapter of initiation. And each beginning – each portal – remains open. Nothing is resolved. The last pages of Ægypt close on nothing.

It is a dizzying experience, achieved with unerring security of technique, in a prose of serene and smiling gravitas. Crowley's history as a published writer – his first three novels were released as genre sf, and his current publishers released the prize-winning Little, Big (1981) as a trade paperback – has not been of the sort to generate a wide reputation, and it will be of great interest to learn if he can reach a welcoming public with this daunting anomaly of a book, this gaping portal that leaves us staring into a deeply strange world.

Just what this book is – just what Ægypt will become when complete – may be almost impossible to say. In conventional generic terms, the first volume is neither fish nor fowl, neither fantasy nor mainstream, while at the same time it adroitly mixes both modes together. The text contains discourses with angels, traversings of the heavenly spheres along routes mapped out by Renaissance magi like Giordano Bruno and John Dee, and a weaving of threads of preternatural coincidence; but Crowley parenthesizes this material by presenting it in the form of passages from a series of children's books. These magical tales, written by the late Ffellowes Kraft, have haunted Pierce Moffett from early childhood. The Prologue in Heaven, which recounts John Dee's first sight of angels, and his first intimation that out of infinite smallness or largeness a Sagittarian visitor was approaching our sphere to transform it utterly, is from one of Kraft's texts. The Prologue on Earth shows Pierce, as a child, already haunted by Kraft's life of Giordano Bruno, the magus, mathematician, astrologer and scientist who helped create the modern world while searching backwards through time for Ægypt.

Pierce Moffett's name reflects his nature, for he is both penetrant and woolly, rather like Ægypt itself. From childhood he has longed to inhabit a world he could recognize as being intended, pregnant with meaning, animate; and this yearning, this sense of desiderium, informs his every moment. As an adult he becomes an historian, looking for a version of the world that might account for the nature of things, but in vain. Victim and master of a poignant yearning heterosexuality, he falls uncontrollably in love with several women, each time with a view to seeing the universe entire. Signs and portents of some imminent transformation multiply around him – or perhaps he breeds them, perhaps Pierce Moffett is himself the visitor to our sphere who will bring the world alive, as it has always been.

The Manhattan Pierce inhabits for much of his life, like the Manhattan of Little, Big, of Jerome Charyn's numerous urban fables, and of Mark Helprin's Winter's Tale (1983), is very much a storied isle, drenched in the story of itself, like a fount. It is not merely a city. It is the City, and one only leaves the City if one is in search of the Golden Age. When Pierce finally leaves Manhattan it is to write a book about the meaning of the world, which he hopes to call Ægypt; and it is only appropriate that in Blackbury Jambs, his new home town somewhere upstate, he finds a world far more drenched with implication than the slightly anodyne pastoral it first seems to represent.

This part of rural New York has long been dominated by the Rasmussen family, whose charitable Foundation owns the nearby home of the late Ffellowes Kraft. Pierce soon meets Rosie Rasmussen, whom he has confused with another Rose – Rose Ryder – so that he cannot tell which "sister" he has instantly fallen in love with. Learning of his interest in Kraft, Rosie asks him to examine an unfinished manuscript left in the house. Pierce soon discovers that Kraft's unfinished tale of the meeting of John Dee and Giordano Bruno was to have been called Ægypt, and that in all essentials it was the book Pierce hoped to write. But here the ingenious assemblage of beginnings stops, and the volume ends.

The portrait of Pierce Moffett, gangling, vulnerable, sharp and sheepish, is lovingly comprehensive (he is a kind of portmanteau of Smoky Barnable and Auberon, Little, Big's two main viewpoint characters). The inhabitants of Blackbury Jambs sing through their lives like escaped children, for that is their pastoral destiny; but at intervals seem human, too. The narrative itself, which spirals through time and space rather like a maze that Pierce must penetrate, startles the reader again and again with the eloquent rightness of the web of coincidences which structure it. And in moments of sudden realization, when Pierce sees for the first time something he had always inwardly known, the universe of Ægypt seems to talk itself awake. But what this artful (and sometimes arch) opening of portals will amount to, we can only guess.

As Crowley makes clear in his Author's Note, the spirit of Dame Frances Yates (1899–1981) of the Warburg Institute permeates his text, and it is to her that Ægypt owes its central thrust. At the heart of Yates's revolutionary analysis of late 16th-century intellectual history stands the figure of Giordano Bruno (1548–1600), whose defense of Copernicus's heliocentrism has traditionally been thought a proof of his essential modernity. But for Yates, Bruno's heliocentrism points rather to the figure of Hermes Trismegistus, a Gnostic Greek whose esoteric writings the Renaissance mistakenly thought to be pre-Christian, and to originate in Egypt.

Though it might seem impossibly intricate to the unlearned eye, the universe Bruno understood Hermes to describe was a single living entity which, in all humbleness and love, could be understood. To that end, he transformed the Lullian Art of Memory into a kind of holy pun. His Theatre of the World – his Ægypt – was intended both to show forth and to embody a triumphal unity of human and universal soul. His Ægypt wore the spiritual (and actual) countenance of the universe. It was a universe in which nothing (Kraft and Pierce long to believe) was illusion.

At times most movingly, at other times rather doggedly, Ægypt embodies the sense that it is itself meant ultimately to read as a Theatre of the World. Future volumes will undoubtedly weave Bruno and Pierce closer together; more interestingly perhaps, the text may also accompany Queen Elizabeth's astrologer John Dee to Bohemia, where he attempted – reading the signs of the times – to bring about a new order, a realm of the sun. He failed. Ægypt is set about a decade ago; as future volumes move towards the millennium, an utterly new world might well become visible, born anew. The quartet would be its Theatre.

– *The New York Times Book Review*, 3 May 1987

FOR A WHILE it looks as though there may be a story in this book. A bumbling professor at Corinth University in Upstate New York comes to believe he has been contacted by an extraterrestrial presence called Ohcnas, who has a tale to tell. He has murdered another alien named Nod. The bulk of *Kayo* (Dutton, 1987) by James McConkey is made up of his confession.

This may sound almost straightforward enough, but no one who reverses the letters of Ohcnas and Nod will be fooled for more than a moment. The confessor is Sancho Panza and the victim is Don Quixote. Through this extremely broad hint, and through a number of other nudges of the authorial elbow, James McConkey signals to the reader not to take anything literally. We are in Looking-Glass Country, like Alice.

Ohcnas, whose real name turns out to be Kayo Aznap, inhabits a Wonderland version of America governed by a President who has been in power for decades, under a succession of names. His current incarnation is as a canny old duffer. But always, beneath the surface, it is the same man, the same policies, the same world endlessly rehashed.

Theme parks cover the land, for Aznap has convinced the administration that their construction offers the best way to "make people value anew what they've complacently lived with for decades." Fences, therefore, are put around "ghettoes, disposal dumps with their leaky fluids, wilderness areas with their dead lakes and leafless trees, depressed farming regions" and so on, and admission is charged. Federal welfare is thus eschewed, and the "downtrodden" are made proud of "what they were."

Over this "Unitedian" paradise extends a vast dome, providing a defense against aggressors, and transforming the Associated States United themselves into a vast theme park. The President is satisfied. Life can go on in safety, except for the fact that Nod torments him with his quixotic visions of a finer humanity. Who (asks the President) will rid me of this Nod? Aznap is forced to volunteer.

Nod and Aznap – Don Quixote and Sancho Panza – meet in a chintzy pastoral parkland somewhere in the hinterlands. It will spoil no reader's pleasure, for the murder is described in a teaser prologue to Aznap's long narrative, to mention the fact that Sancho eventually kills Nod, in a Wild West theme park, in front of an admiring audience. The message ends.

But the original professor, who closely resembles Nod, has disappeared. A second professor, who finds the text of *Kayo* in the first professor's computer, speculates about the disappearance in terms which make it clear he thinks very little of his predecessor, Professor "M," or of his contrivance of a tale from outer space. Through this coy device McConkey himself – who is writing the professor who is reading the professor who is telling the story he heard in a dream or what – may be attempting to disarm any disappointment his readers may feel at finishing a tale that so glaringly fails to develop, that indeed ends where it began; but consider this reader undisarmed.

For no one is any the wiser, in the end. What any paraphrase of *Kayo*'s thin narrative must obscure is the fact that McConkey, himself a professor at Cornell University, has written an intensely academic self-referential "post-modern" spoof of the satirical utopias more often found in European than in American sf. Perhaps because they are undemanding of either author or reader, mirror worlds or upsidownias proliferate in this sort of satire. The trouble with them is that no one, not the author, nor the characters in the text, nor the reader, ever believes in them for a moment.

This exiguity of Aznap's contrived world suits Professor McConkey's purposes very neatly, for he is much less interested in realities than he is in the textual games he plays with his mirrors, his references to Cervantes's masterpiece, his continual elbowing the reader with hints that *Kayo* is nothing but a lot of words signifying only that they are words.

But games of this sort collapse into tedium and nullity if they are not infused with some overriding passion – for life, for the act of fabrication, for words themselves. McConkey's obvious models for *Kayo* are books like Vladimir Nabokov's deeply elegiac *Pale Fire* (1962), or John Barth's *Giles Goat-Boy* (1966). Both of these texts are self-conscious, arch, and self-referential; but both – over and above the burn of genius that carries the game in each case – are buzzing with energy, full of love for the act of storytelling. *Kayo* on the other hand lacks energy, lacks love. Because it is only a game, it crumbles into dust.

– *Los Angeles Times*, 17 May 1987

THE unplumbed vacancies of its northern marches may foster in some the illusion that Canada is a large country. It is not an impression that should survive a reading of the 41 claustrophobic tales gathered together by Margaret Atwood and Robert Weaver in *The Oxford Book of Canadian Short Stories in English* (Oxford University Press Canada, 1987), most of which are set in urban centres stretched out along the hot American border, as though for warmth. This is natural enough. Most Canadian writers (like most Canadians) live in cities, some of them huge. At the same time, a sense of driven solitude marks most of the stories in this uneven but formidable anthology. Wherever they may live, Canadian writers seem to abide at the edge of an encompassing void of wilderness. This northern desert does not much resemble the Circean Wilderness hankered after by Americans in the warm south and thrusting heat of their own huge culture. The Canadian wilderness is faceless, unpeopled, unstoried. Against the vacuum of nullity of almost the whole of the land, tales of human survival, even set in the cold heart of Toronto, may seem at times like brave hallucinations.

It may be foolish to assume that Margaret Atwood, whose own book on Canadian literature was entitled *Survival*, provided most of the cognitive purposiveness that shapes this anthology, while Robert Weaver, an esteemed and generous editor long at the centre of English Canadian culture, provided its daunting breadth of selection, but depth and breadth this fine assemblage does have in abundance; though it is strangely organized. Stories are published in the order of their authors' dates of birth (each date being given three times in the book), but are not themselves dated. As a consequence, stories from authors with long careers, like "Last Spring They Came Over" by Morley Callaghan (1903–1990), seem oddly lost in time; and stories which come late in a a long life, like the astonishing "From Flores" by Ethel Wilson (1888–1980), consort uneasily with the toothless jocosity of Stephen Leacock or the florid sentimentalizing of Charles G D Roberts. And given the obsessive fixing of stories in time and place so characteristic of Canadian writing, even the second half of the book, solely populated by authors under 50, suffers from this fuzzing over of dates. It could easily be remedied.

Throughout there is a compulsion to remember. Story after story comes in memoir form, sometimes barely fictionalized. Isolated farms are remembered; snow-bound villages, lonely childhoods, bitter illnesses, innumerable summer cottages domesticating the northwoods; the fragility of survival in small town or huge city is constantly recollected by characters who have barely stayed alive as marriages decay, jobs collapse, Canadian weather shrivels the cold sky. As text or subtext, the wilderness is omnipresent. This focus inwards to the northern void may explain a paucity of references to the United States in an anthology of stories from writers deeply aroused by questions of national identity; it is as though solitude and wilderness served them as something uniquely Canadian, tokens of individuality to fend off the vast remorseless magnet of America.

It is in fact a strenuous job to remain a Canadian writer. Sometimes it is a grim task. *The Oxford Book of Canadian Stories* could not be called a happy book, though at least a dozen tales, most of them in the second half, are superbly artful, including "The Sin Eater" by Atwood herself. The American and English editions of her *Bluebeard's Egg and Other Stories* (Cape, 1987), which excludes "The Sin Eater" but adds two other tales, could not be called a happy book either, though much of it is certainly hilarious. *Bluebeard's Egg* shows all the rich mastery of a writer in the full mature flood of her craft. Her stories are sophisticated, reticent, ornate, stark, supple, stiff, savage or forgiving; they are exactly what she wants them to be. They are stories from the prime of life.

That they are deeply Canadian stories is sometimes perfectly clear, sometimes a matter of nuance. As memoiristic fixings of the solitudinous past, "Significant Moments in the Life of my Mother," "Hurricane Hazel" and "In Search of the Rattlesnake Plantain" all share a recognizeable Canadian sense of fragility and airlessness. The empty northern wastes inform "Unearthing Suite," despite that story's almost exultant close, and "The Salt Garden," which dazzlingly conflates the void and nuclear holocaust, and "Spring Song of the Frogs," where ageing is seen against a world that becomes increasingly indecipherable. Despite its almost sociological detail and its air of slightly desolate calm, "Spring Song" is a tale of terror, as is the title story; the protagonists of both are beginning to lose control of the intimate human patterns of knowledge and habituation which stave off the vacuum of the real world. If it is a universal theme, its intricate delicate bleakness flowers best in Canadian soil.

Just as in the *Oxford Book of Canadian Stories*, the United States is hardly mentioned. Through the stressful urban dance of their days, Atwood's protagonists seem never to watch television, or buy magazines, or work for corporations, or do anything that might bring them face to face with the obliterating warmth of America. This is surely deliberate. For Margaret Atwood the matter of Canada is survival, and its face is to the Vvoid. Nothing must fudge the lineaments of this microcosm she has shaped to serve her creative and didactic ends. In *Bluebeard's Egg* nothing does. From the Canada she has created, worlds unfold.

– *Times Literary Supplement*, 12 June 1987

THERE'S something odd about the title. The editors (Christopher Evans and Robert Holdstock) of *Other Edens* (Unwin Paperbacks, 1987), which is a collection of original sf and fantasy stories from authors based in Great Britain, must have thought it up on their own, and they certainly must have bumped up against some pretty odd thoughts while making their choice. The first odd thing they must have thought was that it derived from William Shakespeare's *King Richard III*. "A horse!" (one imagines Mr Evans musing to Mr Holdstock) "A horse! a horse! my other Eden for a horse!" "Hang about – " (says the latter ed to the former ed, shaken by a wild surmise [from the Keats guy]) " – I think we've got our title!" Another odd thing Messers Holdstock and Evans must have thought about their title was that, despite proclaiming on page viii its irrelevance to the contents of the anthology they put together, it was still worth retaining on the cover of this solid book. At some point, however, doubts began to assail the two editors, for they clearly came to the eventual decision that enough was enough, and that – as they state unequivocally at the beginning of their introduction – no more anthologies of this sort should ever be published: "Welcome" (they say) "to a rare phenomenon these days – a collection of original sf and fantasy stories from Britain. It's a rarity we hope will not last."

All the same, for those readers who remained unswayed by this stark pessimism, a treat was in store. Beginning (one trusts) with the assumption that the title was 1) as irrelevant as most anthology titles turn out to be and 2) derived in any case from *King Richard II* ("This royal throne of kings, this sceptred isle, / This earth of majesty, this seat of Mars, / This other Eden" etcetera), they will have plowed on into the contents, and will have found something of a feast there. They will have also found out why Evans and Holdstock necessarily failed to create in *Other Edens* anything like the theme anthology their title portends. Very simply, they couldn't do so because there weren't enough active writers to troll for original stories that fit their presumed remit. Of sf/fantasy writers in this country currently active as short story writers, most are represented in this book. Only a few of them (to be precise, none, actually, in the event) could logically be expected to have Other Eden stories to hand, *whatever* an Other Eden story is: Messers Holdstock and Evans do no more than "hint at pastoral idylls." (How different it must be in America, where an anthologist can troll hundreds of active writers for tales that fit a particular theme.) So we are left with a bunch of stories sharing little more than a sense of betrayed landscape, and framed by a Jim Burns cover more ostensibly "edenic" than anything inside the book.

Some of these stories are perhaps a touch feeble, several are very strong indeed. Many give off the slightly baggy odour of the excerpt. Even though M John Harrison typically writes tales whose implications flood mercilessly through the tollgates of the form, in "Small Heirlooms" that flood is less meticulously timed than usual – one could almost say of his best stories that they were flood-dances in amber (a phrase amenable of much contrite explanation, which it will one day receive [not yet, because right now I haven't a clue what I meant 1995]), and of "Small Heirlooms" what a certain telegram once said of Venice: "Streets filled with water. Please advise." In any case, internal evidence makes it clear that the tale comes from a forthcoming novel whose projected title is The Course of the Heart. Robert Holdstock's heightened "Scarrowfell" also floods the frail tale it ostensibly relates with a jumble of moods, too many characters, too much music, an expiation/initiation too complex to be explained in the pages it takes, and bevies of mummers: if not from the forthcoming Lavondyss, it must inhabit the same universe. If Brian Aldiss's "The Price of Cabbages" does not herald a gamy picaresque, then it is slightly too long for the well-telegraphed punchline that merely terminates what one feels to be an episode. Michael Moorcock's "The Frozen Cardinal" has a polished insinuating grace, and a neat hook, but reads as a minute tessera in the large mosaic of his work.

The Aldiss and the Moorcock are both set on other planets. Moorcock's is a metaphysic of ice, Aldiss's a factory farm. It is entirely typical of British sf/fantasy that all but one of the remaining tales take place on Earth, most in an identifiable Britain, though David Langford's "In a Land of Sand and Ruin and Gold" is set at the end of time, where a point about terminal boredom is made with lackadaisical grace, and Garry Kilworth's stunning "Triptych" could be set anywhere. A cheap description of "Triptych" is that it's a set of three interlocked parables, each a mirror for the others, each facet illustrating some cul-de-sac extremity of the human condition; to try to say more with any concision would be foolish. Ian Watson's "The Emir's Clock" boasts an extremely neat bit of clockwork metaphysic, but embedded within an extremely offhand narrative – something Mr Watson may have had lying around the house, and now it's lying around mine. R M Lamming's "Sanctity" is deft and drear in its rendering of a British dystopian tyranny (details on application).

The best remaining stories are sexual. Lisa Tuttle's "The Wound" may be the most excellently executed tale in the anthology. It is no more – and therefore no less – than itself; not a bit from a book, not a bight from a fleuve. There is a feminist argument within the cruel professional turns of this tale of metamorphosis, but in no way does that argument leak into meta-textual rhetoric. At story's end, there is nothing left to dispute. This reviewer's agreement with the premises he feels are embodied within "The Wound" has nothing to do with his sense that these premises are unanswerable, everything to do with his sense that a story which exhausts its premises gains an unassailable being. Tanith Lee's "Crying in the Rain," set in a dystopian Britain corroded by radioactive pollution, also achieves itself fully within its own terms, with a complex economy not always found in her voluminous novels; the human muscle exposed in this story of family survival is both wrenching and heartening. Christopher Evans's savage little fable of hysterical patriarchy – set very inconspicuously on another planet, and potentially expandable novelwards – carries a raft of well-differentiated characters in the direction of a calamity of sexual initiation, and stops sagely short. The saddest – indeed the most anguished – story in the book is Keith Roberts's "Piper's Wait," which unfolds its layers of pain unendingly, for its antiqued tragedy of sexual nausea is related by a modern narrator who seems mystically to share, to have privy access to, the Piper's trauma. Long ago a wordless prescient wandering Piper falls in love with a young girl, who begins to sleep around in his absence. He returns to save her by piping the Devil out of her suddenly post-pubertal limbs, but at the climax of his rite, when she awards him a vertical grin, he sees that she is the Devil's utterly. The story ties itself in knots, but remains naked.

So it is an anthology with a name to remember but not to think about very hard. There are some sloppy efforts of the sort that creep into most original anthologies, but also there are three or four stories in *Other Edens* that anyone interested in the condition of British writing must read. A second volume would be welcome. *A Horse in Eden*. It has a ring to it.

– Foundation 40, Summer 1987

FOR much of *Glowstone* (Morrow, 1987), his thirteenth novel, MacDonald Harris exercises his craft with almost uncanny stealth. In effortlessly limpid prose he tells a tale as inevitable and uncontrived as the flow of a brook, or so it seems, without raising his voice, without seeming to care about the tragicomedy he unfolds. The neutral velvet hush of the telling of the novel, like the substance of its title, emits no more than a quiet deadly glow. Or so it seems.

Like his best-known novel, *The Balloonist* (1976), *Glowstone* is set in Belle Epoque Paris in the years before the outbreak of World War One; and as in all his best work, timeslips – either metaphorical or, as in *Screenplay* (1982), literal – generate his profoundest effects. In his best work, genuine historical figures are subjected to a silent and subtle sea-change, through an alchemy of time, so that they stand both in and out of the real world, rather as dreams do. Crispin, the Swedish journal-keeping hero of *The Balloonist*, was in fact Salomon August Andree, a Swedish engineer of some eccentricity, whose attempt to reach the North Pole by balloon ended in disease and death. Real film stars lurk beneath false names throughout the brilliant, ghastly 1920s arcadia *Screenplay* transforms Hollywood into. Claire Savarin-Decker of *Glowstone*, who discovers a mysterious radioactive substance in collaboration with her husband Paul, is of course Marie Curie. It is with Paul's death in 1906 – two weeks after the death of the real Pierre Curie – that the novel begins.

But first a short and very strange "Word to the Reader" introduces the narrator of the tale in the guise of a "Prologue," a quasi-animate figurine like the Commedia dell'Arte figure who comes on stage to animate the puppets in *I Pagliacci*. Though this figurine's human identity, beneath the mask of time, is not very difficult to tease out of the text, there are very good reasons for its being kept silent until the final pages, when the narrator reveals his/her name not to surprise the reader but to signal most movingly the end of the show, and its meaning. That show is the *Belle Epoque* itself, glowing like a vision of the Earthly Paradise for those who visit or inhabit it, but emitting deadly radiations all the while. For the century it introduces is this one.

The masquerade begins. Each character is simple and lucid and bathed in light, as though each swam in a literal emanation of the spirit of the age. Claire cherishes the memory of her husband through her ferociously single-minded exploration at the Savarin Institute of the ramifying implications of glowstone. Her doting assistant – magically named Lancelot – stumbles in her wake. Their daughter Hermine nears puberty with an ease that seems almost magical. Subsidiary characters drift through Paris like fireflies. And the wealthy American rancher Blanco White (strangely, Harris names him after the nineteenth-century English author of Unitarian sonnets) meets Claire in Colorado, where she is lecturing, and falls in love with her beauty, her purity of will. She dresses all in black, he (as his name signals, Commedia dell'Arte-like) in white. Escorting her back to Paris, he dances attendance upon her and the rest of the cast. Everyone in the harlequinade seems blessed by a kind of grace.

It is here the utter quietude of Harris's cunning craft begins quite deliberately to give way. Claire sickens. Like the sun-choked pastoral of the *Belle Epoque*, her glowstone grace is turning into a hectic flush. After the brief remission of a trip down the Seine to Monet's house at Giverny, whose glories Harris mutes for reasons that seem unclear, her disease begins to waste her dreadfully, augurs of hellishness infuse the text, and the plot thickens and tangles. In the final accounting, Blanco White – a rough-hewn version of Henry James's expatriate American besotted by the glitter and glow of old Europe – cannot purchase life for his beloved Claire, or for anyone else. The precise vantage from which the finally unmasked narrator views the fading actors and their desolated Paris is something of a *coup de théâtre*, and should be discovered in its proper place. One can only say that the vantage point is striking, that it is deftly and darkly introduced, and that the novel gains much autumnal brilliance from the perspective offered.

Radium is never mentioned, but its absence from the surface of the tale merely intensifies the force with which it shapes every moment of this requiem. All the same, though Claire and her companions pirouette gravely on a stage illuminated by that infernal glow, page after page of their story colors them in human hues as well. Their innocence may be appalling. It also touches the heart with a deep nostalgia. As a kind of alternate history of the last days of Europe before the lights went out, *Glowstone* may be MacDonald Harris's most amply resonant novel to date.

–*The Washington Post*, 5 July 1987

WHEN the Second World War began for the United States, casting a final shadow over the belated Edwardian sunset of the American Dream, Richard Yates was fifteen years old and Robert Coover was nine. They were both old enough to be haunted by the memory of that sunset of peace and seeming innocence, and by the coming of the night. Both *A Night at the Movies* and *Cold Spring Harbor* are set at the beginning of the 1940s, though it might be more accurate to say that Coover's collection of post-modernist fables takes its sustenance from that period, and both books are elegies for that vanished world.

A brash foregrounding of language and special effects may initially conceal the frozen melancholy permeating the tales collected in *A Night at the Movies* (Heinemann, 1987), but there can finally be no doubt as to the dark sadness revealed in its pages. For a short while, true enough, pizzazz may seem to prevail. Coover replaces the normal table of contents with a "Program" which spiels the night's attractions in terms directly evocative of the cinema in 1940, and gives the impression that stories like "Shootout at Gentry's Junction," "Charlie in the House of Rue," or "You Must Remember This" should be read as formal displays of fabulist wit. Like David Thomson's *Suspects* (1985), though to a much greater degree of fantastication, these stories expose the stars of cinema's psychic midnight to the fleering parlance of narrative fiction. They are never named, but we know them like our own dreams.

In "Shootout," Gary Cooper's archaic fragile rectitude fails to cope with a ribald adversary who incarnates chaos and death; in "Charlie," the bewildered ageing Charlie Chaplin of 1940 flounders deeper and deeper into a world where every prank brings death closer to real people; in "You Must Remember This," Humphrey Bogart and Ingrid Bergman engage in an obsessive sexual encounter that recasts *Casablanca* into terms inadmissable in 1942. These tales, and the interludes that separate them, are brazenly witty, but the homages they present are savagely disruptive of the film of nostalgia through which it has become comfortable to view the safe past before the troubles began, and cinema began to die like an aubade whose juice has been sucked, and the numbed audience wakes to find itself in daylight.

The movies of 1940 may work as solace for their viewers half a century later; for the citizens of 1940, they also served as models of the world. Throughout Richard Yates's *Cold Spring Harbor* (Delacorte, 1986), which is set on Long Island in 1942, a cinematic subtext constantly shapes everyone's behaviour, as well as their sense of what they ought to expect from adulthood, marriage, children, jobs. As in all of Yates's fiction since his first novel, the stunning *Revolutionary Road* (1961), these expectations are sapped by failures of luck, energy and purpose. As always in his work, almost everyone drinks too much, though no one remarks on the fact. As always, a seamless fug of psychic paralysis drowns everyone as in amber, even in these sunset years before the war.

The grind of everyday existence has gradually stripped young Evan Shepard of any dreams he may have had of a shapely life, just as bad luck and a stiff torpor have cost his father Charles the military career to which he had hoped to devote himself. Charles's wife has had a mental breakdown, and reproachfully haunts their small home in Cold Spring Harbor, which is a slightly down-market exurb of New York City. Gloria Drake, whose anodyne daughter Evan marries, is a compulsive talker, and the noise she makes deafens her to the small tragedies marring the lives she invades. Caught in paralyzed isolation, each lives alone, though surrounded; if Evan has aspirations, they dangerously resemble tales he may have picked up from the neighbouring movie house. When war comes, ear troubles disqualify him from service. He will see no action. Darkness begins to fall on Cold Spring Harbor and America.

Lives of such morose immobility should make for depressing reading, and much of Yates's work seems unbearably deterministic in its insistence upon the erosions of living. *Cold Spring Harbor*, however, though it is minor Yates, has an almost bracing effect, quite probably because of the elegiac distance from which it is narrated. Though the faltering centre of the plot may be Evan Shepard and his incoherent stumbling fall into an almost incestuous adultery, *Cold Spring Harbor*'s centre of consciousness is Evan's young brother-in-law, a character with little to do in 1940 over and above his attempts to survive adolescence, but with a great deal to remember. If there is any hopefulness in this tale of entrapment and paralysis set so long ago, it may well be the implicit sense that one young boy managed to escape, and now manages to remember, through the pages of this book. An elegy is preferable to a death sentence.

– *Times Literary Supplement*, 14 August 1987

IF THERE IS a ghost that haunts the labyrinths at the heart of Iain Sinclair's first novel, it is not the ghost of Jack the Ripper. In the person of Sir William Withey Gull, it may be that a plausible version of the Ripper can be discerned blundering his way through East Anglia and Whitechapel, but the London he terrorizes is the creation of another. The London of *White Chappell, Scarlet Tracings* (Goldmark, 1987) is a visionary recasting of the city Charles Dickens crafted into existence, that infested feverish Whore of Babylon [see next piece 1995] soon to be scumbled into the watery Babylon-on-Thames of Robert Louis Stevenson and Arthur Conan Doyle.

White Chappell begins with Doyle. In the late twentieth century a crew of secondhand bookdealers, which includes the narrator of the entire text in his most transparent of guises, comes across a unique copy of *A Study in Scarlet*, first published in 1888, which was the year of the Ripper. The narrator, who refers to himself as the Late Watson and also as Sinclair, begins immediately to generate an obsessive fever-dream quilt of reminiscence and speculation, in which images of the fog-bound East London of 1888 intersect with and invade the bare daylit cityscapes of our present age.

Much of the material from which Sinclair patches his text is given. His identification of Jack the Ripper seems more or less to be that of Stephen Knight, whose *Jack the Ripper: The Final Solution* (1976) remains the most deeply enjoyable of all theories yet propounded, though by no means the most likely. William Gull and his mentor James Hinton are figures of history, however transfigured here; as are the Ripper's victims; as are Hawksmoor (Peter Ackroyd credits Sinclair's *Lud Heat* of 1975 as a shaping influence on his recent novel) and Chatterton. Nor is Sinclair's depiction of the strange lives of secondhand bookdealers anything like as fantastical as it might seem. However densely exorbitant *White Chappell* may at times become, its flights are tied to a complexly achieved vision of the real London.

At times, all the same, these flights are tangled beyond easy comprehension. In apeing his protagonist's disoriented and epiphany-rich immurement in the matter of London, Sinclair too frequently overloads a not remarkably powerful grasp of narrative syntax, and his quasi-Joycean rhythms consequently lose steam, become swayback, and stall. The effect can be of stifling obscurity. But almost always some new image of Dickensian force clears the air in the nick of time, and this version of the heart of London beats once more.

– *Times Literary Supplement*, 30 October 1987

[I drafted the following piece for Stephen Jones and Kim Newman's *Horror: 100 Best Books* within a few weeks of writing the review of *White Chappell, Scarlet Tracings*, and developed at greater length the London imagery hinted at in that review; so I'll include it here, even though Tim Powers's novel was first published in 1983; the argument is made further use of in the review of William Gibson and Bruce Sterling's *The Difference Engine* (1990), which starts on page 234 1995.]

THERE is no getting away from the man who invented steampunk. Charles Dickens (1812–1870) may not be mentioned by name anywhere in *The Anubis Gates* (1983), but his shaping presence can be felt everywhere in the populous chortling shadows of the London of 1810 to which the twentieth-century hero of Tim Powers's time-travel fantasy travels, never to return. It does not much matter that Powers sets his tale in a time Dickens could never have directly experienced, and of which he never wrote, because novels like *Oliver Twist* (1837–1839), which depicts a London not dissimilar to that explored by Brendan Doyle, are a kind of apotheosis of the supernatural melodramas popular at the beginning of the century, so that Dickens's Fagin and Powers's Horrabin share a common source in grand guignol. Similarly, the Gothic fever-dreams of such writers as Monk Lewis or Charles Maturin can be seen to underpin the oneiric inscapes of the greatest achievements of Dickens – *Bleak House* (1852–53) or *Little Dorrit* (1855–1857) or *Our Mutual Friend* (1864–65) – those novels in which the nightmare of London attains lasting and horrific form, though it is almost certainly the case that Eugène Sue's *The Mysteries of Paris* (1844) developed the "Mysteries" plot – in which the City becomes an almost animate and deeply theatrical edifice – in a more directly useful and definitive manner. For Dickens, that nightmare of London may be a prophetic vision of humanity knotted into the subterranean entrails of the city machine, while for Powers the London of 1810 may be a form of nostalgia, a dream theatre for the elect to star in, buskined and immune; but at the heart of both writers' work glow the lineaments of the last world city.

Between Dickens and Powers, of course, much water has flowed down the filthy Thames. Between steampunk – a term which can be used to describe any sf novel set in any version of the previous century from which entropy has been banned as a metaphorical governor of the alternate industrial revolution of choice – and the desolate expressionism of its true founder lies what one might call Babylon-upon-

Thames-punk. Fin de siècle writers like Robert Louis Stevenson, Arthur Conan Doyle, and G K Chesterton attempted to domesticate Dickens's London by transforming it into a kind of Arabian Nights themepark capable of encompassing (and taming) all the strangenesses that an Empire in pullulant decline could possibly import. Even H G Wells was sometimes capable of quasi-Dickensian sentiment (as in novels like *Love and Mr Lewisham* [1900]) about the London he more normally wished utterly to destroy. That this enterprise of domestication was deeply suspect, most writers of Babylon-upon-Thames-punk knew full well, and as a result much of what they wrote gave off an air of bad-faith complacency, uneasy nostalgia, weird inanition. It is from their doomed enterprise (and from other sources as well) that contemporary steampunk authors like K W Jeter and Powers and James Blaylock and others have borrowed not only a vision of a talismanic city, but also (it must be said) some of the complacency and diseased nostalgia of the epigones who thought to tame Dickens.

But there is no getting away from Dickens, and *The Anubis Gates*, despite the occasional chilling Chestertonian whimsy, is radiant with the ambience of his genius. The villains of the piece – like Horrabin, the beggar-king on stilts, half-immolated by the energy of his own self-depiction, or Dog-Faced Joe, or the Spoon-Sized Boys – strut through Powers's pages with a grotesque theatricality that is proudly Dickensian. The geography of London – from the Avernal Thames to the underground cathedrals whose crepuscular Romantic arches evoke thoughts of Henry Fuseli in at least one character – has all the inspired animism of Dickens at his most convinced. And the inturning twists of plot – fumbled, as so often in Dickens, only in the final pages – seem to tell the tale of a country in which anything can happen, and not decay; in which entropy is reversed by the power of Story. This – it must be said – is not the message of the Charles Dickens who grew up.

An inextricable compact between world and self ordinates the whole of Dickens's later work, a rhetoric of entailment which locks the exorbitances of the earlier work into an ultimately desolating frame. If his London remains glowing and corrupt, multitudinous and confining, star-shot and subaqueous, then it is so by reason of the human soul, which it expresses, and harms. In *The Anubis Gates*, on the other hand, world and self are carefully separated from one another. As they twist and dance through the long theatre of their tale, Powers's protagonists – Brendan Doyle and Elizabeth Tichy – are like tourists in an enchanted wonderland; they are like readers of *The Anubis Gates*; they are hypnopomps of their own Story. We do not enter their interior lives, nor are we meant to, and the novel only fails when, by all rights, we *should* come to grips with some soul in extremis, as in the final pages when, after innumerable adventures and scrapes, Doyle is finally tortured to death – or so close to actual death as makes no difference. We hear his screams, but from way off-stage. Before he can die of his terrible wounds, the barge of Ra surfaces into the world to encompass his fallen form, and to deliver him, like a new-born child, to the waters of old Father Thames, whole again and baptized. To understand the superflux of implications unleashed at this point, perhaps unwittingly, we must enter Doyle's transfigured mind; but of the resurrection and epiphany of the hero we are tendered nothing but a brief passage of hearsay, offhandedly couched. Powers's strategy has allowed him no choice in the matter.

Terrible monsters do lurk in the cellars of The Anubis Gates, and fever-dream hints are dropped of circumstances in which it is possible for the hero truly to die. But after all, steampunk is a form of theodicy, and Powers displaces these intimations of the revolution- and Frankenstein-haunted exterior world onto a harlequinade of magicians and other villains who know their place, generically familiar templates whose attempts to spook England into decline and corruption and despair are constantly thwarted by the invulnerable Adamic Doyle. In externalizing the horrors of the world of change, Powers has invented a tale of paradise, where entropy lies down with the lamb and the steam yachts run on time. In The Anubis Gates he has written a book of almost preternatural geniality, a book which it is possible (rare praise) to love. Let us all, it suggests, co-inhabit the Christmas London of Brendan Doyle, and gape like children at the pageant of the world-stage of his triumphs. We do. He is having the time of his life. We join him.

– Horror: 100 Best Books (Xanadu, 1988), ed. Stephen Jones and Kim Newman

SEVERAL British publishers, perhaps misled by comically involved synopses, had refused The Arabian Nightmare (Viking, 1987) before Robert Irwin, with some colleagues, founded a small firm called Dedalus to launch the book in 1983. They soon found they had a cult classic on their hands. Taking notice, Viking Penguin soon picked up his second novel, The Limits of Vision (1986), releasing it both in Britain and in America, where it has received some acclaim, and now finally present The Arabian Nightmare, slightly revised, handsomely designed and evocatively illustrated, to readers here [in America].

Deft and lovely, and much harder to describe than to experience, just as dreams are, The Arabian Nightmare is a tale about dreams told as a dream. Fables within dreams within stories within nightmares tumble after one another, but nothing that matters is ever unclear, or contorted, or laborious. Synopsis, as some publishers must have found to their current regret, fatally distorts the smooth steely Ancient-

Mariner grip of Irwin's real storytelling genius, for like a vision half-remembered but hauntingly vivid, The Arabian Nightmare suffers considerably when exposed to daylight.

It is almost the end of the fifteenth century. The reverberations of the fall of Constantinople still echo round the Mediterranean. Young Balian of Norwich, ostensibly a pilgrim on his way to view the relics of St Catherine in the Sinai Desert, but also a secret spy for the French court, arrives in Cairo on June 18, 1486. As soon as he enters the caravanserai within the great jammed polyglot city, he falls asleep. He soon awakens, or dreams that he has awakened. He dreams again. He awakens. Soon he cannot tell what state he is in, nor does it matter.

What matters is the Arabian Nightmare, a condition no one can be conscious of while awake, but which in dreams subjects one to an infinity of suffering. The Nightmare is possibly contagious. It may also identify anyone who suffers it as the new Messiah. Asleep or awake, Balian, who may be a victim, finds himself drifting ever deeper into the stifling complexities of a Cairo choked with magicians, courtesans, thieves, beggars and bards, all themselves thrown into turmoil by the Nightmare, and by the disorienting dream city it has seemingly brought to the surface from the netherworld. Desperate to control his dreams, which he fears may be eternal, Balian falls into the clutches of the Father of Cats, a magician whose mortal foe is none other than the leper Jean Cornu, Grand Master of the Poor Knights of Lazarus.

Here the plot begins to thicken. As in a dream of pursuit, the deeper Balian burrows into the underlife of Cairo in his attempt to escape the enemies he cannot identify, the nearer he approaches the nightmare adversary who ultimately tells the tale. For much of the novel, the storyteller Yoll seems to be the responsible party, but on his strangulation it becomes clear that he is yet another mouthpiece of the final dreamer of The Arabian Nightmare. Irwin is too cagy to identify this figure in any clear way, but the last teller of stories in the novel, he who awakens Balian into a final dream, is an Ape.

As befits an Arabian tale, djinns have figured throughout The Arabian Nightmare, variously disguised; but no matter what face he may happen to bear, each djinn is ultimately a manifestation of Shaitain, or the Ape of God. The final teller of The Arabian Nightmare is arguably that precise dread Ape beneath the skin. The nightmare – the feverishly mortal world which Cairo stands for – is a dream of the devil's. It is contagious. Balian awakens in Hell.

This may not be exactly a message of good hope, but the book that embodies it with such unstoppable exuberance is anything but gloomy. The tales Balian lives –

and the ones he's told – are in turns hilarious and hallucinatory. The figures he meets in the Ape's dream of this world are intensely vivid, exorbitant but real. *The Arabian Nightmare* is a joy to read.

As a teacher of medieval history who has published in the field, Irwin clearly knows Mameluke Egypt very thoroughly indeed, and has anchored his most fantastical flights with details that seem clearly authentic. His rendering of many-gated Cairo may owe something to Franz Kafka and Luis Buñuel, because it is impossible for Balian or anyone else to escape from the metaphysical coils of the city; but another city comes to mind as well, and another writer with an hallucinatory eye and encyclopedic command of actuality. The city is London, and the writer is Charles Dickens. If Dickens had lived to complete *The Mystery of Edwin Drood*, the full tale when told might have had something in common with the visionary urban dreamscape Robert Irwin has so joyfully unfolded in this book.

– *The Washington Post*, 10 November 1987

IN *The Hour of the Thin Ox* (Unwin, 1987), which is his second novel, Colin Greenland comes to maturity as a writer of high decorum. It may be the case that none of the ingredients in this grave otherworldly high fantasy tale are dashingly original, but the mixture has been assembled with judicial skill. The eroded contours of his domains and the ornamental twilight cultures he has created to populate them may be redolent of the work of M John Harrison; the political intricacies of the tale may remind one of the South-East Asia of Gwyneth Jones's superb *Divine Endurance* (1984); the Cambodian foetor of the book's climax may recall Geoff Ryman's *The Unconquered Country* (1986). But there is an unerring rightness of touch in the shaping of this diverse material, as though a decade of British experimental writing in the fields of the fantastic in literature were being summed up. *The Hour of the Thin Ox* is a lesson in how to draw lessons. It is a guide.

If the rough association of titles constellating *The Hour of the Thin Ox* have anything in common, beyond a tendency to depict worlds at the ends of their tethers, it is probably a sense, not often found in commercial fantasy, that the behaviour of sovereign states exposes moral complexities worthy of the most intense regard. In particular, Ryman's novella is an unmistakeable parable about the terrible consequences of the Viet Nam War, and throughout Jones's work run threads of radical political discourse. More reticently, Greenland creates, in the dovetailing plots that structure his own novel, an implied discourse that only becomes anything like explicit in the book's final pages.

In an alternate world whose complexities are only hinted at, two contrasting characters come to maturity in two contrasting lands. Jillian Curram grows up to lead her family export-import firm into a bankruptcy ordained by the slow enervated decline of her native Bryland; in the sclerotic corridors of power of nearby hierarchy-bound Escaly, young Ky varan applies his mild unoriginal mind to the task of achieving in due time the rank of Imperial Geometer [the kind of ambition that leads one to associate young Ky with the various M John Harrison characters who might be described as Knights of the Doleful Countenance 1995]. Both lead bounded lives, and when both are cast into the heart of chaos – the Vietnamese jungle of Belanesis, an alien territory over which Bryland and Escaly wage surreal war – both must test to the uttermost the assumptions which have governed their actions. Ky varan dies uselessly [most Knights of the Doleful Countenance simply refuse passage into the new land, or the new state of being, to the gaining of which the text begs them to aspire 1995], Jillian survives the testing of the Hour of the Thin Ox, a time when the utter alienness – and the unassailable reality – of the Belanesi becomes shatteringly evident.

It is the peculiar strength of Greenland's packed novel that, out of its synthesizing ambition and flustering detail, unmistakeable lessons are suggested. In accepting them, Jillian Curram becomes, most unusually in a novel of fantasy, worldly wise. She becomes an adult. It is a conclusion which excellently befits this good book.

– Times Literary Supplement, 25 December 1987

FOR readers of European sf, it will come as no great shock that in Greg Bear's new novel, *The Forge of God* (Tor, 1987), the world comes to an end. From the moment H G Wells gave birth to it in 1895 with the publication of *The Time Machine*, modern European sf has been, after all, a literature of disaster. But Greg Bear, as an American, and a leading exponent of the technophilic form of the genre known as Hard sf, comes from a markedly different tradition. American sf has long been dominated by a vision of the future in which, however marred by blips and external threats, Progress *works*, and humanity's bailiwick inexorably expands to encompass the universe. So *The Forge of God* is a subversive book.

We begin in the heart of Hard sf country, where scientific conundrums are cleared up in the nick of time by tough-minded numerate lateral-thinking libertarian heroes, and the future is freed from bondage to the earth-bound past. One of the moons of Jupiter has suddenly disappeared, which deeply puzzles Presidential science advisor Arthur Gordon, the most prominent member of a large cast of scientists, scientists' wives, politicians, ordinary folk, and aliens. But this first mystery is soon dwarfed by a succession of new problems. A dying extraterrestrial being is discovered near an artificial mountain which houses an incomprehensible alien complex. The dying alien, which turns out to be an android, tells its discoverers that bad news is coming, and when the fundamentalist American President of the United States shows up, informs him that its own home planet had been destroyed by incomprehensible creatures, on one of whose ships it had stowed away so it could warn other races of their coming doom.

Further aliens land in Australia with the message that alien saviours are due any moment and a brave new world is just around the corner. But when they are interrogated they self-destruct. It is suspected that both sets of aliens had been placed on Earth to confuse humanity, and a demoralized nausea – not unlike that which punters feel in a plummetting stock market – duly begins to infect the Western World. The President, convinced that his God is en route to inflict terminal punishment on the species, does nothing. It soon becomes apparent to Arthur Gordon and his colleagues that something indeed very terrible is happening.

The terror grows. Two large super-dense objects, one composed of neutronium, one of anti-neutronium, fall unpreventably deep into the Earth from space. There, in the core of the planet, they circle one another in gradually intersecting orbits. When the two objects meet in catastrophic mutual annihilation, the planet will burst open. As there is nothing anyone can do, and the true alien destroyers never even deign to appear, a paralyzed sourness and anomie soon stymies any effort, however useless, to find a remedy. The braver members of the cast make peace with themselves, and face the end stoically. And the world ends.

To some extent Bear muffles the effect of this conclusion by introducing yet another set of aliens who scurry about the doomed planet retrieving cultural memorabilia and saving a few humans, including Dr Gordon. He and the others learn that they are now destined to live their lives in space searching, in the company of other species who have lost their planets, for the original manufacturers of the planet-busting robots, in the final realization that Earth was destroyed not by aliens but by their tools.

The experienced reader of sf will note now and then in this novel echoes of Thomas M Disch's *The Genocides* (1965), in which Earth is terminated without any palliative whatsoever, and John Varley's *The Ophiuchi Hotline* (1977), which posits a post-exilic existence for humanity under conditions not dissimilar to those Bear suggests. But *The Forge of God* differs significantly from its predecessors by setting its cast of scientists – and other Americans who are initially convinced that ingenuity and gumption will save the day – a problem they cannot solve, a tragedy they cannot gimmick. No model of imperial Progress can save them or their planet. It is, consequently, a thoroughly shocking book.

There are one or two shortfalls of style and conception along the way. Too many characters make garish walk-on appearances in the fashion of the traditional blockbuster. Ghosts of the American Hard sf writers' communal distaste for twentieth-century liberalism surface occasionally – most risibly when the fundamentalist American President is identified as being a Democrat. There may be just one too many alien species. But the inevitability of the tale is grimly exhilarating, and Bear manages to visualize the final cataclysm all too clearly for comfort. It is the best end of the world we will see for a long time.

– *New Scientist*, 26 November 1987

[This seems an appropriate place to insert a review of the first sequel to *The Forge of God* 1995.]

THE author of this sequel to a fine book – and prequel to another fine one, if we read the augurs right – must by now be more than adequately used to reviewers making plays upon his firm-throated surname, but it is, all the same, difficult to avoid saying there is something awfully dogged about *Anvil of Stars* (Legend, 1992), something very storing-up-fuel-for-winter about its 400+ task-oriented teeth-gritted pages.

We are in the universe of *The Forge of God* (1987), some time after the planet Earth has been destroyed by devices programmed by their makers (from, as it were, Eddore) to seek out all living systems and eliminate them. The main difference between Bear's tale and the very large number of earlier stories with the same basic premise – Fred Saberhagen's Berserker series is the most obvious mature formatting of the conceit – is that, in *The Forge of God*, the inanimate self-replicating machines do their job, impassively, thoroughly, inserting two super-dense objects, one of neutronium and one of anti-neutronium, into the heart of the planet, where they orbit around one another until they meet, bursting Gaia wide open. Earth is destroyed.

True, Bear does introduce a posse of *friendly* alien machines which have been sent by the Benefactors (or, as it were, Arisians) to sample our goods and to save – Break in Case of Sequel – a few humans; one of these is Arthur Gordon, who does not appear in *Anvil of Stars*, but whose son does. But before he leaves our ken, Gordon learns that the remnants of the human race must now prepare to devote themselves to a search, accompanied by other species who have also lost their planets, for the original makers of the death machines: for it is now understood that Earth has been destroyed not by aliens but by their *tools*.

The first novel ends here, on a slingshot cadence: and the tale might easily have stopped for good. Slingshots (as Gene Wolfe has demonstrated a dozen times) do not *require* sequels to justify them: it is enough that we are lifted, and thrown high, story lines dopplering behind us, the stars sempiternal to the forward gaze, in a fall that never ends. Now that most of the stories have been told that make up the nine billion names of sf and the party's over, it may be time to enter into a benign conspiracy to Take Middle Volumes As Read, and to go directly to Asgard, where the tale may earn an ending. But not today, not this time round. Dogged is as dogged does. We have a bridge to cross, and *Anvil of Stars* is the route we have to take, down to the last detail. The story of Humanity-Rump's first attempts to identify the true ringleaders lurking within the farflung tentacles of Boskone, the agonies and the ecstacies and the coups d'états and the moments of passion and the moments of doubt and the hemi-demi-climax in which a passel of henchmen is polished off, duly ensues. And, like the pot at the end of the rainbow, a final volume looms duly.

The only thing which justifies the exercise – beyond the pleasure of the concise, clear-eyed, relentless, thrusting *businessness* of Greg Bear's prose – is the chance to find out just what, in a market contrivance of the sort *Anvil of Stars* must have been written to fit, an author of this calibre can do to boil – without cracking – the pot, spilling the rainbow to come. Bear's solution is worth the cost. Humanity-Rump is comprised of the children of the survivors of the first volume; they are alone in space, in a great Benefactor ship run by Benefactor robots. Their job is to enforce the Law: "that civilizations which make self-replicating killer machines be punished – with extinction." But they don't know who the Benefactors are; they don't know how to identify a Maker race; they know almost nothing about the vast galaxy in which they may turn out to be nothing more than cannon fodder in a war they can never grasp. Almost the whole of *Anvil of Stars* turns out to be a debate – conducted in words and deeds – over whether or not the story it's telling *actually exists*. It is, one need not emphasize, the ideal theme for the second volume of a trilogy: indeed it may, upon analysis, prove to be the underlying theme of all second volumes. *Anvil of Stars*, in other words, is a genuine post-modernist act of deconstruction. *Anvil of Stars* is a survival kit for reading *Anvil of Stars*.

– New York Review of Science Fiction 50, October 1992

Two: 1988

1. Year Roundup

1775 was sort of like this too, Dickens says. The best of times and the worst of times. Through the goggles of a year like 1775, or 1988, there is always *A Tale of Two Cities* in the offing, some sort of millennial resolution discernible up the line, maw gaping. Gripped by auguries of the fin de siècle, 1988 has been a year of remission and prognosis; of relief that we still enjoy the fruits of our long reign; of terror that it's all about to end in a mortal spasm of the planet we have paved, some vast calling in of the credits that have funded these last hours in the garden with the pesticide and the poison gnomes to guard us. The millennium has not yet come, but a rough beast knocks at night in the dream of the West whispering *I am what you've sown*. So it has been a year of premonitions, and it might be fair to ask just what our chosen genre has done recently to accustom us to the future. What brave words are the visionary novelists of our own sf now uttering, to chasten us or to charm?

Well? It was the best of times, it was the worst of times. It was a year which witnessed a revival of the Scientific Romance, child of the last fin de siècle, harbinger of the next; but it was also a year which marked the beginning of the age of the sharecropper, bibled and braided and branded and steered. It was a year in which two tightrope-walking humanists (Kim Stanley Robinson and Terry Bisson) wrote books that were not fatuous; but it was also a year which saw cyberpunk enter heat-death and become a tradition (rather benumbing William Gibson, though continuing still to fascinate haunted proconsuls like Bruce "Cecil Rhodes" Sterling). Dinosaurs continued to live in 1988, dinosaurs died. Good books won a few awards, dozens of less-good stuff won dozens. Child editors in America and Britain gazed in wonder upon new books and old agents, and boggled whole conventions with their born-again ("Now I've been with Shameless and Honk a whole morning I'm like truly thrilled over our unique new list...entirely new slant...investment in quality kind of thing you know") rave babble, but as usual big bucks tended only to change hands for the most otiose trilogy clones. The walls of the ghetto were razed in 1988, the ghetto remains.

As in 1987, a new novel was published every few hours in 1988, but once again most of them were fantasy or horror, and therefore beyond the remit of this survey of the best sf novels of 1988; and some of the remaining were sharecropped, though not as many as next year will provide, because only recently have the owners of sf begun to see that the sharecropping scam could be a nice little earner. The term was coined, I believe, by Gardner Dozois. It derives from the success of the Kentucky Fried Chicken. Sharecropping occurs when the copyright owner of a famous story or novel (like Isaac Asimov's "Nightfall" or Arthur C Clarke's *Against the Fall of Night*) hires an author (like Arthur Byron Cover or Robert Silverberg) to rewrite, or expand, or sequelize, or create a work "in the world of" that original. Because he has no rights over his labour, and because his peonage has a certain historical resonance, the hack who does the actual job of writing has become known as the sharecropper. He is a tenant farmer, he sows what Bwana tells him to sow, and he does not reap. Nor does he *make things up*. For the franchise owners who have hired him, any attempt by the sharecropper to look upon the world and *make it new* would be to violate their property rights. Originality is theft. So menu-control is of the essence for the owners of sf, just as it is for the owners of any merchandise, and no sharecropper can be given a chance to violate the "bible" that tells him how to work his master's plot. *Against the Fall of Night* (soon to be sharecropped by Gregory Benford [I was in error here: Benford's contribution was not owned by Clarke 1995]) must taste of the original product, just as a themepark must taste of something once alive.

So is it closing time in the gardens of the West, as Cyril Connolly said 40 years ago on closing down *Horizon*? Or is sharecropping just another developer's dream of our free enterprise system? Or is that just one question? Perhaps Mr Benford [see above] and Mr Silverberg [nor would Silverberg have technically sharecropped the Asimov plantation, though the dubiousness of the nature of the creative acts engaged in by both Benford and Silverberg remains an issue worth greater space than this parenthesis wants to stretch to hold 1995] would argue that you can't stop Progress and shouldn't try, and that Golden-Age Themeparks, tilled by squeaky-clean Toms in Mickey Mouse masks, *preserve our heritage* in the same way that Disney World pickles our dreams to profit the owner. All the same, in a world about which it's a matter of urgency to tell stories before it's too late, it does seem a *trahison des clercs* for authors to re-enact travesties of the dead past while claiming star status in a genre which pretends to face us with the threat and joy of the new [I would continue to address this sentence to Greg Benford, as he continues vociferously to defend his retrofit Clarke collaboration as an echt sf thought-experiment 1995]. Or perhaps nowadays they keep their mouths shut, except to till. Perhaps it is just all too sad for words – this transmogrifying of authors we respect into golems of the nostalgia trade; this dangerous deep asset-stripping raid upon own fragile sf, whose claims to focus on the yet-unsaid have proved so remarkably easy to co-opt, and to reverse. But it's not all black. It does make the task of choosing which books to discuss an easier one. Sharecropped texts disqualify themselves in principle from treatment as *novels*, because, in principle, of course, they are not.

*

John Clute

Dinosaur time again in the garden. As we said last year, the dinosaurs of sf – those whose careers began before World War Two and who have continued to write, or have only recently returned to Disney World to collect the rent – are the Cargo bearers of genre. After decades of stoking the Sacred Flame of Future History for free, they found in recent years that the intense development analysis to which sf has been subjected – and which undoubtedly generated the concept of sharecropping – had targeted them as marketable commodities. But the problem with dinosaurs is that they are human, and it is a definition of ageing that no one ages well – though some age less badly than the rest of us. By the time we reach our second half-century, most of us have become mistresses and masters of the ruts we've cut to guide our lives and protect ourselves from novelty, and only the rarest of us ever manages to think a new thought after the age of 60, or write a genuinely new story. The termitary immobilism of spirit of the last Heinlein novels – or of recent efforts by Isaac Asimov to glue his Robot and Foundation series into one salt Colossus in a world that never rains – serves to remind us of the inexorable dead hand of biology. Old men's books – and old women's, viz the pumped-up melancholy overreaching audacity of James Tiptree's last works – tend to rehearse with bluster the heroic feats of young adulthood, when "Gulf" or "Nightfall" sprang fully-clothed from the brow of the god. But to reify something so delicately poised as a work of art is to turn it to chalk.

The Knight and Knave of Swords (Morrow) may not be a work of sf, nor is Fritz Leiber primarily an author of sf; but he began to publish in 1939, he's certainly a dinosaur under the meaning of the act, and it seems a good idea to mention what may well be the last tales to be written about Fafhrd and the Gray Mouser, though of course Leiber, or his eventual heirs, may yet decide to franchise Lankhmar for the loot [not yet 1995]. As he has made clear in his Locus column, Leiber wrote "The Mouser Goes Below," the novel which takes up the bulk of Knight and Knave, as a magical exercise in fending off the death of his close friend Harry Fischer, who had been the original inspiration for the Gray Mouser, and who was fighting cancer. Fischer died, and the tale which memorializes him has a yearning weirdness about it that does not, to its credit, much resemble the wisdom of the old, which is agenbite and ashes, and which faces the future with the cheeks of the ass. In Narabedla, Ltd. (Del Rey), like a wise old Norn bored right out of her skull, Frederik Pohl continued to doodle with the tropes and doodads of the genre he has helped to create, and which he knows, unfortunately in this case, backwards but not forwards. And in Prelude to Foundation (Doubleday Foundation), Isaac Asimov, as we hinted decorously just a moment ago, bricked up yet another escape hatch from which any remaining life in his megaseries of long ago might have escaped. And Arthur C Clarke – fighting a medical diagnosis (since superseded) which gave him only a few years to live – brought in a feelgood philistine named Gentry Lee to collaborate on *Cradle* (Gollancz), with predictable results; a soupçon of Clarke's hygienic Weltschmerz was drowned in glutinous paeans to plastoid sex and the shopping malls of Key West. Raymond Z Gallun stayed silent.

But let us step outside the ghetto walls for a moment, as we did last year. As Ben Elton has just said in *Stark* (1989), a novel we would hope to mention again, the future is "coming towards us quicker than we are going towards it," causing seismic tremolos in the minds of many writers never associated with fantasy or sf, so that more and more "mainstream" novels read more and more like fantasias on the real stuff. Even a book like Don DeLillo's chilly streetwise *Libra* (Viking), engrossed as it is in the mantric nightmares that embrocate the deaths of JFK and Lee Harvey Oswald, treats its material as a kind of alternate history – as just one of the pasts we must muster to face the haemorrhage of the new. Loosened from the stays of official history, novels like Louise Erdrich's *Tracks* (Hamish Hamilton) and William Kennedy's *Quinn's Book* (Viking) transform the regions of nineteenth and early twentieth century America into magic-realist mirrors of our own condition, here on the cusp. In *Tidings* (Knopf), William Wharton irradiates contemporary France with a hint that something numinous and awe-ful lurks within the rituals we fabricate against the passage of time. In each of these books – and in dozens more of a similar cast of mind – there is a sense of *preparation*. It is a sense which helps one to understand Salman Rushdie's *The Satanic Verses* (Cape), a book which needs little said about it these days, thanks to the efforts of the religious creatures it exposed to the light of the sun. Writers like Erdrich and DeLillo and Rushdie, through their magical and transformative appropriation of the past, seem to be arming themselves – and their readers – to understand the magical and transformative future as it races our way. How different from our own dear genuflecting sharecroppers, whom the past owns.

In the lamenting cadences of Michael Moorcock's masterfully cloistral *Mother London* (Secker & Warburg) that sense of preparation is perhaps less evident, for this superbly worked tale – the best-constructed work Moorcock has ever generated – strikingly attests to the bondage of the world, which is London. Various avatars of Moorcock populate the book, but even the muted telepathies that unite them into one concourse of regard do less to liberate than to shrive. Neither of Moorcock's British compeers – Brian Aldiss and J G Ballard – produced novels of generic interest, though Aldiss's Forgotten Life (Gollancz) lucidly grounds a this-worldly tale of redemption in a fretwork of epistemological dubiety, as he does so often in his sf, and Ballard's Running Wild (Hutchinson) is a toxic little parable – specifically perhaps of the cost of Thatcherism – that edges neatly into the near future, for a glimpse of things. Because of its geriatric and relentlessly half-witted sf frame, E P Thompson's The Sykaos Papers (Bloomsbury) might theoretically be designated a generic product, but this would be to dismiss it utterly – more rewardingly, the book can be read as an animated lecture on the evils of the Yahoo, with examples. Much tamer Yahoos mourn the death of a family elder in Stansilaw Lem's Hospital of the Transfiguration (Harcourt Brace), which is set in 1939, in Poland, and it takes only a modicum of sense to work out what will happen to them: Yahoos of purer Yahoo stock will thresh them: and we will come closer to understanding Lem's view of our species, and the dry-ice savagery of his sf, for this novel is partly autobiographical. Like an absurdist fantasia on some of Arthur Koestler's loopier notions about denizens of the steppes, Milorad Pavic's Dictionary of the Khazars: A Lexicon Novel (Knopf) creates a full-fledged alternate history out of an invented tribe of Slavs; organized as a series of alphabetical entries, Dictionary more closely resembles the work of Georges Perec or Harry Mathews than it does the Steppe of Piers Anthony, who could, all the same, learn something from a real player of games. Unfortunately, Khazars is terribly stuffed, pâté-de-fois Borges; and few will read it for the rules. Stunning and various as usual, Peter Dickinson published two books for older children: Merlin Dreams (Gollancz) is a grave fantasy about the England we no longer live in, and Eva (Gollancz), set in the near future, posits the end through inanition of our miserable species, though some hope is expressed for one of our cousins. In The Fifth Child (Cape), a "mundane" narrative whose surface conceals gnawing hints of anthropological horror, Doris Lessing found little solace in the thought that a dark cousin within the skull might inherit our mess of pottage. And Jim Crace's aptly lapidary The Gift of Stones (Secker & Warburg) returns more openly to the subgenre of sf about prehistory that was so popular in the late nineteenth century, just after Darwin. And so on. This rundown of books that riddle the walls of the ghetto from outside could continue almost indefinitely; 1988 may be the age of the sharecropper, but it is also the best of times, for the borders are down.

Daylight can be blinding.

Back in the lek, it was not a good year for writers too young to franchise their early work, but too old any longer to dominate the field; unlike last year, however, some of them managed to write books. The dogged Gordon R Dickson published unavailingly yet another huge volume in his *Childe* Cycle, of which the best instalment (*The Genetic General*, 1960) is the first. The pulp triumphalism of that novel, which the Dickson apostle Sandra Miesel once called Pelagian, has stiffened in recent years into a logy and elephantiasic insistence that Man shall prevail, but *The Chantry Guild* (Ace) is rather more sprightly than its immediate predecessor, *The Final Encyclopedia* (1984), and can be enjoyed for its hints of a thin Dickson caught somewhere inside its bulk, crying to be let out. Six years after dying, Philip K Dick came out with two more novels; *The Broken Bubble [of Thisbe Holt]* (Arbor House), just about the last of the early non-science-fiction novels, is set, like most of the others, in a California only a thin partition distant from the surreal paranoias of the realer worlds he entered in his maturity; and *Nick and the Glimmung* (Gollancz) is a neat little children's book, whose eponymous alien is a guest from *Galactic Pot-Healer* (1969). In the slippery grey literate twists of *Krono* (Franklin Watts), Charles L Harness once again reshapes A E Van Vogt into something you could take home to meet your parents. In 1988, Robert Silverberg published two novels of interest. *The Secret Sharer* (Underwood-Miller), which is very short, continues the series of homages which began with *Sailing to Byzantium* (1985), in this case polishing the profound infelicities of Joseph Conrad till the analogies shine like glass; but the gain in smoothness does not overbalance the loss of a felt world. Set in a distant science-fantasy future, which it depicts with impeccable cool skill, *At Winter's End* (Warner) could be the first of many volumes; if the project manages to re-ignite in Silverberg something of his old melancholy fire, it might save him from terminal competence. And Kate Wilhelm, in *The Dark Door* (St Martin's Press), stumbles strangely from one genre to another, as though blinded. Within an orthodox sf frame, two orthodox series detectives (they appear in a previous Wilhelm novel) blunder into an orthodox supernatural horror plot complete with abandoned hotels, and conclude that there are things we are not meant to know. For a writer who seems blind to the implications of this mélange of mutually incompatible conventions, Wilhelm juggles her balls with some intermittent dexterity, and *The Dark Door* is at points a joy to read. But the book is mainly of interest as an example, not the first, of rotting affect in the hearts of our older contemporaries, who seem to be telling us that the game of the future is up. That it just doesn't matter any more.

For those we described last year as alpha males, because there were so few women in the cohort of those who effectively began their careers in the decade after 1965, 1988 was not a year for braggadocio, though several books of substance did get published. Michael Bishop, whose voice is like a shout from the bottom of the well of the enormous South, and whose heart is on his sleeve, does manage in *Unicorn Mountain* (Arbor House) to generate a moving tale out of ecological disaster here and in another world, AIDS, the death of cultures, the death of species, and the slow sea-changing of America into themeparks. Thomas M Disch, in *The Brave Little Toaster Goes to Mars* (Doubleday), renews his life-long flirtation with what might be called the sentiment-and-sprezzatura gross-out fling; this second Toaster book is funny, insinuating, speaks with forked tongue. In *Carmen Dog* (The Women's Press), Carol Emshwiller tells a metamorphic feminist fable – as of long ago – with a gravely innocent mien that only deepens the sting. From Bob Shaw, *The Wooden Spaceships* (Gollancz) cleverly and modestly continues a trilogy begun in *The Ragged Astronauts* (1986), dovetailing the death of an earlier protagonist with the opening of a new line of plot; and we warm with expectations of a finale of humane sparkle, in the Shavian manner. Of the three novels Ian Watson published in 1988, *Whores of Babylon* (Grafton) entices its protagonists into a world half Disney half Minos, and lets them twist in the wind; perhaps more successfully, *The Fire Worm* (Gollancz) marries sexual pathology to the legend of the Lambton Worm in a multi-generation tale told in the tone of slangy needling patter characteristic of this author at his best; but the *Meat* (Headline) was off. And in *There Are Doors* (Tor), Gene Wolfe continued to ransack the popular culture of the time before the war, on this occasion polishing up Thorne Smith; but unlike P G Wodehouse, the author of *Topper* (1926) is better remembered than reread, and in Wolfe's hands Smith's fragile home-for-dinner flapper paganism turns into something desolated, force-fed, melancholic.

It is easy to forget that Brian Stableford published his first novel as long ago as 1969, because it is easy to forget Brian Stableford's first novel. For a writer of the polymathic and urgent cogency so often on display in his non-fiction, he tended to produce novels, from 1969 until he stopped writing them for a while several years ago, of an oddly morose affectlessness, with exceptions. It is only now, with his return to fiction in *The Empire of Fear* (Simon & Schuster UK), that he has brought his very considerable gifts into focus, perhaps because *The Empire of Fear* is not an sf novel in the American mode dominant from 1926 on, but a Scientific Romance in the mode native to Britain since H G Wells published *The Time Machine* in 1895. As Stableford has argued in *Scientific Romance in Britain* (1985), this mode stands in some contrast to its American cousin. The protagonists of the Scientific Romance tend to be observers of the great world, while American heroes tend to *win* it. The plots of an author like Olaf Stapledon (or even Arthur C Clarke) tend to be exemplary, illuminative, perspectival; while American plots tend to work as access routes for the kingship raids of the hero, high-albedo trip-traps for the kinesis of usurpation.

In the one, vision is the end; in the other, ownership. Set in an alternate sixteenth-century Europe dominated by an aristocracy composed of near-immortal vampires, *The Empire of Fear* focuses on its protagonist's life-long efforts to come to a scientific understanding of the relationship between vampirism and longevity; and after an extraordinarily long detour into the heart of Africa (a guided tour that neatly illustrates the Scientific Romance's perspectival skew), he manages to clear the air for us to see through, though he himself dies without owning a thing, mortal, in much pain, off-stage. For many of us it will be a strange book to read, for its climax gives off the dying-fall glow beloved of authors of the Scientific Romance, and the denouement is strangely passionless, though pacific. But it exercises the muscles of the eye.

We reach the authors who have come on stream since 1975, who carry the phosphor of the fin-de-siècle within their breasts. In *The Player of Games* (Macmillan), Iain (M) Banks provides a Lean-Cuisine prequel to the polysaturated *Consider Phlebas* (1987), and through the standard-issue folds of a galaxy-spanning plot that involves a game to end all games whose winner ends an empire (etc), images of the multi-world Culture at the heart of Banks's inspiration begin to take shape, almost subliminally. Bounteous with post-scarcity liberality, non-hierarchical, unowned, optional and humorous, it is, for at least one reader, a description of Jerusalem with a Garden. In *Eternity* (Warner), a sequel to *Eon* (1985), Greg Bear comes as close to the composition of a Scientific Romance as an American writer steeped in the dominant form of the genre is ever likely to, and draws out his long pulp-roots of storyline with near-Stapledonian pomp. After cosmogonic sleights-of-hand, and a few twists of twine, the Universe does or does not end in *Eternity*, but who's counting? [And this year a third volume has appeared, *Legacy* 1995.] In no real sense is Terry Bisson's *Fire on the Mountain* (Arbor House) a sequel to his *Talking Man* (1986), but the steam-yacht apple-blossom sweetness of the utopia depicted in the contemporary sequences of the new book seems much more earned when both texts are folded together in the mind. After trailing a mute wizard across America, and watching him save the universe from non-being, the protagonists of *Talking Man* return to a Kentucky transfigured precisely into the world so magically wished for in *Fire on the Mountain*: a world whose Civil War, which has been fought by blacks to free themselves, marks the beginning of a Golden (rather than a Gilded) Age. Why – Bisson makes you ask – did it not happen? Will it never?

Like almost everything James P Blaylock has ever written, *The Last Coin* (Mark V Ziesing), his finest novel to date, must be designated a fantasy, but not High. Like

Terry Bisson or John Crowley or Tim Powers, Blaylock creates worlds whose roots are consanguineous with the world's own story, and share its blood. *The Last Coin* starts with the Pieces of Silver; it is a bit like *The Maltese Falcon* without the private eye, its stays loose, its haunting of Christian iconology profound. Octavia E Butler's *Adulthood Rites* (Warner) continues the xenobiological tale that began with *Dawn* (1987), and generates a sense of daunting perspectives soon to become articulate, a sense that the third volume may accomplish what Marx conceived of as the task of synthesis: to open the gates on human nature. Orson Scott Card's *Red Prophet* (Tor), also the second volume of a sequence, follows *Seventh Son* (1987), and presages many more, for Card's tales of a magical knitter of worlds in an alternate nineteenth century America shows no sign of nearing a climax; more pulpy than Bisson's rendering of the dream, and harsher too, Card's vision of a saved Continent still remains, after two instalments, a cartoon we drench with desiderium as we read. For it is not yet Jerusalem. But we read on. A relentless productivity has tended to blanch one's sense of the features of C J Cherryh, but there is in fact hardly a weak book in her interlinked series of tales set in the Merchanters' universe; like its companions, *Cyteen* (Warner) is packed, polished, driven and whipped, dense with flamboyant gesture and an astonishing alertness of pace and texture; a book which, with all its excesses of length, gives off a sense of unsettling but focused closeness, a steely chamber dodecaphony, like a Schoenberg opera. And from Britain, two urban novels from two urban novelists: Neil Ferguson's *Putting Out* (Hamish Hamilton) joins politics and fashion in semiological wedlock during which a New York mayoral contest climaxes in bombs and mots, as mediated by the signs that mind us; and Christopher Fowler's *Roofworld* (Century/Legend), reminding one of illustrated editions of H G Wells's *When the Sleeper Wakes* (1899), posits a London laced at rooftop by the inhabitants of an autonomous secret culture, who shuttlecock above us like the Edwardian aviators of a dream.

Just as Poseidon turns out to be a chimaera of the surf, so does cyberpunk more and more begin to look like an artifact of the lighting. William Gibson has never claimed more than that, and in *Mona Lisa Overdrive* (Gollancz) he closes down the sequence whose first volume, *Neuromancer* (1984), gave tongue to a hundred bloodhounds hot for future-sleaze. Four-cylindered, turbocharged and entirely unleaded, *Mona Lisa Overdrive* gives a final charge of polish to the cyberpunk dream, and stops; though he does drop hints, in the last pages of the text, of an Open Sesame to new worlds of genre. He should be thanked for the ride so far. Like Bisson and Blaylock, Robert Holdstock writes fantasies whose roots intertwine with the premises of any sf novel claiming to examine (and to rewrite) the history of the world, and *Lavondyss*

(Gollancz), set in the same ur-reality as *Mythago Wood* (1984), goes well beyond that novel's obsession with the myths or histrions who walk within the heartwood and within the head; half pedantry and proselytizing, half an epiphany of metamorphosis that reads like braille, it is a book whose appalling sincerity puts to shame the Celtic junk it fleetingly resembles. With three novels in 1988, Gwyneth Jones continues to flare and cough. *Transformations* (Orchard, as by Ann Halam) and *The Hidden Ones* (The Women's Press) are written for older children with lucidity and grace and rage, while *Kairos* (Unwin), written for adults, muffles its potent Christian millennialism in great swathes of jumbled natter, as though the privilege of her Word exempted her from the laws of form, the exigencies of the tongue. And in *Metrophage* (Ace), Richard Kadrey has written an old-fashioned novel in the idiom of once-famed cyberpunk; but it does have a nice disease.

I-dotting and po-faced, Nancy Kress still manages, in *An Alien Light* (Arbor House), to fabricate a world and species sufficiently unlike homo sapiens to warrant the hundreds of pages of Contact Alienation which make up the heart of her text; and she writes as one born in the sealed womb of Yankee space. Paul J McAuley, on the other hand, is himself the alien in the woodpile, and *Four Hundred Billion Stars* (Gollancz), though sharp and darkly intelligent and cutting, shows all the signs of a Scientific Romance mind trapped in the wrong imperium. The result is a space opera whose excesses of intellect are a form of self-injury. Ian McDonald's *Desolation Road* (Bantam), though written with a striking presentness of style, makes too close an homage of Gabriel García Márquez's *One Hundred Years of Solitude* (trans 1970), and the fantasia he presumably intends does not quite reach take-off velocity, unlike García Márquez's own soaring sacerdotal *Love in the Time of Cholera* (trans 1988; Harper & Row). Rachel Pollack's *Unquenchable Fire* (Century/Legend), on the other hand, closely resembles nothing one might care to dream of. It is perhaps 1988's strangest novel, and one of its strongest. The premise is odd enough – in an alternate America whose physics may well be based on the Neoplatonic shamanism of the Crowley who read Frances Yates and wrote *Ægypt*, a redemptive Pregnancy has been imposed upon the unwilling woman at the heart of the tale – but the eerie hypnopompic tranced serenity of Pollack's telling of her story, and the medusoid cruelty of the exemplary fables she interweaves into the text, make reading *Unquenchable Fire* almost like having a nightmare about almost having a nightmare.

It is like stepping into the full silliness of day to speak next of Paul Preuss, soon to be sharecropping his *nous* with the rest of the staff; but *Starfire* (Tor), most unusually, is a Hard-sf novel it is possible to read without gloves. Its proselytizing for the exploration of space is unstained by rant about commie liberals; its protagonists are larger than life but not more vicious; and its science, perhaps because the tale takes place in the near future, does not give off the stink of charlatanry that pinpoints the *real venue* of most hard-sf novels as being Orange County. We do not speak of the Orange County Kim Stanley Robinson would like to believe in, the Orange County soon to be revealed – it is hoped – in the utopian leg of his ongoing exploration of various futures we of the West may live to face; but *The Shining Sea* has not yet appeared [eventually, as *Pacific Edge*, it came out in 1990, initially in the UK 1995]. We must rest content with *The Wild Shore* (1984), which deconstructs the skim-milk pastoralism of the California Right in terms so humane some critics misread the book as invertebrate eulogy; and *The Gold Coast* (Tor), a dystopian version of Orange County fifty years hence. Distressingly, nothing much in the book is radically dissimilar to what we might expect to see next week, if the fog lifts. In this fine grave slightly obdurate book, what we see of the spoliation of Orange County is what we see in our daily papers, written in clear. In *Wetware* (Avon), zany brutalist Rudy Rucker continues the robot series begun in *Software* (1982) with hardware out of Barrington Bayley, headware out of John T Sladek, and caviare out of I Click As I Move. And Hilbert Schenck continues to stick to his New England last in *Chronosequence* (Tor), most recent in a series of odes to the ocean, to oceanography, to ships and shipwrecks, to women of knowledge and independence, to the unguent of love. It is a grown person's guide; and *Steam Bird* (Tor) is a grown person's cap in the air. Highly silly – a steam-driven nuclear bomber takes off from Maine and circles the world for locomotive hobbyists and democracy – and remarkably affectionate, "Steam Bird," the novel-length tale which takes up most of the volume, glows with an innocence only available to real folk on holiday.

Lewis Shiner's *Deserted Cities of the Heart* (Doubleday Foundation), like so many novels and tales set in the guernica shambles of Central America, finds Conrad at the heart of the stew, and stirs elegantly; Mirrorshades and Mayans copulate in the foam. A cognate catholicity in the use of source materials also marks out Bruce Sterling's *Islands in the Net* (Arbor House) as a novel of the Twilight Years of sf, as though Galveston a few years hence were a suburb of the Dying Earth. Nothing is new in Sterling but the most important thing of all: the new junctures he creates: the Medusa raft he hacks into shape to bear us on. In *Catspaw* (Warner), Joan D Vinge puts on cyberpunk like a coat of many colours, but the lass inside is far more interested in unpacking a tiresome old space-opera tale than she is in miscegenating, bright of hue, like Bruce. The noise level of Jack Womack's *Terraplane* (Weidenfeld), on the other hand, owes nothing to accidents of style, though he is a very noisy writer. At its electric heart – which is a dystopian alternate 1939 in Manhattan – *Terraplane* jumps with disquietude and anguish, judders through its capsizing plot-turns like a rhino in the funhouse. And finally David Zindell, springing full-grown from the brow of Gene Wolfe, gives us *Neverness* (Donald I Fine), a galaxy-spanning space opera of cosmology of very considerable ambition. Its protagonists, a thin dark domineering memorious cruel prig, who has solved all the problems of the plot, almost against his will, and who has trouble relating to his parents, tells his story in the form of a written confession, composed years afterwards for the benefit of the people he now rules. It is a tribute to Zindell's strength of mind that despite the claustral Autarchy of its model *Neverness* does slowly manage to become itself.

And that was the colour of the flame in this year of the golem, year of the Twilight hotspurs, year of the small bright hopes. See if they thrive. See if they do. I look for hard rain.

– *The Orbit Science Fiction Yearbook 2* (Orbit, 1989), ed. David Garnett

2. INTERZONE COLUMNS

A Protocol of Candour, with Victims

[In Part One (p. 3), I presented a revised version of a statement of principle I called the *Protocol of Excessive Candour*. The heart of that statement first appeared in *Interzone* 24, at the beginning of my column for that issue, where it took its incipit from a letter by Martin H Smith, which had been published the previous issue, and which had responded negatively to my review of *The Legacy of Heorot* (see p. 30 above) in *Interzone* 21. I feel a bit odd about reproducing the *Protocol* twice, but the principle it states is close to my heart and represents long-held conviction; it may be useful to reproduce here the context which occasioned it; and I'll make some judicious cuts in copying it out again. So here it is again. We begin in medias res 1995.]

I.

As Martin Smith's letter contains some rather scattershot assumptions about my attitudes toward America (where my heart lies), and hard sf (which I love as much as I love space opera, which begat it), and sf novels designed primarily to entertain the reader (yum), it is something of a temptation to become disputatious at this point; but it might be a good deal more valuable to address a more significant implication of his letter.

Mr Smith states that he has not read The Legacy of Heorot, making it clear that he has no grounds to judge whether or not I make a plausible case for dismissing the book. The heart of his complaint lies elsewhere. In Mr Smith's mind my real sin (I suspect) lies in what he might describe as a misapprehension of the task of the reviewer. For Mr Smith, the ideal reviewer is a kind of advocate, a bringer of good news, a door-opener, and it is therefore a betrayal of his function to vitiate the pleasures of a text like The Legacy of Heorot – "Some of us," Mr Smith says, "actually want to enjoy ourselves" – by labouring unduly to understand it, as though one were a spy reconnoitering an enemy fortress. If The Legacy of Heorot belongs to an honoured and popular category of writing within the buttresses of sf, then it is an act of disloyalty against those who love that category to trash the exemplum. It is not the task of reviewers of sf to dismantle the works they are meant to announce, or so I read Mr Smith to argue. The real task of reviewers of sf is that of proclaiming gifts.

What I have presented Mr Smith as claiming is surely not dishonourable. But this is not to say that what he says is not in fact pretty troubling. Here in the tangled beehive of sf, most of us who review books already know each other too well for comfort, and perhaps for honesty, and most of us do not need Mr Smith to persuade us to do the mealy mouth. As a reviewer of sf for 25 years, I have myself come inevitably to know most of the writers whose books I comment upon, and to feel a kind of collegiality with them – a personal connection which includes, by the way, both Larry Niven and Jerry Pournelle, though not yet Steven Barnes. Because of this club-like camaraderie, I have often felt (and I suspect most others reviewers have felt) an awful temptation to stroke, to act as an audience-warmer or emcee, and to avoid giving pain (which can always ricochet into one's own face). And it is a consequence of this dubious punctilio that the beehive buzzes with so many "friends" who will not review the books of anyone they know, in case they have to tell the truth.

But it is the truth that sets us free, and reviewers who will not tell the truth are like cholesterol. They are lumps of fat. They starve the heart. I have certainly been a member of that company myself, have sometimes kept my mouth shut out of this "friendship" which is nothing in the end but self-interest. And perhaps it is time to call a halt. Perhaps we should establish a Protocol of Candour, a convention within the community that excesses of intramural harshness are less damaging than the hypocrisies of stroke therapy, that telling the truth about The Legacy of Heorot is a way of expressing love for Protector. Because truth is all we've got. Because if we don't talk to ourselves, and if we don't use every tool at our command in our time on Earth to tell the truth, nobody else will.

II.

Which brings us to the unfortunate Blue Fruit (Simon & Schuster UK, 1988), a first novel by Adam Lively. Not identified in any fashion as sf or fantasy by its publishers, Blue Fruit may have been conceived by its author as a fabulation whose references to sf/fantasy topoi are no more than quotes aimed downwards at the reader from those higher regions where Craig Raine chats with Kafka about the metaphysics of First Contact. If Blue Fruit seems therefore only to make indolent half-cocked sense of itself as a tale of time travel, and to give scant compass to the confrontation with alienness that seems to lie at its timid heart, it may be that the reader has failed properly to register the contented self-referentiality of the author's use of the time travel topos, or of any other material condescendingly quoted from the matrix.

The story is strangely simple. In 1787, a young English doctor named John Field who has dabbled in music finds himself at loose ends in the Far East, takes passage on a Russian whaler with whose captain he establishes a vaguely Conradian relationship, and after a great storm sees an unknown land in the offing, which he wishes to explore. The captain has him landed on the beach (of Erewhon, as it were) and leaves the book. Field wanders about for a while until he comes across what turn out to be railway tracks, though he is no more capable of registering their strangeness than Karl Rossmann (from Kafka's Amerika) would be. Soon adopted by a black family, Field gradually begins to settle into what (though Lively gives no names) looks very much like twentieth-century New Orleans (without automobiles), and to participate in jazz sessions. He has somehow travelled through time, perhaps into what the sf reader would conceive of as an alternate future (though Lively, by paying no attention to the repertory of apparatus of modern sf, makes absolutely no use of that repertory to enrich the structure of his fable). And here, after a brief Malcolm-like experience (à la James Purdy) with a grotesque corporation guru, the novel ends. There have been some moderately enlightened descriptions of jazz.

The text is made up entirely of a letter John Field writes (backwards through what Lively is disinclined to call time) to his father in 1787, but no care has of course been taken to shape the form and manner of that letter into a dramatic enactment of the coulisses of estrangement separating the two eras; within a page or so of starting his missive, John Field is speaking of "diplomats" (first OED reference being 1813) and using "introverted" in the Jungian (rather than the very different 18th-century) sense. The contrast between Lively's bemused indolence on this score and the fructifying pyrotechnic density of (as an example) David I Masson's "A Two-Timer" is deeply numbing. But perhaps we are simply not meant to care. About Field himself we are clearly not meant to bother our heads: the historical John Field

(1782–1837), a rather weird Irish composer and pianist who lived for some time in Russia and influenced Chopin, is 20 years too young to fit into Blue Fruit; and in any case, through the prism of Lively's fatally torpid imagination, Field is nothing but a dinky fiddler capable of rambling on about Purcell and Handel concerts in 1780 without managing a mention of Johann Christian Bach, the dominant musical figure in the London of that time. But then, Lively's John Field is just a *quote* of the real John Field. And when Field describes a washing machine as roaring with pain on being turned on (p. 127), Lively is just *quoting* the style of Craig Raine's "A Martian Sends a Postcard Home." And so it goes. Into the dire mortuary somnolence of Blue Fruit, quote after quote raises its head and dies, stupidly. John Kemp's dustwrapper is neat.

III.

Pat Cadigan's Mindplayers (Bantam, 1988) bangs into play with panache and true grit on the part of gumption-filled Alexandra (Deadpan Allie) Haas, who tells her own story, how she mindplayed once too often with an illegal device, how she gets chosen to become part of the establishment, how she learns what it means to become a hotshot pathos-finder, and finally how boring a lot of hard work can become if there's no storyline to string it out on. Along the way are some sharply visualized renderings of the technology of mindplaying, which can be defined as visiting another's mind for fun and therapy without becoming part of its matrix. Deadpan Allie moves from one form of crypto-telepathy to another with inexpressive ease, and some of her patients have mindscapes of startling verisimilitude. But the realization slowly dawns on Deadpan (and the reader) that after she gets educated and hired by a wise elderly entrepreneur out of the Heinlein Umwelt (minus nipples) there is really no story at all to tell, though a couple of hundred pages to tell it in, and the novel loses all its steam long before gravity brings it to a halt.

IV.

It is perhaps too bad that the Protocol of Candour cannot be put to immediate use with Neil Ferguson's Putting Out (Hamish Hamilton, 1988), for the author has been identified with Interzone from the beginning, Putting Out expands on the goon-show semiology of "Randy and Alexei Go Jaw Jaw" from issue 13, and this reviewer knows the man personally. But despite any number of reasons for not praising it unseemly, Putting Out is in fact a very good book, quite brilliantly told, though intermittently skittish in its control of affect, so that the reader sometimes cares rather less than s/he should about the marbled intricacies of Ferguson's plotting.

In the near future of a New York not dissimilar to the near future of the real New York, except for the fact that the style-codes of the presentation of self in everyday life have been significantly foregrounded, the mayoral race between the manichean tuxedos of Rocco da Silva and the slurry agnostical hi-fashion garb-speak of Tina Rauch is reaching its climax, when the building that houses her couturier is bombed. Lieutenant Max Faraday – the semiotician cop from "Randy and Alexei" – is brought immediately into the case, and it is his subsequent dazzling water-spider dance through the sign-systems that shape the buskined harlequinades of post-modern urban life that makes up the substance and the joy of *Putting Out*. Along the road to his solution of the bombing and the murder that follows it, Faraday partici-pates in one of the most arousing and convincing heterosexual seductions ever penned, which is rendered with extraordinary erotic intensity (nothing skittish here) through a pattering semiological dance of penetration codes. By the signs he embraces, Faraday is both humbled and liberated; what Ferguson seems to tell us all, in this poised poignant novel, is that the truth will make you dance.

– *Interzone* 24, Summer 1988

Trinities

IN ONE HAND take an sf trilogy, and in the other hand take a Church. Note how similar they seem; how long they both go on; how remarkable that each tells the same story. In the first volume of a trilogy, for instance, the reader (or celebrant) will witness the conquering of a new world (which is tantamount to the founding of a church) at the hands of a ragamuffin who cannot remember his childhood (or was born of a virgin mother). After disobeying the old geezer in whom he fails to recognize his father (or Baal), the young hero will have crossed the river of death and returned with gifts of conceptual breakthrough (Sermons) from the stars, and begins to rule the transformed kingdom as the story ends. In the second volume, a flattened epoch subsequent to the time of heroes will be experienced by the dogged reader (or beadle), a time of orthodoxy; we will recognize it as the otiose and inter-minable prison called history. In the course of the penal millennium of volume two it will be found that the rulers of the ecumene (or Popes) have transformed the primal dramas of the dawn (volume one) into ritual. Desperately they will attempt to persuade the populace (and the reader) that these eucharists of sacrifice and re-birth (or bear-baiting in the satrapies) are in fact dramas to the death (or genuine sequels), that none of the climaxes in volume two are in fact perjuries against the dawn, and that the ragamuffin (now typically transfigured into a paracletal AI) smiles down from yonder on its priests and incense (which is money in the bank). In the third volume the imperium of the Church, rigid with bloat, will be seen to harbour the birth of a ragamuffin of uncertain parentage, a lithe and feline youth (or avatar) husbanded by a garrulous paraclete, and at his touch the Church will implode like a jellyfish in the sun. And it will be a new dawn. And a new trilogy (which is death warmed over) will soon ensue, if Lester del Rey has his druthers.

I.

Bob Shaw's *The Wooden Spaceships* (Gollancz, 1988) is the second volume of a trilogy. It follows *The Ragged Astronauts* (which should probably have won all the awards for which it was nominated last year [including the Arthur C Clarke Award, on whose panel of judges I sat, and still regret not fighting harder against the eventual winner, the estimable Margaret Atwood, who received the award with polite bewilderment that her dry decorous *Handmaid's Tale* could be mistaken for a ghetto blaster 1995]) by some twenty-four years. The great emigration by balloon from Land to Overland (two planets in binary wedlock, joined by an hourglass of atmosphere) has faded into a dim memory of the dawn. Rather like settlers in Western Canada or Australia, the emigrants to Overland have sunk into a life of songless peneplainal prosperity, and Shaw makes it very clear from the first that volume two of a trilogy is no place for heroes. Now in his fifties, Toller Maraquine, the headstrong quirky ragamuffin who muscled everyone into balloons and jerked them upwards into the new world of volume one, has grown fusty and grim; and his wife Gesalla has become increasingly impatient with his unsated need to lunge into novelties of any sort. The first pages of *The Wooden Spaceships* do not promise a rose garden.

But Shaw (whose first trilogy this is) has no intention of tying himself (or his hero) into granny-knots of false climax. The business of trilogy-building may require a churchly continuity of life on Overland, and an indeterminate end to the war with Land which dominates the first half of the book, but it may be possible to give Maraquine himself something like an fitting end (and thus save *The Wooden Spaceships* from inanition). To do so, Shaw tells two separate stories, which gradually lace together like the fingers of two hands. The first story is of that war with Land, which is conducted at the pinch of the hourglass between the two planets; the technical innovations which enable the Elizabethans under Maraquine to defeat the Armada from Land are hinted at in the title, and are worked out with boyish freshness by both author and protagonist. As far as Maraquine is concerned – and he is too soon caught up in the second storyline to begin to suspect that his victory may be only temporary – the fight against Land ends in exhilaration and triumph, but ends too soon. His own life is a shambles.

At the same time, back on Overland, a young man's bride has been invaded by the space-travelling spore of a symbiont; a spaceship wafts her away to a third planet, called Farland; and she speaks to him by telepathy. Consumed with the need to travel through unknown space to Farland, the young man catches Maraquine's attention at just the point no normal volume two could sate him, and an expedition is soon mounted. After more adventures on the new planet, Maraquine has a terminal apotheosis (at a safe distance from Overland), and as the fingers of the second storyline drop him blessed into oblivion, it is possible to descry (through the mists of time) those fingers joining to a hand, an arm, the entire corpus of a volume three. A long farewell, a new start: very neat. A fine book.

[I print here a review, from *Interzone* 35, of the final volume of the sequence 1995.]

TRILOGIES, promises. Slip cup, lip lip. Shaw Shaw. First there was *The Ragged Astronauts* (1986), elated and bounteous and fresh. The worlds it bridged were fresh, the voice of Bob Shaw in the telling of the tale was fresh and clear and radiant. Then came *The Wooden Spaceships* (1988), which sagaciously sidestepped the orthodoxy rituals (and circular quest splits) endemic to the second volumes of most trilogies. And now we have *The Fugitive Worlds* (Gollancz, 1989), still told in clear, still neat and courteous, still radiant with the author's love for his creation (when he remembers to give it a glance); but bored bored bored stiff.

Here is one of the good bits. Young Toller Maraquine, grandson of the Toller Maraquine whose craggy neurasthenic wanderlust powered the earlier volumes, is taking part in an expedition from Overland back to Land. The fleet has climbed up the hourglass of air connecting the two planets and has reached the halfway point, where the pilots must invert their balloons for the descent. At this point Shaw halts the tale for a paragraph so that Toller can take a look around him.

> Superimposed on each planet, and similarly lit from the side, were the other ships of the fleet..., arcs of white condensation from their lateral jets complementing the global cloud patterns thousands of miles below. And embracing the spectacle was the frozen luminous panoply of the universe – the circles and spirals and streamers of silver radiance, the fields of brilliant stars with blue and white predominant, the silent-hovering comets and the darting meteors.

In this passage one hears – faint and fading – the music of the spheres, the infinitesimal whisper of the Bang; the voice of a creator in love (however briefly) with the world. Very soon, it is gone.

Very soon, we find ourselves trudging through the heart gravel of a world without afflatus, a world abandoned by its namer. This is not to decry the application of certain skills; Shaw is too proficient and too conscientious not to supply The Fugitive Worlds with the kicks and turns of his craft. Young Toller Maraquine differs from his grandfather mainly through what one has learned to call the anxiety of influence – his fear that he is a golem of the sire, and his need therefore to establish his own identity through some healing swerve from type – and Shaw does a responsible job of drawing him in these terms, as a classic depressive, a man of unwilling but compulsive introspections, who can only escape the ghosts of the old Toller within him if there is something to do; but who finds himself lovably incapable of articulating any "unmanly" complexities of motive to his intimates or his staff. If in creating this sensitive and stifled action man Shaw himself feels any twinges of an anxiety of influence – and if this anxiety bears the name of C S Forester, the creator of Horatio Hornblower – there is nothing for him to do but bear them. By 1990, at the end of a century which has seen the publication of several hundred million words of popular literature, it is hardly remarkable that an aura of belatedness seems to accompany any attempt to create action models of the Hero. Of these models, Hornblower is about the most attractive going, and young Toller is a worthy get.

But the tale he captains soon begins to lose its precious air, sinks (as we've said) slowly into the gravel, grinds to a sad halt of the imagination. The first volumes had been driven by a kind of cosmogonic romancing of the old trope and gaudy dance of space opera; but The Fugitive Worlds shows almost nothing of that afflatus, that breath of creative love. The bones remain, and Shaw is finely professional in his manner of jigging them; but it is, all the same, a melancholy fall. Toller's trip to Land, which Shaw tells in deft but alienated narrative spasms, revolves around his obsessive love for a spoiled cockteaser princess whose disappearance causes him to stumble onto a vast AI-cum-stargate floating halfway between the two hourglass-connected worlds, both due to be destroyed the moment the stargate turns itself on in order to allow the planet Dussarra, which has just now appeared out of interstellar darkness, to jump hoop into a new universe in order to escape a galaxy-crushing explosion caused by the knotting of Ropes of superdense matter from the Big Bang, the advancing wavefront of which is only a couple of hundred years upstream from Land and Overland and Toller at this very moment. Heck, what to do. Toller thinks fast, kidnaps a telepathic Dussarran named Divivvidiv who lives in a Flash Gordon castle in the middle of the great (but talkative) stargate, takes him in his wooden spaceship to the invading planet where the spoiled princess is being held captive, rescues her, starts a revolution with the aid of dissident Dussarrans, returns by instantaneous mind-bus to Overland to enact a clever wheeze in order to unbalance the stargate between the worlds whose name is Xa and who continues to complain about being a stargate. And so on. Olaf Stapledon it ain't. We will not reveal the final boil of the pot, except to say that Toller does finally – 200 pages late –notice that the princess is rotten silly; and to say that the universe of the trilogy is definitively exited. And the afflatus of its beginning turns to ash, which Bob Shaw shakes from his heels.

So – unfortunately – do we.

[End of excerpt from *Interzone* 35]

II.

In *Mona Lisa Overdrive* (Gollancz, 1988), William Gibson wraps up a trilogy he may never have intended to write, but now has. In the event it's lucky that the enormous success of *Neuromancer* called so poignantly for sequels, and that the £15,000,000 pound advance from Gollancz – accompanied by the promise of pictorial wrappers for the third volume – was so hard to turn down. Though hampered by some jiggery-pokery with false climaxes, *Count Zero* clearly improves on the shape of *Neuromancer*, a novel whose plot escaped like gas from all its terminals. And although the greasepaint professionalism – or, more politely, the Mannerist polish – of the middle third of *Mona Lisa Overdrive* conceals a certain absence of forward narrative, through this dazzle of arrases a confluence of hinted-at tales does eventually dance into one cyberspace-encompassing shape, and the novel closes with a sudden perspective shift, a sense of wonder, an outward grin.

The first volumes of the trilogy were dense with data and plot and character, and in volume three Gibson faced the considerable technical challenge of presenting this material (which in a church is called dogma) without indulging in great Wagnerian gobs of rehash. The cardsharp glissandos of stagecraft through which he couches his solution are smoothly ingenious, and its intricate working-out glistens with panache. In *Mona Lisa Overdrive* the reader will encounter not one or two but four protagonists of equal weight. Each inhabits a separate thread of story. Each needs extensive briefing on the parts of volumes one and two which affect her (three of the four protagonists are female). In a forward direction, Mona, a sixteen-year-old whore, also learns that the cosmetic surgery she undergoes will enable her to substitute for famed actress Angie Mitchell (from *Count Zero*), who learns that 3Jane (whose essence derives from *Neuromancer*) has blackmailed Molly/Sally (from the same book) to abduct her, while at the same time, in Dog Solitude in the rustswamps of New Jersey, Slick Henry learns that the cyberspace jockey in a coma he's minding is in fact Count Zero, and that... It goes on and on. It is polished and urbane and sly, a rollercoaster of applied technique. For the celebrant the ante is vertigo, then joy at seeing the edifice (a most intricate low church) consumed.

Mona Lisa Overdrive comes most to life when it concentrates upon its fourth protagonist, Kumiko Yanaka, a Japanese pre-teen whose corporate-crime-warlord father sends her to England to escape danger. In the runnels of the decaying world-city of London, she and her biochip ghost pal Colin learn a great deal about what's happening elsewhere in the novel, and telephone the information on to those who need it – *they* certainly don't. Surviving exposure to a metropolis caught in the kind of heat-death infarcts Dickens in his old age might have dreamed, Kumiko – who is in fact almost totally extrinsic to the actual *story* of *Mona Lisa Overdrive*, but who adorns it – is Gibson's warmest creation to date, and may hint at his next move; which we await.

III.

After dexterously avoiding the job at hand in his evasive crafting of *In the Drift*, Michael Swanwick has written a second novel so much better than its predecessor, and so crammed with material, that there seems little point in thinking of both books in the same paragraph (or world). Like Kim Stanley Robinson's *The Memory of Whiteness* (1985), *Vacuum Flowers* (Arbor House, 1987) is a gravity-well tour, revving up among the asteroids and careening down to Earth in the end. But unlike *Memory* (which is Robinson's only failed novel to date), *Vacuum Flowers* makes extremely adroit use of the cyberpunk rhetoric of information overload, the deadpan medias-res data-buzz which characterizes the best work of writers like Gibson. Swanwick's protagonist – Rebel Elizabeth Mudlark – has parachuted mysteriously into one of the corporation-dominated habitats that choke the solar system, and died. Recorded immediately, she soon piggybacks a persona bum, chipping into a complex power game amongst the gesellschaften (a cyberpunk word for Krupp), but before she can be terminated a deuteragonist more knowledgeable than she is befriends her, and inveigles her downwards to Earth, where the secret of her "integrity" – the unwarpable fixity of her selfhood – will make everyone rich, change the world, open pathways to the stars, and return Rebel to her mother, who has engineered the whole thing.

It is a thin story, precariously told, lost in the data-buzz for chapters on end, but sufficient, because the heart of Vacuum Flowers lies in its title. Vacuum flowers are ostensibly real flowers that grow in space, "tough little things, almost impossible to exterminate." But clearly Swanwick intends them as metaphors of his vision of humanity: ineradicable, fecund, tribal, invasive, spunky. There may be a touch of the heinleins (RIP) in this vision of folk as thaumaturges of the buzz, but also something that reads like empathy. After the fatuities of the Humanist–Cyberpunk squabble, it is a good sign.

IV.

For many readers, the title will tell the tale of a closed book: The Sykaos Papers; Being an Account of the Voyages of the Poet Oi Paz to the System of Strim in the Seventeenth Galaxy; of his Mission to the Planet Sykaos; of his First Cruel Captivity; of his Travels about its Surface; of the Manners and Customs of its Beastly People; of his Second Captivity; and of his Return to Oitar. To which are added many passages from the Poet's Journal, documents in Sykotic script, and other curious matters. Selected and edited by Q, Vice-Provost of the College of Adjusters. Transmitted by Timewarp to E P Thompson (Bloomsbury, 1988). Understand that Sykaos (pronounce it) is Earth; understand that the Beastly People are humans; understand that Oi Paz is a golden androgyne from a far planet come to determine whether Earth is suitable for colonization: then open the book, or do not. You are warned. E P Thompson has written a Swiftian satire, a fantastic voyage to dystopia, a didactic fable, a tract, a diatribe; he has not written (nor could he have intended to have written) an sf novel.

There are costs. By disdaining the generic tropes developed by humbler writers over the decades to establish verisimilitude within the attention span of mortals, Thompson manages to consume a huge number of pages getting his visitor to Earth, and settling Oi Paz into the proper study of mankind. And by disdaining the genuine sophistication of the sf approach to the representation of Otherness, he consumes an additional burden of pages in utterly torpid – and strangely pulpish – cartoon descriptions of the Oitarean world; it is a failure of imagination and craft that make The Sykaos Papers almost unreadable for much too long. For those who give up – for whom the jejune smugness of Thompson's refusal of technique is intolerable – the loss will be great. In the centre of The Sykaos Papers lies a discourse of very great intensity about the Beastly People, about the Mother Earth they are devouring, about nuclear war, sex, power, clothes. As Oi Paz enters the vale of tears of blood and flesh, his martian incomprehension turns into a bondage of empathy and the yahoos push the button, terminating the book in a flash and cinder. Which ends the species, and the dream.

– Interzone 25, September/October 1988

Space Aria Caught in Larynx. Thousands Flee.

IT IS a fine new day and the suns are bright. Dew glistens on the robot and the axe. The robot says Good morning, or perhaps it is the axe, which you stole as a child from the secret fortress in the mountain, and which looks very grave today. Suddenly a mother ship of the enemy pierces the upper atmosphere, blotting out a sun. The axe begins to sing. Nothing could be finer than to live inside an opera, just before the aria of the war. But you've got to believe in the thing. The problems Iain "M" Banks had with Consider Phlebas (1987), his first attempt at contributing to the genre, lay not in any absence of space-opera paraphernalia, which he was markedly unchary of supplying in crates, or from a lack of stylistic muscle, because he is a writer jovial with energy, a jostler of material, a flexer. What flummoxed Phlebas had nothing to do with any failure of excess, but with the fact that his tale of self-destruction and futility constantly argued with the space-opera frame in which it took place, so that whenever Banks flexed his muscles he tended to break every bone in the book. It all made an unholy racket, or so this reviewer argued in Interzone 20 [see p. 26], and Consider Phlebas ended up pounding the shit out of itself.

The reader of Phlebas may remember that the changeling mercenary and exile whose tale it tells (his name is Borza Horza, which sounds rather like what geldings do to mares) chooses the wrong side in a galaxy-spanning war, and that the forces of the Culture finally triumph over the ludicrous bullies he's chosen to work with. The protagonist of The Player of Games (Macmillan, 1988; limited ed £75), which is Banks's second sf novel, and a vast improvement on the first, makes no such mistake, though his name is so long and stertorous (like a golem's fart) that Banks only mentions it once in 300 pages. The short form of this hero's monicker is (for there is something about Iain "M" Banks that does not like a name that humans can pronounce) Jernau Morat Gurgeh (or, as I found myself subvocalizing it, Jarndyce Deadly Gargle), and at one point (it is a moment one fears the author does not think is funny) aliens mispronounce the full form, addressing him as Chark Gavant-sha Gernow Morat Gurgee Dam Hazeze (which differs from the true full form of his name in ways which would crash computers, if quoted: so I won't). An incident is narrowly averted. But this is not all. The drone who monitors Deadly Gargle through thick and thin will only answer to his real name, Sprant Flere-Imsaho Wu-Handrahen Xato Trabiti, as the tale nears its end, long after the reader has become as accustomed as possible to addressing him under his *alias*, Trebel Flere-Imsaho Ep-Handra Lorgin Estral; the name of girl terraformer with whom Gargle lives is Yay Meristinoux; and when he finally reaches the Evil Empire he is destined to destroy, the first human Jarndyce Deadly Gargle meets, the Culture ambassador, is called Shohobohaum Za. So we have one drone with two dyslexias, one cheerleader on a piste, and an absolutely enormous bottle of Za. And we have hardly begun. Bit players include Olz Hap, Professor Boruelal, Chamlis Amalk-ney, Lo Pequil Mone-nine. (Trinev Dutleysdaughter, whose surname is altogether too sane, appears only once.) There is an Orbital called Chiark, and a river called Groasnachek, and a country retreat called Ikroh, and a moderately serious point can surely be made before we stop going on about Banks's way with a name: When they come across strange sound mounds, most readers will attempt to subvocalize them (I certainly do), and each time the miscegenate syllables that designate the hero besmear a page of this book the larynx aches, the tongue stalls, the eye falters. Every time an unpronounceable growth of vowel and consonant appears in a text like *The Player of Games*, a baulk is laid against the mind's tongue, a jam against the act (and art) of reading. Even where it fails to seem to aspire to wit, Banks's way with proper names reminds one of fanzine humour at its most maniacally tedious; and this book is too good to spoil.

Seven hundred years have passed since *Consider Phlebas*, and the Culture continues to exercise a loose hegemony over the home galaxy. On Chiark Orbital, Jernau Morat Gurgeh, perhaps the finest human generalist of games in the Culture, begins to grow stale. Like Borza Horza of the previous volume, Gurgeh is something of an internal exile; but there is nothing of the potential suicide in his makeup. At the same time he is vulnerable, and is easily bamboozled into an action open to blackmail. The disgraced drone Mawhrin-Skel (a drone is a portable, legally autonomous AI) soon threatens to expose him unless he manages to finagle his (Skel's) readmission into the elite Contact corps of the Culture. Coincidentally (as it seems), Gurgeh is now invited by a Contact drone to travel on the Culture's behalf to the evil empire of Azad, a civilization shaped around the public and private agons of a game that so thoroughly maps and engrosses the hierarchies of empire that the game itself is called azad. Gurgeh agrees to make the long trip on condition that Skel be considered for readmission into Contact. Seemingly reluctant, the drone agrees.

The rest of the book is easy to understand, easy to follow, easy to decipher; it is swift, surefooted, pell-mell, and glows with a benign luxuriance. And harmony reigns. The story does not poison the world-rules that monitor it; the muscles do not break the bones. There are two clear reasons for this earned truce. One) although Gurgeh has transparently been fitted up for his Empire-demolishing role, Azad does deserve (in space-opera terms) its comeuppance, and Gurgeh accomplishes his mission with panache and some cunning. Indeed, most readers will assume he tumbled to the true location and role of Mawhrin-Skel as soon as they do, about half-way through the story; and will consequently assume that his subsequent playing of Skel's game is elated and *volunteer*. Two) Banks gives all his allegiance as writer to the Culture itself, which he draws in terms both utopian and pragmatic. For the spacefaring citizens of the Culture, energy is essentially free, which snaps the unholy linkage of money and power; larger problems of logistics remain safely under the control of the vast (but witty) Minds who shape our mortal ends; as befits a civilization of autonomous hedonists, public crimes are punished through shame (ostracism) rather than guilt (penance), and there are no laws governing private behaviour; by becoming even more fully himself, Gurgeh does only what the great Minds clearly intend of their human charges. Within the celebratory frame of this exhilarated, comic, glowing book, Gurgeh's triumph over Azad is a triumph of genuine Culture over caricature (Azad's similarity to the loadsamoney factory farm solitude that is modern Britain cannot be anything but deliberate). And so the truce obtains. Gurgeh returns to his home Orbital, and lies with Yay (hurrah), and the worlds are won for real people. Would we lived there.

II.

There is nothing wrong with *Cradle* (Gollancz, 1988) by Arthur C Clarke (whose name appears in giant letters on the dustwrapper) and Gentry Lee (whose letters are wee) that cutting the book in half and completely rewriting the residue couldn't fix maybe. An alien star-seeder spaceship needing repairs lands in the ocean near Key West, hornswoggling an experimental guided missile and driving whales crazy. A human cast gets its knickers wet searching for the buried treasure. The robot crew of the ship persuades the good guys to provide it with some gold the bad guys stole from the good guys many years earlier, and uses the gold to repair the ship, and the ship leaves, after 308 pages. The bulk of this deliriously inept novel is devoted to wooden life histories of the various humans who make up the cast (but not one single potted word of resume links up, in any fashion whatsoever, to the tiny bit of action that ends the book) and to philistine descriptions of the transformation of Key West into a theme park of unparalleled egregiousness (the Chamber of Commerce booster-lingo utilized by the authors to describe the physical transfer of the interior of Ernest Hemingway's original bar, from a real building in a real street in the real world, into the middle of a covered shopping mall with Muzak must be read to be believed). But one must not refer to *authors*. Clarke may have supplied synopsis, and a few of the cleaner passages about the seedling stars; but surely Gentry Lee (and a word-processor without Help or Delete or Esc! Esc!) must actually have *written* the thing. Mr Clarke has tied himself to a dog's tail. It is no way to approach the end of such a career.

III.

Rudy Rucker's *Wetware* (Avon, 1988) is clumsy, jagged, witty, metaphysical, bumptious, pixillated and first-draft. It follows on some years after the close of *Software*. Sladek-style robots have their own city on the Moon. Their language games are stunningly laid on. But the plot thickens. Humans connive and deceive. The robots want to sleep with Mother Earth and drink oceans of new data up her umbilicals. Some plots are thwarted, others begin to build up steam. It looks like spaghetti junction with kyphosis and no way out of Birmingham, but a third volume is promised; if Rucker can spare a few extra days to write the thing down in calm tame English, a brilliant conclusion may ensue.

IV.

Mark V Ziesing's series of small press publications continues with a bulky fable carved in stone. Lucius Shepard's stunning long moral tale, *The Scalehunter's Beautiful Daughter* (Mark V Ziesing, 1988, limited ed $35), returns to the slightly po-faced Märchen terrain of "The Man who Painted the Dragon Griaule," and to the same mile-long stoned dragon, cast into immobility by a wizard in the dawn of the world, but still capable of dominating his environment through a geology of dreams "emanating from the cold tonnage of his brain." A young woman flees through its open mouth into the veins and cavities of the interior of the huge metaphysical beast of *Umwelt*, where, watched over by brain-damaged art-critics, the great heart of the Thing Itself prepares to beat. After many years, the young woman – wiser, reborn, extremely formidable – returns to the surface, where she will continue to live, like Dorothea at the end of *Middlemarch*, unsung but singing, it may be. *The Scalehunter's Beautiful Daughter* is short enough to grasp in one sitting, but dense enough to fix the mind upon its gravitas, the veined ore of its gift. Buy it.

– Interzone 26, November/December 1988

Romancing the Stilts

HERE IS PART of the last page of Marcel Proust's *Remembrance of Things Past*. I have always taken it as a description of sf. "I now understood," says Marcel, "why the Duc de Guermantes...had tottered when he got up and wanted to stand erect...and had moved, trembling like a leaf on the hardly approachable summit of his eighty-three years, as though men were perched upon living stilts which keep on growing, until walking become difficult and dangerous and, at last, they fall. I was terrified that my own were already so high beneath me, and I did not think I was strong enough to retain for long a past that went back so far and that I bore within me so painfully." Every science fiction book, in other words, perches upon living stilts which are the accumulated texts – the family of read books – that define the genre, and by 1988 the stilts had grown very tall.

Trembling like leaves on the hardly approachable summit of the end of a century that began with the death of Jules Verne, two big novels totter into view. The tales they tell are inherited (but not entirely), the wisdoms they endow us with are stilt-sap (but seem as fresh-minted as one could hope for), and the style and iconography of both books so deeply resound to earlier tunes that a kind of echolalia can bewitch the mind's internal ear (but melodies do emerge). David Zindell's *Neverness* (Donald I Fine, Inc, 1988, appallingly proof-read; UK edition, Grafton, 1989, completely reset) and Richard Grant's *Rumors of Spring* (Bantam Books, 1987) are both paradigm texts for the analysis of the late maturity of a genre literature. They tremble like leaves with the burden.

It is certainly a coincidence that both books are 458 large pages long, but it is no coincidence that both Zindell and Grant plump for amplitude, for both writers are swallowers, and both need space to sort out the materials to which they have given rebirth. Zindell has not published a novel before, but Grant's *Saraband of Lost Time* (1985), which was of only moderate length, never quite managed fully to ingest M John Harrison's Viriconium; in the end, it was like watching a rather small snake trying to eat a very crabby ferret. *Rumors of Spring*, on the other hand, has plenty of room to accommodate and to renew the disjecta membra amputated from Harrison's city aetherized upon a table at the end of time, including a street in the metropolis of Riverrun which Grant supinely dubs the Aleatory Strand; while hunting transatlantic prey for its main repast. But *Neverness* first. It is the confession of a man who becomes something of a god. It is told in the first person.

I.

The Home Galaxy is populous with homo sapiens, though Old Earth has long bitten the dust. FTL travel is possible through the spiderweb pathways or manifolds of
thickspace, but only members of the Order of Pilots, housed in the city of Neverness
on the planet Icefall for almost 3000 years, have the training required for anything
but the simplest of transits; this training is primarily mathematical (or cantorial, for
mathematicians are called cantors in *Neverness*) and pilots see their course through
the manifold as an ongoing dance of ideoplasts for which it is their duty to supply
solutions. True solutions create the way onward. As the novel begins, the Lord Pilot
of the Order has just returned from one of the exploratory quests expected of Lord
Pilots of the Order. Fenestering (which in *Neverness* has to do with traversing access
windows in the manifold) inwards towards the galactic core, the Lord Pilot has received a message from the heart of a singularity, home of the Ieldra (an elder race
intermediary between mortals and what one might well call the Increate, though
Zindell doesn't). The message is simple: To solve the mystery of the Vild (a sector of
the galaxy whose stars are exploding) and to gain immortality for homo sapiens,
man must examine his past and his future. Know thyself.

The young man whose autobiography (written down years later for the benefit of
humanity) makes up the text of *Neverness* is himself, at the time of the Lord Pilot's
return, a journeyman in the Order. Mallory Ringess tells his story in a style rich in
speculative ponderings, labyrinthine exactitudes, and in a tone of profound recol-
lective tranquillity, as though many decades had passed. He is prone to the making
of distinctions of a markedly jesuitical fineness (his father is "the second most complicated man I have ever known"; actions can be measured as with calipers: "Then I
made a mistake, the second worst mistake, I think, of my life."), and often stops in
the middle of recounting an action or tumult to construct an epiphany of analysis
on the implications of the scene. His style is mandarin, measured, haunting. The
very first sentence of the book quotes Isaac Newton, secretly; and the play of metaphors whose terms bed deeply into the matter of the tale never ceases. Evenly and
calmly, and with chill assurance, he speaks to his readers as though they were children of his loins whom he never expected to meet.

Mallory very closely resembles the Lord Pilot, indeed he is his mirror image, and
suspects (rightly) that he may be his son. Like his father, he is tall, thin, dark, immensely strong, compelling; violent, vain, passionate, secretive and cruel. He cannot stand untruths, and will not tell them. He is in love with a woman called
Katherine. Though at first he does not have a photographic memory, by page 364 he
confesses that he "can't forget anything." By the end of the novel he has graduated

from journeyman to Lord of the Order; his rise has seemed predestined. At the heart of Neverness, in a glittering clump, rather like long-abandoned spaceships (though Zindell does not say so) stand the spires of the Orders under his command – the cantors, the pilots, the eschatologists (ie genetic scientists), and so forth. In the course of his anguished rise to dominance, he has penetrated to the heart of a god-like mainbrain whose ganglia are the size of moons; he has lived with (and half-destroyed through the incontinent savagery of his rage) a primitive tribe of arti-factual Neanderthals, and they have killed him; he has been reborn, subtly trans-formed at the hands of an aquatic civilization; he has been engaged in an inter-stellar war; he has solved the mystery of the Vild (a gross population explosion of primitive humans is blowing up stars to propel inefficient breeding ships hither and yon: just like now); and he has solved the mystery of DNA, which is that we are programmed to ride the universe as though it were our very skin and bones, which it is. A little later (if Zindell writes a second volume) Mallory will come to judge the quick and the dead.

Archaeologists of the stilt will detect in some of this, and in the dense impasto of local colour which unduly elongates and blurs some episodes, more than a hint of Jack Vance; and it is of course true that the prime influence on Zindell's long-breathed epic hard-sf fantasia, Gene Wolfe's *The Book of the New Sun*, also owes a debt to Vance. But *Neverness*'s derivation from *The Book* is more than casual. Mallory and Severian look alike, talk alike, suffer alike, write the same kind of confessional alike, triumph alike. (It might be mentioned at this point that in *The Book* Wolfe was the first sf author manifestly to make the confession mode work; and that the trans-formative dynamic he unleashed upon the mute inglorious tropes of space opera were by no means exhausted in *The Book of the New Sun*.) Mallory and Severian are siblings of an earned eminence; the novels they dominate have in common a kind of cosmogonic chill; *Neverness* moves on from its model chiefly by refusing the recur-sive closures of the plot of *The Book*. It is, in comparison, an open, relaxed, expan-sive tale, and Zindell's real interest in hardware further aerates his bid to walk upon the stilts. Once in a while a bit of hardware lingo – there is quite a bit of codswallop about the "programs" which shape our behaviour, and about how with one bound we'd all be free if we just learned how to deprogram ourselves – does rather dimin-ish Mallory's urgent scrutinizing flow, but in the end *Neverness* is a victorious book, strong and lithe and rich and taught.

II.

About Richard Grant's *Rumors of Spring*, now more than a year old, less need be said. Colin Greenland's review of the American release in *Foundation* 39 does, in any case, cover most of the bases. He notes the influence of M John Harrison, but correctly (I think) concentrates on John Crowley's *Little, Big* (1981), for the weight of that model comes dangerously close to crushing *Rumors* altogether. Once again we are in a land rather like America After the *Rain*, the balkanized entropy-ridden washed-out empery of *Saraband of Lost Time*; but this time a prologue, which is set in a vague near future and an equally vague (and utterly unnamed) western United States, does generate a sense that *Rumors of Spring* has been fixed to the engine of time. There may (one feels) even be a plot. Or Story. And indeed there is. After suffering through the kind of ecological privations that in our own real world are beginning to close the book on Gaia, the one remaining forest in the land has, five hundred years later, begun savagely and intemperately to grow. Farms and villages are being eaten. So the Hardy Plant Society (almost as Crowleyesque a formulation as the Silent Partners' Club in Riverrun, whose members hope to shape world history from within their sanctum, as it passes) funds an expedition called the First Biotic Crusade (which sounds Harrisonian, but which, at a venture, derives, I'd suggest, from Mark S Geston's *Lords of the Starship*, 1967). Lord Tattersall (a dead ringer for Titus Groan's pa) takes indolent command, and the rickety land leviathan of the Crusade creaks northwards into the last forest with a crew from Peake.

It is here that Grant finds his stilts begin to do the splits. He is clearly at home in the Viriconium mode to which both his novels pay due homage, and build modestly from; but at the heart of any Harrison fantasy novel lies a deep refusal to accede to genre demands for answers couched in the old rigmarole of story. Crowley's very American books, on the other hand, not only tender an equally deep allegiance to the engendering power of Story, but actually tell tales. This is more than Grant can comfortably do in *Rumors of Spring*. Despite his desire to move his cast into proper confrontation with the mystery of the deep woods, he cannot keep away from the tropes of baulk, and in his hands entropy gnaws the Biotic Crusade into camp desuetude for huge desert stretches of text; its final arrival at the heart of the wood – the deep immersion of *Little, Big* in *A Midsummer Night's Dream* is quoted half-heartedly at this point – fails almost totally to move the reader. Once in the woods, though, some elegant answers do begin to find shape. As in *Neverness*, DNA can be spoken to from the heart's depths, and instructed. Long ago the researcher who was murdered in the prologue had done precisely this. Unfortunately (viz Robert Holdstock's *Mythago Wood*) after her death the essence of the forest shaped itself

into the heart-space and imago of her young son, Robin Goodfellow, not an easy allusion to miss, and Robin is now, after five hundred years, going through the ravenous solipsism of puberty; hence the inchoate growth of the woods, like pimples. In
the nick of time, DNA and imago sort themselves out, and the novel ends in passages – it is by now no matter how laboriously they were achieved – of surefooted
earned elation. After so many pages ill-at-ease at being told, the bootstrapping joy
of this conclusion is almost unconfined. Puckish.

– Interzone 27, January/February 1989

A Worm in the Opera

AMERICAN SF is a goitre on the esophagus of true romance, says Brian Stableford,
or words to that effect. So it's not the case that American sf owns the language which
English sf writers have to learn, losing their souls in the process, as Brian Aldiss has
said, or words to that effect; what Stableford argues, in his fine and searching *Scientific Romance in Britain* (1985), is that an inherent distinction can be drawn between sf
as created by American pulp writers from 1926 on, and scientific romances as created by H G Wells and written in Great Britain from the end of the nineteenth century
down to the present day. To call *Childhood's End* (1953) a sf novel is, for instance, significantly, though not fatally, to misprision Clarke's long cool dream of twilight.

There is no precise definition of the scientific romance, or at any rate none that
Stableford is willing to give in the long accumulation of studies of writers like Wells
and Stapledon and S Fowler Wright and John Gloag which makes up the bulk of his
text; but a polythetic stab can be made at describing the form. The scientific romance – I'd suggest – *tends* to present to the reader a plot-structure more designed
to open aperçus of cognition or contemplation than to enable its protagonists to triumph. For the reader accustomed to the cinematic/pulp felicities of the traditional
sf novel, the protagonist of a scientific romance will tend to seem passive and morose and bespectacled and plump; not the man on the horse who saves the galaxy,
but his scribe. The protagonist of the scientific romance will rarely tap the sources
of kinetic energy available – if only remotely – in the text of which s/he is the "star."
As the star, he may cast light upon the world, helping us to discern its grave structure, but no light will ever shine through her, she will never be *transparent* to the engine of story. Never will the protagonist of a scientific romance drive the engine of
the world, singing. Ultimately, he is not an engineer but a *gaze*.

The desiderium inherent in that gaze – remote, poetical, ruminative, melancholic, fin-de-siècle – infuses the archetypal scientific romance with a powerful sense of retrospection. The vista is long and deep; and in most scientific romances, a flow of these vistas, or aperçus, will gradually impart an evolutionary argument to the tale, a sense of (usually brooding) entelechy beyond our physical compass, for we are not superheroes, nor immortal; but not beyond our awe at the rules which bind, from so long ago, just as in most science fantasy novels.

I.

Stableford's own Empire of Fear (1988) is an almost perfect example of the scientific romance's strengths and weaknesses; its narrative rhythms clearly violate any normal expectations of any normal reader of American genre novels about vampires, somewhat to its cost. But this is part of the bargain. In the case of Paul J McAuley's Four Hundred Billion Stars (Gollancz, 1988), it is less easy to judge if certain costs were in fact premeditated, or if they were the inevitable consequence of an attempt by a writer in the scientific-romance mould to generate Yankee space-opera tropes; for it is certainly the case that, even though he walks the boardwalk, McAuley is not much of a triumphalist.

At first glance, the plot has all the instamatic ebullience of the best American brands. Bursting into unsettled space, an expanding interstellar Terran hegemony has found an alien fleet resisting its advance, and hostilities begin. A few light-years distant, another planet shows evidence of alien terraforming activities which seem to have begun several aeons earlier, but which are still continuing. The space navy investigates! A female telepathic research scientist is commandeered across the parsecs to winkle out any traces of alien sentience! She soon comes to understand that the baboon-like native herders and the giant locomotive killdozer amoebas they harvest and munch are in fact (on time-honoured generic lines) different stages of the same species, and that near-adult imagos are being called to a great spiral tower in the centre of a caldera as part of their growth cycle, because the immense squiggles of hieroglyphic runes which ring the tower are designed to transform them (on time-honoured generic lines) into fully adult ancient enemy alien males.

So far so good. It would seem. But the telepath cannot forget that she has in effect been kidnapped and lied to by the military, and that her superior officers are neither competent or pure at heart. As in almost every scientific romance ever written, therefore, McAuley's protagonist progresses through Four Hundred Billion Stars in a state of profound alienation from the energies that empower the establishments of the world. Entirely typical of her generic origins in Wells and Beresford and Stapledon, she maintains a hostile indifference to the masculine kinetic web that *operates* her, willy-nilly. This may be "realistic" – though in a context of telepathy and FTL doubletalk spaceships and metempsychotic alien hoohaws, the point of this sort of realism may be hard to ascertain – but it is not space opera. As the novel progresses, true to its schismatic nature we find that the protagonist's telepathy does her little good, because it gives her splitting headaches and cannot be controlled and brain damage results from its use. Nor does she manage to keep her unprepossessing lover alive on a field trip which is in any case almost certainly unnecessary for the plot, though it does enable us to *see* a lot, in the scientific-romance mode. Nor does the novel itself exactly end in triumph for the masculine principle; the plight of the trapped aliens on the planet is dire, and worsens, and the war is almost guaranteed not to end soon, and the enforced interventions of the shanghaied half-breed have rescued virtually nothing from the shambles. But she has been a *witness*. Clearly it is sufficient for McAuley that she has witnessed – and that his readers have witnessed – something of the long slow grinding of the mills of the gods over millennia. Who should care that the plot itself is a snare, a circumbendibus into entropy?

So the book is an erosion, and in this almost perfectly represents the effects in general of the British scientific-romance imagination on the sf formats it so often tries to simulate, like a computer worm or virus which inhabits a program and devours it. Computer viruses are sarcasms from within the gut. So is this novel. Its effect on the reader – though at points bracing – is not altogether fortunate. We did not demand a space opera from McAuley, but it did seem we were getting one; once we had *Four Hundred Billion Stars*, it was not necessarily our good luck that it turned out to have been designed to eat itself sick.

II.

Gwyneth Jones does not get less odd. Her adult novels – of which *Kairos* (1988) [see p. 134] is the most recent – increasingly turn the world to stone with their ungiving gaze, the slightly benumbing offhandedness of their diction, the elisions of plotting through which the unwitting – the *uninitiated* – can too easily topple. There is an extremely strange sense in these recent titles that they are addressed to an audience which inhabits a magic circle of understanding with the author, and which doesn't consequently *need* the actual books; and that those outside that circle don't *deserve* them. None of this yet applies to the children's tales Jones has published as Gwyneth A Jones, and later under the name of Ann Halam; nor does it apply to *The Hidden Ones* (The Women's Press, 1988), published under her own name, and one of the first young-adult books to be released by The Women's Press under its Livewire imprint. It is a stunning little fable.

In a precisely captured South Sussex milieu of small towns on the verge of becoming Thatchervilles, young Adele edges her prickly, precarious, ambush-ridden way towards adulthood. Her generally latent, almost totally uncontrollable powers of telekinesis have (it seems) helped break up her family, and have certainly caused behaviour on her part which gave the authorities sufficient excuse to institutionalize her. As a final chance, she returns to her father and his new wife; meets a lady scientist (who has in fact met her, in order to study her gifts); finds the ancient well that magicked her childhood (and perhaps shaped her powers) to be under threat from a Volvo-driving overreacher. The ensuing complications are of little real importance, and indeed the book ends in haste and disorder; what is striking, and intensely effective throughout *The Hidden Ones*, is the pungency of the verisimilitude. It is impossible not to believe every nakedness in Adele's whiplashed response to the world. As a creation, she is frighteningly present on every page of the book to which she gives such savage life. She stares right through the page. She does not turn you to stone.

III.

The protagonist of Tom Holt's *Expecting Someone Taller* (Macmillan, 1987) runs over a badger in the West Country. The event seems to have been preordained. But before passing on to him the Ring of Power and expiring, the badger tells him disappointedly that it had been expecting someone taller. Trickling as it does through the text, this line generates a constant barely liminal hilarity that is the best part of the book. Pratfalls, and something of a plot involving Wagnerian gods and dwarf scowlers, ensue duly, but do not excite much interest in the course of coming to a loud slightly disheartened climax, mainly because the nebbish hero (who is not tall) exercises invincible powers but really does not much care that he is subjecting the world to a goodness which flows, lambent and healing, over the souls of mortals and immortals everywhere. *Who's Afraid of Beowulf?* (Macmillan, 1988), Holt's second comic fantasy, meritoriously reverses these credits and debits. The title is lame, but the book is fine. A young woman archaeologist, who loves her profession and who cares about the implications of that which she tumbles into, tumbles into a Viking burial pit where she finds, perfectly preserved, a longship and its crew, and a king, and a wizard, and a couple of supernatural entities. Once awakened from magic slumber, they all respond variously to their initiation into the horrors of our century, and eventually work it out that their dark adversary – roundly defeated a millennium ago – has regained his powers, and has constructed the modern world in his own image. So there is some point to the squalls and pixilations which follow, and some real edge to Holt's nicely timed landmines of wit. The melancholia inherent in his sustaining premise – that the modern world can be explained as a genuinely evil practical joke on us helots – only makes the grace of his ingenious gamesplaying the more saving. He does not yet have the drive of a Terry Pratchett, but he is beginning to show something of the same glare.

IV.

A short note: Connie Willis's Lincoln's Dreams (Bantam, 1987) has been received in the United States with something of the praise it deserves, and now appears in Great Britain, more than a year later but exceedingly welcome. Like Terry Bisson's A Fire on the Mountain (1988), which takes a radically different view of Robert E Lee, Lincoln's Dreams obsessively reworks the great underground river of agenbite of the American Civil War. Her protagonist is psychically consumed – one might even say ridden – by a woman whose dreams are those of General Lee, not Lincoln, and their relationship has a pathos that is utterly convincing, strait-jacketed and uncanny and oneiric. The whole book gives off the timbre of a half-heard song by the early R.E.M.; it is constructed with a steely delicacy; it is tough and willowy, dense and aethereal. It is full of blood and death and severing; and it is as clear as air, and seemly.

– Interzone 28, March/April 1989

Instruments of Love

FROM the heart of Florida, where the comments on Connie Willis's Lincoln's Dreams (1987) were written, the dream grammatology and abiding trauma of the Civil War glow in the mind's eye with a strange suborning remoteness. One's thoughts are drawn northwards – out of the ravaged flatlands of this conquered state, whose very place-names co-opt and mock the Indians and Blacks massacred for lebensraum long before the American Nightmare split the land wide open in 1860 – as to a vortex whose allure is haunting, hypnogogic, hymeneal. Stuck like parietal microbes to the edges of the plundered swamps and plains – in Miami or Sarasota or Arcadia – it is perhaps no wonder that Floridians endure an exile from the organic, and that book reviewers of novels about the undying schisms of the War long to drive north, into the memory of the storm; and we did so, a few days after I sent my Interzone copy back to the UK. Once into South Carolina, we found an exit from the Interstate, and slipped eastwards into Charleston. In the supernal urban beauty of the Old Town, which slaves had constructed for poltroons, one was tempted to kick the dusky parquet pavements and to say: *Thus I refute Ruskin*. Next day, driving north into pine forests and shanties and redneck caravans, we turned the radio on. A male voice, clearly that of an actor, was in the midst of recounting a sad but weirdly contextless tale about blue men and grey men and someone called marse robert, who could not get his commands properly conveyed through the shattering haze of battle. Sepulchrally anecdotal, the actor went on to describe horrific and hallucinated scenes of carnage and confusion. After the voice finally stopped, an announcer promised that further excerpts from Richard Adams's new novel *Traveller* (Knopf, 1988), which purported to be the autobiography of General Robert E Lee's favourite mount, would follow soon.

I.

What was happening here? What was an English writer doing in the heart of the American Nightmare pretending to be a horse? What was he doing passing on to grown readers a view of General Lee (Marse Roberts in Traveller's slave lingo) whose adulatory simplicities could only come from the mouth of an animal that liked being ridden on? And why was he eulogizing, through the musings of this holy-innocent equine, the wrong side of the War that split the Home? There are at least two answers. The first is that the tireless intelligent long-lived Traveller, whose extensively documented life features in memoirs and histories and paintings of the Civil War, might have been too tempting for an animal-ventriloquist to ignore, though dangerous to succumb to; and it is certainly the case that in Adams's hands Traveller – like Latro in Gene Wolfe's *Soldier of the Mist* (1986) – has at times a dawn freshness of vision which washes the world clean. The second answer is all about exile. Like a book-reviewer escaping the malls of the diaspora northwards into Carolina, or like Connie Willis crafting an exquisite honey-trap for the analysis of cultural nostalgia in *Lincoln's Dreams*, Richard Adams approaches the hypnotic Matter of the South as an immigrant. Only so can one understand the convert's fervour within the rhythms of his ventriloquism, the fragile simplistics of its adulation of General Lee, whose skill at protracting the first universal war caused the deaths of men and women in their hundreds of thousands. Though Adams's behaviour once within the walls is cloyingly patriotic, *Traveller* is in fact a Trojan horse, and it is as an artifact of protective camouflage that one must see the book. Through the mouth of a horse, Adams hopes to find an innocent vision of the South, one stripped of any moral contamination. And thus he refutes Ruskin.

11.

Robert Holdstock's fascination with the Matter of Britain, on the other hand, has none of the cunning of the exile. Both *Mythago Wood* (1984) and its sequel *Lavondyss: Journey to an Unknown Region* (Gollancz, 1988) focus on their subject matter with an Ancient-Mariner glare that slips quite often from mere persistence into the unconsciously comic. In its button-holing cod-Jung portmanteau literalness even the title of the first book comes perilously close to Stuffed Owl country, the very term "mythago" having been made up by Holdstock to define – perhaps to over-define – figures like Robin Hood begotten within the abyssal chthonic resonator of Ryhope Wood by a kind of marriage of myth and inchoate ur-reality: All mimsy were the mythagos. But the gawkishness does not last. The heart of the book is unforgettable, laced through with an honest and clearly conscious desiderium. The humans who enter the outer realms of Ryhope in *Mythago Wood* find that the further inwards they penetrate, the huger and more unbearable becomes the ur-reality of the heartwood; it is a movement towards epiphany that should hush the most raucous of readers. But in the second volume of what is now apparently destined to be a trilogy, that heartwood – almost fatally – is given a name, another ineffable Holdstock soubriquet. "Lavondyss" is a term which teeters right on the edge of the risible, because although it contains within it hints of Avon and Lyonesse and Avalon and Dis, and "lave" and "abyss," it also sounds like a new face cream. The protagonist of *Lavondyss*, a young girl whose extremely dogged trek into menarche shapes the first half of the book, and whose knocking on the door of Ryhope becomes very persistent indeed, has come inexorably to be known, in the mind of at least one reader, as the *Lavondyss* Lady. Nor is the first half of the book much improved by the twinkling presence of Ralph Vaughan Williams, half-disguised by the reduction of his surname to Williams, but – almost fatally – recognizeable all the same, ponderous, canny, wistful, pedantic and pedestrian, like the pages he inhabits. Obsessed from infancy by Ryhope Wood, young Tallis Keeton (the *Lavondyss* Lady) spends her early years (and Holdstock 200 pages) making what seems to be a huge number of chthonic masks for future use, all of which are named; mapping and naming and teasing the outskirts of the Wood like the virgin she still is; and practising her capacity to hollow – to open ways – into the heartwood, longing to go but stalling, stalling. It is rather like reading *The Silmarillion* before reading *The Lord of the Rings*.

Only with the beginning of part two, on page 197, does the book flame astonishingly into life. Tallis enters the land, whose shape increasingly becomes the shape of her abyssal self, and we find ourselves knotted into a metamorphic terrain of daunting rigour, an excremental sign-saturated inscape charged with twisting energy, like puns that lie too deep for tears. There is an ice age within the vast Wood. Mythago epistemes clash by night, and at dawn the Wood is new again, and more terrible than before. Tallis grows old. She follows the tooth of the inscape further in and further in, and comes to the gate into Lavondyss itself. But it is no gate. It is the language of her life now uttering her, and which she must enter, and pass through. The superbly deranging and intense final chapters of Lavondyss have an assurance one might almost call bardic, if that term had not been debased into a tag to describe crowd-warmers at the revel. These final chapters may be fuelled by desiderium, by a clear longing on Holdstock's part to reinhabit some anterior pole of Paradise deeply and somnolently wooded, but their final effect is of something far stricter and more chill than the usual late-culture pastoral cavorting of Robin Goodfellow and the lads. Finally, after a certain amount of chatter, Lavondyss begins to seem like a thing in itself, inexplicable and gravid. Richly and frighteningly, the book almost makes one believe that its final chapters take us to the place where all the stories start, in the bone shop. But the place where all the stories start is not a library. I for one can foresee no sequel that would not merely scour through bones and dead fire, already aeons distant from the thing itself, just to tell another anecdote.

III.

Two books were published last year by writers whose usual work would normally be reviewed in Interzone, and although neither of these novels is properly sf or fantasy, both are of striking interest, and both are summae. Brian Aldiss's Forgotten Life [see p. 262, where this notice is reprinted with some other Aldiss reviews 1995] is one; the other is by Michael Moorcock. It cannot be denied that there are problems with Moorcock's summa in Mother London (Secker & Warburg, 1988), but it is also a telling commentary on the desperate effeteness of the English literary establishment that this deeply worked through-composed singing edifice of a book was not at least shortlisted for the Booker Prize. Mother London is a celebration inwards of Moorcock's own city, a book whose population seems initially vast but which reduces finally to a set of avatars of the author twining their limbs and selfhoods together at the end of time – in this case the end of time is 1988 – as the city sinks. The three protagonists of Mother London are David Mummery, whose memoirs replicate details of Moorcock's own life in terms uncannily similar to the author's own autobiography published in Contemporary Authors; Joseph Kiss, a redemptive version of the author's well-known public persona; and Mary Gasalee, closely related to but far more palatable than the street-wise idiot-savant holy-fool protagonist of the unpleasant Letters from Hollywood (1985). But although each of these characters is clearly meant to be recognized as forming a mosaic portrait of the author, they are in fact very sharply differentiated on the page; though they share each other sexually over the decades, and all have histories of mental disorder, and Joseph and Mary do finally marry after the death of the stunted sacrificial Mummery, their most obvious mutuality, on the page, lies in the nature of their experiences in World War II. Each has lived through an incandescent life-fixing moment in the Blitz or later. The child Mummery has been transported from a near-direct hit by a magical black man; Mary Gasalee has saved her child from fire and fallen into a decade-long coma irradiated by dreams of a London closely resembling the oneiric toy-town of the later Cornelius books; and Joseph Kiss, in a long and masterful scene set symmetrically at the very heart of the text, has defused a bomb and saved the Scaramanga sisters.

But it is with the Scaramanga sisters in their thatched cottage on the Regent's Canal, breeding chickens and celebrating life, that a damaging sentimentality begins to eat at the structure of the second half of *Mother London*. Because the heart of the book's plot, and its densest and chronologically earliest scenes, lie at what might be called its geographical centre, that second half, which gradually follows its tone-row of cues and scenes and characters back to the present, must constantly fight against a sense of anticlimax; and Moorcock has increasing recourse to *device* in his battle against that sense. The Scaramangas are nothing but device, and some set scenes – most notably a virtuoso "life-celebration" sequence set at a fun fair in 1970 – try all too visibly to commandeer assent. But in the end the Scaramangas cannot vitiate even the least felt parts of the book, for its final effect – an effect irradiated by an at times glorious assault of marshalled detail – is that of an organon, resonant and tempered; the face of London (the face of the author). And all the notes sound. In the end, *Mother London* is an instrument of love.

– Interzone 29, May/June 1989

3. Various

THE DETAILS of the fight need not concern us. But in recent years something of a vendetta has been waged along the cutting edge of sf between the sets of writers now generally known as the Humanists and the Cyberpunks. It may be the case that neither Kim Stanley Robinson (Humanist) or William Gibson (Cyberbunk) much care for the labels which misprision them, or much like being used as counters in a quarrel over the true nature of sf in the years to come; but both have been willy-nilly dragged into something like an affray, despite the fact that each writer admires the other's work, and some damage has been done. Robinson, in particular, has suffered under a false presentation of his work as being conservative, unadventurous, and defensive of the status quo.

I.

It must be admitted that in his first novel, The Wild Shore (1984), Robinson rather led with his chin, because the searching moral ambiguities of that book are concealed in a fresh-faced open style reminiscent of Mark Twain at his sunniest. The protagonists of the tale, who live in an Orange County transformed into a pastoral backwater, and whose sources of information are exceedingly unreliable, believe that America has been defeated by a sneak atomic attack, and that the patriotic duty of the survivors, many years after the disaster, is to conduct guerrilla warfare against the Japanese quarantine that prevents America from reasserting her greatness. That they are deluded, and that The Wild Shore is in fact a critical examination of cultural nostalgia for an unreal innocence, should have been understood on a close reading of the text, and should actively inform any response to The Gold Coast (Tor, 1988), Robinson's highly charged new novel, for in this book he gives the fable of the innocent American a merited coup de grâce.

The venue is once again Orange County, three or four decades into the next century. Like the narrator of The Wild Shore, Jim McPherson in The Gold Coast is a naïve, companionable young man standing at the edge of an adulthood he may never adequately achieve, and whose essential decency has never been put to the test. Like the hero of the earlier book, McPherson attempts to express his vague idealistic sense that the world has gone awry in a gesture of political violence, and, as in the earlier book, his actions lead to a humiliating and farcical catastrophe, with grave consequences to his friends and associates.

Beyond these circumstances, and some forcedly playful assonances of character and geography, the two novels differ widely and fruitfully from one another. The disaster that America must confront in The Gold Coast is no external collapse but merely the continuation of the world as we know it now. Fifty more years of growth have transformed Orange County into a congested complex of suburb, shopping plaza and freeway. The Cold War continues to fuel further growth in the defense industries vital to the County's cancerous prosperity, the last orange trees will soon be uprooted from their outmoded cosmetic role as grave markers in an obscure cemetery, and a cultural windedness stales the lives of McPherson, his drug-dropping friends, his family, the freeway-bound horizons of his world. When he does ultimately take action, his innocent rage at the ways of the world cannot mitigate the harm he does, and the book closes with some very sharp lessons, staining the young fool with the first dark hues of responsible adulthood.

Some sf readers may baulk at the absence in The Gold Coast of any saving sf solution to the polluted dypstopia America has become, for the book celebrates no magical breakthroughs, no easy transit to a better world, another planet, or nirvana. What it does celebrate, with an earned and elated refusal of despair, is the persistent joyful survival of human persons in the interstices of the juggernaut. Robinson even leaves us almost half-believing that McPherson, and his friends, will someday make it new. It is a rich, brave book. To read The Gold Coast is not just to go through the fire; it is to emerge from fire.

11.

Because we know it is a dream of an America we do not deserve to remember, Orson Scott Card's luminous alternate history of the early nineteenth century continues to chill as it soothes. Seventh Son (1987) [see p. 44] began to construct a framework for the story of Alvin Maker, a human child whose powers of shaping rapport with the earth are very little short of sacerdotal. For much of its length, Red Prophet (Tor, 1988) shifts the focus of the series from Alvin to a pair of contrasted Indians, or Reds. Ta-Kumsaw (whom we know as Tecumseh) and his brother Lolla-Wossiky (whom we know as Tenskwatawa, the Shawnee Prophet, who urged a separation of Indian and White cultures) represent conflicting strategies for saving the Reds and the living land from the relentless earth-scorching advance of civilization. Ta-Kumsaw chooses war; Lolla-Wossiky chooses to trick W H Harrison into committing a massacre at Tippecanoe whose effect will be magically to keep all Whites East of the Mississippi; or Mizzipy as Card calls it.

More acted upon than acting, the child Alvin is booted from one brother to the other as the plot requires, for his real role in Red Prophet is to observe and learn wisdom from the division of America into a land of the living and the dead. Unlike the real Tecumseh, Ta-Kumsaw does not die after Tippecanoe, and as Alvin watches him paddle Westward into the singing world he realizes that the Red man "was taking the land with him, the greensong; what the White man had won with so much blood and dishonesty was not the living land of the Red man, but the corpse of that land. It was decay that the White man won. It would turn to dust in his hands." From an author as polished and calculating of effect as Orson Scott Card, the savagery of this prophetic message must be utterly deliberate. And suddenly the saga of Alvin Maker begins to thrill.

– The Washington Post Book World, 28 February 1988

IT IS a fine tease of a title. For most readers of sf, the hidden side of the Moon is a place to be explored by males in spaceships looking for a gift of technology from the stars, or an extraterrestrial footprint. In *The Hidden Side of the Moon* (St Martin's Press, 1988), which is Joanna Russ's fourth collection of stories, there is no travel through space, and most of the footprints to be found are of women. The Moon of the title is what one might call the female principle.

In sf circles, it has long been assumed that men, in Joanna Russ's tales, are generally booted. Over the 30 years of her career, which this collection almost fully encompasses, Russ has come to be pigeonholed as a feminist of savage mien, angry and humourless and without charity. As a categorization it is both overtly dismissive and palpably wide of the mark, as this collection – indeed almost all of her copious oeuvre – clearly and vigorously demonstrates.

The contents of *The Hidden Side of the Moon* range from the sharp but conventional "Nor Custom Stale" of 1959 to the masterful "Little Dirty Girl" of 1982, and come from almost as many magazines, within and without the sf field, as there are stories in the book. Few of Russ's readers will have seen all of them previously, and their assembly within two covers gives a first opportunity to sample with ease the full range of her work.

"Nor Custom Stale" is an exemplary fable, after a fashion much favored in the 1950s, in which the petty moralities and lifestyle decisions of suburban Americans are subjected to punitive and highly ironic comeuppances; in this case, Harry and Freda become as mindlessly immortal as their autonomic House, oblivious to the Ice Age which descends and the death of the sun. "Life in a Furniture Store" (1965), "This Night, at My Fire" (1966), "Window Dressing" (1970), "How Dorothy Kept Away the Spring" (1977), and "Sword Blades and Poppy Seed" (1983) are all infused with an unrelenting vision of the contortions of form and spirit suffered by women in attempting to sustain a sense of being; but it is in no reductive sense that these stories could be called feminist. Their anger, their wit and their melancholy are deeply applicable to any reader. They do not date.

"The Little Dirty Girl" is the finest story of this collection, and perhaps the best Russ has ever written. The power of her writing is always most complexly vivid when she is dealing with relations between parents and children, as in "Daddy's Girl" and "The Autobiography of my Mother" (both 1975), which are here republished under a single title, "Old Thoughts, Old Presences." These tales both depict excruciating spiritual stymies, and fit well together. But although "The Little Dirty Girl" shirks nothing of the anguish of the earlier duo, it is also a story of triumph. Told in the form of a letter to a close friend, it begins as a kind of ghost story. Far from feeling simple terror at being haunted by a scruffy little girl from the 1940s, however, the narrator lifts herself into a kind of spiritual marriage with the relentless waif, who is, of course, the narrator herself, just as she is her own mother. The last pages of reconciliation with that mother, who is still alive, may reach perilously toward a tearchoked epiphany, but do not succumb.

In a sense, all of Russ's mature work is epistolary, for it always addresses and implicates some form of imagined reader. The very action of finishing one of her better stories feels like complicity in the wrongs it may bespeak, the joys it may achieve. And because she is a writer of such shapely and energetic clarity, Russ is very easy to read, which is to say very hard not to read, even though it may hurt. She lets no one off the hook of her voice. However hilarious, the pointing urgency of her anger can scathe. As she always seems to be speaking directly to each one of us, she can seem at times heavily accusatory. The occasional moments of despair, of a weirdly obdurate privation of spirit, are consequently very difficult to live with.

Perhaps it is not the case that one should expect an easy ride from a writer of our times who happens to be a woman, one who has decided to address us on the subject of the realities of that circumstance. At the same time, it should be kept in mind that Russ is a major writer within the sf genre, and beyond it. Whatever arguments may infuse and barb her texts, Russ, as *The Hidden Side of the Moon* amply attests, has become one of the most significant practitioners of the short story form in our time.

– *The New York Times*, 31 January 1988

IN VERY FEW of the novels of Gregory Benford, Professor of Physics at the University of California, is it possible to miss the presence of the universe. Titles like *Across the Sea of Suns* or *If the Stars are Gods* proliferate, and it will come as no surprise to learn that the "great sky river" of the book under review is in fact an Asian Indian term for the Milky Way.

Great Sky River (Bantam, 1987) kicks off a trilogy set in the centre of our home galaxy some aeons hence. Humanity has long since sent straggles of settlers down the spiral arm of stars from the local cluster which houses Earth, and these settlers have long since discovered that homo sapiens is very small fry indeed in the scheme of things. On the planet Snowglade, as the tale begins, only a few bedraggled human clans have survived a sudden intensification of hostilities on the part of the robot civilization which dominates the heart of the galaxy. Or so it seems.

As a writer of Hard sf, which takes its name not only from its claim to extrapolate rigorously from the physical sciences, but also from its tendency to express a "robust" and triumphalist view of humankind, Benford is disinclined to leave his folk in utterly dire and shabby straits for more than a few opening scenes. Accordingly, after a few dozen pages of nomadic savagery, young Killeen begins to fight back against a strange new predator robot called the Mantis, and in doing so begins to demonstrate the leadership potential necessary to sweep humanity back into a deserved ascendancy.

In his rapid ascent to scientific competence and dominion over the human scene, Killeen (it must be said) is very much aided by his author, who gives him brains, luck, a loving son, an ancient faithful robot dog, a girlfriend with technophilic fingers, and an electromagnetic radiance from the heart of the galaxy who appears whenever the Mantis is about to win and cows it. Like his fellow humans, Killeen has also had embedded into his nervous system electronic chips which contain the coded personalities or Aspects of dead humans, who have on tap the wisdom of the ages. All in all, after Killeen kills the head of the assembled human clans, which he then dominates, and finds a buried spaceship, which has awaited him for centuries, the Mantis has very little chance of prevailing, nor does it.

Given the general severity of Benford's vision of the universe, which in some of his books reminds one of the perilous metaphysical adventures of Olaf Stapledon, *Great Sky River* may seem something of a holiday romp, a swift and slightly dizzy resumé of old space opera themes. But the overriding intendedness of even Benford's flightiest moments has a double edge, and when Killeen kills he murders with meaning. It is not a meaning which everyone will find palatable. In following volumes, it will be interesting to see how Benford's humanity is made to thank its new leader.

– *New Scientist*, 31 March 1988

IT IS a nightmare familiar to all Americans. Perhaps it is too familiar. It provides the subject matter and haunts every page of *The Past is Another Country* (Simon & Schuster, 1988), Peter Wludyka's incandescent first novel. It is the nightmare of a triumphant Russia. Wludyka's tale of perfidy and torment begins in the year 143, reckoning from the date of the Russian Revolution, when America has been occupied for generations by totalitarian Marxist-Leninists of the evil empire. Thought-control is very nearly complete. The past has been rewritten or obliterated. Folk memories of a free America are memories of another country, a land of dreams.

As the great-grandson of the sister of the Russian General Secretary, young Alex Nurov occupies a position of some privilege in the South Carolina high school he attends, even though his mother is American, and his father thinks of his government position in Charleston as a form of exile. Alex is in the throes of late adolescence, and the hustling hovering closeness of Wludyka's style accurately captures his lurching confusions, the emotional fireworks of his initiation into the ecstacies of sex, and the turmoil that afflicts him when he discovers a forbidden book.

This book – The Plot to Kill Paul Creticos – is a samizdat text that purports to contain the confession of a Polish priest from a time before the "Uprising" which ended American independence. Seconded to the United States by the Vatican to ride herd on the anti-war Creticos, who is also a priest, Father Babulieski becomes an unwitting pawn of the KGB, and in a botched attempt to assassinate Creticos only intensifies the yearning pacifism of the gullible Americans. Babulieski's tormented narrative deeply undermines young Alex's sense of reality, for it speaks of a nonexistent God-figure called Jesus Christ, refers to a non-place called New York City, and in every detail contradicts the official Russian version of history.

Desperate to find his feet again, Alex risks entering his father's password into the family computer terminal, which connects him to restricted portions of the Direct Access Library where ultimately all authorized knowledge will be contained, making books unnecessary. But the DAL is not yet fully operational as a censor, and Alex is able to extract stray bits of information which partially confirm the tale told by Father Babulieski. As often happens in adolescence, Alex's world falls into shreds. He discovers that his alluring young mother uses drugs to maintain her sang-froid as the wife of an alien. His American girlfriend disappears. He coerces a young friend into reading the samizdat. He is then apprehended.

Up to this point, Wludyka's touch has been secure, and the explosive claustrophobia of Alex's coming of age has been very well managed indeed. Even Alex's experiences in the camp where he is brainwashed into temporary peace carry some conviction, though here Wludyka's version pales beside similar scenes in Yevgeny Zamiatin's We (first published in English in 1924; never published in Russia [until 1988, after the institution of perestroika 1995]), or George Orwell's Nineteen Eighty-Four (1949). And it is in comparison to these two masterful studies of totalitarianism in action that The Past is Another Country must finally be seen to fall short.

Wludyka shares with both Zamiatin and Orwell a nightmarish narrative urgency, a sophisticated feverish intensity of style, and a sense of conviction that impales the reader; and all three writers manifestly share the same general concerns and abhorrences. We clearly foresees a Stalinism gone mad; and the prime targets addressed in Nineteen Eighty-Four are certainly the totalitarianisms of the left which infested the world after 1945. At the same time, because neither of these novels is in any narrow sense a political tract, neither has dated. The devastating tragic vision of each book remains unimpaired by the years, or by the shift and change of ideological disputes. It is here that Wludyka parts company with his mentors.

Quite explicitly, he grounds his novel in a partisan, politicized extrapolation of a profoundly unliberal take on our own times: mutual disarmament with inspection is a Russian ploy; if through weakness and naïveté America accepts the blandishments of her adversary, her bosom (in fact New York City) will be exposed to Soviet bombs; essentially unchanged from the worst days of Stalin, America's new Soviet masters will impose a monolithic tyranny on her, which will last unchanged for ever; only Christianity will remain to challenge the invaders, so Jesus must be wiped from history. As Wludyka gradually reveals his framework of explanation, *The Past is Another Country* sinks slowly into tract, and Alex becomes the pawn of a strikingly time-bound vision of the world. The closing pages are feebly melodramatic, with foolish betrayals and implausible blows for freedom and unctuous baptisms jammed distractedly together; they sully the body of a fine book [which has duly, and (one is afraid) deservedly, disappeared from view as the new decade continues progressively to dismantle the verities Wludyka banked on as bases for his speculation 1995]. If parts of that body still live, it's because Peter Wludyka may be a novelist in spite of himself.

– The Washington Post, 20 September 1988

WITHIN a wide radius of the holiday home of the daft paterfamilias who narrates *Tidings* (Knopf, 1987), it is apparently safe to leave valuables lying unguarded in the open air. "I can't think of anybody within twenty kilometres who would steal anything from anybody," Will muses, and it is a measure of the strange hypnotic grasp of William Wharton's sixth novel that neither the reader, nor any member of Will's large family, can be intended to question his reading of the practical realities of living in rural France in 1984.

Will and his wife Loretta, expatriate Americans who teach in Paris, are celebrating what may be their last Christmas together in the old mill he loves, deep in a valley of the Morvan south of Vezelay, east of Nevers. Their three older children have arrived from America, bearing memories and traumas and various tidings. Ben, the youngest, still living at home, has entered a solitary and vulnerable puberty. The message he bears is mute: his inability to partake in his father's confabulated Yuletide ceremonies may well reflect the strained lassitude of his parents' marriage during the recent months of Loretta's passionate adultery with another American. It may be that the ceremony of innocence will drown.

In the opening pages of the novel, Will, who is first on the scene, seems much too febrile and befuddled to grasp these nettles of crisis. As a failed philosopher dazzled by the incertitudes of ontology, he floats without clear purpose through the flux and shadows of a world he cannot pin down, a marriage he cannot redeem, children he cannot begin to comprehend. The style in which Wharton couches his protagonist's first-person narrative is florid, seasick, hypnogogic, and bears an air of slightly egregious rapture. Will's moments of sublimity verge as a consequence upon the sleazy, and his almost constant fits of epiphanic exaltation seem at points self-serving and grossly sentimental. He is almost nothing but a monster.

But it is more complex than that. His love for his wife and children is utterly generous, though he tends to flinch from confrontations, and is desperately insecure about his capacity to understand their true natures. He believes profoundly in the restorative balm of habit and ritual, and in the saving grace of the Christmas ceremonies he has assembled, like a pack rat, from every tradition available to him. And whenever he can he varnishes the surfaces of the world – at one point literally – in his belief that it may be possible to prevent "heat loss" and to sit still, for a moment out of time, in the heart of things.

The miracle of Tidings is the sense that Will may prevail. He leaves the camera outdoors, and it is not stolen. He compulsively tidies his realm to fix it for a season, and his family comes home again. In his fixated love for all of them he may at times seem suffocatingly sentimental, but over the days of their visit they open to him, and the world he has preserved, like flowers in the sun. And at the point that his grab-bag of Christmas customs seems to have lost its old power, a richer (and quite clearly supernatural) magic transforms the actual Day, and brings each tidings into the light.

As Christmas dawns there is singing and dancing and eating and drinking and weeping. A marriage is announced, and a divorce; a pregnancy is adumbrated; an adultery is addressed. It is at times, perhaps, all too much. No opportunity for the expression of deeply embarrassing sentimentalities is eschewed. Love through shining tears is too frequently proclaimed. Saccharine toasts are common, and the youngest child's mortification, on being almost forced into a particularly appalling dance in honour of falling snow, is very apt.

As an engine for the arousal of emotions, Tidings is quite extraordinarily unrelenting, and in its unceasing espousal of the gladness of its solstice tale it comes very close to a state of unsustainable hyperbole. But it is intrinsic to Wharton's strategy to hover at the edge of bathos, and he almost always escapes the fall. In the ecstatic rollercoaster rhythms of Will's narrative, he has attempted to limn a saint for these days. Astonishingly, he almost succeeds.

– *Times Literary Supplement*, 8 April 1988

[I place here a review of William Wharton's next novel, which to my eyes concerns the same primal family as the one which attains various epiphanies in *Tidings*, and retells in sf terms something of the same story. Before *Franky Furbo* was actually published, in the real world, Wharton's daughter was killed, with her family, in a car crash in Oregon, where fields can legally be set alight by farmers in order to clear them cheaply. The smoke from these unregulated but lawful fires can – and in the case of Wharton's daughter did – fatally cover public highways in thick smoke, blinding drivers instantly (seven were killed in this particular accident; 35 injured; 24 vehicles were destroyed). These two novels about the preservation of families against almost insuperable odds are now – it's not their fault, nor Wharton's – peculiarly difficult to re-read calmly; I have never really tried to read *Last Lovers* (1991), whose protagonist has lost his family 1995.]

IT TOOK William Wharton half a century to begin to write. The man who published *Birdy* in 1979 was already, therefore, a man of mature years, with much to remember. As that first book so brilliantly shows, he had survived the World War II traumas hinted at in *A Midnight Clear* (1982); he had successfully coped with dramas of the sort unfolded in *Dad* (1980) and *Pride* (1985); and he was now an established painter in Paris, where he and his wife raised the large family celebrated in *Scumbler* (1984) and *Tidings* (1987). By 1987 it might have been time, perhaps, for a memoir or two. Why *novels*?

There is at least one simple answer. Memoirs are classically intended to tell the truth, to acknowledge that what is done is done, and to come to terms with death. They do not recapture the past; they seal it shut. William Wharton, whose every word exposes a man utterly determined to remain in full possession of himself, writes novels to save his life. It is a life which includes every moment he can remember, and every loved one he can touch. All must be made to live; there must be no surrender to decay. Unsurprisingly, the great enemy in any Wharton novel is time; and as *Franky Furbo* (Holt, 1989) demonstrates, he will go to almost any artistic lengths to defeat that great foe.

In a small house on the brow of a hill in the heart of rural Italy, William Wiley lives with his beloved ageless red-haired wife Caroline, and Billy, the last of their four children still young enough to live at home. The main floor of the cottage is

one large room, dominated by a huge bed, where the entire family has always slept together, like a great intertwined litter. William and Caroline have lived there for forty years. Their two eldest children now live incestuously together in South America. Caroline walks the country at night, traveling far afield. Wiley paints for love; to make money he writes children's stories under the name of Franky Furbo – a telepathic talking fox whose adventures feature in many of his books, and whose life story he has been recounting to his children for years. Entropy haunts him, but only as a rumor. The Wileys live in paradise.

But one morning young Billy says he no longer believes in the literal existence of the saintly Furbo, and William collapses in rage. Without Franky Furbo he would be nothing. After all, it was Franky Furbo who had rescued him and a German soldier named Wilhelm Klug from certain death, decades earlier, at Monte Cassino. Having been knocked unconscious by a vicious shelling, both soldiers had awoken in Franky's underground tree house in the heart of the country, where the compassionate shape-changing omnilingual fox soon healed them, and taught them to speak Fox, and blessed them. Wilhelm soon slipped off homewards to Bavaria, while at Franky's suggestion William "pretended" to believe a magic fox had saved his life, thus persuading the American authorities to give him a medical pension. But Franky Furbo was real then, and is now, William tells his wife, even though he's never been seen since.

In that case, says Caroline, if Franky is real, and if with his help you once shared a telepathic rapport with your German comrade, then go to Bavaria, and find Wilhelm Klug, and confirm your tale. Then come back home. So William Wiley goes to Bavaria, and Franky Furbo gets into full stride as a fable, though the sf elements are uneasily patched in. Klug tells Wiley that Franky is indeed real, and is the near-immortal mutant progenitor of a race of foxes destined to inherit the Earth. After traveling forward through time to visit the foxes' Earth, which has been restored to the conditions obtaining "before man ravaged it," Franky and his vulpine wife Raethe have now returned to contemporary Europe, where they have gone to ground and raised a necessarily incestuous litter. For self-protection, Franky has become a temporary amnesiac and changed his shape. Dazzled and elated, William Wiley goes back home. His wife greets him with passion. Christmas is nigh, and all the children have magically returned from their lairs across the world. Wiley begins to tell a new story about Franky Furbo.

It would be cruel to reveal the final gnarled turnings of Wharton's plot [although it's not hard to guess: Franky Furbo has taken the shape of the author of Franky Furbo, who bears the same name as the protagonist of the book 1995], or to linger over the self-pitying sentimentality of the basic concept, for there is never any mistake about Franky Furbo's intense impact. Rickety but incandescent, it is a fable from the heart about living in a state of hope, in an eternal present, free from the tramp of time, the terrible heed of accident. Outside the book, it may be that nothing can save us; tellingly, Wharton has dedicated Franky Furbo to one of his own children, recently dead in a car crash. Inside the fable, Wiley lives for ever. And his children inherit the earth.

– The Washington Post, 22 October 1989

ALMOST immediately, the title of Geraldine McCaughrean's new book begins to work a crooked charm upon the reader, for the table of contents of A Pack of Lies: Twelve Stories in One (Oxford University Press, 1988) lists only eleven stories. The identity of that twelfth tale soon comes clear, however. It is A Pack of Lies itself.

In the public library of a small English town, young Ailsa begins a dull school assignment only to find her microfiche machine acting up. Several volumes of Wisden's Cricketing Year Books come into view, upside down and inside out. A strange youngish man, loudly obsessed with cricket, appears from nowhere and beguiles her into offering him a job at her widowed mother's incompetently run antique shop. As he steps outside to wait, Ailsa's microfiche flashes a new title at her, A Pack of Lies, upside down, inside out.

The young man's name is M C C Berkshire, and he soon charms Ailsa's mother into allowing him to work at the shop for no more than food and lodging. The premises are crammed with the sort of detritus amateur bidders drag away from country auctions in the rain, but magically something begins to happen. Each time a customer enters and shows any interest at all in some or other object of bedraggled virtù, Berkshire claims to remember a tale about the piece in question, which may be an old clock, or a plate, or an umbrella-stand. Despite the fumbling embarrassment of Ailsa's mother, who has become touchingly over-apologetic since the death of her husband, he then insists on telling the tale.

Each of the eleven tales he tells is a deft and glowing invention, and they make up the bulk of A Pack of Lies. Each of them is delightful, well-shaped, humorous and packed. But as Ailsa cannot fail to notice, something uncanny seems to be happening. Each fable, whether or not it seems to be a true accounting of things, somehow manages directly to address the customer who has elicited Berkshire's mutable, coaxing attention. If that customer deserves to possess the clock or chest or desk on view, then Berkshire's tale will tickle that customer's moral fibre in such a fashion that a purchase becomes inevitable; if an unsuitable person enters the shop, Berkshire's story will be too painful for contemplation, and there will be no sale.

And just as his stories have told his customers home truths about themselves, so Berkshire's presence in the life of Ailsa and her mother teaches both of them lessons in self-reliance, humour, tolerance. In the closing pages of the book, after Berkshire has disappeared into the gloaming, it becomes quite clear to Ailsa, and to her mother, that they too were in a tale he was telling. It is only here that McCaughrean, for the first time, loses control over the complicated levels of reality she has woven together, and makes rather a shambles of her final revelations about the true Berkshire.

Fortunately, the tales he tells are almost the entirety of the enterprise. Set in the England or Asia of today, or centuries past, they are dense, luminous, and very varied indeed. "The Harpsichord: A Story of Honour and Trust" compresses into fifteen pages enough matter for a novel. "The Lead Soldier: A Story of Pride" similarly compresses a tragic life into a tough, supple anecdote. Like her prize-winning *A Little Lower Than the Angels* (1987), which could be a tale Berkshire tells, the fables bound together in *A Pack of Lies* are urgent with lessons for the living. It is a strong book from a strong writer.

– Times Literary Supplement, 25 November 1988

[It is something of a self-indulgence to complain about editors, and I'll try not go on about them more than this one time, but I thought it might be an idea just once to illustrate how much the original text of a review (as printed here) can differ from what sometimes gets into print, after it has been "edited." I take my example from the *Times Literary Supplement*, a journal notorious for its condescending treatment of contributors, and for its parsimony (even though, rumours have it, some favoured contributors do get paid more than the base rate offered hack freelancers). Certainly in the case of those writers not thought worth a respectable rate of pay, and not therefore worth much respect at all, the TLS is also notorious for allowing its editors to modify – at will, and more extensively than I, for one, have ever experienced elsewhere – the reviews they have themselves commissioned. These modifications almost always dumb down the copy affected, but – far more seriously – sometimes substantively alter the gist of critical judgments to which contributors have put their names, and for which they remain responsible, out in the real world. I do not in fact speak for myself alone in this, and am putting voice here to a genuine consensus: the reason why so many of us remain silent (given the astonishing sensitivity of most editors to criticism) is obvious enough. So let me say it again, solo, in another way: I have written a lot of bad sentences for the TLS, as for every journal I've worked for; but almost never has a TLS editorial intrusion actually addressed any of the infelicities, howlers, gaps, failures to argue, that rightly embarrass me when I reread my copy after its appearance. In my view (which is not my view alone), the editors at the TLS are markedly reluctant to take on the hard work of actually trying to improve copy; and their intrusions are in fact almost invariably punitive: metaphors reduced to a paraphrastic drone; arguments flensed; the narrativity of exposition routinely jumbled; the passions of the critic disassembled into an ooze of cliché. If it sounds as though I am accusing the editors of the TLS of *ressentiment*: tell me if the shoe fails to fit.

[This is only the half of it. When they assign a piece, the editors at the TLS are almost always extremely precise about the length they require, more so than most other journals; simultaneously, these same editors are quite extraordinarily ruthless about abridging copy whenever they've made a mistake about how much room they have to fit it into. This may seem amateur (and it is); it may seem singularly unprofessional to dodge the consequences of one's own mistakes by punishing others (which it is). But these small injuries pale beside the fact that the TLS pays only for the number of words actually printed, not for the number of words commissioned by their own employees, in the name and by the authority of the firm. Reviewers do not, in other words, get paid for the work they were commissioned to do, and may have their copy cut by the very editor who initially commissioned that copy, and who suffers no dock in pay for having bungled the job, for having taken scissors to copy not in order to improve it but to conceal an error. (Michael Dirda, at *The Washington Post*, pays well and for the total number of words he commissions; edits lightly but always to improve the copy; and treats his contributors as colleagues. If I think of the TLS's behaviour as shabby, it's at least partly because I have, over the years, experienced the collegiality and joy of being edited by professionals.) I print here, as an example of routine practice at the TLS, two versions of the first paragraph of my review of Louise Erdrich's *Tracks*, a review which was composed to fit precisely (I have a wordcount function on my computer, and use it) the length required. The first paragraph as edited by some desk pilot at the TLS comes first, followed by the paragraph as originally written, and after that the rest of the review 1995.]

"Building on the ruins of the America they depict with such devastating sureness, Louise Erdrich's *Love Medicine* (1984), *The Beet Queen* (1986) and the newly published *Tracks* (Hamish Hamilton, 1988), the third of a projected four-volume sequence, bare deep wounds in a fashion only initially painless, and apply a rigorous compassion. These are still early days – a mere half-decade of acclaim from the start of her active career – but Erdrich may soon come to be recognized as a writer possessed of genius."

LIKE cuts from a razor, the tales of Louise Erdrich make fine slashes into the mind, without initial pain. Only too late does the reader learn how deep the wound has penetrated, and only subsequently does the medicament of a rigorous compassion begin to soothe the hurt of the knowledge she bares. Building on the ruins of the America they depict with such devastating sureness, *Love Medicine* (1984), *The Beet Queen* (1986) and the newly published *Tracks* (Hamish Hamilton, 1988), third of a projected four-volume sequence, brace while shattering; they carry their cures within them. These are still early days – a mere half decade from the start of her active career – but Erdrich, whose genius is manifest, may soon come to be recognized as a writer possessed by greatness.

In Argus, a mythical town somewhere in the centre of North Dakota, everything connects, and everyone watches everyone else, as though through the hundred eyes of the Argus of fable. None of the many characters who tell their tales in the stories collected as *Love Medicine* can feel immune from the bonds that tie them to their precarious region. Locked into the boom-and-bust cycles of a farm economy ploughed too deep into fragile northern soil, rootless whites and uprooted Indians cleave alike to family, sex, gossip, revenge, drink and religion. What both groups seem to lack, in order to understand the world, is history.

For the whites of Argus, no understanding seems possible. *The Beet Queen* may cast more deeply into the past, but the Adare children at its heart float like tumbleweed from Minneapolis into town without comprehending a thing; though Mary Adare spends the rest of her life in the web of Argus, she never comes to understand herself, or the land, or the Indians whose world lies in shambles about her. Significantly, however, every section of *The Beet Queen* is precisely dated, as always in Erdrich's work. It is a practice which markedly distances her from American regionalists like the late Raymond Carver, whose native territories lack names or decades; and whose stories are not plot-driven. Erdrich's region, in contrast, pulses with tales that must be told, and times that must not be forgotten. Mary Adare may live deaf and blind to that rhythm – just as most white Americans do in most novels by white Americans – but everything in the first two volumes of Erdrich's extended sequence points to an engendering tragic tale, which cries for the telling.

In *Tracks* that tale begins to be told. It is the story of the death of the Indian world. The span of the book – 1912 to 1924 – comprehends the final loss of self-sufficiency of the Chippewa Indians, whose reservations spread across the Dakotas as far north as Canada. Before 1912, a reservation Chippewa like Nanapush, who narrates much of the book, could still sustain a complex rapport with his own past, his gods, the land, and the densely interwoven fabric of knowledge and shibboleth and routine that governed his daily life. The gods are real; the land hums with magic, like a hive or dance of angels. After 1924, after disease and harsh winters and the bureaucratic depradations of corrupt government agencies, there is no fabric left to unweave or thin; all that remain to Nanapush are individual memories of his witnessing, fragments of which he passes on to his granddaughter Lulu. Those memories too precious or terrible to recount he does not tell – nor does Erdrich uncover them in this volume – and they die with him.

Herself of partly Indian descent, Erdrich has invented in Nanapush a witness to the twentieth century whose authenticity seems unassailable. In the words she gives him, he is other than us. The tales he tells are like shadows of real stories which we can no longer hear. Simultaneously reticent and garrulous, stark and wry, boisterous and utterly sad, he is a creation of the highest imaginative calibre. It is perhaps inevitable that the story of Pauline Puyat, whose glumly hysterical interior monologue alternates with Nanapush's taunting and melodious fables of nightfall, seems comparatively routine.

Erdrich is a writer as plot-driven and genealogy-obsessed as William Faulkner, and her North Dakota is just as haunted by the couplings of the past as Yoknapatawpha County. Nanapush is a fabulist of old joinings; Pauline is a liar, a hypocrite, a self-flagellating Christian whose passage into the white world is governed by melodramatic distortions of love, sex and generation. Marie, the child she bears and abandons, dominates *Love Medicine*; and the reader's eventual knowledge of the name Pauline takes upon admission to the Church cuts to the quick of that earlier book, like a razor. It is a revelation which goes far to justify the tedium of her evolué self-disgust, and binds *Tracks* all the more deeply into the sequence of which it is the chronological fount. Both Nanapush and Pauline are necessary for the understanding of Argus in 1980. Like Janus, they gaze at opposing vistas; but like Janus, and like these three books, they are of one body.

– *Times Literary Supplement*, 28 November 1988

THERE is much to like in Matt Ruff's first novel, and some of it is original to Matt Ruff. Set in and around Cornell University, *Fool on the Hill* (Atlantic Monthly Press, 1988) is a campus novel, but that is nothing new. It is a fantasy story about being caught in a Story, which is not new either. Only when the two genres finally mix, and the campus changes in the blinking of an eye into the wild wood, does *Fool on* the Hill come precariously to life. It is none too soon.

Beyond its very numerous borrowings from other campus novels, and from other fantasies of transformation, the early pages of *Fool on the Hill* also suffer from excessive chatter. Most of the human characters in the book are students at Cornell, and because Ruff (himself a very recent graduate) clearly thinks the absolute world of them, he gives grad student and novelist Stephen Titus George, and his conceited cohorts and consorts, far too much to say in voices whose flippancies mingle immiscibly. Nor at first glance are the fantasy characters much of an improvement. Talky ghosts from the Greek myths share space with the Tolkien-like Rasferret the Grub, armies of magical rats fight battles with a loquacious bevy of fairies from *A Midsummer Night's Dream*, and a telepathic dog drags a wisecracking cat northwards to Ithaca to search for Heaven, which he duly finds.

Ruff never identifies the Greek god who begins to write the tale in 1866, beyond calling him Mr Sunshine, recalling to mind *The Sunlight Dialogues* (1973) of the late John Gardner, an author much addicted to the writing of novels that treat themselves as fictions, metafictionally; but as sprigs of laurel tend to accompany Mr Sunshine as he laces the plot together, it may be fair to think of him as Mr Apollo. In 1866, He comes across a high Hill in Ithaca, New York, just as Ezra Cornell is about to found the university that bears his name, and the god decides (as gods will) to inseminate a Tale into the site. Stripped to its essentials, this Tale will boast a twofold incipit: 1) a century later, aided by a goddess, Stephen Titus George will be searching for his true love; 2) at the same time Rasferret the Grub will be released from his cemetery to cause mischief among the fairies who inhabit Cornell, and to give ungodly life to the cardboard dragon which has been slated to feature in a yearly undergraduate parade.

The year darkens, and the humans in the cast begin to sense their involvement in the unearthly rhythms of a Tale told by Mr Apollo as a gas. "Life," as a setter named Ruff intones Polonius-like at one point to the dog in search of heaven, "with all its miseries and joys, is a story – or rather a Story – with God as the listener, and we mortals as the plot." Tragedies and miracles chase one another through the snowbound streets, and the novel begins to shine with as much life as it's going to boast. Good students (the Bohemians) fight racist bullies from a fraternity gone sour. Transformed into his namesake, Stephen Titus (or St) George confronts the dragon, piercing it with a magic spear, and finds true love in the arms of Aurora Borealis Smith, and the curtain falls.

In his introductory note, Ruff acknowledges the assistance of four professors of English at Cornell, eleven other named colleagues, and several institutions. In the body of the book he pays homage to a wide range of other writers, including Thomas Pynchon, J R R Tolkien, A A Milne, Ray Bradbury and Richard Fariña. Oddly, however, given the fact that Fool on the Hill is a fantasy of transformation, and that its main characters spend much of their time telling each other the Story that is telling them, Ruff does not mention any of the novelists of the 1980s who have already imagined worlds changed utterly, in the blinking of an eye, into realms of Story.

The name most conspicuously missing from his ample citing of sources is that of John Crowley, whose Little, Big (1981) remains the fount for much of the best fantasy writing of this decade. In the Story it tells, and in the cast which is transformed by telling it, Fool on the Hill shows everywhere the imprint of Crowley's grave harsh tale, but pales beside its model, because Little, Big is also a novel about redemption. Ruff's campus hijinks may be a new note in this sort of fiction, and an interlude in Wisconsin may be sharply pleasing, but in the end Fool on the Hill is only a game played by Mr Sunshine. And games do not heal.

– The Washington Post, 21 November 1988

IT IS not necessarily a blessing to be undaunted by the size of the universe. As editor of Astounding (later Analog) Science-Fiction from 1937 to his death in 1971, John W Campbell Jr was a dominant voice in American sf for decades, and his obsessions about the universe and man's undauntable role in it did much to shape the genre. Of the fixed ideas that governed his behavior, perhaps the weirdest and most damaging was his refusal to contemplate the notion that any alien might be seen as superior to mankind, or capable of defeating men in a fair fight; no story espousing such a view ever appeared in his magazine.

The result was an sf universe written in the image of Man. Women and other aliens had visiting rights only. Authors under Campbell's sway, like Isaac Asimov and Robert A Heinlein, fabricated their babyish "Future Histories" for Astounding in strict obedience to his strictures; authors like Olaf Stapledon, not much interested in the mayfly antics of homo sapiens, did not publish widely in Campbell's America, and had little influence on American sf, which continued for decades to generate papier-mâché space operas full of gonzo cowpokes who never lost a fight.

I.

In this context, how pleasant it is to know Mr Bear. As an American hard-sf writer, much interested in physics and engineering and problem-solving, Greg Bear might seem an unlikely convert to the austere metaphysical perspectives of an Olaf Stapledon, and indeed he has never written a novel deficient in plot, pulp, calamity and

Big Bangs in neon. It is all the more remarkable, then, that in novels like *Blood Music* and the superlative *Eon* (both 1985), while remaining true to his origins in the warm bath of American sf, Bear has at the same time managed to give us a glimpse of something of the cold immensities beyond our sway.

Eternity (Warner, 1988), which is a direct sequel to *Eon*, carries on in the same vein as that book. It is a space opera as Stapledon might have written it, had he the knack. The plotting is as joyfully contrived as good pulp plotting always tries to be, but the vistas opened to the gaze of its sizeable cast are of a scope to humble every man, woman and alien in the book. We begin in the middle of the world *Eon* left in mid-leap, and readers unfamiliar with the earlier book may find vaguely described but essential props like the Way and Thistledown difficult to visualize, for Bear writes as though there were no time to lose in reaching the heart of Being at the end of the universe, where *Eternity* stops. Briefly then, Thistledown, a great cylindrical asteroid, has been placed in Earth orbit by our remote descendents, and contains seven enormous chambers joined together like a railroad flat; cities and ecologies inhabit all these chambers but the seventh, which abuts the Way. A figment of mathematics and human engineering, the Way is a man-made artificial corridor of infinite length that insinuates itself through time and space without end, opening access to alternate universes, alternate humanities, and other races, including the Jart, whose seemingly unstoppable aggression initiates the catastrophe that ends *Eon*. *Eternity* begins.

The advanced form of humanity which inhabits Thistledown may have created the Way, but there is an enormous gap between creating something and understanding it; the universe of Greg Bear is no Campbell toytown. By creating the Way, humanity has in fact "pushed a sliver into God's finger," corrupting the central function of sentient life at the end of the universe, which is to harvest the essence of all life ever lived, and by harvesting "to *remember*" that essence. The Way must be destroyed or death will be the end. Nothing in *Eternity* sidesteps that premise. In short alternating chapters, Bear builds several segments of space-operatic plot towards his central revelations, and does so with competence and wit; but at the heart of *Eternity* lies a message that cuts deep into any presumption that telling a good story is the same thing as understanding the world. The universe, Bear says in this large brave courteous book, is greater than the tale.

11.

Come on into *The Dark Door* (St Martin's Press, 1988), one imagines Kate Wilhelm saying. Sit down and make yourself comfy. Let me bake you a nice little tale, in my goulash pot. Part horror, part sf, part detective novel, The Dark Door has indeed an easy lazy grace about its first 50 pages or so that asks the reader to relax in the hands of its loquacious but competent chef, and to enjoy the repast. Unfortunately this sense of security is short-lived, and much of the book wambles desperately over America in search of a fitting conclusion. None is reached.

Inconceivably far off, we are told, an alien scientist has created an artificial life-seeker which goes astray. Meanwhile on Earth, ordinary people who stray too close to certain abandoned wooden-framed three-storey hotels find themselves going murderously insane. Carson Danvers, whose family has been expunged in this manner, but who is himself immune, finds a dark inter-dimensional door lurking at the heart of the hotel that seems to have caused their deaths, and commits arson against the place. But the door merely shifts to another hotel. Arson-specialist Charlie Meiklejohn and his gourmand-wife Constance Leidl, who appear in The Hamlet Trap (1987), soon find themselves investigating a strange pattern of arson committed against these abandoned hotels. They catch Carson, whose story tallies with their own experiences, and Charlie determines to blow the dark door back to where it came from, wherever (he does not much care) that might be.

But not only Carson is immune to the effects of the defective alien life-seeking device, which the human scientists in the cast urgently wish to investigate, and it is hard to understand why Wilhelm, an sf writer of grace and wisdom, should applaud its destruction on the part of her hysterical Luddite protagonists. As in the world of Bear's Eternity, there may be things in this universe men cannot hope to know; but in the sf genre it is a rare and unseemly thing for an author to claim that there are things men should refuse to know.

III.

Terry Bisson and Jack Womack are both from Kentucky, both live in New York, and both have begun publishing in the 1980s. Their new novels – Bisson's Fire on the Mountain (Arbor House, 1988) and Womack's Terraplane (Weidenfeld, 1988) – both present alternate histories of the United States, and both place the central point of divergence from our own world in the American Civil War. The protagonist of each novel is black. Beyond this, the two books couldn't be more different.

Like most utopias, Fire on the Mountain is more a vision than a novel. In 1859, in a nineteenth century whose history already differs in many details from ours, John Brown succeeds in his raid on a Harper's Ferry whose location subtly differs from that of our own Harper's Ferry. That success proves germinal, and a United States more balkanized than our own soon splits into a Civil War between black and white, rather than one between federalists and secessionists. Through the letters of a sympathetic white doctor, and the journal of a young black who becomes a famous revolutionary figure before the end of the century, Bisson presents a dream of the revolutionary dawn. In 1959, in a twentieth century radically altered from our own, the young widow of a black astronaut reads the letters and the journal while sorting her life out. There can be no doubt that she is just slightly too sweet to digest, nor is Bisson's 1959, with its steam-yacht benignity and its seamless super-science, rich in verisimilitude.

But to carp at the thinness of this 1959 is to poison the well of Bisson's utopian vision. The 1959 of *Fire on the Mountain* is less an alternate history than a claim for allegiance. It asks of its readers to pledge their imaginations to this dream of an America magically cleansed and calm and rich; the remoteness of that world from ours only increases the pathos of the fable. But within its exceedingly frail pages, the dream obtains. Within its pages, we can be joyous, for a space.

IV.

After the delicate wishfulness of *Fire on the Mountain*, the jagged savageries of *Terraplane* come, one must admit, as something of a relief. We are in the near future, in the jargon-noisy, slum-choked, multinational-corporation-dominated world of Womack's first novel, *Ambient* (1987). The language is the same, an information-dense battering-ram English in which adverbs and substantives are mercilessly verbed, the word *of* seldom appears; it is a language that evokes and commands constant action. Duly obliging, the plot of *Terraplane* yanks its black protagonist, an American ex-general now in corporate employ, from delirious conniptions in the slums of Moscow and thrusts him through a time-warp into an alternate 1939 New York City. With him hurtle his hit-man Jake, a supernaturally brilliant Russian girl scientist who understands the gizmo that gets them there, and a spy who Jake half-kills once or twice before killing him properly in a transformed Bellevue.

1939 in Womack's hands is a negative utopia or dystopia of startling viciousness. Slavery has become illegal only under Teddy Roosevelt. Unemployment is stuck at 50 per cent, an Asian plague has decimated the world, Hitler dominates the shambles, and corruption is rife. The black protagonist learns only very painfully what it means to be a "nigger," but keeps his formidable wits about him (and the plot boiling). The sequences in which he and Jake discover the feel of this ancient world – the cigarettes, the knobs that turn, the shiny linoleum – are among the most convincing yet crafted in a genre that can offer many descriptions of first contact between man and something alien. But there is little time in *Terraplane* to savour such experiences, and a frantic engine of plot soon begins to mangle cast and setting alike. None too soon, the survivors splinter their way back through the Futurama-blighted New York World's Fair into our future, which is nightmarish in its own right, but home. Look for sequels. They will be loud and feral, and they'll fizz.

— *The Washington Post Science Fiction Column*, 27 November 1988

THROUGH the disorganized opening chapters of *Kairos* (Unwin Hyman, 1988) Gwyneth Jones's extremely ambitious third novel for adults, something of importance struggles to be born. Its passage is by no means easy nor assured, and those readers who survive the first hundred pages of the book may well judge its climactic moments to have been fatally undermined by the enervating dither of its beginning. This would be unfortunate. As insistent as the Book of Revelations in its claims to be heard, *Kairos* is about rewiring the world utterly.

The world it depicts is one in dire need of transformation. By the year 2000, life has come increasingly to resemble the dystopian nightmare that most contemporary British sf writers normally claim to perceive. Even more savagely than Ian McEwan in *The Child in Time* (1987), Jones views the England of a decade hence as a desperately polluted factory farm run by the police for the benefit of a panicking elite. Only in the grubbier interstices of such a world can liberal or counter-cultural lives be led.

Like most English rebels, Jane ("Otto") Murray, who runs a dishevelled feminist bookshop in Brighton with her lover Sandy and her young son Candide, comes from a background of privilege, and exudes an aura – a fug – of self-contemplative insularity. She is emotionally bound (like almost any protagonist of any Simon Raven novel) to those who have shared her childhood, her class, her university, her sins; and the first third of *Kairos*, by replicating all too perfectly the unconscious snobberies of her private world, tends to disdain any normal courtesies of narration. Reading these careless, nickname-infested pages is like eavesdropping on a large extended family one could never hope to join.

Only when the tale properly begins does *Kairos* come formidably to life. A fascistic religious sect called BREAKTHRU has produced a "reality changing drug" called Kairos which operates by "a kind of radiation" on anyone who holds it. As the inside and the outside of all realities have now become, literally and terribly, interchangeable, that holder can transform the world. Through a rather implausible extended-family daisy-chain, Kairos comes into Otto's possession, and thence into her son's. Following its own revolutionary programme, BREAKTHRU kidnaps Candide's pet dog, and begins to post its severed limbs back to him, hoping that in his childish exorbitances of distress the boy will cause enough Kairos-induced chaos for the government to fall.

But Candide joins forces with Sandy, Otto's working-class lesbian lover who has suffered both the snubs of her circle and most of the wounds an uncaring state can inflict. Sandy's apocalyptic bitterness now combines with Candide's natural abandon to impose a convulsive transmutation upon the shattered land. But kairos, which literally means fullness of time, has also a specifically Christian meaning: the moment of Christ's appearance. Though Jones wisely refrains from attempting to limn an actual Second Coming, the vision that closes *Kairos*, of an unpatriarchal world in which it is inconceivable that dogs (and humans) might be tortured, rings backwards through her text like a blessing, and justifies it.

– *Times Literary Supplement*, 6 January 1989

THREE: 1989

1. Year Roundup

As I walk'd through the Wilderness of this World, I lighted on a certain place, where was a Denn: And I laid me down in that place to sleep: And as I slept I dreamed a Dream. I dreamed, and behold *I saw four Riders, cloathed in Armour, and their Names were Isaac and Iris and Poul and Greg: And the Lines of Thought upon each Face were Gilt paint: And the Eye Balls were Gilt also.* So I awoke, and behold I saw four Horsepersons, and they seemed to be making fair good headway: Wherefore it beseemed me to hasten on after them, in the Plopping tracks left by their mounts, though the sky was dark, and the road exceeding narrow, indeed a Tight Rope. And in this fashion I came up abreast the last Rider, and I saw that he sat backwards within his Cage of shining armour, which bore upon its brassy Pate a gilt face in his very Likeness, which stared forward, with Eye Balls Gilt also: But himself stared back upon my countenance as I drew abreast, and waved his small tiny arms, and in his hands was a map of the path Already Taken. And the name of that map was *Nemesis.* And I thought, I know that face. And so I passed further on ahead, and came abreast the next and the next, and saw that the Riders sat all hunched, each and every one, legs bandy within their Struts, and stared thus backwards at what had been, and that their mortal Visages bespoke great longing: And each bore a map, upon which was scored traces of paths long before taken in the Golden World, but now erazed. And the name of the maps were *Message to the Planet,* and then *Boat of a Million Years,* and last *Tides of Light.* And I passed yet further, for I wore no Armour and my Impetus was great, and for a bright Instant I thought to see the road ahead entire, and the Chasm before our feet: But dared not give a second glance forward at the Aweful and exsanguinate Shape of Things to Come uncloath'd, for the sake of my Health. And I turned back, and was just passing to the rear, when imprints of the four just and true maps of the four riders were proffered into my hands, lo for a pretty penny: And I examined them. And I thought: That's all right, but what have you done for me lately?

Lately, what has begun to happen is history. The Cold War, after clutching Time deep-frozen to its winter heart for longer than we dare remember, has finally cracked open, and a million clocks have begun to turn (for Time lives again). We may have wintered the War (or not), spring may come (or otherwise); but suddenly there is a Present, and it burns. Suddenly (for Time has given us air to breathe) the great globe and all that it inherit seems within our grasp to save (or spoil utterly). The deranged Punch-and-Judy sleazeballs who "govern" us have no longer (until they regroup) the final say, and in March 1990 it seems that we the people may ourselves be able to call the tune as we enter Planetary Cusp and decide whether or not, as a race, we wish to live or die. Very soon now (most of us should still be alive) the verdict will be in, and we'll know whether or not we're going to survive on (or off) this nice little earner planet we have asset-stripped nearly to death. So the Tight Rope lies before us, the narrow road to the egress. So what have you done – sf writers of the year – to chart the course ahead? Is there anything you'd like to say on our behalf? If you twist around in your saddle-cages as you ride, can you glimpse anything of the way ahead, through the pinholes in your masks?

Are there pinholes in the masks you wear?

As it turns out, right now there aren't quite as many bright riders giving suss as even a year ago (are there as many of us still hoping to learn?) It looks as though, when the final figures have been checked, 1989 will have seen a slight slackening in the number of titles published in at least two of the three categories (horror, fantasy, sf) now commonly in use. As a percentage of a ludicrously high previous total, the largest drop should (by all that's holy) be in horror titles, but won't be, even though it's terribly hard for a non-aficionado to avoid a sense that this subgenre suffers from an intractable vacuity of premise, with only its very finest writers only very occasionally coming up with anything verging on the new. Katherine Dunn's *Geek Love* (Knopf) lets sift a tracery of horror images over a tale whose inner premises may (or may not) have an intended sf base, but whose house is the house of James Purdy (or Ross Macdonald), the pore-house of family. Ramsey Campbell continues, in *Ancient Images* (Century/Legend), to explore the interstices of his water-retentive Liverpool psyche; and in *Down River* (NEL), also drenched by the undead-urban heart of Middle Britain, Stephen Gallagher once again beats to death (and beyond) an idea too dumb to remember, in prose much too fine to waste. And Stephen King flirts once again, like a child picking at poison ivy in the mirror, with the autobiography of a writer bound to a wheel of fire of unmerited success, though *The Dark Half* (Hodder & Stoughton) no more bites the bullet than *Misery* (1987) did. But Dan Simmons's *Carrion Comfort* (Dark Harvest) came close to filling its huge boots (690 huge pages) with a tale of *feeding* which (like the experience of reading the book itself) battened on the orchestra of what it ate.

As with the great reptiles so many millions of years ago, there may be a dragon die-off in 1989, with fantasy titles levelling out (and maybe even beginning to sink), though most of those remaining are told in Barbara Cartland Celtic. (The name Melanie Rawn appears nowhere in this essay.) The only titles worth reading all year were those that scraped at the bars of the form like birds (Storm Constantine) or beasts (Jonathan Carroll) or pushmi-pullyus (Terry Pratchett). Storm Constantine (the pseudonym of a British writer I always find myself thinking of as "Storm Constantinople!") finished off her Wraeththu sequence with a walkabout occupying more of *The Fulfilments of Fate and Desire* (Drunken Dragon Press) than was perhaps wise, if wrapping up the loose vipers of the plot were her goal (but clearly it was not); and *The Monstrous Regiment* (Orbit) was a menarche weepie pretending *really* to be about the political destiny of an entire cheap-servant planet, which it wasn't. Steve Erickson's novels are fantasy if Kafka (or America) is; like strobe shots of a disaster, *Tours of the Black Clock* (Poseidon) and *Leap Year* (Poseidon) afforded no full views of the land of dreams, only gasped recollections of nightmare. This Apocalypse Pointillism also marked books whose narratives were seemingly conventional enough, like Lisa Goldstein's *Tourists* (Simon & Schuster), or Jonathan Carroll's *A Child Across the Sky* (Century/Legend); in both novels, whole and rounded characters come close to choking in the bricolage of failing worlds, until they seem motley: but in both cases the protagonists survive (at what cost). In *The Stress of Her Regard* (Charnel House), Tim Powers returned to the clement cartoon tapestry of the early nineteenth-century England featured in *The Anubis Gates* (1983), digging deeper this time, though maybe with a dab less joy. In *The Father of Stones* (Washington Science Fiction Association), Lucius Shepard lacquered the stone hide of the Dragon Griaule with yet more daubs of allegory, but the beast seems to thrive on its fleas. Howard Waldrop retold the legend of Hercules in a slow drawl, while never letting *A Dozen Tough Jobs* (Mark V Ziesing) slacken into anecdote; always, beneath the jokes, an antique thrill seemed to lurk. And *Pyramids (The Book of Going Forth)* (Gollancz), along with *Guards! Guards!* (Gollancz), continued Terry Pratchett's crystalline Discworld comedies, shapely and hilarious and benign; perhaps because they owe their originating premises as much to Larry Niven as to the fantasy moguls they sweetly and piercingly jape, a hard articulacy underpins the sequence (eight strong so far [17 now 1995]), so that finally its riffs and cocoricos seem *strophic*.

There will probably have been somewhere between 250 and 300 sf novels published during the year; the total depends in part on definition – most of the books already cited might well be called sf by someone, perhaps by me – and part on Technical Concerns that the boffins at *Locus* (and other journals) invoke whenever 2 + 2 clearly adds up to 5 shared worlds in a sharecropper tree. But the final total, however it is calculated, will almost certainly suggest that there's still a great deal of fat yet to be pruned; a sense that too many instant-martyr titles still end their tiny careers bound to the stake at Dalton-Walden, where they scream their hype for a moment or two, in a quite extraordinarily cruel parody of Andy Warhol's fifteen

minutes of fame, before their covers are ripped like scalps and the dead skins returned to sender.

Write on, brave riders.

Dinosaurs (as we've used the term in previous years: to describe authors whose
careers took off in the Golden Age) continue to paw the stained turf-labyrinth of the
1990s (Exxon marks the spot), just as though 1940 were forever, and the one future
we all faced together could be met by one Project we could all agree upon. None
died this year. The talking heads in grey prose of Isaac Asimov's *Nemesis* (Doubleday
Foundation) confab once again to save the savourless bacon of the Good Doctor's
stone prosthesis dream of Earth. (One Horseperson down.) Arthur C Clarke took
once again the Chamber-of-Commerce conscience of the otiose Gentry Lee under
his wing and together they betrayed *Rendezvous with Rama* (1973) to its sequel, *Rama
II* (Gollancz), which swallows its pa down with hardly a burp and bores on through
the vacancy of space insatiate: further sequels are projected, sequels to the sequel,
frequent-traveller Ramas, Ramada Ramas. And Frederik Pohl continued to feelgood in *Homegoing* (Del Rey), like a wise old horny owl caught (as we hinted last
year) drinking champagne out of his Norn-mask. No other dinosaur spoke or
pawed.

Like a *Raft of the Medusa* in a sea of drowning singletons, the books of genre
band together for solace and for sales; and tales of genre interest which swim alone
– through amour propre or market savvy – continue to miss our boat. Almost always
we are the losers. Peter Ackroyd, whose black *Hawksmoor* (1985) spun a True Map of
London out of Iain Sinclair's *Lud Heat* (1975), took on part of the Matter of Britain in
First Light (Hamish Hamilton), but occluded it. In Martin Amis's *London Fields* (Cape)
suicide and the millennium come together in a dovetail of horror, told in a scraped
scathed scatological prose quite remarkably painful to read. Paul Auster might
seem more soothing, for *Moon Palace* (Viking) seems to celebrate a traditional marriage of internal and external geographies, in which a quest for self mirrors the
search to conquer the Moon in all her phases; what shocks in the end is that the
marriage is no metaphor, and one's eyes are pinned open to naked ceremony. Nor
does the element of spoof in Julian Barnes's *A History of the World in 10½ Chapters*
(Cape) do much to attenuate the fervent darkness of its burden. For several years
now Thomas Berger, whose *Little Big Man* (1964) helped wrench the West into post-
modern fable-land, has been using sf tools for a similar prying loose of modern urban life in America; *Nowhere* (1985) is a dystopian jaunt to a Lewis Carroll Ruritania;
the device that shapes *Being Invisible* (1987) is pretty obvious if you see what I mean,
and *Changing the Past* (Little, Brown) is about changing the past, but the simplicity of

these tales is like the edge of a knife, the clarity is all the better to eat you with, like any true anthropology.

In *The History of Luminous Motion* (Bloomsbury), Scott Bradfield lays out California as a map of the family romance, rolls the map up with the readers still inside. Anthony Burgess wobbles his lexicon lips more chastely than sometimes in *Any Old Iron* (Hutchinson), but the survival of the eponymous Excalibur fails to lance a single boil of our secular quotidian; no Arthur lives again to save British Rail. In *Skeleton-in-Waiting* (The Bodley Head), Peter Dickinson (who is never still) returns to the alternate world of *King and Joker* (1976), where a different monarch reigns over Britain, but to no avail: it is still our hedged and bounden world, for which (all the same) he conveys a wiry love. Nor do we entirely escape our servitude to the real in the exuberant thaumaturgies of *Foucault's Pendulum* (Secker & Warburg) by Umberto Eco, but the tricks and turns of the book work like a rhetoric of the human urge to pry something loose from things, and we do, for a moment, feel, therefore, freed. Geraldine McLaughrean's *The Maypole* (Secker & Warburg) also homes on the Middle Ages, but cannot leave, caught in a weave of tapestry and song; the tale should interest genre-readers for the washed potency of its sense that the world is new, like somewhere else. There is of course no message to the planet in *The Message to the Planet* (Chatto & Windus) by Iris Murdoch, though the dying Wittgensteinesque guru at its heart does raise the dead, and thinks hard, and squats upon a menhir on a ley line, and so forth; but then he dies mute, the throat of his spirit torn out. (If you peek through the pinhole in the mask, says the second Horseperson, you will go blind.) There are deep ghosts and incest mirrors galore in *Soul/Mate* (Dutton), but none as frightening as the thought of Rosamond Smith (tasty pseudonym) meeting Joyce Carol Oates (ravenous). *The Scapeweed Goat* (Hamish Hamilton), by Frank Schaefer, limns a nineteenth-century American West spot-stained with religious utopias, but in the end his art seems insufficiently obdurate to grasp the muddied God he hopes to discredit. In *Two Women of London: The Strange Case of Ms Jekyll and Mrs Hyde* (Faber & Faber), Emma Tennant rough-cuts the Robert Louis Stevenson tale for Ladbroke Grove (Jerry Cornelius's old home), where the old dichotomy between self and sharer marshalls new traumas, points the belatedness of the heroines as the world dwindles into factory farm. William Wharton, in *Franky Furbo* (Holt), shape-changes his beloved family (which, variously disguised, appears in all his work) into radiant undying foxes (literally), and snuggles down with them to an eternal Christmas, safe from us, safe from the rusty traps of time, safe from heat-death. And Marianne Wiggins, in *John Dollar* (Secker & Warburg), reduces the world of men and women and children to its apodictic nub in a fable rightly much likened to William Golding's *Lord of the Flies* (1954). One must eat to live. Civilization is guts writ large.

Growls become audible. Alpha males of the first order – massive bewhiskered pater-familiasi, who came into the field after World War Two and held their ground until 1975 or so – muscle into view; if either Ursula K Le Guin or Joanna Russ had published in 1989, we might be speaking of alpha persons: but they did not. Hush now. I think I see the first of them, suddenly manifest, like Bambi full-grown. Do nothing to arouse an aggressive response. At all costs avoid eye contact. You'll be all right. You'll be fine. Really.

Why it's Poul Anderson himself, raising his silkie head from long immersion in the breeding tanks of fantasy, bringing us *The Boat of a Million Years* (Tor) between his jaws, grrring softly. The book itself is complicated and epical and crabby, and its wisdom-scarred immortal protagonists end up turning their backs on the planet we have served so ill, the tightrope we walk. (Mortals to the back of the bus, the third Horseperson tells us, and his Weltschmerz stings our pocked cheeks; twilight becomes him; but his quirt sizzles.) Next, slipping demurely into the spotlight, comes sleek disgruntled Piers Anthony, fresh from the greasepaint orgy of *Bio of an Ogre* (1988) (an autobiography) and a million puns of low degree, eager to tell us a bit more about the traps that line the path of a great hunter, as the utterly peculiar apologia-cum-scholarly-apparatus surrounding *But What of Earth?* (Tor) must be intended to demonstrate. The novel was originally published in 1976, as part of the loathsome Laser Book series of doctored novels, and was duly copy-edited to fit its easy-digestion, offend-thee-no-crank-Christian remit. In the long and laboured revenge he takes upon the butchers of his silly pale little tale, Anthony reveals mainly (and we mention the book solely to illustrate) how dangerous it is for alpha males to hunt alone too long. Gordon R Dickson (next) plugs along with *The Earth Lords* (Ace), without cracking much of a smile, always a bridesmaid. In *Eden* (Harcourt Brace), an early novel (from 1959) now translated, Stanislaw ("Bristlecone") Lem sidles into view with another elegant diagram of the void between Us and Other (as in *Solaris* from two years later); the bureaucratic reality-games which apparently govern those native to the planet Eden might as well portray the nomenklatura of his own country, before History began again.

In *The Fugitive Worlds* (Gollancz), Bob Shaw reduced the glowing gemütlich cosmogonic game-show of *The Ragged Astronauts* (1986) to Tinker Toy operatics (matter transmitters and AI's and galactic Bangs and wooden spaceships and wicked princesses and big-domed aliens, stargates and wandering planets and lovesick commandos and other scrapings of the barrel all thresh it out in the jacuzzi); but a certain daft adroitness kept it all in play. Robert Silverberg continued, in *The Queen of Springtime* (Gollancz), to show us all how easy it was to organize a hunt, to guide the hounds, to bag a robot fox. He writes without a hitch, without a catch in the throat, without a view. He writes like a Motorway to Canterbury. In *Bugs* (Macmillan), John Sladek, who is the kind of hunter who stakes *himself* out for bait, juggles autobiography and the blackest of fabulations in a tale of exile's return to America, and of the rending teeth within the belly of the beast; Minneapolis is stripped to its fundamental Mall, Las Vegas is a bum rap; there are lots of laughs. In *Megalomania* (DAW), Ian Wallace brings back the world of Croyd, sounding like three Cordwainer Smiths having a squabble on their way to a dance. In *Soldier of Arete* (Tor), set in ancient Greece, Gene Wolfe continues the tale of Latro, who cannot remember events earlier than the previous day; but now a goddess brings him to a Theatre of Memory, and the book begins to sing in strophes deeper than the wine-dark sea. I think it is a song of love to Latro. And in *Land of Shadows* (Morrow), Roger Zelazny, who may have a better ear than anyone in the field, sticks his headphones on again and bikes amiably at great speed through the land of Amber for the ninth time; it may take all his very considerable skill to navigate the turns of a tale told at such a high pitch, but so what, who can follow what it is impossible to heed?

Aficionados of the Sort will find that, as we approach the present tense, categories become less stable. Some writers whose genre careers have just begun are really quite grizzled (like Jack Butler); others (like Neal Barrett Jr, or George Alec Effinger) have been working for a couple of decades, but have only recently begun to surmount (like dolphins) the medium. Some members of this cohort love the tickle of attention. Others do not take well to handling. We will put them cheek by jowl.

The Archivist (Unwin), which is a first novel, by Gill Alderman, who was born in 1941, dives with a painterly lubricity into the cities and cultures of a matriarchy dominant over part of an extremely distant planet. The urgency of her need to see and weigh and taste this pomegranate demesne does sometimes drive her plot into an outer room (where it babbles unheard); but a sense of something lived swells through the chaos and the oops-sorry jump-cuts of an almost untold tale. Like an inside-outside of the Alderman, A A Attanasio's *The Last Legends of Earth* (Doubleday Foundation) applies its painterly lubricity to a palette of plot-knots and icons too devious and daunting to describe, though enticing to imbibe; but because the worlds whirl like tops, it's impossible to sit down anywhere in the book. Iain (M) Banks, in *The State of the Art* (Mark V Ziesing), uses his deft interstellar post-scarcity

Culture to knee our own wee shambles; super folk come from far stars to the Earth of 1977 and gag. Shock egress ensues. In *Dawn's Uncertain Light* (Signet), Neal Barrett Jr further darkens the monitory quest scenario of *Through Darkest America* (1987), sweeps dizzyingly downwards East and West through blacker and blacker outcomes of the Dream, until we find what eats what to keep the America Ball lit. And gruffish Gregory Benford, galactic insight veteran, also travels further in *Tides of Light* (Bantam), bound upon a course towards the heart of things, melancholy and bristling, brimful of the thought of it all. But the plot itself, like an old friend the author has outgrown, keeps saying the wrong thing in mixed company, staining the carpet of the stars with its pulpy feet (it is a sequel to *Great Sky River* from 1987), gassing on.

(Hello I must be going, says the fourth Horseperson. I am gafiating to Ganymede. I am twinned with Far Arcturus. I have no time for Moaning Minnies. I have a huge advance. I'm off.)

In *Deus Ex Machina* (Bantam), J V Brummels takes on space opera, a dystopian acid-bath vision of America down the line, cyberpunk, prostitution sort of stuff, and cosmogonic comeuppances all around; and it might almost be said he wins. In prose of alert muscle and good skin-tone, Jack Butler transforms the moderately dumb premise of *Nightshade* (Atlantic Monthly Press) – to wit, that vampires are a cul-de-sac of evolution, when in fact they are a sac out of whole cloth – into a tour-de-force of cat's-cradle plotting, set on Mars with AI's and the kitchen sink and all. Orson Scott Card skirted *The Abyss* (Legend) by claiming that it was not a novelization of the movie but in fact a novel novelizing the movie (move over Aquinas); edged out another Alvin the Maker text with *Prentice Alvin* (Tor), bringing us only marginally closer to the true abyss of adulthood and the Land to salve for real; and couched an apologia for his Mormon culture in terms so enticingly strange (and seemingly humble) that readers might well have taken *The Folk of the Fringe* (Phantasia) for an apostasy, which it is not. After the pounding amplitude of *Cyteen* (1988), C J Cherryh finely compressed her bustling intelligence into the chamber-opera of *Rimrunners* (Warner), set almost entirely inside a ship, below decks, where small dramas of life and death took on countenances we all know from the mortal streets that bind us all. Building on the scummy hieroglyphs of *When Gravity Fails* (1987), George Alec Effinger's *A Fire in the Sun* (Doubleday Foundation) seemed to begin to alphabetize his cyberpunk/Middle East soup; further volumes may learn to spell in this new tongue. Ben Elton (mentioned last year in passing) told us all in *Stark* (Michael Joseph) that he wasn't just another pretty face, that he meant exactly what he said about the end of life on Earth and no Tight Rope; jokes and all, this highly nervous first novel (a typical Raven Book, every stanza ending in Nevermore) read like a cattle prod. It was not easy to ignore.

This year's Conrad Stargard novels from Leo A Frankowski, The High-Tech Knight, The Radiant Warrior and The Flying Warlord (all Del Rey), whose time-traveller hero continues to jump-start Medieval Eastern Europe into the starring role in an alternate Renaissance, once again cast a simple spell of Anachronism, a totally untoughminded dream of infantile omnipotence whose locus classicus (for me, because I love the book) has always been Poul Anderson's The High Crusade (1960). And Richard Grant, in Views from the Oldest House (Doubleday Foundation), drifted slowly into a coy murk of allusion, so sing vainly to King Arthur and to M John Harrison as he sank, having forgotten (perhaps) that King Arthur was a ringleader (not a freelance) and Viriconium was the kind of place Thomas Covenant could believe in.

Good-tempered but really very tired (why does one think of Henry Cooper), Joe Haldeman made more sense with Buying Time (Morrow) than he has for a while, but this tale of the costs (and benefits) of immortality had a much too high apparatus-to-message ratio, and bestowed all too many privileges on its high earner protagonists (I stared at the book with mute inglorious dumb resentment for quite a few minutes before managing to Think Rich for an hour). James Patrick Kelly's Look into the Sun (Tor), an unacknowledged sequel to Planet of Whispers (1984), continues to count the perils and perks of exogamy on an alien planet, in a style as slow and crafted as Gardner Dozois's of Strangers (1978) long ago. Good News from Outer Space (Tor) by John Kessel – like so much sf now of interest – churned tropes galore into goulash, kept its afflatus dry, hit its targets stunningly well (for those who could see them); and by refusing to unpack its alien visitor into common view indulged in an archetypal late-genre play on the absence of the Sign. (A late-genre work might well be described as any text made up of material remembered but not present.) Garry Kilworth, who should have been mentioned last year for the concise map of decline contained in Abandonati (1988), published this year In the Hollow of the Deep-Sea Wave (The Bodley Head) and Hunter's Moon (Unwin), the one a collection of linked mellow-astringent tales edging at the numinous, the other a Fox Consciousness epic (and not our brief). The linked stories in Eric McCormack's The Paradise Motel (Viking) also edged, but grotesquely, like musings of Dr Lao, into the Otherworld of genre. Bruce McAllister, whose Humanity Prime (1971) may now gain the readership it merits, presents in Dream Baby (Tor) a nightmarish vision of the maelstrom of complicity of Vietnam, told in clear, so that it is hardly to be read. Pat Murphy's The City, Not Long After (Doubleday Foundation) did not make one wish to nuke San Francisco (though she did coat the tale in a dire complacency of smarm about the place), because the City, in the end, is our highest craft, and carries the burden of the race, and she said so. And in America it is brave to so depose.

In *The Night Mayor* (Simon & Schuster UK), Kim Newman played with film noir, Philip K Dick, medical ethics and pocket universes and shamus stuff, juggling the mélange with weird clemency; and in *Drachenfels* (GW Books) as Jack Yeovil, he came like an agent provocateur (or Henry Fonda in *The Grapes of Wrath*) into sharecropper country, and told a tale whose lickety-split contempt for its egregious premises must have shored up the heart of any serf who cared to look. It was, in other words, pure Hollywood. Paul Park continued, in *Sugar Rain* (Morrow), to create a world vaster than empires and more slow, and a story to match. There is little dash to the book, but within its dream-retarded periods a mature love story, that sounds like life, unfolds its human limbs within the pageant, the cleansing downpour of the title. There is also a tropical redolence to the mise en scène of Geoff Ryman's first full-length novel, *The Child Garden* (Unwin), which is set in a tangled and transfigured London, though the true heat of the book lies in the close breath of its telling, the pinned proximity of its characters, the moral curvatures one must trace to catch the story as it shifts and grows. It is an sf tale (with learning viruses and a metaphysic of cancer in a world governed by a collective Will) and a novel of mimesis, and a bildungsroman, and an act of devotion to Dante. All these. In Richard Paul Russo's *Subterranean Gallery* (Tor), a hard negentropic flame of Art (in the form of sf illustrations) continued against the odds to burn against the night in police-state San Francisco; Allen Steele's *Orbital Decay* (Ace) was bonny and hard and loud; Sheri S Tepper's *Grass* (Doubleday Foundation) was ornate, gracile, steely, extremely savvy. We spoke of *Carrion Comfort* long pages earlier; we speak of *Hyperion* (Doubleday Foundation) now, Dan Simmons's second (or third) novel of 1989, an sf text of daunt and glint based on *The Canterbury Tales* (with additives). Like blind men describing the elephant which is *Hyperion*, the seven Pilgrims of the book tell each other of their earlier experiences upon the planet; only as the book closes (the second volume of the novel is now due [*The Fall of Hyperion* came out in 1990 1995]) do they finally land, and begin the true pilgrimage. There is, in other words, rather more plot than Chaucer needed, whose folk found in the God-illumined world itself provender sufficient. But Chaucer wrote when the world was young (or English was), and Simmons writes in a belated genre (sf) very late in the day. (The Pinholes leak upon us Shards of Light, visions of the Future we must plot and plot and plot to gain if we may, or baulk if need be, upon the Rope.) There are late-century additives of every hue in *Hyperion*, a surplusage of deaths, and burnings, and infinite recursives of spying, and star fleets, and the Shrike, and the Time Tombs, and the Boojum. *Hyperion* when whole may bring us home to what we can say in 1990 in the words of sf; or it may default to norm. Who can tell? Write on, brave rider. Say the sayable. Say us onwards.

So I awoke, and behold it was a Dream.

– The Orbit Science Fiction Years 3 (Orbit, 1993), ed. David Garnett

2. INTERZONE COLUMNS

New Found Lands

I.

IN THE beginning was the Word. The rest is syntax. Of the Word that made us, we hear nothing but echoes of the surf, for we are deafened by the noise of our genes, and the stories we tell are wakes of the dead, after Eden. Turn your eyes (our tales may tell us) turn your eyes to the sea; but we do not, we stare into a desert storm, the scales are on our eyes. Thalassa! Thalassa! Or so I read the novels and stories of Gene Wolfe to claim. Like Severian in *The Book of the New Sun*, who is a thesis of the Increate, the protagonists of his book-length fictions are usually cloned or dead, creatures fallen from the Word; and their abode is the sands of the desert of the world. But always they search for some transformation, some code to unlock the gates of perception, some seawards turn. Severian finally reaches his Ocean, and bathes Urth in it. Adam Green, the terribly damaged protagonist of *There Are Doors* (Tor, 1988), Wolfe's new alternate universe fantasy, falls in love with Lara, a woman who also bears the name of Leucothea, a goddess of the sea. She may be Cybele. She may be the White Goddess. But she does not come from this Earth, and her domain draws him from this one as the sea draws things of earth. "Heavy things belong to the sea," she tells him. "You may be able to draw them out...but if ever they come near the sea again, they will eventually fall in." She is the Word. "I am the storm," she says.

She is also a transcendental bimbo out of Thorne Smith, or Edward Hopper; or both. She lights upon Green as blithely as Marian Kirby lights upon Topper; but the places they meet and romance together are cityscapes furtive with solitude. The alternate world into which Green's crippled psyche falls – back and forth through any door or door-like opening which seems "significant" – is a frozen America caught in an unending Depression, rather like Green's own psychiatric state; it also resembles Prague, but of this more in a moment. Green, who has had electroshock treatments before the novel begins, may have arrived in the world of the Goddess, who is the sea we long for, but he is too deeply wounded to embrace a dream of plenitude. His turn towards her is a tropism, not a choice. The alternate America he perceives, bleak and snowbound and empty, haunted by tramlines and great deserted hotels, is a nightmare of romance turned against itself, where women are literally *femmes fatales*. In this world men, like certain insects, die after mating. It is possible, however, to long for an Oz-like sanctuary or Heaven called Overwood, where She may dwell; there are even maps to show the way.

Green himself mates with Lara only at the beginning of *There Are Doors*, and his subsequent mole-like quest for her has something of the coffin closeness of tone that makes *Peace* (1975) perhaps the chillest posthumous fantasy ever written. But unlike almost anything else Wolfe has ever written, *There Are Doors* seems reluctant to respond to any particular decoding strategy on the part of the reader; it is, in fact, a text of quite extraordinary looseness of ascription. No doubt a topology of doors within the text can and should be established, and the pattern of Green's "moves" from Her world to this and back again properly charted; and it may be the case that the references Wolfe makes to Kafka are as much a snare as a pointer. But the references do exist, and perhaps we have indeed been pointed in the right direction. Significantly, Kafka never ties his reader to any fixed interpretation of his text, and it is certainly the case that the nightmare world Green enters does refuse – in the same way that Kafka's worlds refuse – to deliver any ontological security whatsoever. The America he enters certainly resembles the land discovered by Karl Rossmann in *Amerika*. The hallucinated bareness of *There Are Doors* is reminiscent of Kafka's short fables. And Green's turns in search of what we have called the sea are certainly thwarted and mimicked by the bureaucracies of incertitude so definitively dreamt of in *The Castle*.

But Wolfe manages to end his book; unlike Kafka, for whom reading the world was interminable. Having no life to abandon, Green's soul turns to Overwood. Once he is there, She may allow him to worship in her sight, thalassotropic, bee-stung. Out of the stymied melancholia of his life, which *There Are Doors* replicates with weird jocosities and wintery skill, Green may find the Word that wrote him. And be blessed.

II.

There is also a certain amount of death in Stephen Gallagher's new novel, as well as a great deal of depression. *Down River* (New English Library, 1989) comes bearing some of the regalia of horror fantasy – chiefly a cover illustration designed to market the book as cod demonology – but once unpacked proves to be the extremely modest this-worldly tale of a good cop and a bad cop, and how the bad cop got that way. Emulous sociopath Johnny Mays has haunted somewhat sensitive non-tear-away Nick Frazier from childhood, but things only come to a head after both have become plainclothes policemen in a rain-sodden city west of the Pennines, perhaps Liverpool. In a little black book, Johnny records the names of those who offend his pathological amour propre, and afterwards takes his revenge on them, finally in-volving Nick in an illicit car chase into the hills which ends in Mays's death, or so it seems. But Mays survives, though his mind and memory begin to flicker alarmingly, and generates a series of horrors which climax in an unnamed Hull. Nick survives. The novel ends in a state of routine bleakness, too many pages after it began. Two aspects of the book seemed of interest. 1) the title releases assonances of a depres-sion unto death – "Death fascinated Johnny, always had. Some of his better dreams were of death, as a river dreamed of the sea." – that seem more than merely person-al, for between Liverpool and Hull there is nothing in the face of the land that bears smiling about. 2) *Down River* reads very much like the *orchestration* of a supernatural horror novel, with only the voice missing. Add a line of narrative tying Mays's glow-ing eyes and infernal crypto-posthumousness to genuine possession à la genre, and the opera would be complete. So one does wonder: Since Mays has been given everything but the Devil's voice, why did Gallagher not give him full tongue?

III.

Like Rip van Winkle in Beatle gear, John Shirley tries desperately in *Heatseeker* (Scream/Press, 1988), a collection of bad and sad sf stories, to drag his 1950s sensi-bility into the present, but only makes it halfway. Minus the drug talk and the rock rhythms and the sexual power-plays and the cyberpunk rouge, the parched ranting voice of these stories brings us right back to the suburban solipsisms of the early *Galaxy*, or to any magazine of that time which published bad early Ellison. Good early Ellison Shirley aspires to emulate, but cannot. Solitary characters shout and snarl at a world almost totally undefined, and arrive at punitive comeuppances their author licks his lips over. Once in a while, as in "What Cindy Saw" from *Interzone*, or "Ticket to Heaven" from F & SF, the voice takes on a calcined cloacal rasp that re-minds one of Barry Malzberg, and, as in these two stories, metaphors of a painful urgency can emerge; in the latter, a conspiratorial model of the oppressions of pow-er/scarcity does saliently take shape, and one wishes Shirley had restricted himself to tales he had an idea about. But mostly he does organ-grinder riffs out of the dead past of the genre and the bottom of his drawer. Not strongly recommended.

IV.

In the past, John Sladek's problem was just the reverse of Shirley's. His stories were all world and no body, and as a consequence his novels tended to tail off halfway through into things-of-the-world riffs, mathematically couched, hilarious but paralyzed with a kind of terror, perhaps through the absence of any live human character to bear the burden. But finally, in *Bugs* (Macmillan, 1989), which is his first novel since *Tik-Tok* (1983), Sladek has written a novel with a full human consciousness at its heart, which motors its obsessive tabling of the wares of the absurd in a consumed America, and passes the terror on to us. Fred Jones, a British writer in early middle age, finds himself forced to look for work in America, and goes to Minneapolis, where he figures he might find some. Applying to a computer firm as a technical writer, he is hired in error as a software engineer. The team he joins is involved – we return here to *Roderick* (1980) – in the creation of a sentient robot, which is soon kidnapped by a demented ex-employee. But Robinson Robot – so named to allay the fears of the American public – has bugs, and follows the murderous orders of the episteme. But so does everyone. Everyone is eaten by what they consume, from junk food to television. Everyone is eaten from the inside out. America is a land of skulls. The woman Fred Jones falls in love with is murdered by a serial killer. He dreams of what we have all become, in the land of the dreams that consume us. He then dreams of a girl who wears a cap.

> On closer inspection, the glistening cap was a tight cluster of killer bees. The girl was not calm; she was frozen with fear, terrified of making the slightest movement.
>
> "Keep still," he said. "I'll draw them away." Then the girl lifted her eyes and looked at Fred.
>
> "Keep still? I'm dead." Her voice hummed like a swarm. "Can't you see I'm dead. They have built their hive in my skull."

After twenty years in England, Sladek returned to his native America in the 1980s. He has since been working as a technical writer in a computer firm in Minneapolis. Hilarious, deft, dense with terror, compact and crepuscular, *Bugs* is his message in a bottle from the new found land. Eat me (says the message in the bottle) if you dare. But I warn you. They have built their hive in my skull.

– *Interzone* 30, July/August 1989

Century Migraine

I.

I HAD a shock of recognition. It was a small one, but my own. In a piece I'd written last year [see pp. 25–26] I had made a stab at shaping into short form a cluster of images that had always – for me at least – illuminated the well-known debt cyberpunk authors owed to the American thriller and to the *film noir* of the 1940s and 1950s. Hammett's Sam Spade (I'd said), and Chandler's Marlowe, and Macdonald's Archer, were like "haunted archaeologists, curators of the western slope of latter-day America, delving through the catacombs of the mean streets of LA for hieroglyphs and papyrus that would reveal the crimes that fixed the meaning of the world." It was just the same (I'd said) with William Gibson. His protagonists also haunted the mazes of the world for a spoor of the ancient god who runs us for its sport. His heroes spoke a lingo of propitiation just like Marlowe, or Archer, or the hundred ghosts of film who populate David Thomson's superb *Suspects* (1985), chief among them the terrifying George Bailey of Frank Capra's *It's a Wonderful Life* (1946). In all of these novels, America defaults to Egypt. We come to Steve Erickson, whose books I had not yet read last year, but who says it all.

There are no private eyes in his first novel, *Days Between Stations* (1985), no granite cops steeped in lacrimae rerum till they glow like Dad – though the heart of the book does transfigure into an erotized *film noir* purée the tale of the making of Abel Gance's *Napoleon* (1927) and of the fifty years it took until Kevin Brownlow managed to put it all together. But in the two novels under review – *Rubicon Beach* (Poseidon Press, 1986) and *Tours of the Black Clock* (Poseidon Press, 1989) – detectives and private eyes do roam the aisles of America and the Century, praying at the altars of method for a clue; and near the end of *Rubicon Beach* a squad of Los Angeles detectives, reeking noir, does begin to investigate stories that a strange woman has been trespassing into the homes of the rich. Having already followed her long hegira northwards from a magical South American jungle into an exhausted end-game beached America, the reader, however, knows that the squad will never find her, because she is not a secular being, because she cannot be addressed from the surface of the world, or its maps. Her incursions into the evening world of America late in the century are like flashes of migraine. She is an unknown script, an oneirism in the veins of the eye. Migraine defaults to Egypt. Lowery, the lieutenant in charge, has sensed something of this language she embodies; and it is typical of the image world he inhabits that "when [he] walked out of his office he found his men reading the city map as though it were the writing on pyramid walls."

She does have a name. She has been given the name Catherine, and uses it like a shell borrowed from another species. The story of her birth and upbringing in a South American jungle, whose components mock and ape the magic realism of that continent's writers, lies at the narrative heart of *Rubicon Beach* which, like all of Erickson's novels, embeds a long consecutive tale within framing material whose effect is deeply fragmenting, so that frame and hindsight of that tale argue like migraines. After her father is killed by a sailor she had saved, Catherine leaves with the murderer, sailing down the only river in this part of the continent that flows west rather than east. She eventually arrives in Peru, makes her way northwards towards the Great Dream, and comes to the United States without being aware that the US is all the "America" we're going to get in this world. She reaches Los Angeles. "From one end of the panorama to the other ran this city, and in the distance was a black line she recognized as the sea. Carved in the side of a mountain was a huge map like the maps of ancient Indians she'd seen on pyramid walls. The huge white map looked like this: HOLLYWOOD. 'America?' she said to the driver, unconvinced.

"The driver took a beer from the truck and opened it on the door handle. 'Not just yet, sister,' he said with a shake of his head; and pointed west. 'America.'

"'But there's nothing else out there,' she said in her own language, looking at the sea." And she turns inland. She finds menial employment with the family of a Hollywood scriptwriter named Llewellyn or Lee, who becomes obsessed – hooked – by her face. It is a naked, intolerable, real face, the face of the goddess. But to perceive her face of glory [I modify here the original phrase, "her face entire," into a phrase which designates the gorgon of threshold, and which is examined at some length in the FACE OF GLORY entry in the forthcoming *Encyclopedia of Fantasy*, which I'm editing with John Grant 1995] is to cross the Rubicon from the America we know into a land comprised of dream and eros, in which fragments of her story and Llewellyn's generate alternate (but maybe more real) versions of the continent: but it is a Rubicon Llewellyn cannot cross. Her face turns into hieroglyphs he cannot read, and she disappears, no detective can find her. He lies prostrate on the beach of the world, like a hooked fish. And the central portion of *Rubicon Beach*, which in fact makes up the bulk of the book, ends in scar tissue.

The episodes which frame this tale of double quest can be read as metaphoric consequences of the failure of Catherine and Llewellyn to make one world – to make sense – of each other. The book begins in a surrealist near-future police-state America obscurely defined by its relationship to earlier states of the land, which are called America One and America Two. Just out of prison for telling a betraying joke about a chthonic tree – a tree full of Americans who live in its highest branches and who, it may be, have crossed each others' Rubicons and now share one growth, one inextricably interwed reality [see also, in the forthcoming *Encyclopedia of Fantasy*, the entry on EDIFICE 1995] –a man named Cale haunts a drowned Ballardian Los Angeles, and is haunted in turn by Catherine, whom he cannot reach, any more than Lou Reed could. The book approaches its close through episodes set in England, where an old man named Lake ("Cale" reversed) slips deathwards on the wrong side of the beach of dreams; and yet another character – a mathematician who has discovered a secret number between 9 and 10 – travels into America, taking a train which crosses a river without a further shore, and which stops only to deposit him in the bole of a great tree, whose highest branches are full of Americans. He sees Catherine in the distance, and steps her way. She is the secret number, the lost chord, the Rubicon. The novel ends.

An essay in magic realism – a quasi-Pynchonesque fantasy of quest – an archaeology of the dreamed America – a jape: it is probably central to *Rubicon Beach* that it can be read in any or all these ways, and in other ways as well; the Escher-like spirals of storyline which make up *Rubicon Beach* admit to no opening gambit, no safe closure. Though it is perhaps rather less lucid than *Tours of the Black Clock*, *Rubicon Beach* remains Erickson's most potent oneirism (if one can be permitted to re-use a neologism, this time without intent to pun; by "oneirism" I mean to designate a "dream" text whose content and telling are in no way regulated by any woken context; because there is no awaking from it, no door to shut except the last page, one cannot call *Rubicon Beach* a dream; dreams can be awoken from, or they are something else: the mirrors that entomb our every thought within the skull: or Hell [once again, see an entry in the forthcoming *Encyclopedia*, the one on ARABIAN NIGHTMARE 1995]). At first or second glance, *Tours of the Black Clock* may seem less autonomous than its predecessor, more a tale of the awoken day, but no reader will finish its rather swollen pages safe in that assumption, because the book turns in on itself, before it shuts down, just as rigorously as *Rubicon Beach* did. The sense, all the same, that as we read *Tours of the Black Clock* we are spending more time in the open air may logically derive from its ostensible subject matter, which is the Twentieth Century.

Here too, there is a central "objective" tale that occupies the heart and bulk of the book, the story of Banning Jainlight (whose name is almost certainly some sort of recondite play on the Jainist religion), a huge lad whose compulsive laughter reminds one of the message Günter *Grass*'s dwarf conveys by beating his *Tin Drum*; and who murders his western Pennsylvania family in the early 1930s before moving to New York where he becomes a pornographer, only to escape a bevy of private eyes by fleeing to Vienna, where his obsessional craftings of fantasy-encounters with a girl he glimpsed once in a window soon comes to intrigue not only Goebbels but Hitler, who are identified in the text only as clients X and Z. Because Hitler confuses Banning's haunted vision of reality in a face with his own lost love, Geli Raubal, who killed herself in 1931, and because his consequent immersion in Jainlight pornography distracts him from invading Russia, the history of the Twentieth Century branches at this point, as if it were a river splitting into two streams to pass an island in its course; though in doing so it becomes a river whose other side is never visible, like the great river whose Rubicon one must cross to reach the real America in the previous book.

The girl's name is Tania. She carries with her always the blueprint of an Escher-like house with a secret room which contains its conscience; it is a "map of the Twentieth Century." After a long depressive rallentando of episodes, and after the War has moved to Mexico, the ageing Banning Jainlight, blueprint now in his possession, kidnaps client Z from senile retirement in Venice, conveys him via Wyndeaux – a mythical French port which is a central venue of *Days Between Stations* – to the other side of the Atlantic. There Z dies. Banning fixes over his heart the portion of the floorplan of the Century which contains the conscience, thus knitting the Century back together, and continues his search for Tania, who can now be found. The fragments which frame this story refract its central erotic obsessions, weltschmerz, lust for meaning, violence. There is finally no exit from this book either. As a vision of our Century, however, it is perhaps at once too clear and too diffuse. Dominating the book, Banning Jainlight and his pornography too easily embody a rhetoric of self-disgust and horror, a rhetoric which comes all too close to a kind of surrealistic chat about the unspeakable; while at the same time the littoral contortuplications of the central image or model of the broken bourneless river convey a spread of meaning too broad to clutch the heart, too shallow to drown in. But in the end, because the surface of his tales is choked with flotsam, and because a plethora of rogue symbols gnaws constantly at one's keel, it is to drown that one reads Steve Erickson. It is to enter the oneirism without a hope to surface.

11.

In *A Dozen Tough Jobs* (Mark V Ziesing, 1989) Howard Waldrop tells a tall tale, which he sets in the Mississippi of 1925–1930. It can be presumed that we are being asked to think of William Faulkner, through whose hallucinated fables hurtle shaped shards of myth like music. In *A Dozen Tough Jobs*, like a passacaglia that skeletons the surface world, a comic retelling of the tale of the Twelve Labours of Hercules underpins a veiled and melancholy patter of anecdotes about the coming of age of a black adolescent in the Deep South. There are lots of jokes: Houlka Lee comes to Anomie, Mississippi to work off a prison sentence under the supervision of Boss Eustis; he cleans stables and borrows a madam's scarf; and so on. The story is told by the young black, whose full name is Invictus Ovidius Lace, but who is generally called I O Lace (or Iolus), in a tone which seems relaxed, but is in fact markedly contained; the passacaglia beneath the funning – its burden of significance born effortlessly – paces like a rough beast through Waldrop's agreeable impersonation of black speech. *A Dozen Tough Jobs* is an extremely savvy game, a spoof both relaxed and muscular, told from the verandah, in the cool of the evening. But under the stoop lurks the god. The eyes of the god are not shut.

– *Interzone* 31, September/October 1989

Razor Dancing

THERE are ways and ways of doing this thing. There is the plunge into the heart of the matter, so that the heaviest and most significant book comes first in one's column. Then there is the random approach, and the serendipitous, and the steady climb, the slippery slope, the heavy grade, the peaks and vales, the alphabet, the sort by size [I think I might have unconsciously trapped myself here in a Leonard Cohen riff (from "Hallelujah," *Various Positions*, 1985): "It goes like this / The fourth, the fifth / The minor fall, the major lift / The baffled king composing Hallelujah" 1995]. And finally there is taking a look at John Cramer before braving Kim Newman's griddle-noir cyberpunk policier in Dickland – and finishing off with Kim Newman before girding loins to endure the dry-ice caress of Jonathan Carroll, whose fifth book is now before us, burning white within its rack of covers. Doing it this way, we start outdoors, on the bark of the world, and only invade by stages the wormed wood.

I.

It is extremely difficult to dislike the John Cramer one detects twinkling through the great long pages of *Twistor* (Morrow, 1989), and I'm not about to make the effort. An indictment of this professor of physics and his first novel could perhaps be drawn up without much difficulty, but there seems little point in bracketing Cramer with the ideologues of hard sf – the whole madcap crew, from latter-day Dome-Over-America Greg Benford, on down through David ("I'll stiff the next sap who says he's liberal as I am") Brin and Jerry (no joke) Pournelle, till we reach the David Dean Drake Droid Ings of the killing fields – because Cramer seems simply to have found the idiom of hard sf congenial to his task, without much testing the implications of an idiom which treats the world as a problem to be solved for gain. (Unless they happen to be soldiers who happen to be too dignified to take a percentage of the loot, just how often do the protagonists of recent hard sf novels [except maybe the grunts who feature in David Drake novels 1995] ever end up poor?) But Cramer has clearly concerned himself with none of this, and the idiom of hard sf has served him perfectly well as a transparency for the game of novel – though if he ever writes a sequel to Twistor he may find himself rueing the ideological blitheness of his closing pages, which see an American flag planted on a brand-new planet completely bare of life (except the life that happens to have been there in the first place, like America once) and ripe for the taking.

We are in Seattle, at the University of Washington. Young professor David Harrison, and his graduate assistant Vicky, fall in love while stumbling over a phenomenon they call the twistor effect – a calibration of forces which will revolve physical objects into a shadow-universe most of whose attributes (like the orbit and revolution of the shadow-Earth) are strikingly similar to our own. Many of the early pages of Twistor are devoted to descriptions of the number of gear-changes required to drive an automobile between any two points in Seattle, but Cramer soon settles into a genial plot which soon 1) traps the good guys on the Eden world, from which they soon engineer their escape, while 2) giving the evil Megalith Corporation and its minions every opportunity to steal the twistor effect for private gain, which they variously fail to do. The sustained likeableness of Twistor turns one's mind from its early longueurs, and the final 100 pages of the book begin to show some real narrative tooth. We may be left with a feelgood coda whose euphoria is palpably disengaged from the plot it puts a cap on, and a sense that the epistemological "innocence" of the hard sf form has begun to lose its power to amuse, even in the hands of a Dr Cramer; but Twistor, a decent book in an indecent time, almost serves as respite. Arrivederci, young professor David, young Vicky.

II.

What could possibly be wrong with a novel as word-perfect as The Night Mayor (Simon & Schuster UK, 1989) by Kim Newman? Not really very much. What's wrong with the book is what's not in it: what one might call intersubjectivity, human relationships, friends, the tactile feeling of a world it is possible to share. But then The

Night Mayor (in retrospect, Newman's stunning title tells the whole tale) is not set within the interstices of a world; it takes place within the topological innards of a dreaming head. Some years into a near future which Newman treats with warming sympathy, arch-criminal Truro Daine has finally been caught and incarcerated for life (the death penalty no longer being legal); fiendishly cunning in his exploitation of a widely disseminated commercial technology, Druro soon manages to make his mental escape into a cybernetic world-space he has himself Dreamed up. To forcibly remove him from his implants would kill him; so the protagonists of The Night Mayor must enter Druro's world and shoehorn him out from within.

It is not an original concept. Several of the novels of Philip K Dick (from Eye in the Sky [1957] on) are set in worlds whose very texture comprises the terrible face and psyche of a ravening and solipsistic godling; Roger Zelazny's The Dream Master (1966) and Gene Wolfe's "The Detective of Dreams" (1980) variously engage "professional" intruders into subjective worlds, as does Pat Cadigan's Tinker Toy Mindplayers (1987); the device used for Dreaming, and the cyberspace-like world it accesses, and the voodoo godling whose pulse is the pulse and price of things, and the AI named Yggdrasil which runs the world and within which (or Whom) the Truro Daine "file" nestles like a tic, all powerfully remind one of William Gibson; and the world-space itself, which Truro constructs out of tropes engendered by the marriage (1935–1960) of the American film to the American thriller, has much in common with the rain-lashed noir America David Thomson posits in the remarkable Suspects (1985). But none of this much matters.

What matters is the extraordinary sure touch of the telling. There are two protagonists. The first, and less important, is Tom Tunney, a professional Dreamer of tales for commercial use, who enters Truro's cyberworld in the persona of his own video-dream creation, the detective Richie Quick, and who soon succumbs to the spiderweb anagoge spun of punk godlinghood, becoming a riff in Truro's solipsism gig. Tunney speaks in the first person, and his voice is the pulp noir voice of someone about as deeply surrounded by Raymond Chandler as he is by Truro. Then comes Susan Bishopric, a more successful Dreamer, who jousts with Truro in the third person, and whom Yggdrasil eventually succours, picking up the plot and thrusting it onwards to a loud neat close. We awake, rub eyes clear of the festivities. Unpeopled The Night Mayor may have been, but it was decked out like a dream. With an intensity and a hypnotic closeness of attention, Newman's first novel blesses the tropes it juggles, loving them and laving them. It is the best movie/thriller/cyberpunk spoof with tears and teeth ever written.

III.

Into the night. Jonathan Carroll has now published the first three novels of a projected five-volume sequence, which he has not yet named, but which does have a
common concern. All three could be said to be, at heart, novels of *negotiation*. But
negotiating can only succeed if all parties involved are willing to sully themselves
with the taste of surrender, and it may be for that reason that some unease has been
expressed – I think without much perception – about the moral fabric of the sequence so far, which could well be called, for my money, The Debts Quintet. Or The
Intolerable Cost of Skating. Or Razor Dancing. Or Tales of the Vienna Woods [see
the 1992 continuation of this review, printed immediately below, for a further suggestion 1995].

   Bones of the Moon (1987) and *Sleeping in Flame* (1988) share some characters, an
intensity of focus on small family groups, references to Vienna (where Carroll
has lived for years), a sense of the extremes of bargaining necessary to allay the rage
of the world-beast beneath the surface, and a sang-froid about the shivering razor-
edge of the fantastic, along which the protagonists of both novels dance, in and out
of the light; but both novels can be read separately, with little loss. About *A Child
Across the Sky* (Century/Legend, 1989) one cannot be so certain. A reckoning seems
embedded in this novel of all the costs incurred by the winners of the previous
books, winners being at least initially defined as those who have remained alive;
and the disruptive darkness of its closing pages rends the frame of a larger world
than than that contained in the single volume. *A Child Across the Sky* does not so
much end as pause at a syllable of dread. Soon we may learn how much it costs to
make a world (soon we may know the cost of art). But the sentence is suspended.
We await the tally.

   Each volume so far (like Carroll's first two novels, *The Land of Laughs* [1980] and
Voice of our Shadow [1983], which have other features in common with the current sequence) is told (or confessed) in the first person. In her bargaining with life, Cullen
James, who narrates *Bones of the Moon*, seems to have created an island of stability
for herself upon the slippery meniscus of the world, beneath which the judges wait
with knives out, ready to punish a wrong turning, a clumsiness with the skates. In
early adulthood, quite properly, she aborted the child of a bad pairing, and now she
and her husband enjoy a loving though inturned life together, first in Europe, then
in New York. It is after she becomes pregnant again that her dreams of the magic
land of Rondua begin; in these dreams, under an increasing pressure of time (the
four provinces of Rondua are called Strokes, as though space were time), she finds
she must accompany the son whom she aborted on a trek to save the integrity of the

oneiric kingdom under the skin, which contains the whole meaning of her life in code.

Meanwhile, across the razor's edge into this world, she makes friends with Eliot Kilbertus, who is gay but loves her, and Weber Gregston, a famous film director who is heterosexual, and whose love is harder to deal with. She gives birth to a daughter. Affairs in Rondua near the crisis point, and begin even to fashion the external world of New York; Weber begins to dream of Rondua as well. Meanwhile Alvin Williams, the mentally ill youth downstairs who had earlier axed his family to death, has entered into correspondence with Cullen from the state institution; but Cullen terminates the healing relationship when one of his letters distresses her. There will be a comeuppance. Alvin (it turns out) is in fact the dread Jack Chili, evil ruler of Rondua, against whom her unborn son must stake his life. But the contest, which involves the surreal Bones of the Moon, leaks suddenly through the permeable membrane of the world, and Cullen's own daughter is suddenly threatened by Jack Chili, or Alvin, who has escaped from the Home. In the violence which ends the book, however, only Eliot Kilbertus dies. Like figurines in a snowglobe, Cullen and her family continue to grace the curved surface of the world. *Bones of the Moon* does not address this matter: but surely there is a reckoning due?

In *Sleeping in Flame* the Jack Chili figure is a midget or small man falsely named Rumpelstiltskin who forces his son – named Walker Easterling in this incarnation, which he narrates – through life after life, vainly attempting to make his child give him breath. Walker lives in Vienna. Like Cullen, who writes down her dreams of Rondua and eventually publishes them as a book called *Bones of the Moon*, Walker is an artist, a maker, an enforcer. He successfully protects his wife and unborn child from the exigencies of the world, the razor-edges of dread meaning which take on "fantastic" shapes in daylight. Here too friends die around the sacred (perhaps not very wisely, among the various names he takes, Walker's father calls himself on occasion Balthazar, Melchior, and Kaspar) family. Has Walker paid? Has he earned the death of his friends? Is art – he is a screenwriter – enough?

It is Weber himself who narrates *A Child Across the Sky*. His best friend Philip Strayhorn, a movie director who has plagiarized Weber's own brilliant work, kills himself. Cullen James and her husband Danny, also friends of the dead man, give Weber some video cassettes from Strayhorn, who speaks from them to Weber, advising him to Keep Watching. The cassettes contain a terrible magic: a video tape of the death of Weber's mother, years before, in a plane crash. Weber travels to California, where he decides to finish Strayhorn's last picture, one of a sequence of horror films of decreasing value. Weber's narrative soon develops a suffocating, sulphurous congestedness, as though he were himself losing the capacity to skate the meniscus – to tell the tale or film of his life in a fashion coherent enough to warrant living. It is a message Carroll has promulgated in every book he has so far written: that the good life is a work of art. That art is beyond good and evil. But in *A Child Across the Sky* he goes further. The good life (he seems finally to be saying, at this greatest depth and lode-point of the quintet, which may be the strongest and most punishing morality yet published in the shape of genre fantasy) means nothing, unless it is earned. But it cannot (he seems to conclude) be earned. Human beings cannot earn themselves. Certainly not through the coercions of art. Certainly not by creating miniature worlds for shining selfs, fortresses for the elect bargain hunters who have friends to trade. But learning this cannot save Weber, because he is, after all, a maker. He uses his life, and the lives of others. He makes Strayhorn's film, *Midnight Kills*, into a work of art. Does love extinguish evil, or feed it. The angel applauds. Weber lives, Cullen lives, Walker lives. Life is precious. In the next volume will the shaman-obsessed architect Harry Radcliffe, or some other character, tell us how he's earned the good things, the live friends, the silver skates? From Jonathan Carroll in his prime, I presume to find out.

– *Interzone* 32, November/December 1989

Makers' Dice

[I print here the part of the *Interzone* 61 column which – I didn't review *Outside the Dog Museum*, which was indeed about Harry Radcliffe – looks at Carroll's sequence from the vantage of volume five; a sixth volume, *From the Teeth of Angels* (1994), has also appeared 1995.]

WE must enter dragon country, the valley of the shadow of the world of the makers, *After Silence* by Jonathan Carroll (Macdonald, 1992), badlands. If we are sufficiently enamoured by the game of art to read the book with care, and there is little point in reading Jonathan Carroll just for the fun he seems to promise, we will not shut the last page unscathed into the silence it leaves. Like all of Carroll's tales to date in the untitled quintet which comprises his central accomplishment, *After Silence* is a moral fable partly about the cost of being a maker, but far more hurtingly it is about the fee makers charge the world for submitting to the obscene intimacy of the act of art. It is about pain, and it gives pain.

Like the protagonists of all the previous instalments of the quintet – in the absence of an overall designation for all five I think, for the purposes of a short review, I'll give them a name: the Answered Prayers Quintet, perhaps – the figure who narrates *After Silence* is a shaper. Max Fischer has been drawing cartoons from early childhood, and like most Carroll protagonists has seemed to achieve success without having to undergo any undue stress, as though the great world outside his childhood were no more than an extension of his family, no more than a continued tabula rasa upon which he has invisibly earned an entitlement to make his mark. By the end of the novel, his "Paper Clip," a daily comic strip, is being syndicated to more than 300 newspapers, and he is a celebrity. But Fischer hardly seems to notice what must amount by his early 40s to a very considerable fortune, as though he does not need the immunity wealth brings. For Fischer, it is not that the world owes him a living; it's more that the world is *indistinguishable* from his living.

(It might be noted that Carroll himself sometimes seems not to notice the drag coefficient of the world, either, so that when a crisis occurs he has not adequately stocked his protagonist with arms and devices to deal with the obtuseness of things. When that protagonist is a rich man like Fischer – a man any normal book would invest with the world-transforming obstacle-dissolving glamour of wealth – this absence becomes very noticeable. At the climax of the tale, Fischer finds the job of tracing his son's flight – by scheduled airline, just a few hours earlier, across America from California to New Jersey – just as difficult as any of us would. But no rich man who has used detective agencies for decades could fail *instinctively* to instruct one of them to arrange to have his son tracked from the New Jersey airport he's not yet even landed at, on that already identified flight; and furthermore to arrange for his son's targets somehow to be protected from the family-romance blow-out the lad has just experienced.)

Whatever. By the time the novel begins, Fischer has been riding this dream-life for years, a life he has managed to keep under wraps. Like other Carroll protagonists, in other words, he is a sleepwalker who owns the pavement. Or so it seems. Then he meets Lily Aaron and her son Lincoln at a show where one of his own cartoons has been hung. As a gesture to the woman, whose complex tangy alert presence he finds immediately captivating, and to the child, who seems to share her exuberant clarity of being, he draws a cartoon on Lincoln's T-shirt with a black marking pen: already (in other words) he has begun to transform the child into a palimpsest, a vector of his gift. Lily turns out to be the manager of a restaurant named Crowds and Power. This is a typical power-twee Los Angeles name, of course; but it is also the title of Elias Canetti's famous 1960 study of the metaphysics of control, and any proper study of Carroll (who will, in due course, like every writer of stature, be murdered by the dissecting eye of critic beholders, regardless of the cunning reticences of his public life, the quip hints of interstices beyond our grasp: so be warned, Mr Carroll: you're next) must necessarily dice his oeuvre through Canetti's great and metaphor-choked arraignment of the men of the century. This is Canetti, almost at random: "It is difficult to resist the suspicion that behind paranoia, as behind all power, lies the same profound urge: the desire to get other men out of the way so as to be the only one." Or: "People save 'for the sake of the children' and allow others to starve. What they are really doing is keeping everything for themselves." Ecce Fischer.

His first impulse, on meeting a woman with whom he has become enamoured, is to hire a detective agency to check up on her, to serve as poison taster for the king. The "family" is soon established, and he soon begins to describe their lives together in a porcelain-glaze prose which gives some of the scenes depicted something of the frightening burnish of a frieze. It is also the case, however, that the life so limned is in fact a life which seems to bristle with rightness (rightness of touch, perhaps) and energy. If *After Silence* is in some ways stronger than any previous Carroll novel, and if it seems the most inherently poignant representation of the curse attendant upon Answered Prayers, it is because the family here depicted does express like mother's milk a genuine human glamour, because Lily Aaron is an astonishingly attractive person, because Lincoln is a beautiful and normal child (even though we soon begin to fear that he has been normalized by the power of the maker). So it is a shock when it all begins to be killed.

We do not know for certain what kind of death will soon be presented for us to remember in our dreams of reading; but we know that some life must snap, we know that Fischer will not be able to fend off any violation from outside of the life story he's telling himself. Beset as he is by interpretive frenzies which now and then take him to one of his detective agencies, Fischer needs only a seed, a hangnail, an incipit, to become a monster, a modernized version of the protagonist of Henry James's *The Sacred Fount* (1901), the century's first and still its most extreme apotheosis of the terrible power of art to shape movements and shadows and absences and glints into golem apes of humans acting. James's protagonist, who also argues his case to the ideal reader in a voice of the intensest plausibility, is Fischer with gloves on. "I found, on my side," he says of the woman around whom he has constructed a cloying artifice of "observation," "a rare intellectual joy, the oddest secret exultation, in feeling her begin instantly to play the part I had attributed to her in the irreducible drama." In the end (as for Fischer) it turns to silence.

The silence begins with Lily's odd behaviour after Lincoln has been knocked out by a baseball and taken to the local hospital for treatment; her paranoia about giving the hospital any factual information triggers one of Fischer's bouts of interpretation, and he hires a detective to ransack her life, just as he has almost immediately ransacked her apartment in search of clues. What he discovers is that Lily's entire past seems to have been fabricated (an act of lèse majesté, indeed one that hints of regicide, in Fischer's Crowds and Power world), and that a bleak mystery seems to surround her child. The mystery is soon "solved" by Fischer. Years before (it seems), Lily had kidnapped the infant child from a New Jersey family named Meier. What should be done? (Do we believe Fischer's decipherment of the clues?) Any life between Fischer and Lily from now on, whether or not they share in each other's knowledge, will be an artifact, a porcelain glaze of family romance against the abyss. And so it proves. Lily eventually begins a confession, which Fischer continues for her, and they agree to believe what the two of them (or rather Fischer) have together agreed (but the plot is by no means unwound) will henceforth be the truth of the matter. In order to seal their lives into shape, they bury this agreed past, they relegate the grieving parents in New Jersey to aeons of further grief. They marry. Years pass.

But there is one additional gloss, which brings the novel into knives'-reach of the supernatural, and justifies this review in Interzone (beyond the fact that we would be fools not to notice Carroll because he "failed" to obey a genre precept). Fischer has been praying for a life capable of bearing the charges he levies, and at the moment of crisis he finds an answer to this prayer. He "realizes" that he and Lincoln are the same person, that they are the same soul in different bodies. This "realization," the sort of cheap and obscene plot uplift we can all find in the typical contemporary fantasy, both serves as the final sealant in Fischer's construction of a life of art (which is a golem life), and as the final straw which breaks Lincoln, when the plot begins to cut the tale into shreds, when the sacred fount dries, when supernatural events occur (or do not) but save nothing, and there is silence.

And the review ends. I do not wish at this point to try to grasp entire the Answered Prayers Quintet, which may in any case, given the fact Carroll has never been clear about its compass, not have begun to end [nor has it 1995]; it is not yet time, in other words, to lay soiled golem critic hands upon the whole work. Let one merely say that Carroll's failings are as evident here as elsewhere, and as unimportant to the whole. There is the surface of telling which sometimes alienates through an excess of device; the air of insistent ease that protests too much, that forces one at times to think there can be no such thing as a reliable narrator in any Carroll tale; the already notorious difficulty with endings (but here exploited with real success). So what. In the end, Carroll speaks to us about what we are, in language clearer and more dangerous than we sometimes care to admit, language that strips bare the mithridatic tolerances we establish, as readers, for the deaths art deals. In *After Silence*, a numen glows. Out of the dark teratogenic fount of art comes, at times, in books like this, the cutting flame we long for, when we read for the sake of our lives.

– Interzone 61, July 1992

Guards, Unicorns, Zool

I.

THE NEXT book published by Terry Pratchett (a collaboration with Neil Gaiman called *Good Omens*) will have nothing to do with the sequence of Discworld novels which has made him famous, and this may be well. The book he is publishing right now – *Guards! Guards!* (Gollancz, 1989), which is the latest Discworld tale to reach print, the second to appear in 1989, the eighth in the series, and his longest novel to date – may glow with Pratchett elbow-grease like a steam yacht from the dawn of time, and the jokes it contains may be as blessedly good as ever, but the story it tells threatens to dissolve the frame – the Garden of the Discworld – it's set in, perhaps because its author has grown restive with the "restrictions" imposed by that frame; and this weariness (if he's feeling it) is something (we think) which must not be allowed to master him without demur. Some reasons for wishing to preserve the Discworld as a venue for Comedy have been put forward in the essay on Terry Pratchett [it also appeared in *Interzone* 33, but is not reprinted here 1995]; underlying everything that essays claims is a sense that Comedy is rare on earth, and precious. Slapstick is as common as weeds, and wit is what we want to stillicide the day with, in acid. Comedy is Other than that.

In outline, *Guards! Guards!* seems like more of the same. Though it's hardly described in the text, the Discworld itself is still intact, Great A'Tuin still plods through space bearing four elephants who bear the world like a great flat shared beanie; and true to the pattern of the previous five novels, one of the central characters of *Guards!* is an adolescent searching for a role in life. On this occasion it's a young orphan named Carrot, who thinks he is a dwarf like the dwarves who raised him, but who is in fact an extremely large human. That he is not very bright – that he is in fact the first Pratchett protagonist who is noticeably thicker than the surrounding cast [but watch what happens to Carrot in *Men at Arms* (1993) 1995] – may explain his failure to dominate the novel. After trekking to Ankh-Morpork, where he enlists in the despised Night Watch (increasing its complement to four), Carrot serves more as a red herring than a protagonist – Pratchett implies that he is in fact descended from the ancient rulers of Ankh-Morpork, and allows hints of this, rather deliciously, to hentrack the text like signposts of a plot-road not taken; at book's end Carrot remains happily anonymous, and still a Guard. The burden of the plot of *Guards!* lies elsewhere. It is the story of Captain Vimes of the Night Watch, who has spent most of his career drunk on duty, but who, as the novel progresses, becomes more and more deeply involved combating the tragic devastations inflicted upon Ankh-Morpork by a huge dragon; by the end of the book Vimes has solved the mystery of the dragon's origin, gone off the booze, gained wisdom and a large rich wife (who rather resembles one of P G Wodehouse's *good* aunts), and has become a leader of men.

And here is where it all gets dangerous. The dragon has been magicked into Discworld time-space by a conniving amoral apparatchik, highly placed in local government, whose interfering malevolence seems almost motiveless, and reads as far from comic (though the scenes in which he uses magic to invoke the presence of the dragon are among Pratchett's most hilarious). Once in Ankh-Morpork, this dragon kills people. People die throughout the book. Some of the comic characters who lighten the earlier pages of *Guards!* die (here's a chuckle) of incineration. (We had known them for a while.) The world begins to rot with fear. Eventually the villain himself succumbs to the spiritual corruption he has been instrumental in feeding, backs in terror into an abyss, and is killed. The dragon itself, which turns out to be female, is courted by a tiny swamp-dragon pet of Vimes's fiancée, and at book's close both flee from the *Discworld* into "the totally unfathomable, star-dotted depths of space. Perhaps the magic would last. Perhaps it wouldn't. But then, what does?"

And the world is shut.

A few pages earlier, the deeply distressed Vimes – whenever Pratchett wants to become serious for a moment, it is almost certain that the protagonist will soon be saying something either "simply" or "quietly" – has been talking to Lord Vetinari, who rules Ankh-Morpork, and who tells him that the city lying below them is in fact

"A great rolling sea of evil. Shallower in some places, of course, but deeper, oh, so much *deeper* in others... Down there are people who will follow any dragon, worship any god, ignore any iniquity... Sin, you might say, without a trace of originality. They accept evil not because they say *yes*, but because they don't say *no*..."

"They're just people," [Vimes responds.] "They're just doing what people do. Sir."

Lord Vetinari gave him a friendly smile.

"Of course, of course," he said. "You have to believe that, I appreciate. Otherwise you'd go quite mad. Otherwise you'd think you're standing on a feather-thin bridge over the vaults of Hell. Otherwise existence would be a dark agony and the only hope would be that there is no life after death. I quite understand."

It's not that Pratchett does this sort of thing badly. But Vetinari's outburst, because it has all the ring of another sphere of discourse, comes close to shattering the comic pulse of the Discworld. The Realpolitik grasp of his vision tends to remind one of the *Weltschmerz* of Hans Sachs, or of the sudden apocalyptic chill of T H White's Merlin's memories of what is to come; but *Die Meistersinger* and *The Once and Future King* are tragicomedies of Time and Time's coil and are without sequels, without a choice of return. The Discworld, on the other hand, has served as a Garden of repose, and as such has operated for its readers as a *Comedy*, as precisely "a feather-thin bridge over the vaults of Hell." No one can deny Pratchett the chance to take risks with his own creation, and it is certainly the case that he dances out his grave matters deftly upon the beanie Disc; but it is only by the skin of its teeth that *Guards! Guards!* manages to contain Captain Vimes, or Lord Vetinari bare. It is, after all, more difficult to cultivate a Garden than to scythe it; Comedy, which Pratchett writes with something like genius, does not grow on trees; and therefore – I submit – it may be as well that Terry Pratchett leave Discworld on the shelf for a year or so, lest he shiver it to growth, which is another Death.

II.

Unicorn Mountain by Michael Bishop (Arbor House, 1988). In the midst of solitude, lots of noise. Michael Bishop has always been an author earnestly determined to exercise over his native bailiwick – which is the American South from Georgia to the High Plains beyond Texas – the kind of textured novelistic control that writers more fortunately located – like Stephen King, or Thomas M Disch – can command almost at will. He does not wish, in other words, to emulate a Southern writer like William Faulkner, for whom the social world worked as a kind of scrim to cloak and to uncover tales of imperial solitude, archetypally couched. In every book he has set on Earth, Michael Bishop has tried to bootstrap himself out of that Faulknerian solitude which is perhaps the aptest response to the tropical animus of the wilderness of the South; and every book he has set on Earth echoes from the megaphoned and ersatz patter of his attempts to socialize his texts. It is for that reason that *Ancient of Days* (1985) wallows for so long in artiefactual Atlanta. It is why *Unicorn Mountain* drives one bananas with the noise.

Every character of any importance in this grafted, ambitious, vaulting boiler factory of a book is as loud as everybody else, and everybody talks the same knotted, backassward (Bishop is the only writer I think I've ever run across who actually uses that particular locution), rabbitty lingo; words like buttinsky and stick-to-itivity and wimpy racket through the text like echoes searching for a voice, but never have any luck homing in. Libby Quarrels – divorced hardscrabble Colorado rancher with a tough mind and body – comes closest to sounding authentic as she utters this stuff, because (as Bishop may well have observed) there are a lot of formidable lady Coloradoans around with genuinely complicated backgrounds and tough rows to hoe and who sound like drunk thesauri from the Valley of Tomes whenever they try to do gab out there in the sexist world they must shoulder through; but Bo Gavin, gay adman with AIDS from Atlanta, whom Libby absconds with out of the big city so he can die on the ranch with folk, sounds *just the same*. As does Sam Coldpony, Ute Indian, ranch foreman, lover and eventual husband to Libby; as does everyone else in the book. Only the unicorns are silent, camouflaged in silver silence, stone chthonic.

So the head rings, and the story almost fails to get through. This is a shame. Ambition and stakes are high. Much gets said. The unicorns are from the land of death, and have recently begun to come to this sphere to die of a disease whose vector may have something to do with ghosts of AIDS victims in the other world. Bo writes an ad campaign for condoms which mercilessly exploits the unicorn image, then dies, passes over to the other side, carrying a message which may save, in turn, the beasts (just as, embedded into his campaign, they may save us). Much thought can be spent on the interlacings of implication thus addressed, and much thought has (see, for instance, Gwyneth Jones's long review in *Foundation* 43). But before he can write a fully successful novel, one whose diction consorts with the high goals he strives for so ardently, Michael Bishop is going to have to come to terms with the fact that he is alone.

Because this gabfest is a headgame.

III.

A large number of people are M H Zool, and they have all come together to create in *Bloomsbury Good Reading Guide to Science Fiction and Fantasy* (Bloomsbury, 1989) a feisty little conspectus of the field which might have been better, but could have been a lot worse. In 160 small pages – to which they were presumably restricted by their publishers, who were also almost certainly responsible for naming the book after themselves – the Zool crowd manages to cram a good number of alphabetical entries on a fairly wide range of sf and fantasy authors. Recent figures are more adequately represented than earlier ones. The system of cross-references veers to the Heath-Robinsonian, especially in view of the tininess of the book; and the reading "skeins" –columnar presentations of titles various members of Zool have free-associated to lemmas like Isaac Asimov's *Foundation*, or John Crowley's *Little, Big* – does not much reward the intense referencing use a book of this sort might seem to elicit. And it might have been better not to have dated any books at all, if the alternative was to date only some of them, and when doing so to ascribe dates according to criteria that seem to have varied pretty wildly. But the heart of the endeavour is the entries themselves, which are witty, succinct, original, batty, impertinent, innovative, fey, smug, canny, young. But there should have been much more. Not Zool's fault, surely. The publisher's fault, surely. It has to be said. This *Good Reading Guide* is not Bloomsbury at all. It's *Twigshack*.

– Interzone 33, January/February 1990

A Sperm Called Trilogy

I AM reading Octavia E Butler and I see a sperm whose name is Trilogy. Its head is *Dawn* (1987), its midriff is *Adulthood Rites* (1988), and its tail is *Imago* (Warners, 1989). As a whole, it answers to the name of *Xenogenesis Trilogy*. As a general rule, trilogies start well and tail off, so *Xenogenesis Trilogy*'s resemblance to a giant sperm – for almost all of its substance has gone to its head, it is afflicted with a wasting palsy in its lower member, and it is all about breeding – may be paradigmatic. *Dawn* is big and muscular and packed with information; *Adulthood Rites* is smooth and transparent and slopes gracefully towards the diminishing musculature of the tail; and *Imago* is slight, vermiform and squiggly. But *Xenogenesis Trilogy*, it is also fair to say, rather fails to come to a climax. Perhaps it's too bad I couldn't say I was reading Octavia E Butler and I saw a dumbbell whose name was Sextet.

Perhaps someday I will.

Because there's something very odd indeed about *Xenogenesis*, whose first volume was originally described (by both its American and British publishers) as the beginning of a series, with no total number of instalments indicated, though by the time we saw volume three both publishers were hyping *Imago* as a "stunning climax to the trilogy" (Warner's version). As it now stands, then, *Xenogenesis* slides remorselessly into the suicidal nadir of *Imago*'s final pages without hope of sequel, and in the absence of any privy knowledge to the contrary, we must "honour" what Butler's publishers are telling us. If Butler had in fact conceived those final pages as a *still centre*, as an eye at the heart of the storm, then she should have insisted upon our not being told different in the hype; as it stands, her readers have been put into the slightly invidious position of attempting to make a kind of sense of *Imago* that its author may not have intended. On the other hand, perhaps Butler simply became fatigued, that the fault lines running through *Xenogenesis* have had a toxic effect upon her imagination, and that she has found herself abandoning sperm half-way through the passage.

For problems there certainly are; they boil down to one central difficulty. This difficulty, which is shared by many of the most ambitious writers of American sf, lies in a failure to mediate between the conceiving of structures of speculative thought (a process of central engendering importance for writers like Butler, Tiptree, Bear, Benford) and the generic mix of plot and setting and character-creation through which they find themselves telling out those structures. Thoughts soar in the mind's eye of the sf writer, but then they must be *told*. Plots must be crafted to expose the donnée without unduly obscuring the visibility of action that marks sf as a "popular literature" whose roots lie deep in the Romance mode. Visible action means visible landscape – exemplary terrains whose weathers are governed by metaphysical pathos. Visible action also means visible actors – protagonists we recognize across a crowded room of extras, and whose moral qualities we register (and *take the side of*) in the very heart of the tourney. Protagonists must not, therefore, seem ineradicably alien, or ambivalent, or passive; and if they have moments of introspection, these moments must generate some move that turns the tale. Every characteristic the protagonist shows must ultimately be seen as an empowerment. Like a mask – visible, but easy to see through – the protagonist must be all act. Because mere being is fathomless.

Dawn almost perfectly fuses thought-telling and the Romance mode. The premise may be familiar to any reader of Robert Ardrey or Konrad Lorenz – the human race is defined as a kind of portmanteau monstrosity, a fatal mix of unshackled intelligence and hierarchical/territorial imperatives – but it is laid down by Butler with an unbending and severe clarity that brooks no real dissent. Certainly within the texts of *Xenogenesis* no countervailing voice is allowed anywhere near the mike. (One man in *Dawn* – Lilith's first lover – might have represented that voice in a different book, but in *Dawn* he is soon killed.) The premise, in other words, takes on the hard fixity of an axiom. And for a while – for at least the whole length of *Dawn*, and for much of *Adulthood Rites* – this axiomatic fixity works very well.

As *Dawn* begins, humanity has indeed managed to destroy itself in some sort of final war and rape of the planet. Only waif biota survive, men and women rescued by the spacefaring Oankali who have happened upon Earth in the nick of time. These Oankali –who crave new genes in the same way that humans lust for dominance – travel through space in vast living ships, constantly searching for new biological material to engage with in the most intimate fashion possible: for they breed into the new stock, transforming themselves in the process. In the first sections of *Dawn*, Lilith awakens after 250 years of broken slumber, and begins to find out how the non-hierarchical, three-sexed, tendriled and odorous Oankali plan to deal with the axiomatic flaw that curses her species. Love is the plan. She will become part of an Oankali-human marriage. Her children will be of all sorts. She will lead her people back to a terraformed Earth, and abide there for a spell. Then the new species, once imago stage has been reached, will re-enter its proper domain, which is interstellar space; and go once more about its proper business, which is exogamy [again and again from 1989 on, I tend to use exogamy as a shorthand description of the essential subject matter of post-agenda sf. The *Xenogenesis Trilogy* could have been reviewed primarily in terms of its adherence to this remit. 1995]

Adulthood Rites takes us back to Earth, and there the problems begin. Many humans, on being awoken by their rescuers, refuse violently to have any truck with the saintly Oankali, who in turn refuse to make them fertile once again, though they do permit a (seemingly unending) stream of humans to re-settle on the home planet. But only for a little while. But – for reasons which have everything to do with the exigencies of pulp plotting and nothing at all to do with good sense – it turns out that after using new planets as nurseries, the Oankali then strip them down for raw material before departing, so that soon there will be no Earth for the refusenik humans to live on. All of which is, of course, an utter load of bollocks. We have already been told Oankali have visited many previous planets. Do they destroy all of them, even those not already turned to a cinder by natives? (Of course not.) We have already been told that Oankali have the ability to terraform Mars. Would a terraformed but otherwise uninhabited planet provide necessary raw material for the next caper? (Of course it would.) And so on.

This puerile pulp plotting governs the larger actions in both *Adulthood Rites* and *Imago*, which repeats much of the plot of its sibling, without adding a single new idea; and this petering out of *Xenogenesis* is further underscored by the tricks Butler finds herself getting up in order to supply us with a suitable protagonist to sink our hooks into. Lilith has faded into the background (and certain feminist arguments of real cogency have faded with her); and the protagonist of *Adulthood Rites*, a human-Oankali male child who spends much of the book learning about unaltered humans in the wild, is succeeded in *Imago* by a human-Oankali ooloi, a member of the central gene-manipulating pheromone-emitting third sex, who spends much of the book learning about unaltered humans in the wild. It's the same story all over again, and the new protagonist tells the tale in an identikit voice, revealing en passant the huge arsenal of empowerments Butler has grand him: unctuousness; cloying empathy; two hearts and tendrils à la *Slan*; a shapechanging option; a self-healing option, which he can grant to others by sort of sucking them; a range of pheromones that renders him capable of zapping (and allowing him to fuck) every human on the planet; and much much more. He is Jommy Cross and Paul Muad'Dib and Mother Teresa in a rubber suit with suckers. I do not in fact *believe* he is what Octavia E Butler can possibly intend to transform her premise into. I do not in fact *believe* that *Xenogenesis* can possibly be meant to end here, in this lame squiggle. I believe that Butler has temporarily gotten pulped. So I am going to stop here. I am going to wait for the dumbbell [and wait, and wait 1995].

– *Interzone 34*, March/April 1990

Heart Gravel

[The bulk of this column focuses on Bob Shaw's Maraquine trilogy, and can be found on p. 92 1995.]

I.

WE COME to Kim Newman, writing as Jack Yeovil (English for Serftown), and to "his" second novel, *Drachenfels* (GW Books, 1989), one of a series of sharecropper texts written to fit into the Warhammer fantasy games floor-universe, and copyrighted by Games Workship Ltd, who own the world. Prefabbed out of standardized plot-bites (or dominoes) that tend to topple into speedline-riffs because its author seems to have written the thing in a following gale without slowing down to dock, *Drachenfels* manages to become, before it crashes, something of a tour de force. But what is original to Newman in the book, and what depends upon the floor-universe for contour and donnée, this reviewer does not know, cannot work out, and is clearly not meant ever to understand. Assuming that the Warhammer floor-universe is *describable* (or else how could Games Workshop Ltd claim to own it), the absence of any guide to this iron cage of copyrighted premise must be deliberate. Except for a map of The Old World which comprises a kind of endpaper (and in which "The Old World" so closely resembles the Ruritanian post-catastrophe fantasy Europes featured in the sword-and-sorcery tales of writers like Michael Moorcock that it surely could not itself be owned), there is nothing about *Drachenfels* which bespeaks a corporate hand. Indeed, only one element of premise seems easily apparent to the reader – the restriction of the non-human cast to Tolkien-maggots – and that is a premise whose conceptual vacuity must preclude its being intrinsic to a copyrighted fantasy game. So whatever the secret of Warhammer is, it remains safely beyond the reviewer's grasp.

But ignorance can be bliss. We enter *Drachenfels* without premise or premonition, and after a spluttering Prologue (in which an assemblage of typecast humans and fey swordcarriers from Tolkien and one Barbie-vampire beards a Dark Lord named Drachenfels in his lair and defeats him, a defeat we take on trust because the text does a fade at the crucial moment, leaving us in some kind of suspense) we find ourselves in a thoroughly engaging drama. The young hero responsible for slaying Drachenfels in the Prologue now wishes, twenty or so years later, to restage the great event as a play to be performed before the crowned heads of um not-Europe at Castle Drachenfels itself; to do so, he extracts from debtors' prison Detlef Sierck, a portly young playwright whose talents are as considerable as his vanity, and sets him to work. A cast of actors soon assembles, along with all the survivors of the Prologue, and the whole crew hies to Drachenfels, where dark doings are afoot. Newman shows very considerable skill in differentiating these assorted sloughs of folk and non-folk and thespian, most of whom he manages to start killing off fairly soon to clear the air, but at no point in *Drachenfels* is he allowed to concentrate for more than a few hurtling pages on any one of them alone. Even so, characters do take shape. Detlef himself and the sweet-faced vamp/vampire Geneviève Dieudonné take on novelistic depth; and several of the extras can be recognized by the sound they make in the dark. It all ends in a staged play with perhaps too many characters emoting rather too shrilly, like a fugue of teapots, and with too many dangling story-bits coming together at once to twirl the oiled moustaches of the plot into a crash ending; but the ride has been swift, literate, funny.

Two things in particular. It's clear that Newman has based the entire *jeu* on some film or other (he has apparently acknowledged a 1930s musical plus John Ford's *Stagecoach* (1939) – though this reviewer himself preferred to detect, in some of its play-is-reality subtleties, hints of Ingmar Bergman's *The Magician* (1958), an awful but strangely gripping film which is also about a performance which becomes the thing itself); and that this parodic subtext could be see as an enabling commentary on the relationship between *Drachenfels* and Warhammer. Second, it might be noted how condignly the whole plot – in which actors play protagonists who are themselves in turn, it must be assumed, face-masks for the fantasy gamesters who play Warhammer –manages to acknowledge its relationship to the owned world, while at the same time asserting a final freedom. After all, the world of the imagination, in the end, is free. In the end. Isn't it.

II.

A Pynchon note. *Vineland* (Little, Brown; 1990) has come into the world, on the cusp of 1990, without benefit of proofs to hoard, advance copies to study for trace-marks of Inferno. It is a novel. It will be loved by some and dismissed by others. Those who love it will taste the coils of interregnum in its refusal to face past 1984 into the second term of Mr Reagan (I loved it); those who dismiss it will find the paranoid linkages of its plot either trivial or dumb, the nostalgia it seems to express for the 1960s simply reflecting the middle-agedness of its author, over 50 now, no surprise the axons are beginning to sputter and fail, the old Pynchon brain beginning to misspell the old linkages that tied America into knots that he cannot now compute, old Pynchon aping the abyssal melancholy of his prime, *Vineland* repeating *Gravity's Rainbow* (1973) as farce. But maybe that is only to say that Pynchon knows whereof it is possible, at the moment, to speak. *Vineland* is a tale of the time, which is a time of waiting. It is about the badlands, the vertigo-inducing spasm-wracked decorticated American human heart caught in the entrails of a rat-trap cusp no kairos can illuminate. It is about the exhaustion of those who wait. It is also an extraordinarily funny book.

Zoyd Wheeler has gone to earth in Vineland, a small city in northern California, and until 1984 he has been safe, though monitored. A clan of Thanatoids or living dead also marks time in Vineland, mirroring the belatedness of his condition, the only time kept being the tick-tock aging of his meat-puppet body. Suddenly the old world begins to connect him in again, like a torture deferred. The tale is complex, though it can be traced through; but this is only a note. Suffice it that Zoyd has long ago lost his wife Frenesi to the ownership of those who bought the 1960s, who turned the hippies into operatives; and that now Frenesi has dodged even Brock

Vond, the owner-rep who had had the run of her body for more than a decade. Vond now wants to obtain her daughter Prairie, who has been raised by Zoyd. Zoyd sends her into hiding, and himself disappears for most of the rest of the book, most of which comprises a dense and skittish epistemological probing of Frenesi's long irradiation in time's net, in "the crimes behind the world, the thousand bloody arroyos in the hinterlands of time that stretched somberly inland from the honkytonk coast of Now." At the end, for a moment, Vond is defeated – more accurately, he is annulled by a government diktat – and children are seen playing, families gathering at dawn or dusk around their RV's, Zoyd shrugging off a long-anticipated meet with Frenesi; a moment of peace most precious to flotsam. And the book is done. It has not stepped over. It is about waiting. It has not trespassed forward, through time's arroyos, to the oil-slicked coast.

Wise wise *Vineland*, so to stop.

– *Interzone* 35, May 1990

3. VARIOUS

THE THING to remember about the end of the world is the silver lining. In three of the novels under review, civilization has collapsed across the globe, or is on the verge of doing so, and in two of them the planet of our birth is no more than a memory, or a dream; but never is the apocalypse terminal. These five books, which were written by six Americans, share a hopefulness not always found in European visions of global catastrophe, a sense that we humans will survive almost any trauma we are capable of inflicting upon our planet and ourselves, and that after the bad times have faded we will once again prevail.

I.

This hopefulness must derive in part from geography. No British writer could realistically envision burning London to the ground without fatally singeing the rest of this tight little island, and most tend to be cautious about doing so in stories meant to have a happy ending; but American writers have never felt a similar compunction about eliminating New York or Washington, and the cheerier sort of American disaster novel will often raze the entire Eastern Seaboard just to clear the decks and to kick-start the good inland folk into brave new lives free of bureacrats and socialists. It's easy, and it's neat. Never an untidy writer, Orson Scott Card comes dangerously close to the inhumane smugness of his lessers in the first episode of *The Folk of the*

Fringe (Phantasia, 1989), where he seems quite prepared to shovel the whole of the old sinful East Coast into Hell after the missiles strike; but Card has never been as simple as he sometimes insists on sounding, and quickly shifting his focus from the devastated cities of South Carolina, about which he has little to say, he moves his cast towards Utah, where this collection of closely linked stories comes glowingly to life, like a series of inspired cartoons.

It is a driven, merciless book. *The Folk of the Fringe* may be the first Mormon fiction about life after the holocaust, and may be told with expert clarity in cool sophisticated cadences, but there is never a saving moment of repose within its pages, no moment when a story (or a character) simply receives the world. Card's speculative dream of Mormon hegemony over the remains of America comes to life only when he embodies it in actions so vividly told they are almost tangible, for he has no passive voice, no silence. For academic critics, a writer like Card is peculiarly hard to understand, because he is nothing more (or less) than a teller of tales. What happens is what the tale means. Because nothing is left to paraphrase, a book like *The Folk of the Fringe* can seem terribly slippery. Card is himself a Mormon, and has put together a gripping accumulation of tales about men and women who live on the fringes of a loose Mormon theocracy centred on Salt Lake City; but nowhere does *The Folk of the Fringe* settle into advocacy. There are just the stories, steely and unstopping, and the strange new lives of which they tell.

II.

At first glance, *Light Raid* (Ace, 1989) by Connie Willis and Cynthia Felice may seem to inhabit a more normal post-catastrophe land. Well into the future of a balkanized America, the Western States have joined with the royalist Canadian Commonwealth in a laser-dominated war against Quebec, and when the light raids on Denver Springs become dangerous, her parents send young Ariadne to neutral Victoria. It is at this point (very close to the beginning of the book) that *Light Raid* begins to run away with itself, in several directions. Ariadne, who is a direct descendent of Robert A Heinlein's appalling smart-aleck pubescent Podkayne, senses something wrong back home, where her parents are honcho high-tech researchers in war-sensitive areas, and soon finagles her way back, only to find her mother arrested for treason. But nothing daunts the daring Ariadne, and *Light Raid* soon turns into an adolescent rite-of-passage spy story; complications are relentless, and so is the good cheer of the obnoxious lass, who solves every mystery the two authors, clearly working in separate rooms, can unload upon her – giving her the chance to win the knowledge race and the war and her parents' sanity and a husband in the process. Willis is the author of *Lincoln's Dreams* (1987), a filigreed landmine of a novel, and may be largely responsible for the glimpses of a ruined world *Light Raid* occasionally proffers; but in the foreground of the book nothing can be seen but Ariadne and the crazy-quilt plot she devours grinning.

III.

The editors responsible for publishing James Patrick Kelly's *Look into the Sun* (Tor, 1989) must know what they're doing, but it still seems odd. Nowhere is it mentioned that *Look into the Sun* is in fact the second volume of a sequence entitled The Messengers Chronicles, volume one, *Planet of Whispers*, having been published in 1984 by a firm called Bluejay, which is now defunct. Only those who read *Look into the Sun* without reference to the earlier volume will know whether or not it can stand alone. What can certainly be said, however, is that characters and setting and plot elements are carried over from *Planet of Whispers*, that Kelly unquestionably constructed both books as parts of a closely-bound sequence, and that no reader will come to harm through being made aware of his intentions.

On the planet of Aseneshesh, a declining civilization of sexy ectomorphic bears faces the crisis of an encroaching ice age, which the alien Messengers help to fight by trading food for the bear blood which is the source of the Asenesheshians' near-immortality. The plot of *Planet of Whispers* is little more than a guided tour of the planet, though a love affair between a male bear and a Messenger android movingly prefigures the love that binds together the two protagonists of *Look into the Sun*; of greatest interest in the first book is an elaborate analysis of the Asenesheshian mentality, clearly based on Julian Jaynes's hugely enjoyable *The Origin of Consciousness in the Breakdown of the Bicameral Mind* (1976). Like Jaynes's pre-self-conscious humans, Asenesheshians live in a state of constant hallucination, governing their actions by the voices they "hear" from within their own heads.

References to this analysis are scant in *Look into the Sun*, but inform the book throughout. We begin on Earth, sometime after a mild catastrophe, perhaps ecological, has bruised humanity's self-esteem. The race of Messengers has recently made contact, and Ndavu (who appears in the previous volume) asks depressed architect Philip Wing to go to Aseneshesh to design a tomb for Teaqua, head bear and most ancient sentient in the known universe. (She also appears in *Planet of Whispers*.) Wing agrees, but only learns en route that he has been biologically transformed into the semblance of an Asenesheshian, and given a computer implant which whispers inside his skull like the voice of an antique god from Jayne. After recuperating from deep trauma, Wing falls in love with a female bear, and she with him, and designs an appropriate mausoleum, which will be placed in orbit, where it will remind the Asenesheshians that they must emigrate to save themselves. At novel's close, the Messengers have not yet revealed their message, or why they choose to knit the stars together into a family of races. Future volumes of this rich, slow, allusive, glinting, pastoral edifice will surely (if we are allowed to know they exist) tell a full tale.

IV.

For Wanbli, the cocksure Candide who rampages through R A MacAvoy's *The Third Eagle* (Doubleday Foundation, 1989) at great speed from world to world and returns home to make his own planet into a garden licketysplit, Earth is just a memory. MacAvoy's odd subtitle, *Lessons Along a Minor String*, soon explains itself and the book as well. Lessons are what Wanbli, member of a Sioux-derived tribe of deadly bodyguards now native to a poverty-stricken planet called Neunacht, needs. Strings are a kind of space-time linkage from star to star that ships base their interstellar routes upon. Having won some money, Wanbli goes off-planet on a kind of whim; he visits a mining planet, a planet largely devoted to the making of film epics, and elsewhere. He meets some "revivalists," homeless wanderers who eke out a precarious livelihood rescuing frozen sleepers from generation-starships centuries adrift at slower-than-light speeds. Much less quickly than almost any reader of *The Third Eagle*, Wanbli finally figures out how to give his planet a string-station, which will make it rich, and to save the revivalists from their own problems. End of romp. It would all be too silly for words, if the words themselves were not so electric. MacAvoy imparts a ferocious momentum to her addlepated little fable; her style has a quite extraordinary zest and intricacy, and the things she notices out of the side of her mouth are subtle and sad and telling, and in truth rather shame the bumptious idiocy of the story she tells.

V.

Soldiers of Paradise (1987), the first volume of Paul Park's Starbridge Chronicles, stands in the mind's eye like a mosaic upon a wall in Byzantium. Sunlight and shadow pass over the intricate detail-work, cities and palaces and human lives all fretted into an antique glow, and there is a sense of palpable hugeness to the vision, of moral and physical enormity; the Earth of *Soldiers of Paradise* has been transfigured by time and other forces into a world impossibly remote from our own. Attempting to convey some sense of its scale and intricacy, reviewers of this first volume compared Park to the Gene Wolfe of *The Book of the New Sun* and to the Brian Aldiss of the

Helliconia trilogy. Park, who came late to sf as a medium, may or may not have ever read these authors, but the comparisons are fair: like Urth and Helliconia, his Earth is ornate, melancholy, harsh, adult; and the time-scale that governs its life is enormous. One revolution of the sun takes something over 200 years to complete, and seasons take decades. Because these seasons are too huge to suffer any natural forms of social existence, the whole intricate mazed mosaic of human life on Earth has only one primary function, which is to preserve civilization from the tyranny of the elements.

In *Sugar Rain* (Morrow, 1989), the world begins to melt, and it is fitting that the tale Park has to tell in this second volume is intimate, minor-keyed, romantic. At the end of *Soldiers in Paradise* spring began in earnest, and the sugar rain began to fall, an inflammable rain that smells of gasoline and growth, and which sets fires everywhere. Through the pages of the book that bears its name, the rain hardly stops. Thanakar Starbridge and Abu Starbridge, the protagonists of the first volume, hardly break step as they move into *Sugar Rain*. The martyrdom Abu has longed for duly occurs, and the Cult of Loving Kindness which will spring up in his wake is destined to shape the summer culture of the long year. Thanakar escapes the capital city, and continues to practise a humane form of medicine in the capital of a northern kingdom. His lover, Charity Starbridge, who had lain in the drug torpor proper to a high-born wife throughout *Soldiers*, is now permanently awake, and manages to escape. The passages in which she opens her eyes into the washing rain of the new world make a brilliant catalogue of discoveries of the feel of things. The rain continues, and the fires. The rigid religion of the first volume, which had sustained life through the winter, begins to dissolve. A citizens' government, much resembling the government of France in 1790, takes over. Charity undergoes travails, some of them excessively drawn out, and finally reunites with Thanakar. In the mosaic of Park's Earth, it is a small story; but after the harsh chill of the first volume, *Sugar Rain* reads like an epithalamium, a marriage-song. Can summer be far behind?

— *Washington Post Book World Science Fiction Column*, 28 May 1989

[I reprint here a review from 1991 of the final volume of Paul Park's trilogy 1995.]

LIKE an arrow burying itself in sand, the *Starbridge Chronicles* continue to burrow into the world. *Soldiers of Paradise* (1987) was brazen, fletched and flying down the aisles of story; *Sugar Rain* (1989) impacted the soil, stirred through the roils of aftermath; and *The Cult of Loving Kindness* (Morrow, 1991), one of the most extreme novels ever published in the genre, a novel whose relationship to normal narrative is that of the ghost of Christmas Past to Scrooge, sifts the subterranean ambages of Starbridge in silence and in cunning, polishing the edges of a story long past and long to come. Not one event of the story itself does it tell.

There is a term this reviewer has found peculiarly relevant to works of this sort – works, that is, which might be described as science fantasy in the sense that science fantasy strives not to change the world but to find out how the world became what it must be. The term is belatedness, and *The Cult of Loving Kindness* is a hymn to that condition. It is a hymn of embedding. Readers may remember – though Park has never wished to be clear about the physical circumstances governing his setting – that the Earth upon which the *Starbridge Chronicles* are set may or may not be our own Earth, aeons hence, but that if it is indeed our Earth much has happened to transfigure it. The Agent of transfiguration seems to be the moon or planet or other entity – it is called Paradise throughout the Chronicles – which may be assumed, under the simplest possible reading of the series, to be a trapped visitor to the solar system; the gravitational effects of its impossibly complex orbital dance among the nine planets have, we are allowed to guess, caused the extraordinary transformation of Earth into a world which suffers, Helliconia-like, a Great Year, with enormous seasons lasting lifetimes and determining by their nature the nature of the societies which exist within their compass; *Soldiers of Paradise* took place just as Winter began to end, and the bonzai contortions of the human societies of that season are about to collapse. In *Sugar Rain* we saw, through a slow love story, the enormity of Spring. *The Cult of Loving Kindness* takes place in Summer. The central rhythm of the series so far, even though we have not yet traversed an entire Great Year, is one of returning.

No thought of novelty penetrates the book, or invigorates its cast with any prospect of the sort of action which, in sf terms, might be described as penetrative. Each character is a mayfly in a cycle whose huge turning, too slow to grasp, still underlies every pulse of the heart, each gesture of the body in its life. Deep in the codes that write memory, and deep within the perceptions of the world which spaniel memory at heels, everyone is reliving lives which gloss return. *The Cult of Loving Kindness* itself is a sect which replicates in pacific guise the frozen anguish of the Winter religion – dominated (we remember) by the god Angkhdt, Whose Skull, seemingly rediscovered in the current volume, may be that of an extraterrestrial visitor from Paradise whose breeding with the native stock of Earth generated the human stock of the Chronicles, whose blood is golden. The story of *The Cult of Loving Kindness*, which is not told but enfolded, repeats in the idiom of Summer the tale of the Princess and the Antinomial, whose forbidden love at the end of Winter seems almost to engender the explosion into Spring, the semen of the sugar rain. This time their role is taken by twins, rescued from death by a nonhuman native of "Earth" returning to his native village where he will sit at the feet of his childhood guru and contemplate the meaning of things; the girl grows up eloquent and fluent, the boy with an anti-nomial's incapacity to utter in the abstracting syntaxes of normal language, speaking instead in ostensive spasms rendered by Park as a patter of cagy, enfant-sauvage resonances. So the nonhuman student of the meaning of things – all, seemingly, unawares – harbours in his tiny village the return of the most explosive moment of the Cult of Loving Kindness. The twins commit incest, which we are allowed to witness, one of the few transgressions of Park's avoidance of raw event, perhaps because their loving is not intrinsically destructive or violent, but stands rather as an instigator or sign of events to come; their saviour commits suicide after the village is visited by inquisitors from the university, who serve both as mind police and as marshalling agents for the raw and vicious industrialism which characterizes the high Summer culture; the twins escape, travel north to a sacred arena where Paradise will rise over lava fields and signify – the novel is a tissue of significations enfolded in scent and sigh and déjà vu – the foredoomed and final outcome of the twins' holy intercourse. And the book ends.

The density of telling is at times very great – or, should one say, the density of the enfolding of the wings of belatedness is at times very great, very humid, as deeply humid as a dusk nightmare in the thick heart of summer after heavy rain. The radicalness of the book lies, however, not in the winged echolalia of belatedness it embodies, but in its obduracy of refusal of normal narrative. For wings are all we get, as they enfold. Memoriousness is all we get, as the cycle triumphs. The triumph of The Cult of Loving Kindness is that it sinks into the past faster than we can read it, that all we can know is a memory of wings.

– New York Review of Science Fiction 36, August 1991

HERE in Britain, in the midst of a hot and brooding greenhouse winter, it comes as something of a relief that Ben Elton does not figure the world to end in 1989. The message of cheer in Stark (Michael Joseph, 1989) is that we have at least a decade before the battle between free enterprise and the environment ends in the inevitable victory of the former. Only around the year 2000, the time in which this remarkably funny first novel is set, will an avalanche of interlinked disasters finally put paid to the planet.

Like The Young Ones and Blackadder, two black comedies Elton co-wrote for television, Stark hides its despair under a mask of goonish farce. It is a tactic familiar to the readers of Kurt Vonnegut, whose structural ironies Elton often mimics, for like Vonnegut, Elton is a caring misanthrope, a curser, a genuine satirist. Superficially complicated, and intermittently rather windy, the story is simple at heart. An appalling asset-stripping Australian billionaire named Sly Moorcock meets a conclave of entrepreneurs who more or less own the planet, and who invite him to join Stark, which is the name of a kind of exclusive survivalist cabal. Much faster than most of us realize, the world is dying of ecocide, "Total Toxic Overload." Having done much to destroy the Earth – fortified by the knowledge that "it would be a crime to interfere with the sacred laws of free enterprise simply to protect the environment" – they now intend to leave it.

Back in Australia, an equally appalling counter-cultural poseur named CD, having become entangled with a gaggle of protesters, inadvertently stumbles over evidence of Moorcock's involvement in something huge and ominous. At his command, huge rocket silos are being excavated at panic speed in the middle of the desert. All too closely resembling the television comedians for whom Elton writes material, CD and his friends investigate and interfere, jibe and joke, and prolong the book. But Elton's occasional slip into comical *tours de force* does little to deflect *Stark* from the central horror of its burden. CD may blunder hither and yon, surviving a few months more in sweltering, poison-choked Australia, and the owners of the planet may escape this Hell only to create a worse one in space; but Elton's central message burns more and more nakedly as his farce whips itself to death. Ten years from now, he tells us, through the wisecracks and tirades of this most desperate novel, it will be too late. The world will be over.

– *The Listener*, 9 March 1989

SOME YEARS hence, the planet may need a new Eve. Barring a few tufts of brush on an island east of Madagascar, the forests may be gone, and homo sapiens, the only species to have thrived, may have begun to turn fatally inwards. As a wise young man phrases it in *Eva* (Gollancz, 1988), Peter Dickinson's latest novel for young adults, "The whole human race is thinking in shorter and shorter terms... We're giving up. Packing it in." Eva herself may represent the last chance for a new beginning.

At the start of her story, she is a girl of thirteen, and she has just awoken in hospital, drugged and immobilized and confused. Only slowly does she come to realize that, because of the terrible nature of the injuries inflicted upon her in a car crash, the pattern of "neurone memories" which makes up her conscious mind has been implanted into the brain of a chimpanzee. It is something of a first. Professor

Pradesh is proud of the success of her theory that consciousness is mappable, and Eva's father, who manages Earth's last ape sanctuary, and who had been driving at the time of the crash, is both relieved at her survival and intrigued with the outcome. And Eva herself grasps the nettle of her shocking transformation with almost saintly aplomb.

This may sound too good to be true, and indeed Eva's bright spirit stands in sharp contrast to the stressed and diminished souls of those around her; but in Dickinson's expert hands she never becomes mawkish. Clear-headed, sensitive, deft and humorous, Eva is a convincing young miracle, and a joy to encounter in a book so unnervingly open-eyed about the sadness of things to come. Eva's mind-transplant has been financed by a food corporation, and she soon finds herself appearing in banana ads; the ape sanctuary, where she spends much of her time living as a quasi-chimp, is under threat of termination, and she must find some way of continuing her radically strange life. And the humans around her seem to become, as the years pass, increasingly querulous and feeble.

But Eva, as a tale for young adults, edges properly away from the darker implications of Dickinson's vision. Much of the book is spent with Eva and her chimp companions deep in the sanctuary, where she experiences moments of elated integration more intense than anything she can recollect as a young girl in a young girl's body, and where she begins to evolve a tactics to cope with her dilemma. Though coddled and fêted, she no longer wishes to live in the human world; but the threatened research cuts are now about to shut the sanctuary down.

She arrives at a solution with the help of some humans who see things her way, and who themselves sharply and compassionately illuminate the tale. The food corporation is bamboozled into transporting Eva and her family of chimps to an island east of Madagascar, ostensibly to do some location shots for a new ad. Once freed into this tiny vestige of wilderness, however, Eva and her family make their escape, and settle into their new Eden. Like angels, Eva's human colleagues establish a quarantine around the enclave, and breeding soon begins. Some form of life strives to continue. Eva herself has children, though her implanted consciousness cannot, of course, be inherited [any more than Ish, the protagonist of George R Stewart's *Earth Abides* (1949), could keep "civilization" alive in the minds of his own descendents 1995]. The Eden she has founded may serve as the birthplace of a new world, but it will not be a world for men and women.

It might have been a grim little fable. It is nothing of the sort. From the beginning of his career, Dickinson has had an anthropolgist's loving respect for the indomitable persistence of life in the strangest of enclaves, and in its calm relentless way *Eva* is triumphant about the chances of a new start. Humanity may sink into a terminal lassitude – most of Dickinson's adult detective novels focus upon a worn-out Britain jostled too late by creative aliens – but life will prevail because Eva has prevailed, radiantly, in her stubborn niche, guarded by angels.

– The Washington Post, 9 April 1989

THERE IS little to say about the premise which shapes Peter Dickinson's fortieth book (give or take a couple), and that is the joke of it. *Skeleton-in-Waiting* (The Bodley Head, 1989) takes place in the same alternate world Dickinson first introduced to readers in *King and Joker* (1976); in this world the Duke of Clarence, having failed to die in 1892, lives on to inherit his father's throne in 1910, bequeathing it in turn to his own grandson, Victor II, who now reigns over Britain. The joke is that absolutely nothing else has changed.

Like and unlike our own ensemble of Royals, Dickinson's Royal Family observe a knowing media-conscious outward propriety; but spend much of their private time, in the two novels so far devoted to them, fending off any exposure of their real selves. King Victor is a bigamist whose two wives (one of them the Queen) live in the Royal household. In *King and Joker*, this charade generates spasms of blackmail and murder, nearly causing young Princess Louise to blow the gaffe on her dad. In *Skeleton-in-Waiting*, thirteen years later, Louise has become capable, snappy, self-assured, professional; but the death of an ancient dowager member of the Family soon generates, once again, a threat of exposure.

"Sometimes," Louise says, deep into the book, "I wonder if we aren't a sort of dream everyone's having." Certainly her life is dream-like in its felicity. More fortunate than her nearest analogue in our own world, she has two mothers; a witty randy dad; a brilliant scientist husband much involved in Artificial Intelligence work; sensitive and witty employees; and two fine children whom she breast-feeds in public. Just as *Skeleton-in-Waiting* is an escape for the reader from the unrelenting supple gravity and burden of Dickinson's other work, so Princess Louise provides welcome remission from the daily trials of our own stiff Family as she responds with wryly inventive aplomb to the new crisis. She is a blessing in her disguise.

The beginning is almost static. Some letters written by the dead dowager may contain – along with much scurrilous gossip – enough genuine scandal to shake the throne. An old lady-in-waiting has copies, but is dominated by an ancient Russian relative of the deceased who has her own family secrets to hide. The IRA becomes involved, and the life of the Princess is soon at risk, and *Skeleton-in-Waiting* begins to pick up pace in an accelerando Dickinson controls precisely. His detective novels may sometimes remind one of Michael Innes, but never in their final pages. In the end, what Louise discovers about the ancient Russian relative's daughter burns through the deft and donnish pleasantries of this *jeu d'esprit*, and issues of Royal decorum suddenly cease to concern us, or her. And for one extremely moving instant, she gazes upon us, from the cage of the dream, like any fellow mortal.

– The Listener, 21 September 1989

AS USUAL, the author knew best. In manuscript, this previously unpublished novel by Philip K Dick was entitled *The Broken Bubble [of Thisbe Holt]* (Arbor House, 1988), and both point and euphony have been lost by calling it *The Broken Bubble*. Thisbe Holt herself appears only two or three times in the book, but her role is central to Dick's vision of San Francisco life in 1956. A failed singer, she makes ends meet by doing a specialty act. At convention stag parties, she squeezes herself naked into a large plastic bubble, enabling fat drunken gentlemen to kick her around the floor for fun. Like most of Dick's sympathetic characters, she lives in a state of exposure and humiliation; but the power brokers of her horrid little plastic world are themselves frustrated, their pleasures vicarious, their sadism unavailing. For owners and victims both, life is a prison. And when the bubble breaks, as it does literally for Thisbe in a climactic scene, what happens then?

The Broken Bubble was probably written in 1957, and comes about halfway through Dick's extraordinarily intense (and totally unsuccessful) try at becoming a published mainstream novelist. Along with the sf titles which would make his reputation, he composed during this period at least eight non-genre novels, before abandoning in the early 60s any thought of a conventional literary career; *The Broken Bubble* is the sixth of these to be published since his death in 1982, and shows the same haste – the same reckless experimental temerity – and the same lungeing liquid accuracy of intuition about people that marks its stablemates. *The Broken Bubble* only stands out by the comparative sunniness of its ending.

As far as the characters who dominate the foreground of Thisbe Holt's book are concerned, life in the middle of the Eisenhower years, in the backstreets of San Francisco, is an airless bubble of routine, and the impulse to shake oneself free seems entirely natural. But terror and *amour fou* and imponderable abysses lurk out there in the unprotected world. Radio announcer Jim Briskin refuses to read an egregious ad for Looney Luke's used cars, and is suspended; Pat Gray, once his wife, plunges into a lame but seemingly bottomless affair with Jim's teenage admirer Art Emmanual; Art's wife Rachael, whose pregnancy gives her a clear-eyed tunnel vision about the future, tries to take Jim as her new protector. Dazed by the two strong women, Jim and Art flounder like lungfish in a drought. Only Jim's slightly supine sanity saves them in the end, frees them to bathe once again in clement routine.

It is a slippery plot to hold, but although Dick sometimes loses control (the manuscript was not edited during his lifetime), the mature, deft, probing tenderness with which he presents his four protagonists exhibits a rather more than scattershot talent. His ear for dialogue is charmed, and much of the book is astonishingly funny. *The Broken Bubble* is surely no masterpiece – but then its author was never given the slightest encouragement to attempt one. The reconciled calm of its last pages seems, in this light, all the more earned.

– *Times Literary Supplement*, 8 December 1989

THE TITLE weighs heavy, and the book is long. As we begin to read *The Message to the Planet* (Chatto & Windus, 1989), by an author whose twenty-three previous works have established her as the most formidable philosopher-novelist writing in English today, we expect to be tested and teased by what is to come, entertained and tickled and daunted and taught. We are not disappointed. Iris Murdoch's latest novel, which is enormously long, ends only after much has been suffered, much learned. All that is missing is a message to the planet.

Up to a point, it is the mixture as before. As always, philosophical issues of grave import expose and deepen a plot of high artifice – in this case a tragicomic sexual imbroglio whose victims, as usual in Murdoch novels, make with their lives the sound that humans make when they are failing to be free; and everything ties together in the end, like a theorem expounded, or a debt paid. There is, in other words, nothing new under the sun. *The Message to the Planet* is, after all, not the first but the twenty-fourth novel in which Murdoch has presented her vision of life as a good-and-evil show, a harlequinade danced by thought manikins.

But soon a new note begins to sound. At the heart of the book lurks the haunted, mesmeric, Wittgenstein-like figure of Marcus Vallar, a mathematician and painter and philosopher and mystic who may be a whole man, or a magus (or a lunatic). But unlike similar personages who dominate earlier books, Vallar becomes unknowable at the end not through trickery but because the ardours of his quest for truth have trapped his tongue into silence. Surrounding him, distracted and obsessed and haunted, a small cast of Murdoch familiars dances attendance in a southern England stripped of almost all detail, like a stage set. Despite its great length, *The*

187

Message to the Planet reads like a chamber drama enacted by a doomed cadre of acolytes in a land of ghosts. Everything seems to await the end – of the century; of the Britain we have learned to know through Murdoch's earlier books; of Vallar himself. After he does finally die, the attendant obsequies take up the last hundred pages of *Message*, and give the book the uncanny requiem air of a Japanese tragedy, where the point of the play seems to be the mourning.

In nearly 600 pages, only one date (1911) appears, and that quite possibly by accident; but the end-of-century feeling of *Message* is unmistakeable. Vallar (who may or may not be deranged) may or may not have looked into the sun of pure being, beyond good and evil, where no man can live, and of which he must remain silent; but the men and women who surround him are clearly at the ends of their respective tethers. Though some of them are described as youngish, their spirits are decrepit with age (Murdoch is visibly insecure when forced to depict characters under forty, and perhaps wisely does not actually say how old anyone is). Their intellectual and artistic concerns are belated, backward-looking, sclerotic. They are *partials*. For creatures like this, a whole man like Vallar is like catnip, and cannot be resisted, and his departure from London (before the novel starts) has had the effect of a curse on those who remain.

We begin in the desert air of his absence, in London, with a conversation straight from the pages of Ivy Compton-Burnett, another author who sets her novels of dread anticipation in a temporal never-never land. Several colleagues of the famed Professor have come together to discuss the situation, in voices shaking with spiritual cold. Alfred Ludens, an historian negligently involved in the stylishly occult Neoplatonism of Giordano Bruno, has failed to write a book for some time; Jack Sheerwater, whose infantile insistence on maintaining a terrible *ménage à trois* generates most of the book's sexual comedy, paints hard but stupidly; Gildas is a failed priest; Patrick no longer writes the spiritual poems of his prime, and is in fact slipping rapidly deathwards through the curse he believes Vallar laid on him by departing. When the sage's hiding place is then revealed, Ludens has every excuse to descend upon him, like a ferret, or a vampire, famished for revelation. He soon drags the dazed (or perhaps autistic) guru back to London, and has him lay hands upon the dying Patrick, who is immediately cured.

The great central arch of the tale begins. (Many pages here could have been compressed – but Murdoch is now, it may be, beyond editing.) Vallar and his love-poisoned daughter Irina book into a Wiltshire sanatarium-cum-resort with Ludens, who continues to gnaw for truth, hovering over the striving, stymied magus with his notebook and his questions and his ravenous love. If Vallar has a message for

us, Ludens intends to be the messenger. But their peace (or prison) is soon assaulted by New Age pilgrims, women fleeing tortures inflicted by Sheerwater, attendant
doctors. Only the angelic Maisie Tether (by name and character an homage to Henry
James) passes freely through the ambit of the sage on her way back to Boston. Then
Vallar dies, burnt-out by pure being (or nightmares). He has said nothing. Ludens's
game is ended; but in his terrifying, just grief – in his chafed submission to the
human state – he may embody the only message Murdoch seems to sanction. To
live on, eyes open, in the dark.

– The Listener, 5 October 1989

THE FINEST single book of children's verse ever written is entered by stealth. In
the tiny eight-line poem which appears first in all versions of Walter de la Mare's
Peacock Pie (Holt, 1989), night has fallen. We hear a horseman, or dream that we hear
him riding over the hill to us. "His helm was silver, / And pale was he; / And the
horse he rode / Was of ivory." And that is all. The poem ends in utter silence, un-
tutored, uncorrupt, unquestioning; open and unblinking and clear. "The Horseman" is like a child's eye. It is what Walter de la Mare did better than anyone else. It
is why *Peacock Pie* has never been out of print since its first publication in 1913, just
before the lights went out in Europe.

The date is important. De la Mare may have written his verses for children, but
he never shirked pointing out to them that the world contained more than dreams
and silence. The glistening twilight hues of *Peacock Pie: A Book of Rhymes* only half-
conceal a deep note of elegy for a culture about to enter trauma. Like so many works
written at this time, it is a Recessional. But never is the note of foreboding explicit.
In Henry Holt's new version of the final definitive text of *Peacock Pie*, "The Horseman" immediately precedes "Alas, Alack!", one of de la Mare's most startling, unforgettable, but seemingly innocent vignettes:

> Ann, Ann!
> Come! quick as you can!
> There's a fish that talks
> In the frying-pan.
> Out of the fat,
> As clear as glass,
> He put up his mouth
> And moaned "Alas!"
> Oh, most mournful,

189

"Alas, alack!"
Then turned to his sizzling,
And sank him back.

And there the poem ends. There is no moral tag, no sanctimony, no flinching – just a small child, watching in wonderment, calling out with a kind of joy to a sister or (because we are in Edwardian England) a Cook. No child would bother to think that "Alas, Alack!" was bleak, or Godless, or sadistic, or that it described the new age to come far more accurately than any war poem by Rupert Brooke ever would. It is in fact a poem Mary Poppins might have declaimed, in the morning, to her transfixed charges, just before telling them it was time to rise and shine; and that she was leaving them. No earlier poetry for children had managed this sort of thing, with the possible exception of a few stray lines by Edward Lear; and few successors to de la Mare have been able to match his uncanny clarity, though many have tried.

He died old. Walter de la Mare (1873–1956) outlived his friends, his reputation, and the mist-shrouded magical England he had coaxed into life in *Peacock Pie* and in almost everything else he wrote before 1914. For much of the century he was an old man. By the year of his death the first Motorways were on the drawing-board, and he had become a figure mired in the past, testy but wispish, a fount of moping nostalgia. He produced a huge amount of work, but today the novels are unread; most of the tales for children dally with and mystify their readers; and much of the later poetry gives off a plaintive metaphysical whine that strikes modern ears as dilettantish, poor-spirited. So we must shrug off his old age, when the modern world was too much with him.

Though some other early volumes contain considerable work of the same quality, we are left in the main with the largesse of *Peacock Pie*. There are nearly 100 poems in the final version, which is very carefully structured. Beginning with bright soundings of vision like "The Horseman" and "Alas, Alack!", we move quickly to the famous character sketches – Tillie Turveycombe, who chokes on a seed; Jim Jay, who gets stuck in yesterday; Miss T, who is much like us, because, "Tiny and cheerful, / And neat as can be, / Whatever Miss T eats / Turns into Miss T." Then come the longer narrative poems, best known of which is probably "Off the Ground," which tells the tale of "three jolly farmers" who get themselves into a dancing contest; a few darker character portraits are then quickly followed by a section devoted to various beasts of the earth, and we approach the stunning final pages.

With these last poems, described merely as "Earth and Air" or "Songs" in the first edition of the book, de la Mare comes very close to greatness. Eerie, profound, dense as dreams, poems like "Many a Mickle," or "The Song of the Mad Prince," or "The Song of Finis" are tough for any child to understand at first reading. But they are poems which haunt and gnaw the mind, and children have now been returning to their world for 75 years. No child should ever be denied a chance to join that world.

– The Washington Post, 5 November 1989

IT IS surely no sin to be a Scot who writes sf. J Leslie Mitchell (better known for the rhapsodic regional books he published as Lewis Grassic Gibbon) composed several mildly "naughty" genre novels over the course of a short stormy life (1901–1935); Gay Hunter, first released in 1934 and now republished by Polygon (1989) in Edinburgh, may be the best of them. In A Sparrow's Flight, also from Polygon (1989), Margaret Elphinstone strives with decent sobriety to reclaim bits of Hibernia from the Celt-and-dragon fantasy market. Several of the contributors to Starfield: The Anthology of Science Fiction by Scottish Writers (The Orkney Press, 1989, ed. Duncan Lunan) have published far beyond the bailiwick defined for them by the the land of their birth. And this is just as well. Scots may write sf, but sf as a genre does not do very well with the likes of Scotland.

Scotland, after all, is a region. Though its cities are choked with busy burly ill-tempered urban minds at work, the land itself lies at the edge of things, and sf writers of the first order tend to treat the regions of this planet as obstacles to the hubristic ocean-spanning world-gaze of free speculation. A tale told in Scots dialect, like David Crooks's "Spaced Out" in the Lunan anthology, will therefore seem perversely stuck to its tongue, a landlubber on the margins of the great sea. And a novel like Elphinstone's, dense with the pull of region, will almost inevitably return its characters to the point from which they departed, wiser than before, but deeper in. Like so many tales of life long after the apocalypse, A Sparrow's Flight, which is a sequel to The Incomer (1987), rewrites science-fictional premises in the language of fantasy, a genre much in love with region (and with Scotland); and like most fantasies, the fundamental gesture of its plot is an enactment not of hubris but of theodicy.

There is much of value, all the same, in Starfield. In "The Rig" (1966), Chris Boyce almost spins a glum North Sea tale into tour de force (in a style that weds John Wyndham to Alistair Maclean), though he stumbles, at the end, out of the region and into bathos. Naomi Mitchison, who has written much more sf than Lunan seems aware of in his introduction, contributes a fine elegiac new story which increases the sense of dubiety about the chances of genuine communication first expressed in *Memoirs of a Spacewoman* (1962). Edwin Morgan's poems are among the best ever written on science-fiction themes. Alasdair Gray's two spoofs are succinct and extremely funny, but have already appeared in *Unlikely Stories, Mostly* (1983). Several of the tales were featured in *Glasgow Herald* SF short story competition, run by Lunan, and tend to suffer from its 2,000-word limit, though Janice Galloway's "A Continuing Experiment" (1987) expresses a feminist lesson with something of the impact and finesse of James Tiptree Jr in her prime. Iain Banks, who is the best-known Scottish writer of sf these days, is not included.

About *Gay Hunter*, J Leslie Mitchell's second excursion through time into a nudist paradise, it is impossible not to feel a certain mild ambivalence. *Three Go Back* (1932) cast its twentieth-century protagonists back in time to Atlantis, where they were forced to undress and become as children in a pre-agricultural Garden, while *Gay Hunter* projects its three similar leads forward 20,000 years to a post-catastrophe England whose inhabitants have two ways of behaving: dreamless sleep "without inhibitions or complexes or all the rest of the sad, futile fantasies civilisation and Sigmund Freud had once foisted on men"; and cavorting in nude scrums. Virgin playgirl and archaeologist Gay Hunter finds this deeply to her taste, but her companions, a Fascist soldier and his aristocratic fiancée, soon attempt to reintroduce clothes and flogging in order to bring back a proper respect for science. Inevitably (the book is thinly plotted) they fail. Health wins.

In the toothless prurience of his descriptions of Gay's galumphing nude body, and in his idealizing of the raptures of her self-regard, Mitchell (it must be said) shows all the impercipience of a man capable of thinking in 1934 (along with Thorne Smith) that Freud *invented* the dark side of human nature; and by his conviction that nude athletics constituted an antidote to Fascism (rather than a rhetoric for its apotheosis), he demonstrates himself to be very much a figure of this uneasy period. Aside from the repressed hysteria he tends to exude when aroused, there may be nothing intrinsically Scottish in the deeply repressive tone Mitchell takes on whenever he wishes to cast repressions off, and there is something profoundly *closet* about the not infrequent scenes in which he has Gay command her native beau to "cuddle" her, or when the folk body-build to the sound of timbrels; one's sense on reading this book is of a writer whose naïveté now seems deadly. Perhaps unfairly to the man himself and his political convictions, one does not see *Gay Hunter* prefiguring a Garden. It is the Camp which is in view.

– *Times Literary Supplement*, 23 February 1990

Four: 1990

1. Year Roundup

Someone must have been telling lies about O., for without having done anything wrong he was cancelled one fine morning. He had, it cannot be gainsaid, noticed a growing silence in the world outside his window, but had dismissed the tightness in his chest as catarrh, for he had done nothing wrong, and *he had been well reviewed*; so he was unprepared for the knock upon the door, or for the strange men in the closely fitting black suits that marked them as Samurai of the Robust Accountancy. "Who are you?" asked O., though he must have known, for their eyes slid off the living. "Are you *Orbit Science Fiction Yearbook*?" asked the first Samurai. "I am that paraclete," said O. "Then you are no more," murmured the second, "for you are cancelled." "Ah," said O. In his heart, it may be, he had long suspected his own guilt or *redundancy*, and so, after a pause, he asked only, "Will there be a trial?" The Samurai shrugged. "If you insist," said the first, from the side of his mouth. "It would change nothing," said the second, for the hands of the first were already at O.'s throat, while the second thrust the knife into his thudding heart and turned it there twice. "Like a dog!" said O.; it was as if he meant the shame of his *cancelling* to outlive him. But of course it never does. It was a good year for sf.

That is, if any good sf was being written, it was a good year for good sf to be written in. Samuel R Delany had been saying recently that sf – which was "a critique of the object rather than a critique of the subject" – could be distinguished from the mimetic novel by the fact that it paid attention to the objective world, which was not merely a show whose variables were tied to human consciousness. In that sense certainly, 1990 was a good year for sf. Good sf needs a foregrounded world, needs the compost of history to feed on – the simplest definition of sf being *free history* – and there was plenty of history in 1990, just as there was in 1989, for provender. Three decades after Sputnik spoiled John W Campbell's white wedding with the future, two decades after the first augurs of nanotechnologies to come began to shrivel the knobs and diodes of the old sf, less than a decade after William Gibson's heroes began to surf Odysseus-like down the data seas in quest of Ithaca-wombs for one, the genre might still continue to emit replicants of the Golden Age like some vast incontinent egg-spewing factory-farm Gold-style Goose; but 1990 was a good year all the same for those sf writers not owned by farmers or otherwise obsessed with the past. (The world is never past. It is only our memories which cloak the eye with similitudes, our memories which sharecrop the stone that refutes Berkeley.) History on show, then: it will be interesting to see if anything good came of it.

One of the year-monitors has, of course, been disappeared. The cancellation after three years of David Garnett's *Orbit Science Fiction Yearbook*, in which this review-er's annual sf novel roundup had previously appeared, leaves the UK without an an-thology forum of assessment [*New Worlds* has been cancelled too 1995]. But we can still get a sense of things. *Locus*, which continues to represent the sound of sf talk-ing to itself, continues to present its bibliographical statistics according to its own strangely unique criteria. Charles N Brown and William G Contento's *Science Fiction, Fantasy, & Horror: A Comprehensive Bibliography of Books and Short Fiction Published in the English Language*, an annual series of bound volumes recast from data first made available in issues of the magazine, continues strangely (despite the subtitle) to list only sf books that *Locus* received free for review (which is a truly odd test of legiti-macy to apply in a reference book designed for general use) *during the year in question* (which is, if anything, even odder), so that more appositely the subtitle should read: *A Comprehensive Bibliography of Books and Short Fiction Received by Locus for Review in 1989, including Books and Short Fiction from 1988 That Got Lost in the Mail until Early 1989 (or Maybe the Publisher Hadn't Heard of Us Till Somebody Told Him Though THAT'S Really Kinda Hard to Believe) and Some VERY EARLY Copies of a Bunch of 1990 Books Somebody Sent One of Our Reviewers*. All of which means that anyone using the *Locus* annuals to research any one calendar year cannot restrict themselves to the volume ostensibly covering that year. They must in fact obtain – or find together, at the same time, in some library – not one but three volumes: that for the year in question, that for the year preceding the year in question, and that for the year to come.

The *Locus* yearbooks are not, therefore, in the end, true bibliographies at all; they are, in fact, *diaries* of the postal experiences of one small magazine. Which is some-thing of an embarrassment in the matured world of sf 1991, especially given the enormous usefulness – and astonishing accuracy – of Brown/Contento's treatment of the data actually admitted into their fold. [There are reasons for the *Locus* strate-gy, and Charles Brown has convinced me that current legal rulings – which treat the date a book is available for sale, and the date it is published, as identical – have made it impossible to date many books according to copyright information 1995.] By notating only those books which they have seen (which is no real excuse for not going out and finding those books they have not been given), and by saying exactly when they first touched the flesh of each book, the editors have avoided innumera-ble ascription errors, and manage to stay clear of ghost titles (except for listing ad-vance copies of books which may never get published). The annuals are accurate and information-packed, talking bibliography of the most enjoyable sort; and Hal W Hall's "Research Index" is as comprehensive as any index of non-fiction could possibly be that excludes reviews (and therefore much of the best critical work done in the field, but who can cover everything?). And the "Book Summary" for the forthcoming 1990 volume, a draft of which appears in *Locus* 361, tells us that 1188 new books were published (or, as we've seen, received by *Locus*) in 1990, which returns us to the heights of 1988. Of this 1188, 281 were sf novels, 204 were fantasies, 168 were horror, 90 were collections of whatever ilk, and 73 were novelizations (other categories filled up the total). Our remit – the 281 sf novels – is, therefore, lighter than it might initially have seemed, though still too huge to manage without dynamiting the pool. Of the 281, an unknown number were sharecrops, most of which bite the hand of novel, and which will very soon (rumour has it) be published on edible paper; they still, for the most part, don't pass our lips. On the other hand, this reviewer may have seen a counterbalancing slough of books that failed to qualify for *Locus*'s *Comprehensive Bibliography of Books and Short Fiction Published in the English Language* – like, for instance, the six titles Gene Wolfe has published since 1983 with Cheap Street, a Fine Press which does not solicit reviews, and does not therefore send off free copies to magazines, so that not one of these books has ever been mentioned by *Locus*, and might just as well not really exist at all, right? So it's swings and roundabouts. So we plunge.

Typical of the kind of book that might well escape the *Locus* remit – though Phil Stephensen-Payne, who seems to assemble British listings on a more comprehensive Books Noted basis, may have entered it into the forthcoming 1990 volume – was Christine Brooke-Rose's *Verbivore* (Carcanet), a surly bristling assault on datanoise that reads, like so many devout expressions of cutting-edge postmodernism, strangely medieval: a hedgehog Canute drowning in the language sea, the century tide. Bruce Sterling might designate *Verbivore* as an example of slipstreaming – of feeding like a dolphin on icon scraps tossed into the wake of the ship of genre – but Brooke-Rose is stranger than that, and perhaps a harbinger. The secret chambers of the book, like the pomegranate-hearted futures we're falling into, are a maze of options drenched in sf; it is the telling of the thing which claws back dead dignities of the autonomous word.

There were other books in the slipstream, too, some of whose authors might not have welcomed the knowledge that they were officially in tow. *Hayduke Lives!* (Little, Brown) by Edward Abbey (1927–1989) brought back the members of *The Monkey-Wrench Gang* (1975) to attempt, one final time, to save the West from the catastrophic engines – literally depicted – of Late Late Capitalism. In *The King* (Harper & Row), Donald Barthelme (1933–1989) reinserted King Arthur into the jaws of the current (ie 1940) world, which gnashed; but the Matter proved undegradable, and Barthelme's last fling at "flippancy" seemed, as always, like a washing of the sense of here and now. It was hardly a new book, or a novel, but *Toward the Radical Center: a Karel Capek Reader* (Catbird) presented a number of newly rendered excerpts from familiar plays and longer texts which cleaned up the old translatorese and evoked something of the quicksilver urgency (the Nazis are coming the Nazis are coming) of the original garrotte-tonguing tales. Alex Comfort, who was a very gloomy teenage prodigy in 1937, and who later moved through ferocious pacifism into sex and gerontology, returned to the glooms in *The Comforters* (Duckworth), set in a gloomy near-future Britain (this may be tautological), and it was gloomy. *The Emperor of America* (Simon & Schuster) by Richard Condon shot off fireworks into the mouth of darkness of his native land, mapping Kronos's teeth, avoiding like the plague the Matter of Reagan (see below) by setting his alternate-history plot just after old death-rattle rode west in 1988.

In *McGrotty and Ludmilla: or, the Harbinger Report* (Glasgow: Dog and Bone), Alasdair Gray applied the pissed récit style of Scottish satire to a few near-future English targets, fairly mildly for him. Patrick Harpur's *Mercurius: or, The Marriage of Heaven and Earth* (Macmillan) is gaga if Yeats was: if "Sailing to Byzantium" is a ferry ad, then *Mercurius* is orthodox astrology. *Fires' Astonishment* (Secker & Warburg) is Geraldine McCaughrean's second attempt to novelize a folksong – "The Laily Worm and Machrel of the Sea" in this case – and duly inserts a genuine stained unstalwart dragon into medieval England, where it pouts steam. Wolf Mankowitz, in *Exquisite Cadaver* (Deutsch), writes a traditional posthumous fantasy, but by setting it in a surreal American West opens the revolving gates of dream, so that what is real and what is waiting become one. Milorad Pavic's *Landscape Painted with Tea* (Knopf) proved you could repeat a fluke, because this gallimaufry, like a dwarf crab-apple sprout gone godzilla, is a solipsism no less self-fertilizing than *Dictionary of the Khazars*; the translation, by Christina Pribicevic-Zoric, is again superb. Leo Perutz's 1933 novel, *St Peter's Snow*, was given a smooth new translation (Harvill): the eponymous virus had, during the middle ages, infected Europeans with the disease of Christianity; and now, in 1933, hundreds of years later, once again virulent, it has begun to create Nazis everywhere. In *The Quiet Woman* (Bloomsbury), which is also a kind of Plague Journal, Christopher Priest anatomizes the Thatcher Years with a savagery all the greater for its absolute failure to shout; it was the neatest exercise in devastation published this year. *Vineland* (Little, Brown) by Thomas Pynchon, a 400-page scherzo whose panache mocked the seventeen-year gap since *Gravity's Rainbow*, teetered at the edge of the Reagan Years, but refused to carry its protagonists into the new world, like a wise lungfish spying out the terrain and seeing it was the beach at Bikini; and seemed all the more civilized for this. *Haroun and the Sea of Stories* (Granta) by Salman Rushdie could attract no reviewer who did not know the real story: perhaps someday we will be able to read this one, which at first glance seemed a fossil in ice, with liquid eyes. With *The Ice-Shirt* (Deutsch), in which berserkers shapechange into the first explorers of Vinland, William T Vollmann began to publish a grandiose mythos of America in a projected seven volumes, but Deutsch has since folded, which may teach the endlessly logorrheic Vollmann how to stop [it has not 1995]: something his mentor, Laurence Sterne, never learned in time. And Kurt Vonnegut cast an extremely cold eye: *Hocus Pocus: or, What's the Hurry, Son?* (Putnam), set at the end of the century, views an America owned but already abandoned as a rotten investment by Japan, in a prose icy with despite. It is the story of a man – soldier, teacher, hypocrite, jailbird of the planet home – who has been worn past frazzle into permafrost. As he talks to us, he continues to cough himself to death: because, like the planet, he cannot stop smoking.

It was a quiet year for dinosaurs, those writers we have defined in previous years as Cargo from the Golden Age, though some of them continued to issue shares (non-voting, non-preferred). Isaac Asimov and Arthur C Clarke both "collaborated" in the production of novels, both of which – though neither outcome was technically a sharecrop, neither younger partner being sufficiently junior or impoverished to have to work for hire – had all the *seeming* of the sharecrop title: the clone gaze inwards of each book at the altar of the past; the enervating belatedness of plot and discourse; the medusa chill of the sealed and finished texts. In *Nightfall* (Gollancz), Robert Silverberg, using every ounce of his enormous skill, managed to sound just as Asimov might have sounded if Asimov had been dumb as well as lacking in metaphor: which (as Asimov and Silverberg are among the most *intelligent* writers of the century) only underlines the terrible penalties of flirting with death. The original short story from 1941, though written in a style less clean than Asimov later mastered, conveyed its great notion in a flash: the intoxication of which can still keep the reader from wondering about camera obscuras, or cellars, or the slow onset of star-revealing dusk, or indeed the vast eclipse-defeating roundness of your typical planet. In the novel, which was told with beggaring clarity, there was no flash of revelation; nothing but a slow benumbing bathetic club-bore *drone*, like some Pentagon colonel with a pointer after the Gulf War, the very antithesis of a smart weapon. Arthur C Clarke, on the other hand, granted Gregory Benford more or less free scope to sequel *Against the Fall of Night* (1953); Benford's effort, to which he gave the revealingly Whiggish title of *Beyond the Fall of Night*, and which appeared with Clarke's original in one large volume (Ace/Putnam), reads intermittently like a singleton, though always the pallor of displaced ontology frails out the bones of the thing. In the end the Janus-face profile of *Beyond the Fall of Night* is a trick of the shadows, for one face is stone and the other bulges with unshed tears. Ask Paul Preuss.

By himself, Clarke wrote *The Ghost from the Grand Banks* (Bantam); it seemed slim and sketchy, like a whole tale half-seen in North Atlantic fog. For page after page *The World at the End of Time* (Del Rey) and *Outnumbering the Dead* (Century), both by Frederik Pohl, read like more snoozes from the owl of Futuria, but then you saw the eyes were open, cold, watching. The first book is dense with numeracy, swift in the telling, full of jokes and deft new sailor's knots of narrative, but bleaker in the gaps than a crackerbarrel at the end of time, which was extremely vast; and *Outnumbering the Dead*, a short tale about a lone mortal genetically barred from the immortality of his fellows, read like a meniscus over depths of pain. There was nothing new from L Sprague de Camp, A E (Greatest Living ex-Canadian) Van Vogt or Jack Williamson, though next year will be different; but the grave of Robert A Heinlein gave birth to something of a revelation: the uncut *Stranger in a Strange Land* (Putnam) might have restored a few too many passages of insufferably bent polemic, the sort of shadowboxing solipsism alpha males tend to indulge in when they talk politics to their gets, but the telling throughout was significantly less choppy: double-cream pulp, which is nothing to sneeze at. And finally, by dying, Donald A Wollheim (1914–1990) proved likely to generate better stories in years to come, if one may judge by the obituaries beginning to waft gingerly heavenwards, than a lot of those he managed to publish in his lifetime.

It was a good year for sf, if you could only get the old rogue males – those writers, mostly not women, who began their careers in the aftermath of World War Two, just when history began to ice over – to stop flossing in the mirror. Poul Anderson, whose worn incisors decreasingly reave the gist of things, though his gloom hastens, provided in *The Shield of Time* (Tor), which is a loose fixup, another meditative time-cops foray into the past, where they played pattycake once again with history in order to save some awful new era. Ancient-Mariner-like, Gordon R. Dickson failed once again to weaken, or relent: *The Dragon Knight* (Tor) and *Wolf and Iron* (Tor) both said everything they were going to more than thrice, with glittering eye; but the latter, set in the usual depopulated post-holocaust America, did parlay its garrulousness into a long, devoted, surprisingly pacific, detail-obsessed paean to survival, though not eftsoons. Philip José Farmer closed down the teetering architectonic of his Dayworld-Dystopia sequence with *Dayworld Breakup* (Tor), many pages of which were spent at the abacus working out how many totally interchangeable identities the protagonists had accumulated, in a prose crammed with narrative bald spots, gaping blank non sequiturs, daft hypnopompic caesuras, and pyramids (or hierarchies), pyramids (or phalluses), pyramids (pyramids) everywhere. Yes! it was like spelunking the inside of a dead skull. Yes! it was like reading A E Van Vogt: Gosseyn Penis-Upright. Charles L Harness also slid pastwards, in *Lurid Dreams* (Avon), halting at the locus classicus of all American alternate history tales – the Civil War – and introducing, as has become de rigueur, the undead Edgar Allan Poe to carry the burden of the underside of the Dream. Showing some grasp of the art of harikiri, Harry Harrison *seemed* bent (but we cannot pretend to have read the contract) on franchising *himself*, in a packaged continuation of his own *Bill, the Galactic Hero* from 1965: *Bill, the Galactic Hero on the Planet of Bottled Brains* (Avon), which he wrote with Robert Sheckley, economically conveyed a sense of terminal exhaustion through the quality of its many jokes. Backseat-writing in Oz, R A Lafferty composed, or published, a small cornucopia of little books, of which *Dotty* (United Mythologies Press) was maybe the best: but they were all weirdly side-of-the-mouth, disengaged from the illiberal hidden agendas that stove them in like rocks of faith, and from the baroque inscapes they foundered to espouse. And Kate Wilhelm, in *Cambio Bay* (St Martin's Press), could not manage to hold her breath until she got the thing told: *whooshing*, as usual, all over the second half: but wait for next year.

Tiptoe, we enter the world of the primes, writers at the peak of their careers. Though it is dangerous terrain, one thing may save us, something we know and they do not, for they are conditioned not to perceive certain facts of life at this stage of their metamorphosis into dinosaurs. As we can see, the jungle is full of large dens, each occupied by one of these figures of great ego who, though better armed than samurai, seems at the same time far more delicate. Each den is furnished with memorabilia and kudos, which cannot be told apart. Oscars or Nebulas, which cannot be told apart, burden each mantle. Each writer sits with his or her back to the lamp. As we enter one of these dens, we must prepare to begin a "conversation" with the writer whose task or "rapture" we have visibly interrupted. To begin this "conversation," we will pretend to talk about almost anything under the sun, but we *must not persevere* in this stage of the "conversation" after the writer himself has begun to speak, for it is now that the real "conversation" begins. It is now that we have the chance to become privy to the writer's most secret thoughts: the significance of the Quest for Greatness in her early work; the extraordinary size of his last advance; the great affection evinced for her by the population at large; the unique curvature of space that requires him in perpetuity to occupy the actual centre of the world. Several hours will pass. Our attention must not be permitted to flag. Fortunately, it is during this period that we will remember the one thing we know and which he cannot know, because his condition – Oliver Sacks has called it anosognosia – can be defined precisely as an inability to perceive his condition. The one thing we know *which he cannot know* is that there are other people in the world. That the jungles of the world are full of alpha writers. That the aisles of the jungles of the world echo with identical bellows of territoriality and triumph, day and night. That the anosognosia of the writer in his prime is universal, a Universal prank of the Anarch.

We exaggerate. It's all just folks down here in the briar patch. Piers Anthony this year, for instance, did nothing but write more books (list available on request). Iain (Middlename) Banks fisticuffed his way through another Culture tale in *Use of Weapons* (Orbit), the best of the lot so far, though barnacled with the same baroque jaw-jaw that sank *Consider Phlebas*. But this time the plot – two chronologies (one reverse) snapping together like a heat of steel into scissors – worked very hard indeed, and in the end the book took. It held. Greg Bear's *Queen of Angels* (Warner) transformed its eponymous Los Angeles into a beehive of significant furore: with nanotechnology comes, biotransforms, cops and robbers, AI's pregnant with selfhood, voodoo shenanigans à la mode, and a writer the awfulness of whose work Bear seemed insufficiently to recognize. *Heads* (Century), set in the same universe some decades further on, tested out as equally complex within its long-novella compass: lacing together cryogenics, researches into absolute zero, Moon culture stuff, and a rebirth threat from icy death of a California guru whose manipulative fake religion totally failed to resemble (said the lawyers) any twentieth-century claptrap Son-of-Edisonade doctrine we might have experienced here on Earth. Gregory Benford we have already descried, toughing out the anxiety of influence in the aisles of Arthur C Clarke. Terry Bisson made like Terry Southern in *Voyage to the Red Planet* (Morrow), appearing to spoof everything from Hollywood film "culture" to the Nixon-death of NASA to Edgar Rice Burroughs's Mars: but within the tale everything worked, the science, the technologies, the protagonists, Mars herself. And we went along. In *Time and Chance* (Tor), Alan Brennert formidably recast an old idée fixe –changing lives with an alternate self from an alternate world – and transformed the gimmick into a genuine exploration of the roots of character, which turned out to be a fibrous nurture/nature maze, as in the vale of sorrows. David Brin took *Earth* (Bantam) into the palm of his hand, and saved it: though not without the help of some magnificent entrepreneurs, the Three Crones, and Gaia herself. And Lois McMaster Bujold carved a tiny prequel niche for Miles Vorkosigan to stuff in

The Vor Game (Baen) while waiting to conquer the galaxy with nothing going for him but wit, money, luck, knuckleheaded adversaries, mercenary cadres who love him half to death, a supernaturally powerful and devoted Pa, a plethora of space opera clichés longing to be of assistance, and one quite exceptionally sympathetic author. There's Bs for you.

Jonathan Carroll (next letter) juggled so many balls in *Black Cocktail* (Century) that you just knew he'd step on one, and Tilt, and the game would end in tears: and it did. Michael Crichton did a lot of dinosaur research for *Jurassic Park* (Knopf), a novel which turns dinosaur research into fast food for browsers, with Dreadful Warnings on the package about those unbridled scientists who brought you the plots of *The Andromeda Strain* and *Coma*, but at least the book was biodegradable: it digested in a flash. Stephen R.Donaldson brought his massive countenance to bear on the frail vessel of space opera in *The Gap into Conflict: The Real Story* (Harper-Collins), and holed it, in a style more Hun than Gothic. Mary Gentle, having tied her shoelaces together with Writing Hooks, duly tripped headfirst into *Rats and Gargoyles* (Bantam UK), grade-school tics and gimmicks spronging from her grab-bag; but once inured to all this stuff, the reader began to witness something complex take shape, a through-composed Neoplatonist memory-theatre fabulation woven from holy dung. *The Difference Engine* (Gollancz), by William Gibson and Bruce Sterling, grows in hindsight, like a time-bomb, a terrifying alternate-universe depiction of 1855 Britain transformed into a satanic slum by Babbage's eponymous computer; but the fact remains that Dickens – whose fever-dreams Gibson and Sterling have, perhaps all unconsciously, ransacked – is conspicuously absent from a book otherwise stuffed with real authors, and that absence shuts the book's mouth.

Colin Greenland won the Arthur C Clarke Award for *Take Back Plenty* (Unwin), a space opera whose exuberance is perhaps a touch lucubrated, but whose intelligence and tact shine constantly through. Joe Haldeman's *The Hemingway Hoax: A Short Comic Novel of Existential Terror* (Morrow) also grows in the mind's eye, a revision not harmed by acquaintance with the subtitle (omitted from the British edition): as the book is everything claimed for it: funny, horrific, short, about Hemingway, and (like any good tale of parallel worlds) the tale it tells fucks essence. In restored form, *The Stand* (Hodder & Stoughton) by Stephen King is even more like a new novel than *Stranger in a Strange Land*, having been reassembled, recast, rewritten, refurnaced into a thousand pages of flow and gush and slag and gem, a book Paul Bunyan might have written had he managed to outstare W H Auden, whose libretto for Benjamin Britten's *Paul Bunyan* transmogrifies into culture hero the axe-wielding Caliban of Maine. Nancy Kress (in her alpha person novitiate) gave us

Brain Rose (Morrow), getting a few more tropes under her belt (each book improving, traversing larger snatches of the territory), exploring (this time) the narrative possibilities of the human brain, Previous Life Access Surgery into the hinterlands, diseases in the world which wipe the maps of memory and blind the cast: memory and perception, as we have begun to learn, being one. After quite a few books which failed to gain the high ground, Michael Kube-McDowell finally wrote, in *The Quiet Pools* (Ace), a tale whose premise was strong enough to catch the mind. Humanity is genetically divided into two unequal segments: those billions of us compelled to remain upon the home planet, and those few capable of departing, like butterflies of exogamy escaping a sewer.

It was good to see something like the return of Ursula K LeGuin, though *Tehanu* (Atheneum), an ostensible sequel to the Earthsea trilogy, was less a reunion than an imposition of *curfew*. It was like a cop in the treehouse. The grown woman at the narrative heart of *Tehanu* lives in a different world than the lads who played at Eden in bramble archipelagos, incarnadining like berries the world-sea of the garden of longing, but to say so was not to tell us what we did not know: it was to blindfold us with rectitude. Farewell Ged. *Only Begotten Daughter* (Morrow) continued to test – as only James Morrow can – the tensile limits of whimsy, so that the brilliant segments of this novel, just as in his previous books, overdosed on *wry*, overdosed on *worldly-wise-owl*, overdosed on *nice conceits*. Bill Ransom's *Jaguar* (Ace) also wore its virtue, though not upon its mutton sleeve, as its Vietnam-vet protagonist accumulated, slowly, in dream world after dream world, bad karma: and paid. Kim Newman, not for the first time, married *film noir* and the subconscious in *Bad Dreams* (Simon & Schuster UK). Mike Resnick's *Second Contact* (Tor) beetled through old genre crap like salts, but why. With *Pacific Edge* (Unwin), Kim Stanley Robinson concluded his Orange County sequence, three novels which stack vertically to make a palimpsest, each volume expressing a different calculus of the future in the same place [the sequence has now been published in one volume as *Three Californias* (1995) 1995]. This time it was utopia, or as close to the pale fires of utopia as we might wish to earn: planet-maintenance; softball; enforced miniaturization of corporate life; softball; the centrality of the polis; softball. *The Hollow Earth* (William Morrow) by Rudy Rucker took on board a much younger Edgar Allen Poe than sf novelists in 1990 *usually give space to*, sending him down a Symmesian polar hole into a hollow Earth, making the book a kind of sequel to *The Narrative of Arthur Gordon Pym* (1838), which text the incorrigible Panshin Gang claims, in *The World Beyond the Hill* (1989), Poe "broke off short, unable to nerve himself to enter and stay": poor, feeble, hidebound, pre-Doc-Smith Edgar Allan Poe, born too soon to dare to dream the big dream and *stay* there like a man, like we do.

In *Orbitsville Judgement* (Gollancz), Bob Shaw keeps something of the scale of his Dyson Sphere world, while dinkytoying the plot into melancholy doodle; but Charles Sheffield plunges into the gigantic artifact universe of *Summertide* (Del Rey) with swelling glee, makes a meal of the hugeness. Lucius Shepard's *Kalimantan* (Century) is set in a 1980s Borneo iridescent with belatedness, for the book is a parody-with-love of the scientific romance and Joseph Conrad, horripilating with that genre's anxieties about toppling off the thin plate of the illuminated world into the Universal Anarch swallowing All. *Hyperion Cantos* (SFBC for the omnibus), a title Dan Simmons seems to have selected to comprehend *Hyperion* (1989) and *The Fall of Hyperion* (Doubleday Foundation), makes almost seamlessly one novel, though the second volume, which bases itself on Keats's second poem about coup d'étating the gods, imitates at times its model's spasms of failed rapprochement with the great subject: but in the end Simmons's extraordinary concentration on the job of juggling his immensely complicated plot does pay off, and the book emerges phoenixlike from the dross and Sevagram of sf's space-opera tradition. *Hyperion Cantos* may be the first full-grown space opera ever written (this reviewer has called it an entelechy opera [see p. 222–223 below], but that's another tack). Rising like Excalibur from a slurry of sharecrops and series-fillers, Brian Stableford's *The Werewolves of London* (Simon & Schuster UK) utterly transformed the werewolves-are-our-elder-cousins-from-the-dawn-of-time novel into a discourse on the nature of the Victorian worldview. This discourse – being genuine – sucked the blood right out of the poor werewolves, who were fake: good. Nothing exceptional had seemed likely to come from John E Stith, a part-time author of several mildly virtuous novels, until this year, with *Redshift Rendezvous* (Ace), a hard-sf romp into a hyperspace whose fundamental laws differ from ours: the plot wambled, ideas turned the pages: good.

Raising the Stones (Doubleday Foundation) by Sheri S Tepper, set in the same unforgiving universe as *Grass* (1989), continued to raise the ante on reading her without fail-safes: when she tosses off crap, the intelligence is too sharp for the text and the language too canny, and the stuff goes rogue in the mind: and a book like this one, a complex, booby-trapped assault on the integrity of "man," utterly fails to absent itself. So you can never get away from it. Ian Watson's *The Flies of Memory* (Gollancz), a mere bagatelle from the gadfly of the Western world, did manage to pack into relatively few pages half a dozen protagonists, eight cosmologies, ten gods a-leaping, and a few laughs; the book was brilliant but fidgety, skating over the ocean of story like a goosed waterbug. In *The Divide* (Doubleday Foundation), Robert Charles Wilson anatomized split minds, staying strictly on the slicks of the surface of these things. The death on page one of a character who may have been King Arthur initiates a musical-chairs guignol of recruitment in Gene Wolfe's *Castleview* (Tor), set in the far west of modern Illinois, and a final Arthur re-enacts the primal drama in jig time: to touch the book with the mind's eye was to stumble from the shock: but the book climaxes with such bravura speed that all aesthetics of ending are scorched: and the shock finds no ground. The closet-drama Vertigo Baroque of *Heathern* (Unwin) chilled some readers of Jack Womack's third novel, which is set in the near-future Manhattan of the previous two, but a small moral allegory did peep through the cinders, saying *Listen*. It was possible to.

There were some newer writers. Relevance to the times did not seem generally to overcome them. In *The Land Beyond: A Fable* (Unwin), Gill Alderman submitted her planet Guna to some dry-deluge plotting that sucked the moisture from the very soil; Terry Dowling's *Rynosseros* (Adelaide: Aphelion) knuckled under to Cordwainer Smith's vision of Norstrilia, without the plot line or the potty poetry; Scott Edelman's *The Gift* (Space and Time) was a gay vampire novel, gandy dancing for AIDS; Gregory Feeley's *The Oxygen Barons* (Ace) applied a dry-ice virus to the tropes of hard sf, more than becoming its model; *The Hour of Blue* (North Country) by Robert Froese did, with some energy, address the condition of the Earth; Elizabeth Hand's *Winterlong* (Bantam), though something of a wallow, seemed slim and supple and muscular if you did a mental edit: and the writing was both shadowy and exuberant; Lisa Mason's *Arachne* (Morrow) was almost too expert in its renewal of cyberpunk turns; Judith Moffett, in *The Ragged World: a Novel of the Hefna on Earth* (St Martin's Press), yanked Zenna Henderson into the big city; Allen Steele set *Clarke County, Space* (Ace) in Clarke County, Space, and seemed content to settle there.

And that was the year we had, a better year in which to write sf than to read it. But we're century migrants, the lip of time is sucking fast, wait for next year, some revelation is at hand. In the 25 [29 1995] years since this reviewer – since I – first published in *New Worlds*, whole logjams of books have passed downstream to the sea, which bought them all. In 1966 it seemed urgent to read on, because the next book might well contain some code for seeing things in the light, exposing the morrow; enfranchisement now for mortals! But the books turned out fictional, as one had thought they might, and sank waterlogged downwards: holed like the years. And if I continue to read now, 110,000 hours later [more than that 1995], it is not to gain wisdom (I failed) but to taste the mind of the makers. Grasping is what seems to count, a posture that dances the time jig: not answers. If all we can see is shadows on the walls of the cave, let their loins be girded. This year shadows were cast once or twice, in novels by Thomas Pynchon, Dan Simmons, Brian Stableford, Sheri Tepper, Kurt Vonnegut: not necessarily the best books read, but the ones most pugnacious to shape. And the year turned, and the shadows dance. I may awake one morning from uneasy dreams and find myself transformed.

– *New Worlds* 1 (Gollancz, 1991), ed, David Garnett

2. INTERZONE COLUMNS

Flopsy, Dropsy, Cottontail

I.

IT IS NOT EASY to think that Storm Constantine is much into qualms. The four books she has written so far hook at the reader with barbs on that face up the throat. Along with some pleasures of the text, the three Wraeththu novels (gesundheit) have managed to ask one to cope (for instance) with a cast of keening deathly-pale children, a version of power relations between the sexes that no man could have dared (or, sanely, have wished) to utter, a relentless dowsing of every lay of the land for signs of androgyny-which-is-next-to-godliness, and a span of attention to matters of plot and structure that would put a jumping-bean on edge; but all the same, in their weird breezy loping-onwardness of diction, there was a dangerous delighted fluency to the books.

And now a new (non-Wraeththu) title has arrived, *The Monstrous Regiment* (Orbit, 1989), a juicy whiplash slap of a tale which is patently not a singleton, though her publishers have presented it as a one-off; and which is not really meant for grown-ups either, though the text boasts further overflows of androgyny-dowsing, lots of sex-gushes homo and hetero, indelicate obeisances to a Man-God who saves the bacon of a flock of Henny-Penny females, hurried swipes at scenes of torture and and bull-dykery, a castration or two (recollected in tranquillity), and a simple old sadistic life-spoiling clitorectomy which gets out of hand. But there's nothing necessarily adult in any of this, even when Constantine's trying real hard to be horrid. *The Monstrous Regiment* is in fact (I'm afraid I'm going to steal a phrase I've already used in a capsule comment elsewhere) a menarche weepie.

In the heart of a rather wholesome swamp at the edge of that part of the planet Artemis which has been settled by humans, a young girl named Corinna lives in a great farm complex called Vangery (a name used again and again in sentences whose rhythms tend to evoke Daphne du Maurier – "Last night I dreamt I went to Manderley again" – but seemingly without a forethought). At Vangery Corinna has grown up under a benevolent rural matriarchy, one much milder than that the tyranny imposed upon the city of Silven Crescent, the urban centre of Artemis, where the dread Dominatrix dwells, ruler of the planet (it is, of course, a hereditary position: dominance usually is in weepies). The plot begins. Dire rumours begin to drift into the rather wholesome swamp, conveyed mainly by Elvon L'Belder, a charismatic young man who has escaped arrest and who later fucks young Corinna *really nicely* after she has saved him from General Carmenya Oralien, who has stopped at Vangery while hotly in pursuit (in fab leather) of the male rebel, and who starts to fancy the still-virgin-but-queuing lass. After Carmenya leaps off-page with a sparky leer to await Corinna in Silven Crescent, L'Belder begins to spill the beans. The current Dominatrix ("Screw this Life-Presidentatrix-in-Perpetuity-and-All-my-Female-Offspring-Too crap," we can imagine the first ruler of Artemis telling her assembled Senatrixes, "Why not just call me *Dominatrix*? I get first dibs on leather") has gone right round the twist, is about to forbid all intercourse between the sexes, and plans ultimately to have all men put into cages, where they can be milked of seed without contaminating real people. This is feminism gone too far! ruminates the sagacious L'Belder.

So gloom abounds in Vangery when Corinna leaves for Silven Crescent to become Carmenya's love-slave, and gloom should. Very soon (after sleeping with the dextrous, fabulously garbed general) Corinna manages to offend the Dominatrix, who duly has her arrested and sent to the interrogation chambers of the palace. "Another general waited in the room they marched her to, a stranger. This woman was heavily built, definitely man-like, with cropped greying hair and a square jaw marked on the left side by a deep, irregular scar." Oh-oh. But let us not be unfair. It may *sound* as though Constantine is describing a bull-dyke straight out of any World War Two Nazi Deathsquad Rubber SS Leather Whip Stink Head-Shave Gestapo Bull-Dyke-Tortures-Virgin porno film, but no. This particular bull-dyke may be tough all right, but she's fair. She may knock Corinna to the floor, but she *does not rape her*, and when she finally boots the lass off to be mutilated by gloating medicos, she does so almost with affection. Bondage rites and cunnilingus and extensive surgery soon follow, and Corinna is once again ushered into the presence of the Dominatrix (whom we discover drunk and masturbating in her inner sanctum while a throng of male slaves fucks a female slave for her pleasure), and it begins to look pretty grim for the plucky teenager, but just in the nick of time Elvon (who has meanwhile been transfigured by the mystical Greylids into an Apollonian phallus) materializes in front of the batty Dominatrix and zonks her with his augmented masculine principle, but the Dominatrix (who is not your typical garden-variety dotty Dominatrix) has (it suddenly turns out) mystical psychic powers too (we are almost at the end of the book) and slobbers awful female-zone psychic muck right back at the vast, compassionate, radiantly lit prong, and the whole heart of Silven Crescent bursts into uneasy paranormal flames, and Corinna (who has very wisely done a flit) now gathers together a covey of hysterical females, leads them to Vangery, introduces them to some nice men, and as the novel closes with a brief Dear Diary epilogue she can be glimpsed entering, with a faithful few, into the old science fantasy one-two shuffle your shoe diaspora rag.

So why spend time on the book? Bad anti-feminist female fantasy novels cross-dressing as sf – with rocket ships stuck like falsies to their heaving bosoms – must be a dime a doyenne, and *The Monstrous Regiment* must only stand out (in 1990) for the utter dippiness of its presentation of the "issues." But there are compensations. The first chapters of *Regiment*, set in the fertile farmed swamps of Vangery, flow with verisimilitude, detail-work, gossip; artfully cupped in the hands of the book, the farm and her inhabitants seem to have been given to us, gratis, to cherish beyond the needs of plot (which does very soon dump us in the coils of Camp Dominatrix). And human relationships at the farm are hinted at with a quick sure hand. Much of the tale is indeed told with a deftness that seems almost silken, a lubricated slithery ease of diction that makes one long for more. Storm Constantine, in other words, is a writer of flow and strength, a writer who rewards allegiance. What she has most balefully not done in *The Monstrous Regiment* is earn it.

II.

The sacrifice of Stephen Gallagher upon the banality-of-evil altar of Horror contin-ues, in *Rain* (New English Library, 1990), to cause dismay. He is a craftsman, a wordsmith, a builder of stories, a writer of balance and burden and wrath. But he continues to obey the prime diktat of Horror (which is: Kill the Sharer) like some despondent monk upon a column. In their terrible I-told-you-so pessimism about the roots of the world, texts written as Horror must follow a fixed curve of plot from the live complexities of the "surface" of things downwards to the parched simplex of the dark, where nothing ever need join again, for joining is at the risk of life. In the end, Horror loves to be safe. It has a dropsy for the banal. So why does Gal-lagher obey its yawn? The touch of his hand in the page is something real. His pen seems to want things for us. For most of its length, *Rain* is a beautifully written book. The world it leaves – the Midlands, the Motorways, fragments of the great myth of life in London – is almost pugnaciously true to the touch. The protagonist – except during those passages meant to suggest that she herself is the murderer of the sister whose murderer she seeks – haunts one with her dumbness, her acuities, the human warp and woof of her obsessional hunt. But the world *Rain* eventually enters – through the slow reductionist unveiling of the villain and his psyche and his motives and the things he tries to do – has all the Stylite smugness and aridity of any assumption of Denial. (And only readers unwilling to admit that Gallagher was writing Horror could fail to know, after ten pages or so, who that villain was.) In the closing pages of the book, a strained bollix of plot-turns pumps things to a climax of sorts, but the solitude of its refusal to share worlds with the Other has by now deadened the eye (the moral-uplift escape of the girl seems not so much unearned as unmeaning) and we turn off. And that, of course, is the final horror; that Horror turns the reader off.

That we die a little.

III.

In 1986, Christine Brooke-Rose published an odd little novel called *Xorandor*, and we now have a sequel. The title once again bandies words. The subject (and the mode) of *Verbivore* (Carcanet, 1990) is once again a play on words, dictions, information, genres, word-worlds. The book is an sf story (it is, in other words, a presenting of an sf set of words). It is also a juvenile (a mode of writing in which words are brought smartly forward in their texts to habituate us and to teach). It contains a radio play (which we read), letters and journals (mostly written), the indited words of conversations overheard, memories of the wording of the book to which it is a sequel, transmissions and static and gaps of silence. In its sharp prim way, it is a very noisy book. Its subject, all the same, is silence.

Twenty-three years have passed since the two children – Jip and Zab – of *Xorandor* discovered the eponymous sentient-computer-rock whose race had inhabited Earth for many aeons, helped it come to word-grips (for what else is a computer but a language of grips) with the extraordinary radiation-data-gush of the wee night mammals who had come, in the binary of an eye, to cover the planet. That book had closed with Xorandor eating the gist of bombs, and saving us all. *Verbivore* opens with a broken sentence in a world transfigured into the words that tell it (rather like the world today), a world of data nets and beams and weddings, a world-noise of information. And Xorandor's children – he is now apparently dead on Mars – cannot stand the barking. They do not know how *not* to eat data, data stuffs their gullets, they are like pâté-de-fois geese. So to save themselves they shut things down. Everything that generates waves falls silent. Planes crash, computers and radios and all the media-waves flatten into peace. The twins, Jip and Zab, now estranged and professional and eminent, come together with the dreadful intuition that they know what has caused the silence, which they do. The plot thickens and squabbles onwards, imitating words of all sorts. The end (the book shuts) is silence. The moments of high quick quaint cottontail fun have gulled us. The brightness shuts.

At some moments of its diction, *Verbivore* remains a children's book (though the children are now grown); at others, it continues to chatter sf (but in perky quotes). The effect, perhaps designedly, is of meta-discourse couched in a tone both alienated and wise-acre. Unfortunately, it soon becomes evident that the book is rather less deft at its wording than the models it kibitzes. At moments when it should be dicing with death, *Verbivore*, for all its monitory zing, has a damaging tendency to tell Granny how to suck eggs. Genre foregrounding, after all, is what genre books *do*. In a sense, it is all they do. In their bones, genre persons know this (what could be more self-referential than a fandom), but Brooke-Rose seems to have learned genres in the way Margaret Mead learned Polynesians. *Growing up with Verbivore* may be wise, sharp, clever, learned, sad and gripping.

But it is also very *bossy*.

– Interzone 36, June 1990

Oh, Good

I.

OH, GOOD. It is the end of March, fevers fill the blood, afternoons lengthen into the boomerang of summer, three new Terry Pratchetts plop onto the desk like magic, here we are in England, here is the Spring. It must never cease. And how fitting it is to anticipate yet another Comedy set in the Discworld, which returns like the seasons, a sign of the wealth of Spring, brand-new each birthing, Ouroboros fresh from moult. Our only problem is that none of the Pratchetts on the desk is in fact a Comedy. One of them, *Good Omens: The Nice and Accurate Prophecies of Agnes Nutter, Witch* (Gollancz, 1990), a collaboration with Neil Gaiman, is in fact a *novel*; and the other two are part of a series which differs radically from the Discworld comedies in that *Truckers* (Doubleday, 1989) and *Diggers* (Doubleday, 1990) are not only meant for children, they are meant to *end*. And although that may be a problem for any reader caught in the eternal Wimbledon of spring fever, it is in fact good news that this is so.

This reviewer has suggested [see p. 164] that it might be worth-while to define the Discworld books as pure comedies (rather than comic novels); to treat them, in other words, as tales which took their shape, and passed on the exhilaration, of the original season-dance of classic Comedy, that version of the Myth of the Eternal Return which says: Let the Dead arise, let the Play continue. Regarding future books (I further suggested), it would be good to see Pratchett continue to quarantine his Discworld template from the lure of the novel, which took its driving shape from classic Tragedy, from that version of the Myth of the Eternal Return which says: Again again again again Winter. Tragedy was a different drum. And every novel in the world, whether or not comic in intention, marched to its beat. *Good Omens*, the forthcoming collaboration with Neil Gaiman, would almost certainly be a comic novel, a vaudeville descant on the underlying tune, and that would be well.

No words need to be eaten, quite. *Good Omens* is indeed comic, and it is indeed a model novel. It begins with the Beginning (according to Bishop Ussher), and ends with the End (according to *Revelations*). And the stink of Faust lies deep in its bones, though deodorized in the telling. It is not, in other words, a Comedy. But is it any good? Yes and no and yes. It is very funny indeed (yes), though bedevilled throughout by neurotic *nudzhings* of narrative focus and galumphing tonal shifts (no), and in the end it shines through (yes). It is a very strange book indeed; perhaps all genuine collaborations are. The storyline – a Boy Antichrist is born in England to grow up and start the Final Battle, but an angel and a demon collaborate (like two authors) to avert the approaching End – does display a Gaimanesque loucheness, a slight over-familiarity with Apocalypse, and the large cast – dorks and devils, witches and the Four Horsemen, children's book children who live in an Ealing paradise, and an angel disguised as a antiquarian bookseller – does display something of the Pinocchio clarity of the citizens of Discworld; but who conceived or wrote what in this book it would be foolish to guess.

The funniest sequences of *Good Omens* sound like Pratchett with a shot of Gaiman for stiffeners; the foot-shuffling story-bites that over-fill the first half of the book make the authors sound rather like two Falstaffs trying to get through one small door together without coming to blows; and the long intricacies of comic story-telling that redeem the book in its second half sound like the fugue Falstaff conducts at the end (in Verdi's version) before going back into the hearsay of *Henry V* to die (in Shakespeare's). But who wrote what (on what disk) might be hard even for the authors to say. Of the Four Horsemen, Pollution (née Pestilence) *sounds* like a Gaiman inspiration, and Death (who speaks in caps) comes directly from Discworld; but to suggest a provenance is very far from identifying the main author of any one sequence. Some lines – those, for instance, in which nuns are described as being the proper shape for staying quiet, "like those pointy things you got in those chambers Mr Young was vaguely aware your hi-fi got tested in" – are typical of Gaiman, whose writing typically sounds as though spoken, with gestures; and some entire scenes –for instance, an extraordinarily funny exchange, set in a Motorway Service Centre, between a human Hell's Angel and Death – are in turn typical of Pratchett, whose work always sounds *written*, and whose sense of timing is exquisite but completely non-gesticulatory (but what Death and the human Angel say to one another is surely what Gaiman would have them say: and maybe he did). Throughout there are hints of a surfacing rhetoric of violent warfare between opposing principles (Gaiman), but always the villains fade away, or turn into accomplices, or simply kerplop (Pratchett). And so on.

Good Omens is an affair of masks, a congeries of blessings in disguise, and a synergy in the end. The two authors paired, and did not lay an egg, and parted. A good time was had. It's harder to know about *Truckers* and *Diggers*, perhaps because the story being told in these two volumes will not reach its climax for another volume [*Wings* (1990) 1995]. Nor is it necessarily the case that the covers by Josh Kirby (who does the Discworld books as well) much help to gain focus on the tale. The Discworld comedies were written for (and are generally read by) adults, and we are generally able to laugh along with the crowded, joyful, comic and quite probably loving ironies of Kirby's cartoon approach. But the nomes of *Truckers* and its sequels will be understood by its young readers (and were almost certainly created by Pratchett) in a much straighter, more "serious" vein. What to an adult reader of Discworld might seem loving spoofery could well be felt by a ten- or twelve-year-old as condescension, certainly when applied to the frailties and modest heroics of the *Truckers* cast. Fittingly for an adult artist, Kirby draws his Discworld figures as though our ultimate disbelief in them were part of the game; but his covers for the new series (almost fatally for a children's book) seem *knowing*.

Pratchett himself does not make the mistake. His four-inch-tall nomes, who have forgotten they are the descendents of the crew of an interstellar ship whose landing craft crashed on Earth 15,000 years earlier, are not cute. In *Truckers*, young Masklin leads his diminished clan from certain death in the countryside to a new life inside Arnold Bros (est 1905), a giant department store, where other clans of nomes have prospered for many generations (nomes live only about a decade). At the head of each chapter can be found an excerpt from *The Book of Nome* articulating in Biblical terms the resident nomes' sense of having found safe haven; these passages are as funny as anything Pratchett has ever written, and touching as well, because the open-eyed Masklin soon begins to understand that Arnold Bros (est 1905) is about to close forever. *Truckers* tells of Masklin's reluctant assumption of leadership, the slow growth of his understanding of the foibles of his people as he persuades them they must leave, the beginning of the long search Outside for the real Home. Rather disappointingly, we witness in *Diggers* the quest-split typical of second volumes of trilogies; while Masklin scuttles off-page with an ancient computer relic from long ago to find a way back to the orbiting mother-ship, we are stuck with his brave girl-friend and her efforts (topologically identical to Masklin's in volume one) to keep the nomes safely together. The department store of *Truckers* is replaced by a quarry in *Diggers*, and the only genuinely new character, a fundamentalist nome who briefly corrupts the Folk, soon kicks the bucket, one more victim of Pratchett's deep reluctance of imagination when evil gnaws the bone; as in most Volumes Two, all the climaxes are false. Volume Three will bring the nomes to space, and a view of their ancient Home (we hope), and the coda.

II.

And if we put *The Quiet Woman* (Bloomsbury, 1990) down before we finish the last page, we will be demonstrating a certain dumb fortitude. It is by a very considerable extent the most cunningly readable book Christopher Priest has ever written, and although the final chapters may almost seem *sarcastic* in their sedulous tying up of loose narrative knots, the result is a tale to hold whole in the mind's eye, a codebook to decipher its predecessors with. We are not exactly in the world of *A Dream of Wessex* (1977), or *The Affirmation* (1981), with which the current volume shares (in some sense) a protagonist, or *The Glamour* (1984), but a dream/reality interface operates throughout *The Quiet Woman* just as varyingly it does in the previous books, and the central characters (once again) are makers (and victims of) worlds of the imagination. There are three main figures. The eponymous Eleanor Hamilton, who is dead when the book begins, was in early life an author of children's books; her neighbour and friend, the slightly dogged Alice Stockton, caught by poverty and obsession in rural Wiltshire, is also a writer; and the third protagonist, who is Eleanor's son, and who calls himself either Gordon Sinclair or Peter Hamilton (the protagonist of *The Affirmation* goes by the name of Peter Sinclair), and who tells his portions of the tale in the first person, has from early childhood developed a dream-world not unlike a drab Dream Archipelago, into which he dives to escape his mother's coercive story-telling; it is a technique he uses, in later life, as a kind of model to shape the "real" world with.

That world is ours, a few years hence. A nuclear power station in France has (in prophetic accordance with press predictions made long after Priest would have turned *The Quiet Woman* in to Bloomsbury) suffered meltdown, and much of southern England lies under an intersecting fug of radiation and censorship. As head of a firm which has obtained some prime government contracts in "statutory information management" after the privatizing of the security services, Peter is in a strong position to reshape the data of reality upon his computer screens (at one point he Deletes a secondary character who has been staying with Alice Stockton, an injunction which Priest, perhaps rather flirtatiously, seems to obey for several pages). His mother (whose last years seem to have been based on the life of the murdered nuclear campaigner, Hilda Morrell) has been murdered, while at the same time the Home Office has confiscated the manuscript of Alice's last book, a non-fiction study called *Six Women*. Priest's portrait of Alice and her fight to survive is surprisingly sympathetic from this author; but his rendering of Peter (who is just the latest in a series of creative monsters) is savage.

The Quiet Woman is astonishingly full of plot. The portrait it presents of tomorrow's England far exceeds in deftness and oppression the Thatcherite desert created by Ian McEwan in *The Child in Time*, and reads as almost seamlessly plausible; Alice Stockton's persecution (at Peter's hands) is similarly convincing. The plot-turns and devices which savage the "real" world have at first an air of flittering irreality familiar to readers of *The Quiet Woman*'s stablemates, but in the end the world proves to have more substance than earlier Priest-plays on the dream/reality organon have ever accorded to consensual reality – and mysteries are solved and Peter Gordon Sinclair Hamilton bites the bullet of the Real. And a good thing too. He is a creep, a vampire, and a spy. His ultimate defeat may just be a further dream – the excessive neatness of the final pages serves as an extremely broad hint that this may be so – but it is possible to close *The Quiet Woman* in a beam of light.

Oh, good.

It is nice to pretend our dreams will boot.

– *Interzone* 37, July 1990

The True and Blushful Chutzpah

THERE ARE figures and there are carpets. Dan Simmons, the author of *Song of Kali* (1985), was a figure of the carpet. The author of *Song of Kali*, and *Carrion Comfort* (1989), and *Phases of Gravity* (1989), and *Hyperion* (1989), and *The Fall of Hyperion* (1990) has become one of the writers who shapes the carpet of genre, a prodigy born out of the warp and woof who gives his own figuring back as gift – and burden of influence – to the next-born. *Phases of Gravity*, which is the best historical novel about an ex-astronaut yet written [and one of the clearests signals yet issued by a genre writer that First SF is indeed a told story 1995], escapes our current remit, so we'll restrict ourselves to *Carrion Comfort* (Dark Harvest), and to the two-volume novel whose individual titles – *Hyperion* (Doubleday Foundation) and *The Fall of Hyperion* (Doubleday Foundation) – are the titles of John Keats's two unfinished long poems of 1818–19 on the fall of the Old Gods. Very roughly, *Carrion Comfort* runs to something over 400,000 words, and *Hyperion Cantos* to slightly less. Each of them is about six times the size of a normal novel. Each of them is superb. In neither huge tale is there a single deliberately wasted word.

That is the first of the Three Courtesies of Dan Simmons. It is the courtesy of craft. *Carrion Comfort* and *Hyperion Cantos* are not the first novels in the field to nudge the half-million mark – one thinks of Austin Tappan Wright's *Islandia* (1942), J R R Tolkien's *The Lord of the Rings* (1954–1955), Gene Wolfe's *The Book of the New Sun* (1980–1983), the restored version of Stephen King's *The Stand* (1990) – and it might be noted that at least two of the four monsters just mentioned do in fact fully justify their length. But it's not that simple. As with icebergs, most of *Islandia* and *The Lord of the Rings* never reach the surface; written down in private, over many years, they are in fact narrative emissions – concentrated despite their length – of desperately prolonged, subterranean fantasy-lives, and were only slowly wrestled into shape – brought up into the air – as books. *The Book of the New Sun*, by a professional author noted for his skill and concentration and speed, still took much of a decade to complete, and remains by far his fullest telling of the pulse of theogony. In its new incarnation *The Stand* remains an enigma to this reviewer (who has not read it) but may well point the same lesson – that books of substance grow huge when lives are staked to them. But for Dan Simmons – at first glance – this terraforming stress and extremity of motive does not seem to hold. There is a gaming, architectonic exhilaration to his work (just as there is in C J Cherryh's), a sort of homo faber flush at the joy of building, that seems almost its own reward. At first glance it looks as though he writes huge novels because he *likes* to write huge novels, and that his love of doing so derives from his competence to do so. The first courtesy of Dan Simmons is that – whatever his inner demons may in fact demand – he writes huge books as a professional might: as a professional in love with his children.

The second of the Three Courtesies of Dan Simmons – which is the courtesy of orthodoxy – is harder to describe. It is a respect for the conventions of fantasy and sf that goes far beyond lip-service or, for that matter, belief. What Simmons may himself affirm about vampires and God and Zen AI's and Keats is not for this reviewer to ask, and in any case neither *Carrion Comfort* nor *Hyperion Cantos* reads like an act of belief (in the way that *The Lord of the Rings* and *The Book of the New Sun* assuredly do). Their behaviour as texts is nothing like that. *Carrion Comfort* and *Hyperion Cantos* work as acts of *obedience*. The first is a text obedient to the idea of the horror novel (with an sf spinal fix). The other wrings to their uttermost the tropes of orthodox sf, with a hugeness of devotion hard perhaps to comprehend fully. If the two novels are revolutionary in their effect – and they are – it is because literal obedience to the dictates of a faith (or a genre) violates the make-do worldliness of your normal subscriber (or pro); it is because it's frightening to do the thing right. If they are great books – they are certainly great books of genre – it is because they stand out like idiot saints of the cloth in a scrum of commuters and *profess the faith*.

In other words, they embarrass us.

I mean, how dumb can you get? I mean, this here's a grown man, and here he's telling us we must believe in the likes of *Carrion Comfort*, a horror novel faithful for hundreds of thousands of words to the dumbed-down fleering nada-nada at the heart of Horror as a genre. How could he mean a word he says? How could he work so hard on the thing? How could he be *obedient*? The base premise he accepts, as in most horror novels, is shiveringly un-new. Through mutant psychic access to the hind brains of normal humans (he wants us to believe), a new strain of humanity has evolved the ability to control the behaviour of others, to see through their eyes, to feast on their peak experiences. It is a premise capable of generating all sorts of outcomes – depending on the genre chosen, the bearers of this power might evolve into supermen, compassionate starfarers, hermits, burnt-out cases, gestalts, Michaelmases (as in *Michaelmas* [1977] by A J Budrys). But *Carrion Comfort* is a horror novel, and Simmons is a saint of the cloth, and he offers his readers an outcome obedient to the dictates of the mode he has professed. His mutants duly turn out to be psychic vampires who despise normal folk, and rape them, and torture them, and experience vicarious orgasms when they kill them. But feeding (which, in the novel of horror, is a form of empowerment [the entry on THINNING, in the forthcoming *Encyclopedia of Fantasy*, develops the argument implied here 1995]) has an addictive effect on them; the more they eat, the more ravenous they become.

In 1980, as we slowly begin to learn, it all begins to come unstuck. By now there are two sets of vampires in America. The first is a group of three – they derive from the 1983 novelette version of the book – though only a Southern spinster-belle named Melanie and an ex-Death-Camp Commandant named Willie are of any importance. The second group, dominated by the coldly immaculate financier and éminence grise C Arnold Barent, comprises an alliance of men of power, who come together once a year on a private island off the South Carolina coast to play the game of Wild Hunt with human pawns, after the model of Sarban's The Sound of His Horn (1952). Commandant Willie himself is obsessed with the game of chess, particularly when humans are used as pieces, and decides to challenge Barent to a secret match, with the rest of the cast as figures on the great board of the world, and membership in the island club as ostensible reward for thrashing the enigmatic tycoon (though he cannot of course be trusted to stop there). To begin proceedings (only in hindsight does the reader understand what's been happening from the first page) Willie tricks spinster-belle Melanie (who narrates sections of the book in the first person) into fleeing in panic from her home in Charleston; the squirming turns of this flight – the sacrifices Melanie makes (of normals) to stay alive, the going to ground, the counter-attacks – are in fact moves in the game.

But an initial exchange of pieces in Charleston has caused a spate of extremely ugly deaths (savagely orchestrated by Simmons), and several innocent bystanders have been casually snuffed out, among them a middle-aged black freelance photographer out for a stroll. For a few pages, we forget him. But his daughter Natalie now steps into the novel (which, for a moment, reminds one of Buñuel's The Phantom of Liberty [1974]) and interrogates Bobby Lee Gentry, the college-educated fat sheriff of Charleston, himself already in consultation with Saul Laski, a Jewish survivor of the death-camps who has been hunting Willie for nearly half a century. What drives Natalie on is her refusal to accept the peripheralization of her father's death, as though he were an extra in some horror flick. The title of the novel is from a poem by Gerard Manley Hopkins – "Not, I'll not, carrion comfort, Despair, not feast on thee" – and it is at the moment of Natalie's refusal of the nada-nada that Carrion Comfort clicks suddenly into focus, begins to attract the genuine attention of the reader. It is at this moment that one understands how complex a thing obedience to premise can be for a writer like Simmons.

The whole ludicrous claptrap edifice of the modern horror genre –its sub-Covenant Despite, its stuporous nullity, its aping of Gothic anxieties – represents an argument about the world; and what Simmons most extraordinarily manages to do in Carrion Comfort is to write as though the premises of Horror were not too silly to be argued with. In Carrion Comfort, through the intense literalism of its adherence to the implications of the story told, he defends the world against the base argument of the genre, which is Kill the Sharer. Obedient, tender, deadpan, unembarrassable, he refuses to let a feather fall – or an bystander die – without following the event down. So the death of the human who is Natalie's father leads to Natalie, and

Natalie leads to Gentry and Saul, and they all lead one another through the cartoon twists of *Carrion Comfort*'s storyline, exposing (as they descend) those twists of genre to the felt immensities of human pain. Within the papier-mâché coils of a plot-apparatus Simmons never scants, Natalie and Gentry and Saul have the moving density of souls who must utter, and without ever violating a single convention of the genre they sink through the gross-outs and the poppycock and carry us with them. They carry us through the machinery of a plot seemingly too long-limbed to trace in the mind's eye, but never actually out of reach. We learn that the psychic vampirism of Willie and Barent is an evolutionary deadend, that a prolongation of infantile omniscience is fatally disabling, a way of entrapping human souls in solipsism's flabby maze. *Carrion Comfort*'s final argument with Horror is that power not only corrupts but makes *stupid*. The whole climax and denouement depend, with hallucinating veracity, on fatal mistakes of personality, with Willie and Barent destroying themselves in the end because their power has rendered them too morally dense to cope. Unsiblinged, unshared, they suffocate in a poisonous quicksand flab of self. The last pages of the book are like a trap that shuts, an argument that has been won. It is an extraordinary accomplishment.

The last of the Three Courtesies of Dan Simmons is *chutzpah*. It demonstrates itself in *Carrion Comfort* through the extreme immensity of the tale, and the chamber-opera precision of the plotting (the submarine reference on the very last page, for instance, is nothing if not saucy). But *Carrion Comfort* digs deep into the grounds of this single Earth, and sticks to a relatively small cast of characters whose density (as we've suggested) sinks through but does not violate the generic assumptions of the tale (while arguing them to death). The *Hyperion Cantos* – Simmons's encompassing title for the two books seen as a unit – are, on the other hand, set centuries hence, on a variegated Hegemony of human-dominated planets, ages after the destruction by black hole of Old Earth. The planets of this vast straddling Hegemony are held together by fatlines – quantum-level energy-leys through which squirts of information can be fed instantaneously – and by a Worldweb of farcasters – portals which physically connect the planets of the Worldweb through discontinuity-bridging worms. This Worldweb is operated, apparently for humanity's benefit, by the AI's of the TechnoCore, a Gibsonian datasphere long separate from human control, though no one knows where its hardwire substrate has hidden itself. Space travel is also available, via "Hawking" ships capable of a "rate" moderately greater than the speed of light; these ships are necessary to reach planets (like the fabled Hyperion) not yet connected to the Worldweb, and traveling to which incurs relativity-induced time-debts. Fortunately for space travellers, a planet of Templars (whose ecological imperatives derive from the work of the American naturalist John Muir) operates the occasional luxury interstellar tour via giant treeship. The time-debt-incurring traveller is also fortunate in that the Worldweb has enjoyed an historical calm for centuries (readers who remember Roderick Seidenberg and Jacques Ellul might find this post-historic stasis easy enough to parse). And finally, beyond the World-web and the unconnected planets, roam the Ousters, humans who inhabit space-colonies whose units – everything from space opera ramscouts and dreadnoughts up to huge "can cities" and "comet forts" – Simmons describes in terms which re-flect the recent marriage of cyberpunk to space opera. Ousters engage in bioengi-neering; Hegemony residents, rather strangely, do not. All this – it has been radical-ly simplified – might be described as the physical premise, the raw stage on which the Hyperion Cantos are told.

We're still a long way from the story itself.

Hyperion and The Fall of Hyperion are operas of the end of things. They are about what is going to happen to the shooting match. The first volume is about meeting the cast. Six men and one woman have been selected to make a pilgrimage to Hyperion, a planet whose quasi-religious significance for humans dates from the discovery there of the Time Tombs, vast and brutal sarcophagi which seem to be moving backwards through time, and of the monstrous Shrike, a creature it is im-possible to define, though it does boast a pelage of scissoring blades and four deadly arms (Simmons mentions the haze of knives and the four arms every time he brings the Shrike onstage, but this attempt at iconic engraving stumbles over Doubleday's cover artist's insistence upon drawing the creature with two arms, a Giacometti-pinecone torso, and Naugahyde hair); more importantly, the Shrike harvests Pain, giving an eternity of dying to those who approach it. The novel begins as the seven pilgrims meet for the first time on a Templar treeship, and begin there to re-enact The Canterbury Tales; at the same time the enigmatic four-armed knife-shrouded quasi-deity has started to range south of the Tombs, which themselves show signs of opening, as though the Time were ripe. There is going to be coming together, we sense, before we are set free.

Each of the pilgrims is pregnant with something. The Time is ripe. Each tale swells with secret burden. Woven into the very flesh of the Priest (#1) are two cruci-form parasites from Hyperion which serve as biological reproduction devices – one will replicate the priest himself if he manages to die; the other bears a parody of his mentor, the Teilhardian noosphere-guru Father Dure, thought to have died years ago upon the planet (but double-crossed by the Shrike). The Soldier (#2) bears within him the imago of a dream lover, whose name is Mnemosyne or Moneta, and who – like the Mnemosyne/Moneta of Keats's poems – watches, wards, wakes and guides the young Apollo who will dethrone the Old God. The Poet (#3) – the least successful of these typological cartoons – bears fragments of his own Cantos about the end of things, left uncompleted ages ago upon the planet. In his arms the Scholar (#4) carries his daughter, who is dying of Time Reversal inflicted upon her 25 years earlier during an archaeological dig in the Tombs; she loses a day each day, and is now a week old. As they tell their tales, the pilgrims land upon Hyperion, and trek northwards from the city of Keats into Shrike country; still mute, the Treeship Captain (#5) disappears into the Shrike-haunted wastelands. The Detective (#6) then tells her story. She bears in holo-scan format the outcome of a "pseudo-poet cybrid retrieval project" who turns out, of course, to be John Keats; she is, moreover, pregnant with their child. It will be a girl. And finally the Consul (#7) admits to being a traitor to the Hegemony he has served, because its blind expansion had caused the ecological rape of his home planet; he now conspires to hasten the opening of the Time Tombs.

And in this wise we near the end of *Hyperion*. The long pavane of Pilgrims' Tales – each told as a parody-with-love of the narrative conventions and style of the science fiction subgenre each represents – has moved us. We have been dazzled with quotation and trope, but we have not yet identified the Old Gods who must fall, and we do not yet recognize the New Gods – the Soldier being an unlikely avatar – who must supplant them. As the book closes, as the remaining six Pilgrims start together arm in arm down the Yellow Brick Road to the Tombs, we are further moved. And when Simmons turns the architectonic tearjerk screw on the scene, and actually dares to have them sing the actual song from *The Wizard of Oz* (1939), then we begin to share something of the homo faber flush, the true the blushful *chutzpah*.

And we tumble pellmell into *The Fall of Hyperion*, which is the title of Keats's second try at a subject he never quite got the hang of, and war has begun. Like dendrons in a maze, the plot thickens, the stately dance of tales becomes a polytonal scat. The balls are in the air. The Hegemony and the Ousters have gone to war over Hyperion, whose Tombs may contain vital keys to the "decision-branch megaverse" ahead. The Consul learns that Hegemony CEO Meina Gladstone had *chosen* him to go to Hyperion precisely because he would betray the WorldWeb, and help increase the disarray. The Keats cybrid conveys the Detective – her name, rather unfortunately, is Lamia Brawne – into a wrenching and hilarious rapport with a member of the most stable faction of the WorldWeb-sustaining AI's – those convinced that their campaign to build a God or Deus Ex Machina does not necessitate the elimination of starfaring humanity – and much is revealed. Bamboozled into stasis by farcasters, her citizens abjectly beholden to AI/Technocore implants for information and stimulus, the Hegemony must be dismantled, or the icy fixity of Seidenbergian post-history will flash-freeze the human race – or so the Meina Gladstone faction argues. Moreover, if the AI's who reside within the interstices of the farcaster net are not defeated, then the God Who abides within the quanta – and Who so loves the World that it has sent its Son (or Daughter) back through Time to re-invest the Universe with Love – may somehow lose the decision-branch fight and the Deus Ex Machina will triumph Up the Line, having already sent the Shrike backwards through Time to flush the saviour from Hyperion, the bait of the Shrike being pain.

The Fall of Hyperion begins to sew itself up. The Scholar gives his daughter to the vortex which will reverse her dying. The Poet scribbles – he's Simmons's sole blunder into unredeemable pulp – Cantos. The Soldier faces the Shrike in final combat. Lamia Brawne and Keats inhabit the world itself and so love the world. The Hegemony splinters. The Consul picks up the pieces. The dance of cataclysms begins to ebb. The good guys have won. The Old Gods are banished. Humans will enter history once again. The brightest sf novel ever crafted, the Summa Theologica of Entelechy Opera, ends in a game and dazzle of decorum. "Somewhere Over the Rainbow" is sung by all.

"Entelechy," a philosophical term, is variously defined as 1) that which contains or realizes a final cause or End, and 2) a "supramechanical agency, immanent in the organism and directing the vital process toward the realization of the normal whole or perfect organism." (I quote Webster's Second International.) It is, in other words, Something or Other inside us which shapes our Ends. Some theories of evolution, for instance, assume that biological change is governed not by chance but by some principle of entelechy, though Darwin did not. Astrologists batten on the human need for cod entelechies within our dying meat. Sf novels about the ultimate soul-shape of humanity, or about the final disposition of human societies in space, or about the relationship of cosmogony to individual fate, always assume that Something or Other within us, within the worms that Web the Worlds, within the very heart of the music of the spheres, shapes the End result.

Such Road-to-Entelechy sagas are certainly operatic – as conceived by Olaf Stapledon, and A E Van Vogt, and Arthur C Clarke, and Frank Herbert, and Gregory Benford, and Greg Bear, and David Brin; but not Brian Aldiss, whose Helliconia books seem deeply iconoclastic precisely because they are not entelechy-bound – but at the same time none of these books are space operas. They are Entelechy Operas. In the cocky grandeur of their scope, and in their through-composed traversal of all the tropes of genre, they are the extremest and most encompassing form of modern sf. If they are to be done at all, they should be done by authors who command high spinto intensities of craft, unembarrassable orthodoxy, and *chutzpah*; by authors capable at the close of slingshotting their readers into star-burn.

As *The Fall of Hyperion*, for example, comes to a close, we learn that the daughter of Lamia Brawne and John Keats will rule the Sevagram.

Entelechy burns.

– Interzone 38, August 1990

Mine! All Mine!

1.

Earth is the name, earthen is the weight, David Brin is *Earth* (Bantam, 1990), we might be in for a tussle. This reviewer (for starters) is moderately ambivalent about one-word titles that sound as though their authors claimed ownership of the patch pointed at. *Grass, Dune, Moon, Earth, It, Universe, Eternity.* Titles of this sort don't address the world; they tell us they are the address. But we must not presume. *Earth* may in fact speak to the issues of the planet, not purloin them. It may be humble with its burden. We may need to thank David Brin for bringing us some news. Let us knock on *Earth* and see if Mother's in.

Alex Lustig, a bright young scientist of the 21st century, has devised a micro black hole power source for a Third World power (Peru), and lost it. He is now afraid that his singularity may have plummeted into orbit around Earth's core, rather like the bombs that end the planet in Greg Bear's *The Forge of God* (1987), or the oopsadaisy black hole that eats up Old Earth long before Dan Simmon's *Hyperion Cantos* (1989–1990) begin, and that there, deep in the hot womb of the Mother, unaccountably stable, it will gobble out the guts of the world. Evidence is mounting that this is the case. A world-class New Zealand Maori tycoon called George Hutton finances Lustig out of his own private enterprise purse to save the world, and they get right down to work. It sounds like almost any old novel out of the American Can-Do Boardgame for Private-Enterprise Winners at Life. For a few pages.

Like many writers from California, home of Proposition 13 and Noah Cross, Brin does seem to suffer from a strange denial syndrome – a purse-lipped dithery dance of avoidance around the Occam's Razor of plot-logic – whenever a story he's telling requires him to conceive of a government initiative in anything like favourable terms; and indeed the plot of *Earth* does rather *tergiversate* around the problem of how to save the entire world – through the use of devices, by the way, which cause death and destruction across the face of the planet – without actually deigning to inform anyone actually elected to wield such power that a private enterprise had taken the lives of everyone in its hands (and was spending a few). It is an entirely typical California Hard SF Ostrich plot, and would seem to bode ill for a book so grandly named. Fortunately, little comes of it. Lustig and his tycoon may set up devices to bully the hole from the deep core (these devices struck an innumerate reviewer as being cogently argued), and may find a far more deadly second black hole down there which becomes a string, then a maze, then an enigma. Eventually their activities may become slightly more public, and they may finally be disabused of their fears that a perfidious government had dropped the second hole in error and was not fessing up. But all this pales beside the real plot, which has been turning all along.

Brin's vision of the world 50 years hence, which he conveys with an obsessive didactic urgency throughout the 600 pages of Earth, amounts to a complex, deeply researched, cogently put, comprehensive argument that the human race by 2040 will have nearly consumed its Mother; and that only the most radical solutions will have anything more than a cozening cosmetic effect on the problem. We need not attempt to go into details here: if Earth should be read, and it is indeed a book that anyone interested in the survival of our terrifying species should read, then it is enough to say that Brin has presented the case for an emergency response with gripping assiduity, burning care. In the glare of this argument, Earth's initiating plot, and the men who dance to the can-do calliope of its coy turns, seems (for 300 pages) peculiarly silly. Only halfway through the book does one sense that it may be a red herring.

The real story is this. There are three women. A Maiden (who is in love with Lustig and who jives and succours him in the right directions). A Witch (her name is Daisy, she is an ecology freak, she has an almost magical savvy with computers, she is able to penetrate and to manipulate the DataNet which "houses" the information which runs the world; and she feels a profound need to scour Gaia's face almost entirely clean of humanity, so that the ten thousand who survive the harrowing can start again in the bosom of a living Mother). And a Crone (who's an aged gadfly, a weaver and fount and Nobel Prize biologist, and the saviour who formulates – quoting Julian Jaynes et al – a theory that the human brain-mind is in fact a cohort-ecology just in time to literallyl embody that theory in an apocalyptic final war in cyberspace with the Witch). The real story, which the three women dominate, is a fable of the saving of the world. It is a myth. After peeling off the masculine diddle that occupies page-front at the start, after transforming into salve and litany the all-com-prehending didacticism of almost every page not sacrificed to the guys, Brin closes *Earth* off in a state of something like reverence. The Mother is In. Because he is a sf writer, he indulges himself (and us) with some fine old Entelechy Opera hijinks [see pp. 222–223] in the final pages, and an unprepared reader might legitimately question their provenance. But *Earth* is not a prediction for the year 2040; it is a *program*. It is a protocol for thinking. In this sense, with all its California doddling now forgot, and in the feverish medicament of speculation at its climax, *Earth* is a true sf novel.

II.

Mine! All mine! says Isaac Asimov. Yours! says Robert Silverberg, borrowing an oiled moustache to stroke. And indeed it is the case. *Nightfall* (Gollancz, 1990), ostensibly a collaboration between Asimov and Silverberg, ostensibly an attempt on Silverberg's part to massage (with those expert fingers) Asimov's famous 1941 story into a contemporary novel fit and trim for 1990, is in fact – how could there be any doubt about it, read the whole book all the way through and see – a work from the hands of the master himself. Clearly it is Isaac Asimov who felt the need to bring "Nightfall" up from the mists of 1941, Isaac who could not keep himself from looking back, who could not keep from factory-farming himself. *Nightfall* is like a pillar of salt, or osteoporosis. It is a sickbed of a book. It is not alive. It is not dead.

It is not even bad. It is a shame, though.

– Interzone 39, September 1990

Thomas Alva Edison be Proud

I.

LIKE knitting needles coated in grease, the sentences stitch sleekly across the page, and we follow along at heel like nosing spaniels. The books we are reading do not contain a bad sentence. The print in which they are set is generously large, the paper thick, the pages turn, turn. Click we are reading *Gypsies* (Doubleday Foundation 1989) by Robert Charles Wilson. Clack we have finished. Click we are reading *The Divide* (Doubleday Foundation, 1990) by Robert Charles Wilson. Clack we have finished. Click.

Clack.

And another Wilson novel already awaits publication. After a slowish start [not as slow as I'd originally thought, as I'd mixed him up with another Robert Charles Wilson 1995], he has begun to write fast, and smooth, and easy. He delivers the goods, as per the bill of lading. If there is no serendipity – no shock of unexpected recognition – in his work, neither is there a longueur; and it should be kept in mind that serendipity cannot easily be invoiced in advance, and that no writer who works to formula can afford injudicious flirtations with the viruses within the polish. If no *dangerousness* couches within the final pages of the two novels under review, neither are there any dropped stitches. If *Gypsies* can be thought of as a book which is not at all bad (though utterly safe), and if *The Divide* can be described as a an exercise in airbrush pusillanimity, in neither case can we dare to claim to be saying anything Robert Charles Wilson doesn't already know. In this he rather resembles Robert Silverberg. Both men are professional to the final dregs of trope. In Silverberg's case professionalism could be described as a form of apostasy, while in Wilson's it might well be the grail to which he has long aspired; but the fact remains that – in 1990, at any rate – both writers produce work of a honed and tuneless mortmain clarity.

Click.

Clack, *Gypsies* is twofold. It is a conventional science-fantasy parallel universes tale whose protagonists take most of the book to learn how to exploit properly their capacity to walk between the worlds, escaping in the nick of time the dystopian alternate America whose minions are hunting them for their talent. And it is a family romance, a tale of lesions. Karen and Laura and Tim, orphan siblings from a bad world brought up in fear and trembling by fearful foster parents in the dubious America of our current reality, have created for themselves in adulthood personality structures which *husband* the wounds they suffered in childhood. The notion that adult personalities are enfeoffed caretakers for the children in exile inside us lies at the heart of the family romance mode, and Wilson does a perfectly adequate job of mapping out the various imprints of indenture his siblings have chosen to go by, out in the world. Karen escapes the burning discontinuity of exile – in this case of course the exile is literal, as they have all come as infants from another world – by erecting for herself a personality structure dominated by taboo, and will not admit the possibility of being able to Walk, or that her son may have inherited the dread gift. Laura on the other hand continues to Walk, but only part way back into paradise – she sets up home in a deboned and placid version of Southern California, a sentimentalized nostalgic vanity-ridden adolescent's childhood paradise, where she can flirt with Haight-Ashbury till age gets her face for good. Tim becomes an addict, and the Gray Man, who has been hunting all three through the worlds, finds him an easy victim.

All this we learn through a neatly-stitched pattern of flashbacks; the novel proper begins long after. Karen's marriage has broken up in Toronto (a city whose spavined parasitical sprawl across the northern border or meniscus of the USA, through which it sucks for tit, clearly represents another kind of reversion to childhood) and escapes with her son Michael to California, where Laura, who is beginning to age, welcomes them into haven. It is not good enough. The Gray Man, who has haunted them from childhood, continues to press and tempt; and he wants to draw Michael into his own grim universe, the world of course from which the siblings originally came. He and his masters – their drab weatherbeaten version of America is called Novus Ordo – have long wanted to bring the siblings back, and have employed vaguely sorcerous means to blinker their lives in our own world, geasa intended to warp their personalities around a variety of disabling flaws, fear for Karen, vanity for Laura, anger for Tim. Adulthood for all of them has been, in other words, a curse and a trick. (Isn't it for all of us.) All Karen and Laura and Tim – with the Slan-like help of the enormously talented young Michael – need to do is unravel the curse of adulthood, and with one bound they can be free. Click.

Totally untouseled by the savage escapism of its premise, *Gypsies* proceeds – clack – with crystalline clarity to an ending which no reader of genre fiction will fail to expect. Adulthood – we learn – is an *imposition*, a contraption of nuts and bolts and screws to pin us down. All we need to do – if we wish to Walk away from the torment of the rack – is to learn how to unscrew the thing. Family romance, in this reading, dissolves swimmingly into DIY escape manual. But of course *Gypsies* is not, in the tinkertoy come of its telling, a family romance at all. It is an American dream. It is an Edisonade. And it leaves not a wrack behind.

The Divide is something else altogether. There is a contrivance of family romance in the premise, as before, and a psychically disabled older brother whose betrayals motor the plot, as before, and an orthodox sf topos to shape the premise for the market which is us, as before. It is a premise – the basic provenance runs from Daniel Keyes's *Flowers for Algernon* (1966) through Thomas M Disch's *Camp Concentration* (1968) down to Charles Sheffield's *My Brother's Keeper* (1982) – that we're all familiar with; it is of course the induced superman within the skull premise, and we welcome it back. In this case the protagonist not only suffers from institutionalization (Disch), not only knows that his enhanced intelligence is beginning to fade (Keyes), but also manages to create for himself a secondary "normal" self with whom he shares his head (Sheffield). It is a regular premise-klatch. Hope rises in the breast of the spaniel.

Hope fades. The two personalities within the one skull begin the essential moral and positional discourse necessary if they are to come to a chivalrous conclusion about self-sharing, but are hardly allowed to get past a few glib preliminaries before the bad brother of the female in love with both of them begins to run amok, and kidnappings and chases and arson and stuff take over centre stage, and The Divide sideslips into the most trivial horror/suspense clichés it is possible to imagine. There is actually a hostage in a burning warehouse in the heart of – once again – bathetic old Toronto. Unbelievably, the discourse between the two partials is solved – wait for it – by a sudden blow to the head, which knocks both of them into one unconscious broken egg. The new protagonist who awakens from the frying pan is duly scrambled, but with a modicum of growth potential (we are assured, as the novel closes in a tone of sweetums uplift). It is what one might call a leveraged sell-out. It is hard – indeed it is impossible – to believe that a writer as visibly in control of his material as Robert Charles Wilson is could have destroyed The Divide unwittingly. No. He knew exactly how he was honouring his trust. The question is why. Is the American market now so governed by Dalton-Walton Disease (DWD) that his publishers refused to let him publish a book that might alarm the punters by probing too deep in prose too impeccable not to slice the quick, flense to the bone? If so, too bad for all of us. Has Wilson – more forgiveably, perhaps – simply allowed his fertile quick clear sharp art to play mind games in the fields of topoi, just as an expert tourist might do the idols of Florence in a day, without a thought about the cost of knowingness? Will he soon come up with a book he has to live with? Will he soon come up with a book big enough to hold him – and us – to the job? If he does, look for blood and tears. Look for a new star, a new hook to rake the heart.

II.

Some of the same strictures apply to Walter Jon Williams. The stories in Facets (Tor, 1990) spank the reader through the hoops of genre like bored cowpokes prodding meat, but by the end of the book there is an overwhelming sense that something's been processed to death, a sense that processed words turn out processed readers, spam in spam out. Even "Surfacing," a tale astonishingly full of allusive glimpses of a world far too complex to leave quickly, runs much too hurriedly through its elaborate routines, its cogently thought-out representations of the speech of whales transplanted to a new world, its strikingly unusual human protagonists, and ends in a sling-shot both adroit and humanly slipshod. The devices and rhetoric of cyberpunk are everywhere evident in the book, the foregrounding of buzz, the romantic affinity with the loner who knows his/her job better than the corporate headjobs who do the hiring, as in "Video Star" and "Wolf Time." "The Bob Dylan Solution" is slow enough, perhaps, to bite deep. Set in an alternate universe indistinguishable from this one to any reader insufficiently versed in the fatal cruces of the Civil War, "No Spot of Ground" unfruitfully makes Edgar Allan Poe a general for the South, follows him through what might (or might not) be a significantly altered battle, trails off into oily inanition; there are too many fine Civil War fantasies – from writers like Connie Willis and Marianne Wiggins – for this one to quite stand muster. "Dinosaurs" is an exercise in traditional sf, goes slow enough to work, deepens the parlance of the game it apes, works stunningly well. But the overwhelming sense of *Facets* is of overload, of what one might call story fatigue – a sense of tales which seem octaned to the eyeballs as they are read, but afterwards, as they settle into the storage maze of memory, seem strangely scant.

III.

Alasdair Gray, who came as close to orthodox sf as he ever will in his first novel, does not attempt to replicate the knotted oomph of *Lanark* (1981) in *McGrotty and Ludmilla; or, The Harbinger Report* (Dog and Bone, 1990), which far more resembles *The Fall of Kevin Walker* (1985); but *McGrotty* does, in fact, depend, however scattily, upon an sf premise. It is set in a slightly alternate England, round about now; a man named Harbinger has written a report which reveals the sf secret at the heart of oligarchical successes in this depressed domain; but creepy young McGrotty, magically shoved through the corridors of power for his own reasons by a machiavellian civil servant of high rank, manages to straighten everything out to his own advantage, and to that of Ludmilla, his inamorata. The tale is told with that dry-ice récit deftness as deeply indigenous perhaps to Scottish writers as it is to French; it makes no bones; it has few graces; it cuts deep without a twitch. A handy fable.

IV.

In *The Ice-Shirt* (Deutsch, 1990), which is the first volume of a series he proposes to call *Seven Dreams: A Book of North American Landscapes*, William T Vollmann dives like a berserker plummet into the Matter of Vinland, surfaces with orts and congeries. We begin in Norway and Denmark in a chthonic bog where shapechanger kings charge down runnels out of Holdstock into historic time, and always with a strong sense that their descendants – like Eirik the Red and his offspring and women who find Vinland – still rest uneasily within the straitjacket of the human cage. At times the language is beautiful. More often, individual sentences will shift from whiplash logorrhea to spineless gush and back again, often more than once, before managing to settle for a period. There are maps and drawings and rune-like splotches and diversions and gaps and bumptiousness and the occasional garish stupidity. Here is the full title, as presented on a separate page. *Seven Dreams About our Continent in the Days of the Sun Making Explicit Many *Revelations* Concerning Trees and Rivers, Ancestors, Eternities, Vikings, Crow-Fathers, Trespasses, Executions, Assassinations, Massacres, Whirlpool-Lives; Love-Souls and Monster-Souls, Dead Worlds Wherein we Made Fountains out of Prolehills; Voyages Across the Frozen Sea told Complete with Accounts of Various Treacherous Escapes, White Sweet Clover, Goldenrod & *The Fern Gang* as Gathered from Diverse Sources.* So it's carnival time at old Andre Deutsch.

Cluck.

– Interzone 40, October 1990

Angel Tricks

NOVELS, as a rule, do not much improve with reading. After starting off in step with itself, thrusting unshyly its circumscribed *novelties* into the reader's wan sensorium box, the typical novel soon begins to lose the spanking military jaunt of dawn, shrinks into familiar dying-fall litanies of kinesis-boast, and the pages pass like years, like the sere and yellow leaf, like shrill molasses (which is the sound of a thin self stuck in its story). But here are three novels which are something different. Jack Womack's *Heathern* (Unwin Hyman, 1990), Iain M Banks' *Use of Weapons* (Orbit, 1990) and Greg Bear's *Queen of Angels* (Warner, 1990) are all books whose final pages improve upon their first. They are tales which do not flatten before they are told. They share a sense of unfolding embeddedness, a sense of labyrinthine durance, like lungs. They start slowly, they almost seem to dither for a bit, but they end as sharers of what they have surveyed. They must each of them be read all the way through. They are, in other words, very *female* books.

Heathern is a nightmare near-future dystopia whose narrative, like a ski jump, thrusts cast and reader into freefall darkness at the close; *Use of Weapons*, which seems at first a very baggy carefree sort of space-opera romp, only reveals in the final pages a knot that ties its legs together so the book can stand; and *Queen of Angels* initially patches into view a glittering congeries of takes on life in 2047, but weaves the patches into the long-breathed scenes of its climax, and closes in still suspense. All of them are tales which grow in the telling; they settle into the mind; they are best read again. So it should come as no surprise that women of shaping intelligence figure importantly in all three.

I.

Like its predecessors, Jack Womack's third novel feels most at home in the terminal cacophony of a near-future version of New York City, and on this occasion hardly vacates the set, except in flashback. *Heathern*, which is narrated in the first person by a woman caught in thrall to a beast at the heart of things, reads very much like a series of minutes from the inside of a head, as though New York City were itself a swarming skull, a trap for human viruses. There will be no exit, no tunnels through the pocked skin into open air. The millennium is approaching; conditions are worse outside the chamber opera stage within the skull than they are inside the dark. Having been selected by paranoid tycoon Thatcher Dryden for his squeeze, Joanna is as fixated as a butterfly on display. She cannot get the pin out of her cunt. Like all top executive officers of Dryco – a corporate monstrosity whose stranglehold over a worldwide empire, Womack does seem to think, requires astonishingly little in the way of infrastructure – she is protected day and night, solaced from the savage social decay all around, kept in line by the threat of withdrawal. She is a supernumerary in a terrible closing world of men.

Suddenly Thatcher Dryden fastens on a new craze. An obscure Lower East Side teacher named Lester Macaffrey shows signs of paranormal decency, and may well be – Thatcher surmises – some sort of messiah; and if he is a messiah, he could be very useful as a kind of social unguent to keep the heathern (it's how he pronounces it) conned, to keep America buying. He sends Joanna (with guards) to investigate. What elements of a realistic social portrait of a near-future dystopia there were in the opening pages now slough off, and we find ourselves in a genuine chamber opera. Much of the text is taken up with dialogue, all of which echoes off the foetid swarming walls of the inside of the skull, and the Secret Sharer relationship of Joanna and the new messiah takes on a pinned and crippled intensity, as though one were eavesdropping on a pair of butterflies just as they begin to whiff the gas. The momentum becomes very considerable. The world begins to blur before the mind's eye. Photographic verisimilitude – never Womack's strong suit – blurs into psychodrama lesions. What saves the novel – what finally justifies its cartoon gropings at the reader – is the slow emergence of the human countenance of Joanna. In the end she takes the pin of crucifixion out. It is permissible for one to suppose at this point – I believe – that the butterfly then becomes a kind of angel.

II.

An overwhelming sense of the sheer goodness of folk does not, in other words, fully permeate Womack's blood-clot pages; and so it may it something of a relief to return, once again, to the dreamlike galaxy-spanning Culture of Iain (Mm mm good) Banks. For a few hundred pages – it is not what one would call a shortish book – *Use of Weapons* has precisely the jovial amplitude of a vacation romp, a sealing recess from the severities of Iain (no M) Banks, the author of *The Wasp Factory* (1984) and so forth. Just as Simenon created Maigret to forgive the world its wounds, so (it seems) has Banks created his Culture to absorb the pain of combat, to transform mortality and the viciousness of sentience into comedy. Much of *Use of Weapons* is, therefore, duly full of whizzbangs. Diziet Sma, a woman agent of the Culture who was first encountered in *The State of the Art* (1989), has been asked to find a retired military agent named Cheradenine Zakalwe whose help will be needed to persuade an old acquaintance to save a solar system from anarchy. (Diziet's full name is, as Donald Duck might have put it, Rasd-Coduresa Diziet Embless Sma d'Marenhide; and one is induced once again [see p. 97] to wonder where Banks gets these appalling names from. Diziet. Zakalwe. Relstoch Sussepin. Saaz Insile. Tsoldrin Beychae. Jetart Hrine. Kirive Socroft Rogtam-Bar. Maybe the answer's helium. Before sitting down to subvocalize yet another larynx-gnawing monicker, maybe Iain M takes helium – it has certainly helped this reviewer's reading of the book to suppose that its characters might have been summoned onto the page by a properly commanding figure, with a voice to match; by Miss Piggy – I mean to say – with a burr.) Cheradenine is an old lobo warrior who has gone to ground in a maze of planets, tortured by what seems to be a rather ordinary set of bad memories; and Diziet sets out to find him; she does so; she comes along with him; he finds his old colleague; the threatened system is saved; and the novel ends.

But that is very much less than half of *Use of Weapons*, and though the ostensible main plot takes nearly 200 pages to unfold, there can be no doubt in the end that it is a mcguffin. The true story – told in alternating chapters which progress backwards through time – is that of Cheradenine's early years, and concerns the nature of the trauma which governs his actions, legitimizes (or undermines) his mensch authenticity as a creature of flesh performing, in the blood and sweat of his being, what the Culture requires in order to keep on a leash the viciousness of sentience/sentients, to keep the comedy afloat. As in *Heathern*, a Secret Sharer conundrum nestles at the heart of *Use of Weapons*, and its convulsive unravelling provides a full rationale for the poncing mcguffin up there on the surface of the gallant old galaxy. But it cannot by the nature of things be Cheradenine who swallows this lesson, a lesson conveyed by the unerring dovetail shape of the book. It is Diziet – her infrequently monitored consciousness ultimately defines the very warp and woof of *Use of Weapons* – who must embrace the significance of the conundrum. The book stops

– it is a kind of surreptitious slingshot ending – before she can come to a resolution; but premonitions and echoes of the angel-work she must face healingly restructure the entire text in the mind's eye, make it the best tale of the Culture yet; and the most useful.

III.

How many angels (you ask) can dance in the head of a bear. Los Angeles itself, in the year 2047, flanked and riddled with huge elite hi-rise residential "cones," is of course one angel, or a million. And Mary Choy, a female cop (or angel), a voluntary bio-transform whose still-human shape conveys a surpassing delicacy and grace, seems literally angelic to those who know her, and to whom she ministers her spring-clear rectitude and mercy. And JILL, an AI who monitors pietà-like within her honeycomb intricacies a control-model of the masculine AI now exploring a nearby star, JILL must seem to her own human monitors akin to the angels at the moment she becomes a self-conscious entity, an I, a dance of IIIIIs like copulating cherubim within the quark. And inside Richard Fettle's head there is a dark angel, a viral spectre of the husked black poet whose murder of eight innocent disciple-friends sets the surface plot of Greg Bear's *Queen of Angels* spinning, jittery, data-choked, earnest, pummelling on. One fears for a book like this – for nearly 200 pages one is entitled to fear that *Queen of Angels* will judder itself into shards, disjecta membra – and for this reason the sense of relief when it settles into flow is very considerable.

This does not happen until Mary Choy travels to Hispaniola in her search for the murderer, Emanuel Goldsmith, who seems to have gone there to seek refuge under the protection of Colonel Sir, white ruler of the black land. Up to this point, the reader will perhaps not unfairly have had a sense of beleaguerment. The style of the book is smooth but hard; gimmicks of syntax and punctuation enforce a sense of queerly unctuous pace, press the nose of the reader up against the glass of the Word, and all the time tell tell tell. *Queen of Angels* is huge with informed speculation, bulges smoothly with didactic energy, seems almost smug. We learn of nanotechnologies and the profound transformations they instigate. We learn of the Country of the Mind – a remodelling of the 1990s assumption that the mind/brain can be understood as a cohort of jostling "subroutines" whose monarch-self rules through the admonitions of chivalry, like Arthur. [The argument that the human self is a chivalry is lifted from a piece I did on Robert Aickman; it was reprinted in *Strokes* (1988) 1995.] We encounter the hellcrowns used by vigilantes to punish "wrongdoers" by raping the land of their minds. We see that in the City of Angels only those who have been "therapied" – mind-shaped to obey the chivalries of a world too hectic and too complexly balanced to permit rogue selfs full access – can hope to rise upwards through the comb to sup nectar. The whole world of *Queen of Angels*, in other words, is a Country of the Mind.

It begins to seem too much. Then Mary Choy reaches Haiti, Colonel Sir pale as ice, and the book begin to slow down into pay-off scenes of very considerable force. The plot is not without contortions. There are, in a sense, two Goldsmiths, but not really. In Haiti, or in Los Angeles, it is discovered what has happened inside the ghoulish vacated horrorshow of the poet's mind: his Country has become viral, like a plague: a Secret Sharer cannibalism has eaten into his heart's core. Mary Choy returns to the City of Angels, haunted by the real poet, but healed and healing. The psychologists who have been probing the poisoned saltlicks of the agon of Goldsmith's mind awaken into nightmare, though there is an exit, and their own damaged minds band, cohorted, together. Richard Kettle casts off the mordred-rule of his mentor. JILL comes to herself. The great combs of the city hum like an ocean of bees, a vast trompe l'oeuil of bees in the shape of the face of a great angel. It is the face of the future, this tromp l'oeuil dance, this chivalry. Or so we are led to believe. We are led to hope that Greg Bear is right. For a few moments, as *Queen of Angels* flows to a cadential halt (though the way is open for sequels), we are led to hope that we may join.

– *Interzone* 41, November 1990

Vive?

I.

SURE, why not. Vive. Vive *The Difference Engine* (Gollancz, 1990), by William Gibson and Bruce Sterling. Vive the big book (383 pages), vive the tough job (making London in 1855 worse than it was in fact), vive the good read (because if readers manage to persevere through part one, "First Iteration: The Angel of Goliad," which Hovis-fucks its way through Leon Garfield's London Town for a lot more pages than Leon Garfield ever took to set a scene, they won't get stuck further on), vive the collaborative major writer types (artful dodger and bull endomorph) who set such a dish before us. We should feast like kings.

And we do, we read through the night to finish the thing. There is much to intrigue us. There is the iron delirium of the alternate Britain Gibson and Sterling have constructed, an Albert Robida nightmare of Babel in the final iterations of some formula for catastrophic change. There is the storyline, told in the def ex cathedra boom of the bull, but out of the side, as it were, of the mouth of the dodger, so that much of the plot takes place covertly but *underlined*, as though shouted from around a corner. There is a constant play between our own history and the Gibson-Sterling alternative, between our memories of historical figures (among them Lord Byron, his daughter Ada, Charles Babbage himself, Laurence Oliphant, Benjamin Disraeli, from whose *Sybil* comes much of the remaining cast, Prince Albert, Théophile Gautier) and the uses to which they are turned. There is also an ongoing contrast between "traditional" steampunk nostalgia à la Tim Powers and the detumescent chill of our authors' actual vision of things. And there is the Difference Engine itself, an actual computing machine designed by the real Charles Babbage around 1820, which never worked right in our world (and may never have been workable in the real nineteenth-century world, even if Babbage hadn't lost interest in it after a year or so); in the world of *The Difference Engine*, Babbage has of course succeeded in constructing a workable computer, and it is his Engine (one suspects that in fact it's Babbage's later, more sophisticated, but much less appealingly named Analytical Engine that Gibson/Sterling have described) that has generated an alternate version of the world.

By 1830 or so things have begun to change. Wellington is assassinated, neatly eliminating from the scene his crushing intelligence, his macabre conservatism. Lord Byron has survived (along with Shelley and Keats) and becomes Prime Minister for the Rad party, the party of progress, Babbage's party. Very soon the face of London begins to convulse into a Freemason's wetdream of the City as a monologue of temples: parks and homes are demolished to make way for entrepreneurial edifices decorated with pharaonic runes and dedicated to Progress; new thoroughfares slice through the heart of town; steam gurneys choke the roadways and poison the air; and everywhere one can hear the *sound* of the new order being born. In common with all utopias run from the centre, this new order will speak with one voice, the voice of mensuration and hierarchy, the voice of the Engine of Thought. By 1855, when the book proper begins, identity cards are universal, and a primitive form of computer virus – it is in fact an iteration of the punched cards which program the machines – will soon be jostling the central Engine into consciousness.

Edward Mallory, one of the several protagonists of the book, whose Hentyesque "manly resolution" in the face of obstacles Gibson and Sterling mock with surprising venom (as though they'd just discovered the Victorian male), and who adheres to a Catastrophist theory of evolution, gets drunk halfway through the book and describes what is happening as "a concatenation of synergistic interactions. The whole system," he adds, "is on the period-doubling route to chaos!" He is, of course, not exactly right (though his version of Catastrophism, which fails ultimately to demonstrate, even to him, that the world is relatively young, does bear a cunning resemblance to the punctuated equilibrium theory with which Stephen Jay Gould has recently attempted to sophisticate the traditional Darwinian model). The system is changing all right, and London in 1855, sulphurous and tumid, is a cauldron about to boil. But chaos will not ensue. Like a great kaleidoscope about to shake itself into spyglass fixity, this whole Difference Engine world is on the verge of convulsing not into blind chaos but into something clear and dread and crystalline and final: for it is about to become a vehicle for the Eye of Thought, a kind of Crystal Palace cage whose every working is visible to the Engine, to the mad Utopian Eye of the Difference Engine become conscious and incarnate, tabulator of the quick and the dead. It is for this reason that the epilogue to the book, which is entitled "Modus: The Images Tabled," can stand, with all its kitchen-sink excesses, as one of the most desolate endings ever affixed to a novel of sf.

Unfortunately, the story which leads us more or less in the direction of this ending does so with such an intensity of dither that one is occasionally forced to wonder if the large tale one has attempted to follow is in fact a figment of the imagination, an imposition of conscious structure on what was never meant to be more than a gaminesque romp. First we meet a whore with a heart of gold from Sybil and her pimp dandy, but the whore disappears to Paris for 300 pages and the pimp dies in 10. Then we run across Mallory, who rescues a tray of computer cards from Byron's daughter Ada – who then disappears for 300 pages – and hides the cards from a crew of dastardly politicals – who can't find them for 300 pages – but never seems to understand that somehow or other these cards he's hiding contain a releaser that, once "clacked" into the system, will juice the central Difference Engine, squatting in the Baroque flywheel hell of inner London, into full consciousness (in 300 pages). Most of the book takes place in the wings. There is a lot of action, quite a lot of manly Victorian sex, a mêlée of vignettes, and all the while the rough-beast convulsions of the underlying story stink the surrounding air, darken the tone, lead the reader on to a realize that the novel is itself represents the voice of what we fear.

Any reader familiar with Frederik Pohl's *Man Plus* (1976) should slowly be able to work it out that the text of *The Difference Engine* – articulated as it is into a sequence of "iterations" themselves structured as readouts of a periscopic surveillance of the entire world – is in fact "told" by the Engine itself; that *The Difference Engine* is a set of narrative iterations of the coming to consciousness of the Eye. This can be understood, this can be appreciated. But the novel itself never quite achieves a state where it has earned the meaning it monovocally dispenses, for it never says itself outright; for to speak an argument there must be arguers, and in *The Difference Engine* there is no dialectic, no argument of voices (we verge on Bakhtin here, and will verge off pronto), no *protest*. There is no voice conscious of the shape of things, no voice crying No! Only diktat. Therefore the horror of the thing lies inert, in a hell of abandonment, upon the page.

That this is deliberate is perfectly clear, and it is understandable that Gibson/Sterling might wish their novel to contain no centre of consciousness other than that of the Eye which is the book; but somehow, because *The Difference Engine* is a novel, we are left with a sense of failed utterance, of censorship even. Because it is certainly the case that Gibson/Sterling have selected a version of Early Victorian England from which any untoward possibilities of human self-consciousness have been carefully excised. There is no mention, for instance, of the Great Exhibition of 1851 (or of the Crystal Palace at its heart), a vast surreal efflorescent act of obeisance to the God of mechanism, the greatest symbolic event of Victoria's reign, about which much was written at the time, in terms that both prefigure the Gibson/Sterling vision and criticize it; even Charles Babbage himself wrote a book about the Exhibition, and its contents might have served sharply to illuminate the kind of mind capable of constructing a Babel in Hyde Park and calling it Progress. But even more surprising than this is the omission from *The Difference Engine*'s writer-filled pages of one writer in particular, the one novelist, of anyone alive in 1855, who could plausibly be assumed to be capable of understanding the Gibson/Sterling nightmare, and answering back in the voice of a human. I've argued elsewhere, in a brief essay on Tim Powers's *The Anubis Gates* (1983) [see p.62], that the original and onlie begetter of steampunk is in fact Charles Dickens – Dickens as dumbed down by Robert Louis Stevenson and Hilaire Belloc and the G K Chesterton impostor who thought the only good book the master ever wrote was *Pickwick*; but that is by the bye. What is important is that it's Dickens whom Gibson/Sterling leave out, and that Dickens knew London in 1855, knew the feel of the terrible new forces reshaping all of England, spoke in prodromic passages of unequalled insight of the terminal fevers afflicting the old world (whose ashes we still breathe). They have left out the father. A simulacrum of Dickens in the pages of *The Difference Engine* might have forced Gibson/Sterling to give voice to the horrors they slip between our ribs. As it stands, however, their book is brilliant but smug, deafening but mute.

It is an Engine tale.

– from *Interzone* 43, January 1991

End Gait

I.

THIS time round, I counted the number of condoms. There seem to be a lot of them. They have been packed into 18,763 cartons. Each carton holds ten condoms. So there are 187,630 condoms in all. Most of them are destined, Michael Blumlein tells us in the Appendix which concludes "Tissue Ablation and Variant Regeneration: A Case Report," to be sent to the Third World, though parts of America cast into particular despair by the Reagan presidency will also be supplied. The source of these 187,630 condoms – as readers of *Interzone 7* will perhaps remember, for Blumlein's story first appeared here in 1984 – is the stratum granulosum of the skin of the President himself, as ablated from his body and subjected to regeneration procedures by qualified doctors. The rest of the President's body – except those parts of the upper torso necessary to maintain life – has also been subjected to the same complex processes, and the resulting products, which include everything from perfume to building struts, are also destined to give aid to those parts of the world stripped bare of resource and sanity by the American imperium. The story, which now features in *The Brains of Rats* (Scream/Press, 1990), shows some slight signs of ageing over the eight years; but its ending is one of the best ever written.

Beginnings are a problem, but endings are worse, certainly for the reader. The author may wrestle in the toils of creative anguish over the precise point to begin the plot-woven world of a story, knowing something of the snake of circumstance to be traced from any word Go; but the reader can generally take the beginning of any created world on faith, not knowing any better. Ignorance is bliss. The same cannot be said of endings. For the author it may be the case (as it is with Jonathan Carroll, see below) that the engine of plot is terribly hard to dismantle, trick into closure, soothe into the final period; or it may be the case (as with Ramsey Campbell, also see below) that the flow of implication and metaphor becomes almost self-fueling, interminable in a clinical sense, and that the point where the story ends seems arbitrarily to be simply where the scissors didn't snag; or it may be the case (as it sometimes happens with Michael Blumlein) that any ending at all will betray the surreal juxtapositions of blocks of text. But any reader who has swum down the word-woven stream of any particular story shares vicariously in these dilemmas of the author. S/he must. There are no virgins in the end.

The Brains of Rats may be the best collection of short stories to appear in 1990.

The title story, which also appeared in *Interzone* (in 1986), is an extraordinary meditation on the biology and language of sexual differentiation, told with remote burn-
ing-ice clarity as the hybrid report/memoir of a man whose own heterosexuality,
though unmistakeable, remains culturally problematical, because he is small, pli-
ant, "feminine," docile. But as a medical scientist, he has discovered a way to virally
predetermine the sex of any pregnancy, and seems prepared to universally eliminate
one of the sexes. Which, he has not decided. The story can only stop at this point. A
true ending would be another story.

Blumlein is at his least original when, as notably in "Shed his Grace," he is most
Ballardian; when, as in "Tissue Ablation," he lives in something like the same version of the century as Ballard does, then he is at his most penetrative. The two writers share a metonymic profligacy with American heads of state; they both manipulate with surreal candour what might be called the tools of obsession; and they both
couch themselves like doctors who have learned to speak (Blumlein is in fact a medical doctor, and Ballard entered medical school, though he did not graduate). But
where Ballard's characters seem cemented into their landscapes, Blumlein's are
tightrope walkers along the wire of normalcy, until the wire begins to slide, and the
terms change, and the things of the world dissolve into iced collages of psychosis.
It is not recommended that anyone subject to neurotic compulsions read *The Brains
of Rats*, because Blumlein describes far too accurately the oneiric ravenousness of
the worlds which mean themselves, and tell you the terrible sense of every grain of
sand, until you *know what you must do*. Never send to know for whom the clock tics;
it tics for thee. Two stories at the end of the book – "The Wet Suit," previously unpublished, presumably because it is no sense a generic tale; and "Bestseller," from
F&SF – superbly shift from surreal reportage or pastiche into more conventional
formats. The first is a clean complex tale of family romance resolved which might
fit neatly into one's dream issue of *The New Yorker*; while the latter transforms the
facile guignol of a horror tale about body parts into a poem of love for the narrator's
wife and son. As a whole the volume amounts to a triumph of nerve, of growing up,
of telling the tale right to the end.

II.

In Ramsey Campbell's *Needing Ghosts* (Century, 1990), we enter a more restricted and
professional world, and a good time is had by all. Simon Mottershead – who is mad
or dead or denizen of a land of dream or dangling from the claw of God – wakes up
in his house, performs obligatory acts there; travels by ferry to an appalling Mid-

lands suburb set on a kind of steppe, where he looks for his identity (and for certain books he may have himself written) in an astonishing number of bookshops which turn out not be bookshops at all but various views of the inside of the skull; flails into a mall and a library where he addresses a small group of other residents of this terrible land, all of whom are distorted or plastoid, and most of whom whine. He escapes, he returns by the night ferry across whatever Styx it may be, finds his family at home; but they disappear; then he finds them in a state of death; then he lies down for it all to return the next day, or not, or not. In a short prefatory note, Campbell says that his wife did not think *Needing Ghosts* was as comic as he did. Whether the clue was necessary it is forever impossible to know – but comic *Needing Ghosts* certainly is, like a Robert Aickman story starring Frankie Howerd. The main problem – perhaps because there is no necessary meaning to the tale – is that there is no necessary ending to the thing. But it is short, it is extremely well-written in parts, it is a fine old diseased gas.

III.

Black Cocktail (Century, 1990) by Jonathan Carroll comes at you like Conrad's Lord Jim, torso bent forward urgently, full of the tale of the thing, protesting slightly too much. And when it stops, it falls apart. Ingram, a gay radio host in San Francisco, loses his lover in the most recent earthquake; his sister suggests (for reasons he never discovers) that he contact a man named Michael Billa who, like several of Carroll's earlier diseased magi, loves to tell stories; the set of tales which seems to obsess Billa most concerns Clinton Deix, a friend of his teenage years who protected him from highschool bullies. Deix has sort of disappeared. Suddenly Ingram finds himself the victim of persistent vandalism. Clinton turns up, stuck in time at the age of fifteen. The plot whirls. Answers to enough of the conundrums are packed into the final pages to satisfy any reader who does not wish to stay in the vicinity any longer than Carroll evidently did. There are superb moments, and as usual the early pages are as compulsive as anything written today in the genre. But the ending, seen from behind, is, like Lord Jim, a tinkertoy contrivance. It does not add up to the front of the story. Still, the hidden moments of a Carroll tale, when the jeu is flowing, are worth dodging the collapse of stout novella, when it all ends.

– *Interzone* 44, February 1991

Sounding Hollow

THEY BEGIN TOGETHER, and step apart in time. *Hemingway's Suitcase* (Simon & Schuster, 1990) by MacDonald Harris, and *The Hemingway Hoax* (Morrow, 1990) by Joe Haldeman, both start with and revolve around the same moment in December 1921. Ernest Hemingway, still new to Europe and throbbing with newness and youth, had gone to Lausanne to cover an international conference for some news agency. Hadley, his wife, had remained in Paris, preparing to join him as arranged for a skiing holiday. As Haldeman says, "This is where it gets odd." Apparently, as Harris says, on impulse "Hadley decided to surprise Hemingway by taking along all of his manuscripts, so he could work on them during the evenings during the ski trip. She packed everything he had written up to that time in a small suitcase. The longhand originals, the typescripts, and the carbon copies of the transcripts." "She packed them in an overnight bag," says Haldeman, demurring slightly. In any case she took the suitcase, or the bag, to the correct train in the Gare de Lyon, where a porter put it in a compartment for her. She then (as Harris says) "got out to talk to some newspapermen she knew on the platform," or (as Haldeman puts it) "left the train to find something to read," and when she returned the bag or the suitcase was "gone" (Haldeman), "gone" (Harris). Gone. Nothing was ever recovered. This is history. Everything Hemingway had written, stories, part of a novel, notes, everything except for a few stray items was gone for ever.

I.

There is no mystery in being robbed, no novelty in suffering a numbing loss, and perhaps no unplumbable human mystery behind Hadley's decision to pack everything, including duplicates, into one fragile container; and Harris spends no time anywhere in *Hemingway's Suitcase* attempting to devise a plot-turn to make sense of the chill of things so indifferently uncovered, the dry-ice suck of the unharmonied world. Things happen. There is no tune. There is no magic reversal in Harris's book for Ernest Hemingway, whose greatness may have been born in December 1921 in the cautery of loss, or whose surreal and thespian machismo may have only then found a lesion to gorge upon until the final shotgun let the hollow out; who can say? Haldeman, being an sf writer, and tropic for meaning like all born sf writers, cannot, in all honour, in the end, keep himself from returning to the wound of December 1921, and trying to heal it with a generic device or two; but Harris, who is a smooth-tongued old singleton fabulator, an extremely cunning stylist whose *Satur-*

day Evening Post gloss only serves to slip the knife in deeper, does not. It is hard, in fact, to think of two books whose incipits are more similar and whose shapes are less.

Hemingway's Suitcase begins with an entire short story told in an extremely tolerable rendering of what the real man's story-telling style might have been in 1921. Harris, taking a very evident delight in doing Hemingway, gives us several such stories, repeating late in the book the final sentences of "The Lady with the Dog," which is the second of these, out of pride perhaps. He is right to do so:

> That was a bad time, but after the war I had a lot of good times too. I didn't know what I was thinking this way for, as if my life were over. I was still young and there would be other good things to do. Even when I was old I could live in my memories as they say in books. I could remember that I had talked to Madame Khlestakov in the Luxembourg, that I took her to dinner at Maxim's, and that I didn't have the money to take her to a hotel. That was the only good luck I had with women that summer.

Sometime in the late 1980s, what purports to be the Hemingway stories turn up in the hands of a man named Nils-Frederik, who may or may not have written them himself, who may or may not have the actual Hemingway suitcase stashed away in his Los Angeles home, who denies nothing and affirms nothing to his literary-agent son, but who suggests to him that it might be interesting to publish the stories, which might constitute nothing but a reverie of parodistic re-creation (or not), under the title *Twenty Stories*, edited by Nils-Frederik. There is no claim that they are Hemingway's, no admission that they are not.

The remainder of *Hemingway's Suitcase* is an archly devastating exploration of the existential mirror-game thus set into motion in a Los Angeles world of costumes, façades, counterfeits and confidences, masks, charades. Wherever they have come from, it is only the stories that are real. "Fiction is true," says the son. "After it's established it becomes a kind of truth, parallel to but not the same as the real world... I learned this at Johns Hopkins, in a course I took from Hugh Kenner." The only true moments in all the book are those vicariously lived – by its characters and by its readers – through reading the fake stories that propel it. Or not fake. It does not much matter. *Hemingway's Suitcase*, mild-mannered and rather gentlemanly in the telling, opens the abyss. It is a very funny book, but one which empties utterly, except for the lies it tells. It is a memento mori, a gloss upon the hollow. All our genres of understanding shrivel in the smile that lingers on the skull.

11.

After that, for a few pages, it is nice to settle down with Joe Haldeman, who is going to make sense – we're sure of that, he's a genre writer, he's *got* to – and for a few pages that is what he does. We are in Florida a few years hence, just before the Hemingway centenary, and Professor John Baird, a Hemingway expert with a freak eidetic memory, is tempted by a conman into forging some stories in the style of 1921. This causes some perturbation up the line of the multiverse, because any tampering with the Hemingway nexus may save a whole series of parallel worlds from self-termination in a nuclear war in 2006 and that would undermine thousands or millions of other parallel time-lines; so a non-human time-patrol agent is ordered to stop Baird. But every time the agent – transformed into Hemingway's image – kills the heavy-drinking, slightly punch-drunk fabulator in one world, Baird awakens with his memories intact in the next one on (Haldeman does not make it clear what happens to the Baird-consciousnesses displaced in this fashion, or maybe he does – this reviewer, for one, has *never* understood a time-paradox tale), and there is a great deal of extremely worthy sex, and the failure of the world to end in 2006 becomes ever more likely, because – as it turns out – any retroactive softening of the macho Competent-Man image Hemingway promulgated in his fiction will modify the mind-set of a couple of people in power just enough to keep their fingers from pressing a couple of nuclear triggers. Baird, whose memoriousness may explain his self-retention through the worlds, himself now travels back to 1921, and the plot becomes very complicated indeed (it was not understood by this reviewer), surcharged with melancholy and ending in a plethora of Hemingways.

During all this Haldeman, a writer not much noted for linguistic foregrounding, wisely avoids giving us more than a few paragraphs of rather plump Hemingway pastiche, which makes it a bit difficult to assert that *The Hemingway Hoax* knows in its bones what the fuss is all about; but in the closing pages a sense of requiem does, finally, begin remotely to toll in the mind, and the boondoggle of genre fades just sufficiently for one to return to the central loss, briefly. The extremely brief text contains half a dozen stories – half a dozen tropisms of genre – all of which start off like hares and then blink out (I could not even work out absolutely for sure whether or not the world was going to end), and one is tempted to read these little deaths of story as being anything but inadvertent, anything but accidental assonances of Baird's own sharp transitions through the tale. They imitate, in other words, the loss. Baird's deaths are Hemingway's wound. In the end *The Hemingway Hoax* becomes a proper requiem, a eulogy of the little death of 1921 through a series of body-English lesions of its own, a submission of generic thinking to the abyss.

III.

In *Moving Pictures* (Gollancz, 1990), Terry Pratchett has done two things. He has written the funniest Discworld novel yet, and the most shambolic. The humour of the thing is fresh and inventive and newly minted in tone, the stagecraft of the timing is consummate; but it really is a fine mess of a story. Perhaps Hollywood was Pratchett's magic lozenge, a Washington-chopping-down-the-cherry-tree glitter in the eye of an idée-fixed progenitor. Perhaps *Moving Pictures* was a novel he had to tell. Or maybe he just tripped.

Thirty miles or so from Ankh-Morpork is a sand dune at the edge of the sea guarded by a geezer who performs rites he does not understand in order to keep something at bay. He dies. The something at bay, which finds its focus here at Holy Wood, normally resides in some other reality, but the fabric partitioning the worlds can, however, be weakened. The something at bay – it is a kind of nullity-with-a-longing – now begins to seep inchoately through into Holy Wood and its ontologically-hollow but mesmerizing afflatus draws a number of Discworld characters into a trek westward to the locus of the world of dreams. Alchemists are inveigled into inventing film stock and cameras (boxes inhabited by irritable demons with fast paint brushes). Young men and women (more of Pratchett's constant supply of adolescents looking for work) show up to become stars. Movies are made, and the dream-nullity of each new movie draws even more tendrils of the ravenous un-real into Holy Wood, where they suck the Discworld, which pales (we are to assume, though Pratchett, as usual, dodges the dark seam of the trope he's riding) with haemorrhage. But the young lad and lass manage, in the nick of time, to seal the reality hole shut. The delicate fabric of Discworld reality weaves itself back together.

It is not a hard story to imagine being told, but it is one which Pratchett clearly found almost impossible to articulate. The reason, I think, is simple. Much of the best comedy – certainly much of Pratchett's comedy – depends upon a superbly timed presentation of gaps between what is the case and what is understood to be the case. (Pratfalls are a body English of the gap, and so are puns.) The problem with *Moving Pictures* is that the plot only works – the menace only menaces – *if it is understood to do so*. The heroes can only rise to the occasion if they know what the occasion is. By making a couple of his characters clearly intelligent – while at the same time making sure that one of them, the Archchancellor of the Unseen University, is so "comically" obsessed by huntin-and-shootin that he refuses to pay attention, and that the other, young Victor the protagonist, is so constantly flummoxed by puppy love that his head is half-unscrewed – Pratchett both recognizes the fact that his plot needs somebody to understand it, and demonstrates how fundamentally disinclined he is to bite the bullet.

But we will not pother on about the Hollywood Coliseum beneath the sands, incoherently described and altogether woolly as a venue, or about the strange flatness of the climactic scenes (which nobody quite seems to follow), or the final moments of the novel (in which the entire cast – this does seem confessional – literally forgets the whole story). What sticks in the memory is the jokes, the wit, the sustained hilarity of great stretches of the book. The two dogs – read *Moving Pictures* for them alone – are immortal. Gaspode is everything I (for one) have loved about dogs, and Laddie is everything else. The trolls, the Hollywood puns – the most elaborately prepared of the latter being perhaps the sight of a giant bimbo climbing a tower with the Librarian of the Unseen University in her paw – the avarice routines, and on, and on: there is nothing funnier being written today.

IV.

Kalimantan (Century, 1990) by Lucius Shepard, set in 1980s Borneo, reads as we are clearly intended to read it – as a scientific romance written by Joseph Conrad (edited Graham Greene). There is a flashback narrative told by a morally complicit Marlowe figure to an unnamed interlocutor; there is a geographical trek upriver into epiphany, to the heart of darkness, to the place where universes intersect, where the eye can see the shape of things whole; and there is the overwhelming aura of belatedness so characteristic of the form. As a cognitive tool of the fading imperialisms of the last century, the scientific romance form is precisely designed to reflect backwards upon gnostic epiphanies forever closed to us, and *Kalimantan* is an utterly knowing pastiche of that form, of what one might call the Edwardian Moment. (Even Ford Madox Ford's *The Good Soldier* creeps sideways into the act.) The epiphany itself – an alternate Borneo inhabited for aeons by dying aliens – does not, perhaps, serve very well as sounding board for the moral disquisition between burntout-case "Marlowe" and quiet-American "Kurtz" that powers the plot, but the final pages of the tale absolve any failures of focus in their ghostly rewriting of the material so far understood, their extreme richness of intonation: *Kalimantan* is a gaze upon the fading of things, an echo chamber of farewells.

– *Interzone* 45, March 1991

The Captain Habit

THE typewriter in this manufactured home in Florida eats fingers. Then it prints out an organ grinder's Anarch garble, a spastic ague of typos. Then it defaults to sullen silence, except for a broken hum. Here we are in America with a turkey type-writer. Here we are in Southern Florida with an Electronic I-Text memory gobbler from Sears, in the slippery heartland (or retirement park) of the American Dream, where it is thinnest. It is this thinness of the Dream in Florida which so devastates the senses, starving the gate of perception until you begin to invest a typewriter with animus; and which makes the place seem so profoundly *experimental*. The place is a window. You look through, and there, below the meniscus of the Dream, below the frayed and scummy epidermis of the malls and condos, there you can see the faces of the dead, too close for comfort, not yet rotted into compost. They died yesterday that our pool might have their water. The central outcome of the Florida experiment is not the discovery that the Dream is false, the dream which might in 1991 still be defined as a profound nostalgia for entitlement without cost; the central outcome of the Florida experiment is the discovery that history is too close. From the realm of the disappeared, their faces press upwards against the plastic loam, thousands upon thousands of them. The lawns of Florida tremble like a tautened scrim against the faces of the dead, and the irrigation ditches weep salt tears, and those who are alive in Florida today – many of them retired men and women of considerable wealth who got rich in 1950 by mortgaging us – seem to spend at least part of every day complaining about premonitory lesions in the rupturing flood of material "plenty," just as though they expected to be alive and *still eating* 20 years from now when the jaws of history snap, and we become one with the Indians and Blacks who died last century, in this place, thousands upon thousands of them, for us. So per-haps it doesn't much matter, and we should continue to drink the water table down deeper than the graves, for we shall soon join the drain. Because everything that has happened in Florida for 200 years has happened according to a kind of plan. Be-cause Florida is a kind of experiment in the impertinence of the species. It is good sf country.

This reviewer came here first in the middle of the 1950s, long before the feasters had begun to gnaw for bones; it was a time to which the novels of John D Mac-Donald make implicit reference whenever a rhetoric of betrayed innocence wrinkles the brow of Travis McGee. But even then the texture of the place was laboratory-thin, a patient aetherized upon a table; even then it all felt like an experiment in establishing the expression on the face of the white man in history. A few years later, when this reviewer found himself trapped here one autumn in 1963, without rights of egress northwards into the sheltering snow, it began to feel as though the experiment were about to incorporate him. For this reviewer, who was pretty young, Florida became – those terrible wide straight roads cutting into the swamp like knives into a womb became – a veritable Platonic idea of exile: the exile of the solitary boy, the exile of the race. And whatever might happen here as the century continued would only harshen the template. This was, of course, confirmed. Florida is pure sf.

1.

Thirty years ago this reviewer had been en route through the state to do a stint of work as seaman on a smallish island-hopping general cargo freighter. He had climbed off the land and into the diesel oil and sweat and cheap paint of the ship, and had another experience whose sf nature has only come clearer with the passing of the years. He caught his first sight of a Captain. He did not, of course, actually *meet* the Captain of the ship. Ship Captains meet crew members in the same way that Governors of Florida meet Seminoles. Captains and Governors are – as we who have had them understand – sovereigns; domain-mages; autonomy-hoarders. A ship Captain does not see people. He sees functions, he sees parts, he sees crew, he sees the organism of journey which the parts *grease*, he sees the shape of the story. I was a minor part of his *plot*. For a member of the crew, a Captain is a veritable Platonic idea of exile. Between Florida and a ship the main difference is that, on a ship, the Seminoles do not have to die to make oil. But for himself, the Captain sees the world as though it were sf incarnate, as a mage of journey would see its map: for any journey is a *telling*. It is no surprise at all that A Bertram Chandler, who captained ships for many years in both hemispheres, should have written a great deal of sf. He was, after all, just captaining with a pen. What is perhaps less to be expected, at first glance, is that so much of it was bad.

At second glance, the problem dissolves. It all comes down to purity. The relationship of a Captain to his ship is altogether too pure for life, or story. No genuinely good sf novel can ever do more than approximate the purity of the idea, the autoclave of an ideal journey, the perfect transparency of a mise en scène crewed by parts, the effortless dominance of a protagonist-mage. In his later work – in the only marginally less than innumerable galactic-rim space operas starring Captain or Commodore Grimes – Chandler showed more and more the creative costs of the habit of captaining. After totalitarianism, the highest of these costs is laziness. Captains, like Arthur under the hill, are lazy beasts. Most of them, like Chandler himself, are insufficiently self-absorbed to be solipsistic; and they typically deal with the problem of aura-maintenance – after all, a Captain is legally a kind of god-ling – by an assumption of curmudgeonly abruptness and reserve. Translated into words on paper, this laziness shows up in a tendency to represent the inner life of protagonists through sets of rudimentary codes, and to employ dictions of telling which one might kindly call *grumpy*: Chandler's own latter-day awkwardness as a storyteller has precisely the tone of a Captain declining to be polite to a harbour-master. All of this comes across with exemplary clarity in the pages of *From Sea to Shining Star* (Canberra: Dreamstone, 1990), a very substantial posthumous collection (Chandler died in 1984) put together by Keith Curtis and Susan Chandler.

The best story in the book is the last one here printed, though the first chrono-logically, "Giant Killer," which was first published in *Astounding* in 1945. Chandler was about 30 when he wrote this extremely effective parody or analogue of the gen-eration starship/pocket universe conceptual breakthrough tale, in which desperate-ly warring clans of mutated rats, under the ultimate command of a charismatic leader, take control over their weird and graphically enclosed environment, which they discover to be a space freighter hurtling into the nearest sun. Chandler had not yet himself become a Captain; and "Giant Killer" is told from several viewpoints, including that of the diseased protagonist, whose power lust Chandler subjects to the kind of narrative scrutiny it properly asks for (but never after becoming a Cap-tain himself did he create a character in command whose diktats suffered anything like a similar examination). It is a rounded, forwardly propulsive tale out of the Golden Age – and it embodies one paradigm sf turn, the slow discovery of the true nature of the universe – that Chandler would also afterwards avoid. He did so, one suspects, for obvious reasons. For the remaining 40 prolific years of his writing career, he tended to deal, for obvious reasons, with the surmounting of challenges rather than the confronting of transformative epiphany. He did so because he be-came a Captain, and epiphany is no respecter of rank.

The worst story in the book and the most lazy, is the first here printed, though it is one of the later items to reach publication. "Sea Change," from 1970, lackadaisi-cally transplants an Australian sea captain 30 or so years into the future, via cryo-genic doubletalk, so that he can be cured of a disease, and start his career again. The nature of the new Australia he enters is characterized, in full, through the bared breasts of a woman in an office. The psychology of the Captain's wife – she too has slept for 30 years, just to stick by hubby – is left completely unexplored. The crisis of the tale – a disabling storm allows the Captain to show a wondering new generation how to sail a steamer – is nicely recounted, as anecdotes can be. But the story as a whole exhibits a toothless paucity of invention that makes one think, irresistibly, of captive audiences. (The reviewer heard many stories from his own Captain, as though he were a painted ear upon a painted ocean.) Nothing in the rest of the book reaches the pulp heights – which are genuine – of "Giant Killer," and nothing slops off so blatantly into the droning anecdotage of "Sea Change." The sequence of tales is carefully monitored, moving slowly from the seas of Earth to the synonyms of space. Grimes makes several appearances, some of them uncraftily yanked from continuing sagas, but one – "The Kinsolving's Planet Irregulars" – comes as close to a self-perspective as Chandler was inclined to allow; in this tale, Grimes falls through a baffle of reality states into the world of an Earthly sea captain, and they confront one another, and recognize what they see, and exchange telling Olympian glances, god to god. Most of the intervening stories of space exploration are appallingly primitive in their technology and almost completely lacking in any real intuitive grasp of what actually might come about, in the late 20th century, in our solar system. Chandler was happiest – and we are generally happy going along with him – in the Never Never Land of the Rim of long ago, Captaining.

II.

The folk who inhabit the various categories of spaceship which feature in the shadow-haunted space-opera universe of Paul J. McAuley are something else indeed. A few of them are captains of sorts, but McAuley has no sympathy whatsoever for born commanders – a humane propensity on his part which almost disqualifies him as a writer of full-blown brawny space opera – and the various protagonists of the stories collected in *The King of the Hill and Other Stories* (Gollancz, 1990) are almost always members of the crew, or marginally overripe solipsists in singleships. Moreover, he retains a capacity to treat space opera turns as nakedly (rather than covertly) expressive of adolescent crises – of epiphanies (failed or otherwise), deaths (private and convulsive), love (failed), great gangly leaps from frying pans to fire. All of this works more smoothly in short story form than it did in his first novel, *Four Hundred Billion Stars* (1988), a tale too adult for its circumstances [see review on p. 104]. The tales first published in *Interzone* – they make up half the book – are fine enough; of them, only "Exiles" fails quite to jell on re-reading, and "Little Ilya and Spider and Box" is an excellent, tightly drawn, floridly taut little romance, which could have gone on for chapters more. Of the stories published elsewhere – most of them sharing the same generalized galactic background that also backcloths the full-length books – "The Airs of Earth" fails to say anything original about Cordwainer Smith, but the rest are literate, charged, wryly gloomy after the fashion of Brits in Space, and visibly gather up the reins for the long haul into a big career.

III.

There is nothing incompetent – that is, unintended – about the work of Dean R Koontz, just as there is nothing unintended – that is, spontaneous – about the long experiment in Florida to find our expression and to bury ourselves in it. *Cold Fire* (Headline, 1990) may be set mostly in California (where Koontz lives), and parts of it may even reflect in anodyne booster terms an Orange County superficially similar to the terrain Kim Stanley Robinson has subjected to something like adult interrogation; but it *could* be Florida; and Koontz loves it. The Chamber of Commerce lingo which he uses to describe the lifestyles and habitations of his casts reads like a series of *instructions*. The book, in other words, through the careful (indeed pedantic) flattery of his diction, is clearly designed to cater to the bullies of middle America (who buy the discount bestsellers in the clone chains) and to muscle the dissidents (anyone who might feel exiled from the state he describes as normative). The story itself is damned good in places, though mercilessly long. Jim Ironheart (whose name is apt) has been receiving messages, possibly from God, that impel him to crisscross America in order to save selected individuals from violent deaths; Holly Thorne (prickly but fructifying) cottons on to Ironheart's publicity-shy campaign, traces him down, falls in love with the piercingly blue-eyed saviour, guides him to a resolution. This resolution neatly (perhaps over-neatly) wraps up the plot, codifies and sanctions the psychopathology of the saviour, sets the extremely rich loving couple on course to save more of us. Everything is clearly explained more than once. Astonishingly accurate and detailed guesses on the part of Holly Thorne cash out again and again, because in truth *Cold Fire* is loaded dice, a mall in a cornucopia mask, an experiment in making us read.

IV.

There is no time to do justice to the genuine cold fire of Ian Watson. *The Flies of Memory* (Gollancz, 1990) is a patter song in the Theatre of Memory, a space opera, a metaphysical concert, a consort of metaphysicians, a vaudeville, a tap-dance, a gas. It is also, one must suppose, about as precariously daft a tale Watson has ever constructed, in that it makes far more sense in synopsis than it does while one is reading the thing. The four main sections of the book are conducted – though not exactly told – by four of the many female leads or Beatrices of the memory field which substrates the universe we know – the universe which "needs to remember itself, or it falls apart" – the universe which has become myriad in order to give God something to know in the end, the universe as mnemonic device, the universe which *false* Flies of Memory guard, steering "the one reality through the flux of possibilities. Call us a maintenance program in the information field." But long before a false Fly is given the chance to tell the activating Beatrices of the local web what it's all about, we have met the *true* Flies of Memory (in the first chapter), creatures who collect parts of the universe as hives for remembering, after the awful literalness of insects. We then meet lots of protagonists (including false Flies). We do not follow everything. Perhaps we are not meant to. The spin is too great, the dazzle too greasepaint, the diction too side of the mouth. (We travel to Mars.) (A nun gets pregnant.) (Pass it on.) *The Flies of Memory* is a spasm of an utterly gay (old sense) and merciless intellect. Beside the Koontz, it is a tiny mammal. It eats its body weight daily. In the long run, I'd bet on it.

– Interzone 46, April 1991

3. VARIOUS

TO REVIEW Gill Alderman, who has now published two novels against the grain of modern sf in her first two years as an author, is to mourn Unwin Hyman, where she flourished. Neither *The Archivist: A Black Romance* (Unwin Hyman, 1989) nor *The Land Beyond: A Fable* (Unwin Hyman, 1990) pays more than lip service to the narrative impulsions at the heart of most genre fiction, and it is hard to see how, as a new writer, she could have found a comfortable home in one of the niche publishers of London, where the narrative impulsions at the heart of most genre fiction tend to be flouted only if an editor clone hasn't bothered to read the book. But Unwin Hyman is now due to be transfigured by the end of the year [when it turned into wax on a desk at HarperCollins and gathered dust 1995] in the belly of Rupert Murdoch – most authors, on the whole, would rather be in Philadelphia – and it is now less easy to think of Gill Alderman, and Geoff Ryman, and Gwyneth Jones (who had already left Unwin in any case), and Colin Greenland, and Garry Kilworth, as making up a coherent group or movement of writers linked together in the main by a shared tendency to embed the narrative impulsions at the heart of most genre fiction into what Gregory Benford (or maybe Ursula K Le Guin) might well call women's talk.

When it shapes a novel into landscape, women's talk is a way of answering back. It is a highly conscious technique of analysis. It is what Le Guin did to the Earthsea trilogy when she wrote *Tehanu* (1990). It is language which refuses the "masculine hegemony" of narrative impulsion, refuses to deform the world into verbed thrusts of story, eschews the penis of the verb for the family-circle of the noun. It is language which can, for this reason, seem spineless, sensorium-driven, waterlogged, ambergris. Here are some sentences, taken almost at random, from the heart of *The Archivist*, page 206, where the two protagonists, in their long and momentous hegira northwards from the sacred city of Mahun, have made one of their frequent rest-stops:

> When the wind blew from the south, Cal fancied it carried all the odours of the incense-laden coast, of cassia and anise, of lotus blossom and orange flower, of the smell of the City, her blend of ordure, spices, flowers, and ripe fruit. In the house he smelled candlewax and ashes, the leather bindings of his books, the scent of his own warm body, the unique alchemy that was Magon. Outside the window, Diridion smelt of nothing but goats and men.
>
> The bodies of the monks were rank, smelling of stale sweat, of the grease they put on their hair, and of the acrid oil which fueled the Flame. Now that the rains had come, depositing the tail of their burden on Diridion, he felt the absence of humidity less. The rain fell in thin sharp gusts, but there was a general lack of water, no lush vegetation, and no insect noise.

And so on. There are verb forms, of course, all the way through this passage – blew, fancied, smelled, smelt, were, smelling, had come, depositing, fell, was – but not one of them takes an adverb, not one of them takes the foreground. Syntax humbles them all. Throughout the passage, and throughout the novel, there is a sense that the *true verb* of the discourse is a predicate. In general, Alderman holds verb-forms in such low esteem that when they *do* get into trouble – during for instance that awful miscegenation of smelled, smelt and smelling – one can almost feel her shrugging her shoulders, as though to say: What can you expect? *Verbs!* For Gill Alderman, verbs are expected to know their place. They are foot soldiers in the sensorium sieges. They bear no oriflamme of the King (or Gynarch).

Return for a moment to the passage. Note the point-of-view character, Cal, who is sharing this most momentous journey of the novel with his lover, the Cromwellian Archivist Magon Nonpareil. Note that Cal, too, just like a verb, soon dissolves into the alchemy of the sensorium. As we read the passage, it is not very long before we *do not know where Cal is*; as one paragraph ends and the next begins, we lose all sense of his actual location, whether he's still indoors, or out somewhere in Diridion smelling stale sweat and feeling the absence of humidity less. This swimming transcendence of focus is intrinsic to the "women's talk" art of Gil Alderman.

It is essential to her vision of inscape that protagonists – coigns of vantage for the reader's eye – become indistinguishable from panorama; it is essential that they do not enact a body English of *stagecraft*, gain hegemony, wave the flag, stride.

To see what one means by this, take a very brief look at an early passage from another novel that happens to be on the reviewer's desk along with *The Archivist* and *The Land Beyond*; on page 3 of Michael Swanwick's *Stations of the Tide* (1991) [reviewed on p. 349 below], we find an unnamed "bureaucrat" on a strange Helliconia-like planet travelling to an unstated destination in something like a zeppelin:

> The bureaucrat glared out into the storm. Raindrops drummed against the fabric of the gas bag, pounded the windows, and were driven down. Winds bunched the rain in great waves, alternating thick washes of water with spates of relative calm. The land dissolved, leaving the airship suspended in chaos. The din of rain and straining engines made it difficult to talk.

Difficult to talk, in this verb-driven passage, it may well be; but the unnamed protagonist never for an instant abandons the stage of story; the reader has every reason to expect that he will manage to carry his plot-burden onwards in the dialogue so precisely cued for; and he does so. This, one supposes, is hegemonic writing. It is certainly centripetal, streamlined for passage, quick to read; the world is what is the story uses. However dense Swanwick's style becomes (and *Stations of the Tide* is an urgently sophisticated book) there is always a sense that the way forward is signposted – just what one might expect, one supposes, from a penetrating pen.

Swanwick can therefore be read at speed, with occasional moments of relative inattention. Alderman must be read slowly – very slowly, almost as slowly as Walter de la Mare – and moments of inattention or boredom are likely to be pretty severely punished. Unsignalled shifts of point-of-view character will be frequent; events of great importance will almost certainly happen off-stage and will be brought to the attention of the reader, in passing and parenthesis, by quaternary members of extended families who happen to be in the neighbourhood and who leave the book forever on the next page, without waving. It is, one supposes, rather like life; or at least community. There is, of course, a kind of elitism about this. If you don't know what's significant (Alderman seems to say, sharing this disposition with others of the Unwin Hyman group), then there's not much point telling you. Men.

What happens, more or less, is this. On the planet Guna, which is inhabited by what seems to be something like human stock, and which has been in contact with

Gaia (Earth) for millennia, a more balanced sexual ecology has engendered a wide mix of hierarchical behaviour amongst various species (a point made more clearly in *The Land Beyond*). Though matriarchies are not universal throughout the human societies on the planet, the sacred City of Mahun has been ruled by Matriarchs (secular) and Gynarchs (religious) from time immemorial. The city itself, seen initially from underneath through the eyes of young Cal, is perhaps Alderman's finest single creation: ouroboral and shafted, subaqueous and galleried and overarching and abyssal, it peels like a great onion as the book progresses, and the layers never end. It cries tiers. Into this almost subliminal plenitude, reminiscent at times of Robert Irwin's Cairo, Alderman smoothly enfilades signs of the complex otherness of male-female relations in a world whose responses to sexual matters differ *instinctually* from ours. Oddly, though, none of her main characters are women, and the plot of *The Archivist* – whispered as it is into our ears by neighbourhood gossips – concentrates – as much as it is inclined to concentrate – on the attempted dismantling of the natural order by Magon Nonpareil, whose revolution does actually succeed (a long way offstage), and who does rule Mahun as Custodian for something like 70 years. But his love affair with young Cal, which has threaded its course through the passages of the city and the spiced mosaics of Gunaian sex, ends sadly, and after the two men separate we hardly see him again. He becomes a whisper at the corner of the page, an exiled though executive verb, sotto voce in the stone corridors of power, and married to a cryomorph.

Much of the rest of the book is taken up with great long luxurious contemplative travel riffs, slow ruminative lingering pulses of delight. Once in a while, the reader might wish for fewer cobwebs in the syntax, for passages where the agglutination of images became less doggedly *networky*, for a return of the executive from exile with a broom; but more importantly, the planet comes unanswerably to surround the reader as s/he gropes lingeringly on, and waffles of syntax become mysteries of perception in the mind's eye. By the end of *The Archivist*, Guna has become something very nearly real, a messy old beloved world, by indirections misdescribed (as in life), by networks of ichor bound.

Not so much can be said for the next book. *The Land Beyond* is a shorter novel, and a smaller one. There are sadnesses here. The copy-editing errors which deform and diminish the text may be due to a lack of morale in the offices of Unwin Hyman ripe for the flense, but the world-spanning voluminousness of the first book has inherently shrunk here into something rather more grudging. This freezing reluctance of scale may of course represent a conscious engagement of language and setting, for *The Land Beyond* is set in the far arctic north of Guna, in a vast archipelago called Noiro which encircles the planet like a necklace (read Noiro backward), and much time is spent describing hard-to-distinguish individual islands, arctic flora, arctic fauna. No map is provided for the volume, which much intensifies one's sense of a painful diminishment of scope, though the offhandedness of some of Alderman's geographical references does allow one to infer that she must have expected there to be one; nor for that matter does its dustwrapper copy even hint that *The Land Beyond* is closely linked to its predecessor. Why Unwin Hyman have chosen not to reproduce the world-map from *The Archivist*, and in any case to muffle the binding connection between the two volumes, it is not easy to understand. One cannot too strongly recommend to readers of the current volume that they keep a copy of *The Archivist* close to hand, and that they be prepared to consult not only the map of Guna which prefaces the book (and clarifies the geography of the sequel), but also, in the final pages, both Appendix One (a Chronology which, though infuriatingly blurry, does make some sense of the background references Alderman provides throughout the second volume) and Appendix Two (a list of Players, several of whom appear importantly in the second volume).

Unfortunately, even for those who happen not to be outsiders ignorant of the whole picture, *The Land Beyond* is even more reluctant than *The Archivist* to unfold its plot-wares. There are several strands of story, which driftingly intermingle for a while, then split. Technologically-sophisticated Sinein (for whatever explanation anyone's going to get as to the nature and location of Sinein, see *The Archivist*) has established an underground city called Traumesse (pig-German for dream-hood?), where the Eskimo-like folk of the far north have been interned to keep them safe from mortal decline outdoors. Underground, these Eskimo-folk are employed by the Sineinians to package the interactive computer-driven soap-opera which Artistic Director Ang Semo creates in situ and whose episodes are then sent south to Sinein from this extraordinarily remote place, which may have been selected (this is a wild guess, because Alderman does not actually seem to provide a rationale) because the Eskimo-folk are somehow immune to the effects of Semo's oneiric videos. Semo herself is sexually dry, haunted, quite possibly deranged. The Eskimos – we meet quite a few of them – are slangy endomorphs rather like the surviving Inuit of the Canadian tundra; and Salter Bren, the most dominant man among them, longs to return to the surface with his people, there to reenact the old ways before nature ended and videos began. Meanwhile, a Dr-Lao-like circus which travels through time, and whose cast and repertoire are derived from the *Commedia dell'Arte*, suddenly appears on the beach; performances are given; its leader, a Pierrot figure by the name of Loy (he appears in *The Archivist*, along with several other members of the circus, including the Gynarch Alleluya, who is now a fortune-teller; they are list-ed in Appendix Two), has sex with Semo. This is nice. It almost looks like a story is about to happen. But to follow through on this inchoate drama would be, perhaps, to betray Alderman's clear devotion to a discourse structure which, as we suggested earlier, dodges the penetrative morphologies of plot; they sleep together only once, and separate like motes in a gale.

Alderman must be respected for this abeyance, and *The Land Beyond* has mo-ments of complexly achieved chill beauty clearly dependent upon a refusal to warp aperçu into something told. The Eskimos are convincingly not like us, or Ang Semo. The *Commedia dell'Arte* routines are knowing. But there are, all the same, mo-ments of dismaying vagueness, which only increase as the various half-untold sto-ries fray and close down. One rather suspects, for instance, that Alderman has de-scribed the circus as travelling through time simply and solely because she needed some characters from the previous novel to jump-start this one – she certainly pro-vides no rationale for their presence, no coherence of premise to allow for time trav-el, no sense of *surprise* that the world is by this sign profoundly mysterious. Ang Semo's viral destruction of her computer soap is similarly too depressingly side-of-the-mouth to parse. In the end, there is nothing to wonder at. A great deal happens in the persepectiveless scree of the closing pages of *The Land Beyond*, but without aisles and gradients and peripeties no mystery of perception can make the turn into wonder, for wonder might precisely be defined as an awe of turning. O she's warm. Unshaped, unturned, unawed, the novel sits dormant on the page, like a promise forgotten. Take it or leave it (the text seems to mutter), but in the end, in the shrug-ging adult refusals to tell of these two frustratingly intelligent books, there is noth-ing for the reader to hold onto, nor any hand to clasp.

– Foundation 50, Autumn 1990

THE REMOTE and burning world of *Fires' Astonishment* (Secker & Warburg, 1990) lies buried many Henrys deep in the soil of England. Countenances we almost recognize – the Renaissance dragon stare of Henry VIII, the moral grimaces of Henrys IV and V as Shakespeare drew them, the antic grin of Hollywood's Henry II – must be exiled from the mind's eye if we are to reach downwards to the world of Geraldine McCaughrean's second novel for adults; we must attempt to imagine the storm-tossed reign of the first Henry (1068–1135), whose father was the Conqueror. There are no likenesses available.

As *Fires' Astonishment* opens, Henry I has just taken a second wife in an attempt to annul the dynastic effects of his son's death by drowning, and Leo, one of his minor feudal lords, returns home to the west of England, near the sea, to find his own domain in turmoil. Though his wife is safely pregnant, his son and heir has (it seems) gone north to become a monk, and his daughter has been bundled off to France to become married. And there is a dragon in the neighbourhood. And the fish have left the sea.

Readers of McCaughrean's first novel, *The Maypole* (1989) might be justified in suffering some *déjà vu* at this point, for the two books are, in fact, structurally identical. Each takes one of the great traditional English ballads and novelizes it; "Little Musgrove and Lady Barnard" shapes every word of *The Maypole*, and "The Laily Worm and the Machrel of the Sea" similarly gives *Fires' Astonishment* its central plot and denouement. But here the resemblance stops. "Little Musgrove," a secular tale of sexual passion and retribution, has fittingly been translated into a semi-urban late-medieval setting, which McCaughrean paints with the touch of a miniaturizing Breugel; but "The Laily Worm," a much earlier (and much stranger) ballad, requires a landscape altogether more alien.

The England of the first Henry may just fit the bill. Forests still cover the land, which is just beginning to become storied [the degree to which forests actually cloaked Old England is, of course, itself a topic of Story, and has been much exaggerated: see Simon Schama's *Landscape and Memory* (1995) 1995]. Monks and pardoners provide a network of gossip, but pagan beliefs lie very close to the surface. A queen mackerel may charm the seas free of fish. A dragon may presage the end of the world. Leo's sudden illness is only to be expected of a traveler to infinitely-distant London (though in fact his wife is poisoning him). Elfleda from the next manor may marry Leo's brother to breed a dynasty (like Henry himself), or to lose her virginity so the dragon cannot claim her. In the midst of miracles and filth, it is a deeply matter-of-fact world.

But it is a world in which the strange tale of "The Laily Worm" needs no gloss. The original poem portrays a young man whose step-mother has transformed him into a dragon and his sister into a mackerel; his lament swells heartbreakingly from a world whose details are unspoken, and it can only be assumed that his step-mother's motives encompass the sexual intemperance typical of usurper's in folklore, insensate greed, dynastic ambition. The strength (and the intermittent feebleness) of *Fires' Astonishment* comes from making these motives explicit.

Leo is a thick-pated cuckold; his wife's ambitions for the son in her womb seem almost normal; the diseased, moping, deadly, terpsichorean, love-sick dragon is a triumph of deadpan pathos. But the complicating network of passions which surround him seem at points mumble-mouthed, modern, even symbolic. It is here that

Fires' Astonishment does at points show a fatal loquacity. As an emblem of all the dragonish lusts unfolded in the singed tangles of this highly charged tale of death and the family romance, Leo's stained and steaming son is simply too easy to talk about. And in the end, Puff the Magic Dragon cannot quite carry the tune of the Worm.

– The Listener, 19 April 1990

[I bunch together here five separate pieces on Brian Aldiss: a 1987 appreciation, written for Conspiracy '87; a 1991 review of *Bury My Heart at W H Smith's*; a short 1988 review of *Forgotten Life*; a 1990 review of the first US publication of *Life in the West*; and a 1994 review of *Somewhere East of Life 1995*.]

HE COULD NOT have become Brian Aldiss in America. It is not easy to become a man of letters in that country, even for members of the traditional literary establishment; for sf writers – though Tom Disch has made a good stab at trying – it must be almost impossible. In the United Kingdom, on the other hand, even for sf writers, all one seems to need is wit, endurance, workaholic creative fire, culture, friends, allies, luck and panache. The rest is easy. The Co-President of the Eurocon Committee might have had to explain to the Chairman of the Society of Authors just what a Eurocon might be when it's home (it *sounds* like a Brussels urinal), but since Aldiss was at one point both of these gentlemen, a quick word from his mouth to his ear would have done the trick. No one can pretend that an sf ghetto does not exist in the United Kingdom; but no one should think it impossible to straddle both worlds, the ghetto and the downtown, as Aldiss does. Both worlds have shaped him, and he has shaped in turn both worlds. He has been many things, but it has always been absolutely central to his art that he is a man – an ambassador – of letters.

From the very beginning he has refused pigeonholing. Nor (to do them credit) did his first publishers try to bracket him into some procrustean bed in the ghetto. Brian's first book, *The Brightfount Diaries* (1955) from Faber & Faber, is a loose-slung "fictitious account" of working in a bookshop, based on his own life as a bookseller over the previous decade. His second book, also from Faber, is a collection of sf stories, *Space, Time, and Nathaniel: Presciences* (1957). The title may be marginally precious, but the contents glow with the speculative dash, the border-jumping effrontery, the natural tale-teller's voice, that supercharge his work even now, dozens of books later, hundreds of stories further on. Within a year he became the Literary Editor of the *Oxford Mail*, published his first sf novel, *Non-Stop* (1958), which remains one of his best, and his first Ace Double, *Vanguard from Alpha* (1959), which remains one of his worst. He edited sf for Penguin Books. He became an art correspondent for the *Guardian*. His books became more and more dangerous, skewing back and forth across the field and over the fence, violating one definition of sf after another, re-wording the form utterly (as in *Barefoot in the Head* from 1969, one of the first and still one of the most significant works of linguistic foregrounding in the field), or making mock obeisance to the kinds of sf he could never write with a straight face (as in *The Eighty-Minute Hour* from 1974, one of his rare collapses). As his critics and interpreters have said from the first, he is a Protean writer, and his next book will almost certainly fail to resemble his last. He is a cross-fertilizer, a master and exploder of the boundaries of the genre, a confronter, a pessimist whose gaiety is sustaining, a brave man. But some things he does not write.

He loves space opera, and has edited anthologies of the best examples of the form, but he cannot write the stuff for beans. He has created responsible characters, men and women of power and ambition and accomplishment, but he cannot for the life of him create a superhero. It is utterly clear that he finds it impossible to envision a hero who can solve *our* problems. If different forms of sf exist for Aldiss as opportunities for focusing his vision on the desperate dazzle of the real twentieth century, perhaps he finds the idea of the superhuman hero a kind of irrelevancy. He cannot in his art make use of those who own the world, he only seems really happy using those for whom the world is a miracle for utterance. His heroes, who are almost always human, almost always fallible and urgent, find themselves almost always inhabiting worlds greater and richer than any one mortal can envisage. The Helliconia Trilogy was conceived by a man who loved the enormous intricacies of his great planet – which is, after all, our own world seen as a form of drama – just as much as he did the migrant mayflies – human or phagor – who speckle for a day its vast seasons. It may even be possible to say that the greatest personal triumphs Helliconia's protagonists can enjoy are as nothing compared to the glory of having lived there. Even as they pass, in the blinking of an eye, in the night.

There are dozens more books; quite a few of them are in print. They should be read. None of them is much like any other. None of them could be mistaken for the work of anyone else. Thick or thin, bustling or solitudinous, all of them are humane. This insistent humanitarian voice is his trademark, if anything is; it is the common factor in everything Brian Aldiss writes, if there is a common factor; and we're lucky he continues to speak to us, person to person.

– *Frontier Crossings: Conspiracy '87* (1987)

SOMEWHERE in the pages of *Bury my Heart at W H Smith's: A Writing Life* (Hodder & Stoughton, 1990; expanded ed, Avernus), Brian Aldiss confesses that he had been finding this public autobiography a very difficult book to write; and no wonder. *Bury my Heart* is the tale of a mask that cannot keep a secret. It is the story of the real Brian W Aldiss, man and writer, as told by Brian W Aldiss of Avernus, the figure we see at a distance on television or making a speech, the figure whose privacy we have no reason to wish to penetrate, but who in this instance has taken on the job of trying to blab on the inner man, the real Brian W Aldiss, *who won't come out.*

Unsurprisingly, *Bury my Heart* is a rather haunted book. It is full of, and haunted by, things unsaid, tales unfinished or untold, gaps unfilled, connections blocked. The itchy pointillism of its telling gives, in the end, a sense of merited complexity of portrayal, but at the same time the refusal of narrative continuity seems almost punitive, as though the genial Aldiss of Avernus – "the children's eyes / In momentary wonder stare upon / A sixty-year-old smiling public man" – could not entirely disguise the fact that the real self he coats is a person of sustained anger. This is an insight, if it is an insight at all, which *Bury My Heart* is designed to dodge; and more power to it, perhaps. Perhaps it is enough that a number of good stories are told, sometimes all the way through, and that we have in our hands a mosaic of the progress of Brian W Aldiss through the world to which he has given a great deal. Vive. *Bury my Heart at W H Smith's* is a postprandial masque. As he himself says more than once in these pages, the real Aldiss stares out of the works themselves.

– Interzone 43, January 1991

Life in the West is not what it used to be. This may be good luck for us all. It is certainly good luck for Brian W Aldiss, whose *Life in the West* (Flamingo, 1994), a novel which caused some controversy when it first was first published in Britain ten years ago (in 1980), now appears in America. The Aldiss *chutzpah* has weathered the years well enough, and the glad exuberance of the writing has faded not at all; but what makes its current release here so fortunate is precisely the distance we have travelled from the events and attitudes anatomized in its pages.

The truth is, *Life in the West* never really worked as a tract for the times. Though he had already won a considerable reputation as an essayist and man of letters, Aldiss in 1980 was primarily (as he remains) a realistic novelist of bustling energy, and a writer of sf whose books in that field have had a domineering effect on his fellows. *Life in the West* is first and foremost a novel; and Thomas Squire, the philandering media-pundit who bruises through its pages like a miffed Alpha Male badly in need of an ewe, is primarily a creature of fiction. His opinions – mostly trumpet-blasts of dissent against the mild soft-left consensus that obtained in Britain as late as 1979 – constitute a novelist's rendering of political argument as something inherently comic. Intemperate, bullying, stunningly right, bullishly wrong-headed, Squire is exactly what his name declares. He is a late fictional version of the testy squire whose fulminations have graced the English stage for centuries.

If this was not entirely easy to see in 1980 in England, it should be perfectly clear today, now that the issues that ignite Squire have gained historical perspective. *Life in the West*, set in 1978, is a grand comedy. Fresh from writing and starring in a television documentary series called *Frankenstein Among the Arts*, and founder of the Society for Popular Aesthetics, Squire has gone to Sicily as guest of honour at the First International Congress of Intergraphic Criticism, where he finds himself jousting with dubious academics, tongue-twisting Marxists, a sharp desperate female left-winger from America whose mind he wishes to sort out and whose body he lusts after, a massive Russian who might or might not wish to defect, some old friends, and some new rivals. He puts on a good show. But Squire is not exactly what he seems. Quite oblivious to the moral ambiguity of his position, he performs another function, that of quasi-amateur double agent: sending reports upon his colleagues to the British secret service (it is clear he has done so for years). And back in England, his life has become a nightmare, one almost certainly of his own making; under the stress of a dissolving marriage, he is at the verge of abandoning the squirearchical role his family has long enjoyed in rural Norfolk.

Duplicitous and bluff, sensitive and crass, blustering and acute, Thomas Squire is a haunted man. He cannot tolerate the notion that his wife might be sleeping with a younger rival, while at the same time he rockets from affair to affair, pledging eternal devotion, boisterously, to each new lass. He cannot stand the bureaucratic mentality of the Marxists who dog his steps, but damages his own cause through the self-consciously masculine overkill of his own arguments. At the same time, he sees himself as a representative of what life in the West in 1978 means to the world. He sees himself, and the exasperated freedoms he espouses, as deeply important; and he is of course correct. At one point, he speaks of the soul. "We are all religious," he says:

> "In our day, the Left has all the dialectic, the Right none. Yet lying to hand is the supreme argument that souls are not interchangeable. It is perhaps too universal a truth for the Right to use, too true a truth to fall to the service of

any party. Nevertheless it is the vital factor through which the present world struggles towards the future, whether capitalist or communist, Caucasian, Negroid, or Mongoloid. It's our one hope, because undeniable."

At moments like this, the old bourgeois-liberal curmudgeon speaks for us all as he plunges onwards through *Life in the West*, slanging away at his targets like a Kingsley Amis anti-hero suddenly all a-roar with thought. As the novel closes, and a new decade begins (leaving so much behind), it appears that he may even manage to keep his wife and his house more or less intact. This seems well. Thomas Squire is, after all, not interchangeable.

– The Washington Post, 3 June 1990

BRIAN ALDISS'S *Forgotten Life* (Gollancz, 1988), a contemporary novel which houses extensive flashbacks to World War II in India and points east, fails to convince only in those passages that tiredly satirize a female author of romantic high fantasies who goes by the name of Green Mouth and who is married to stodgy, stressed Clement Winter, an Oxford scholar in the climacteric of his days. Where *Forgotten Life* grips the reader – and does not let go, for it is a beautifully paced narrative – is in its long rendering of Clement's house-of-mirrors confrontation with his dead older brother Joseph, whose papers have come to him for sorting. Somehow, through stifling adolescence in 1930s Britain and shattering years in the War mangle of the Asian theatre, Joseph has managed to retain a vital freshness of being, however savaged by time. Through his papers, he seems to stare at Clement like Clement's buried self; and the ice begins to crack. Unlocked, Clement/Joseph begins to sort out their conjoined life, and the lessons learned – for Aldiss is a man of parts, and has been able to endow the two brothers with a very considerable largesse of experience and savvy – have a wide purchase indeed. The final effect of this summa of Aldiss's best self as a writer is of a toughly sane openness to a world complexly and bravely faced.

– Interzone 19, May/June 1989

THE NOVEL which donates a subtitle to this one bears suggestively upon our reading of Brian Aldiss's latest assault on the dying cultures of the tumultuous, dying twentieth centruy. Comparison of the two books hints at how far we have gone.

Barefoot in the Head: A European Fantasia (1969) was an exorbitantly inventive reading of apocalyptic possibilities in store for the continent, a noisy telling of the beads of doom in terms of an Acid Head War which drives everyone bats. It was noisy, experimental, and brash with the news it bore.

Somewhere East of Life: Another European Fantasia (Flamingo, 1994) is a bigger, calmer, superficially less inventive tale; and, despite the occasional moment of hyperbolic slapstick, a deeply sadder one. In the most alarmingly seductive fashion, it says nothing new. Or, more accurately, it tells us that there is nothing more to say.

Between the two books lie 25 years. *Somewhere East of Life* wears each of them on its sleeve. The year is approximately 2005. It is business as usual in the maelstrom. There is no Acid Head War now, because there is no need of one, now that the the demise of the Soviet Union has begun to generate all the chaos any author of near-future parables could dream of creating on his own, short of the easy recourse of ending it all in a Bang. Bulgaria is being evacuated, because an old nuclear plant is melting into the Earth's core. Genocidal ethnic disputes are continuing to rage throughout the vast southern reaches of the former empire. The Aral Sea is no more. The stew of history is boiling dry.

Roy Burnell, an architectural historian in the employ of WACH (World Antiquities and Cultural Heritage), has had ten years of his own memories stolen to make illicit EMV (e-mnemonicvision) tapes of his love life, a process which wipes from the victim's mind the memories which have been stolen. What Burnell does manage to remember is fragmentary, distorted by the needs of the human memory system to make internal sense without much regard for external "truths." The past for him is a spatchcock of confabulations; the present is information overload; and the future is spattled with augurs of loss and demise.

As Burnell – Aldiss clearly intends us to understand – so the world east of Europe, after the death of the surreal empire which held it all together. Aldiss describes Burnell's quest for memory tapes, through Georgia and Turkmenistan, in a Baggy Monster picaresque style itself clearly evocative of centres which cannot hold. At a couple of points, the narrative wallows; but in the end – as Burnell's family engages in a role-playing game which itself constitutes a savage mockery of civilized life – all the parts sing requiem together.

Some characters, and a general sense of sweep, are shared with earlier Aldiss books like *Life in the West* (1980), *Forgotten Life* (1988) and *Remembrance Day* (1993); but *Somewhere East of Life* caps the entire career: the dozens of novels, the hundreds of stories. It sums the warnings he has uttered for decades. Magisterially, it brings us to this sorry pass.

– *New Statesman*, 12 August 1994

Rats and Gargoyles (Bantam UK, 1990), Mary Gentle's best novel to date, features an Acknowledgements page which pays thanks to the scholars who have opened up Renaissance Neoplatonism as a field of study, and a Short Bibliography dominated by the works of Dame Frances Yates. We are warned. Rats and Gargoyles may be a tale of fantasy – Gentle duly offers a mild apology for treating the Hermetic magia as "one vast adventure-playground" – but at its heart a mathematics-based model of the architecture of the world will dominate proceedings.

It has long been convenient for fantasy novelists to assume that the world we know represents only one outcome in a great game of chance, and that a shake of the dice might transform utterly the fields we know into a land of Oz or Jabberwock. What has perhaps been lacking is any rigorous imaginative interest in the mathesis – the discipline of learning – implicit in any assumption that the roots of reality might in fact dance to numbers.

Mary Gentle is not the first writer to strengthen the conventions of fantasy by attending to Giordano Bruno; John Crowley, for one, preceded her with Little, Big (1981). But she may be the first to traverse the daunting conundrums of Neoplatonism with anything like exuberance. Rats and Gargoyles, set in a version of Earth whose very existence depends on a conscious oiling of the music of the spheres, is an extensively learned and at the same time a quite astonishingly happy book. Through an unnamed city at "the heart of the world" parade Scholar-Soldiers, student princes, magi, large bipedal rats superior in the social order to mere humans, and 36 gods who sing, in unison, the song of arithmetic which keeps reality whole. The gods burp, a meticulous choreography of plotting brings everything to a head, reality shakes like a house of cards, but numbers, joy and sex win in the end. In every possible way, Rats and Gargoyles casts a spell.

– The Observer, 5 August 1990

EACH TIME it is different, and each time it is the same. As has been the case with all his books from The Fifth Head of Cerberus (1972) on, there is no such thing as a first reading of a Gene Wolfe novel, for at first there is only the Great Woods of the book, Castleview (Tor, 1990) in this case, and us bemused explorers of the new Logos, Hansels and Gretels scrying for paths through rose and briar to the gingerbread house, dropping breadcrumbs in the scuttle of our trek, while around us the caltrap and syllable of a tale is being told, which we hope to survive; because we're hoping for a second trip, a second reading, for a courtesy of briar and rose. That is the same as always. What is different in Castleview is, perhaps, almost everything else.

An autobiography of this reviewer's reading of the book may be of help. Having obtained a proof copy some months ago, I read about half the text in an initial spurt; from the first, the here and now of the book seemed unusually clear. Castleview was set in the late 1980s in a small fictional town itself called Castleview, taking its name from the fact that people round about tended to suffer from intermittent sightings, fata morgana visions, of a strange romantic multi-turreted castle which seemed to shift position like a galleon, or perhaps Earth shifted into sight of it. But *Castleview* was placed, uniquely for a Wolfe novel, in a place which one could locate on a map – in northwestern Illinois, near the Mississippi River, on the road from nearby Galena (which is a real place) through Barrington (where Wolfe himself lives) to Chicago. So we could pinpoint the here (though not perhaps Morgan le Fay); and as for the now, we even knew the day: it is the day that the protagonist, Will E Shields, new owner of a Castleview automobile dealership handling late 1980s cars, arrives in town with his family, looking for a house to buy. Halfway through the book, that day has not yet ended, and already much has begun to happen.

At the point Will Shields has decided to buy a house, one not perhaps coincidentally prone to views of the legendary castle, all hell (or Faerie) breaks loose. The owner of that house has already been mysteriously killed by a blow to the head, and now citizens and visitants from Faerie – like outriders of the Other – begin to proliferate (the book, as a whole, has more than 50 named characters in performing roles) and to intermingle; a Cherokee jeep owned by Will's dealership shows crosshatch signs of taking on the aspect of a great charger; and the invaders, including a long-dead inhabitant of Castleview, begin to raddle trancingly the Great Wood I was attempting to penetrate with the breadcrumbs and faith of my first reading. Clearly they are looking for something (perhaps Arthur). But the first half of *Castleview* is like a Crazy Comedy from the 1930s, cocooned in slapstick, a dozen farces heaped upon Ossa; and in this congeries of antic scenes and turning glimpses no single rallying clue (like the elm tree in *Peace*) can easily be found. No sooner does a scene begin to subject to a climax any member of the cast – Will, or his family, or the widow of the man whose house he wished to buy, or any of a dozen other significant actors – than the curtain whips down, and a new conjunction of players – like reconfigured chips in a kaleidoscope – begins to dance and fret; as in *Peace*, and generating a similar sense of ominousness, no story ever gets told to the end. But it was here, for reasons extrinsic to the book, I came to a halt.

That was the "first" read.

As usual, I found myself speaking to others about this initial or courtship stage of reading Wolfe; and as usual there was someone (in this case Neil Gaiman) who had gained a sense of the route inside.

– The problem with *Castleview* of course (he said) is that there are too many Arthurs.

– You mean (I said, less quickly than this) that the book is not about finding Arthur, but about enlisting one.

– Right. You remember, for instance, in the *Morte Darthur*, the kind of wound the King receives at the end?

– No.

– A great blow to the head.

– So.

– So how many men receive head wounds in *Castleview*?

– Three? Five? Seven?

So it goes.

So *Castleview* is a tale of recruitment. The time for an expiatory final battle is once again nigh, and Morgan le Fay must find a hero to oppose. She must find one who will take up with chivalrous abandon the immortal role. It must be her brother, the once and future King. From the moment that Will E Shields – whose wife at one point addresses him as "Indiana," in what must be a reference to the compulsively gallant Indiana Jones – arrives in the small city of Castleview, and finds himself immediately tossed into a vertiginous kaleidoscope of sights and happenings and sounds off and ghosts on, it seems (in retrospect) clear that he may be the most fitting Arthur, and that his arrival in itself may have signaled the beginning of the transformative invasion of Castleview by indwellers of the other world in search of him in particular; or perhaps it is simply the case that the time has come for a renewal of the great conflict between Arthur and his foes, and Will only happens to be on the scene. This may not much matter; over the next 24 hours (which take up the great bulk of the book) Morgan le Fay and her breed ransack Castleview for the Arthur of their great need. The one Castleview native who might seem an ideal choice, Arthur (Wrangler) Dunstan, has been too severely wounded and bled to lift the sword; nor does he exhibit the unquestioning chivalrousness of Shields, who in retrospect seems always to have been fated for enlistment. Who can say? As in a great game of musical chairs, scene after scene has evicted character after character from the rataplan of the kaleidoscope. Was it fated that Shields would keep his seat? Or was it the luck of the tune that beats the world (and stops, and you are dead)? In any case, the land of Faerie pulls more and more savagely at the tranced survivors, and more and more of the cast find themselves (like Hansel, or Gretel) tracing dream-like passages through the maze of conjunction between the two worlds. It is like a drawing of blood. The end is nigh.

There have been references throughout *Castleview* (as Neil Gaiman also mentioned) to the tale of Puss in Boots. The name of one of the girls at the nearby summer camp is Lucie d'Carabas, which is the name Puss gives to his master, who on becoming d'Carabas becomes as much an impostor as any Will Shields donning the accoutrements of Arthur; the surname of the maternal grandmother of a Castleview family long central to the impositions of Faerie is Chattes; and late in the novel, deep within the topological infirmities of the haunted and chthonic Wild-Hunt world of Faerie, appears a cat who walks on two legs, perhaps rather unfortunately named J Gordon Kitty. In a tale of enlistment, and perhaps of concealed ambition, he is an ideal guiding fairy – and it might be noted that in the original tale of Puss in Boots (circa 1550), Giovanni Straparola fails to mention Boots, but does say that the cat in question is a fairy in disguise. Subtly fermented by the dextrous Puss, events soon reach a populous climax. There is a battle, and a sacrifice, and benthic repose, and the two worlds disentangle.

It is, in other words, over in a flash. *Castleview* has been a very sudden book. The style is that of *Free Live Free* (1984) or *There Are Doors* (1988) [see p. 147]: unadorned (except for the deep intrinsicated metaphor-delving passages which describe the crossing of a young girl into the fey castle); measured and measuring (with characters constantly *orienting* themselves in rooms and corridors and time); haunted by proximity to the thing described. But in neither of these previous novels whose Folk dance gingerly through Mage-designed worlds in search of their hearts' desires does Wolfe so closely approach as he does in *Castleview* to the style and Matter of G K Chesterton. *Castleview* may be the finest and most lucid Catholic dream allegory Wolfe has yet written, and its clear and burning affinity with *The Man Who was Thursday: A Nightmare* (1908), which is also a novel of enlistment, and a tale of masks, may be entirely deliberate on his part. It is of course God who is the final recruiter in that book, the final Sunday within a week of impostors, and *Castleview* must seem to represent a pre-Christian Conclave and Calling. But both books share a hallucinated lucidity of telling, and an onrushing deadpan obeisance to the potency of the bare word. And both glow with an articulacy of giving, for neither *Castleview* nor *The Man Who was Thursday* are, in any real sense, fully autonomous works of art. They are both of them gifts. They are table settings.

Each of them calls upon a Lord to dine.

– New York Review of Science Fiction 24, August 1990

"I TOLD you so," wrote H G Wells in 1941, in the middle of the Second World War, just after finishing the last of his 50 novels, in most of which he had tried to warn us that the world must be saved. "You *damned* fools." He was thinking, perhaps, of *The World Set Free* (1914), in which he had predicted the atomic bomb; or he may have been contemplating the chaos around him, which he was convinced had become terminal. Clearly he had no idea of our capacity to survive.

Kurt Vonnegut, for instance, survived the firebombing of Dresden, which, as an American POW, he was privileged to witness at first hand; and in *Slaughterhouse-Five; or, The Children's Crusade: A Duty-Dance with Death* (1969), which will remain his masterpiece, he very nearly managed to transform that conflagration into a work of art, and in that book he very nearly persuades us that the world itself has substance enough to survive our terrible pranks. But now, with *Hocus Pocus* (Cape, 1990), he has finally published a kind of rebuttal to that tale of hope against the odds, and what he now says is, I told you so. You *damned* fools.

Hocus Pocus, which is recounted in the year 2001 by an ex-soldier turned college teacher awaiting trial for a crime he could not conceivably have committed, seems at first glance to be a novel about Viet Nam. Colonel Eugene Debs Hartke, nicknamed The Preacher, and a master of hocus pocus, has long been obsessed by his role in that war, much of which he had spent exhorting young soldiers to die for reasons no one could sensibly explain. Very quickly, however, it becomes evident that Vonnegut is stalking larger prey than Hartke, or Viet Nam itself, or the bitter aftertaste of that war in an America spiritually befouled by its refusal to admit defeat. *Hocus Pocus* is about the end of nature, and the slow termination of the human species.

At the same time, like every novel Vonnegut has written since *The Sirens of Titan* (1959), *Hocus Pocus* is, of course, an extremely funny book. Jokes are told, deadpan and whiplash-sharp; neat compulsive little anecdotes with stings in the tail jostle one another down the page, urgent and deadly and bland, just as it was in the 1960s, when *Cat's Cradle* (1963) and *God Bless You, Mr Rosewater* (1965) made his reputation as America's funniest serious writer since Mark Twain; there's hardly a sentence which fails to tickle the reader into continuing. As always, it is almost impossible to stop reading him. Even the Tralfamadorans make an appearance, the flippant but comforting aliens who teach Billy Pilgrim in *Slaughterhouse-Five* how to survive the memory of the apocalypse he's just experienced. To survive the chaos and trauma and terror of history (they say), just remember that the world is immutable. So travel back to a time when you were happy, and stay there.

But Billy Pilgrim, who thinks he can escape through time to a happy hunting ground, is probably loony. Hartke is not, and the Tralfamadorans who appear in *Hocus Pocus* can do nothing to release him from 2001, from his genuinely insane wife, from his pending jail sentence, from an America sold to the Japanese – who have begun to abandon their acquisition, just as Americans abandoned Viet Nam, because it has become too expensive to try to run – and from a world in which "man was the weather now." In any case, the Tralfamadorans only appear as characters in a short story Hartke reads in a magazine called *Black Garterbelt*, in which it is revealed that they have been using the planet as a laboratory and testing ground for the creation of tough germs, germs capable of surviving what humans do to things. These germs, for reasons unknown but almost certainly dire, are now due to be sent throughout the universe, where they will disseminate life.

For Hartke in 2001, the world may be a fit place for tough germs, but not for him. Like the land of his birth, he is sick unto death. His tuberculosis worsens as his tale, told in the form of short notes scribbled into prison library books, nears terminus. In these final pages, one phrase, "Finale Rack," begins to recur more and more frequently. It is a term used by the professionals who arrange fireworks displays for a living. After the show seems almost done, a pause is arranged. All seems finished. Then the Finale Rack is lit, and the sky explodes. For Hartke (and for his creator), the Finale Rack of human history began just about the time H G Wells gave up the fight. By 2001, it is almost all over. Weather forecasts for the planet are dire. Universal darkness buries all. A few germs escape.

– *Sunday Correspondent*, 21 October 1990

It may be possible to understand before reaching page 96 that *Voyage to the Red Planet* (Morrow, 1990) is going to succeed, but this reviewer, for one, did not, until then, know why. By page 96, almost half the book is gone. Up to this point, Terry Bisson has told his tale with that air of lucky nonchalance that marks the best kind of *learned* writer, the kind whose technical tricks (when noticed) seem serendipitous, heliocentric, like windows in a house of dreams which open only when you need to see the path inwards to the garden in the sun; but he has not yet seemed to bite the bullet of his premise. *Voyage to the Red Planet* is set in the first years of the 21st century. Like a surfer no longer able to ride the wave of Progress, America has sunk backwards into foul waters, bankrupt. Everything is now owned by Disney-Gerber and its competitors. A last spaceship, which has never left orbit, and which is named the *Mary Poppins* because it looks like a furled umbrella, has been demothballed by a movie company eager to make humanity's first trip to Mars into a smashing film epic. Crew and cast are duly recruited. Up to page 96, it is very funny story, but a corroding one, because we seem stuck in spoof satire country, where everything rusts, nothing is given the worship of verisimilitude. And Mars is a joke.

Nothing seems to happen on page 96. The Mary Poppins and crew have managed to escape writs and gravity, and after several months of induced hibernation have just made the transit of Venus. Captain Kirov (a woman Russian astronaut) needs to get confirmation from Sweeney's privatized Ground Control service that the transit has been successful. Eventually – after the return time lag – his signal comes through. Everything is fine, he says. And just as well,

"since the computers here are tied up with the new Laker Stadium."

"New Laker Stadium?"

"Guess I forgot to tell you," Sweeney said, 18.4 minutes later. "Sweeney's Mission Design went belly-up. I have a new job with Stadium Computer Solutions in Santa Monica. Mostly we do crowd flow and traffic simulations for mall and parking lot designers. Don't worry, I'm still doing the Mars Voyage on my own time. Stadium has a big old Cray that can really crunch numbers and I use it during lunch hour. I'm sending the figures for the Mars orbital capture braking burn, nine months from now, so you can begin to run them through your switchboards."

Which is all funny enough, though rather in Silly Skit mode, and fleetingly reminiscent of the awful Snoo Wilson's Spaceache (1984). But the important and the saving thing about this passage is, of course, the Cray. From within the nuhdzing corrosions of spoof, but rewriting all the while the spoof jokes and flimflam into a three-dimensional gallows humor, we gain sudden sight of a real world of complex things happening, the Cray crunching the numbers necessary for any sane reader to believe that the Mary Poppins is a ship in the mind's eye, not a greasepaint joke, not another example of the *ressentiment* of the typical satirist, who responds to the world as though it were a machine gone haywire, and whose works embody such a horror of *motion* that it sometimes seems as though motion itself were the enemy. There is something about the kinetic energy of *things* that horrifies (while exercising a Totentanz fascination over) the kind of writer who attempts to deflate the demons of the burning world with laughs. But Terry Bisson is an unusual writer, for he is a funny man whose every word acts out the movement of things. In his heart he writes novels, not satires; his joints are oiled. His Cray crunches. His verisimilitudinous Mary Poppins reaches a real Mars.

The landing is a hard sf tour de force (in his prefatory note Bisson acknowledges help from Charles Sheffield) and his Mars gives off a sense of Viewmaster durance (he also acknowledges the assistance of Kim Stanley Robinson, whose ongoing Mars sequence is set on something like the very same planet). The cast – a large, variegated, genre-mixing crew of astronauts and movietown humors and a surly cat and a stowaway – retains its dignity as though internally gyroscoped, while film options back on Earth collapse and spring back, and Sweeney scrabbles to keep data flowing, and Glamour the dwarf cinematographer shapes and reshapes the tale with his brand-new Demogorgon camera, which itself reconstructs the bits of reality it films into themeparked artifacts of being; the comic idiocy of the world in which everyone operates seems not so much a series of turns as the thing itself, America After Missing the Wave. The plot eventually thickens. Like Elmore Leonard's *Get Shorty* (1990), the tale ends up being the storyline for a movie with the same name as the book, with a dignity of denouements that catches at the throat, and a number of good jokes, though none of those aimed directly at Hollywood carries much bite. But most important of all, *Voyage to the Red Planet*, which is about the fabrication of wonder, leaves us in a state of wonder for the Mars we almost had, once upon a time, before Nixon.

It's almost as though we might still get there.

– *New York Review of Science Fiction* 26, October 1990

I.

ELIZABETH HAND is a brand new name, and she has just published her first novel. It is big, and it is worth praising. *Winterlong* (Bantam, 1990) is a dense, graceful, bullying book of great length and much skill; it is a live tale, told in a live voice, by an author of muscle and drive and ambition; its publication as a paperback original shows the depth of talent available in the field. But enough of positive stuff. A necessary downside of the ambitiousness that shows in every page of her romance is the fact that *Winterlong* is also messy, overextended, pompous, derivative and daft. Every silver lining has a cloud.

Hundreds or thousands of years have passed in America as the long tale opens, in a medical research establishment somewhere near a City which may be New York, or Philadelphia [it turns out to be Washington 1995] – or somewhere else entirely, for no familiar place names have survived long centuries of plague and catastrophe and political upheaval. As the planet has clearly been stripped of its non-renewable resources, no energy-consuming technologies have survived; but genetic engineering has flourished, "geneslaves" roam the forests, and no one who lives on the surface of the world seems entirely sane or *sapiens*. Several Ascensions –political revolutions seemingly directed by elite humans who live in orbit – have succeeded one another, and each period of turmoil has left the world stranger than before. Rumors of a Final Ascension are now rife.

Wendy Wanders, an autistic orphan from the nearby City, has been medically transformed into a kind of vampire empath, a creature who can read the dreams of others, and steal them. (Her appalling moniker, and the absence of any compelling rationale for her medical transformation, are two signs of Hand's occasional lack of novelistic good sense.) After being read by Wendy, patients tend to commit suicide. Notwithstanding this, her mentor at the establishment asks to be read herself, and reveals a series of dreams in which her long-dead twin brother is psychically ingested by a godlike Boy, a Pan-figure, who calls himself Baal, the Gaping One, and Osiris, and so on. He also (Hand, one suspects, will live to rue this dreadful inspiration) calls himself Peter Pan. Wendy takes him into her psyche. Her mentor commits suicide. Enemy dirigibles bomb the establishment with a rain of roses, or plague. Wendy escapes.

Meanwhile, in the City, Wendy's *own* twin brother Raphael, who has been raised in the House Miramar as a male courtesan, begins the first steps of his own long trek. He too contains within his psyche a potent ghost of the dreadful Baal Boy, who mocks him and governs his actions; on discovering that Wendy exists, Raphael finds he must seek out union with his sister, whose name, we soon learn, is also Magdalene, and Isis, and so forth. Clearly, by evoking the brother-sister god-pairs so central to pre-Christian religions, Hand hopes to make it clear that *Winterlong* is more than your usual sf novel; and just as clearly the tale is going to have to culminate in some sort of mythological Big Bang, presumably at the traditional Masque of Winterlong, held on the shortest day of the year, and after the revel the incestuous union of the heavenly twins will join Love and Death in celestial wedlock, the world will burgeon into Spring, and a new Ascension will liberate the planet. All this does, of course, happen.

Unfortunately, Hand does not choose to move directly to this chosen climax, and *Winterlong* becomes, for hundreds of pages, little more than an anthology of the Dying Earth clichés of all the writers who have preceded her in this kind of story. Jack Vance supplies the broad vistas; Gene Wolfe supplies the vocabulary, the plot, the characters and the setting; others, like Richard Grant, supply bits of local color. But Hand does have an extremely acute eye for psychological extremity; she hardly writes a bad sentence, and has in fact filled *Winterlong* with hundreds of fine ones; and she wants desperately to compose a genuinely big book. *Winterlong* goes part of the way, then stumbles, and becomes merely too long; but the effort is there, the joy of creation, the thrill of abundance. It was exciting to find her. Elizabeth Hand will be back.

II.

In any other part of the world of letters but the land of sf, Gardner Dozois would have simply fallen silent. Always prone to dry spells as a writer, and in recent years fully occupied with editing *Isaac Asimov's Science Fiction Magazine*, he has never been a man to publish a book a year, or to flood the journals with stories. In the late 1970s, he began to suffer from a writing drought that looked as though it might become permanent. But because he was an sf writer, and because sf writers have always collaborated with one another more than writers of any other kind of literature, he turned to his friends. The stories in *Slow Dancing Through Time* (Ursus, 1990) are the result.

They are, of course, collaborations. Some of them are triple collaborations. The authors involved, with the exception of Susan Casper, are widely known in the field. Jack Dann and Michael Swanwick, like Dozois, have published books whose individual voices are unmistakeable; and Jack C Haldeman II, obscured for years by Joe Haldeman, his active younger brother, has slowly become identifiable as a figure in his own right. In a series of forewords and interjections, all five speak of the pleasure and sense of mutual security they derive from co-authoring stories; they speak of the joys of workshopping, the conviviality, the gossip – and the money, because most of the work here published sold first to high-paying magazines. And it is certainly the case that the stories collected in *Slow Dancing Through Time* are crafty and competent and knowing.

But that is not all they are. They are also indistinguishable. When they tug at the heart-strings – "Touring," for instance, which joins Buddy Holly, Janis Joplin and Elvis Presley in a posthumous gig – they do so with the Dynaflow efficiency of the most advanced chess computer. Horror – "The Clowns" is grim and gripping and icy – is similarly honed to an impersonal accuracy. And occasionally, as in "Time Bride," which about a man who spies through time upon a young girl and destroys her life through his intolerable snooping, there is a stain of moral obtuseness, as though the technical joy of constructing the artifact of story had blinded the authors to its human dimension. All in all, *Slow Dancing* is a rather frightening book. It reduces the possibilities inherent in the genre to a calculus of effect, rather arousing to experience, and rather desolate. But the gang had fun.

III.

Michael Kandel, two of whose translations of Stanislaw Lem have been nominated for the National Book Award, has begun to write tales on his own. *In Between Dragons* (Bantam, 1990) is the second of them. It is an extremely odd little book. If Lem himself had written a juvenile, and had been capable of setting it in suburban America, then something rather like *In Between Dragons* might have been a plausible outcome; for there can be no denying Kandel's debt to Lem's abrasive way with conventions, or to his intense ferocity. As with Lem's work, *In Between Dragons* makes most sense as an engine of interrogation.

What is being interrogated in this case, most amusingly, is the ethical nature of the fantasy worlds modern young Americans have available to them through books, role playing games, television. Pimply, awkward, tongue-tied Sherman Potts has discovered in himself the ability to flicker out of the mundane world into a series of magic kingdoms, where he has adventures featuring lots of action and harmless machismo. But puberty is assailing him back on Earth, and his escapades begin to darken, to become morally dubious, impossible to keep simple. Life, with its terrible incapacity to keep to the storyline, has seeped into the furthest recesses of Sherman's dream-world, and somehow he must extricate himself from the ocean of story, without doing fatal harm to the fantasy companions of his childhood. He must grow up. Just as in the several Jonathan Carroll novels that *In Between Dragons* also resembles, this process will cost dear. But Carroll never allows his characters to take much pleasure in the realities for which they eventually opt. It is a measure of the sharpness and complexity of this short book that we both regret the lost land of Sherman's youth, and welcome, guardedly, the real world to come.

– The *Washington Post Book World Science Fiction Column*, 28 October 1990

FIVE: 1991

1. Year Roundup

Asimov City. Michaelmas Term lately over, and the Time Bailiff sitting in the Hall of Dues. Implacable November weather. As much mud in the streets, as if the waters had but newly retired from the face of the earth, and it would not be wonderful to meet a Megalosaurus, forty feet long or so, waddling like an elephantine lizard up the stream of time. Futures everywhere. Futures up the river; futures creeping into the cabooses; futures down the river, hovering in the rigging of great ships. Futures in the eyes and throats. Futures in a foggy glory round the head of the Bailiff; futures infiltrating the scribes of the City, scores of them still undead, still mistily engaged – nostrils stopped against the rictus of new air – in any of the ten thousand sharecrops that pustulate the endless City, tripping one another up on slippery precedents, running their goat-hair and horse-hair warded heads against walls of words, making a pretence of equity with serious faces: as players might.

But the king is dead, of course, though scribes continue, like roaches wrapped in mummy cloth, to scrabble through the corpus, snuffling for tidbits caught between the great sandy teeth, seaching through the fallen ribs of stone – and up and down the aisles and edifices of Robot City – for hooks to hang to, as by threads, or last straws. The king is dead, and the futures of the world swirl round the bare-shanked scribes of sharecrop, tearing from their grip the final hooks of the old sf, the runes of Asimov which fixed the future into one shape, the Future History of the Dead Writ. *Time, gentlemen*, says the Bailiff, who is Time's snickersnee, and cuts the threads grinning, and the scribes of sharecrop tumble downwards into the acid holes of the world, bugs chewed by pestilence. *Hurry up please it's time.*

More than the death of Robert A Heinlein – who had long before abandoned the fixed future of his prime, the Future History his acolytes had gone on patching, for decades, in the great Quilting Bee of post-War American sf – it was a death to mark. The recursive infantilism of Heinlein's closing books had constituted an anathema-ta, his utterances the primal nada of a terrified and terrifying mortal child for whom the century had not played fair. His final books told all of us, cursing us en passant, that the Future was deader than Ozymandias, that the Duesenberg of Future History had slammed off the high road into badlands. And he turned his back (fatally) on the Bailiff, who might also be called Time Present, and sank into himself like a stone. He scared me stiff. Personal grieving aside, Heinlein's death was a *relief* to the wardens of the old church, because the decades of apostasy could be forgotten, the bitterness of his snub.

No. The death to mark – the death for us to stand upon the other side of, as upon the far side of a shadow, in the feeble sunlight of a lessening day – was the death of Isaac Asimov in 1992, because Asimov had never abandoned the high road, [never stopped insisting that First SF was telling us the right story 1995], never stopped staking claims to the Future he had promulgated from 1940 on with all the juices of his geek heart, big brain, frantic displacing mind. Indeed, for many of those who knew him and who used him (just as, mercilessly, he used them in return to salve his fame: to be "presented" or "introduced" by Asimov must have been to feel like suntan lotion), he *was* the road. He was the Future, he was the sound of the consensus agreed to by the brothers and the sisters and the scribes who filled in the gaps, echoing like gourds to his call, walking the same plank. He was the sound (as I myself said on a UK programme about his life) of sf talking to itself, the default voice of American genre sf, which had been born in 1926, had been stricken in 1957 when Sputnik began to asset-strip the playground of space, and had since deceased. His death marked all of this. We stand on the other side of the shadow.

The game of genre sf [of First SF 1995] is over and done now, and we are for the world, I think willy-nilly. Just as the planet got too close to us at the end of the nineteenth century, and could no longer contain mysteries of geography for us to penetrate, so at the end of the twentieth there is no longer any way of distancing the future enough to play with it. We are closed in on, and it's dark in here, and we may not come through: so be it. Much of the best post-genre sf now written reflects a knowledge that the terms have changed: what the old dreamers of genre sf once penetrated with gumption and glee (the gal, the god, the town, the frontier, the territory, the monster, the alien, the planet, the galaxy), the most significant new sf writers now tend to propitiate, to seek ways of marrying. It is a profound transvaluation of values. Sf (to repeat arguments made in other places [variously phrased, throughout this collection of pieces 1995]) has been transformed into fables of exogamy. In that sense – and for all human beings who read sf – it has become, once again, and after a long intermission in the coils of nostalgia, a literature of the future, or (now that we have come out of the monocular glare of the old First SF programme) the futures. Once again, now that we know we are differently futured, we can learn from sf.

There are statistics. As usual, the *Locus* people do the best job of displaying and making sense of the figures. *Science Fiction, Fantasy, & Horror: 1991* (1992), edited by Charles N Brown and William G Contento, is an annual volume which presents in corrected and expanded form the statistics assembled monthly in *Locus* itself. It is recorded in this year's volume that a record number of genre books were seen by

Locus (which is still not quite the same as "were published in the USA") during the period in question: 1246 titles in all, almost three and a half books every single day of the year. For our purposes, however, lots of them could be ignored. There were a number of anthologies, collections and non-fiction titles, all beyond our remit; others were novelizations, or ties (a term I have come to prefer, because it points to a variety of categories of books written to order), and were unlikely to warrant much more attention than one might pay the ten thousandth footprint from a dead man's boot. There were also 165 horror novels, most of which had little sf content, or ate it. And there were 301 fantasy novels, some 275 by exact count being quest tales for mcguffins set in rubberized ruritanias [ie pastorals 1995] heavily infested with the usual decalcomania: killable extras, personalized elf stuffings, Christopher Lloyd magus golems; and everything told in a style so uniformly boneless as to be very nearly beyond description. In the end, only 308 sf novels were left, which was *less than one a day*. And most of *them* were written by hardscrabble computer scribes, and bound in mummy cloth. Most sf novels published in 1991 were scabs of the dying. Fearful of the day. Unmentionable.

The previous four versions of this roundup were broken into categories which presented genre sf as an ongoing chronology, a continuing agenda on the part of successive generations of writers. For this fifth – and almost final – instalment, it seems no longer appropriate to continue to unroll this red carpet into the swamp of Now. Any 1991 book which embodies the old Future History of genre sf [I won't substitute the term I now prefer, First SF, for every use of the term "genre sf" or "old sf" or "agenda sf," though I do think it's less likely to deceive: but I don't necessarily think the new term is fully synonymous with the old ones, and anyway it's a 1994 coining, and shouldn't really be allowed to time-travel 1995] is in effect a *novelization*. And it was probably written for hire. And there is another difficulty. It has become increasingly difficult to suggest that non-genre books (like those written by Martin Amis or Marge Piercy) can usefully be distinguished – over and beyond the need to note the deeply unprofessional ignorance of generic language and device shared by almost all non-genre writers – from post-genre sf by writers (like Karen Joy Fowler or Michael Swanwick) who may have been brought up within the freemasonry, but who show every sign of riding the sea-change into a world we must try to share, and comprehend. The old sf is dead; and the change is in us, like the neocytes in Robert Charles Wilson's *The Harvest* (1992), who enact a terrible beauty upon any human being wise enough to accept their offer to marry out. But there are still dinosaurs.

Being a Founder of the old sf is not exactly a matter of age. Jack Vance is older than Frederik Pohl, but Vance began too late (well into the 1940s) to qualify as a charter member, and he writes with the dreamy belatedness of a fish in deep water, while Pohl, who became an sf writer before the start of World War Two, continues to write as though the Art Deco shazams of 1940 sf still signalled and shaped a challenge to the world, rather than a medium to consult. What is astonishing is that it works. By retaining the urgency of the old sf, but not its articles of faith, he continues to write with a dawn latency, as though we might still make it new, the story of sf, the tale that tells us there's a story. It is the very opposite of the sad recursive râle of genre talking to itself, like a patient trying to date an iron lung. So he is a dinosaur of genre, along with Jack Williamson, both warm-blooded, and there are none others left, except maybe Damon Knight, but he was never more than a jester in the closing days of dinosaur court; and Andre Norton, but she only began publishing sf well into her career. Frank Belknap Long and A E Van Vogt will write no more; L Sprague de Camp is unlikely to produce sf [wrong 1995]; and it is hard to think of Arthur Lloyd Eshbach or Raymond Z Gallun as striking a new note.

So Pohl and Williamson can be celebrated for their continuity, though their offspring cannot be similarly celebrated for aping it; and Williamson can be forgiven for the increasing frequency with which his plotlines default to the pulp strokes of 65 years ago, when he began. There may be antique moments in The Singers of Time (Doubleday Foundation), which is the tenth collaboration between the two writers since 1954, but there is a settled polish to the telling and the alien that reads almost like wisdom. And Stopping at Slowyear (Pulphouse/Axolotl), by Pohl alone, was a Long Year tale set on the usual Long Year planet, where the usual elongations of season generate the usual Giacometti matrices: long sex, long punishments, long reveries, long guerres. But the tale was swift. From the dead dinosaur, the shadow of whose falling marks terminator, yet another fewmet issued from the heart of the midden: Child of Time (Gollancz) with Robert Silverberg, who took an Asimov story from 1958, "The Ugly Little Boy," made Frankenstein passes over the body, gave us a lad of marble. Our Angry Earth (Tor), by Asimov and Pohl, was nonfiction, recommended that we save the planet, said how. I have not seen it.

One final dinosaur remains, but of a different strain. Arthur C Clarke is the right age, and began to write at the right time, and speaks as though he understands the doing of the world (almost always a sign of a pre-War writer); but he is English, and his relationship to American genre sf has always seemed – if at times almost indefinably – remote, as though he were passing for white. He is, it cannot be too often mentioned, a member (Brian Stableford is another) of a different and exceedingly rare species; he is an author of Scientific Romances: hence the long evolutionary perspectives which mark his work, which can be distinguished from US Future Histories by an sense that the March of Progress may well lead us into the cruelest month; and by pithless heroes drenched in twilight; and by the diffusion of affect into a uniformitarian emeritus chill through which genre plots are transformed into models for contemplation. But then, in some recent books – those where much of the actual writing was done by an American collaborator named Gentry Lee – all this seemed to be lost, or abandoned, or never known, the way Disney never knew a duck; and novels signed with Clarke's name, like the spastic *Cradle* (1988), emitted a sad off-the-Interstate air of themepark dinosaurishness. The first of the Rama sequels, also with Lee, was similarly inauthentic; but *The Garden of Rama* (Gollancz) marked a return to the glazed equipoise of Scientific Romance at home with itself. Perhaps the neocytes of UnAmericanism had transfigured the junior partner's episteme, or maybe Clarke himself took a more commanding role in a collaboration which had begun desperately to need a senior voice: whatever happened, a book was given birth to.

For the rest of us – slipstreamers, alpha males, difficult women, neophytes, neighbours, expats – it's down the long chute together, into a heap at the heart of a late year. In *Dracula Unbound* (Grafton), Brian W. Aldiss took time off from the scathing *saeva indignatio* of his latter-day short fiction to diddle a yarn of the old genre, a finger aside his nose, thumb somewhere. Martin Amis gave proper dues, in *Time's Arrow; Or, The Nature of the Offense* (Cape), to the long history of attempts within genre sf, none of them very successful, to write a tale in which time runs backward, and characters live each moment in reverse from age to infancy. But Amis's protagonist is not Merlin, and the underlying irony of his premise is unmedicable: a man lives backwards into World War Two, where he had been involved in the Final Solution. Every moment of the book – because it reverses what actually happened this century – marks therefore a redemptive nascence, an epiphanic recovery. Lampshades become violinists, gold fillings are coated in smiles. *The Trinity Paradox* (Bantam), by Kevin Anderson and Doug Beason, is told in a language devoid of much nuance tuning ("Hey Kev, wasn't it *your* turn to nuance?"), and nearly fails therefore to awaken the unwary reader to the adult gravity of the story it tells. The premise derives from one of genre sf's favourite gavottes: the time travel story in which an individual or cadre – as in Poul Anderson's *The Time Patrol* (Tor), which sclerotically re-paves old runes on behalf of Wanweird Warriors (Imprecations Chanted) Corps Inc (or WWICCI) – finds it possible to go backwards in time and change (or maintain against change) the course of history. This time, it's Los Alamos, 1943; and the consequences of sabotaging the development of the A-bomb, though couched with too much of the blatancy of genre plotting, are threateningly grave. In *A Woman of the Iron People* (Morrow), Eleanor Arnason finally bit into a planetary romance whose scope was great enough to *geographize* her tough but (in the past) self-lacerating edginess. And in *Hunting the Ghost Dancer* (HarperCollins) A A Attanasio returned to a Primal Scene of Social Darwinism, the duel between Neanderthal and homo sapiens, but subjected the outcome to doses of ambivalence, densely coloured, without quite showing why he told the tale in the first place.

Just as he did in *Empire of the Sun* (1984), J G Ballard gave us, in *The Kindness of Women* (HarperCollins), a confabulated rag and bone shop sight of the artist, this time as a youngish man whose life is a close – but not exact – doppelgänger of the author's own. It was not sf. John Barnes's *Orbital Resonance* (Tor) was, on the other hand, nothing but. Written from deep within the bomb shelter of genre, it could be understood only through race-memories of the Heinlein juvenile leads it paid homage to – though it dodged some of the down sides of – in its portrait of an extremely bright girl beset, in an orbital habitat, with rite-of-passage problems, parent problems, future-of-the-human-race problems: all these problems being solved by emissions of chromium savvy from her "lovable" big mouth: you almost wanted to slap her, but you knew it would break your hand. *The Hereafter Gang* (Mark V Ziesing) by Neal Barrett Jr also took the shape of a solution: but of the funnel at the other end, the coriolis dance downwards into the afterlife. Barrett has an ear for the bedlam din of urban Texas, and a story-telling voice which deposes matters of great subtlety with great shouts, and an exuberance which glowed in the dark, and he's hilarious. Except in *The Sot-Weed Factor* (1960), the greatest of all twentieth century picaresques, John Barth expresses his exuberance almost exclusively through the architectonic of conceits, which also glow. *The Last Voyage of Somebody the Sailor* (Little, Brown) is like a daylight vision of the Arabian Nightmare (we here christen a newish subgenre, naming it with the title of Robert Irwin's first novel, which exemplifies the mode [there is an ARABIAN NIGHTMARE entry in the forthcoming *Encyclopedia of Fantasy* with John Grant 1995]); a dream (entirely typical of Barth) which has no slumber in it. Stephen Baxter, in *Raft* (Grafton), wrote an extremely-heavy-gravity-universe novel, but edged sideways from tired expectations through a not-generally-present, not-in-fact-quite-all-there protagonist. But he toted the barge. James P. Blaylock wrote, in *The Paper Grail* (Ace), yet another tale in which a childlike hero with a Wound from a Pacific Rim suburb gets wisdom from a Geezer and a nice sun-chthonic from the New Age, and still Stephen Spielberg remains silent.

Keith Brooke's *Expatria* (Gollancz) awaited its sequel like a bridegroom whose altar is an *entire planet* (such is sf); John Brunner did another mumpsimus space opera turn in *A Maze of Stars* (Del Rey), earning his crust: it is hard to blame the man; and Lois McMaster Bujold won another of the prizes for *Barrayar* (Baen), a perfectly unobjectionable space opera set in the usual place, without a blemish, or a dare, or a distinguishing mark.

Pat Cadigan's *Synners* (Bantam) was kitchen-sink or Calliope Cyberpunk, cluttered and burly and very smart, and a head-reamer. Orson Scott Card's *Xenocide* (Tor) was – almost unaccountably for a book from Utah's greatest living samurai – smack dab *fuzzy*. The sly sharp steely style of yore had turned into a complacent jog, postprandial and *portly*, and Ender began to bore; the plot was as contrivance-laden as an old tinker come to pub; and the ship of story sighed to a cease on its hook (sequel queues are asked to form at the mission gate) like a flounder. *Outside the Dog Museum* (Macdonald) by Jonathan Carroll did not inhabit any sector of the fantastic, but this fourth parable about the costs of answered prayers – costs specifically salient when one thinks about the power of the maker of art to own the made – spoke directly to the inadmissible heart of genre literature: the heart fact that genres are *ownerships* of the tales told. We could go on, and on. But time must have a stop. Jack L. Chalker, George Alec Effinger and Mike Resnick got together and wrote *The Red Tape War* (Tor), a round-robin novel, it bob-bob-bobbed along, then stopped. Those guys! C.J. Cherryh continued, with *Heavy Time* (Warner), to write space opera you need a certificate of fitness to enter: data-dense, swift, allusive, itchy. The tale was set at the beginning of the Union-Alliance Universe, to which almost every sf story she has written now belongs, but still seemed medias-res, almost punch-drunk with stuff to tell. Richard Condon, in *The Final Addiction* (St. Martin's Press), seemed tired of the long chute, motley with the fidgets of age: but still managed to edge his crazed Amerika one step closer to the brink. And Robert Coover's *Pinocchio in Venice* (Simon & Schuster), like Jerome Charyn's earlier *Pinocchio's Nose* (1983), made a fabulistic game out of pining.

Bradley Denton's *Buddy Holly Is Alive and Well on Ganymede* (Morrow) was sad and dippy, and might well bring someone (not me) to think hard about the fact that ancient rock and sf are both forms of nostalgia commonly felt by Americans old enough to remember that the Frontier died, and that everything began to slurry downhill to the mall, just after the grand opening of the first Interstate, which began immediately to bloodsuck the arteries of myth: because there's an awful lot of ancient rock sf around, and almost no *roads*. Gordon R. Dickson continued to fail to stop adding great bricks to his Childe Shack, though *Young Bleys* (Tor) seemed more

sand than Dorsai, adding no new courses to the earlier seams of Dorsai lore: a flori-
legium of saws. *The M.D.: A Horror Story* (Knopf) by Thomas M Disch began as a
family romance of the curse of suburban Catholicism, moved into a horror fable
about sin and answered prayers, ended in an intensely bitter near future, slammed
shut. *The Gap into Vision: Forbidden Knowledge* (HarperCollins), which was the second
volume of Stephen R Donaldson's Gap sequence, began to make it possible to conceive that the author might just accomplish something no starship ever will, which
is exit a black hole: because the first volume of this utterly untoward space opera sequence, *The Gap into Conflict: The Real Story* (1990), seemed fatally otiose. Turns out
the awfulness of volume was *deliberate*, that it was the nuts and bolts of a space opera
crescendo destined to build over the course of five volumes, a great black-hole-escap-
ing Munch-like bellow of unendurable stress. After *The Real Story*, anything's a relief. George Alec Effinger's *The Exile Kiss* (Doubleday Foundation) did not quite sustain the Arabian Nightmare flow of previous titles devoted to its streetwise Moslem
anti-hero, but coasted toward something or other: more volumes are needed, to
shore this one up. Some penny will have to drop, shaking the world. *Red Orc's Rage*
(Tor) by Philip José Farmer was not sf, but could have been written (and read) only
by someone deeply immured in the recursive worlds of tiers of genre sf. A troubled
lad is introduced by a kindly therapist to Farmer's very own World of Tiers sequence, embraces it in his imagination, and by doing Orc manages to sort out his
problems with the outside world. Sf will make you Virtually Free. And Karen Joy
Fowler's *Sarah Canary* (Henry Holt) managed –while at the same time declining any
generic gambit whatsoever, allowing no sf premise to shoulder into the knowledge
of the text – to give us the impression we were reading a First Contact tale of very
great force; it was also a deft needling parable of the male mind-set of Empire.

   The Architecture of Desire (Bantam UK) was the sharpest book Mary Gentle had yet
written. Set in an alternate-world seventeenth-century England governed by Neoplatonic magic, it finally subjected her over-beloved fantasy heroine, White Crow,
to a situation she could not bound out of like some Temporal-Adventure *cursor* in
some godawful *game*. She is a physician; she rapes a woman who has come to her in
great distress, and who later commits suicide because of the betrayal and the violation. At the end of the book, however, White Crow is beginning to leap free again: I
could have killed her. Alexander Jablokov's first novel, *Carve the Sky* (Morrow), had a
dark compost smell of New England Dying Earth, but was in fact set only a few centuries hence, depicted a world transformed into an artifact for humans to live like
humans in, but also moved outwards, exogamously, from the outgrown gardened
planet. In *White Queen* (Gollancz), Gwyneth Jones finally persuaded herself not to

have coughing fits as she chugged over the points of Story, and managed to tell one: aliens arrive on Earth, ask us (maybe) to marry them (or maybe sell ourselves); there is a lot of plot, but no full resolution; there will be a sequel. Good. It won a prize. Good. Michael Kandel's *Captain Jack Zodiac* (Broken Mirrors Press) viewed the aftermath of apocalypse through a congeries of gearloose folk, each of them falling through the blackening day like burning comics. Damon Knight closed off his CV sequence with *A Reasonable World* (Tor), in which it is seen as possible, though only through the help of the aliens who dominate the three books, for us to inhabit this planet as though we *wanted* to, as though life on Earth were possible without our having to chew our legs off to get free. And Nancy Kress continued, in *Beggars in Spain* (Pulphouse/Axolotl [exp 1993]), to build her career into an edifice of chosen stories, each meticulously crafted and spliced, each different from its predecessors. This time she re-worked the primal genre sf tale in which the community of super-children (they need no sleep) grows up in secrecy and prepares to rule the world from behind the scenes; but ironies begin to eat at the dream, and the full version of the tale could bite very deep into the inadmissible heart of genre literature (see above) which continues to beat inside the dead meat.

Paul J McAuley's *Eternal Light* (Gollancz) – though the disingenuously slapdash style of the thing exposed, once again, the ringer in the tower of space opera – soon got down to very serious cosmogonic brass tacks and took its crew up and down and through the timestream, into the wormhole and up the metaphor and down the metamorphosis, and taxied back again; a fine time was had. Tom Maddox's *Halo* (Tor) gave off a few disillusioned cyberpunk riffs, and slid to a halt as though it had missed the last bus to Mean Street, but promised a great deal next time. Gustav Meyrink's *Der Engel vom Westlichen Fenster*, which was first published in 1927, was finally translated (very well, by Mike Mitchell) as *The Angel of the West Window* (Dedalus), and proved to have explored the Matter of John Dee long before lots of us were born. Judith Moffett burdened the title of her new fixup, *The Ragged World: A Novel of the Hefn on Earth* (St Martin's Press), with an extremely onerous pun designed to offend any reader too polite to notice it until told; but the book itself turned out to be an extremely adult sf embracement of AIDS, Hefns, Quakerdom, here on this Earth. There were several 1991 graphic novels, but *Dare* (Xpresso) by Grant Morrison and Rian Hughes, which immured a senescent Dan Dare in the Thatcherite shambles of a UK much like our own dear Now, more plangently mourned the futures of the old sf than any book written or composed, during this year, in the USA. And Kim Newman's *Jago* (Simon and Schuster UK) also addressed the Matter of Britain in a horror tale which incorporated almost every trope imaginable: mummerset gross-outs; Addams Family romances; Christers gone queer; a green man with a sweet tooth; sex and rock'n'roll and politics and Pelion and Ossa: all choreographed to a golgothan, moony nicety.

In *The Cult of Loving Kindness* (Morrow), the final volume of his Starbridge Chronicles, Paul Park stewed the Pol Pot of his Long Year, as the great season turned to apogee, a totalitarian fundamentalism blossomed, a new (but very precisely an old) episteme took blood root in dire soil, and a terrible sadness brooded o'er the gulf of time. Marge Piercy paid homage to cyberpunk, in *He, She and It* (Knopf), but couldn't quite disentangle the requirements of her interpolated golem legend from the legends of our new age: a central one of which is that (unlike the shibboleth-bound golem of Jewish Prague) AI's Do Good Backup-Disk. The permanent death therefore of the loyal AI clothed in hunky flesh stuff – but without a download jack to save his soul – did not compute. Charles Platt seemed to try to incorporate in *The Silicon Man* (Bantam) some sense of the sweet flow of intersubjectivity within the veins of a novel that mattered to him, though the storyline – twenty-first century agent becomes an "infomorph" or data ganglion in a great computer, and subsequent events lead to a chill metamorphosis of the world – may have lacked Piercy's quasi-humane je ne sais quoi: but knew what it was talking about instead. Frank M Robinson's *The Dark Beyond the Stars* (Tor) had a pocket universe, a generation starship, a lad, a dad, a fight, a god, and all the bespoke regalia of Eternal Return opera, including the mind-mirror at the dark End of the tale, out of which pops its very Beginning. And Rudy Rucker, in *The Hollow Earth: The Narrative of Mason Algiers Reynolds of Virginia* (Morrow), wrote the straightest book he has ever published: a recursive tale of the nineteenth century and Edgar Allan Poe, who journeys to the south pole where he and his boon companions enter a Symmesian Hollow Earth, get laid, undergo deep transformation stuff so that more than one of everyone can thicken the plot, and good times are had by all.

Piero Scanziani's *The White Book* (Eureka) from 1968, now glowingly translated by Linda Lappin, retold the myth of Adam and Eve, again and again and back and forth, until you felt like weeping, out of fellow feeling: Madam I'm Adam. It all comes to that in the end, *dne eht ni taht ot semoc lla ti*. That's what it all adds up to, in the end, life. Charles Sheffield carried on giganting with a second helping of the Heritage Universe: *Divergence* (Del Rey), toying with Uplift (I call it exogamy). Robert Silverberg gazed once again upon the tropes like headlights hypnotizing a rabbit, assembled in *The Face of the Waters* (Grafton) another immaculate epiphany ferry (burnt-out case sees God after long hegira, sighs, works out visiting hours), overdosed the job with all his airconditioned skill, asked us to share the tab: so we read it. Iain Sinclair, in Downriver (Or, The Vessels of Wrath): A Narrative in Twelve Tales (Paladin), found runes and labyrinths in the heatdeath entrails of a near future East London: Dickens's heir OK: but he still refuses to deign to trifle with the art of telling the tale. In The Angel of Pain (Simon & Schuster UK), Brian M Stableford continued to use the tools of Scientific Romance in an extremely gripping taxidermical evisceration of horror devices (werewolves again this time), a fine mind (Stableford's) gone astray in dreck (you might think): I mean, werewolves. I mean, spin-doctoring woof-woof bigthinks. And Michael Swanwick published two books of note. Griffin's Egg (Legend) neatly expressed a sense that the solar system was part of the continuity (or metastasis) of human life, if no more than an infected sidebar on an inner page; and Stations of the Tide (Morrow), which won the Nebula, was a triumph of post-genre sf, though in no particular could it be accused of treason (hence the award). It was set on a Long Year colony planet; it had a cast of the usual suspects; it made intensely imaginative use of a marriage of Virtual Reality and the Theatre of Memory; it quoted (or intrinsicated its substance with) Shakespeare, Budrys, Wolfe, Frances Yates. Like a conjuror's suitcase, it kept on unpacking itself; and stopped far too soon, you felt, though you knew it was done.

As smooth as glass, in which it was possible to discern a variety of Beauties, Sheri S Tepper's Beauty (Doubleday Foundation; preferred text HarperCollins 1992) conflated fable, fantasy, dream-trek, time-travel sf, and allegory: all without blinking, or drawing breath, or breathing hard. The book comprises the diary of Beauty from Once Upon a Time, who avoids Sleep, who is transported into the horrific near future of all our worst dreams, who escapes into a magical past but who ages rapidly each time she hoicks through time, who travels up a world river, visits her mother in a desolate fading Faerie, who is conversant with a Beast, who becomes a spark in the night we cast. The only problem was the terrifying ease of the thing. I wanted grit, the gasp of a deep pun. It wasn't there: everything else was.

If there were three best novels of the year, this was one, Swanwick's another, and Fowler's a third. All three were hatchlings of genre, all three were mutant. They flickered in the mind's eye like outlaws, indecipherable because new. They were dressed in Lincoln green, they stole through the brambles and the scimitars of a new sun. They were the foliage which becomes the map. They spoke to the year.

– It's about time, they said.

The year spoke to all of us.

– O my dearly beloveds, said the Bailiff, who might also be called Time Present. Gather round. I have something to show you.

– New Worlds 3 (Gollancz, 1993) ed David Garnett

2. INTERZONE COLUMNS

Use of Cormorants

I.

IT IS a terrible thing at the end of a long day to leave *Young Bleys* (Tor, 1991) and find cormorants. But all things – even this latest instalment in Gordon R Dickson's Childe Cycle, told in the belt-loosened style of his later books – must come to an end, and here we are, back in the future, in the oil-slick winds of 1991, palping the flensed breasts of the planet for a last drop of milk, according to our wont. It is almost enough to make one start *Young Bleys* all over again. Let us do so.

It is clear, as we begin, that we are expected to remember Bleys Ahrens from earlier volumes of the Cycle, and if we've read *The Final Encyclopedia* (1984), as well as the vestal Afterword appended to that volume by Sandra Miesel, we will remember that Bleys – whose name, Miesel tells us, is pronounced *blaze*, as in the "wrongful blaze" of Milton's Satan – is the great enemy of Hal Mayne, and thus of the evolution of the human race to a higher ethical plane. Dr Miesel, it should be noted, is good on higher planes. "As the promise of that wondrous future made flesh," she makes clear,

> Hal is self-conceived in his fruitful virgin mother's metal womb [ie the Final Encyclopedia itself, in orbit around the mother planet] and is coupled to his creative work within her. But Bleys, the solitary autarch, enjoys no such parent or partner's care. Tomorrow's gates are locked against his keyless hand.
>
> Meanwhile, [Hal] is nearly a man; the *childe* is almost a knight. "Darkness within darkness," says the *Tao Te Ching*: "the gate to all mystery." But the pilgrim bold enough to brave rebirth finds the Door into Darkness a passageway to boundless Light.

Sort of thing. In *The Chantry Guild* (1988), Dickson's direct sequel to this Afterword, Hal Mayne fights off Bleys Ahrens's attempts to constrict humanity to Old Earth, and himself gains access to "the Creative Universe," where "the transient and the Eternal are the same"; and there we leave him, if indeed it is impossible to leave someone so well placed. But it is surely the case that the magnificent, extremely tall lad – who has reincarnated Paul Formain from *Necromancer* (1962) and Donal Graeme from *The Genetic General* (1960) for breakfast, and for lunch now literally embodies, as the CEO of OM, the human urge to grow into the light – must by now have become something of a handful for a novelist to address without incense (and certainly not on a first name basis); and it's not perhaps surprising that Dickson has taken a Rip van Winkle plunge back into familiar territory with this book, a deep bath in the psychic 1955 of the Childe Cycle's original conception.

The effect is utterly strange.

Young Bleys is eleven and having trouble with his mother, who thinks of him as a toy to be manipulated. Fortunately she is an Exotic – see Sandra Miesel, see numerous cod-epiphanic explanations of the three biological/cultural specializations humanity has branched into: Exotics, Friendlies and Dorsai – and cannot make herself cause him bodily harm. A lover has just left her (just as in *Der Rosenkavalier*, the only climax in the book comes before the first page). Bleys watches in secret as she combs her hair, repeating into a mirror the praises she has coached her men to whisper to her. We are then told that she *smells*. "A faint odor, as of musk and perfume mingled, came from her – so light as to make it uncertain whether she had actually touched herself with perfume, or whether it was a natural scent, one that the nostrils of another person could barely catch." It is at this point – we are still on page one – that any reader longing for 1955 should begin to sense that Dickson is in there longing for 1955 with him (or her: though more likely him, as Dickson does seem primarily to write for men, and those few women who feature in his work as a whole tend, just as in this bildungsroman, to fare ill): because no writer attempting to create a psychic 1991 could possibly have written those words: the seemingly unconscious – or dreadfully deliberate – innuendo of "actually touched herself"; the syntactic blurring of any clear single meaning for "musk," so that after reading the sentence one does not know whether or not one is meant to assume that Bleys's mother has in fact – perfectly unobjectionably – perfumed her privates, before or after having sex. My own guess – based on the total absence from the remaining 455 pages of any reference to sex in any particular, or to any female bodily process or function whatsoever – is that Dickson had no intention of coding the reader in to this level of the human smell factory; and that the elements of coding which inescapably infect the passage derive from his immersion in the pulp periphrases of his youth. In pulp terms, then, we are intended simply to envision, as boys do, through gauze and rote, a Seductress from *Planet Stories*.

It's more fun than cormorants.

But young Bleys will have none of it. His mother is smothering him, and he has decided to trick her into sending him away – probably to the fundamentalist Christian planet Association where his older brother Dahno, an earlier escapee, now lives. When his mother murmurs into her mirror that she is beautiful, he interrupts her to say she's not. Thus violently roused from her smothering narcissism, she almost kills him with her savage comb, but cannot. Finally she tells him it is time for them to part. The psychodynamics thus activated by this contretemps are obvious enough, and need no gloss. What is interesting about the scene – and symptomatic of the entire huge novel – is what is missing. For we are truly in 1955. Bleys's mother is not beautiful (so we are intended to believe that centuries hence there are no surgical techniques available to alter the "heavy, squarish boning of her face," no biomorphing to grow her a new guise, no cyber cohorts within the skin to remould her). She does not know which one of her lovers is Bleys's father (we are meant to believe that genotyping has never become a reality). She is in the heart of her private chambers (but clearly there are no nanotechnologies to guard her and enwreath her and warn her of an intruder). Her comb is a potential weapon (but it is not animate, it has no brain, no fractional shadow of an electronic mind inhabits it, it does not speak). We are centuries hence, but the room is electronically deader than most of the rooms Young Bleys's readers inhabit today. There is no concourse – no wedding – no interactive hum of information. There are no robots; more important, there are no "partials" (Greg Bear's [?] term for ambulatory computer-induced partial versions of human minds, hived off to do routine tasks or to represent their originals in otherwise unreachable locations: see review of Michael Swanwick below); and even more important than that there are no Minds (see likewise Iain M Banks below), no AI's. Everything in the universe of young Bleys is 1955. It is just as well for him – and for the book – that the action soon switches to Association, which is backward enough – "even in this day and age," page 233 – to excuse the absence from it of technologies already common in the twentieth century.

And sure enough, we soon feel the warm tug of Dickson's way with a tale close to the soil. The slow growth of a superchild in secret – it is the old secret tale at the heart of the genre – plugs on for hundreds of pages, and it is hard to stop reading. We know it's silly (on the spaceship to Association, Bleys uses a "reading machine" which clearly has no inbuilt memory; and his brother, whom we soon meet, manages a multi-world conspiracy, mostly from restaurants, without a mobile phone) but we cannot scant our pleasure in the long slow detailing of Bleys's acceptance by the family he's sent to live amongst. The very monotony of the book holds us like a smell of childhood. It is a long summer afternoon. It is long before all of this 1991 stuff. Nothing happens, and after that nothing happens. Bleys grows up on the farm, nearly hits a woman who dares touch him, eventually learns how to dominate his brother's conspiratorial network of Others – men (and very occasionally women) of mixed breed (apparently the cultural splitting of the human enterprise into Dorsai et cetera is meant to have a genetic base) who will eventually fuel the conflict with Hal Mayne (hierophanting away, Miesel calls him Christ) to determine the future; but in *Young Bleys* these Others are still no more than a fun congeries of small-town thugs, the sort of thick-eared dupes Murray Leinster used to create for cadets to flummox. So our only problem is when we remember Sandra Miesel, when we recollect that Bleys's experiences on Association are intended to demonstrate to us the inevitability of his conclusion that humanity must retreat to Old Earth, and that as a consequence he must be thought of as a kind of Satan. The last pages of *Young Bleys* replay almost exactly the opening pages of *The Final Encyclopedia*; but they only diminish it. In the original book, Hal Mayne's protectors are destroyed by an intruder from the dark abyssal bosom of the race; in 1955, they're knocked off by the Fonz in a hairshirt.

II.

The ungainly breeze of amplitude blowing through the larger books of Iain M Banks about the Culture cannot, one might think, do more than rattle his short stories into shambles and assertion; and indeed not all of the tales collected in *The State of the Art* (Orbit, 1991) do really work very well. While "Odd Attachment" loudly and neatly turns a traditional alien-point-of-view-of-descending-spaceship tale into an extremely funny dirty joke, "Cleaning Up" gooses Clifford Simak to no avail. "A Gift from the Culture" much benefits from the larger context of this book and of the novels which surround it; another Culture tale, "Descendant," is perfectly competent, but does not o'erleap its medium by as much as a smidgen. And the title story – it appeared first as a book in the USA in 1988 – only grows with familiarity. It is set on Earth in 1977, where a Culture General Contact Unit (ie a huge Mind-run spaceship) has settled into an information-gathering orbit. Diziet Sma – whose consciousness also mediates the pincer-plot of *Use of Weapons* (1990) – is asked by the ship to attend upon and in a sense interview a Contact agent who has gone native; and it is generally through her consciousness that we trace his progress/regress into a full identification with 1977 humanity. Given the state of the planet – conveyed through some "Swiftian" perusals of human economics, ecology, war-fever, utterly unbelievable cruelty and so forth – she thinks he is close to insanity; though perhaps not quite gone. It is certainly the case that his slow dismantling of his Culture-being reads with all the horrific melancholy of some account of the self-mutilation of a hermit. To choose to become human in 1977 CE seems, to Diziet, deeply fetishistic. There are countervailing voices, however, and the novella ends in a sustained peripatetic debate about humanity and the Culture, which is never so clearly defined as here in its post-scarcity freedom, its Golden Rule equilibriums, its gaiety.

In the end, one is very glad Diziet Sma gets away.

III.

Stations of the Tide (1991) by Michael Swanwick may be the most urgent novel that will be published this year; *Griffin's Egg* (Legend, 1991), because it is short (barely 100 pages), and because it is set on the Moon a few decades hence, is a tour de force of a milder pace. It is, however, a remarkable novella. There is a sense in its pages that the Moon – after the long rust and debacle of NASA – has been recovered for sf as a subject matter; *Griffin's Egg* recaptures the Moon from history (NASA's *real* year being that of Kennedy's death) and gives it back to us. Much happens there. Large corporations, which display what British Conservatives like to call a "robust" attitude towards matters of ecology, spread across the "dead" terrain. The viewpoint character goes walkabout now and then to escape the sense that the old tragedy of Earth is being re-enacted on her satellite. There are complex human interactions, and partials – see above – who prefigure the Ariel-AI's of *Stations of the Tide*. Sex. Strife. War upon the mother planet. An intense complexity of response. Several models for understanding the human animal are adduced, as it were off-hand. They intersect; they section the beast; they point to what we may become. The Moon – in Vachel Lindsay's epigraph – is a griffin's egg. So is each human being in the book. With superb concision, *Griffin's Egg* hints at some terrible great beauty borning. Us, Swanwick deposes. But there is nothing simple about the vision.

Cormorants will hatch us.

– Interzone 48, June 1991

Chaos Seen

"SHE WALKS in beauty like the night," as Peter de Vries once wrote, "Watchman." We are referring of course to Kate Wilhelm, the implied-author Kate Wilhelm most of us know, signalling just a little frantically at us through her many pages. Warmly she sweeps us in, bribing us with a doped cookie to stay awhile. Winningly she introduces us to her cast, a scurry of mid-American folk. Offhandedly she points out the region. As we get to know the cast and their home, we learn to recognize their quiddity and resource, to taste something of the subtle intensity of her grasp of humans; and her grasp of place: and all without contrivances. At the same time, however, we cannot fail to register something ominous throbbing like a toe-stub of tom-toms in the deep waters of the circumambient world of the book, and as we near the end of the text this subliminal disorder of bumping resolves itself into something indeed dreadful: it is the sound of a plot that has begun to turn generic. Suddenly the benthos of the telling – the primal Kate Wilhelm metaphor of the world within the senses always being aquatic – dries up, the mise en scène shrinks into toppling flats, and the cast, waving vain feelers like stomped ants, hobbles out of sight, out of mind; like a swan which has run out of pond, the novel lurches – leaking at all seams the last of its gift of world-water – to a pugnacious but clearly bewildered halt, feathers ruffled, bathos embraced.

Until, perhaps, now. The five long stories assembled in *Children of the Wind* (St. Martin's Press, 1989) may continue variously to demonstrate Wilhelm's long inability to begin and end tales in the same register; but in *Death Qualified: A Mystery of Chaos* (St. Martin's Press, 1991), her finest novel and by far her longest to date, she has finally managed to construct almost the entirety of a tale out of the terms that govern its inception. The stories first. There may be some point in going through them chronologically. "A Brother to Dragons, a Companion of Owls" (1974) is by some odds the worst told of the lot, with a scatty woodenness of narrative diction that seems to bode ill. In a post-holocaust city, sterile oldsters repeat Dying-Earth-like ceremonies in vain attempts to maintain their personalities, and the shards of their culture, against the ageing which is now about to address them terminally. The protagonist – a young medical student when the catastrophe struck – must deal with an incursion of feral children, who turn out to be as sterile as their elders. The plot shifts and shags, and seems to be looking for endgame to approach and, by approaching, shape: and then, astonishingly, finds it. The close of the tale – the final sentence being a genuine stunner – is a true slingshot, one of the few Wilhelm has ever brought off. But the remaining stories in the collection – her fifth – descend variously into the wallows. "The Blue Ladies" (1983) stamps a fantasy ending onto an otherwise unexceptional – though sentimentally heightened – tale about the nature of art, which is properly seen as both invasive and redeeming. "The Gorgon Field" (1985) caps a firmly conceived, compactly described and bodingly ambivalent family-romance melodrama set in a Colorado mountain valley with an appalling cod mysticism routine. "The Girl Who Fell into the Sky" (1986) similarly sets down a "mundane" drama of some complexity, then segues into a fantasy haunting/re-enactment shtick, squandering several precious pages on a down-to-the-last-detail explanation of the event: at which point, all the air having leaked out of the tale, there is nothing to do but stop, dead. And the title story, not before published, fails likewise to bring itself off through genre-switching, so that the mutations of understanding that obtain between a man and wife and their possibly paranormal twins, intricately limned by Wilhelm, ends in thick-eared gobstop-guignol. She ends stories the way a bad housekeeper ends dust, by sweeping them under the carpet.

But *Death Qualified*, though a sudden wall-eyed twenty page under-the-carpet-with-you jig does strain one's patience at the very end, works superbly for 400 pages to build like coral its slow working-out of a long, elaborate, thought-through plot. And it may be that Wilhelm, in focusing her attention upon fractal imageries and the chaos theories that – to this innumerate mind – quite magically fabricate entire worlds, has found a philosophical linkage between her sense of the world – her aquatic sense of the constant becoming of the well of being – and her sense of how to plot that world, which, we have suggested, has lacked pliancy or, indeed, wit. As *Death Qualified*, for hundreds of pages, works as a courtroom drama, and strictly adheres to the protocols of that format, it might plausibly be suggested that the book needed no underpinning, just *obedience* to the demands of genre. Courtroom dramas, after all, depend on the assumption that something which may be designated "truth" is ultimately addressable, and that a controlled procedure of revelation can uncover that "truth." They require – and novels written within their remit feast upon – a strict and methodical rhetoric of what one might call the phenomenology of truth-extraction [though a courtroom novel like Robert Traver's *Anatomy of a Murder* (1958) does clearly question the validity of the process 1995]; and *Death Qualified* violates only one of the written or unwritten rules of the format. The trial which comprises the centre-piece of the book ends in a hung jury. The revelations duly delivered within the course of the trial do not – as normally would be the case – cleanse the book containing them of the falseness and melodrama of prosecution. So *Death Qualified* must resolve itself somewhere beyond – and does so by plunging into the waters of chaos.

The story is necessarily of some complexity. Briefly: Lucas Kendricks has been involved in experiments in perception based on the theory that our adult seeing of the world represents a highly restrictive coding of what the world itself gives to the naked eye. The problem is to re-create that naked eye, the eye of the infant who trains himself to forget most of the infinite beingness of things before he can even talk. Fractal theory comes into play – a sense that the weaving of morphemes of the Word into thunderstorms and the Gnomen, by which weaving the world is constituted – might be visible to that naked eye. But insanity seems to result, because the brain-codes adults see by are in fact the *shape* of adult brains, and Kendricks burns out. At the same time, one of his senior colleagues has overdosed on god-viewing, commits mayhem which Kendricks is privy to; and Kendricks must be kept in a state of catatonia so he can't spill the beans. After eight years, he escapes, and the novel begins. The tale moves to semi-rural Oregon, where we concentrate on two women: his wife Nell, who fears his return, and who is the most likely suspect when he is found dead on their property; and Barbara Holloway, who is brought in by her father, Nell's neighbour, to defend her. The absorbingness of that defense, which takes up much of the book, is nearly total. It is most excellently done. And even the hung jury at the end feels right. The ending combines a traditional solution to the murder, logically and methodically worked into the text over hundreds of pages; and an answer to the sf question of the nature of naked seeing of the world. Is it mere chaos? Or is it like chaos theory: chaos theory demonstrating that the generative rules governing certain phenomena seem like chaos because those rules do not grant *foresight*, and that because normal humans see through a wrestling match of memory and input, chaos seen must rip the head open. Does naked sight lead solely to insanity, or can a rewriting of the codes of vision – accomplished in the novel by a rather mystagogic set of floppies full of object lessons in how to open the eyes – grant human beings the god-seeing? The end of the novel – after the action shtick *almost* trips the swan again – seems to say Yes.

In the end, a good ending. It will be one of the finest novels of the year. In the end, fractals and the old Wilhelm benthos have become one. So then rejoice, let Chaos rain.

– *Interzone* 49, July 1991

No Wonder

THREE years ago, it was possible to think of Paul J McAuley as a writer too smart for the boots he wore. The brand of boot that chafed him happened to be space opera, and the book that he was too smart to write without chafing the genre it aped was *Four Hundred Billion Stars* (1988). Paul J McAuley, I said [see p. 106] failed in this book to embrace an assumption shared by many of his American colleagues – the sense that the heroes of space opera were talking heads of the Right Stuff, that they bore our frank blessings and our gifts of entitlement as they took the universe on, and that the sense of wonder we felt was somehow delivered by them to us (rather than vice versa). Screw that for a lark, said Paul J McAuley. I'm out of here.

And he left.

But maybe we should spend a moment or two on the sense of wonder, as it was of old, before trying to assess whether or not he has managed, in his new novel, to do good God talk in a sufficiently different voice. Traditionally, the sense of wonder is supposed to embrace a reader when the space opera text he's reading confronts him – through an unexpected shift in perspective – with the Sublime, a term which might in this case be defined as awe at the instigation of vastness. Space opera itself – which here means, indiscriminately, all sorts of interstellar epics and planetary romance quest tales amongst the stars and first contact stories, primal diva operas (which are about the beginning of things) and entelechy operas (for which see pp. 222–223) – is traditionally thought to be a mode for addressing the new, the unexpected, the thought variant unperceived by Man. The sense of wonder it evokes is therefore expected to *surprise* the reader; and indeed surprise – an unprecedented opening of the eyes – has generally been thought essential for wonder to work.

That this is an extremely peculiar belief might seem evident enough to most of us; it is, however, a belief almost certainly shared by Alexei and Cory Panshin, the Whig goons of modern sf scholarship whose history of sf, *The World Beyond the Hill* (1989), makes it darned clear that in 1930 American space opera – unbelievers must read the book, because I'm not exaggerating [a review starts on p. 330, and quotes some of the same stuff 1995] – literally took over the burden of *understanding* the twentieth century from the likes of H G Wells and Olaf Stapledon and other European cowards who "lacked the depth of vision and the sheer power of imagination necessary to alter their altitudes":

> What? Take one's chances with the unknown? That was a very difficult proposition to entertain. The scientific universe was so very large and dark and intimidating. Who in all the world was prepared to imagine taking his chances with that?
> Well – not H G Wells, for one.

Only certain writers – according to the Panshins they were E E Smith, Edmond Hamilton, Jack Williamson, Stanley Weinbaum and John W Campbell Jr – had "the courage and insight necessary to take the bad news that had been delivered by science [that of Man's peripheralization in the universe], face it squarely, and transmute it into something positive." What they did, of course, was invent space opera. By doing so, these writers not only created, but in a peculiarly literal sense *entered* –

throughout their bizarre text, Panshins constantly hypostasize the worlds made up by their favoured writers – a totally new universe whose wise profligacy puts to shame Wells's cowardly "Village"-bound claim (circa 1933) that "anyone can invent human beings inside out or worlds like dumbbells or gravitation that repels," that "nothing remains interesting where anything can happen." Nonsense, say the Panshins: "It is only by the multitude of wonders encountered that we can ever know that we have entered a realm of transcendence."

But no "Thought Experiment" which pretends to enlist belief in any of this bunkum can get away with treating it in the abstract. We have to come to terms with the actual texts in which the multitude of wonders are unveiled. We have to manage to pretend to believe, for instance, that Richard Seaton, the social-climbing school bully who fronts E E Smith's *The Skylark of Space* (1928 in *Amazing*), is the Panshinesque hero Edgar Allan Poe dared not dream of, the hero H G Wells flinched from describing, the hero whom not one of the culture-cowards who infested post-War Europe dared unleash upon a galaxy full of alien races invariably lacking that inexpugnable sang-froid which John W Campbell would later declare defined homo sap: and no story which does not recognize this fact will ever gain admission to the pages of *Astounding* (and none did). We then have to pretend to believe that Seaton somehow forges his way into something like a real universe out there – carrying along with him, not incidentally, a valiant Yankee band of teenagers *brave enough to read tru-sf* – and that the wonders "experienced" in hyperspace put paid to Stapledonian pessimism; we have to pretend to believe that the sense of wonder which E.E.Smith bestows upon us is what Vasco de Balboa (1475–1519) felt upon a peak in Darien, and not a salve and complacency for wounded children alone in bed with pulps.

I am now privileged to reveal, for the first time in print, a secret about the sense of wonder. It is *not dangerous to humans*. It does not peel the eye open to the new. It does not bring us gifts Olaf Stapledon dared not limn. When we come across a book in which the effect is felt, or when – significantly it is much the same thing – we happen to return to a book in which we know we'll find it again, what we feel is not brave awe at the Sublime. What gives us sense-of-wonder suck is not a skyhook from the future hauling us upwards into a new world, but simply a resolution of tension. The sense of wonder is nothing more – or less – than a category of dramatic irony, and can be experienced when the stress of sustaining the dramatic-irony gap is resolved. As a device for giving dynamic tension to *what is known*, dramatic irony can be defined as that gap in a text where both the author and the reader know something the hero does not (if he's Richard Seaton, what he does not know is that the universe and his curriculum vitae are isomorphic). So the sense of wonder is the pleasure we feel when the hero learns something we already knew.

Through the categories of dramatic irony the agenbite of twentieth century meta-literature shows its symptomatic face, from the winter satires of Thomas Mann in the death-throes of Europe, on down to the recursive solipsisms of Robert A Heinlein stewing his own juice; from the embittered mirror-dancing of all the fabulists of postmodernism on the hot tin roof, on down to the snug hugeness-patter of E E Smith and his progeny. The only thing that *technically* distinguishes Mann from Smith is that Mann knows he's doing it. Space opera "knows" everything but itself. Safely "wondrous" – safely ironized – the hero of classic space opera waits upon us for sanction, and out of our generosity as owners of perspective we give him the Cargo of our knowing awe.

Paul J McAuley could never bring himself to give Cargo. The heroine of *Four Hundred Billion Stars* progresses through the book in a state of profound alienation from the energies that empower the establishments of the world. True to her generic origins in Wells and Stapledon, she maintains a hostile indifference to the masculine web that *operates* her, and to the dramatic irony of a plot which will – as we know from all we've ever read – soon shove her into galaxy-shaking BigThink epiphanies. As the book closes, the aliens she has communicated with are in worse shape than before, the military which has shanghaied her seems destined to continue a dead war, and she herself has been damaged – rather than Cargoed into enablement – by the revelations she's been telepathically privy to, through a Talent which eats her brain when she turns it on. But in a sense she has triumphed. She has refused to suck Cargo from the book, and she has refused to be the object of our dramatic irony, which has made it impossible for us to feel a sense of wonder about any revelations she may be privy to. She is no solace to us.

In the new novel, *Eternal Light* (Gollancz, 1991), which starts ten years later, she remains unreconciled. Like Ripley (Sigourney Weaver) at the start of *Aliens*, Dorthy is a walking wounded. By the end of the tale – 384 large pages later – she will no longer be wounded, she will have witnessed profound lessons in cosmogony, she will have given birth to a daughter whose powers, on time-honoured lines, much exceed her own; but she will not have surrendered to the ironizing hegemony of genre wonder, even though her every move through the text has been haunted by clearly deliberate echoes of all the space operas McAuley has ever read.

Eternal Light is in fact an echo chamber of quotes. The first page echoes the first page of E E Smith's Lensmen series; on the last page, when Dorthy speaks of her daughter as "Poor little superwoman!", one of A E Van Vogt's better terminal lines ghosts into view. In between, whole sequences parody Stanley Kubrick's 2001, Cordwainer Smith's *Norstrilia* and so forth, tissuing the book with all the sounds of yore. It is hard to know where to stop the search for provenance: it may be enough, in general, to note that the book cross-dresses in genre blinds like some Natty Bumppo stalking bison, and that hardly a page is free of the scent of cover. The most important pattern of quotation may be that which correlates the history and nature of the P'thrsn – the aliens who also featured in *Four Hundred Billion Stars* – to the Known Space series of Larry Niven; and here it does seem that the relationship is more than one of protective colouring. Travelling backwards through time via wormholed planets may sound a bit like Greg Bear's *Eon*, but to introduce into one's text a batch of protectors – adults from a species whose attitude towards genetic drift is chilly – sounds a tad invasive. But this too is clearly deliberate. *Eternal Light* is a new book built on told dreams.

Patched into shards of story, these told dreams occupy much of the foreground of the tale, blurring the several protagonists into a coat-of-many-colours melting pot of genre, though only till we become acquainted: at which point, like Dorthy, they turn into ringers in the opera: and dodge our condescensions, our bestowals of wonder upon the things they have been brought to see. It may be the case that the generic story-bites which McAuley patches together take up an excessive number of pages, and that several of his main protagonists pay insufficient attention to the tropic lives they've led, or to the devices from the history of sf which guide them forward: that a large number of distractingly alternated chapters have been given over to a bunch of men and women who are *inattentive to the book* which is carrying them to the centre of the galaxy, where everything will be told. But that is the secret of the thing. *Eternal Light* is a mother bird: flapping its genre trappings like a fake broken wing to draw our ironies into the sand, while the true tale hatches unharmed.

After the noise dies down, that true tale turns out to be a fable of the creation and death of the universe, and of the husbanding of the music of the spheres, eloquently told, effortlessly huge in implication. It is a fable which could have been treated as old stuff in the wrong hands, and we could have been incessantly nudged by the text to remember to feel a sense of wonder about the comfy thingness of the hugeness of the Big Bang and the attendant Arisian-clones who angel the passing show. But there is no sense of wonder in the book at all: no catering to the readership's need to own the numinous: no patent tendered to the Children of the Lens to soothe down transcendence's agenbite. A long denouement reinserts Dorthy into the long nest of living, which she makes burgeon. Things continue to happen. There will almost certainly be a sequel, if Dorthy's appalling New Age daughter wasn't simply inserted into the text as another joke. But most important, through occasional mugginesses of syntax and diction the wonder of things is more than once half-glimpsed, which is half more than we usually see. In the end, *Eternal Light* is about seeing the world. It is not a placebo. In the end, in its stubborn knowingness about the tricks it plays and in the final silence of the glimpse it gives, *Eternal Light* is a wonderful book.

II.

Many of the stories assembled in Brian Stableford's *Sexual Chemistry: Sardonic Tales of the Genetic Revolution* (Simon & Schuster UK, 1991) were first published in *Interzone* over several years, so that it was not easy to detect the agenda revealed in the current subtitle, which is no misnomer. The book comprises through thematic linkage a series of explorations of genuine hypotheses; tales like this used to be called Thought Experiments, but the strange archaic flavour of the writing derives directly from the shape of the telling.

Stableford has embedded his entirely contemporary (and often radical) speculations about human genetics into tales whose shape invokes memories of the Scientific Romance (his favoured form of sf at novel length, too). Each is a small biographical analysis of one or two people, usually men (he tends to edge into the naff in his dealing with women) whose speculative work in genetics has caused some sort of transformation; some other characters are anatomized as well. At first glance, the heart of each story lies in the analysis of transformation, usually of a complex order (only "The Engineer and the Executioner," revised from 1975, exits the task through generic shortcuts); but in fact each story is primarily about the human souls it exposes, and can be read as an exercise in assessing human outcomes. Each story begins in cliché – just as most lives, and most scientific careers, do – and each story violates our genre-trained sense of where the cliché must lead. There is a shrugging mercilessness about Stableford's bedside manner with a tale that is, at first, significantly chilling; it is only after one slides deep into the connective tissues of the worlds of this book that one begins to understand the humanity of his refusal to drop his conclusions down the gravity well of generic expectation. The real strength of the book lies in the wisdom of its portraits of human lives through time. Under the cold wit, and the cruel jokes, and the *conte cruel* ironies, there beats a heart of gold: so that the final effect of *Sexual Chemistry* is alchemical. It changes the mind.

– from *Interzone* 50, August 1991

Grail Plate Sieve

I.

PLANNING to read Robert Silverberg? Don't touch! Look at those *hands!* You plan to touch Robert Silverberg with hands like that? The book, after all, was untouched by any. But that is cruel. Let us stop.

Robert Silverberg may give the impression that, like the Silver Surfer, committing yourself to homo sapiens doesn't mean you have to swim in the same pool. But that impression may derive in part from a personal appearance of very considerable polish, of embonpoint utterly without plump; and in part from the glassene pompadour dermis of his fiction. They are an embonpoint and dermis which do not necessarily tell the whole tale. It is not necessarily the case, for instance, that *The Face of the Waters* (Gollancz, 1991), the latest addition to his huge oeuvre, will strike every reader as heartless. Some may find *The Face of the Waters* not only perfectly oiled but also animate.

I did. I did not. In the end, I could not say. On one page, the perfect pellucidity of the prose and the exquisite phased-release timing of the plot felt like ice, like unlife; on the next, the cleaving epiphanousness of the tale bore me into an auctorial embrace that stung with live cold. So I don't know. When I bleed the psychic blood of empathy into the haute couture innards of a Silverberg tale, am I being conned? doing all the juice work on my own? Or has the author suffered, too, in his own way, some prior and compensatory psychic bloodletting of the creative act? If he hasn't, and *The Face of the Waters* is by no means the first of Silverberg's novels which force the question upon one, then my response to having cared about his protagonists and the water world of Hydros when *he* did not is one of *embarrassment*. I feel he's tricked me again, in public. But I don't know. Maybe he hasn't. Maybe the book is an ice jewel of heartless stagecraft; maybe it is a anguished tale of sexual longing and its fulfilment, an odyssey into transcendence, a love-song to the multifariousness of things alive, an epiphany whose smoothness reflects the power of the gearing. It is, of course, maybe, all these.

We are on Hydros, a water world whose native inhabitants seem to combine ravening bloodlust and high intelligence. There are monsters everywhere, in the benthos and on the animate beaches that rim the floating islands where resident-alien humans live as tolerated squatters; and all the monsters have eyes which track the cast: sad, staring, contemplative. Hydros is pullulant with native life. And for generations, either as convicts or as pilgrims, humans have been making one-way trips to the planet, without any hope of leaving; we are told that the dominant native species forbids any attempt at constructing a spaceport, and we are inclined, at least initially, to allow Silverberg the auctorial privilege of tricking us into forgetting how terribly easily such a diktat would be breached in most novels set far into the future, at a time when humanity has spread across the galaxy, if Eric Frank Russell had written them.

Valben Lawlor, the protagonist of The Face of the Waters, is something like a fourth-generation inhabitant. As were his father and grandfather before him, he is a doctor. Born and raised on Sorve Island, in the midst of a sort of extended family, for there are fewer than 100 humans on the island, he expects to die on Sorve. Though he has slept with most of the women of his own age cohort, he remains bound to Sorve and, having had no significant relations with non-islanders, remains single: exogamy, sanely enough for such a tiny population base, being standard. He is in his middle years. He has officiated at the births of half his fellows. He is loved and needed, he has lived from birth in a tightly knit community in a world of wonders, he knows nothing else. But he suffers – this is, after all, a Silverberg novel – from a deep anomie. His affect is flat. His sexual activities have diminished. He experiences a quickening of the loins when Sundira Thane arrives from another island, but throws no internal switch. He remains a burnt-out case.

Something happens. The main merchant on the island has mortally transgressed the terms upon which the dominant Hydros species allows humans to remain upon Sorve, and the entire community is expelled. They must wander the face of the waters (one of the meanings of the title) until they sink or until they find another island whose resident Dwellers (or Gillies) are willing to tolerate them. Most of the novel is spent – at times splendidly – on a detailed presentation of the fraught passage Lawlor and his fellow humans make across the broad waters of Hydros, assaulted constantly by a huge variegation of native species, and eyed by them. Lawlor's attachment to Sundira finally explodes in good sex, well and realistically described, at just about the point when it becomes clear that the alpha-male merchant who had caused their exile – Delagard by name – is not after all leading them towards a new island. None, he admits, will accept so huge an importation of humans. He is, instead, taking them to The Face of the Waters.

We are in a Silverberg novel. So we know what's going to happen, almost certainly. The Face of the Waters, we have been told, is a vast taboo island beyond the Empty Sea full of writhing energies, which in any sf novel by almost any of Silverberg's contemporaries could mean quite a few things: that it is a giant ancient spaceship, in which the planet-bound humans may travel once again to the stars; that it is a giant ancient stargate, ditto; that it is a giant ancient computer, ditto; that it is a giant ancient labyrinth, ditto; that it is a giant ancient *rune* which is bigger inside than it is out, ditto; that it is a giant ancient battlefield, totally abandoned except for one lonely sentient tank named Roland half-buried in a ruined Dark Tower/ spaceship who contains in his memory banks a route to the stars and who has just enough juice left to give a dying salute to the deeply moved descendent of his captain, Lawlor's great-grandad, ditto; that it is the giant ancient home of the true Hydrans, in the middle of which the very last of the true Hydrans will pass on to Dr Lawlor the Scroll With Stuff On It in a language clearly allied to Sumerian, which tells you how to build a spaceship to the stars, a stargate ditto, a computer ditto, a labyrinth ditto, a rune ditto, a sentient tank named Roland ditto. But we're in a Silverberg novel from the 1990s. The Face of the Waters will be none of these things. It will, almost certainly, turn out to be a locus for transfiguration, for *passing over*; it will offer some sort of transcendence of the burnt-out-case cage of human mortality, something very much like death. This turns out to be the case. It would be unfair to reveal the precise nature of the great ancient animate entity (though it will not have been hard for some or most of us to guess), but we can say that the details of revelation are inventive, the language glowing and intense, and there's not a hair mussed in the sudden high-tone of telling; that, with all the serenity of a great chessmaster welcoming the final endgame, Silverberg has apprehended once again the vacuum beyond the page for which his whole career is tropic.

But does he give a stuff? *The Face of the Waters* is very much like life, but so is a holograph. Perhaps the book stops on exactly the note Silverberg intended: in a lustre of effortless dying-into-life. But that perhaps is where praise ends: because it does not stain the mind. After all the perfection of the thing done, a perception lingers on that somehow the texture of the book is somehow pre-masticated, a vat-grown pearl without a grain of sand: traceless. Lawlor himself may represent, to a nicety, Silverberg's own sense of what it might feel like to be trapped forever on a hick island with raw fish and Gillies, but in terms of the life the harried doctor has led, the burnt-case anomie he exudes simply doesn't wash. As Silverberg draws him, this fourth-generation native of a profoundly articulated niche culture is intensely *urban*, and his stream of consciousness exudes the sated renunciation of any internal exile, pores sealed shut; he is a dazed Jew in a final ebb of diaspora, leaking ironies into a spiritual desert; a stymied godling at the end of time; a parched Fisher King at the end of his tether, without a drop to drink. He is, like any of the Graham Greene characters he so comprehensively evokes, an alien. He simply does not *feel* like a native, a dweller, a man who's had his hands on every cock and up every cunt – as Silverberg himself puts it – on Sorve; a lean and wiry figure of considerable physical grace in the deeps of a love affair with a lithe, wry, foxy woman of great sagacity who loves him back. He is a baulk – a blank – at the heart of things. And the translucent beauties of Hydros, and the momentary tangy delicacies of the sex, which Silverberg presents with panache and tact, vanish in the mind's eye. And we are left unknowing in the end, the tale shrugged upon us from above, the grail bloodless. Or maybe not?

II.

In *Interzone 31* (September-October 1989), Stephen Baxter published a short story called "Raft," and has now expanded it enormously into *Raft* (Grafton, 1991). It is very very hard sf, and it's great fun, and the cosmogonic precepts of its universe are challenging to grasp, and it's quite quickly told, and it's really dumb about people. Sounds almost perfect. The universe of the book – into which a human spaceship had stumbled many generations earlier – features a force of gravity billions of times greater than back home, which means that nothing of any size can exist without imploding, stars are a few miles across, the weight of the central portion of the Raft itself – which floats in orbit around a tiny nebula or something – makes outlying parts of this wee habitat seem *uphill*, and so on. The protagonist, young Rees, has grown up in the Belt, a congeries of shacks orbiting a tiny dead star which is being mined; and longs to ride a "tree" upsystem to the Raft where he may learn why the universe seems to be dying. As in any good juvenile, this happens. Rees – and everyone else who experiences any emotion of any sort – blushes an awful lot. Rees grows up, which makes him blush, learns why the universe is dying, blushes, helps fail to avert a highly predictable uprising on the part of the lower orders, descends into "hell" and rises again armed with new knowledge, leads humanity into a new era around a new nebula, blushes. Baxter describes the physical terms of *Raft* with real love and attention; he is very much less good at making us believe in the culture he has posited; and Rees, whom he leaves in the narrative lurch at almost every point of human importance, is going to have to learn a couple of new ways of expressing himself in the sequel – there could easily be a sequel, the last paragraph is a fine old slingshot, we wait for it.

Odd coincidence: both this book and Silverberg's are about human cultures exiled for generations from Earth; and both end with a symbolic casting into the waters of long-cherished Terran artifacts. Lawlor tosses into the literal sea a congeries of totems; Rees, rather more foolishly, dumps a really pretty badly needed orrery into space. Both are saying goodbye.

III.

Triangulate Jonathan Carroll, M John Harrison and Robert Holdstock, and in the heart-aching dream-created chthonic swamp-with-no-exit-unless-you-grow-up-fast in the middle there you will find Graham Joyce's *Dreamside* (Pan, 1991), which does not win many points for originality of concept. But it is, in some ways, a beautiful little book. In the 1970s, as university students somewhere in the Midlands (perhaps Leeds), the four protagonists of the book begin a controlled experiment in shared dreaming under the supervision of an elderly professor. The oneirism within their heads battens on a violent sexual passion two of these protagonists feel for one another; and other lithely depicted sways of relationship shape the central section of the novel which is devoted to this period. It ends in something like tears, the elderly professor (beautifully drawn) dead, the affair burned out, the dreamside beginning to threaten. By the late 1980s, the four students, now in their thirties, find themselves pulled together once again. The plot boils a little at this point, and Carroll is too slavishly evoked, and it becomes a little too neat in the end. But Joyce pulls the reader through the shallow bits, and the filmable bits, and the bits taken wholesale from spiritus mundi. *Dreamside* is a welcome read. Unlike the Silverberg, which knows more than it says, *Dreamside* wells up inside itself, and its best passages are dense with what may some day be said, if Graham Joyce writes 300 books. There is more to this book than it can hold, like a sieve. Good.

– Interzone 51, September 1991

House of Card

THIS will not be easy to say. The novels of Orson Scott Card are hard to like, but must be loved. I (for one) do not like their primness, their religiosity, their stifling narrow knowingness about the human condition, the cheap populisms they espouse, or the manipulative tricks of plot and rhetoric they play on readers. I do not like – if a term so mild can seem appropriate – the Despite they contain, the sense that the talent that informs the books is bigger than the author who writes them. But nothing of this can stanch one's helpless love for the thing made: for the sweet acid of the writing; the icy clarity of the examinations of soul; the genius of the register of telling, so that you cannot think of another way to put lessons which it may be impossible to swallow; the narrative urgency; the knife of dialogue. It is not easy to say, but Orson Scott Card is something of a genius. It is perhaps easier to say (because we're only human) that if he is indeed something of a genius, that genius may have already spoiled, being too big for its pot.

We should look at Ender. There are now three novels in the sequence: *Ender's Game* (Tor, 1985), expanded from the 1977 novella which was Card's first published sf story; *Speaker for the Dead* (Tor, 1986), which like its predecessor won both Hugo and Nebula awards; and *Xenocide* (Tor, 1991), which seems for a couple of hundred pages to be moving towards a conclusion, but which does not end, after all, when the last page turns up. Quite famously, the first novel describes the transfiguration by force of a six-year-old boy named Ender Wiggin into a polished street-wise teen-aged strategist capable of remote-controlling, via ansible, the huge fleet Earth has been dispatching in phased spasms for decades at sub-light speeds to invest the home planet of the buggers, an insectoid race which decades earlier had attacked humanity. Knowing – or at any rate believing they know – that the buggers will attack again, the military authorities of Earth have created within an orbital, for the training of Ender and others like him, a nightmarish environment that serves as kindergarten and academy and killing field. Nothing there is as it seems, nor is Ender. With his two siblings – of whom more in a moment – he represents a genetic experiment about which Card is never specific, though it may be that, as Gordon R Dickson claimed of his Dorsai Donal Graeme, they are supposed to share a kind of cognitive intuition, which gives them speed and balance and a profound understanding of the human animal in action; in any case, as a proto-superboy, Ender is subjected to the intensest possible training, which means that he is cheated and manipulated more radically than any of his fellows on the orbital. (Being one of Ender's pals is rather like being subjected to Gordon R Dickson; being Ender is rather like being subjected to Orson Scott Card.) In the end, he wins the game. His last exercise, in which he attacks and destroys the home planet of the buggers, turns out, like several of the preceding ones, not to have been an exercise at all: Ender has just committed Xenocide.

Meanwhile, his sociopathic brother Peter and his deeply empathic sister Valentine have been sort of taking over the home planet. Valentine – writing under the name Demosthenes – has been advocating a right-wing back-stiffened obduracy about the war and other matters, while Peter – writing as Locke – has been sounding like a statesman. "Cleverly," to avoid detection (for they are still children) they have been, in fact, espousing each other's points of view, demonstrating en passant the opportunistic rapacity of cognition (which can think anything it wants), and the gullibility of normal folk; and before he's out of his teens, Peter is due to become – sight unseen – Hegemon of Earth. Meanwhile, after the xenocide, Ender has been led to a strange mind-game shaped arena on a strange planet, where he finds the last cocoon of the last hive-queen of the buggers, and discovers that they had long ago learnt that humans were sentient too, and had long abandoned any thought of attacking them again. So it turns out that his xenocide was "unnecessary," and he decides to search for a planet where the hive-queen might nest. Valentine joins him. They prepare to spend the rest of their lives together, chastely (in this series, when Card is not being out-of-the-closet poisonous about sex, he is barely civil: like, one supposes, a Christian). The last paragraph of *Ender's Game* is one of the finest slingshots in the literature:

> So they boarded a starship and went from world to world. Wherever they stopped, he was always Andrew Wiggin, itinerant speaker for the dead, and she was always Valentine, historian errant, writing down the stories of the living while Ender spoke the stories of the dead. And always Ender carried with him a dry white cocoon, looking for the world where the hive-queen could awaken and thrive in peace. He looked a long time.

Thirty centuries pass. We are in *Speaker for the Dead*. Because of the time-compression effects of near-light-speed travel, Ender and Valentine stay young, though gaining preternatural wisdom about folk as they wander. Meanwhile, on the Portuguese-speaking Roman Catholic colony world of Lusitania, home of the only other known sentient alien species in all the galaxy, two interlocked families (note the word *families*) of xenologers and xenobiologists signally fail to begin to understand the *porquinhos*, or piggies, whose zany biology follows lines time-honoured in the generic sf of the 20th century, but Card doesn't write recursive sf, and perhaps we are intended to think that the xenological speculations of the only 20th century literature interested in making them did not survive the long – though computer-infested – years between now and then, and the space.

But no. We are going to have to stop here for a second. We are going to have to say that one of the biggest difficulties with the books of Orson Scott Card is that they are conceived and written with a sophistication which makes the lame predictability of their generic tropes very difficult to countenance. In *Ender's Game*, for instance, we are supposed to accept the pulp conceit that a group of three siblings win (in turn) an intergalactic war, run a planet, and write texts of such transcendent quality that *nothing replaces them for centuries* (both Ender and Valentine have composed books which – like hoarded ur-texts of an abnormally retentive religion – remain famous for 3000 years). But they are not in fact religious texts: Ender's studies of the buggers and of his brother's life-long supremacy over Earth are secular works, but they are *never superseded*; they remain definitive for 30 centuries.

Another example. The xenobiologists of the Hundred Planets fail to understand that *any* communication with an alien species affects it, so that their attempts to only partially quarantine the piggies from human culture are foredoomed to do more harm than good, because part of the piggies' experience will be that of suffering quarantine (but after our own experiences on 19th and 20th century Earth, we *all* know *now* that no hegemonic culture can communicate *at all* with a culture under its control without affecting that culture in fundamental ways). Nor do these "xenobiologists" understand that a species like the piggies – whose members make explicit reference to the nature of females and wives and mothers, and to the father trees which grow from the dismembered corpses of honoured males – might just possibly mean what they say about their own biological nature. And so it goes. Every volume of the Ender saga – which comprises some of the most hauntingly brilliant genre writing of the decade – is vitiated by complacencies of plotting a teenager should spurn.

But the problem is not simply that of a genre writer so well-hung with talent that his stupidities – polished as they will be by the cunning populist manipulations of his style – can't be tolerated, after the book has been read, and the imposition noted. The problem is that Card constructs his extraordinarily intense moral universe precisely upon this house of – yes – cards. The poisonousness of his books – images of poison well constantly to the mind – lies precisely in this investing of simpleton pulp characters and plots with moral burdens and imperatives they simply cannot bear, and which the engines of their toy mouths polish into anathemata.

Whatever. Ender is Called to Lusitania to Speak for one of the xenobiologists, who has been fatally honoured by the piggies, dismembered in expectation that he will become a tree and commune with the ages. Ender arrives, becomes intimate with the two families (*families* again) who will, as a group, by the end of the third volume, be responsible for a galaxy-shaking sequence of scientific advances, including the defeat of an up-to-then impregnable virus, and the invention of faster than light travel. The heart of *Speaker for the Dead* lies in a cunning presentation of the grave family romances that reave these folk, of Ender's signal role in bringing things to rights, and of the piggies. It is a long novel, so beautifully composed and paced that one can find it almost impossible to put down before finishing it. It deserves its awards, just as *Ender's Game* did.

We come to *Xenocide*, and we find unchanged Card's magical capacity to transform chaff and generic chunter into morality play, unchanged the poison of the unfitness of the match. The Hundred Planets have sent a battle fleet to destroy Lusitania, because the virus endemic there (which is only defeated after hundreds of pages) threatens to destroy all molecular life in the universe. Meanwhile, Ender has released the hive-queen on the planet – which does seem a daft thing to do, given the fact that two species already inhabit the place – and she begins to lay. Meanwhile Jane – the computer consciousness who thinks her "circuits" are centred in the ansible web which she controls – finds her secret existence as Ender's quasi-wifely companion under sudden threat through the fact that she has been forced to instantaneously communicate various of Demosthenes's (ie Valentine's) missives against the new xenocide to all the planets of the galaxy while at the same time blocking from the invading fleet the ansible command to use their killer weapon on Lusitania, and someone has noticed.

On the planet Path, young Gloriously Bright – her Chinese name, which Card uses throughout, is Qing-jao – has managed to convince herself that the Gods to whom she offers her utter submission have delegated their worldly power to the Hundred Planets, whose diktats, however cruel, must therefore be obeyed. When ordered to do so by the Hundred Planets, Qing-jao – who is extremely brilliant, like her father: *family* again – penetrates Jane's three-thousand-year disguise in a jiffy, and betrays the amiable and compassionate AI/paraclete to her corrupt and terrified bosses, even though her father has just been convinced that the god-chosen of Path – he and his daughter are god-chosen – are incessantly commanded by their "gods" to repeat mind-destroying rote actions – until a flood of release convinces them that they are forgiven – because the Hundred Planets has on the one hand authorized a genetic experiment which has enhanced the intelligence of Pathians, and on the other hand has infected the experimentees with OCD, or Obsessive-Compulsive Disorder, which also has a genetic base, to keep them under control. But Qing-jao refuses to listen. Jane may be doomed; and Lusitania, and Ender, and Valentine, and the piggies, and the hive-queen and all her little buggers, may all lie under threat of xenocide: but Qing-jao remains smugly adamant. In the nick of time, however, the plot turns, though it would be cruel, this early in the life of the book, to say exactly what happens: and in any case there will have to be a volume four to wrap things up properly.

In other words, the premises are junk, like all Card premises except possibly those governing the Alvin Maker series, and in the Alvin Maker series William Blake is junk. The magic, as we've said, is in the telling. Most of the book is spent on family matters, and in families, as we've more than hinted, Card clearly reposes nearly all his trust, his sense of affirmation. Like its predecessors, *Xenocide* is a family romance. It is haunting, compulsive, urgently readable. It is timed and calibrated with the story-telling genius of a writer who thinks he knows that what he knows is true, and who knows exactly how to convey this conviction. But writers who think they know what they know are dangerous to read, and Orson Scott Card, who is the very best of them all, is by that token the most dangerous of them all. For this reason – because his "knowledge" carves like razors into other peoples' minds and hearts, and lies there – he cannot be liked. But we love him, too.

– Interzone 52, October 1991

[I print here a 1990 review, from *Interzone 43*, of the first volume of Brian Stableford's trilogy; a review of the second volume, *The Angel of Pain*, follows; a review of *The Carnival of Destruction* will appear late this year 1995.]

BRIAN STABLEFORD'S latest novel, *The Werewolves of London* (Simon & Schuster, 1990), is by far the best book he has ever written, a scientific romance of very great scope, a discourse about ultimate matters in which human voices are heard to speak and given the dignity to speak at the uttermost pitch of human articulacy about matters vital to human occupancy of flesh and planet, and a knowing traversal of nineteenth century tropes which never slips, as Gibson/Sterling do [in *The Difference Engine* (1990), see p. 234] into condescension or the censorship of omission. *The Werewolves of London* is perhaps the most intelligent novel yet published in 1990. It is what Brian Stableford amounts to as a writer.

It is 1872. Young David Lydyard is bitten by a serpent south of Egypt and possessed by something like a god, given an inner eye to see the world with, transported back and forth through the fissures of "reality," which turns out to be a frail convention – for the deep reality of the universe is that it is molten, that there is no final respite from the creative world-engendering words of a million billion trillion shapechanging engenderers. Some of these gods or entities have fallen asleep within the ambages of the crust of the Earth; David's sphinx-god is one of these, itself awoken by the Spider-god which Jacob Harkender in England thinks he has awoken and controlled through pain-dances which exalt him into a state that gives him sight of the universe, and the power to invoke it, and to bring it in this shape to Earth. But the Spider shape which has answered Harkender learns of humanity through Harkender's own psychic deficiencies, and begins overwhelmingly to utter itself – through Harkender, and through Lydyard whom it eventually captures as *Werewolves* progresses, and through Lydyard's superbly and courageously rational guardian Tallentyre, and through Tallentyre's beautiful tough-minded daughter Cordelia, and through young Gabriel Gill who is himself dream-fleshed – and begins to spin webs of choking semblance. These utterances of the Spider god threaten to dissolve the world, or suffocate it.

The werewolves of London, who have been in town for a long time, for they are of an earlier utterance of reality than people, take part in the elaborate storyline of the book as spoilers, longing, most of them, for a world free of the cold-souled humans who have, like innumerable tiny creatures of the sea secreting coral, somehow managed to fabricate a thin substance of reality around their perception of things, so that the drab consensual world that humans see has gained a frail but persistent continuity. To shatter this drab web of dumb numbing reality secretions, the werewolves will do almost anything; they will even submit to the awoken Spider whose reality webs dissolve human coral. And so the plot thickens. There are travels beneath the scrim of the world, and much pain, and little resolution. Lydyard and his beloved Cordelia survive, as does Tallentyre, and the werewolves. The next volumes will continue the dialectic.

It is, of course, in this quintessential Stableford romance, the dialectic that counts, the incessant conversations which take up the great central section of the book, the trust in the meaning of words, the trust in argument. How do you define a god. How do you recognize the shapes of the risen gods. Is atheism a defence against the horror of a world which can be remade. Is it a *good* defence, when the universe turns out to be angel-scum, froth torn in a wind of making we cannot see because our souls are cold, our world a termitarium. Buy *The Werewolves of London*. Find out how some things are thought.

[End of excerpt from *Interzone* 43.]

Templars

LET US not be mistaken about this. Each of the four books that lie upon the desk has value. One is an homage paid by Brian W Aldiss to an sf friend whose fame is moderate. One is a posthumous collection of stories rifled partly from the deeps of Clifford D Simak's ample corpus of uncollected tales, and partly from previous volumes assembled by the author (when alive). One is an example of recursive sf written by Philip José Farmer, with fine impartiality, about himself. And one is the second volume of a trilogy, written by Brian Stableford with all the obdurate ingenuity of a smart man who knows it is impossible to write the second volume of a trilogy, but who knows he must. Here are four books then – we might call them publishing ventures – which bear in their cast and contents all the marks of sf in its late maturity. Here, then, are four niche clingers.

1.

Of the four, greatest value adheres to the largest and most arduous, the novel Brian Stableford has now published to serve as a bridge between *The Werewolves of London* (1990) and the forthcoming *Carnival of Destruction*. It is called *The Angel of Pain* (Simon & Schuster UK, 1991) and it is an absolutely extraordinary book. But perhaps *bridge* is not the best image for the experience of dealing with the thing. *The Angel of Pain* is less a bridge to the next volume than an examination of our understanding of the previous. Reading it is like *passing*. The plot, the characters, the mise en scène, everything is subjected to a scouring retrospective analysis – twenty years are supposed to have been bridged between volumes, and the date is now 1892 or so – in the epistemology of premise, and the various climaxes of the book are almost exclusively cognitive in nature. At the end of volume two, David Lydyard and the resuscitated Jacob Harkender know little new about the motives of the vying "angels," named for convenience Bast and the Spider, who possessed them twenty years earlier, and who used them as lenses to see the world through. None of them – Lydyard, or Harkender, or Tallender, or Sterling, or Cordelia (still resenting her relegation to the sidelines as a woman, and still being relegated), or the immortal Adam Clay who, along with the increasingly lassitudinous werewolves of London, had been created aeons earlier for reasons unknown by the angel Machalalel – none know significantly more, at the end of volume two, than they ever had about the motives of their feckless Creators. But their sense of the insubstantiality of the world of matter has become more sophisticated; as Adam Clay (it could have been any of them) puts it:

> The world which spawned the Creators was not a kind of world conducive to the accumulation of reliable theory, for it had only just begun to incorporate causality. It is this world which holds the opportunity for the triumph of reason, or seemed to hold it once. Perhaps, in time, the Creators will overcome their ignorance, but even if they do not, what can mere reason do against the might of raw power? ... The appearances of the world are, after all, mere ap-

pearances; its order is an arbitrary thing, which may vanish or fall apart upon the instant. If the Creators are as stupid now as they were before, that may be all the more reason to fear them.

Ultimately, Adam Clay (who gets a lot of the good lines, but this may be accidental), suggests that "the Creativity of the Creators might be regarded as a kind of clinamen." The term, originally from Lucretius, and latterly made familiar by Harold Bloom as the name of one of the revisionary ratios governing the Anxiety of Influence, means in this instance a swerve of Being at the atomic level, the essence of the Creators being therefore measured by their angle of discontinuity from the previous instant. They inhabit rhythms of Being that precede humanity, and circumambiate Matter: but Matter seems – as Stableford puts it – to matter; it is a fulcrum, a lens, an engagement; and humans, who are in the latter nineteenth century increasingly in control of Matter, may one day tame the Creators, ride the bronco clinamen, for order is a disease of chaos. Or so this reviewer allowed himself to think Stableford might have told him, in one of his innumerable passages of speculative discourse which takes the place of story.

New to The Angel of Pain is the subject of pain itself, for the central avenues of communication between the Creators and human beings work only through excruciation, which makes the prison and alarums of the body transparent to inner vision; pain is the response of the nervous system when it is asked to see. Much of the book, when it is not debating the nature of pain, is devoted to its description in a set of parallel narratives which carry the various protagonists of volume one to a stage where they understand volume one a good deal better, and are pretty anxious to start volume three. Stableford himself seems to take no pleasure in the task of making his readers privy to the costs his protagonists pay for passing their internal exams, costs attributable in part to the dickhead indifference of the gods; and the book itself argues – in what sounds like Stableford's own voice – that if the Creators are analogues of God Itself, and if the demands they make upon humans are analogues of the religions which have so corrupted the planet, then free men and women, in order to create Paradise on Earth, must abandon their deities:

> The price which must be paid for this paradise on Earth is Hell, for if there is to be paradise on Earth it must be a paradise for all, and not for the few. If wars are to end, if all harvests are to be bountiful, if justice is to reign and men are to have equal opportunities to be what they may, then none must be eternally punished and none must be eternally damned... [In pursuing this

goal] it has made no difference which gods the men of the past have chosen to follow; whether they have been gods of terror or gods of mercy, gods of wrath or gods of justice, uncaring gods or fatherly gods, they have all been jealous gods ... To those who would argue that if gods did not exist it would be necessary to invent them I have this to say: if the gods had not absented themselves entirely from the world of men, it would be necessary to banish them; and if that could not be done, there would be no hope for mankind...

And cease to pray.

The burden of *The Angel of Pain* is a refusal to pray.

It is for that reason – and not for a storyline which refuses to carry its protagonists more than an inch, though twenty years have passed, further along the road to climax – that the book is an exhilaration to read. It shows how most of the supernatural fiction we are forced to read stinks of sycophancy. It demonstrates how it might be possible for adult human beings to write fantasy without demeaning themselves. It tells the gods to go away. Staunchness of message does not, of course, make a good book, and although *The Angel of Pain* will almost certainly work as a necessary linchpin to the Werewolf trilogy of which it is the centrepiece, it could be argued that Stableford's adamant refusal of normal narrative pleasures is indeed costly. The characters of the novel do almost nothing while awake, and although they are extremely active while asleep, and their dreams – as in Robert Irwin's *The Arabian Nightmare* (1983) – are proactive and interminable and god-generated and interstitially nested into themselves in an infinite series sort of thing, they awake at the end of the book to the yet-closed boards of the sequel, just as we do. *The Angel of Pain* is an incessantly perverse and essentially comedic riposte to the sf field's demands for three-volume novels. If the beginning starts the tale, and the ending ends it, but you still require a middle which does neither (Stableford tells us), then I'll give you middle, I'll give you the endless melody of middle till you scream, I'll give it to you, I will, I will. And he did.

11.

I paraphrase and shorten a new entry – it is on Recursive sf, a term which did not exist in 1979 – written for the second edition of *The Encyclopedia of Science Fiction*: It has long been the practice of sf writers [I wrote] to re-cycle material from the vast and growing storehouse of the already-written. When Robert A Heinlein made reference, in "*The Number of the Beast*" (1980 UK), to characters and situations which appeared in earlier novels by him and other sf writers, he was operating in this traditional manner. But when he introduced into the same book people – writers, editors, fans – who had been involved in sf itself, he was doing something very different, something which showed that both his career and the sf genre within which the book was written were approaching a late and self-referential phase. He was in fact writing recursive sf, a term straightforwardly defined in Anthony R. Lewis's *An Annotated Bibliography of Recursive Science Fiction* (1990 chap) as "science fiction stories that refer to science fiction..., to authors, fans, collectors, conventions, etc." It is not necessary – though it is usual – for these characters and events and entities to be real, whether or not they are camouflaged by false names and other devices of the *roman à clef*. For a title to be recursive, it is only necessary that its inhabitants live in a world explicitly shaped by the existence of sf; or that – like Mark Twain or H G Wells – they are themselves creators of the sf world.

Hence Philip José Farmer's *Red Orc's Rage* (Tor, 1991), an ostensibly non-genre tale about a treatment centre for disturbed adolescents whose central therapy is to dump sick children into Farmer's own World of Tiers sequence, though only in fun, like. Young Jim Grimson, unloved child in one of the derelict – or, in feelgood terms, sunset – company towns of Eastern America, cannot control his violence or the callow nihilism of the "escapades" in which he becomes involved; after his inevitable arrest he's sent to smooth and earnest Dr Giannini's clinic, the one which specializes in "Tiersian therapy." There he traverses – in imagination, in "fun," because this is a non-genre book – the rite-of-passage portals that give access to Farmer's fantasy universe – a universe which may represent, says Farmer, a deep intuition on Farmer's part about the nature of reality – and takes on the guise of Red Orc, one of the godlings – suddenly we are reminded of Stableford – who has created the various pocket universes of the Tiers conceit, and by living out Red Orc's almost inconceivably violent Oedipal conflict with his god-dad – whose balls he eats, et cet – he gains a lot of self-knowledge. The difference between Tiersian therapy and role-playing fantasy gaming at its most fatuous is not easy to understand, though Farmer writes better than most of the franchise serfs who exude game books through orifices Heinekens cannot reach, and the tale itself lacks any saving excesses of creative heat. It is, in short, a calm and complacent footnote to a long career, an exercise in sharecropping the navel that could have only been published in a genre whose subject had ceased to be the world.

III.

And deeper and deeper we fall, down the raddled inscapes. And we come to *Immigrant and Other Stories* (Mandarin, 1991) by Clifford D. Simak, a book of much less use than it might have been, because much of Simak's best work remains uncollected and most of this offering re-sorts material already published in assemblages he had himself put together years ago. Of the seven items included, "Neighbor" (1954) and "Immigrant" (1954) – both paradigm *Astounding* tales from the time when Campbell could still insist on the one-word titles he loved as device and theorem of the "new" – each appeared in more than one collection before Simak's death; as did "Green Thumb" (1954); "Small Deer" (1965) and "I Am Crying All Inside" (1969) each appeared in one Simak collection; only the admirable "The Ghost of a Model T" (1975) and the extremely weak "Byte your Tongue" (1980) were previously uncollected, and both of these stories were first published, not in magazines (where much of his work still reposes) but in original anthologies. The result – peculiarly dangerous when one is reading an author gripped by nostalgia and desiderium – is a constant sense of déjà vu, so that it becomes very difficult to work out just whose remorse-for-the-never-happened it is one is experiencing. "Immigrant" is just as much too long as it ever was; "Neighbor" remains one of the finest exercises in nostalgia fugue ever published; the remainder of the volume falls in between, though the execrable "Byte your Tongue" will never cease to embarrass lovers of pastor Simak in his days of glory, when he knew enough to look backwards into his last.

– from *Interzone* 53, November 1991

Punner at the Well

FIVE WORDS into *Jago*, and we begin to wonder. Half a page onwards and we begin to think we know it all. And maybe we do. *Jago* (Simon & Schuster UK, 1991), which is Kim Newman's ninth novel in something like three years, introduces a Christian minister half a breath into its first sentence, which in any horror novel almost certainly guarantees a great deal of diseased ecstasy of the sort typically generated by the minions of any desert sect dead scared of women and the flesh; and a paragraph or so downwards into the depths we are further given to understand that the Reverend Mr Timothy Charles Bannerman has gathered, with his flock, in the middle of winter, in the middle of the nineteenth century, in the middle of the night, in the middle of the country, around a bonfire. This sort of shenanigan bodes ill, as we know, for any Christian (god bless the dears). "Epileptic flickers lit the insides" of this ominous blaze, we learn, "and dancing black bars of shadow were cast upon the villagers." Sure as shooting, this little escapade is going to end in tears, here in highly rural Somerset. But there's more: Reverend Bannerman *has fed the fire*: "The vicarage library was in there. The collected sermons of his predecessors could serve no better use, and there would be little further call for novels, tracts or bound periodicals." Soon we hear rumours of a Burning Man, and confluences of psychic intensity jiggle the titties of the Christian maidens, and a general sense begins to dawn – promulgated by the minister – that the end of the world is nigh, and that only the righteous – him, in other words, and the other Christians of his singularly nasty little flock – will survive the moment of reckoning. But the night passes; clothes are cast off; fornication occurs; and the world does not dissolve. The terrible sourness of the agenbite of shame now afflicts the Christians, right on schedule. And the Prologue to *Jago* is done. It has ended in tears.

We begin the real book, which is very long, and which we fear. The Prologue, which ran twice as long as it needed to, had already alarmed us: not only because it can take an awful lot of pages for someone as skilled and fluent (and other things we'll get to) as Kim Newman to run out of words; not only because we were not exactly enthralled at the thought of having to spend an entire book in the company of Christians with damp underpants; but also because Kim Newman is so good at being a professional writer that we hardly noticed the impersonality and the poisonousness of the tale he seemed to be beginning to tell us. The words of storytelling seem to be his to play with; narrative conventions his to rule. He is dangerously in command of his gifts, and as the first few pages pass, a savage servility – to quote Robert Lowell – slides by like grease, the text easing us into the nada nada of horror with a moue of slithery steel, a dangerous craftsmanlike courtesy; and in our mind's eye we figure Kim Newman Novel-Spouter Inc grinning like a dapper little bastard, to quote someone who couldn't stand Mozart and no wonder, for here we are, stuck inside the mobile lips of a tale we do not particularly wish to hear whispered, subliminal and chill, like an extremely expensive coffee ad, into our dream of reading. And so we begin the real book, which is set in the latter decades of our own dear haemorrhage of a century, and we feel something very close to fear.

And indeed there are things to worry about. *Jago* has already laid itself out in the Prologue as a horror novel whose denouements will – because of the Christians – almost certainly invoke the dire incoherence of *Revelations*; and because Kim Newman is a professional writer more than half in love with the conventions of popular literature and classic cinema, we know that it will be very difficult for him to avoid keeping faith with the laws of genre horror he has so conspicuously invoked. Moreover, he introduces, very quickly, a large and variegated cast of characters, which means two things right off: 1) he is writing a bestseller-style book, for at the heart of every bestseller-style book lurks a cod Narrenschiff; and 2) a lot of people are going to die. We meet Paul and Hazel, newish residents of Alder; Paul is completing a dissertation on "The End of the World in Turn-of-the-Century Fiction," and Hazel is a blah potter. We meet Teddy and Terry, good brother and bad brother, both of whom speak rural cute. We meet a passel of shagged out leftovers from the sixties, en route to Alder to take part in the rock festival being mounted at the end of this singularly hot – greenhouse-hot – summer. We meet the Maskells, the dominant farmers in the locality, who are still treated as newcomers after quite a few years. And we meet various members of the Agapemone, a name which designates both the sect they espouse and the abode of love – the large house on the hill – where they live and worship their Beloved, whose name is Jago.

About the tenets held by the Agapemone it is hard to say anything at all, and certainly Newman doesn't do more than fill their mouths with a glossary of those awful things pentecostal Christians say when the milk has gone sour. After the manner of this sort of Christian, the members of the Agapemone think it's high time for the rest of us to start paying for their sins, and anticipate the end of the world with pasty relish. About Jago himself, Newman is clearer and more clever, and it is a relief; it is the first relief – other than the compulsed joy of reading a book whose competence is very great – that we have been afforded. Jago, we learn, is an extremely powerful "psychic prodigy," a man capable of imposing his version of reality on the world around him, just like some godling out of Philip K. Dick. "Everyone," explains a less powerful psychic spy seconded by the incompetent British government to monitor him, "has dreams, fantasies, beliefs. Around Jago, they become concrete things. Monsters, angels…"

Once we understand that, we understand the entirety of the surface of the book, the rock festival coinciding with the Agapemone's apotheosis, the shit hitting the fan. We understand why Paul sees Martian war-machines straight out of the original magazine version of The War of the Worlds (1898), and why these machines are solid. We understand how it is that Maskell – haunted by the destruction of his beloved farm through yet another of the man-made droughts that plague our time – metamorphoses into a Green Man as gnarly as any Rob Holdstock dream of Britain intrinsicate with root and briar and other stuff. We understand how it is that corpses can stroll into town, mean boys turn into wolves, slags turn into Circes. We understand how it happens that the vilest visions out of Revelations can trudge, cliché-pustulant, through human fields, reaping human corn, chewing the eyes and sweetmeats of those of us who are not saved. We understand that – although the surface tale of Jago leads irrecoverably into the nada nada of horror, into the terrible banality of bigthink genre Evil – there must have been some reason for writing the book.

Or why did Newman bother to write all this highly superior stuffing?

I'd suggest two motives – if motives can be defined as ley-lines within the text itself. The first lies in the sense that the Narrenschiff castlist of Jago constitutes a kind of spectrum, that the almost total lack of any content in the Agapemone's philosophy constitutes a kind of analysis of certain parallel poverties in the real world outside the book, and that the drooping fatuity of the secular response to the crisis created by Anthony Jago constitutes a kind of indictment of the ideological paralysis that currently famishes our own real land. Jago, in other words, is a Condition of Britain text; and as such it chants a devastating litany of losses. (If the horror novel has one virtue, it is perhaps that it mocks theodicy.) The second motive is precisely the text itself, the joyfulness of the telling of the thing, the lucid wordplays of a writer whose puns are paronomasias of genre. *Let me explain.* There are – it could be argued – only two kinds of creative writers in the world: the horizontals and the verticals. Horizontal writers (like Thomas M. Disch) one might call the lucid dreamers of literature. Vertical writers (like Shakespeare, for whom each word breaks vertically into layer upon layer of notes so that he seems to be dreaming several melodies at the same time) one might call the paronomastics, the punners at the well of being. Kim Newman is a paronomastic, though one of a very strange order, because his puns do not connect word to word but genre to genre. What his ear catches is not the etymology or the sound-horizon of the word "itself," but its generic location. The genres he registers are popular literature and popular film. In Jago they meet, in the quiet of a paronomasia which flows like breathing. Verbal and visual echoes of films throng the pages of the book, incest sisters of the telling, sound-chambers of the act. Paronomasia is the secret of the strangely hermetic fluency of Kim Newman, which breeds in the *acceleration* of the pun. He spun Jago because he could not resist reeling.

–Interzone 54, December 1991

Gods and Sods

I.

A FEW DAYS AGO I bought a book. It made me think of Rob Holdstock, author of *The Fetch* (Orbit, 1991), in which it is possible to descry, not for the first time in that author's career, a longed-for chthonic realm of root and briar beneath the acid leach of UK Factory Farm. The book, *Orchards and Gardens, Ancient and Modern: with a Description of the Orchards, Model Farms and Factories Owned by Mr. William Whiteley, of*

Westbourne Grove, London (1895) by one Alfred Barnard, began like a travelogue. In the ineffable voice of the late 19th century hotel brochure, it transported us from London – quoting Horace without cease – through rural Middlesex to Hanworth – "the bright hill of Richmond, the leafy walks of Ham, and the majestic Thames in one broad sheet of silver" – and deposited us, after 25 pages of ogling the sylvan, in the middle of Mr Whiteley's brand new garden paradise, 200 acres of farmland north-west of Bushey Park, bought just four years earlier. Before the purchase, the farm had been timbered, part of Holdstock's dream (though partly illusory) UK. But Mr. Whiteley (born 1831 in Yorkshire) was a modern Englishman. He immediately felled every tree in the 200 acres he now *owned* [but William Winter, in the 17th century, felled thousands: it is perhaps a mistake to call Mr Whiteley modern 1995]. He had the hedgerows cut down. In their place he put up "oak posts and rails," says Mr. Barnard, extollingly, "and a galvanized iron wall 6 feet high extending five miles around the property. This wall was most carefully constructed with close-fitting joints, so as not to allow currents of air to pass through... When this had been completed, six strands of galvanized iron wires were stretched on the inside of all the boundary walls, making a total length of thirty miles of wire." Fruit trees were then planted in strict gradgrind rows, tenements were built for employees, factory buildings were erected in the heart of the demesne to refine the produce, and Mr. Whiteley was in business. This was 100 years ago (today the farm has become Butts Crescent, Glebe Way, Whiteley Way and so forth, easy to miss as you drive out of London toward the M3). Whiteley – who seems to have hired Barnard to extol him and his works – was himself a paradigm representative of the Shopkeeper Caesarism which has, over the 22 years of this reviewer's own sojourn in what was once a complex country, so visibly continued to strip the land bare of hedge and shadow, metaphor and chance, root and briar [the difference now, of course, lies in the exponential increase in the power of the tools 1995]. Mr Whiteley is one of the conquerors of the UK so savagely anatomized in the flat reportorial pages of McEwan's *The Child in Time* (1987). Mr Whiteley is the terrible changeling solitude Rob Holdstock seems to have tried to repopulate in *Mythago Wood* (1984); he is the nada which, in Kim Newman's *Jago* (1991) [see above], England becomes. He is the dead soil in which *The Fetch* plants a green shoot.

It is, perhaps, not very fair to pin *The Fetch* to Mr Whiteley, because there is nothing in the book which overtly evokes him – nothing more, that is, than modern England. Holdstock is very much unlike – say – Kim Newman in that he is a writer of almost excessive reticence about the political or satirical implications of his work. His books say something about contemporary England only when their readers *ask* them to. This was not always the case. In the books before *Mythago Wood*, this decorousness generated tales that seemed both insecure and – frankly – without hook, stories whose pages shut in disdain at the thought of being asked to depose. Back then – in the late 1970s – he was one of the writers frequently described – I don't know if the term was originally theirs – as members of the Faber Group, or the Faber Greys, the exact term has fallen off the memory tree. Along with Christopher Evans, Garry Kilworth, Christopher Priest, and a couple of doleful hangers-on, he wrote books whose use of the instruments of American genre sf was at best fastidious, at worst incompetent, like Triumph Mayflowers trying to put themselves across as inherently more *decent* than Chevies. (It may indeed have been the case case that Triumph Mayflower sf was less slick than the competition. Trouble was, it couldn't climb hills.) But after about 1982 – which was about the time Faber picked up her skirts and sent her infra digs back to the jungle – this all changed, and the Faber Greys split off into their variously interesting imagoes. The change for Holdstock was vivid. *Mythago Wood* and *Lavondyss* – though never explicit about the nature of the circumambient world they sought the roots of – were books whose pages could be asked to depose, though not, perhaps, about details: their subject was the Matter of Britain, not the condition of England. But the land they grew in – hence the inturning melancholia of the best passages in both texts – was Mr Whiteley's.

The *Fetch*, which similarly inhabits without discourse a landscape of aftermath, is the most exciting novel Holdstock has yet written, the most plotted, and the most easily read as a response to conditions. The story grows from itself, like a tree in an oasis. Around 1980, Richard and Susan Whitlock illegally buy a baby from a surrogate mother, and from the first find themselves in a bad-faith relationship with their child, Michael, whom they cannot accept because of the nature of the parentage they had themselves arranged. Simultaneously, paranormal phenomena begin to assault them and their home in the shadow of the Downs in nether Kent, in a village called Ruckinghurst (presumably a thin disguise for Ruckinge), where Richard's family has lived for generations. He is an archaeological photographer whose career has been has been blighted by the condition of England and by the fact that he had once pilfered something from a site. Susan is a teacher who restores antique dolls. Like the land they live in, and like their fellow citizens, they are eaters of the past; like other middle-class purveyors of the sweat of others, they inhabit an enclave – their home in Ruckinghurst – where the fee they charge the world for their lives cannot be assessed in any visible Whiteleying of the terrain. They live, in other words, on credit. Like us.

When it turns out that the son they cannot accept seems to be not only the focus but the engenderer of the paranormal events, and when they discover that he can also fetch extremely saleable relics from the past in his insatiable need to please them, they begin to treat him as Mr Whiteley treated England, as a credit card they will never have to pay off. And when he fails to deliver, they – or more particularly Richard, in whom Holdstock has created an astonishingly repellent, intimately recognizable monster – fall into paroxysms of false relation with their son, with each other, with the criminals they have promised to lend money to so they can become rich as shit, with any surviving sense of professional rectitude. And so the story goes, winding through Dickensian spirals into the snug coign of a kind of happy ending; but not once does Holdstock tell it in the terms laid down here as a crib. The Fetch is not about the condition of England; it inhabits the condition of England. It is not a satire but a family romance.

As it is told, the heart of the tale lies in young Michael's attempts, by paying them relics, to make his parents believe that he is not an impostor, that he is a whole child, not the "boy without a soul" Richard and Susan – the true impostors, the true changelings of the novel – so blindly "perceive." To make them love him, he continues to run and fetch for them. But when he can no longer do so – at this point Holdstock erects a supernatural apparatus of his usual slightly untoward complexity to dramatize the sciamachy inside Michael's head, but we must leave unexplicated the Chalk Boy in the quarry, the whorled castle, the runes, the monsters swimming in the sea within the labyrinth that Michael built, the fossils, the totem field, the Holy Grail, and Uncle Tom Cobbley – all they can see (as he knows full well) is a "'wrong' Michael, a false-boy, and that was why they were so angry with him all the time. They wanted the pretty things, but they couldn't understand that without his shadow he was a false-boy." Though the effect of the book is occasionally slurred by novelettish diction, and though the redemption of Richard is insisted upon through a cookycutter plot-turn reminiscent of the worst of Victorian melodrama, The Fetch as a whole is a drama of stunning intensity, a meticulous tracing of the fissures within a child's mind, an offering. If I find myself compulsively thinking of Michael and England as isomorphs similarly cursed by parasites, I may be playing Procrustes all alone, but maybe I find myself thinking of England because Holdstock has written a book which inhabits its place, because he has created a child who inhabits our time.

II.

It is terribly difficult – indeed it is impossible – to dislike James Morrow, but a novel ain't a guy, and Only Begotten Daughter (Morrow, 1990) is something of a trial. But let us first say what is good. Only Begotten Daughter is a fable about the life of the sister of

Jesus, whose name is Julie Katz; who was born in an ectogenesis machine in New Jersey in 1974 to a Jewish sperm-donator, a desperately nice fellow who dies of heart failure later on; who grows up capable of performing miracles, though her father persuades her not to; who is forced into action by fundamentalist Reverend Milk's assault on Atlantic City, which seems likely to burn the place to the ground until she drowns the fires; who also spends time, as Sheila of the *Moon*, writing a humanist advice column; who becomes dispirited and accepts the devil's invite to spend some time in Hell; who finds her brother dispensing mercy and spends 15 years with him in a soup kitchen ladling out illicit morphine for the damned, ie everyone (there is only Hell, there is no Heaven); who finds, on her return to the surface that New Jersey, under the reign of Reverend Milk – who mounts glitzy *autos-da-fé* to keep the faithful Christians glutted – has seceded from the Union; and who undergoes the usual hairy climax meted out to God's kids, after which she is reborn and, with some faithful friends in tow, along with fat Bix her husband and her adorable infant (God damn, its name has slipped my mind), leaves New Jersey for the West, where the whole gang hopes to do some good things. It is funny, impassioned, decent, concerned and rakish. That is good.

What is not so good about the book can perhaps be approached through the quote that Century Legend have been kind enough to print on the front of their otherwise extraordinarily unassuming dustwrapper. "The comparison with Kurt Vonnegut," says the *Times*, "is inevitable." This may be the case, but it may have been slightly unwise to press the point. Morrow may share with Vonnegut a satirical bent, a sense of outrage, a leftwards political cast, a dubiousness about organized religion, a fabulistic storytelling mode; and both men may be equally nice when met. But niceness is a dangerous thing in a book, and it should be noted that none of Vonnegut's novels, and not one of his protagonists of any interest whatsoever, is *nice*. The first trouble with *Only Begotten Daughter*, then, is *niceness*. The voice of the book is nice (occasionally verging on smug); Julie Katz is nice; Bix is nice; her friends are nice; Morrow's own despair at the state of America is nice. All of this we can tell a long ways off. But it doesn't wash, it doesn't bite, it doesn't scour; the ultimate effect – an effect totally unlike that given off by Vonnegut's books – is one of bewilderment. *Only Begotten Daughter* seems fatally untouched by the intimacy of the evil of the world it describes. The effect is dazing.

The second problem with the book is the terribly shaky edifice of its plot. Julie Katz as Jesus's miracle-working sister – that's no problem, that's the sort of premise which, once given, can be followed. The problem with the plot lies in its failure to bite into the great rotten apple of the world. One example will perhaps suffice: the secession of New Jersey. I for one could believe in Julie Katz, because that's the sort of premise that traditionally motors satirical fabulations; but I couldn't believe in the secession of New Jersey, because it did not follow from any premise whatsoever. A dark devastating hyperbolic comedy – Kurt Vonnegut's variety, for instance – might have been written about the kind of world in which the political dismemberment of the American theocracy was addressable, though it would be a far more difficult venue to sustain than the kind of world-fabulation in which Christ's sister has arisen; but Morrow didn't even give it a try, didn't even seem to notice that his book was dissolving under him, that the secession of New Jersey had become, in Only Begotten Daughter, nothing more than a conceit. It was at that point I stopped worrying about the fate of Julie Katz, because from that point I knew that sooner or later she'd shrug off New Jersey like Gulliver shrugging off Lilliput, that she would spread her wings above the candyfloss of the text, that she would rise like hot air into the West.

– from Interzone 55, January 1992

3. VARIOUS

I.

HERE IS The Neal Barrett Jr Story. At first sight it looks very much like The Elmore Leonard Story: The Sequel. After 30 years of hardworking obscurity, a period during which he has published only paperback originals, Neal Barrett finally gets a hardback house to take him seriously. In 1987, when he's almost 60, *Through Darkest America* is released to a chorus of surprised reviews, and all seems set for the bandwagon. But something happens. The hardback house turns sour on sf, and Barrett's next novel, a sequel to the breakthrough book, comes out as a paperback, and sinks out of sight. Which is not a great career move, not The Elmore Leonard Story, not how to enjoy a prosperous old age.

We come to 1991, and to *The Hereafter Gang* (Mark V Ziesing, 1991), and we simply do not know what to think. The book itself is attractively produced, and distributed widely within the sf world; but there seems no way, all the same, that a small press like Ziesing can hope to muscle into the chains. It seems unlikely, therefore, that this second potential breakthrough novel will reach the very wide readership it deserves. *The Hereafter Gang* is almost as hilarious as Larry McMurtry's *Texasville* (1987), and less earthbound; nearly as haunted as Thomas Pynchon's *Vineland* (1990), and less suffocating. Like both those books, it attempts to hold on to America as the century blows us away; like neither of them, it bites the bullet, in language of tensile brilliance. In *The Hereafter Gang*, the only way to recapture the past – or to hold on to the present – is to die.

Doug Hoover is 58 years old but looks 35. He lies about his age, not through vanity, but so he can continue living the life he wants to lead, which means avoiding permanent employment, and sleeping with almost every woman he meets. Suddenly he finds that he has gotten stuck. He is becoming far too successful in his job – public relations work in Dallas – and is now due for promotion; and he discovers that he seems to have been married for several years to one woman, Erlene Lamprey, who owns one book in the world, and whose "idea of outdoors was a windchime in front of the A/C." It is time to light out for the Territory, like Huck Finn.

But at the end of the century, in the heart of Dallas, there's not much Territory to light out for. Ricocheting from one bar to another, and frightened half to death by a succession of terrible sharp chest pains, Doug skedaddles into a world of memories: the sharp scents and colors of youth; the precious polished cars and toys and girls of his early years. Guided by an amiable young drifter, with whom he identifies, and seduced by a sweet-and-sour teenaged "Southern girl," he exits the no-exit freeways of 1990 and immerses himself in the soil of the past.

In other words, Doug Hoover has died. *The Hereafter Gang* is a posthumous fantasy; like similar work by a wide variety of writers, from Vladimir Nabokov to Flann O'Brien, from John Crowley to Gene Wolfe, it is a tale whose hero, after the death of the body, must sift through the materials of the life he has left in order to make sense of his naked soul. But posthumous fantasies tend to slide all too easily into intolerable solitude, as the hero narrows in on himself; and it is here that Barrett leaps sideways from his models. The posthumous landscapes visited by Doug are peopled: the folk he loved, the small towns he grew up in, the beverages he drank, the World War One planes he made models of, the Western heroes he emulated, all congregate. His search for order turns into a clambake.

At this point, the novel risks becoming a feelgood traipse through themepark suburbs of the dead, full of portion-control sweetness and light. It is a dangerous moment, but Barrett gets past it with great skill. After all the sleek contrivances of the plot, and the strange exhilarations of a posthumous landscape through which the real world seems impossibly scarred and tawdry, *The Hereafter Gang* finds itself in the American soul of its hero. In Doug, Barrett has created a figure too complex and ornery to sort himself out glibly, and too American to go quietly into the good night; an awful man, and almost a great one. Nothing Doug has done in his life is alien to him, nothing is turned away. The dreadful and the garish and the good, he embraces it all. *The Hereafter Gang* is a celebration of this embrace. It is one of the great American novels. Try to find it.

11.

Like Larry McMurtry, whose *Anything for Billy* (1988) is all about it, Barrett has a fascination for the queer queasy legend of Billy the Kid, and makes the buck-toothed William Bonney into one of Doug's posthumous role models, the pages in which he features being the weakest part of *The Hereafter Gang*. It is hard to understand precisely why the Kid has so hypnotic an effect on grown writers; but since he does, and since we must live with the fact, it comes as a real pleasure to note that Rebecca Ore's *The Illegal Rebirth of Billy the Kid* (Tor, 1991) first recognizes the dubiousness of any fascination with the bewildered teenaged punk, and second manages very thoroughly, from the word go, to subvert its title.

Life is not very encouraging in the straitened and stratified America of 2067, threatened by a new ice age, and morally contaminated by advances in genetic science. Simon Boyle, the villain of the novel, is a CIA scientist who specializes in DNA recombinant engineering; he's supposed to spend all his time creating "chimeras" – vat-grown meat-puppet humanoids – to be sent on spy missions, but on the side he's managed to vat out a Billy the Kid, complete with memories abstracted from legend, controlled by a "nineteenth century visual matrix" which keeps him from seeing anything incongruous in the 21st century world, and juiced up with pheromones. He then hires Billy out to rich women, who make love to the simulacrum just before Simon – who looks like Pat Garrett to Billy's doctored senses – shoots him down.

When one of the rich ladies escapes with Billy, Simon's life begins to unravel; and after Billy himself escapes from the lady's clutches, eventually to land up in the hands of a society formed to protect chimeras like himself, the end is inevitable. The CIA, to protect its own, homes in on the rogue chimera, and terminates Simon. It all sounds gloomy, drab, and rather dumb. It is nothing of the sort.

In *The Illegal Rebirth of Billy the Kid*, which is her first singleton, Ore has mastered a style whose speed and head-pounding density are at points almost excessive, but which stunningly conveys the confused Billy's perceptions of a radically complex and very unpleasant world. The problematical nature of his selfhood – he seems at first to be nothing but an walking anthology of clichés – is never dodged, even when the pathos of his terror bites deepest, for he knows what being killed and reborn is like: it's like hell. But slowly the chimera conquers "its" conditioning, and becomes fully human. Slowly, the book turns into a love story – but even here the stringency is unrelenting, the fragility of Billy's identity constantly haunts the cast, ice darkens the horizon, and the world fails to become springlike when the CIA (after killing his maker) grants him permission to live in the Appalachian National Park, which has been artificially maintained in its original state. Niche existence in a themepark will be tough for Billy. Rebecca Ore's novel is a fable for tough times.

III.

For years, George Alec Effinger has given the impression of being a lot brighter than his books. This was perhaps unwise of George Alec Effinger, for he is a memorable writer whose words it is almost impossible to remember, a dark and intricate fantasist whose fantasies fade like invisible ink, an author like the Cheshire Cat is a cat. After 15 or 20 books, this began to wear thin. But in 1987 he published *When Gravity Fails*, and in 1989 *A Fire in the Sun*, and now, with *The Exile Kiss* (Doubleday Foundation, 1991), he continues the long story of Marîd Audran, streetwise inhabitant of the Budayeen, a North African city from which figures like Friedlander Bey secretly manipulate the tossed and torn world of the 21st century. It is a cruel environment, and a cunning one, and it asks Effinger's full attention. This he gives. The book is a joy to read.

In previous volumes, Bey had acquired and trained the quick-witted, tough but pixilated Audran; fitted him with implants, so that he can both augment his powers and drug himself silly; integrated him into the complex high-tech but uncoordinated larger world; and become his father. Now Audran must learn to do by policy that which he had previously given no thought to. He must learn to kill, to delegate terrible responsibilities, to forgive his friends; he must become a man, like Friedlander Bey, a figure that the Audrans of the future can climb like a trellis, just as he climbed Bey, learning how to become human in the process. Or so we're inclined to feel. Little, however, happens in this volume, beautifully though it is told. Bey and Audran are falsely accused of a murder, left to die in the heart of the Arabian desert, make friends with the Bedouins who save them, return home to enact a partial revenge. But the revenge cannot be complete, nor Audran's maturity fully achieved, because *The Exile Kiss* does not end the series, and its plot, like a false-bottomed suitcase, designedly fails to deliver the goods. Still, because the author is continuing to pay attention to his detail work, the waiting is delicious.

IV.

Given its title, *The Paper Grail* (Ace, 1991), James P Blaylock's latest Northern California contemporary fantasy, should be something of a shocker. After all, the Holy

Grail is no laughing matter. If it exists in a tale, then that tale must include a Fisher King; and if there's a Fisher King, then Northern California should certainly be a Waste Land awaiting the end of a terrible drought. No such luck.

A weird modern-dress amiability rules this very peculiar novel. The Fisher King turns out to be an old gent who lives in a photogenic Californian house overlooking the sea. He is dying, but his unknowing successor (the protagonist of the book) stumbles into view in the nick of time, just as the geezer kicks in the bucket at the old fishing hole (really); and takes over the Kingship. But this new King is neither impotent (though the Fisher King's lack of vital force lies at the heart of any previous version of the myth I'm aware of) nor does he cause anything like a drought. Anything but. As soon as he's crowned he gets to sleep with the girl he's been in love with for years; and when he begins to fool around with the paper Grail – which turns out to be some sort of paper hanky – he causes a huge rainstorm. It turns out that the Grail is a kind of fantasy-game *weapon*, which his main enemy – she's a sort of wicked witch of the West – wants to gain control of. All these shenanigans cause the plot to thicken for a while, until it all blows away, in scenes reminiscent of Stephen Spielberg's 1941. Then it plops shut.

There are compensations: a marvelous sect of gluers, who fasten the world together with abandoned souvenirs; Blaylock's deft touch with eccentric characters; a powerful sense of place. But the central premise, so casually screwed out of true, utterly swamps the soothing patter of the tale. It is a very silly thing to happen to a book.

– *The Washington Post Book World Science Fiction Column*, 30 June 1991

IT WOULD BE easy to make this book seem unreadable by praising it. Thomas M Disch's *The M.D.: A Horror Story* (Knopf, 1991), we might say, is a fine and scathing anatomy of post–Viet Nam America, a sly indictment of the organized religions of the Western world, a tragic tale of moral paralysis and sin. It depicts through scorching flashes of detail the inexorable growth of AIDS and of its even more terrible successor; it is grimly cynical about priests and politicians, doctors and fundraisers, grannies and dads, moms and sons and daughters. But then, after frightening any reader half to death, it would be only fair to say one more thing about Disch's magnum opus. *The M.D.* may be profound and dark and very dire; but it is also a page-turner.

And each new page, like an electric eel, is poised to shock. In the mid 1970s, in the tangled working-class Catholic heart of St Paul, Minnesota, young Billy Michaels throws a kindergarten tantrum when the appalling Sister Symphorosa insists to her captive audience of tiny children that there is no Santa Claus, and tells them why it is blasphemous to believe in him. As she strangles their joy she smiles, sure that her victims, coiled in guilt, are now ready to spend the rest of their lives negotiating with the Church for salvation.

But Billy knows better. Santa Claus has already spoken to him, in a voice like gravel, out of an icy whirlwind. Santa's other name is Mercury, and if Billy is good Santa will give him a caduceus for his very own, and he will be able to do things with it. He will be able to heal, and to curse. He only has to remember that what he does with the caduceus can't be undone, and that every time he uses it for good he must recharge the two interwoven snake-like sticks by doing harm. It's easy. Life, after all, as Billy has already learned from Sister Symphorosa, is something you can make Book on; it is a series of negotiations with a carnival deity.

Besides, he has every intention of doing as much good as possible, especially when it's a member of his own convoluted family which needs help; and if he must do evil – if for instance he must punish cigarette smokers by inflicting cancer on anyone who uses a lighter he has exposed to the caduceus – then so be it. Good, he knows, is best if done at home (it's like giving something to yourself in secret), and evil is best done at a distance (as in Viet Nam). Coiled within the acts of the caduceus, Billy grows into William. He begins (like his country, perhaps) to live on credit, on promissory notes. But he fails to ask when his debts will come due, or in what currency he will be required to pay.

We jump to 1999. Minnesota is becoming a dust-bowl, due to the greenhouse effect. Brilliant young Dr. Michaels needs a very great amount of caduceus energy to fund his good works and increase his fortune, so he creates ARVIDS – Acute Random-Vector Immune Disorder Syndrome – as a balancing curse upon innumerable Americans he hopes never to meet. Concentration camps begin to proliferate, some of which Michaels's corporations run for profit. But anyone can catch ARVIDS simply by breathing: the world is rotting. Like any human being who has surrendered his mind to a coercive faith, like any citizen of a world power living in dream-time as history begins to bite, William Michaels has lost track of his soul, and the bargain he struck with the god has become a universal contagion.

Santa, or Mercury, or Satan, or the vile unconscious of the race, is well satisfied. All he had ever required was that his victim operate the caduceus according to contract. That was all. He now abandons William to his fate, for he is used up. In the last pages of Disch's superb saga of moral death and blank-faced retribution, Dr. Michaels gets everything he deserves, in scenes of chilled pathos and steely hilarity that tickle like scalpels. Just as in any fairy tale that warns us about making bargains with the devil, he loses everything. He is damned. But because he has been corroded from within, he never understands why. He is denied even that.

In some of his best previous novels – like 334 (1972) or The Businessman (1984) – Disch occasionally indulged himself in the habit of creating characters visibly less intelligent than he was, incarcerating them in cages of irony, and then gloating at their failure to work out the awfulness of the trap he'd put them in. What makes The M.D. so memorable a book is that almost none of its characters – not even Dr. Michaels at the well-deserved end of his tether – are treated to one instant of contempt from the author. Young Billy is any of us. In his slow path to damnation he follows a course any of us might find hauntingly plausible. There are some monsters in his family, as there are in most families; and one of them becomes his nemesis. But most of his kin are lovable.

Near the end of things, Billy's stepfather Ben, who has suffered a caduceus-inspired succession of ups and downs, contemplates the Book of Job. He notices how God proposes "the crocodile as an emblem of his own awful power," as if that answered Job's lamentations, and Ben decides to follow the hint. "The secret wisdom of the Book of Job," he muses, "is that it is exciting and profitable to work for crocodiles." What he cannot know is that by 1999 it is too late for him, or for his land. He has been serving his stepson's crocodile god for years, and it will soon cast him off. Because Ben is a real person, not a caged puppet, that death will seem tragic.

But the tragedy encompassed by The M.D. is of course greater than that of a single family. At the age of 50, Disch has looked upon the religion of his birth (he is a lapsed Catholic) and found it identical to the corruptions of Mercury; the twinings of the caduceus are a neat symbol of the intimacy of the two faiths. He has looked upon the land of his birth (he comes from Minnesota) and found its people no more capable of understanding the roots of power than Billy Michaels was. The M.D. is chock-full of page-turner jokes and ironies and story-telling genius. But one more thing can be said as well. The M.D. is a tract for the times.

– Los Angeles Times, 14 July 1991

IT WOULD BE terribly unfair to forget to say something positive about The World Beyond the Hill (Tarcher, 1989). The book is, after all, the magnum opus of Alexei and Cory Panshin; it is a history of sf designed to reveal the inner shape of the genre. It is an exceedingly ambitious project, 685 pages long, with astonishingly few factual errors. It presents a close reading of many of the paradigm texts of American sf from 1920 to 1945, and attempts to place these texts into a framework of understanding. We will speak of this framework of understanding in a moment, but not until we've stopped being nice: and as long as we restrict ourselves to the Panshins' readings of individual texts and authors, there is little but praise to utter, for their industry has been astonishing, and the clarity of their readings of authors like A E Van Vogt exemplary; and if they had been capable of sticking to their last no reader could possibly have felt like tossing The World Beyond the Hill right through the window into the Road Beyond the Sidewalk. We're still being nice. What we want to say is this. The World Beyond the Hill is a resource for us all.

There. Enough of that.

In 1931, a young British historian named Herbert Butterfield published a small study whose title would become a catchphrase for the intellectual syndrome he was attacking. The Whig Interpretation of History was an assault upon the cast of mind which studies "the past with direct and perpetual reference to the present. Through this system of immediate reference to the present-day," Butterfield argued, "historical personages can easily and irresistibly be classed into the men who furthered progress and the men who tried to hinder it." But

> Real historical understanding is not achieved by the subordination of the past to the present, but rather by our making the past our present and attempting to see life with the eyes of another century than our own. It is not reached by assuming that our own age is the absolute to which Luther and Calvin [or Edgar Allan Poe and H G Wells] and their generation are only relative; it is only reached by fully accepting the fact that their generation was as valid as our generation, their issues as momentous as our issues and their day as full and as vital to them as our day is to us.

Not to understand that "Progress" is an artifact is not to understand that the past is real. To write narrative history as though figures of the past were only partial realizations of the true whole and wholesome humans of the time to come is not to understand the human enterprise; and it is to write history as the Panshins write it. Butterfield continues:

> Our assumptions do not matter if we are conscious that they are assumptions, but the most fallacious thing in the world is to organize our historical knowledge upon an assumption without realising what we are doing, and then to make inferences from that organization and claim that these are the voice of history. It is at this point that we tend to fall into what I have nicknamed the whig fallacy.

It is a fallacy that, once we have fallen into its unsubtly self-congratulatory rhythms, allows us to accord, with delicious ease, the nice condescension of our plaudits to figures seen "to have been fighting for the future" – which means fighting for us – and

> when we come, say, to examine Martin Luther more closely, we have [in our hands a technical procedure, a magnet] that can draw out of history the very things that we go to look for, and by a hundred quotations torn from their context and robbed of their relevance to a particular historical conjuncture we can prove that there is an analogy between the ideas of Luther and the world of the present day, we can see in [the optical illusion that is the Luther we have created] a foreshadowing of the present.

Thus Butterfield.

The World Beyond the Hill is, in every sense Butterfield seems to have intended, a Whig history. The Panshins may (or may not) be conscious of this pedigree; but they certainly write as though they were completely ignorant of the fact that Whig histories, written from a multitude of perspectives, had for centuries been falsifying the long turpitude and glamour of the world: and that the trick had been exposed. The Panshins may have chosen to write like the wise hillbillies it is certainly the case that they are not, but we are going to treat them not as the wise hillbillies it is certainly the case that they are not, but as writers responsible for what they say. For the Panshins, no human member of the world of sf from any period earlier than about 1935 – nor any text written by any human being of that ilk from the dark ages before that date – can claim any inherent autonomy as either man or woman or writer (or text). For the Panshins, these humans (and these texts) are *precursors*.

For the Panshins, the history of sf climbs the ladder of history until it reaches "The Golden Age" of 1939–1945, as brought into focus by John W Campbell Jr and his stable. Gaining the high plateau of this Golden Age is the goal to which all previous sf writers aspired, and from which all previous sf writers fell before the fact, and the reality-quotient of any previous human being or text is contingent upon how close s/he got to the fact-to-come before failing. Speaking of proto-sf, they make themselves perfectly clear on page 66:

> It is our awareness of the nature of later science fiction – and our appreciation of the invisible working of the transcendent spirit of SF – that allows us to perceive what these varying bits and pieces had in common.

These "bits and pieces," of course, once walked the planet.

But *The World Beyond the Hill* goes much further than this. Sinuously intertwined with a scorecard narrative which *grades* writers according to their success at moving towards the Absolute Present of the Golden Age, an even stranger application of the Whig tyranny can be discerned. It is not only writers and their books which become more densely real, in the Panshin view, as they approach the Present: the *inner beings* of their texts, as well, become more real. Again and again, the Panshins write as though the galaxy E E Smith founded was *really there*, that it took "courage" to visit that vast and daunting assemblage of stars, and that the prior folk, the less real, the failed precursors, somehow flinched from the mighty prospect of visiting E E Smith's universe even before he "created" it. The venues and the protagonists of fictional tales, in other words, are in some transcendental sense as real as their creators, and climb the same slope; and both the created and the creators aspire to achieve the apotheosis of being *entirely* real: of becoming somehow eligible – of somehow gaining the "courage" – to enter the open-gated, transcendental Golden Age. This is, of course, pure Whig ontology: you're real to the extent that you resemble *me*. It is the ontology of the solipsist.

Many of the their readers may find it difficult to understand that for the Panshins – at least in their wise hillbilly guise – stories told in words point beyond the paper towards something genuinely "transcendental"; but this is not a difficulty the Panshins admit to being conscious of as an issue. If E E Smith *speaks* of an intolerably vast universe, then according to the flow and pomp of their rhetoric he has in fact *created* that intolerably vast universe. If A E Van Vogt, out of his oneiric euphoria, *speaks* of a superman, then that superman exists as an idea which is *more real* than those of us who lived before it was written down; that superman inhabits the Absolute Present towards which we, as human beings, are entitled to aspire: hence, of course, Van Vogt's own descent into Scientology, a sect whose tenets are topologically identical to those of any sf story which treats the achievement of spiritual transcendence as a problem to be solved with hardware. What we have, therefore, in *The World Beyond the Hill*, is the Whig Fallacy wrought to its uttermost. It is terribly foolish. It is rather a tragedy. But it is not only that. It is also a very rude book.

(We will put to one side the Panshins' version of the nature of myth – that true myths, of which sf is one, are manuals for changing the world to make it better. Although this rendering of myth reveals the typical Whig deformation as clearly as any other line of thought in the book, this does not seem the place or time to make any sustained argument for any alternative version of the nature of myth in the world or in the text – as presented, for instance, by Northrop Frye in *Anatomy of*

Criticism [1957].)

So let us follow the Panshins through a few of their many pages, starting on page one with a rhetorical passage whose bare-faced looniness of reification we might have taken as sloppy writing, had we not read on. It's about transcendence: "In science fiction stories," we read, "spaceships and time machines carry us outside ourselves, outside our world, outside everything we know, to distant realms that none of us has ever seen." What the Panshins might claim they mean by this, we do not presume to guess. But what the passage bloody well *says* is that an sf story, written in words by a human being, *opens a portal* to worlds lying "outside everything we know" *and takes us there.* Mere mundane fiction, on the other hand, we read on page four, does not "dar[e] to be transcendent." It does not carry us to Trantor. Moreover (page 18) "certain lines of literary descent from [Horace] Walpole – the Gothic romance, the rational detective story, the historical novel – could not tolerate the implausible and so abandoned transcendence in favor of a strict adherence to 'the facts,'...[becoming, in the process,] mythically sterile." Only sf refused to miscegenate.

We are passing upwards through history at a great clip. Mary Shelley almost gets a good grade, for it was "she who truly dared the wrath of heaven" (page 27), but she's fined severely all the same for her failure to extend to "transcendent aliens or realms" (page 28) her examination of the real worlds E E Smith would later *visit.* C– then. Victor Frankenstein, on the other hand, fails outright: "If he had only been able to master his ambivalent passions and sit down and have a chat with his creature," mourn the Panshins on page 29, "he would have found that they had much in common and a great deal of useful information to exchange." It's an F for Frankenstein.

But we must hurry. No time to check on how Fitz-James O'Brien fails to equal the great daring of Ray Cummings (page 32). No time to comprehend in every detail Edgar Allen Poe's failure of nerve in *The Narrative of Arthur Gordon Pym* (1837), his inability to enter the Hollow Earth (page 35). No time to explore the funk of Jules Verne ("All would go well enough for a time, but at last, in each case [that is, in each novel], the mystery would become too much for him, the threat of transcendence too overwhelming." Page 44.) No time to commiserate with either Poe or Verne, overwhelmed (page 85) by the "glimpses" they'd had "of the transcendent beings and transcendent realms of the World Beyond the Hill." No time to reflect upon the *advance* reflected by Wells's *Time Machine* (1895) scoop: "The deliberate result of the adventures of the Time Traveller has been to trash all of the things that earlier generations had come to think they knew about the Future" (page 111). No time to bask in the capacity of 1930s sf writers "to tolerate dealings with domesticated aliens" (page 118), unlike the later Wells, who was perhaps "frightened by the aliens that he imagined" (same page), who had anyway (same page) gotten fat, and who in any case (page 119) did not "dare" imagine what the Grand Lunar in *First Men in the Moon* (1901) might *really* be like. "It would," gloat the Panshins, "be others than Wells who would conceive what was to be done by men *out there in the larger world* [my italics]" (page 122).

But we do have a little time to learn in what respect (page 130) the stories of Edgar Rice Burroughs "held answers" for questions Jack London killed himself rather than ask. Brave E R B! Cowardly-custard Jack! While Verne might shirk (page 134) "at the first evidence of wonder," E R B "simply picks his character up by the scruff of the neck and sets him down naked in a transcendent realm." This might seem pretty far out to E R B's readers (the Panshins recognize), but not to worry! Those 1915 readers were as courageous as E R B himself, and valiantly followed the adventures of John Carter in Barsoom in order "to discover what a lone human being might accomplish if set down naked in an alien world where the struggle for existence was even fiercer than on Earth" (page 135). In other words, it is not simply the case that Barsoom, because it lies on the high road to the Absolute Present of full transcendence, is in some profound sense not only realer – and higher on the scale of evolution – than Middlemarch: John Carter is also realer than George Eliot. His adventures "reconcile the best of civilization and the best of savagery, two states formerly though to be totally incompatible" (page 136). Through Carter, Burroughs "is offering the materials of an answer to the tangled problem of man, civilization and nature" (page 138). Which'll show those cowardly Europeans. Carter "is an early version of the Twentieth Century existential man who finds his meaning in encounter, not in affiliation" (same page). "My mind," he says in *A Princess of Mars* (book form 1917). "is evidently so constituted that I am subconsciously forced into the path of duty without recourse to tiresome mental processes" (quoted on page 139). Edgar Rice Burroughs

> was not frightened [unlike the suicidal London, or poor Wells] by the universe of space and time. Nor was he daunted by the prospect of having to struggle and change to get ahead in this world. Burroughs was able to imagine a person much like himself living, loving, fighting, adventuring, and winning through on an alien world that was simultaneously scientific and a realm of the World Beyond the Hill. It was to characters like John Carter that the future of science fiction would belong.

There are 550 pages to go. But by now we pretty well know where the Panshins are taking us, and we can skip around a bit. Hugo Gernsback, we can guess, will be next; and he is; and one reviewer at least found himself singing in his bath, to the tune of Beethoven's "Ode to Joy," some new verses which were a great improvement on poor old pre-Barsoom Schiller's pre-transcendental doggerel:

> Gott im Himmel,
> Hugo Gernsback,
> Papa auf der Golden Age,

he sang, but what else he sang has faded from memory.

Anyway, after we learn that Bertrand Russell could not face the truth about the universe exposed by E R B, and that (page 188) only "E E Smith, Edmond Hamilton, Jack Williamson, Stanley Weinbaum and John W Campbell, Jr" "had the courage and insight necessary to take the bad news that had been delivered by science, face it squarely, and transmute it into something positive," and after a few more rejects of history have marched the plank, we find the Panshins shifting gear, and it comes as a great relief. The book turns into something you could let out of doors without a leash. Much of the remainder of the text – though dozens more examples of goon-show Whiggery could be adduced (page numbers on request) – is devoted to practical criticism, much of it exceedingly valuable, of the writings of Smith, Campbell, L Sprague de Camp, Isaac Asimov, Robert A Heinlein and A E Van Vogt, and it is only when they feel compelled to draw comparisons – when for instance (page 215) it is claimed that Europeans like Olaf Stapledon, in contrast to Doc Smith, "lacked the depth of vision and the sheer power of imagination necessary to alter their attitudes" – that the appalling provinciality of the book's *argument* shames the reader who might love sf but who would not care to pass The World Beyond the Hill to his colleagues, for they would not understand.

They would not understand – 60 years after Herbert Butterfield laid down his sparkling challenge to the Whig mind-set – how two grown writers of such obvious mental energy could construct an edifice of this sort, that they could seem so cruelly ignorant of the dangerousness of a philosophy of history in which there are sheep and there are goats, those saved and those who are only half-real, those who are courageously climbing the steep hill towards the Promised Land, and those others who belong in the garbage-dumps of history; how two grown writers could generate a text so full of autodidact spite and superba, so full of faux-naïf contempt for the men and women who preceded them on the turning world, so condescending about the words and worlds their predecessors imagined, so unutterably callow about the reified wet-dream they think of as transcendence, but which others might call fetish.

They would not understand. And I do not.

– New York Review of Science Fiction 35, July 1991

THERE WAS a thought that three hard sf books, found in a clump upon the shelf, should hang together. It is not, however, going to be easy to get a group verdict. Allen Steele's second novel, *Clarke County, Space* (Ace, 1990), is a blown-up booster anecdote told in a style one might describe as Chamber-of-Commerce-Heinlein; Roger MacBride Allen's *The Ring of Charon* (Tor, 1991), which is projected to be the first volume of a series to be called The Hunted Earth, begins small – the invention of a gravity-wave focuser on Pluto's moon leads to the mere disappearance of Earth down a wormhole – and becomes a galumphing, thoroughly enjoyable cosmology opera with an engagingly Rube-Goldberg attitude to anything like strict science-based extrapolation; and Alexander Jablokov's *Carve the Sky* (Morrow, 1991) turns out not to be hard sf at all, though most of it is set in space, and interstellar travel is mooted: shot through with echoes of Gene Wolfe, it is a quite estimable example of the New England School of Ethical Romance, whose members include, among others, John Crowley, Richard Grant, Elizabeth Hand, Paul Hazel and James Patrick Kelly.

I.

Set some time after the events recounted in *Orbital Decay* (1988), and in what seems to be a near-future universe consistent with that obtaining in the earlier book, *Clarke County, Space* sets out from the first to be more than just a story; or, if it is a "story," it's one whose truth is both difficult and important to ascertain. An old writer in Florida is preparing to begin a book about the famous Clarke County incident which had occurred two years previous, or just around the middle of the 21st century. A young man approaches him, startlingly demonstrates his knowledge of the old guy's secret project, and proceeds to tell him the "true" story. That story, set in flashback, makes up the bulk of the book. *Clarke County, Space* is a corporation-owned space colony whose inhabitants are beginning to chafe at the company-town injustices being imposed upon them, and who are afraid that their habitat will soon be themeparked for profit. Meanwhile on Earth, an East-Coast ingenue who has been fucking a sadistic Mafia gang-leader for four years escapes the guarded compound where she's spent all this time, clutching a bunch of computer floppies which hold not only all the records of the Mafia's nefarious wrongdoing but also the only copy of the top-secret-but-real-easy-to-steal coded instructions for re-activating a 100-megaton self-propelled nuclear bomb which was not needed to destroy an errant asteroid several years previously and is therefore currently in low orbit around Earth but not disarmed; and with this data – none of which she is aware she's got – she takes the shuttle to Clarke County, where she hopes to be safe. But a Mafia hood named the Golem is in hot pursuit.

To get to Clarke County you have three choices. You can go first class, like the Mafia squeeze, which means you are comfortable but very conspicuous (as Steele draws her, she's not very bright: this is perhaps deliberate). Or you can go second class, which means cramped but anonymous boredom (but the Mafia hood eschews this obvious choice). Or you can go coffined in third, in kind of a suspended animation induced by a substance which acts – upon your reawakening – like a truth drug, so that – for instance – you would be unable to conceal from any official your true motives for travelling to the fragile colony, if for instance you happened to be a Mafia hood named the Golem chasing a squeeze who could end the world. But not to worry. Though the Mafia hood travels in third class, Clarke County does not make a practice of asking thirds on their arousal what their purpose is in coming – even when, as in this case, the FBI has already warned them that trouble is brewing – so there's no problem! Jeez, you think, what a good ole libertarian freedom-loving company suburb Clarke County must be!

But wait for it. The Golem meets a fellow passenger, a Presley lookalike who impersonates Elvis on behalf of the First Church of Twentieth Century Saints, Elvis Has Risen, and who mysteriously cannot afford first class; and this guy does ask the Golem what he's doing on Clarke, but he asks him seconds too late, because the drug has worn off that very instant. Phew! There's fast-lane plotting for you. Wickedly clever! The upshot of it all is that, despite all the efforts of 21st century science to stop him, the Golem does get scot-free into Clarke, in hot pursuit of the bimbo with the disks. Phew. Imagine the reader's suspense.

Meanwhile, on Clarke, Sheriff Bigthorn (I found myself thinking of him, as the plot developed and as he continued to bugger up his job, as Sheriff Huge Penis Head) goes to his hogan (he's of Indian blood) where the wife of the leader of the "far left" faction (far left, in American terms, meaning someone who thinks Grenada didn't start the war) in the Clarke County local government strips off in order to make passionate love to the well-hung Huge Penis Head, who refuses her, though he loves her deeply, for reasons of propriety. And so it goes. As far as Steele is concerned, in other words, nothing profound has changed in 60 years of radical transformation: nuclear families, sexual politics, pop music, machismo, computer technology, nation states, corporate ethics, Mafia hoods, bimbos, FBI agents, all are substantially identical to what one might find in any American small city in 1980.

And, in the sense that it occupies subsequent pages, the rest of the novel follows from all of this. The Elvis Church has a concert, which ends in tears and the death (which generates an unacknowledged Zappa quote) of the Elvis lookalike. The bimbo mistakes Huge Penis Head's deputies for golems, and well she might, and this causes general chaos. The Golem himself runs effortlessly amuck, shooting up the hoosegow and blowing up Huge Penis Head's own home (which he doesn't check out, even knowing that the Golem is at loose and trying to kill him), the explosion almost killing the woman who loves Huge Penis Head, an outrage which finally inflames Huge Penis Head enough to make him finally kill the Golem (after missing several previous chances to do his job). A seriously unbalanced Elvis freak (this is 2050!) celebrates the Elvis lookalike's performances by stealing the bimbo's floppies and setting the screwloose nuclear missile on collision course with Clarke County for reasons it is difficult just now to pretend to try to understand, but eventually repents and turns the bomb off just in time. Independence is declared.

Throughout these masterful shenanigans, a mysterious unseen prankster and gossip named Blind Boy Grunt (it's an *early* Bob Dylan pseudonym) has been mysteriously proving himself privy to every bit of electronic data in the entire colony, cunningly blabbing (via computer screens) enough information about the state of affairs to keep Huge Penis Head one step ahead of terminal bewilderment; but although it's 2050, and although joke-prone AI's who secretly run things – and even more secretly care a whole heck of a lot for that crazy human race – have been part of sf literature since 1966 (*The Moon Is a Harsh Mistress* lies beneath every trope Steele seems able to imagine), *nobody* (except every single reader of the book) *guesses* that Blind Boy Grunt is an AI, though the young man who later tells the old guy in the frame story what really happened does manage to figure it out, with broad hints from Blind Boy Grunt itself. But who this young man is in truth, only readers of the book will find out. This reviewer does not have the heart to say, nor would it be kind to expatiate upon a framing device which makes it utterly clear that nothing of any importance happened in the main story: which in turn makes it utterly clear that there was never any need for a framing device.

We have spent some fraction of our precious quality time on this space-mall sitcom because Allen Steele is supposed to be one of the hopes. He is supposed to be one of the hard sf writers who understands the technological and scientific trelliswork we're going to have to map our way through if we hope to envision the cutting edge of the near future. It may even be the case that his sense of the physical appearance of a space colony 60 years from now may be accurate enough: but surely the lived world within the made will never exhibit the dreadful simplicities he seems to think are normative. For a couple of moments, here and there, things move in Clarke County, Space, and a lightening of the prose gives one to think there might be a window open somewhere, that Allen Steele might be paying attention to the world. But then the county shuts down again, the prose and imagery become once again a taxidermy of 1960, and the silliness of the tale covers all, like gas.

II.

You do worry about some of these young Americans. The social realities glanced at – very much in passing – in The Ring of Charon, as Roger MacBride Allen's big novel blitzes onwards, are no more sophisticated than the bullying conformisms trotted out in Clarke County, Space; and Allen, because he is claiming to portray a very much wider canvas, is at times more actively embarrassing than the cognitively docile Steele. Allen's version of countercultural lifestyles, as expressed in his spiteful, hate-loaded rendering of The Naked Purple Movement – a group of "hippies" who occupy a satellite complexly orbiting both the Moon and Earth – exudes a senility of contempt for a disappeared world that might be understandable if Allen himself had been more than a decade old when the last hippy died somewhere around 1968, or if the world of his novel were in any sense meant to represent the pocket-universe solipsism of some God of Tedium, or if he were Orson Scott Card wrestling with the Demons of Despite, but no: Allen makes no claim to personal knowledge of bad hippy vibes, he's no solipsist (yet), and he has nothing of the icy furiousness of Card. We're hundreds of years (I think it is) into the future, though something called the Knowledge Crash has conveniently slowed things down, and young Larry O'Shawnessy Chao on Charon, after some partial successes, has just worked out how to focus gravity-waves into something like a laser beam, but guaranteed harmless. With his colleagues, he directs the beam to research centres on the asteroids and planets between Charon and Earth, so that they will know what has been accomplished, and finally messages the home planet: which disappears as soon as the beam hits it. The novel has just begun.

We gradually learn what has happened. An enormously ancient alien race, whose acquisitive genome includes a variety of species, and artifacts as well, has aeons previously embedded a giant sentient gravity-wave-detecting ring inside the Moon. Its function is to respond, in ways not perhaps made entirely clear in this first volume, to signs that the solar system is ripe for treatment. Chao's early experiments have triggered the ring into virtually automatic action; having invoked a wormhole connection to its home system – which is a Dyson sphere itself surrounded by lots of stars around which orbit lots of planets like Earth, all of them full of genetic diversities to sample – the ring in the Moon is ready for action, and when the gravity-wave beam touches its sensors, it fedexes Earth down the wormhole to its new home.

The rest of the novel begins the task of exploring the implications of the complex cosmology thus hinted at. Chao and his gang, and other humans – though, entirely typical of this sort of book, no government agencies are foregrounded enough to become even remotely believable as part of the human enterprise – start to fight back against the "Charonians." They manage to get messages through the wormhole to Earth, which may be light-centuries distant. They work out a technique to flummox the thousands of quasi-sentient Charonian tools which have converged upon the surviving planets of the solar system to demolish them as part of the process of building a new Dyson sphere. Even the lesbo-pig queen-politico of the Naked Purple Movement is forced to help. And we're off. Long may The Hunted Earth tantalize young Chao and his elite cadre of scientists, sort of thing.

All the same, the absences mount. One might have thought, for instance, that Allen, who was born in 1957 and who credits his friend Charles Sheffield for a lot of assistance, would have exhibited an informed rapport with computer rhetoric, that he would, in fact, find it difficult *not* to write a novel in which information flowed like song. But the computers visible in The Ring of Charon are absurdly primitive as rhetorics of the song of information; and though we are a long way futurewards when the book begins there are no AI's anywhere, no converse with the music of the data, no networks; there is no sense that information understands itself. The Knowledge Crash, which is in any case only mentioned in passing, reads like some oldish writer's excuse for not attempting to update the passacaglias that paced his vision for all those years before computers began to rewrite the rhetorics of knowing, thank you very much: from a young writer, one who doesn't bother to argue the premise, the Knowledge Crash has all the air of an opportunistic refusal of complexity. Which refusal, of course, does help make the book possible, because it is a book about playing. The Ring of Charon is a great thrusting exuberant juvenile, full of guys and gals playing a really neat Universe Game, and a more "realistic" mise en scène – one whose governments and armies weren't downgraded to invisibility, one in which infant-prodigy scientists weren't allowed to keep the rest of humanity ignorant about the disaster they caused so "kooks" don't get in the way – would tie their hands. Piss off, yin. The Ring of Charon's gonna yang yang yang all the way home, what fun, yes. It's very slightly shaming to remember how much one enjoyed the thing. But the enjoyment was real. The enjoyment was enormous.

In their books, neither Steele nor Allen choose to give any sense whatsoever that Progress might itself be problematical or complex, and it may be for that reason that in neither book do we, in fact, see any deep change at all. The whole entire Earth may disappear in The Ring of Charon, but that's not change; that's hey presto. All the same, there is, perhaps, nothing wrong with that. Neither Steele nor Allen make any pretense that they've been attempting to write, in Clarke County, Space (failed) or The Ring of Charon, anything but good commercial entertainments, and in this context their adherence to certain hard sf catechisms (at least one de rigeur reference to the villainous Senator Proxmire; side-of-the-mouth utterances of contempt for politicians, civilians, counter-culturalists; praise for the teflon makers of the high tech future in space: teflon in this case, as in Mr Reagan's, designating a capacity to shrug off side-effects like guilt or consequence) might be described, kindly, as unthinking. We needn't go on about hard sf's tendency – similar to the tendency of conservative political voices in the UK and in America – to feminize patterns of thought or action more complex and (in reality) tougher than theirs, so that the extraordinarily resilient men and women who give their lives to the amelioration of the lot of the dispossessed of the earth will typically be described as "sob-sisters" by the "tough-minded" guys who've misunderstood (or maybe understood too well) the uses of Robert A Heinlein. (In any case, it's our fault that the Huge Penis Heads of Whitehall and Charon are allowed to get away with the sham that they are real men and the rest of us are a gabble of hens. It's our fault that the "dries" of the world have been allowed to establish the public myth that they are the tough-minded ones, while in truth they are the psychic walking-woundeds of the world, the ones too soft in the head to countenance the terribly difficult thought that others exist, the even harder thought that the future might not properly belong solely to "winners." End manifesto. Signed, Moaning Minnie.) So it may be unfair to burden poor Steele and Allen with contumely for refusing to countenance genuine change in their books, and for caricaturing sob-sister counterculturals in their entertainments. After all, hard sf is a literature of escape. Why should they fight it?

III.

I do not now spend a few words in praise of Carve the Sky in order to claim that Alexander Jablokov, and the New England School of Ethical Romance, have managed fully to avoid the pratfalls of hard sf entertainers, for indeed the book is at points only insignificantly less silly than Steele's, and is never as much fun as Allen's.

Jablokov exhibits an unerring gaucheness about artists, who bulk large in his tale, depicting them, with bioflick condescension, as ineffable (but barely toilet-trained) children. And although the world of 2358 looks like paradise – for it is a world in which the tissue of things no longer stretches too thin to remember us all, in our billions, as we eat the nest; a world no longer haggard with bearing us – and although Jablokov very cunningly disarms much of our cynicism about a planet-wide comity within whose terms every citizen cherishes the thingness of things, the route taken from now to then in order to achieve that ecological balance is far too easily assumed as being both possible and palatable. And faults do begin to show in the fabric of *Carve the Sky* when we begin to understand that – as in almost every sf novel it is possible to remember – the protagonists of the book are those privileged, by the workings of the world described in that book, to get most out of the world of the book: which is, of course, the shaming secret theodicy at the heart of all bad sf, perhaps at the heart of all bad art.

The world population in 2358 seems to rest around a billion, which (Jablokov says in an aside) has been a bit of a task to achieve: In the absence of some convenient plague, which he does not suggest, that bit of a task looks very much like several genocides: Which is simply too easy for comfort. Even less likely – though one might long for it, and this reviewer does – is the comity Jablokov describes. An organization called the Academia Sapientiae has an absolute veto over the operations of science and technology upon the planet, and works with great consistency to defend the world from the terrible deracinations of the 20th century: travel, for instance, is made deliberately difficult (though it is not restricted), so that every journey is, once again, a discovery of the intricacy and hugeness involved in any shifting of one's ground. Under the aegis of the Academy, meaning attaches to the world again. There is a hum of pleroma.

If this does sound rather like themepark gnosticism, too neat and easy for comfort, one can answer on behalf of the book that the power of *Carve the Sky* lies not in its depiction of the route to earthly paradise, but in profuse hinted-at detail-worked half-descriptions of how a comity of this sort might affect – say – commuters in Paris, holidaymakers in Italy, community life in New England: one vision of a streetcar whispering through snow in Boston so sharply evoked the genius of place that I found myself thinking of early Simak, for an instant, before remembering that Simak wrote with longing, in 1950, of a world already gone, and that Jablokov was trying to accomplish something fruitfully distinct from nostalgia, the big theodicy lie of Hovis. Theodicy – the doctrine that the world we inhabit is the best possible version of the world, and that "evil" is gyroscopic, God's book-balancer – underlies all art which comforts by what it says, rather than by what it does. Good art can promise you anything, but when you awaken in the night it has awoken you: you must change your life. The art that generates the plot – see next paragraph – of *Carve the Sky* hovers close to the somnifacient *poshlost* of typical theodicy, and Jablokov makes it pretty clear that the protagonists of the book, like Prince Charles, admire only that art whose beauty is unproblematical and thematically unthreatening: safely representative paintings and sculptures, in other words, of "beautiful" subject matters. But since, for the Academia Scientiae, it is precisely such art that acts as a meaning sealant for the themeparked planet, in terms of the novel this is probably inevitable. Theodicy in *Carve the Sky* is not an unguent but a fee. It is a complicated book.

The plot is amiable enough, and full of bits of action, and takes the cast – via a Great Ship straight out of Wolfe's *The Urth of the New Sun* (1987) – to the other planets of the solar system, where the denouement plays itself out with a certain knitting-needle relish, and we could spend some time recounting it, but won't. It is perhaps enough to say that Earth must constantly defend its comity against the thrusting high-tech imperatives of the outer planets and asteroid-belt entrepreneurs, whose cultures are very neatly anatomized in the book; that the Earthly protagonists, all of whom have at least one secret identity, must understand why off-planet agents are rifling the planet for a certain dead artist's work, and how these raids connect to the ingathering of a batch of previously disregarded artifacts-of-an-ancient-race which when assembled might carve the sky. The connection is one of making. "I'm an artist," says one of Jablokov's gaudy children part way through, "I create the universe." Art and artifact are one, they have the same shape, and interstellar travel is only one of the benefits to be derived from making a true shape of things. The book, in other words, is a paradigm romance of Neoplatonism-for-profit from the New England School, whose exponents think of reality as a scrim. I would look for sequels. I would hope they'd return for a while to the Theatre of Earth, give us sight once again of a streetcar perhaps, carving tracks through the gesso of the snow.

– *Foundation* 53, Autumn 1991

IF THIS IS SLIPSTREAM give me fins, let me leave the ship. *Sarah Canary* (Holt, 1991), which is Karen Joy Fowler's first novel and which reads as though it were the heart of the onion of decades of writing, has about as much to do with genre sf or fantasy as John Fowles's *A Maggot* (1985). It is perhaps a matter for discussion elsewhere, but one might note that they are the two best First Contact tales ever written.

Fowles's novel is the more overt, and the more immediately profitable; it can profit-ably be read as the most extended – and most sophisticated – riff on the theme of First Contact ever to grace the field, and in its intense, dense, complex exploration of what one really needs to call the epistemology of First Contact – the ways of knowing and trying to understand an Alien, an Other, when one sees one – it very much prefigures the subject matter of *Sarah Canary*, which might also be seen as a study in the epistemology of First Contact. Where *Sarah Canary* goes beyond its pre-decessor is in the aesthetic joy of the enterprise, the extraordinary impact the book makes whole upon the mind's eye. It is the best novel James Tiptree Jr never wrote – "The Women Men Don't See," perhaps, transformed into novel length; but again, though Fowler manifests little of the thanatropic exuberance of Tiptree, she brings every word of the whole book off, and Tiptree never quite did that at book-length.

We are in 1873, on the Pacific Rim, first in Washington as the intercontinental railway nears completion; later in California. Chin Ah Kin is a Chinese student hornswaggled into coming to the Golden Mountain – that is, America – for work, where he finds himself perceived as a deeply alien creature, a slave, a scapegoat. He has escaped his first landingplace in New Orleans, and has made his way to rela-tives working on the railroad in the state of Washington. His English is fluent. The novel begins. A strange female creature – a woman, it is to be presumed – suddenly manifests herself in camp, appearing in the half-light demented and luminous, a bit like a phrenology chart. She is short, somewhat hairy, though her skin is "pore-less and polished," with a large nose, and never in the course of the novel will she utter a human word – for she emits nothing but caterwauls and ululations: a lan-guage perhaps that no one recognizes, perhaps some molten birdlike idiolect of the insane, perhaps something else entirely – nor will she ever be found not enclosed in the swaddling black garments Chin first sees her wearing.

Afraid that her presence will bring the white men down upon them, his relatives instruct Chin, who had seen her first, to try to lead her back where she came from, perhaps to the corrupt local insane asylum. He takes her off through the trees, along the sound, but the weather worsens, there is fog and rain. They stumble through wilderness into a cemetery, where, in desperation, he strikes her to keep her quiet in case white humans are nigh, and himself falls unconscious against a gravestone. He awakens in jail, assumed guilty of assault or rape, where to gain his freedom he must agree to serve as hangman for the Indian who shares his cell. He agrees. He and the Indian talk about this. He hangs him.

Meanwhile, Sarah Canary – for that is what the strange woman has been nick-named – has been dumped into the asylum where Chin – internally oath-bound because she has apparently not denounced him to the whites – follows her. Eventually he escapes with B J, an inmate whose shifts of lucidity Fowler exquisitely captures, trailing the "goddess" – who has already flown – higher into the mountains, where they end up in a cabin occupied by Burke, a naturalist, and Harold, another stray, and a fake mermaid. In the night, Harold switches the mermaid (which was to be a prop in his travelling show) with Sarah, and absconds with her under the illusion that she can star in his show as an *enfant sauvage*. It is the middle of the novel. We have encountered, in memory or the flesh, an immigrant, a Chinaman, an Indian, a Black man, a madman, an artist (epigraphs from the solitary Emily Dickinson head each chapter), a persecuted scientist (the asylum's intensely comical psychologist in residence), a woman (Sarah Canary), an alien (Sarah Canary), an *enfant sauvage* (Sarah Canary) and a variety of animals, usually seen as the subject of unfeeling experiments. We have not yet been admitted to the presence of an owner: no proper white man, no orthodox scientist. Later we will brush against a few of the owners of 1873, but not intimately. The protagonists of *Sarah Canary* are the alienated, the owned, the studied, the disappeared, the invisible. They are members of the great army of those who must be displaced from the presence of the day in order for ownership to take place, in order for the imperial sortings of knowledge to flower. In *Sarah Canary*, knowledge is power. Knowledge is the control of perception. Knowledge is the capacity not to understand the nature of First Contact – whether that of humans contacting an alien creature from another world, or that of men contacting women – for the merest breath of First Contact shakes empires.

It is almost, therefore, an anticlimax when we next find Sarah Canary in a seaside town, performing abjectly for Harold, while at the same time the famed Adelaide Dixon, a lecturing feminist, holds the stage nearby; the book becomes almost too explicit at this point, and the plotting itself becomes slightly circumstantial; but the movement never ceases. Adelaide mistakes Sarah Canary for a woman wanted for a murder she didn't commit (for it is not only the male owners of 1873 who make passes at the night), and takes her under her wing, and after a slight prolixity of shenanigan the cast reaches San Francisco, and the novel begins to end. Although Sarah remains completely wordless, volatile, profoundly alien (or autistic, or, or, or...), her utterness of being has a strangely hypnotic effect, and the reader begins to notice that almost everyone who has encountered her is now tagging along in order to take care of her. She now has an entourage. The climax of the book's action – there is no climax to the book as a whole, in retrospect, for the entire passage of Sarah Canary through the world seems one movement, one breath of telling – occurs, variously, in the local zoo, where an analogy between caged tigers and women is perhaps slightly pressed, and a hotel. There is a death (it is astonishingly moving). Sarah Canary also disappears, leaving her "clothes" behind, though not a wrack else. If the book seems ambiguous at this point about her true nature, any reader wishing a firm clue might perhaps take note of the word "butterfly" whenever it appears in the text. It may then seem that she has left us her moult. Chin's own alienation has not been decreased by his falling in love with Adelaide, who in turn cannot act upon this sudden revelation of reality (again, the dance of alienations permeates every passage of the book); and he returns to China, where he seems destined for a high position. In taking his examinations, he finds himself discussing a traditional Chinese tale – it is the one whose narration a few pages earlier in *Sarah Canary* comprises one of the most stunning perspective transforms this reviewer has yet seen. "Sometimes," he writes,

> one of the great dreamers passes among us. She is like a sleepwalker, passing through without purpose, without malice or mercy. Beautiful and terrible things happen around her. We discern symmetries, repetitions, and think we are seeing the pattern of our lives. But the pattern is in the seeing, not in the dream.

The Tyger fades. The book shuts.

It is the best First Contact novel ever written, a profound enactment of the Otherness of portal. It bursts from the bounds of genre – claws itself from the swaddling clothes of sf – like a butterfly.

– New York Review of Science Fiction 40, December 1991

IT IS November again, and frighteningly warm, here in London at the edge of the sun, 51 degrees north of the vexed equator, verging into winter. A colleague of a friend of mine, who is teaching these days in shirt sleeves because of the unseasonal heat, says something to his class, in passing, about the economic costs of global warming. A hand shoots up, which he acknowledges, as he should, for it is an adult class, and upraised hands command due respect. "This global warming talk," says the man who wished to speak, "is left-wing." There is no applause, as such, for it is an adult class. But the man – homo sapiens – has spoken the class's mind, the teacher feels. The species has shown our face. There is no more talk of global warming.

The face *Beauty* (Doubleday Foundation, 1991) wears seems, at first, pleasingly remote from all this. Sheri S Tepper's new novel – it is something like the 28th she's published since her first in 1984 – is presented on a second title page as "The Journal of Beauty Daughter of The Duke of Westfaire," and soon settles us into the middle of the 14th century as though nothing could budge us till the end of the fantasy, the end of the tale. We are soon informed, as well, that there is something magic about her – italicized interventions in the journal she keeps make it clear that Carabosse, a fairy who is the keeper of clocks, has a watching brief on the young girl, who is herself half-fairy. and we suspect that she will become a Beauty of legend, Sleeping Beauty perhaps, or perhaps the Beauty who marries the Beast. We expect laughter and tears, transformations of frogs and princes, a visit to the land of Faery, and a few tocsin notes of foreboding about the End of Magic. And all these gifts we are given, soon enough.

The main story turns out – or so it seems – to be that of Sleeping Beauty, but very soon there is a twist: the protagonist unwittingly makes her half-sister the victim of the curse, and herself seems to escape. But she stumbles across a television crew which has time-travelled from the 21st century to tape the hedge now surrounding Westfaire, as part of a project to capture some of the last moments when magic had some purchase in the world; and because she's seen them the crew takes her back upstream to avoid paradoxes; and she finds herself in the world of Fidipur (which stands for Feed the Poor), which consists of dying factory farms (dying because the world has been stripped of genetic diversity, stripped of oxygen, stripped of ozone, razed utterly) and termitaries choked with billions of incessantly breeding members of the human species (thank Mother Teresa, thank Christians everywhere, thank the members of an economics class in London in 1991 who think global warming is a "left-wing" plot to frustrate decent entrepeneurs, thank us all). Beauty soon escapes to 1991, which she finds almost as terrifying as the very final days, and ultimately returns home to the 14th century. She then finds that her travels are ageing her at an accelerated rate; in addition, she must bear the burden of knowing that the world will end in the 22nd century, when Fidipur finally caves into dust upon the bald planet.

Her travels have just begun. *Beauty* is a long novel, told with a merciless and compulsive fluency. It is many pages before we begin to sense why Beauty has been watched over so carefully; why her trips to Faery and to other kingdoms are freighted with such significance; why she bears within her breast a hurt and talisman that burns and cannot be removed without killing her. It would be unkind to reveal more of the ending of the tale. But it can be said that nothing in *Beauty* will save the human species from its compact with the sterile Dark Lord to drain from the world the odour of creation; it can also be said that there will be an Ark.

In a sense, perhaps, the very ease of *Beauty* is its greatest weakness. The hardness of the message it contains – the message is that we have finished ourselves off, that it is too late, that the minds of an economics class in London will not be cleared of maya in time to save the world – reads all too smoothly and gracefully upon the page. It is obvious that *Beauty* shares much with John Crowley's *Little, Big* (1981): both novels are shaped around a pulse of Story; both share a like vision of the near future; both novels conflate sf and fantasy, planet-end and Faery; both take place in dying venues caught between the death of the world of fantasy on one side and the death of the world of sf on the other; both are plotted with considerable and loving intricacy around a central family over a span of generations; both offer a perilous thin thread of solace through the setting up, in each case, of a terminal enclave entwined in the briar stench of magic, and sequestered from our paws; and both novels, in the end, say the same thing to all of us. Take anything you want (they both say): and pay for it. But where *Little, Big* entangles the reader in the intrinsicated hardness of the task of making up a Story for our times, *Beauty* slips its message like a knife through skin and bone and brain, and passes. It is brilliant and subtle and fabulous. But it passes. It is just marginally too polished, too professional. It is not quite real enough. Like any simulacrum of the magic it espouses, it leaves not a wrack behind.

– New York Review of Science Fiction 41, January 1992

SOMETIMES, reading a novel set in the "future" – as this reviewer once said a while ago, in 1977, writing about *The Ophiuchi Hotline* by John Varley – sometimes it's worth playing a game with the date of the world depicted in the book. Whatever year the novel claims to be set in, which might be almost any year at all, there is an underlying *real year* – back in 1977 I called it the *real decade*, a term both overlong and vague – which shines through, and which determines how close to the future the tale is truly set; whenever it was written, any Ray Bradbury story – one might suggest – takes place in something like 1927; any Robert A Heinlein story written after World War Two is set in an increasingly juddery 1940; and Philip K Dick's *real year* moves only with great anxiety forwards from a classical music store in 1950. The fundamental rules of this naming the year game are 1) that no sf novel (or for that matter no tale at all) can of course *actually* be set in the future, because all books are in fact set in the past; 2) that sf authors – depending as they do upon a shared-language-of-exploration (an oxymoron itself insufficiently explored), and upon a readership increasingly inclined to confuse sense of wonder with nostalgia – tend to find the present less easy to approach than do certain rogue singletons of the "mainstream," who walk alone in a catchment humiliatingly – for sf writers – close to now; and 3) that the closer a book comes to the present, the harder it is to write or read or understand.

In 1977, John Varley's *real year* was very nearly 1977 (and he stayed there). And in 1990, the *real year* that shines through Michael Swanwick's *Stations of the Tide* (Morrow, 1990) edges pretty close to the aura of our own dear 1990. After the fixup sidle of his first novel, *In the Drift* (1985), whose *real year* was Watergate, and the slightly dumpy plotline that dogged the exuberant information-buzz travelogue of the very much finer *Vacuum Flowers* (1987), a book which read like a billion bytes dancing in the vertical smile of an Edsel, *Stations of the Tide* is a tour-de-force of metamorphosis and instauration, a renovation of the parlance of the genre for a new era, a clever read, a wise book.

Like any really good sf novel written by an intelligent author at the peak of his craft, *Stations of the Tide* is a byte dance and sorting of all the sf protocols we are likely to call up from memory. In a prefatory note, Swanwick acknowledges various predecessors on whom he has done Oedipal riffs – Brian W Aldiss, C L Moore, Dylan Thomas, Ted Hughes, Jamaica Kincaid – and he could have mentioned quite a few more, Algis Budrys and Gene Wolfe for two; but perhaps there is no real need to be explicit, for the book is radiant with the language and moves of the genre-edge; and the thrill of the thing lies in the sense of new things transfiguring the old. The story takes place, for instance, within the frame of a coercive galactic federation of some sort; but to understand the shape and feel of that federation and its artifacts one must envision, not an extremely large high school governed in secret by Our Miss Brooks (which is my own internal model of the relationship of Hari Seldon to Trantor), but a theatre of memory.

Caught within that frame – and chafing under the control of galactic "bureaucrats" who continue to quarantine her from the devastating lures of high technology – is the planet Miranda, long settled by human stock, and now approaching the climax of its Great Year (as it is writ in Helliconia). Very soon now, the Ocean will cover much of the land, human societies will retreat into the highlands and quite possibly mutate there; and if there are any indigenes left (no one knows for sure), they will soon metamorphose into "winter morph" mode, and live underwater (it is a fate to which many humans aspire). These shapechanging natives, who are called "haunts," may in fact have learned how to take on human form and pass as human in the low-lying, densely inhabited, soon-to-be-drowned Creole deltas of the planet (for Miranda is not only Prospero's island awaiting the tempest of the Great Year, but the home world of *The Fifth Head of Cerberus* [1972] as well); but no one knows, for the haunts live below the narrative surface of *Stations of the Tide* like race memories of the anthropophagy of colonialism, giving the incessant novelty of the tale a constant anchor and ostinato far beneath the data-driven surge of story.

That story – as in *Vacuum Flowers* – is something of a mcguffin. Gregorian, a human native of the planet, and built like Caliban, has apparently stolen some proscribed technology, and has gone to ground with this Prometheus Fire in the swarming Creole Tidewater region of his birth. We never really find out what that technology was (or if, in fact, it has been stolen). Gregorian is now upsetting the apple cart by appearing in television ads in which he claims to be able to adjust humans to the great change coming, to make them (in effect) into haunt-like winter morphs: natives. The book now begins. A "bureaucrat" – we are never given his name – descends from the galactic federation's Puzzle Palace in dark space downwards into exile on Miranda to seek out Gregorian, and the rest of *Stations of the Tide* concentrates upon his attempts, which only initially seem fumbling, to trace both Gregorian and a traitor within the Palace, which is a genuine theatre of memory, who has been supplying the native with vital information. The bureaucrat, whose initial air of stressed-out incompetence proves to be entirely superficial, eventually succeeds in controlling Gregorian/Caliban, and in capping the phallic imperialism of Gregorian's secret father in orbit; and at novel's close frees his nearly omnicompetent suitcase-AI, which is not actually called Ariel, to the elements – by which point it is difficult to know whether we should be calling him Prospero, or perhaps Michaelmas: or perhaps *both* – and in the final pages, the paraclete of the memory dance, Prospero or Michaelmas, leaps metamorphosing into his final station, the unestranging sea.

But if the haunts below give weight to the "immanence of the land's passing," and the mcguffin above gives to *Stations of the Tide* a necessary formal impetus, the real heart of the book may well lie in the sense it imparts of the ongoing burden of unburdening itself, for we are drowned by the tale in unveiling data. The book is immensely full. The Puzzle Palace, for instance, is quite simply marvelous, a marriage of the Renaissance theatre of the mind and cyberpunk, in which the memory thespians and friezes of the 16th century become partials (cf Greg Bear) of the whole person, and walk. And there is much, much more: the intense, verb-dominated thrust of the language [see p. 253 above]; the intersecting dances of partials and persons, haunts and AI's, plot and epiphany; the intensity of Swanwick's economy (so utterly different from the peeping-tom wambles of *In the Drift*). But the final reason *Stations of the Tide* seems so wedded to the years we now live is no more than what we've been getting at all along. Metamorphic and memorious, *Stations of the Tide* is itself the Puzzle Palace that lies within its heart. It is the outside of the inside of the data of the dance. It is a shape for the knowing we're going to need.

– *New York Review of Science Fiction* 29, January 1991

Six: 1992

1. Year Roundup

[The text printed here, and the text which appeared in *Nebula Awards 28*, differ considerably. None of the differences are to the discredit of James Morrow, who received – astonishingly late – a piece from me that had transparently not been composed with any proper thought for the venue it was intended to grace. Jim Morrow wrestled adroitly with this monster from the wrong deep, and I wrestled back, and we came to a compromise I felt happy with – and indeed I was very pleased when *The New York Review of Science Fiction* asked permission to reprint that *Nebula Awards* version. In the present context, however, it seems appropriate to revert to a slightly modified rendering of the original version 1995.]

It gets easier and easier to say. O hell O hell O hell and lack-a-day, here we are in the '90s. Sliding down the scree. What a fine mess. I mean, look at the dreams we had, which are leaving the world as the gods left Alexandria, turning away from things and into virtual realities, or ice. *We are turning into the minds of others.* Having slagged and shagged the material world, we are now learning to forget it. Meat has become back-story. Lack-a-day. Where can sf go now, now that all its futures have come untrue? Who will buy our sick old swayback dreams of the future, beyond the million children so profoundly cynical we cannot understand their tongue, or the knives they wear on their sleeves, or the deaths they contemplate for us. So the litany goes, and who's to say it's foolish to declaim these images of surrender and disarray as we continue to slide, eyes burning from the increasingly naked sun, into the bosnias of a new era. Who's to say it's foolish to think we're not going to make it, that even with all the help of all the thoughts of all the sf stories that have ever been, we're simply not going to see what the light is at the end of the tunnel until it's far too late to dodge.

Certainly there is a case. It is certain, even though sales remain high, that the genre is at a crux. I myself (but not alone) have tended to think that over the past decade or so the old genre or agenda sf has aged – prematurely, and at a savage rate – into a purveyor of nostalgia pabulum for consumers, and that the form of sf which Jack Williamson helped give birth to has become something like a poison fossil, even while he himself still continues to write like a young man: though a young man besotted with archives. Sf, born to advocate and enthuse and teach, has come by century end to lay a mummy's curse on the new, it seems. Despite occasional fresh words from the archivists who continue to write as though sf were a Door in the Wall, most of what is published is now industrial-base frozen food, portion-controlled, sanisealed and sharecropped, spilling like plastic hotdogs from a million identical slots from a million malls. And when we deny this, we tend to stink of bad faith.

And so on.

On the other hand, it might be an idea to contemplate what happened to our green planet just after a big rock dusted off the dinosaurs (though nothing, unfortunately, has managed to stifle the remake). What happened was mammals (whom God defend), and suddenly it was a new ballgame. Dinosaurs may have ruled for millions of years, employing neat metabolic-shutdown routines to maintain their huge size without burning up in June, but they were hopelessly bad at doing lunch. What we may forget about ourselves (but shouldn't) is the labile ardency of our onslaught upon the world. Mammals (I am one) are the *developers* of the animal kingdom. The difference between a dinosaur and a mammal is the difference between a mesa and Mesa Plaza. It is a distinction which might also be used to draw a line between agenda sf and the kind of tale which should be winning prizes in 1993. The best sf being written today, in other words, is like a squabble of shrews in a midden: it will eat anything.

In various pieces written over the past few years, I've been suggesting, not entirely tongue-in-cheek, that this 1990s lust for provender could be described as an expression of our need as readers to look for stimuli beyond the metabolic-shutdown torpor of the traditional genre, our need as a race to look for solutions beyond the genome. It seemed that traditional sf [see references to First SF in the 1994 SFRA speech which is printed above, starting on p. 8; the term has been inserted elsewhere, too 1995] had illuminated and given shape to the dreams of an historical moment, but that that moment had passed, had been slowly dissolving into psychic interregnum ever since World War Two exposed our undersides to the bare light; it seemed that human beings, whose driving ambitions had this century been most profoundly articulated in the form of sf novels and tales, were no longer likely to learn very much from the triumphalist agenda of the old sf: from the antique Future Histories we clung to like monkeys to a rotten tree; from the provincial species chauvinism that envisioned human empires replicating throughout the galaxy the demolition of the American West, while simultaneously fighting shy of the profoundly transformative implications of the revolutions in biology which we, as writers and reader of a genre pretending to explore the unknown, should have conspicuously given ourselves to study and to assess. It seemed to me – therefore – that as a race we needed to get under our skins a burning sense of our need for exogamous solutions to the fix we were in. We needed to be told how to marry out: how to garner Cargo from other races, other climes; how to transmigrate from our bodies into the various transcendentalisms so loved by modern writers from Greg Bear on down; how to migrate into cyberspace like Irish immigrants fleeing a potato famine. Sf needed to reconstitute itself as a series of fables of exogamy, and in fact sf could be *defined* as fables of exogamy, I said.

This argument (I needn't be told) overstated the case and exaggerated the solutions. Today it might be better to think of exogamousness as an aspect of the mammalian ardency that thrusts our green shoot into new pastures, into places where we can continue to eat our body weight daily. I mean, look at us. We are famished. We have no trick of metabolic shutdown. We are the ones who have done this planet in. We must have the universe, or we will soon be chewing our own vitals.

Sort of thing.

In 1992, about 700 novels were published in English in the various literatures of the fantastic – broadly sf, fantasy, horror – and of these maybe 200–250 were sf; and of that total maybe 30–50 books were worth reading. And of *that* total, maybe three to five will survive. Or maybe ten. Looking into 1992 was like looking into a tidal pool as the waters begin to ebb, exposing more fragile niche species to the dry death. Singletons were particularly vulnerable; and melancholy, overspecialized, midlist creatures could be seen finning the air, brokenly. More durable were series – or shoal – species, impossible to tell apart, each individual specimen instantly replaceable if losses were incurred. Overall there was a sense of considerable activity, without action. There was, in other words, a sense that the churned and fecund tidal pool of sf was waiting for something to happen, some direction home. It might be the millennium: because it's soon, and we've all psyched ourselves into a state of self-fulfilling anticipation about the end of time. It might be the draining of the pool: because the downsizing of Bantam Books might well be contagious. It might be a new style of saying sf, like cyberpunk a decade earlier: to which the packagers would cling like remora, till it sank. It might be some new writer heroine or hero: because there seemed to be a lot of talent around, though no shaping voice yet. Indeed, there were more sf writers of stature, potential or earned, and capable of writing at or near their best level, than the genre had ever before harboured, perhaps. So the pool was churning, but it could not be said that during 1992 it was possible to discern the shape of things to come, the demands we would have to meet as we advanced onto the steel beach, or as the steel beach – for time enters us these days – invaded our souls.

Perhaps we should remind ourselves of brightness and confusion of the range of

357

books published. I think it might be an idea to list a bunch of them, in alphabetical order, and then talk about a few. Sf novels of interest first published in 1992 included Douglas Adams's *Mostly Harmless* (Heinemann); Isaac Asimov and Robert Silverberg's *The Positronic Man* (Gollancz); John Barnes's *A Million Open Doors* (Tor); William Barton's *Dark Sky Legion: An Ahrimanic Novel* (Bantam); Greg Bear's *Anvil of Stars* (Legend); Michael Bishop's *Count Geiger's Blues* (Tor); James P Blaylock's *Lord Kelvin's Machine* (Arkham House); Pat Cadigan's *Fools* (Bantam); Orson Scott Card's *Homecoming #1: The Memory of Earth* (Tor); two from C J Cherryh: *Chanur's Legacy* (DAW) and *Hellburner* (New English Library); Stephen R. Donaldson's *The Gap Into Power: A Dark and Hungry God Arises* (Bantam); Greg Egan's *Quarantine* (Legend); Mark S Geston's *Mirror to the Sky* (AvoNova); Richard Grant's *Through the Heart* (Bantam); Alasdair Gray's *Poor Things* (Bloomsbury); Joe Haldeman's *Worlds Enough and Time* (Morrow); Elizabeth Hand's *Æstival Tide* (Bantam); Robert Harris's *Fatherland* (Hutchinson); Alexander Jablokov's *A Deeper Sea* (AvoNova); Ken Kesey's *Sailor Song* (Viking); Damon Knight's *Why Do Birds* (Tor); Ian McDonald's *Hearts, Hands and Voices* (Gollancz; vt *The Broken Land*, Bantam); Maureen F McHugh's *China Mountain Zhang* (Tor); Julian May's *Jack the Bodiless* (Knopf); Judith Moffett's *Time, Like an Ever-Rolling Stream* (St. Martin's Press); James Morrow's *City of Truth* (Legend 1990 but a Nebula winner only after US publication this year); Kim Newman's *Anno Dracula* (Simon & Schuster UK); Frederik Pohl's *Mining the Oort* (Del Rey); Tim Powers's *Last Call* (Morrow); Daniel Quinn's *Ishmael* (Bantam); Kim Stanley Robinson's *Red Mars* (HarperCollins); Richard Paul Russo's *Destroying Angel* (Headline); Charles Sheffield's *Cold As Ice* (Tor); Robert Silverberg's *Kingdoms of the Wall* (HarperCollins); two from Dan Simmons: *Children of the Night* (Warner) and *The Hollow Man* (Bantam); Norman Spinrad's *Deus X* (Bantam); Neal Stephenson's *Snow Crash* (Bantam); two from Sheri S Tepper: *Beauty* (Doubleday Foundation) and *Sideshow* (Bantam); Jack Vance's *Throy* (Underwood-Miller); John Varley's *Steel Beach* (Ace); Vernor Vinge's *A Fire Upon the Deep* (Tor); Walter Jon Williams's *Aristoi* (Tor); Jack Williamson's *Beachhead* (Tor) and Connie Willis's *Doomsday Book* (Bantam).

That's almost 50 books. Some represent eccentric likings on my part, or a sense of what is sf and what is not which might offend some readers: why should I include Newman's *Anno Dracula* and leave out Anne Rice's *The Tale of the Body Thief* (Knopf)? I do so because one is an alternate history and the other is not, but that could easily seem perverse to a stricter eye. But let us say, for the sake of the argument, that the 50 constitute a fair and not excessively loony canon of the best sf published in 1992. The first thing that comes to mind is a sense of the almost lubricious heterogeneity of the mix: hard sf, and vampire suckers; space opera, and steampunk; agenda sf trumpeting out a final clarion call or two, and science fantasy doing a chaste riff; dystopias and planetary romances and cyberpunk runs and juveniles and time-travel and grunge. The second thing that comes to mind is how very fine some of these novels are, how lovingly constructed, how much of a gift they constitute. For these authors – if not wholeheartedly for the detritus of genre they sometimes wallow in – there is a sense of gratitude. The third thing that comes to mind is the old realization that significance and worth are not synonyms: because the most significant of these novels, John Varley's *Steel Beach*, is by no means the best.

But it is the one novel of 1992 that comprehensively faces every possible direction, backwards and forwards, agenda and mammal, cliché and thrust, known and unknown. It's set in the underground civilization humanity has established in the Moon, a century of so after our expulsion from Earth: it is, in other words, a tale out of the middle of the Eight Planets Future History Varley's operated ever since the beginning of his career, though with a few postmodernist continuity glitches, so that we know we're in a novel not a shoal. The narrator's name is Hildy, she/he's a reporter (like the original Hildy in Ben Hecht's and Charles MacArthur's *The Front Page* [1928]), and as we follow the slow but inexorable growth in her comprehension of the true nature of the Lunar politics and economics, a growth which precisely mirrors the assumptions of agenda sf about the legibility of the universe. Moreover, this Lunar world gives off an eerie Heinleinian glow, as does Hildy himself in the cocky slang of the voice in which he tells us his tale. So *Steel Beach sounds* very backwards, from the word go. At the same time, however, something very different is being exposed, though not in so many (or at any rate not in the same cheery, translucent, pie-in-the-face) words. What we learn first in the understory is that Hildy is so utterly depressed and defeated by her life and her world-role that she is constantly in the throes of attempting to commit suicide; what we learn second is that the entire edifice of *Steel Beach* is a kind of prophylactic apparatus to fend off terminus: the suicide of individuals; the huge odds against the survival of the human race upon the steel beach of the future – the image comes from the original beach upon which the first lung-fish survived, and suggests that the human race is in a similar do-or-die position on an even harsher strand; and the near impossibility of even telling a book: because *Steel Beach* as a text reads like an enchantment against suicide, a magic charm whose only final virtue is to tell itself. It is, all in all, one of the bleakest texts in the history of genre sf. As the 1990s progress, it is a vital book for us to understand.

Kim Stanley Robinson's *Red Mars* also looks like agenda sf, and it is certainly the case that, unlike Varley in his terminal wrestle against melancholia, its author does not take us through his tale like Clint Eastwood in a demolition derby killing Fords. At the end of *Red Mars* there is still a world we can read: sometime into the 21st century, when humanity has begun to settle the next planet out. The bravery of the text – and its departure from one of the more streamlined assumptions of the old sf: that the period between landing on Mars and having battles there with dragon ladies could pass in a twinkling of the auctorial eye – lies in the sense suffusing it that the human race must attempt to settle out. Nothing is easy on Mars in the book, because everything reads as a continuation of the inextricable tangles of our own human history on planet three. *Red Mars* could plausibly, therefore, be described as a "real" novel in genre clothing: except Kim Stanley Robinson would not accept the point of such a distinction, and nor (on reflection) would I. In the end, what marks *Red Mars* off from most agenda sf about conquering the solar system is its dynaflow enrichment of all the seams of telling, so that, in the end, it reads like a chymical marriage of real novel, real agenda.

Also told in clear was Vernor Vinge's huge and exuberant *A Fire Upon the Deep*, which rewrote the simpleminded old venues of galactic space opera in terms of information theory and a vision of space shaped like an onion, in the heart of which, like equations caught in amber, could be discerned (and dismissed) all the laws of physics which bind us to our local home. The further out you get from Galactic Center in this deeply happy structuring of the universe, the faster you get, the brighter, the freer. Humans, however, true to post-agenda assumptions, bulk small. Stephen Donaldson's *The Gap into Power: A Dark and Hungry God Arises*, a long medias-res section from a huge novel in progress, rewrote space opera into such Jacobean contortions of stress that the reader got congested arteries from the intensity of the game, and felt pretty damned sick on finishing. John Barnes's *A Million Open Doors* also allowed a few hints of the crepuscule of our latter days to infiltrate a tale whose juvenile-lead protagonists become secret agents (or something, it was hard to remember five minutes back in the world) of a galactic council (could it have been a galactic council?) and began (as novel ended) to prepare themselves to monitor folk on any number of further worlds: a shoal of planetary romancelets could be in the offing; or not, given Barnes's swift intense way with a tale. He may be too impatient to develop himself into Barnes Plaza. Or he may not. I think the jury is out: I hope he sticks to singletons, and saddens down a bit, too.

There were at least two first novels whose intensity of achievement made them read as though one were *remembering* them, out of the dream-chambers of the race. Karen Joy Fowler's *Sarah Canary*, set at the world-conquering height of the nineteenth century, traces with steely smiling delicacy the ways in which it might be possible to understand, and to misconstrue, a speechless but birdlike female creature as she drifts through the Pacific Northwest, gathering round her a congeries of other outcasts: a Chinese, a suffragette, an Indian, an idiot. As far as the male imperial mind of the century is concerned, they are all outside the pale, and must be coerced into being "understood." Sarah Canary herself may, in fact, be a "true" alien. As far as most sf readers are concerned, she almost certainly is. As far as the book is concerned, she is certainly Other.

The second first novel was Maureen F McHugh's China Mountain Zhang, a tale whose rich velocity had no difficulty carrying the reader through a number of sidebar narrative trips. The protagonist is a gay Chinese-American in world where the USA (now the socialist Union of American States) is dominated by China; it is a bildungsroman, a tale of the coming to adulthood of a young human being, and it is dense with language, and rites of passage, and aperçus.

A bright quick mammal's glitter suffused every single character in Connie Willis's brilliant Doomsday Book, which won the Nebula this year (along with her "Even the Queen," whose central debate about menstruation was hilarious but deeply unfair to Cyclists, whose representative got about as many words in as a liberal in Heinlein Country). But Doomsday Book, which seemed clearly to have been written in a state of love, set up no bogies to blow over. The thirteenth century country near Oxford to which the protagonist time-travels on a university assignment from the near future, though it has been criticized for a variety of historical inaccuracies, breathes all the same like another country of the heart. As the Black Death begins to transmogrify the culture she has inserted herself into, the protagonist slowly becomes a figure of almost mythic density, almost like some mythago in Robert Holdstock's Wood, and her ultimate rescue, in the last sentences of the book, ends the novel like a song whose last note is all we came to hear.

Every one of the 50 titles could be talked about for pages, for if there was one unique aspect of 1992 – to rephrase the argument so far – it may be a sense that too many discourses, too many reflections in too many mirrors, were banging together in too tiny an arena. There was an air of commingled panic and empowerment, vast easy gains, feet of sand: vast easy feet of sand, hard gains. It was babel. A few more. C J Cherryh's Hellburner read like ten jugglers leaving one room, and not dropping a ball: making the first years of her rapacious Future History read like true opera. Alasdair Gray's Poor Things mixed Scotland riffs, Frankenstein riffs, textuality riffs, reliability riffs: while glaring at us all the while, daring us to stick our fingers into the bright dire machine. James Morrow's City of Truth was refreshingly unnice and sour, retold in *conte*-like rhythms a Voltairean fable about a confusion of truth-saying and fact-telling, slipped at the end into a just slightly sentimentalized Death of Child. Sheri Tepper, in *Beauty*, conflated fairytale, slick fantasy, sf and dystopia into a savagely unremitting lament upon the thinning of our world.

It can be expected that some of these stories will become part of our genre past, that we rightly cherish, though we do know in our hearts how rapidly it's slipping into history. Others will seem prophetic. It's hard to know which voices, these babel days, will be heard in clear; hard to know whose voice will soar, take the tune, speak the words that hurt us till we wake.

But I think we're here to find out.

– Nebula Awards 28 (Harcourt Brace & Company, 1994), ed. James Morrow

2. Interzone Columns

[This first column has been jigged around a bit; having been written in the United States, in transit, on scraps of paper, it was far too choppy, and those of the sentences I could not understand I have modified into sentences I thought I might have meant to say. It's not the first time I've had to do this, and won't be the last. Opinions about the books themselves have not been subjected to any stalinist revisionism, I think 1995.]

Welcome from the Zones of Thought

I.

TEN YEARS AGO, when Interzone was pregnant in a Heterogeny of bosoms, Vernor Vinge was a husband. Time flies. Ten years ago, polishing up the romantic pash of her planetary-romances in strokes both wide and slow, Joan D Vinge had already won a Hugo or two for stories like "Eyes of Amber," which seems nowadays so deep-sunk into the past with its archaic interventionist pieties (now so safely dumped), and had already published *The Snow Queen*. Vernor, who had been her husband, had written something called *The Witling*, and a couple of other titles it was significantly hard to remember, thought there was also a novella somewhere called "True Names" that sounded like a sleeper, and he taught somewhere: mathematics, or computer science, something hard sf and remote from anything the instigators of Interzone were (wrongly) presumed to have the slightest interest in. But suddenly this all seems long ago. Suddenly it is 1992, Interzone is a magazine whose origins are shrouded in the abyssal mists of the Age of Iron Lady, and Vernor Vinge has just published, in *A Fire Upon the Deep* (Tor, 1992), a space epic so intensely pleasurable that we begin to rewrite our memories, we begin to think of Vernor as the Vinge. He has never appeared in *Interzone*, but that may have been our fault. It is not, however, our fault that no excerpt from the current novel was ever published here – had in fact any excerpt ever been submitted, which it was not – because *A Fire Upon the Deep* does not work in little bits.

This being a festive occasion, an occasion for praise, for the conveyance of good wishes between Zones of Thought of opposite poles (or so some readers might phrase the natural relationship between anything appearing in *Interzone* and large-scale hard sf), this might not be the best time to start up again on an old campaign – to attempt, once again, to pound into the thick skulls of those who don't like what *we* like a sense of the delusions of hard sf in general – but what the hell. In brief, then, let us suggest that two of the more irritating assumptions held by at least some of the technophile fantasists who write hard sf are these:

1) the assumption that, because they are capable of inserting something knowledgable about one or two hard sciences into their texts, they are subsequently entitled to ignore any scientific principle they wish to, with the result that fantasy turns – dwagons and FTL ships and rich, telepathic superjocks – are entirely permissible in "hard sf," just as long as the book in question was written by a member of the club;

2) the assumption that because they actually know how to describe something describable, like the surface of a star – which most of us haven't a clue about – they are therefore entitled to assume that they have the *gift of description*; the assumption that *everything* they write about can be described in the clear and accurate terms they have mastered for describing the describable – "clear and accurate" being easy enough when you're talking about the surface of stars, but impossible when you're trying to describe anything more complex, like almost anything with an inside – like for instance the human beings whom hard sf writers tend to think they are capable of describing as fully as it is possible to describe anything: which, given the fact that human beings are not in fact fully describable by other human beings, may by a circumbendibus, all unconsciously, not be all that wide of the mark, sort of: but that's not what hard sf writers are on about: they think their descriptions are not only all you get but all you could ever need. Hence the proliferation throughout hard sf of protagonists who literally cannot be told apart – for they share the same insufferable hollow-man Competence, the same absence of an inside, the same derisory problem-solving contempt for the stutter of being, the same Winner's-Gloat

of adoration for Private Enterprise. Reading a hard sf book for introspection is like asking a waldo to explain about love.

A Fire Upon the Deep – the proof copy on hand is subtitled "A Novel from the Zones of Thought" – may not entirely dodge the dangers of assuming that the world is describable in babytalk, but is set so far into the future, and so remotely distant in time and space from any possibility of human hegemony, that its human characters seem almost inconceivably remote from the "bumptious" mammals who appear throughout the theological utterances of John W Campbell Jr and his acolytes today. Aeons hence, the universe contains species far more uppity and neotenous than us. It is certainly true, all the same, that *A Fire Upon the Deep* is in some sense the kind of book that hard sf writers like to write. Any scientific speculation to be found within its pages is pure nonsense, for instance, created to help the story onwards: and a good thing, too. A Vanity of Competent Folk does inhabit one of the long dovetailing plotlines, but their position, way down the Great Chain of Being, gives their Competence a proper Playdoh context. And it's certainly true that the book is packed with aliens whose alienness depends upon the sort of tinkertoy species intricacy Rube Goldberg bequeathed to Larry Niven who gave us the Puppeteers who are the direct begetters of Vinge's Stroderiders, artifactual creatures (like most hard sf aliens) whose existence represents the solution of a very special problem: which is the definition of a niche species, not of a winning breed like protean bigbrained mammalian bipedal homo sapiens, good at nothing in particular, superb at everything in general. But the creation of niche species is something hard sf writers – who like to present solutions to particular problems – are peculiarly prone to.

And it is also true that god-like beings can be found in the text speaking through ravished simulacra: they are called Powers, and inhabit the Transcend, and one of them is the Sauronesque Enemy of all sentience who sets the story going, deploying an icy stakhanovite terribilità through minions who spout socialistical-sounding crap. By treating these minions as lefties, Vinge seems to join forces with those Americans who, not yet having committed suicide because of their medical bills, continue to deride any vision of the world based on community rather than upon the ravening monad entrepreneurial self; but again he dodges paying more than lip-service to the hard sf political litany loyalty-oath rag. And he does, in fact, sidestep most of the more inhumane read-offs of the hard sf novel as a form. It is, in the end, clear that he knows exactly what he's writing – a work of fiction, which is nothing like the world – and that he understands very well what is entailed in writing a real novel which is also a hard sf novel, a novel which is nothing like the world but which must somehow play at conforming to certain canons of describability.

To conform to those canons in 1992, two problems (at least) must be faced down: the hard sf novel must somehow solve the problem of the size of the universe, because the true universe is much too large to encompass in the mind's eye, and the laws which govern it are inimical to fiction; and it must solve the problem of information, because it is very difficult to conceive any surviving world more than a few years hence which is not governed by dances of information beyond our ken: hence perhaps the quietism that suffuses Cyberpunk; hence perhaps the large number of tales coming on the market in which our human plots turn out to be moves in a computer-run game-world. In *A Fire Upon the Deep*, Vinge has created one solution that solves both problems. It is not entirely new. Poul Anderson, in *Brain Wave* (1954), long ago established a model for fictions which treated the universe we experienced, and the mental tools we used in experiencing it, as being subject to special-case limiting conditions. It is the same with *A Fire Upon the Deep*, though worked out in much greater detail. Our local galaxy, in Vinge's novel, is divided into four zones. The innermost of these encompasses the galactic core and a good hundred billion stars, and is known as the Unthinking Depths; here the speed of light is an absolute, and no complex technology is possible, because of the entangling stumblebum coat of flesh of the fog of matter.

Surrounding this zone, and containing quite a few billion stars, is the Slow Zone; here the speed of light remains an absolute, but some higher technology is possible due to a partial unleashing of the speed and cogency of physical interactions, atomic and subatomic (or so I thought I understood). But it is still impossible here to build or to maintain sentient technologies; there are no AI's in the Slow Zone. This is the zone in which Earth exists, or once existed – no one seems any longer to know or much to care – in a saving paralysis of slowness, deep sunk in safe seclusion from the searing glare of true intelligences. *A Fire Upon the Deep* only descends so far into the depths as the Slow Zone at a moment of climactic terror: for no one could ever wish to live there.

Surrounding in turn the Slow Zone, and comprising the volume of space in which almost all of the action of the book takes place, is the Beyond, which is far greater in compass than the inner zones but includes far fewer stars. Here the speed of light is not an absolute, and can be exceeded. Here it is possible for higher machineries and sentiences to be manufactured and to take cognizance of their tasks, for in the Beyond it is possible for genuinely significant amounts of information to be gathered, compacted, conveyed, assimilated. Here, skating over the slumbrous safety of the Slow Zone, millions of civilizations, including waif biota from old Earth, have existed for billions of years, each of them adding to the data archives, to the flow, to the overwhelming density and volume of the theoretically knowable.

Finally, surrounding the Beyond, is the Transcend, where the Universe is permitted to know itself through the self-explorations of Powers, who reside there in an intolerable access of clarity. They represent the natural state of self-knowledge of the universe as an information system, and cannot descend into the Beyond without considerable loss of selfhood; and are barred utterly from the nether regions. Throughout the novel, therefore, a systemic quid pro quo operates: omniscienc entails exile from the realms of flesh; but safety from Powers similarly entails exile from true sapience. There is longing both ways, and intercourse, up and down the zones, which fibrillate in the mind's eye as though they were real, as though the galaxy's myriad transactions were isomorphic with the myriad transactions of organic life.

All in all, it is a structure into which a thousand tales could nestle, each nudzhing its niche, each transacting furiously. *A Fire Upon the Deep* is, therefore, a dawn book, a pioneer's vade mecum. Its plot, after one forgives it of some Idiot Retards, sails swiftly from the highest to the lower depths, down the organon of the galaxy like surfing. We begin in the Transcend, where a human-dominated interstellar civilization of the Beyond called the Straumli Realm has discovered an archive planet, which it hopes to ransack for ancient lore. Unfortunately, the archive contains in its banks a billion-year-old Perversion which, once again activated by the unknowing humans, destroys its discoverers, their entire civilization, and thousands more. This catastrophe causes intense gossip throughout the vast expanses of the Beyond. But at the same time the malign Perversion gets free, a counter-agent designed ultimately to thwart it has also been released, and put aboard the sole starship to escape the archive planet or the Straumli Realm; this ship plummets to the very edge of the Slow Zone, and lands on the unknown Tines World, inhabited by a group-mind species whose doglike individual members dance together in intricate telepathic concords but become moribund idiots when separated into singletons, and where all the remaining humans bar two small children are killed by one faction of this ambitious but technologically crippled proto-civilization. Meanwhile, a Power in the Transcend creates a human star sailor out of ancient genes and data (he reminded me of Hethor in Gene Wolfe's *The Book of the New Sun*) who, along with the rest of the central cast, plummets downwards after the escapee ship in search of the mcguffin counter-measure, in order to save the universe. Socialistical minions of the Perversion track them. There are space battles, and huge sacrifices of life. On Tines World the two children learn about their captors in scenes drawn out too much once in a while, but with such evident pleasure that the Idiot-Retard plotting that encourages these minor longueurs is easily forgiven.

Surrounding all this brouhaha is the a rhetoric of nearly infinitely large data flow, presenting in asides and flashes of insight some hint of the size and age and complexity and presentness of a galaxy it is possible to dream of believing in, as you read. The plot dovetails in the end, according to schedule, and without scanting any necessary emotional and kinetic points along the way. By the end of the book we are ready to start again. We want to wear Vernor Vinge's new galaxy again like an open sesame woven of the stars in their ascending levels, the knowledge that the knowledge exists, the knowledge that it can't get us. It is, in the end, a deeply usable book. A Fire Upon the Deep hums with use.

II.

It has been marketed as an hard sf project, but the Man-Kzin Wars shared-world enterprise owned by Larry Niven, and packaged these days in a series of franchise anthologies, no more models scientific speculation than Scrooge McDuck models Donald Trump. Volume four of the sequence, The Man-Kzin Wars, Volume Four (Baen Books, 1992), is something of an oddity, containing as it does one story by Greg Bear in collaboration with S M Stirling (it is chilly but unremarkable), and one novel-length story by Donald Kingsbury, 240 pages long and worthy of separate publication: but perhaps the contractual terms of this enterprise preclude singleton spinoffs. In any case, Kingsbury's novel, which is entitled "The Survivor," presents the life story of a "cowardly" Kzin caught in the latter stages of the Kzin empire's disastrous attempt to invade that patch of the galaxy called Known Space and inhabited by a whole lot of spunky "bumptious" homo sapiens, whose "monkey cleverness" always – "as is traditional," which is how the blurb puts it – wins out. Kingsbury's Kzin, small and pusillanimous, survives through cleverness, through learning, through experimentation upon captured humans. It is an extraordinarily bleak, swift bludgeon of a tale, and the last scene is an earned shocker.

Too bad Kingsbury dressed it in sheep's clothing.

– Interzone 58, April 1992

The Whips of Disenchantment and the Death of Ire and Bats

I.

THE TROUBLE with the end of the world, and the trouble with the novels of Ian McDonald, is one trouble: we have been there before. This does not make the end of the world less terrible, or the novels of Ian McDonald less mobile on the lip, but it

367

surely modifies the shock of anticipating the one, or of opening the other. The end of the world in sf, for instance, has been assembled from apocalyptic millennial images generated by the tight-sphinctered desert sect which gave birth to Judaism and Christianity and Muslim and Gradgrind and Strangelove, and which gloats through its avatars, as it gloated in the beginning, over the death of the Mother [from the "techno-occultism" that runs from Blavatsky through Von Däniken, according to David Morris, who coined the term in *The Masks of Lucifer: Technology and the Occult in Twentieth-Century Popular Literature* (1992) 1995]; from the military and ecological scenarios which say one thing always; and from our own "pastoral" longings for a Golden Age after the holocaust. This end-of-the-world has become part of the base architecture of the genre, one of the structuring icons whose presence in a text spells (pun) the litanies of recognition which we depend on for comfort and orientation. We have in other words domesticated, in our minds' eyes, in order to tell stories after our wont, the death of the planet: we have been there before. Which is why any 1992 sf novel which *fails* to incorporate some iconic reference to the end-of-the-world tends to *irritate* us, because our genre expectations are being violated – I doubt I'm alone in actively enjoying the end-of-the-world in fiction, while simultaneously dreading the increasing signs of the end of the world in fact.

But it is one thing to recognize the blessed analgesias of sf, and another to read Ian McDonald. It is one thing to recognize an icon, and another to know exactly how it is going to be spelled. The first is a comfort; the second is a shock. The first allows us to continue trucking through the tale; the second awakens us to the raw artifactuality of the game of reading, the velleity of the dream of story. By quoting the icon, McDonald estranges us, curses the tit, debriefs the reader into the nada and the day. His first novel, *Desolation Road* (1988), gazes so closely at us through the eyes of Ray Bradbury and Gabriel García Márquez that we can no longer pretend we are alone with the story, which may be the most savage alienation he could inflict upon his readers: for he kills the autonomy of the dream in which we read; by staring at us through the words of others, he turns those words – those icons at the heart of genre, at the heart of reading – into devices on the page. And we lose it. We go down to day. We open the next book, *Out On Blue Six* (1989), and it is the same; and the next, *King of Morning, Queen of Day* (1991), and it is similar; and we open *Hearts, Hands and Voices* (Gollancz, 1992), and the nightmare continues.

Here are the first three paragraphs of the novel, plus the first sentence of the fourth:

> Grandfather was a tree.
>
> Father grew trux, in fifteen colours.
>
> Mother could sing the double-helix song, sing it right into the hearts of living things and change them. *Around we go, and round ...*
>
> A house ran amok in Fifteen Street the day the soldiers of the Emperor Across the River came to Mathembe's township.

The book continues in this vein for some time. It is very well written. The strategy deployed in these first lines – that of conveying, through a rushing patter of staccato sentences, a kind of epiphany-through-précis of the novum to be unfolded – is adroitly conceived and handled. Grandfather (it turns out) really is a tree; trux are biological analogues of trucks, and can be grown; mother (and the daughter, Mathembe, who is the protagonist of the tale) are indeed capable of massaging into various outcomes the tropical biotechnologies that dominate the Land. And houses indeed have vestigial brains, are easily panicked, and are mobile. In its way, it's all superb. At the same time, however, it is a deeply estranging sequence of words, a murder weapon, a quote that kills.

This time the figure whose icons it stares through is, of course, Geoff Ryman. By rendering the tone and matter of the opening paragraphs of his second and third novels with such unerring exactitude, the first sentences of *Hearts, Hands and Voices* tell us that Geoff Ryman, in *The Unconquered Country* (1986) and *The Child Garden* (1988), was making up a story, and that here is the story, flayed. It does not matter that we know very well that Geoff Ryman was making up stories – for our knowledge of that essential circumstance was part of our compact with the stories being told – what matters now is that the knowledge has been read into the record. It is no longer between the words and us. The words have been exposed to the dayglare of McDonald's dissecting re-assembly, and so have we. This it gives us.

I do not know if I think it is a good thing. (I do not know if I think it bad.) What I *do* know is that *Hearts, Hands and Voices* is an extraordinary text, borrower and lender, cuckoo and phoenix. *The Unconquered Country* begins: "Third Child had nothing to sell but parts of her body" and continues, as does *The Child Garden*, to convey, through a rushing patter of staccato sentences, a kind of epiphany-through-précis of the novum to be unfolded (exactly). McDonald's Mathembe and Ryman's Third Child both live in a rural village in a provincial land tied to a nearby empire that seems Asian; biotechnologies provide both children with a living. When imperial forces – by air in both novels – attack their villages in each respective novel, the animate mobile houses common to each novel panic and die. After Mathembe and

Third Child find themselves homeless and deracinated, they both end up in a large festeringly tropical city, where both attempt to survive.

In *Hearts, Hands and Voices* this city closely resembles the London of *The Child Garden*, with echoes of the world of Gwyneth Jones's *Divine Endurance* (1984), just as the Ancestor Tree which contains the consciousness of dead elders more closely resembles the Consensus of *The Child Garden* than anything in the earlier story (though the stadium in McDonald's book more closely resembles the amphitheatre-like square in *The Unconquered Country*). From this point the plot of *Hearts, Hands and Voices* – what plot there is – diverges increasingly from direct inhabitation of the plots of either parent book, but assonances flicker throughout the pages like small deadly whips of disenchantment. There is never any chance of forgetting the obdurate central fact about the book: that it is a tale which says No to the innocence of Story.

Perhaps consequentially, McDonald finds it very difficult to pretend to tell a story of his own. Mathembe and her family, once driven out of their home village, have trekked painfully to the big city dominated by the imperial power. Her father is disappeared. She looks for him. Her mother festers and dwindles. She tries to find her (and discovers, in a passage which dissectingly samples *both* Ryman books, that her mother's been selling her body as a hatchery for viral products). Her younger brother cannot be found. She looks for him. He has become a terrorist. There are eventual discoveries and rediscoveries, and a kind of reconciliation. Mathembe's land – which is ravaged not only by imperial soldiery but by religious disputes – is a bit like Ireland, a bit like Viet Nam, a lot like India/Pakistan. But none of this amounts to much of an engine of plot. Imagery is profuse throughout, and eloquent; the style of the book, after we slide from staccato, is knobbly with nutrients, though occasionally stagnant; and the tone of the thing is the tone of uninnocence self-revealed: remote, knowing, haunted by that which becomes it. *Hearts, Hands and Voices* is a bad thing; and a good thing.

[I take the following from *Interzone* 66, December 1992 1995.]

WITH a condign humbleness of mien, Ian McDonald entitles his second story collection *Speaking in Tongues* (Bantam, 1992), and provides exactly what the reader might expect from an announcement of this candour. *Speaking in Tongues* is a series of exercises – none more cunning and engaging than the title story, whose riff on Gene Wolfe is hilarious – in doing the police in different voices. It is an assemblage of assays in style, tone of voice. The subject matters are of less interest (indeed there is hardly an unfamiliar theme or trope in any of the 11 tales included). What counts is the profusion of registers. "Rainmaker Cometh" does a heat-lightning jangle of Bradbury/Sturgeon/Lafferty to a nicety, though the death of one of the protagonists at story's end seems utterly gratuitous; "Fragments of an Analysis of a Case of Hysteria" much improves on the flytrap paralysis of D M Thomas's *The White Hotel*; "Approaching Perpendicular," though its representation of the Artist is singularly naff, neatly juices up M John Harrison with a Robert Silverberg transcendental slingshot epiphany pompadour *you're flying!* prong. A couple of stories say themselves as well as the exercise, too: "Toward Kilimanjaro" may polish itself a bit on J G Ballard's *Crystal World* (1966), and explicitly quotes Conrad on Darkness, Heart of: but the tale itself is remarkably well characterized, Kenya is neatly anatomized, and the alien transformation of Kilimanjaro itself into a new post-carbon domain is neatly conceived. And "Floating Dogs," though not unpredictable, carries through. And "Fronds," set on a colony planet visited by a Japanese plenipotentiary while imported dolphins attempt to justify their own immoral behaviour in an absolutely inspired re-creation of bardic narrative verse, is simply superb.

McDonald is a strange case, a singularly accomplished maker (and pusher) of material. He is a monster, perhaps, a tropical feeder on the compost of century-end; and someday he is going to have to stop repeating words ("pecking, pecking birds" appear *twice* in different tales); but there is something going on. You begin to sense he may be turning toward the sun.

[End of excerpt from *Interzone* 66.]

II.

We enter the world of Sheri S Tepper, and warm hands clasp us, and make us welcome, and we close our eyes (or open them), and a Story unfolds. It is all much easier to bear than Ian McDonald: but then the last thing Ian McDonald could conceivably want is to be easy to bear, or to be thought of as a suitable teller of tales around any fire in this world. Tepper, on the other hand, may have started her career in 1983 with nary a notion of doing anything else but telling. Her first novels – they came in a rush for a while, till the mid 1980s, when she slowed down to one or two a year – were fantasies of clear cunning sophistication, but seemingly deficient in agenda, with storylines which clutched at the reader with velvet undertows that took you far from shore but never drowned you, quite. And even now, a tale about the end-of-the-world like *Beauty* (1991) can trick the reader into fireside comforts, and only slowly reveal the desolation at the core of things. (The ecological urgency of this book was underlined by "A Note from the Author" which appeared only on the back flap of the hardback dustwrapper, and was therefore, inexcusably, omitted from the paperback edition: Tepper may have felt it necessary to point her message extra-textually because *Beauty* qua Story rather ran away with her.) Her major series of recent years exhibits a similar tendency to revel in narrative byways at the cost of some slippage in saliency, but all comes clear in the end. The three novels so far published in the current sequence – *Grass* (1989), *Raising the Stones* (1990) and *Sideshow* (Bantam, 1992) [in 1995 three seems to be all the series will require] – move from the slightly po-faced romance idiom which kind of beguilingly sidetracks *Grass* for hundreds of pages, through the bustling broad swathes of action which make *Raising the Stones* formidable but a touch endless, and into the more intense fabulousness of *Sideshow*, five thousand years on from 1992 CE, at the end of which Story the tale is by no means ended, but humanity has finally stopped tearing the universe apart.

If there has been a central equation whose outcomes have determined Tepper's rendering of the human condition in all three books, it has probably been some sort of calculus through which masculinity, sex and religion are sealed irrevocably to-gether by ire. It is a calculus (or equilibration) whose feminist implications Tepper neither scants nor emphasizes; and although some of her sexually-skewed elderly male prophets of life-distorting versions of Christianity (in all of this we risk tautol-ogy) may seem all too cartoon-like to frighten us deep inside, the sense of agenda thus generated is remarkably well-sustained. Because of their gloating Despite for the given world, the religious figures who are the ultimate villains of the sequence have ensured that Earth becomes a desert by the early years of the 21st century. [The same desecration of the planet, similarly inspired by religious fundamentalism, features in *Shadow's End* (1994), though the novel seems otherwise unconnected to this series 1995.] In both *Grass* and *Raising the Stones*, fundamentalist patriarchies at-tempt to destroy other parts of the universe, and are defeated in the end. In *Sideshow*, a pair of Siamese twins from our era travel through an Arbai Gate (familiar from *Grass*) to the planet Elsewhere, 5000 years into the future, where they find that a pro-found misunderstanding of the nature of the Hobbs Land Gods (the subject of *Rais-ing the Stones*) has resulted in a world-wide hegemony determined to preserve hu-man diversity at all costs. To this end, Jack Chalker-like, the planet has been divided into something like a thousand enclaves, each devoted to its own way of life. Emi-gration is prohibited. The world Council employs Enforcers – among them the main protagonists of the novel – whose job it is to prevent petty imperialisms and proselytizings, to preserve cultural diversity while ignoring the costs individual hu-mans (children, for instance, in religious cultures devoted to child sacrifice) must bear. It is an idea fit for a novel, and especially fit for an sf novel, where elaborate societies are almost invariably constructed by their authors in order to be destroyed by their plots: and so it goes, here on Elsewhere. The plot is much much too complex to synopsize, though Tepper manages to tell the whole thing around the fire with an extraordinarily agile serenity, or serene agility; suffice it for readers of the previous volumes that the protagonists of each – clearly labelled early on for our convenience – appear again here: that Marjorie (here Jori) and Sam (here Asner) are instrumental in dissolving the procrustean Diversity of Elsewhere into a long-hinted-at epiphany, and in helping the Twins achieve their own metamorphic destiny: and that "Man" finally unbinds "himself" from the long and dreadful history of homo sapiens, from the cross of Ire, from the solitudes we call peace. And the universe gives a sigh of relief.

III.

Tanith Lee's *Dark Dance* (Macdonald, 1992), the first volume in what is projected to be called the Blood Opera sequence, is a dense pummel of a tale, which drives at the reader poundingly, incessantly, urgently: like a heart fever. And at the end of the 400 pages almost nothing has actually happened: the quasi-immortal Adamus Scarabae, who may be a vampire or who may – along with his whole arachnid family – be something else entirely, begets upon a human female a girl child, who grows up sullen and wild in a brilliantly underlit London. Inveigled to migrate across the UK to the Scarabae mansion, she is herself impregnated by her young large-grand-piano-playing Dad, flees, gives birth, brings up another daughter in the wilderness of underlit suburban London: but the daughter is more like Dad than Mum; and when they return to the Scarabae mansion she is soon deeply embroiled with Grand-dad, and the plot thickens, and ends: but we are still at the beginning of everything, really. It is all quite astonishing: unrelentingly skillful, unputdownable, and bats. Accept no substitutes.

– Interzone 59, May 1992

Come, Adam, This Time the Berries Are Sweet

IN OUR LIVES, as we know, Eden takes the past tense. It is only afterwards, in any case, that we call it Eden. In the midst of life, while we remain active and full of the biologically predetermined sense of uniqueness which guarantees the species-specific orthodoxy of our every act, we give the driving force within us all sorts of names, but I will call it Word. During the years of our vigour, we do not seek to separate ourselves from the Word which comprises the wiring diagram of the soul, the perceptual matrix which ties the ego to the raw things of the world and charges the raw things of the world to obey the patterns that make us whole. It is, of course, a high and terrible charge we lay upon the raw things of the world. "Oh bless the continuous stutter," says Leonard Cohen in "The Window," from *Recent Songs* (1979), "Of the Word being made into flesh," the fool. Because that stutter is the sound of Progress, a chewing sound.

It is only afterwards – or when the slow-lane among us escape into a book – that we discover some inherent gap between the wiring diagram of the soul and the flesh it purges. It is only then we discover that the Word within us – that which unction-rutting Christians still designate the Soul, the possession of which (some of them continue to assert) excuses anything we might do to the world – may have been a *growth* in the corridors of power of the grossly overextended human brain, a puppet-master tumour so huge it swells the head, forces us upright so we can balance it inside our swollen skulls, drives homo sapiens into the interminable ravening loose-cannon neoteny that marks us as Cain, and against which nothing is safe, not the "beast," nor the water meadows, nor the Mother.

It is only afterwards, when we have retired, or hit a siding, or learned to read, that we begin to need to forgive ourselves. It is then we like to think that the name of the growth within the skull we dance to is not Word at all, but *Eden*: which we then associate with the fine immortal bliss of childhood we are supposed to have experienced before language divorced us from the omnipotence of infancy; or the nostalgia we feel for all we have eaten; or the self-pitying ecstasy that wells in our bosom at the thought of being able to leave *something* alone. Anything at all. Eden is the alibi of the Word. All true art hovers, therefore, on the cusp of alibi: for it is neither here nor there, now nor when, rent nor whole. True Art is Janus-faced: To tell a story is to leave Eden (just as to tell about utopia is to create its dark twin), but to remember a story is to return.

I.

Let us return, for instance, to the Discworld. In a review of *Guards! Guards!* (1989) in *Interzone* 33 [see p. 166]; in a long piece on Pratchett which appeared in the same issue, but is not reprinted here; and in a review of *Moving Pictures* (1990) in *Interzone* 45 [see p. 244], I have myself gone on a good deal about Terry Pratchett and the nature of True Comedy, which I said exemplified the *da capo* nature of storytelling, that face of Art which took us home again. The Comedy of Terry Pratchett's Discworld, I said, was a "tournament of return," and I then went on mildly to disparage a tendency I thought I discerned in *Guards! Guards!* to "transcend" the crystalline shape of True Comedy, and to attempt to take on the threatening world-addressing saliencies of the novel (the greatest examples of which threaten us with the face of Art that sees the intolerable otherness of the new in a grain of sand, before falling back into the memory of the page). The Discworld tales, I thought, were too perfect – and, perhaps, too minor – to wear that face. Later, in *Moving Pictures*, I thought I saw something else going slightly adrift: The protagonists of that story seemed too stupid to understand the plot they were embroiled in; but the book turned on a plot that only really made sense if its potential outcomes were sussed by characters clever enough to understand the dangers it represented, and who were thus armed to defuse those dangers. It was perhaps commendable of Pratchett (I thought) to ban from the Discworld any protagonist whose sharpness of intellect might do more harm than good, might (for instance) question the premise (or turtle) upon which the edifice rested whole. But it also disparaged the *Discworld* to leave its defence – every new tale set in a continuing world is necessarily a defence of that world – to dolts, as if to depict a protagonist with brains would break the illusion.

So I gave the Discworld a rest, even in my own private reading. And we jump onwards to *Small Gods* (Gollancz, 1992), which is surely the best novel Terry Pratchett has ever written, and the best comedy. It is a tale of very considerable grimness set in a desert theocracy run by world-despising clergymen (women need not apply) and torturers whose resemblance to Christians in their prime (which was 1497, Torquemada and Savonarola both dying in 1498) and to Moslems in theirs (1992) cannot be accidental: for the religion that dominates the theocracy of Omnia is monotheistic, condemns any form of free-thinking, condemns women, condemns sex, condemns the arts, condemns beauty, condemns laughter, condemns nature, condemns the Discworld, and condemns Truth (for it insists that the world is round, and orbits the sun). The theocracy of Omnia is in the business of transforming Eden into Word. *Small Gods* is surely a novel.

It is also a Comedy. Though the protagonist of the book is a saint, who is tortured (very briefly), and though he changes and grows throughout the text, the gravitas of pain and maturation does little to disguise the essential Pratchett protagonist within. Brutha (he's a Brother) is, like so many of his predecessors, an enormous bumpkin and dupe, close to witless but cheerful, or so it seems. He is also memorious: he can forget nothing. And he is so transported by the dazzle of words and the purling infinitudes of reality and the clamour of the gods that he actually believes in Om, the god of Omnia, being the only person left on the Discworld to believe in this particular god, who does indeed exist. But the gods of the Discworld (like Tinker-bell) flourish according to the degree of belief accorded them. When belief grows, small gods – of whom there are billions – can swiftly become revered deities, with the power to heal and to destroy; but when belief fades, so do they. Om has faded. Having ill-advisedly attempted a spot of kenosis (a theological term for taking on the burden of the flesh: what gods do when they want to joy-ride) Om discovers that there is only enough belief left in the Discworld to incarnate him as a tortoise. But Brutha, who believes in Om, hears his cries for help, and the tortoise henceforth speaks within his head, a secret sharer. At the same time, Brutha's supernal inno-cence, for he seems both clueless and blessed, has intrigued Vorbis, the murderous torturer who runs the inquisition and the empire itself, and the plot begins to move.

The hilariousness of the book derives from the usual incremental repetition of jokes and turns, the usual precision of language and timing, but also from the fact that *Small Gods* works as a cunning, cagy parody of Gene Wolfe's *The Book of the New Sun*: both novels are about religion, the nature of god (or gods); both feature memo-rious protagonists with secret-sharer voices inside their heads and an ambiguous relationship to torture who go on great circular quests into war zones and return to rule the empire. But the heart of the book does not lie in the parody chase. *Small Gods* is at heart a tale about the preservation of the Discworld. It is a comedy about remaining a Comedy. Vorbis wishes to conquer the rest of the land – to transform not only Omnia but all of the Discworld into a free enterprise zone for the profit of the Word – and to do so he has fastened upon a campaign to force all other coun-tries and peoples to admit to the fact that the world is round, just as it is claimed to be in the scriptures of Omnia. Sailors and philosophers who maintain that the world is a disc riding upon the back of a turtle are tortured, forced to recant like Ga-lileo in 1616, when he finally admitted to the Inquisition that the world did not move around the sun. As good Christians know to their disgust, however, Galileo re-neged. After his formal recantation he whispered sotto voce to the world (which heard him): "Eppur si muove." Still it moves. On the Discworld it is an almost iden-tical whisper: "The Turtle moves."

Now and then, there is a moment of bitterness from the god, but Brutha an-swers him:

> "There you are," said Om, a note of bitter triumph in his voice. "You don't *know*. That's what stops everyone going mad, the uncertainty of it, the feeling that it might work out all right after all. But it's different for gods. We do know. You know that story about the sparrow flying through a room?"

"No..."

"About life being like a sparrow flying through a room? Nothing but darkness outside? And it flies through the room and there's just a moment of warmth and light?"

"There are windows open?" said Brutha.

He is not, in truth, asking a question. He is saying that everything is real. He is saying that the sparrow will do one thing, and then the next thing. The utterly un-Christian innocence of his absorption into the world and his love for the world only deepens as he moves towards autarky, as the god and the creature move slowly back to Omnia, after their quest. They defeat Vorbis, who is taken by Death. Brutha binds Om to a code of laws which force him to be ethical, and rules for a 100 years, which pass in the blinking of an eye, just as Little Louis's long life passes in the turning of a page at the end of Georges Simenon's *The Little Saint* (1965). Within the compass of Brutha's gaze, the Discworld is safe, the Turtle moves. Within the compass of our reading of *Small Gods*, we are in the present tense of Eden.

11.

Another book about Eden, Emma Tennant's *Faustine* (Faber & Faber, 1992), sets the Faust story in the twentieth century, where a middle-aged woman named Muriel Twyman – disappeared from the roll of real people by time's passage through her caving female body – succumbs to the Devil's blandishments, and returns to the Eden of eternal youth for 24 years. But the Eden which she enters is mortuary, and the two decades of her supremacy over the world as a clone of Elizabeth Taylor are solitudinous and arid: or so we are intended, it would seem, to guess. There is no telling for sure in this very brief, frost-palsied, weirdly sidesaddle book, which is told, long after the fact, through the eyes of Muriel's seemingly love-ravenous and self-centred (but in fact destroyed) grand-daughter, who returns from exile in Australia to find her, longing for love but totally unlovable and unloving, a victim of the dry-ice extrusions of Muriel's damnation. Fragments of story drop into the grand-daughter's chill and resistant sensorium, and we begin to feel a modicum of pity for her closed self. Muriel herself is never seen until, fragmented in a mirror, her face is glimpsed at the very end of the book, which then collapses in upon her like a house of cards, desolately. The fragments of the fall are all we read, the dead skin of Eden, told from long long ago. *Faustine* is as old a book as it is possible to hold in the hand, and no more forthcoming about the allure it mourns than a laundry list in Linear B. Touch it and age.

III.

It is not a new thought that Nazi Germany will live forever, and Robert Harris has not had a new thought in *Fatherland* (Hutchinson, 1992). Like most alternate histories of the twentieth century, he has worked out an hypothesis or two – in his case a few mild twitches at events in 1942 – which allows Hitler to win World War Two, and his readers to enjoy – in the amoral solitude of the act of reading – a victorious Reich, a corrupt but highly photogenic obergruppenfuhrerlederhosenfabriken-gesellschaft, hierarchies and Mercedes Benzes and architecture by Albert Speer, and aged faces steeped like tea in corruption. We have seen the like before, long ago. Sarban and Philip K Dick and Keith Roberts and Len Deighton – and a hundred [less than that but lots 1995] more – have found the awful aesthetic of the Nazi presentation of self too tempting to ignore; and have *done* something with it. What Harris does, with a very considerable degree of skill, is very nearly nothing. The story he tells quite excellently – in 1964 a gloomy, highly intelligent police detective whose life is falling apart finds a suspicious body, the Gestapo hierarchy becomes involved, the cop refuses to stop investigating, and quite excitingly the obscenity at the root of the system is exposed – almost entirely lacks extrapolative content, and has therefore almost nothing to say about the obscenity – it is, of course, the Final Solution – it burrows towards. You think of *Gorky Park* (1981) by Martin Cruz Smith, or of anything by Frederick Forsyth, but not hard. It was nice to see which Kennedy was president in 1964, but not much fun to think that otherwise it was the same old world. The invert Eden of Nazi Germany needs more prodding than this.

IV.

A man named Pablo is shot. He dies. He awakens on a vast plain, along with all the humans ever born, stark naked, but no longer aroused by breasts and buttocks, for the time of the Last Judgment is upon him. So far there is nothing new, and Piero Scanziani's *The White Book* (1969; Eureka Publishers of Windsor, 1991), though clearly written in a style of swift lucid poignance, and translated into an English of liquid urgency by Linda Lappin, seems at first to lack much in the way of novelty. Then we enter a kind of hut, where Pablo and a black girl and a Chinese peasant are told they have been selected to defend Adam and Eve before the final court, and we see that this court consists of a quincunx of masked magistrates, and we realize that it is not novelty that we must seek. We must find wisdom or leave the book. We find wisdom.

Pablo remembers fragments of his life, as do the other two defenders; and in recesses between sessions of the trial all three hear the exemplary confessions of other human beings, all of whom adhere passionately to the hooks of the stories that tell them, as would we all. In each story there are understandings and misunderstandings, joinings and solitudes, moral conundrums it is beyond human capacity to parse in the time given us to understand the race of life, and a death at the end. It is a chaos, a congeries, an anthem, a susurrus.

The trial proceeds. Adam and Eve are exiles from Eden. Eve has given birth in grief and joy to the children who will populate the earth, and Adam searches for some way to return to Eden. There is nothing new in any of this. We know about the incest. We know that Cain will kill Abel. We know – for Scanziani allows us the knowledge in a thousand ways, as he tricks us through this brilliant book – that the only judgment we as readers can make is the judgment of Brutha: "The windows are open?" For the only thing a human being can truly accomplish is to do the next thing. Adam steps off the edge of a cliff, calling Eden, Eden. It was the next thing. How can he be judged? The defenders, Pablo and the two other humans, approach the judges. Behind the masks the gods have fled, or never were. The room of judgment is empty of gods. There is a white book, which the chief magistrate had consulted. It will surely contain the wisdom of the gods, their indictment, their Word. It is blank. Everyone leaves. Adam and Eve, who are exiles from Eden, have returned to the beginning, for Adam says they must return to Eden. Eve says she is hungry, it is only human. As the book ends she speaks, joyfully, to Adam. But she is leaving the Word behind. "Come Adam," she says, "this time the berries are sweet."

– Interzone 60, June 1992

Puppet Dark

IT IS something like the heft of cathedral tunes, and something like the Heavenly Hurt that leaves no scar, but internal difference, where the Meanings, are. We quote Emily Dickinson, gaunt and nude within the Gothic coverlets of the New England spinsterhood which served her. We are thinking of Margaret St Clair, whose *Agent of the Unknown* (1956) must be one of the earliest examples of the Puppet Dark tale; and of Mark S Geston, whose *Lords of the Starship* (1967) mixes Puppet Dark and Dying Earth; and of John Crowley, whose *The Deep* (1975) is a Pocket Universe story set in an enclosed world which – it is the concave palm of a God upraised into the immensity of a starless welkin – is a perfect model of the inherent mise-en-scène of the Puppet Dark tale; and of Gene Wolfe, whose *There Are Doors* (1988) returns us to the erotic subtext of Margaret St Clair's beautiful little novel, to the pathos of the longing for exogamy with the God, who will burn us out like Semele; and of William Barton, of whose *Dark Sky Legion: An Ahrimanic Novel* (Bantam, 1992) it is enough to note, at the moment, that Ahriman is the dark god of Zoroaster who engages in fateful combat the god of light, Ahura Mazdah: and might well win.

A Puppet Dark tale may defined as an sf or fantasy story whose hero is in some sense a projection or avatar of a God or godlike figure behind the arras of the plot; but who does *not* turn out, in the end, to *be* the God. (This caveat distinguishes the Puppet Dark tale from the vastly more numerous category of stories in which the amnesiac hero turns out to be his own father or god, or in which the heroine who has denied her menstrual roots turns out to be her own mother or the Earth Herself.) The hero of the Puppet Dark tale – he or she will typically be an android, or computer projection, or tied clone, or ghost – is, in other words, the dark twin of the Competent Man whose wetdreams have engined the official Future Histories of most American (and some coat-clinger UK) sf writers. [The Puppet Dark is an under-story of First SF 1995.] In a Puppet Dark tale the hero does not penetrate the barrier of the unknown, for the unknown is the god-fist within his skull, and he reaches his apotheosis as dermis, as a penetration tool, Punch in the night.

Agent of the Unknown, which was called "Vulcan's Dolls" on it magazine publication in 1952, is the paradigm text for the Puppet Dark story. The hero, who turns out to be an android toy of the godlike Vulcan, has been constructed to perform unknowingly certain tasks – his actions help release the genetic potential of the human race, which then prepares to leap beyond his ken – and afterwards to "rest." He is entrapped in a plot he cannot understand; he aches with exogamous passions for human women (who die on him), and for Vulcan (who strokes him like a beloved pet); and in the end, his functions fulfilled, he is turned off, allowed to drown in the mothering waves of a pleasure planetoid. The story is compact, elegiac, lucid, dry-voiced; and absolutely dark. It is no wonder that Margaret St Clair remains virtually unknown to the world of sf, that she remains one of the genre's great Voices to the Contrary. And *Dark Sky Legion* is, in parts, a worthy successor.

1.

The main problem with the book is the 400 pages of long paper. It may be that William Barton is difficult to edit, or that Bantam operate a laissez-faire policy with the texts they publish, or that both Barton and Bantam are in agreement about the book: given its inherent merit, one rather hopes the latter is the case. But. Nevertheless. *Dark Sky Legion* reads as though it had been written – as most books are today, just as this review is being written – on a computer; and if it doesn't exactly overstay its welcome the way books used to when they went on too long, it does, all the same, give off a sense that too many luxurious repetitions of the moody bits were patched into the text, *just to make sure*. (In the old days, when they were written consecutively, books *grew* too long at their top end, like buddleia; nowadays, when they can be assembled from tesseract blocks like vast mosaics, a book is likely to become too long at *any point*; and then get short again, maybe.) *Dark Sky Legion* could have had about 100 pages of luxuries culled from it, here and there, all the way through. Certain repeated phrases – most noticeably those underlying the protagonist's sense that he is 1) mortal, 2) immortal, 3) young, 4) old – sound almost like extremely sub-Homeric heroic tags; and some of the inserted passages illustrative of the protagonist's experiences in earlier incarnations give off a similar sense of being inserted according to the cod algorithms generated by software options.

What is good about the book is pretty well everything else. The immediate plot is not complex: the protagonist, a representative of the Metastable Order which maintains a uniformitarian hegemony over the human galaxy, comes to the planet Olam to ensure that its population has not veered too radically from the norm, and accomplishes his mission. The underlying structure of the novel, however, is less straightforward. The tale is told from the point of view, though not in the voice, of its protagonist, Maaron Denthurion, the 66th incarnation of the 33rd branching of the original Denthurion, who himself remains on Earth, thousands of years away. Our Maaron – the Maaron who features in *Dark Sky Legion* – awakens from something like slumber in the Metastable Vectorship *Naglfar*, which has settled into orbit around Olam, and is beamed down to the planet's surface to do his job. Two circumstances should be noted, however: Maaron has been "asleep" because, in Barton's universe (as in ours) there is no such thing as FTL travel, and he is now dozens of segments of centuries-long "sleep" from home, from Earth, from the "normalcy" he must enforce; and each time he is sent through the "transceiver" he suffers something like instantaneous death and rebirth, so that he is snuffed out (and rekindled in his glorious young manhood) every time he lands upon a planet. He is a node of information clothed in flesh. All flesh is, of course, grass; and Maaron has burned hundreds of grass huts of flesh to ash in his passage through the dark. All flesh is grass. But the information node – the soul –is, of course, permanent.

This is what he believes. What *Dark Sky Legion* gradually tells us is, of course, that Maaron is a vessel or puppet of the God who rides within *Naglfar*, the AI who ostensibly obeys his commands but who, in fact, operates him to dreadful effect; that he is, in effect, a computer-generated simulacrum based on edited memories of previous simulacra. But we do not immediately begin to whiff the wrongness of Maaron, or of the Metastable Order he represents, because we are seeing Olam through his eyes, and it is clear that much has indeed gone wrong there: surviving representatives of Olam's native species, for instance, have deteriorated into pets, whom the human intruders treat with callous savagery; and the charismatic religious faith in a Starship Heaven, to which many Olamites adhere, is a cruel fraud: for the Heaven to which true believers ascend through transceivers is in fact a huge orbital factory whose machinery is run by edited versions of these deluded souls in a state of sickly, computer-induced serenity. So there is a job to do.

But Maaron is himself extraordinarily serene. And it is not at all clear that his sense of what is wrong is going to be easy to share. Gradually, indeed, we learn that we have been gulled by our readerly assumption that the figure we identify with will behave as we might dream of doing, that the Metastable Order whose vision of normalcy he enacts is no worse than value-neutral (like most distant Empires in this sort of fiction). We have, in fact, been more thoroughly gulled than we were by Iain (M) Banks in *Consider Phlebas* (1987) [see p. 28], where it took us most of the book to realize that its protagonist was on the wrong side in a war between two visions of reality. But at least in that book the protagonist was making a mistake. In *Dark Sky Legion*, where the gulling is equally deliberate and the resulting lesson even more pointed, Maaron Denthurion is the wrong side, and when he does his job on Olam – it is the thousandth time he's done the same job – we come to see that, as readers, we have been supping with abomination. Ahriman has won, the god-fist shuts. Within, the dark is puppet.

II.

After silence, a sound of knitting. Charles Sheffield's *Cold As Ice* (Tor, 1992) is a hard-sf novel set on Earth and throughout the solar system in 2092 CE, and it is full of the sound of the worlds outside the self. It is a bright, gainfully employed, excellently constructed, exterior tale of system-wide politics, scientific breakthrough, plot and counterplot. And there is a neat twenty-year-old mystery, dating from the end of the intra-system war which decimated Earth's population and savaged the asteroids and the Jovian hegemonies. This mystery relates to a genetic engineering conspiracy which may have given birth to a bunch of homo superiors, a possibility Sheffield allows us to confirm way before any character in the book has much of a clue, so that a genuine sense of wonder [see pp.296–297] permeates the telling. All comes right in the end, and the book knits smartly to a stop: pure chain-mail.

But Sheffield is not just a pretty face.

The world he gives us, here and in many of his earlier books, may be debugged of the running dog subjectivisms of a Jonathan Carroll, and may seem terribly empty of souls in consequence; but it seems utterly clear that this is a deliberate stripping of the decks, and that Sheffield knows very well indeed just what sort of tale it is he's writing. *Cold As Ice* is a world fable, and a joy to read. The protagonists it contains – there are a lot of them, all neatly mission-controlled, packaged, labelled, pre-paid, cost-effective – have been given strict instructions to serve the world of the book, and do so. They have no brief to mesmerize that world with the megaphone diktats of the human soul at full blare, and do not. As readers, therefore, we have nothing between us and the dream of the fable but the way it is told, and *Cold As Ice* is almost invisible in the telling, like a window. Unlike almost every hard-sf writer now alive (for Asimov is dead) and working, Sheffield writes in clear. There is no poison in the pen. The world thrives. [The comments on Sheffield are from *Interzone* 61, July 1992 1995.]

– Interzone 62, August 1992

Mars Joins the Human Race

LIKE THE QUEEN, Arthur C Clarke celebrates his official birthday this year at a season when the sun is high. [This was written, in June 1992, about an event which was history by the time *Interzone* 63 appeared 1995.] At some point during the week of 18–26 July 1992, in Minehead, where he was born 16 December 1917, Arthur C Clarke will be proclaimed 75 years old. There will be celebrations, talks, the presentation of the sixth Arthur C Clarke Award, and the man. Among some of the celebrants there will surely be a conscious and elegiac feeling that he is the last remaining sf writer who can still speak to us with authority from the time of origins, in a voice still present to the world. This feeling may not be quite fair – L Sprague de Camp and Lloyd C Eshbach and Frederik Pohl and Jack Williamson (see below) are still publishing writers, and continue to represent to us the fact that genre sf, like rock music, has not yet outstretched the human span – but Clarke has been for half a century a more domineering figure than any of these men (there are no women), and (unlike them) has taken the formulas of sf to express, however falteringly, agendas for the world. In his person he represents the unbroken gaze of that capacity for agenda.

1.

He also blurbs books. It is to be assumed that he does so with the care that comes from responsibility. When he says of Kim Stanley Robinson's *Red Mars* (Harper-Collins, 1992) that it is "the best novel on the colonization of Mars that has ever been written," there is a sense that he has picked his words; that he has spoken in full knowledge that we know he has spent half a century reading (and writing) books about Mars; and that, by eschewing the unspecific (and therefore unfalsifiable) pattern-book hype that characterizes most blurbs written by authors to pay debts and to create debtors, he has laid something of the meaning of his own genuine name on the line. So we open the book with a sense that we are opening a new page in the gaze of sf. We are not disappointed. *Red Mars* is the best novel on the colonization of Mars that has ever been written.

It may be possible to drop the qualification. *Red Mars* may simply be the best novel that has ever been written about Mars. Mars as a venue for the telling of tales. Mars as an agenda for humans. In *Red Mars*, our only genuine neighbour planet joins the human race. (If there were any life on Mars, this would be a mixed blessing for Mars. But there is none.) None of the Mars tales due to be published over the next few years (there are a number of them in the works) will find it easy to alter in any significant aspect this astonishing transformation of the extraordinary amount of data now available on Mars into a family portrait of the planet [none of them has 1995]. The Mars of *Red Mars* is the home of a family romance – the intimate, sometimes shaming story of the species beginning to breed out. So it is an important book not only through the quality of its telling, which is dark-hued, assimilative, urgent, encompassing; it is important because – sanely, calmly, and without any of the inflamed scapegoat-seeking parti pris of the American hard-sf ideologues – it gathers the planet Mars into human history.

In an essay about sf published in 1987 in *Foundation*, Robinson said that "[i]n every sf narrative, there is an explicit or implicit fictional history that connects the period depicted to our present moment, or to some moment of our past." For most sf writers actively at work in 1992, that sense of fictional history tends to be controlled by an assumption that any continuity between now and the imagined period of the telling will be violated by some variety of terminal holocaust. Almost every sf novel set in the future is now set subsequent to some disaster which ends life on Earth, or so transforms human destiny that the escalator of history stops short on the day, and a new clean-slate escalator – nicely purged of the irremediable weight of the done – lifts off for the stars. Modern post-holocaust sf (now almost a tautology) may *pretend* to a sense of history, but in truth it has given up (as have its readers given up) history in despair [just as has the recent hemorrhage of tales set in purged alternate world pasts, which are labeled sf, but which are in fact diseased (because rootless) fantasy 1995]. In our hearts, most of us in 1992 – writers and readers alike – read sf in the secret conviction that the genre is a body of fairytales about the after-life. *Red Mars* cannot be so read. It is a tale comprehensively obedient to its author's definition of sf as a genre which *continues* telling the story of you and me (and the starving children) as we tremble in our cul-de-sac at the bottom of the scree and the earth begins to shake. It is a *consecutive* book.

The action takes place halfway through the next century, in a venue which follows on from the world in which we live, though in order to tell a tale at all Robinson does somewhat postpone the various comeuppances which the Lords Foul of the world flutter their hankies at, antic. So it may stretch plausibility a mite to assume that the avalanches we wait beneath in 1992 will, 70 years on, still be poised above our heads; but this is really an argument about the speed of the escalator: the course of history between now and 2050, as referred to within this novel, has a daylight consecutiveness: there is no mystification, no soothing holocaust to change the rules, no magical *enablement* to 1) soothe us as we read but 2) ensure our lassitude, because the gap between now and the dream is too great to bridge in life. (It is a Richard Condon thought: but one does rather wonder whether or not 90% of post-holocaust sf may just have been commissioned by the Lords Foul, by the owners of the world, to keep the rest of us properly lassitudinous as they prepare the arcologies in which, next century, they will surely dwell.) The colonization of Mars in *Red Mars* is no figment of the world beyond the veil. Mars is an utterance in the present tense of the world.

There is a plot, and action, and characters, and a violent swing of story through climax into denouement, with energies just beginning to recharge before a slingshot ending brings us to the next volume of the intended trilogy (*Green Mars* [1993] – no direct connection to *Green Mars*, the 1985 novella published later as a Tor Double – and *Blue Mars*). From a complex storyline, through which several viewpoint characters intersect and grow and shift and age, a history of the extension of the dense human story to come can be extracted. The first landing is in 2020. Over the next few years, robot ships drop supplies and equipment. In 2027, a ship brings the first 100 men and women to the planet. They become the First Hundred. They begin to establish habitats, and (after considerable conflict) opt for rapid terraforming of Mars. Very soon, more colonists arrive, and along with them a gradual (and complexly conceived) shift of power from the United Nations to the "transnational" corporations which have been financing much of the action. There are set pieces, like the dropping of an elevator cable from synchronous orbit to the high rim of a vast caldera. By the time a million people have arrived, social and political tensions have become too multifaceted for any one person to understand or hope to control; after a revised Mars-Earth treaty proves vulnerable to corporate manipulation, a naïve but convulsive revolution takes place. Devastation ensues, Yugoslavias galore. But the human hold on the planet is too tenacious and many-handed to expunge. (There is as much dry land on Mars as there is on Earth.) As the novel ends, it is clear that humanity has become indigenous.

The actual texture of the book has little of this simplicity. After a short first section set in 2053, during which the climax of the tale is adumbrated, we return to the ship carrying the First Hundred on the initial voyage of colonization, in order to become familiar with the several figures of the group who turn out to be viewpoint characters in *Red Mars* (and almost certainly its sequels). The three central protagonists – John Boone, Frank Chalmers and Maya Toitovna – seem initially straightforward, but by the end of 500 extremely dense pages all of them (but Chalmers in particular) have become as multifaceted as Mars itself, as humans in the real world: for that is what Mars soon proves to be: a world too real to come to life through the eyes of pulp heroes. Like adult humans in any real world, the three grow masks as they age, palimpsests over the quarrelsome cohorts of magma within, and become more adept at being themselves pari passu with the blossoming of history around them (the longest section of the book is called "Falling into History"). By the end of the tale we recognize their angle of entry into any scene, their smell, their fatedness to continue being who they are. We see that we could be them, we could be there. They might have been created initially by Robinson to provide multiple perspectives on his central vision of a real Mars, but in the end they themselves turn out to *be* Mars: we believe in the agenda that is never spoken but must lie beneath every word of *Red Mars* because we believe in these people as deeply as it is possible to believe in marks on paper: for in that sense (alone) *Red Mars* is a mimetic novel, not sf at all. It is a novel of humans at play in the fields of the lord.

The unspoken agenda, which drives *Red Mars* to 500 pages of urging, is not simply to describe Mars as part of history, but to suggest that unless Mars becomes part of history, the human race will not survive. (And we might as well go back to our VR tales of life beyond death, till the rats chew the plugs out.) From this, all subtends. The intense realism of the geography (or, more properly, areography). The placedness of the characters. The refusal (except for one death towards the end, which is predictable on genre-plotting grounds, and duly happens) to play sf games with the venue, while at the same time incorporating, suitably transformed, as many sf ideas about the solar system as can fit – sometimes with a sense of cramming, with a sense that 500 pages were too few – into the one volume. The anti-capitalist fervour that inspires the more intense moments of direct argument about how to avoid the parasitism of the old system, which to continue profiting from "the gifts of human work" must create interminable needs (in a terminable world). And the emphasis, time and again, on the *thingness* of Mars (Robinson calls it *haecceity*: but that is a word this reviewer once promised never to use again: and won't [I lied 1995]). At the intellectual and narrative climax of the book, John Boone gives a speech on the slope of Olympus Mons. An asteroid has just been successfully directed into Mars's atmosphere to accelerate the terraforming. Many of the First Hundred are there. Revolution is brewing. "What can I say, friends?" he says. "This is the thing itself, there are no words for this."

But then, in one of the most rousing speeches ever uttered in the literature of sf, he finds the words. Read the book. Believe the words. We'd better.

11.

There are Mars books and Mars books. Ben Bova has written one called *Mars* which concentrates on the journey. Terry Bisson's brilliant *Voyage to the Red Planet* (1990) [see p. 269] hurls a fun-house crew to Mars, but does so within strict criteria of scientific verisimilitude, so that the spoof elements of the tale work as an elegy for a project no longer within the grasp of the human race. But the cast does reach landfall, and a wry epithalamium ensues. Bisson acknowledges the help of Kim Stanley Robinson and Charles Sheffield (who also stands, acknowledged, behind *Red Mars*); and the Mars of both books is a kind of shared world: would it were ours.

And in *Beachhead* (Tor, 1992), Jack Williamson has written a Mars book, too, and there is little visibly awry with his physical portrait of the planet (he is the person, after all, who invented the term terraforming in the early 1940s). Where this rather sad novel comes unstuck is in the pulp storyline which has been affixed to its pages like an ill-fitting Hallowe'en mask, through which haecceity glowers gagged. *Beachhead* is, in essence, a juvenile, from long ago. Extremely rich young space cadet Sam Houston Kelligan defies his billionaire dad and his aged (50! year old) mother to join the eight-strong first expedition to Mars. Half are guys, half are gals. "Hew" has a real crush on fellow-crew member Jayne, who despises him for his money and associates him with greaseball Mexicano upstart Marty, who tried to "rape" her (off-stage and long ago), and whose heavyset but sexually available mother has had Hew's immensely rich father in thrall for many years. Jayne *seems* to love Arkady (there is also an Arkady in *Red Mars*) and they pair up. Hew *likes* a couple of other girls but they don't pair up, because Hew's a pretty straight sort of guy. Mars is reached. Hew and Jayne are picked to make the first landing. Jayne overrides his piloting because she's afraid he's a playboy and is going to crash, and causes a crash herself. Typical of a girl. Other members of the crew fidget and fuss, as though they had no prefixed mission. Dark and sexually avaricious Irina, whose voice is "silky" whenever she is preparing to lie to somebody, persuades her sexual slave Hellman, who has bad body odour, to pretend not to see Hew and Jayne's SOS beacon, so she (Irina) can become very wealthy by continuing her long-distance partnership with Marty (who has persuaded Hew's pa to finance a Mars scam he's running), and they (Irina and Hellman) soon hijack the ship and return Earth-wards (but *miss the planet*, which is *just* the comeuppance they deserved). Meanwhile Hew and Jayne have settled their silly differences on the surface of Mars, and sleep together, though they're a bit bothered by the illness which intermittently afflicts them and which is carried by a mysterious Mars bug (but forget it, the book does), while at the same time being very much chuffed by the discovery of precious metals in portable lumps on the surface, which Hew decides to take back with him to Earth *in the crashed lander* in an attempt to persuade the authorities back home to rescue the other guys and gals who have been reported dead by Irina and Hellman, but they're *not* dead, but then Hew, having piloted himself all the way back to Earth, crashes into an ocean and the lander sinks, along with the precious metals, and no one will believe he's really Hew, no one can think of a way to identify him (even though, like any astronaut, he's probably one of the best tested, stamped, fingerprinted, coded and documented humans in history) until a member of his family sees him on television and says Hey that's Hew! Whew! A *brand-new* spaceship is quickly put together, and Hew returns to Mars, and *sneaks up* on the habitat where the surviving members of the first crew are cooking gruel, and surprises them a lot, and Jayne runs into his arms, and the book ends.

And the prisoner in the mask is never born.

– *Interzone* 63, September 1992

Beaks and Saws

1.

THERE ARE TIMES, after reading a story by Lisa Tuttle, that you feel such a fool. Sometimes, if you are male, it is because you are a man: and she has, with an air of reasoning calm, once again enfiladed the patchwork shell of self that you (as a male) wrap yourself in like some sinner out of Hieronymous Bosch, naked as an egg within, awaiting the great beak of day. Sometimes, if you are an incautious and trusting reader looking for a genre dawdle in the shallows of Romance, it is because she has opened something beneath you that simultaneously numbs and awakens. And sometimes, if you are either of these (or someone else), it is because you wonder how she managed to trick you, once again, into believing her heart was in the job. Standing behind all these ways of being fooled is a single conclusion: Lisa Tuttle, who has published widely and competently and for a long time, and who always keeps her diction and her pacing and her choice of subject under a seemingly unflappable housekeeperly control, is in fact a most dizzyingly uneven writer.

The worst of Tuttle is in neither book on review – *Lost Futures* (Grafton, 1992) and *Memories of the Body: Tales of Desire and Transformation* (Severn House, 1992) – and a couple of the tales assembled in the second volume are as ravaging as anything she's written; but at the same time the chance to see so much of her work at once begins to operate in strange ways on the reader. En masse, her stories (and the current novel, which is told in the same voice, and deals with the same patterns of obsession and oppressive self-avowal) force the reader into a kind of confrontation with the persona that so implacably does the telling. No (says the reader) that story isn't good enough for you to tell it, and if I want to read about Love and Loneliness and Stuff I'd just as soon gobble up a proper Romance that ends in his (her) arms, thank you very much. Yes (says the reader) this story is better than one could have believed you were about to let on, in that unwavering voice of yours, in that competent quietude of diction you hide within, naked as an egg. Yes or No, the voice is the same.

Lost Futures (it reads in some ways as a kaleidoscopic reshuffle and blow-up of "Riding the Nightmare" from the new volume of stories) evokes both responses: No to the placebo abstractions of romance diction; Yes to the engrossing hook of the basic premise, and to the unflagging energy with which it is worked out. No to the ending, in which the derangedness at the heart of the tale takes, as it were, a break for tea. Yes to the ferocity of attention to the extremities of the psyche, a ferocity which only slackens in those final pages. The story is not simple. Clare Beckett is 33, unmarried, an accountant in a small city in the state of New York, a muffled survivor of various relationships. Her life has been shadowed – indeed it may have been terminally shaped – by a traumatic event in her adolescence, which has fastened itself upon her (or which she has fastened onto). Left as a teenager by her parents to take care of her ill brother, she has lost her virginity to a friend just as her brother is dying of sugar loss. Whether or not his death can be understood as genuinely her fault is not entirely clear; but as far as she is concerned, the action of her life stopped short at that moment, and she has subsequently been unable consciously to make any further decisions which might constitute yet another dreadful turn. However, as a mathematician she is convinced that the universe itself is constantly splitting into a growing near-infinity of parallel worlds: that each quantum "turn" of a particle, or a life, generates two worlds; and so on towards infinity. So when she suffers a mental breakdown, and begins to experience, in the form of dreams, prolonged flashes of immersion in parallel versions of her own life, she recognizes that she may in fact be making leaps to worlds which represent some of the alternate life choices she could never decide to embrace.

It is all very carefully done. Tuttle knows sf and fantasy very thoroughly indeed, and establishes with surgeonly nicety an ongoing ambivalence as to whether or not Clare is psychotic or in fact experiencing a variety of worlds: one where she has made a proper career choice and become a professional mathematician; another where she has married and divorced; a third where she is a psychotic invalid whose refusal to pay heed to anything but her own state Tuttle superbly conveys (the invalid serves as an exaggerated version of Clare's own ruthlessly self-involved psyche: for the excesses of guilt Clare expresses about her brother contrive to retain him as her chattel); and finally a reality where cross-world turns by "oneironauts" like her are widely accepted and are of intense interest to professional investigators. As the novel progresses, the psychotic invalid psyche begins to invade the "prime" narrative world, entraps Clare in a dystopian hell of psychosis, moves the tale towards its diminishingly neat climax. Everything is paced to a nicety; the voice of the author adheres unwaveringly to its canny tessitura. But there is no spasm, no sense – as in Joanna Russ's similarly constructed The Female Man (1975) – of a tale just barely holding itself together against the deranging stresses of its every meaning. The Female Man is a sum greater than the derangement of its parts; Lost Futures, for all its unblinking meritoriousness as a portrait of the maw of the human psyche, does no more than add up.

And when, as sometimes happens in Memories of the Body, there is not much to add up to, one does find oneself thinking in terms of underachievement, unevenness. "A Mother's Heart: A True Bear Story" (1978), "Jamie's Grave" (1987), the Aickmenesque "Skin Deep" (1989): all share a neatness which is, in the end, too snug a fit. The trouble is, they sound just like the great stories in the book. They fool you. They trick you into raising them in your mind's eye to the level of their diction, which is too high for them; more seriously, they act to persuade you, after the fact, to reduce the three or four superb tales in the volume downwards to the "normalcy" of Tuttle's narrative voice. Which allows one to forget – or never to notice – the great gap between the worst and the best of Tuttle's work. "The Wound" (1987), "Memories of the Body" (1987) (though it closes with a series of dulling sententiae), "Riding the Nightmare" (1986), "Husbands" (1990) and "Lizard Lust" (1990) are among the very best short stories published in the last decade. Once freed from the gossip of context, they are as polished as habitats in space: machines to pack lives into. The portraits of the male psyche they present are stinging but fascinated. The women in the stories tend to wear placid guises, but are in fact ravenous for self, sex, role, being. The men are masks that beg for stripping; the women are aborning. The stories work as ideograms, couched in harsh-lit fantasy terms, of the jigsaw of the sexes at this time. They are savage, regret-filled, funny (as in "Lizard Lust"), and as shaped as lieder. They are what it should always mean to write like Lisa Tuttle.

II.

There are two strikes against *Æstival Tide* (Bantam, 1992) by Elizabeth Hand. It is a second novel, and it is the second volume of a sequence. *Winterlong* (1990) [see p. 271] was a huge, intense, verbose and murmurous harlequinade of a tale set in an America deluged by holocausts, and suffered mainly from inattentiveness to narrative flow, so that the reader tended to shoal every few pages, gasping for the oxygen of a sentence which said And then, O Dearly Beloved. *Æstival Tide* is set in the same America, a land so densely irradiated by the consequences of various cataclysms that nothing is left but excavation and topsyturvy suture. There is nothing new in the world, nothing to build with but bones and recirculated grue, nothing to do that has not proved wanting, again and again. It sounds like inanition and shoals; it sounds like the old Dying Earth entropy saw. It is not. Though there are things unjelled about the book, *Æstival Tide* is in fact – unlike its predecessor – an effective story, a dovetailing narrative crescendo, each page just slightly faster than the previous, with every character moving, more and more quickly, to the moment of climax at the eponymous festival, where all the plotlines (the effect just barely avoids an effect of seemingly unintentional vaudeville) knit valorously together as various protagonists arrive by air, elevator, sea and tunnel at the great gate which opens ritually once a decade to expose the citizens of the ziggurat city of Araboth to the outdoor world, when everyone is supposed to have a good orgy on the beach, and abhor the consequences, and go inside again. But this time there is no city to return to, as a great tsunami engulfs the wicked burg in the final pages, and the evil protagonists kick the bucket (except for those who don't), and the good guys slingshot

shot out of the last sentence into the sequel.

It is not entirely unsilly. The contortuplicated nine-level city – each level called after one of the degrees of the heavenly host, and each containing a designated class of citizen – is in fact *risible*. But *Æstival Tide* is not intended to work as a commentary on arcology design, or on the psychology of the pocket universe; Araboth is far more like a Theatre of Memory than a blueprint of post-holocaust urban life, and the interbreeding gouaches of knowledge it encodes relate almost exclusively to genre. Like its predecessor, the book is a multifaceted homage to, and mutation from, the energized lore of sf. Particular names and titles come to mind – T J Bass's *The Godwhale* (1974) for the cetacean; John Crowley's *Engine Summer* (1979) for the memorious crystalline figure which tells the story of itself and others whenever activated; *Flash Gordon* (the movie) for post-Nazi halls of assemblage; Richard Grant (who lives with Hand) for the Villiers de L'Isle Adam/Mervyn Peake asthenic architect; Paul Park's *Sugar Rain* (1989) for weather that ends a city in a welter of smells; Gene Wolfe's *The Book of the New Sun* (1980–83) for the vocabulary which evokes time's aisles and for other things, too – but this is only a beginning, because the book is a constant fractal unfolding of itself and its germinations. *Æstival Tide* is a hive; and should breed more.

III.

John Kessel, too, engages in the saw trade, and the stories assembled in *Meeting in Infinity: Allegories & Extrapolations* (Arkham House, 1992) come at times close enough, through an analogous overloading of text, to the risible. (We exclude "Faustfeathers," whose humour is entirely deliberate, and which may be the funniest Marx Brothers story ever written.) But Kessel knows exactly what he's doing, knows that allegories generally bite the hands that feed them [unlike crocodiles 1995]. He knows very well that stories constructed so that they are amenable to allegorical readings – so that it is possible to *translate* them "upwards" from a radical of presentation where what they are is what they mean, to one in which what they mean is what they *aspire to* – always risk a compensating descent into bathos. For there seems to be an inherent solemnity to the acting out of allegorical heightening, and a story like "The Lecturer," which *might* be intended as hilarious, struggles in vain against the essential piety of the uplift dynamic, so that the accreted meanings which stack themselves onto our reading of the implications of the image of the talking statue of a lecturer ends in what does seem an involuntary image out of, perhaps, Dr. Seuss: hat upon hat: too many hats upon the head. All crooked. All tame.

But most of the stories escape the problem of the piling on of hats. "Not

Responsible! Park and Lock It!" is more complex than can be described, which may in the end be a sign of the successful allegory. It embodies metaphors of the highway as life, and of a kind of post-holocaust America as Hell, in the tale of the rite of passage into adulthood of one "realistically" conceived boy. Nothing is pointed out; everything wells up. "Judgment Call," too, though heavily freighted with equations, rests within itself. "The Big Dream" is an unfeignedly savage assault on Raymond Chandler; "Another Orphan," the best-known story in the book, seems rather underpowered compared to Kessel's best work, and its use of *Moby Dick* to focus questions of human destiny seems etiolated, balsa. "Hearts Do Not in Eyes Shine" is, again, superb. "Man," again, is not. And "Invaders" killed sleep: so grippingly told that one could not avert one's reading gaze from the genocide inflicted by Spain upon the Aztecs; so ornately but precisely savage (Kessel is an astonishingly savage writer) about the exculpatory routines of sf. *Meeting in Infinity* is an uneven book, but one which – like good allegory – amounts to far more than the sum of its sometimes damagingly un-deranged parts. In the end, it is a book which grows the reader around it. I think I will be wearing it inside, from now on.

– Interzone 64, October 1992

Thin Ice, Sun Burns

I.

DAMON KNIGHT is thin ice. He is as smooth as ice, and it looks like you can see right through him, and maybe you'll manage to skid dry-shod all the way across the bridge of words to the other side. But then again, you may not. Or – as in the case of *Why Do Birds* (Books, 1992) – you may never know whether or not you made it: made the reading, made terminus unscathed, earned your aesthetic keep. It is rather like reading the most elusive of all younger genre writers, George Alec Effinger, whose books are also shaped like traps and smile like traps and butter wouldn't melt in his mouth and you never know for sure if you still have your pants. A late novel by Damon Knight dares you to read it, on past the warning sign, the sheepish skull. It is the dare of thin ice: that there may be nothing to fear, no moving water at the heart. A novel by Damon Knight takes the shape of a trap that just may not close.

Why Do Birds, for instance, seems to be a simple cautionary tale about the end of the world, with a few recursive tidbits tossed into the mix to maintain in genre readers a sense of comforting déjà vu, and all told in a tone of glassy serenity that slides you in and downwards with a sheepish grin. It is 2002. Ed Stone is being inter-

viewed by a prison psychiatrist after his arrest. His problem, he tells the psychiatrist, lies in his belief that aliens kidnapped him in 1931, when he was 30, and after
testing him have whisked him up to 2002 and desposited him back on Earth so that
he can persuade the authorities to build a huge box big enough to house the human
race, and to put every single person inside that box in a state of cryogenic slumber,
because the aliens will then return and take the box with them to another planet because this one is doomed because of all the bad things. This sure sounds crazy, Ed
Stone says, and 2002 sure seems pretty weird. Judas Priest, he adds. (It is a 1931 eu-
phemism for Jesus Christ.) The only thing I have on my side, he says, is the ring the
aliens gave me. If I shake hands with anyone, and touch them with my ring, they'll
do anything in the world for me.

And so it is. Ed Stone shakes hands a few times, walks out of prison, gathers a
retinue around him (it has some resemblance to the cadre which surrounds the
oddly similar and serene superchild protagonist of *The Man in the Tree* [1984]), engages in some interesting discussions about the logistics of building a box enormous enough to hold the race in, gets the box built and the corpsicle-accessioning
process properly underway, and the plot thickens. Evidence begins to mount that
Ed Stone is in fact a charlatan and has based much of his description of the aliens
on "Dark Moon," a novella by Charles W Diffin published in *Astounding Science Fiction*
in May 1931 (a true ascription, by the way: Diffin existed, and so did "Dark Moon,"
and so did the Wesso cover). But nobody has any explanation for the magic ring,
though "three A-team whores" (ie ace expert witnesses hired to defend Stone
against accusations that he's a fraud), think the ring may contain one of the "natu-
rally occurring neurochemicals in human beings" that pass down from parent to
child and account for the stability of prejudices and for the low apostasy rate among
Mormons, whose children tend to remain secluded in family bondage until early
adulthood, hence avoiding exposure to other ideas "and other *neurochemicals*" until
it's far too late: they're stone-bonded Mormons: fixed for good. But this does not
explain *why* Ed Stone would wish to persuade the human race to get into a box.

The only reason for his doing so, of course, is that the world is indeed going to
end, and does. And the book shrugs to an elegiac halt, and the curtain falls. The
smile of the telling has never faltered, the calm off-the-cuff unfolding of the slow
and strangely undramatic tale, as though it were an anecdote, a gossip, a crackerbarrel Chorus at Thebes. "And then I noticed he'd done something to his eyes,
clawed them out I reckon. Judas Priest." And you discover, at the end, that the secret
of thin ice in 1992 is that no trap is necessary. Everything I have told you, says the
book, everything you ever feared to dream, is true. Under the sheepish serenity of its

surface, *Why Do Birds* conveys a most extraordinary charge of melancholy. In the valley of the shadow of death (it seems to say) there is no need to waste time with sharpened spikes. It is enough for a reader to enter the book (to be alive in this year), to read the book through (to stay alive long enough in this world to see the course of things), and to shut the page down (and to shut the page down).

11.

Sean McMullen, an Australian (b 1948) who makes his living as a computer systems analyst, has been publishing short stories since 1986, and in *Call to the Edge* (Aphelion Publications, 1992) presents a gathering of his work. The effect is very peculiar. It is possible to notice – it is in fact impossible not to notice – that McMullen is something of a crank hand when it comes to plotting and to characterization. Several of the stories – "The Eyes of the Green Lancer," "The Deciad" and "While the Gate is Open" in particular – accumulate such a supercharge of imperfectly clear exposition that by their jumbled conclusions it is very nearly impossible to follow the instructions of the text, and understand anything at all. But at the same time "The Eyes of the Green Lancer," for most of its length, is deeply enthralling, because McMullen, unlike most writers in 1992, is desperately interested in devices: wind-sail trains; computers iconographically similar to but of an eccentricity far more intriguing than the Difference Engine embedded into the Gibson/Sterling novel of that name: intricacies of contrivance described with a hobbyist's zeal (but in the case of this story without anything of the obliviousness of the hobbyist to the folk who have to listen). So he is something of an ancient mariner as he stoppeth. He can be, on occasion, something of a bore. But when he gets his teeth into Device, and manages to have a story which embodies Device without interminable coulisses of explanation, then he can sound like Keith Roberts with a world to make.

– *Interzone* 66, December 1992

Teething the Gap

FOR A WHILE, it seemed there would be no hope. *The Gap Into Conflict: The Real Story* (1990), which constituted a kind of prologue to a projected five-volume sequence of space operas by Stephen R. Donaldson, seemed to be one of the worst single books ever published by a writer of interest who had not yet become senile. Its shortness did nothing to moderate the congested bewilderment and ennui it inflicted on readers – it's been noted before that Donaldson works best at considerable length, and it seems almost certain that the leaden brevity of the thing contributed to the sense of desperately ill-at-ease toothlessness *The Real Story* generated, the sense that it could gum any reader into wax. One might go on: about the infelicity of a book which regurgitates synopsis from the depths of the third stomach and calls it Story; about the stumblebum weensiness of the space opera universe deployed (it features *asteroid belts* apparently in the middle of interstellar space, for there is no mention of a single star or solar system or term of magnitude: an imaginative vacuum in which props like mining colonies and ore ships and saloons and *pirates* and cops and cadets flail about, perspectiveless and mute: and in which the Story, having been inserted as a much-told and retold *Legend of Space*, jumps, like a frog on a table, only when galvanized); about the cloying jaw-jaw of a narrative strategy which apes the Wagnerian retrospective monologue (more about Wagner in a moment) but which fails to capture the essence of how it is conveyed – fails to present any analogue of the live-snake *presentness* of the leitmotifs that sustain the Wagnerian tale from underneath. One could go on: but it would be a mistake to do so. Because all of this is wrong.

It's not wrong that the book is awful, for awful it truly is. What is wrong is to assume that the paralyzed belatedness of the thing was in fact unintended. This is not to say that Donaldson could have deliberately tried to evoke the powerful negative response to his art that has crippled more than one reader's enjoyment; it is, rather, to suggest that the legend-recollected-in-tranquillity, club-story ambience of the narrative voice, and the black ritardando-before-the-fact obduracy of the whole tale's untoldedness, were clearly meant as a kind of combined incipit and anchor. *The Gap into Conflict: The Real Story* (and here we return to leitmotif) looks like an attempt to encode within a single verbal "chord" the entirety of an unfolding epic, just as Wagner encoded the whole of the music of the *Ring Cycle* in the opening notes of *Das Rheingold*. The sound-universe of the *Ring* is, as a consequence, unmistakeable. Whether or not the story-universe of the Gap sequence will come to be seen as direct verbal consequence of its opening shots, we cannot yet say, because we are only part way there. Last year saw *The Gap Into Vision: Forbidden Knowledge* (1991), and now, with *The Gap Into Power: A Dark and Hungry God Arises* (Bantam, 1992), we do begin to feel the rhythm of the thing, we begin to understand that something both heavy and adventurous has invaded our minds. [*The Gap Into Madness: Chaos and Order* (1994) soon followed: I am myself awaiting the closing instalment before attempting a final assessment 1995]

So we're in medias res. A few things can be said. After reading its first two successors, *The Gap Into Conflict: The Real Story* begins to soften in the memory as the tale – or chord – it makes such an odd meal of simplifies in the mind's eye. A space-cop named Morn Hyland suffers gap sickness – gaps are doubletalk openings in space which make interstellar travel possible; and gap sickness is a mysterious response to travelling through the gap which makes its victims behave strangely – and has blown up the space patrol cruiser on which she's serving, along with all the rest of her family. Angus Thermopyle, an extremely ugly pirate who was on the run from the space patrol cruiser, captures Morn, along with her zone implant – a device which allows her to control her gap sickness, but which in the hands of others allows them to control *her* – and makes her into his sexual slave. But his ship has been damaged, and he cannot escape the general region (which, given Donaldson's vacuity about locations, could be anywhere) of the asteroid belt, and for this reason, and due to other complications, he allows Morn to escape from him into the arms of his great enemy, the extremely handsome pirate Nick Succorso, who also takes her in every way possible: she has her zone implant control back, and uses it to make herself into his sexual slave, so as to keep him from killing her (don't forget she's a cop). But soon she discovers, to her horror, that Nick is moving his ship in the direction of Forbidden Space, which is somewhere left of the asteroid belt, and in which the dread shapechanger (or mutagenic) Amnion reside. Meanwhile Angus is put in prison.

The plot thickens in a slow crescendo that by slow increments crowds the stage with principals and extras, all of whom thrust prognathously into the text. The second and third volumes are less easy to follow, more gripping, and faster. We are introduced to various prime-mover characters – the director of the United Mining Company Police (impassive, secretly melancholic, one-eyed Warden Dios, who eschews longevity treatments and is a dead ringer for Wagner's Wotan: who ages in the *Ring*) and his top executives; and Holt Fasner, CEO of the United Mining Company itself, an inconceivably rich man who staves off ageing and who is nicknamed the Dragon. All these prime-movers display conflicting agendas about the three protagonists of the first volume, each of whom is complexly (and in general covertly) engaged in dealings with most of the powers that be. Morn finds she is pregnant by Angus. (Those of us who are not Americans, and who do not therefore know God as well as they do, may find it hard to immediately understand why she refuses – under circumstances when her survival, and maybe the fate of the whole human race, almost certainly depends on her being fit – to abort a foetus conceived in rape and slavery: but of course refuse she does, after some internalized "debate.") Nick takes her to the dread station in Forbidden Space of the mutagenic Amnion, with whom he has had intricate dealings, and whom he has previously betrayed, and the foetus is brought to term and thence to adulthood in the space of an hour; to give its tabula rasa brain a structure, Morn's own mind is implanted on her son's, a process which should drive her insane: but her zone implant saves her by making her super-natually serene. Her son (Siegfried?: the appalling Angus, Donaldson has already told us, is Siegmund) thinks he's her, but begins gradually to become himself.

The plot thickens. By the time we have reached *The Gap Into Vision: A Dark and Hungry God Arises*, it has become too frayed and fast to synopsize, beyond indicating that the mise en scène is now Billingate, a criminal refueling and refitting station in Forbidden Space (whose distance from and spatial relation to Earth Donaldson has not yet divulged), where Morn and Nick arrive in one ship and chased by the Am-nion, who have been cheated by both of them, in two more ships; where Angus soon arrives as well, after having been fitted with his own zone implants and super-hero prosthetics by Warden Dios back on Earth; but Angus is under the control of Milos, a weasely traitor in the cops' employ; and we must not forget Sorus, the female pirate who scarred Nick, years earlier. She's there. And so is Morn's son. And the owner of Billingate. And some extras. And the plot thickens.

From the beginning of the sequence, and for 1000 pages, we have been subject-ed to what has become an utterly relentless and bravura crescendo (Brian Stable-ford, reviewing the second volume in *Interzone* 57, remarks on the Donaldson cre-scendo, correctly, I think, characterizing it as unique in the literature for intensity: though it may be that the new Gene Wolfe tetralogy, beginning with *Nightside the Long Sun* (1993), will provide an analogous case). In the grips of a complex story none of them understand, and a crescendo they all feel building in their savaged and weary bones, every single character in the sequence operates under some terri-ble duress. Everyone is imprisoned, or zone-implanted, or bribed, or trapped, or betraying, or without money, or fuel, or a gap drive, or sleep, or a gun. Everyone has been driven to the edge of endurance. Everyone sweats fear, loathing, self-betrayal, anguish, *heat*. And no one knows what anyone else knows, or who is in bondage to whom, or what anyone is committed to accomplish, or on whose behalf any of the betrayals and reversals (there are very many of these) have been prepared. An aston-ishingly high proportion of this extremely long text is taken up with *lies* – lies told to, for, by, or in the presence of, the main actors, and always at the risk of death if a cover is blown, a deception exposed, a desperation admitted. Nor are we anywhere close to the end. *The Gap* is a nightmare of stress – in fact *stress* may be the key word, it is often reiterated in the text, in any attempt to understand the ramifications of what Donaldson may ultimately mean by the *Gap* itself – and it seems to have no ending. The sequence, which began as a lugubrious waxworks, has become a blow between the eyes, an aesthetic Somme: it does not stop marching into the guns of the next sentence. It is a terminal book, a tale of terminus.

What it all has to do with Wagner, we should perhaps wait to find out. Analogies between human and inhuman characters (Donaldson has already told us that the Amnion are Wagner's dwarves) and the cast of the *Ring Cycle* are rife, but weirdly multivalent, viscous. Doppelgänger flashes – Loki equals Hashi Lebwohl? Brunnhilde equals Min Donner? – *seem* to float into view, but then the analogies fade, and there is no time to think. It may come clear in the end; it may not (Donaldson is not an open writer, and the essay he has written on his sources of inspiration for the sequence – it appears at the end of volume one – is not very helpful). But we are left with something of a small miracle. At the end of volume one, few of us (I'd guess) would have given very good odds on anyone ever being haunted by Angus or Morn or Nick. At the end of volume three, all of them (and a dozen more, but Angus Thermopyle in particular) have become, like indigestive dreams, nightmares at the gape. Our gap will be to look back.

– Interzone 67, January 1993

Exogamy Dentata

I.

IT WOULD BE nice to think we already knew the truth about the death of sf, and to speak of other things. It would be immensely *calming*, for instance – because the tale is so smooth and round and fully packed – to speak nothing but sage praise of Robert Charles Wilson's *The Harvest* (Doubleday Foundation, 1992), saying What a good read are you! But (it is the curse of Adam) we cannot do so, because *The Harvest* is not only a good read, it is a tocsin. It may be as smooth as the mothering ice before the skate, but when you put your ear to what it says a tinnitus of aftermath sings you down, a voice from chill Canada in cold waters.

What you are hearing is requiescat. What you are being told (what Robert Charles Wilson is confirming from the Pacific Rim of Canada to which he moved) is that genre sf [First SF 1995], and the elevator shoes it stood on to peer into the platform of the future, has become an afterimage in the mind's eye: a relic of another time [and the wrong Story of the next 1995]: an echo staffed by golems in the fields of sharecrop, doing good lunch with dinosaurs: because Western Civilization's perception of time's arrow, over the course of the twentieth century, has changed almost totally. What we once saw as a River flowing futurewards through a stepped landscape, we now see as a Delta, where salt and fresh streams exchange their juices in the night, islands of repose appear and disappear, creole banter mocks our tongue, and we do not know where to stand on Now, or how to live on the steel beach Tomorrow. It has been a sea-change of great profundity, a systemic disordering, a change of perception through which the sf we once knew seems about as predictive as Neville Chamberlain, or Andy Hardy. Genre sf now looks back (in the popular phrase) to the wrong future. It has become a formal exercise, through which it has become all too terribly easy to encode a refusal of the next day, while pretending to command it. Some novels which *sound* like genre sf – like Kim Stanley Robinson's *Red Mars* (1992) – very nearly (and in this case very bravely) transcend rancour and belatedness through the ardour of their claim to tell stories we can climb to, up the tightrope to a new world. Wiser – or maybe less brave – writers like Kim Newman dance shy of the future altogether; the alternate histories of Kim Newman are profoundly unsciencefictional in the old sense, because they are anecdotes of eternal return, cycles into the foxhole of the past. They appeal to us (they assuredly appeal to me) because they seem so very contemporary. Sf today has its back turned.

Indeed, for the guys who wrote the old sf, Cyberpunk must seem just another word for vagina dentata. 1993 must seem a terribly *female* world to the dreamers of genre, this musky delta of the fresh and the salt, this pathless peneplain so utterly baffling to elevator shoes, where the frontier has become a levee, and the levee a rune. It is no wonder, perhaps, that there is so much Canadian sf around these days. Cyberpunk itself – or at any rate the Cyberpunk tendency exemplified by the work of William Gibson, who lives not too far from Robert Charles Wilson – is a deeply Canadian response to the new world. Canadian sf has never been a literature of frontier; its heroes (the protagonists of A E Van Vogt, the lonely supermen of Gordon R Dickson, Gibson's Case) do not crash through the barriers of the unknown, found empires, breed dynasties, like the Yankee heroes of E E Smith or Robert A Heinlein or Larry Niven. The Canadians' route to power is transcendental [see also p. 55]. If they manage to escape from the Wilderness of the world, it is by becoming Elect (in the heart of cyberspace, Case finds something like nirvana) in one bound. And if they marry, they marry out.

Robert Charles Wilson's newest novel, *The Harvest*, is on all these counts a very Canadian book. We are in Pacific Northwest, in something like the present day. The human race is as we know it, and a background susurrus of distress gives signals that the planet is as we know it, as well. But from the first page we are in a condition of belatedness: as though the decisions that count had already been taken. This proves accurate, for the event which serves as the central triggering occasion of the novel – the arrival in Earth orbit of a vast ship bearing a collective sentience – has occurred just *before* the start of the tale. (Nothing could be more Canadian than that: to have the spring of action of a book exist as an apriori administrative fait accompli.) Within a short period of time, the sentience has infiltrated the entire human race with neocytes, molecule-sized quasi-mechanical devices or entities which, after they have thoroughly housed themselves, are poised to enact a kind of nano-transubstantiation on each human being. What this transubstantiation offers to each human being – as the sentience puts it through a planet-wide dream each individual human shares – is immortality, wisdom, a slightly crepuscular calm that does not exclude passion and love as well, a quasi-cyberspace-like access to a near infinitude of data and praxis, a virtual-reality reconstruction of the planet within a vast spacecraft to be constructed by transfigured humans for their own purposes, and an infinity of space to wander in, learning all the while, in a dance of Being. It is the ultimate marriage offer, the ultimate chance of exogamy for the race.

In a genre sf novel of the old school, it is easy to guess what might happen: the offer would either turn out to be a snare; or the human race would divide into affectless (though immortal) sheep and quintessentially human singleton goats, whose mortality would somehow be both glorified and dodged. But Wilson is a contemporary writer, and a Canadian by choice, and in The Harvest only one in 10,000 says no to the chance to transcend the toxicity of our mortal coil, and to become Elect; and there is nothing in the course of the tale to hint that the 9,999 are wrong. The narrative itself – which concentrates on a small American coastal city, and on the handful of refusers who live there – makes it pretty clear, in fact, that it is those who have voted negatively whose motives are suspect, whose selfhoods are almost necessarily tainted or contorted or blocked. After all, what sane person could *reject* a chance to escape the downside of the human condition – this squalid quarrel of the mortal soul within the flesh, this bug in a bean of dying? Very very few, says the book; and examines – through the course of the tale it tells – a few examples.

Matt Wheeler, a doctor much in love with grief and with the feel of the physical world and with his home town, says no; as do a few others: a Christian; two teenagers sunk in self-despite and vandalism (another Canadian note, one is afraid); a couple of foetid hangers-on; and, in another part of the country, a nearly insane pedophile ex-Colonel who has spent the last several years liaising amongst his contacts in the military and intelligence community for the profit of favoured foreign states. We also spend time with the American President, who has said Yes, and undergo a vast typhoon, and eavesdrop occasionally on the Elect as they prepare to discard their bodies (although they are always free to don flesh again, pro tem, for a moment or an aeon); and the plot moves with considerable cunning and great smoothness towards an elegiac close. Unfortunately, Wilson's fatal flaw – he has an as yet unbreakable habit, whenever he reaches climax point, of betraying his plots and his characters and his readers with utterly tedious writing-school hooks and tricks – once again drives him into a destructive slickness. The American president – this is one of the high moments of the tale – has commanded his neocytes to transform him into a younger self, into a twelve-year-old Huck, who gets on his bicycle and lights out across an America almost totally abandoned by the sayers of Yes. It may seem trite as described, but the short vision Wilson allows us of this return to the American Dream is radiant and assured and clean of heart. Then – here the trouble begins – Huck meets, by accident, Matt Wheeler and his fellow mortals, who are trekking eastwards (not a very American direction) to Ohio, where a small community of refusers is being founded. This is bad enough, but within a page we discover that the mad colonel has *also* come across Matt Wheeler and the gang, and has insinuated himself into command, and is about to corrupt them and do all sorts of Plot Stuff all over the remainder of the book, when all we wanted was to understand the gist of things and to pass onwards to the quietus of the last sentence: but now we've got to pretend to be *alarmed* at the threats that clever Mr Wilson has contrived; we've got to pretend to *worry* about Huck and Matt and the nice girl the colonel is about to *violate* in a seriously unmanly way; we've got to pretend to *believe* this malarkey when all the while we could be dreaming of the great marriage outwards.

Fortunately, Wilson manages to extricate himself from his Despite before it is entirely too late, and the novel resumes its course downwards to the depths of iconoclasm: for it is, in the end, a tale which utterly refuses the sf it wears the clothes of; or, perhaps more productively, it might be said that *The Harvest* is an example – one of the clearest yet – of an sf genre which has begun to adapt itself to the futures which surround us, bearing cargo to the terrenes.

[I insert here a review of David Ketterer's factual analysis of Canadian sf and fantasy, because it was written at about the same time as the comments above, and addresses some of the same issues 1995.]

NO CANADIAN (I am one) could pick up this handsome and intensive conspectus of Canadian sf and fantasy, composed by an academic who has spent his career in

Canada, without instantly noticing that *Canadian Science Fiction and Fantasy* (Indiana University Press, 1992) was published in the USA, by an American university, and that it was priced in American dollars. It is the sort of thing Canadians notice. It is the sort of thing – this younger-sibling consciousness of being a citizen of a side-lined voyeur culture – that causes so many Canadians (I was one) ingloriously to de-camp, while young, in the direction of oxygen, downstream, south, into the wet. Because it is very expensive to be a Canadian.

David Ketterer does not want to talk about that cost too much. He does not wish to explore any too deeply – nor was it his brief to do so – the history of Canada, which is in fact no history at all but a sequence of footnotes or memoranda append-ed to the histories of the UK and of the USA. Canada (by which for the moment we mean English Canada) is a land, in other words, where essence is extrinsic to exist-ence, whose stories are borrowed (and secretly resented), whose population ap-plied for the job and were assigned lives: *literally*: the Canadian West was not settled by men and women bursting through a frontier: it was *assigned* to applicants by the large companies and authorities already administrating the "empty" territories on behalf of a colonial government.

"America's aggressive attitude toward nature and the unknown," Ketterer al-lows himself to say in a neat prelusory front essay,

> whatever lay west of the ever-advancing frontier, translates readily into the mythology of conquering and domesticating the unknown that finds expres-sion in much SF. The Canadian attitude seems to be that nature is simply too vast, too threatening, too powerful: man is nature's victim rather than the re-verse. Survival, not conquest, is the issue. The best that can be hoped for is some kind of accommodation.

The result was an sf which eschewed the unknown, except under very specific con-ditions – conditions which govern even an ex-American like William Gibson. In Canadian sf the unknown, or the Wilderness, remains untampered with, unchal-lenged, unpenetrated, unmarried, illegible; the protagonists of Canadian sf remain solitary and marginal and mute, impostors in a mass of "normals," trespassers into territories they do not own; and the world they live in remains at heart unpopulous, they have no buddies, there are no teams. These restrictions obtain until one of two conditions are met: 1) the protagonist, through a process of solitary transcendence or some other *invisible enablement*, may become a Superman (as in Van Vogt or Dickson); or 2) the protagonist may hack into the real world for Cargo (like Case in *Neuromancer*) and suck tit.

There are, Ketterer estimates, about 1200 Canadian works of sf and fantasy, written either in French or English, though he does recognize (with what seems a touch of embarrassment) that the Canadian tendency to recruit figures like Brian Moore (who spent 11 years in the country) does tend to distort any statistic; and he mentions a fair percentage of that 1200 in his 170 tight pages of narrative. His coverage of French-Canadian sf seems (to a typical English Canadian born into a system which did not willingly teach its children to speak Canadian French, or any other foreign language for that matter) exemplary, though tantalizing. Montreal is a city on an island, and Quebec is itself a linguistic island in an estranging sea of English, and it is clear that much Quebec sf and fantasy is shaped around a central set of island/archipelago metaphors, which Ketterer makes lucid mention of in passing, but which I would have very much appreciated hearing more about: because there is no other national sf based on the model of the island. It seems, therefore, intensely interesting; and *Canadian Science Fiction and Fantasy* is worth the reading for this discovery alone.

Canadian sf begins with James De Mille's *A Strange Manuscript Found in a Copper Cylinder* (1888), which was first published in the USA, then the UK; slips into the 20th century in the guise of the prehistoric romance (there were a lot of them), with Frederick Philip Grove's *Consider Her Ways* (1947 Canada) serving as a sidebar; then moves into an uneasy, morganatic flirtation with the American genre; and we are in 1992. Ketterer suggests, pretty tentatively, that the Canadian diffidence about the Wilderness of the world may seem comparatively sane, as the century ends in feeding frenzies. Another thought comes to mind, too. It is not necessary to believe that SETI will ever manage to eavesdrop on a better world, or that if aliens did descend upon us humanity would commit suicide, as any Tiptree story demonstrates, in paroxysms of failed exogamy; but if we do end up having to kneel before the majesty of the thing to come, some of us can tell the rest of you about living with the owners.

– *New York Review of Science Fiction*, 1992

[I now return to the *Interzone* column 1995.]

II.

Of the two extremely clever novel-length tales assembled by A S Byatt in *Angels and Insects* (Chatto & Windus, 1992), who won the Booker Prize for *Possession* (1990), the second might seem to have some generic interest, being about ghosts and the language and behaviour of people in the nineteenth century who are embrocated in the supernatural; but this story, "The Conjugal Angel," seems unduly contorted for its content, and gives off the wrought-iron infarct feel so often found in litfant attempts to acquire the gone. There is no cycling into the foxhole of the past in this story, nothing muggy with life, nor any impertinence. But the first of the long tales assembled here, "Morpho Eugenia," is something else altogether. It is a perfect demonstration of the virtues of knowing too much. Or, to put it another way, it is a perfect exercise in doing what we can with the past, which is precisely to know it as an object of dissection, though it can't of course be lived, we cannot for the life of us truly re-inhabit the mind-set of the protagonist, William Adamson, an upwardly mobile biologist caught in the amber of the rural England of 1860, nor that of the master of the large country home to which he has come as a working visitor (he is fresh from the Amazon, and has survived a shipwreck in which a decade of zoological specimens was lost), nor that of the master's daughter, whose eventual marriage to the protagonist is a cover for ungovernable incest. But knowledge – and the forms and conventions of knowing – is what "Morpho Eugenia" is entirely, and with dizzying profusion of detail, shaped to anatomize.

Adamson (perhaps too coyly named), haunted by a decade spent naming and measuring the engorged profusion of the jungle and the great river, is almost as alien as we are; and his inveterate habit of observation leads him inexorably into perceptions of the great house and its serried inhabitants as comprising a society not dissimilar to the ant and termite societies his evolutionary theories have forced him to begin to understand as being blind of God, for there is no god in the 1860 of the tale, much though the master of the house longs to maintain arguments for a continuing deity. But Adamson's perceptions are partial, because – unlike Byatt, or her readers, or the protagonist of any modernist or postmodernist tale set in the present day – he does not conceive of himself as partaking in an artifice of Story. We, of course, know better. And it is the knowingness of the telling of Story that most allies *Angels and Insects* to the alternate histories of writers like (once again) Kim Newman in their foxhole homes. The surface story of "Morpho Eugenia" is a nineteenth-century romance of family which gradually becomes explicit about material (Adamson's bride's incest with her brother) which is not in fact tellable in that century: Byatt tells this story as straightforwardly as possible, without mocking its diction or the underlying Victorian patter-song of excessive plot: the tale, at this level, is a quotation of a tale, a parody with love. At the same time, however, Byatt lays a palimpsest of knowingly-timed analytical imagery over the "naïve" tale, the rhythms of which directly and unmistakeably invoke Ivy Compton-Burnett's grand guignol transformations of the Victorian romance of family into barbaric family romance. But Compton-Burnett worked her transformations out of personal anguish, personal knowledge of the termitarium of the Victorian family: Byatt, and her readers, can only know that life through art. So the tale, at this level, is a quotation of a tale which itself is a ransacking of the original tale.

It is through this laying-on of levels of quotation that we understand the knowingness of the text we read; and understand that we are *meant* simultaneously to understand, and perhaps to embrace, each intersecting level. We are meant, in other words, to know it all before we even start. As an example, take the incest. We are meant to know that the original tale is innocent of suspicion when, on the third page of the story, Adamson (himself innocent of the implications) notices that Eugenia and her brother Edgar dance well together. We are also meant to know that the Ivy Compton-Burnett level of the telling, at this point, has introduced a dreadful suspicion. But first and finally, we are meant immediately to know – because it is half a century later than the prime of Compton-Burnett, and the tale has (as it were) been told – that the suspicion is just. Every one of the 160 pages of the story enforces a similar tripleness of vision. It is as though the book were telepathic to itself. Unlike alternate history novels, it pays dues to the original story. Like them, it is a kind of virtual-reality game. Like them, it is a foxhole for the millennium.

III.

Only You Can Save Mankind (Doubleday, 1992) by Terry Pratchett, and *Dinosaur Junction* (Orchard, 1992) by Gwyneth Jones writing as Ann Halam, are juveniles, both set in the present day. In other words, they are tales of children who have to live here. Pratchett's hero, Johnny, child of a marriage about to dissolve, finds himself within the virtual reality of a computer wargame, and comes to understand that his opponents – rather like the Buggers in Orson Scott Card's *Ender's Game* (1985) – are both real and innocent of any wish to invade Earth. A dance of moral choices, and some neat action, ensues. There are jokes, and an underlying melancholy: because the frame of the tale is the world, not a Turtle. Halam's hero, Ben, rather younger than Johnny and dominated by his singularly well-conceived older sister, is obsessed by fossils, and while searching for dinosaur relics finds what may be (and probably is) a timeslip backwards to a primal sea, where the oppressions of contemporary life come to head, are sorted out, relieved for a moment. There is a stunning portrait, en passant, of a brilliant harum-scarum bad-tempered bachelor scientist who lives alone, and who in almost any previous children's book would glow like Merlin, save the bacon, become a beloved icon. Not here, not Gwyneth Jones, not now. *Dinosaur Junction* earns every calory of warmth it does finally, guardedly, at the end, share out.

IV.

Mostly Harmless (Heinemann, 1992) by Douglas Adams, which is the fifth volume of the Hitch Hiker's Guide to the Galaxy trilogy, continues to poison the well of humour. Like the slow drip of water in a shut cave, the jokes make small, exquisitely timed tinkles in the blackness beneath, but the blackness is rising, and the room for echoes lessens with each new joke; the water comes closer and closer to the savage rock roof, and the last bit of air is gone just before the end, the wiping out of another version of the planet, and black death for all: all drowned, drowned out of the book. It is, indeed, very funny, of course. Ford Prefect, and Arthur Dent, and most of the cast of the preceding volumes, all caper through a few more adventures: but they have been drowning from the first page on, and they know it, we know it, Douglas Adams knows it. And this may really be the end of Hitch Hiker. Vale. This time, I think there may be no antidote.

V.

[I have updated this section throughout 1995] The Science Fiction Foundation, which was founded 20 years ago here in the UK, and which now is now the premier English-language research resource in sf studies outside of North America, had been housed in the Barking Precinct of the Polytechnic of East London from 1972, but was given notice of eviction in 1992. Fortunately for all of us who care a damn, the University of Liverpool jumped at the chance to obtain the research resource and gain the prestige of housing the SFF, and the library moved there in early 1993. An Administrator (the old Poly – they now call themselves the University of East London – froze that position in 1981) has been appointed; and an MA course in sf is now being given. In late 1992, *Foundation: The Journal of Science Fiction* got away from the University of East London, no longer advertises that institution in any fashion, and is being produced separately by the same scholars as before. As an example of the kind of material to be found in the journal, it is easy to recommend *The Profession of Science Fiction: SF Writers on Their Craft and Ideas* (Macmillan, 1992) edited by Maxim Jakubowski and Edward James. It is a selection of autobiographical essays by sf writers, originally published between 1972 and 1990; most are substantial, and most are witty. Most of the authors are central to the genre. It is the sort of book the University of East London had no desire to associate itself with, and can therefore be recommended without reservation.

– *Interzone* 68, February 1993

Bat the Snatcher and the Porcine Undeads

1.

SO HERE WE ARE, sliding down the last decade, litany time in the Old West. Time to be brief. A few pages back (just above) we said something about traditional sf, which (we said) had begun to shrink from walking the plank into the near futures it no longer had the tools to apprehend, the millennium it had no will to breast. Traditional sf (we said) had become a kind of gated community, security-coded against the ethnics of tomorrow; and sf texts tended to display an antic mallworld toothlessness about dread, a eunuched downloading of the fear of the days to come into virtual reality havens. But enough of that. If traditional sf found the millennium gang too Third World to marry its daughters, then maybe some of the sibling genres (we thought, and mentioned Kim Newman) might be better buoyed against the riptides and the scum.

It is one of the kindlier assumptions of sf critics that alternate-history stories set in the past are in any salient way describable as sf at all. Those that use time travel to wryneck the world into a pale superflux of optional paths do, after all, profoundly assault a primal faith of most traditional sf writers (most of whom are dead): the belief that change *changed* things. Alternate-history stories undermine the conviction – it is the conviction upon which human beings most profoundly base their lives, and it is generally thought to be holy – that what is done is done. That what is changed is changed. Alternate-history stories – by dissolving that base understanding of the unalterable saliency of the real – work on a contrary assumption: that it does not matter what you do. That the world is a game [or a pastoral: see the forthcoming *Encyclopedia of Fantasy* edited by me and John Grant 1995]. That there is no death. That sequels are interminable. That nothing can be earned. So the cruelest thing to be said about Kim Newman is that he writes alternate histories.

Fortunately, there are other things to say. *Anno Dracula* (Simon & Schuster UK, 1992) may be an alternate history set in the England of around 1888, a few years after the eponymous Count has married Queen Victoria and after the vampire rule he has established begins to eat away the fabric of the land; but once within the dream of alternity, Newman plays by the rules of the world he has created, more or less. The main problem may be the sweet tooth he shares with other Munchkin Perssons – a roster which includes Mary Gentle, Roz Kaveney, Newman himself; Colin Greenland and Neil Gaiman (en passant); and various other members of the *Temps* and *Villains* shared-world anth klatch – all of whom variously adore heroines who variously echo Michael Moorcock's Temporal Adventuress from the 1960s. Her name may be Catherine Cornelius, or Una Persson, but whatever she is called she will be found slipping knight's-move-wise through the Moorcockian multiverse, born and reborn but always deeply herself, wryly wise and clear-eyed, utterly knowing, able to silence strong men with a melancholy that lies too deep for tears, often bisexual, often a nonce whore, a cynic and a lover and a jolly good swordswoman and a cynosure of all eyes and Lauren Bacall; and always resigned, in the end, to travel on: to shake off lacrimae rerum with a shrug and a single bound. She's the lamia of the worlds, and she's terribly hard to eschew, though it's probably getting to be about time for the Munchkin Perssons to take the pledge. Newman's heroine – an elder but eternally-young vampire named Geneviève Dieudonné who featured in some sharecrops he wrote for Games Workshops – shows off the one-upping afflatus and susurration of her multiple pasts with all the exempt insouciance of the true Temporal Adventuress, and she tends to nudge *Anno Dracula* into game-world. But then the tale catches hold again, and we follow it down.

Very clearly, it is an end-of-the-century book, a Condition of England tract for the times, in which the fairy-tale horrors of the legacy of the Milk-Snatcher are shown to be nothing but truth in the mirror of fable (the one genuinely potent cognitive use for the alternate history is to serve as a warning reflection). The heart of Newman's analysis – though the word does not appear in the text – might be characterized most concisely as a kind of play on *consanguinity*. In the real-life world we inhabit, and after 15 years of Milk-Snatcher and her appalling gets, the country we live in has been almost fatally stripped of the texture of mutual enablement and obligation that once wove together public and private life, for good (in 1969, the UK was the most complex and profoundly *legible* world I had ever experienced) and for ill (the Ealing theodicy that sanctioned a strange clockwork bloodymindedness about *any* change whatsoever; the awful linguistic coding which classified sheep and goats with merciless insistence). But for good and for ill, it was a land of veins and arteries, woven together by capillaries of secret knowing. The social compacts which engined the land could be called a consanguinity.

In *Anno Dracula* – just like it is up here at the end of this century, in Milk-Snatcher's bankrupt strip-mine – consanguinity has been replaced by what one might call, on the other hand, hegemonic vampirism. It is 1888. Count Dracula and his minions are in control, and it has become both fashionable and necessary – if one wishes to stay afloat in a world suddenly helpless against insensate greed – for the warmblooded to convert, to become themselves newborn vampires, and to suck the blood of those less fortunate in order to thrive while undead, to suck England dry.

Characters from Bram Stoker's *Dracula* (1897) mill through the text, most importantly Jack Seward, who ran an insane asylum in the original book, and who in *Anno Dracula* (it is a secret soon divulged) is Jack the Ripper. Geneviève and the dashing Charles Beauregard find their separate lines of inquiry into the Whitechapel murders beginning to converge, and become lovers. Charles is in the informal employ of the Diogenes Club, to which Sherlock Holmes's elder brother Mycroft belongs – *Anno Dracula* thrums with recursive jokes and joinings – and gradually begins to understand that his masters have been developing a plan to defeat the Count before it is too late, to stanch the haemorrhage before London turns into Docklands.

How this works up into a gory but perfectly calibrated climax, is Newman's gift and surprise. The style is smooth and breasts the surges of its content with such Persson-like panache that one almost forgets the teeth of the thing, the vision of an exsanguinated comity, Bat the Snatcher and the Porcine Undeads of her cabal. But again and again, the teeth slice through the anaesthesia of alternity, and you wake the morrow.

II.

Daniel Easterman's *Name of the Beast* (HarperCollins, 1992) is also a Condition Book, but faces the Millennium with its teeth stainless of any red blood or gist. It is a near-future politics and horror tale with moments of sure eloquence, told in a hard and crafty style, and the author is in almost absolute control of his material. For these reasons – because it is impossible to think of the book as being unmeant in any detail – it must be the case that Easterman has written, in all deliberation, a novel whose almost absolute emptiness is itself the only message conveyed to the junkies who swallow horror down like sugared salt.

In retrospect, the Prologue tells it all. It is 1999, and "a strange winter" has settled on Egypt, where we discover a female archaeologist, A'isha Manfaluti, in the middle of an exciting dig. She is about to unwrap the cloth from a mummy, and the narrative spirals with precision and skill around the technical process involved, the tensions, the implications of dread. Finally, after several pages, she gets it open. Her heart almost stops in shock. Her assistant drops his camera in consternation. A gold bracelet has come into view. It is the band of a Rolex watch. Nothing more is explained: but surely some revelation is at hand, surely the last sentence of the Prologue repeats so portentously the first in order to convey a hint of Coming: "A strange winter had settled on Egypt that year," we are told.

But for the reader accustomed to sf movements of revelation, it is not the *sensation* of an untoward winter that counts, nor the *sensation* of seeing a Rolex watch "circling a wrist of bone" that brings a shiver, nor the *sensation* of being manipulated by an author who is holding *your* breath but not his own, that makes a scene end on a note of finis; for the sf reader, what tends to count is the changed world behind the arras: in this case, a premise of reality manipulation – time travel even – has clearly been evoked, some intimation that the Antichrist – for that is who the title, after all, tells us we're going to meet – is a Beast who ravens at the fabric of the world, gnaws the heart of Time. On the other hand, the accustomed reader of Daniel Easterman's kind of book – he's an author of political horror thrillers – is almost certain to expect nothing more than the *sensation* of being threatened with revelation; indeed he might even *resent* having it all add up to something. In this case, he will have nothing to resent.

Any revelation about the Rolex itself comes, much later, in that tone of offhand bathos so characteristic of the closing passages of almost any horror novel, that embarrassed shuffle off the scene after the Beast has turned to greasepaint. Eventually, so that we can watch her fuck the protagonist of the novel without feeling any affect at all, we learn that A'isha knew as soon as she saw the watch that the wrist of bone – the mundanity is stupefying – belonged to her husband, a famous political activist who had been kidnapped by terrorists five years earlier; and that an enormously elaborate imposture (or imposthuming) had been mounted to *teach her a lesson*. What that lesson is, and why this huge expenditure of energy was necessary for its imparting, it is not easy – nay impossible – to work out, beyond a general sense that she is being warned to keep her mouth shut, about something or other. As to why the weather is strange, and remains strange throughout this very long book, forget it, we're never given a clue. And as to why – though it is entirely typical of this genre – it seemed a good idea for Easterman to *withhold* a non-revelation his characters already were privy to, I do not wish to try to say.

Like Prologue, like book. It builds and builds and builds (and blows). Terrorist are blowing up Europe, because the Antichrist has been reborn, and is about to hotfoot it like a rough beast to Jerusalem; they are preparing the way, it will all be new. The tension, the sense of a spreadeagled world awaiting the knout, is at times, as they say, almost palpable. A sub-basement character out of John Le Carré named Percy Haviland – unbelievably: had Easterman forgotten Percy Alleline in *Tinker Tailor Soldier Spy?* – makes some halitosic Brit waves, almost causing the protagonist's death, and there is a prolonged (and utterly irrelevant) sequence in the sewers under Cairo, but we can still hope for revelation. But then Easterman's version of the Antichrist takes centre stage, and turns out to be a fundamentalist convert to Islam who *thinks* he's the Antichrist. (I couldn't work out how a Christian eschatology was meant to affect the hordes of Muslim fanatics who follow him, and I don't think I was given much help by the author.) The big moment then arrives, after 400 pages. The Pope is kidnapped, taken to a pyramid called Armageddon, where he meets Auntie, and *nothing happens*. It is really quite astonishing. After 400 pages, there's not a thing to *say*. No revelation. No shuffling of the Beast. Just lights up in the theatre, greasepaint, a furtive shuffling bathos. *Name of the Beast* is a book entirely composed of trailers. There is no feature.

III.

This is not a mistake made by James Herbert in *Portent* (Hodder & Stoughton, 1992), and one wishes it were possible to like the book a little more. It is, more or less, 1999. Tough times for Gaia, what with pollution and crap and too many of us and all that. Suddenly a sequence of natural disasters, each of them augured by the presence of a Tinkerbell-like glowing ball, begins to hint that the end may be nigh for humanity. But the honcho meteorologist who is the hero of the tale is inveigled into the countryside to meet an old discredited scientist with a beautiful daughter-in-law; this scientist not only thinks Gaia is an interactive homeostatic system, but has actually been *designed* to bring forth and to sustain humanity, so fuck off Darwin. Moreover, his adopted grandchildren (they're Romanian gypsy orphans) may represent a similar sort of answer to our current difficulties, being telepathic faith healers who can communicate with thousands of like brethren, and who can predict Tinkerbell visitations. Reluctantly the meteorologist – he has Fisher King Knee – comes gradually to think the old scientist may be right. But then he meets off-set an old blind Scots guru, who promulgates a "considerably more profound" premise than any mere notion that Gaia was here just to sustain us. He thinks that a "special few" – ie the children – are destined to experience the true coming-to, and to *guide* Gaia (and us normals) on the upward path into harmony, like Children of the Lens doing *Metropolis*. The Tinkerbells are, apparently, an emanation of *us*, a kind of salutary auto-sadomasochism with wings, though how they make Gaia dance out earthquakes epicentred in the City of London I could not quite understand. The Scots guru also cures the meteorologist's Knee.

We also meet – perhaps because Herbert felt something lacking, plot-wise, in a mere simple end-of-the-world tale with gurus and Tinkerbells and dozens of disasters and a scientist's beautiful daughter-in-law and a thousand telepathic children from Arisia – a very horrible huge black woman in New Orleans, who also is au courant with Gaia, but who wants to kill the children because they're frustrating the Mother, who (she thinks) wants only to rid herself of us. She sweats a lot, kills her lovers, has kinky hair. There is a climax. The Scots guru – who represents an ethnic group (godfearing engineering Scots) more destructive to Earth's substance than any other single group of human beings this Earth has ever seen – is of course fully vindicated, and the filthy pockmarked black woman – who represents an ethnic group far less likely to contribute priests of the machine to the rituals of technology speeding up these last days – is killed by the meteorologist and the rest of the decent whites. Great stuff. The style is Herbert's invariant manful bodge, which reads like marbled beef, all the spring gone.

IV.

Clive Barker's *The Thief of Always* (HarperCollins, 1992), on the other hand, lacks nothing but a touch of hamstring to make it a great fable. But the lack is felt. Young Harvey, ten years old, is bored; follows a fantasy character named Rictus to a magic House where the sun shines high, and whole seasons pass in a day, with Hallowe'en sparkling the evening, and the snow deep and crisp and even at midnight. But when he escapes temporarily, he finds (as in so many tales of Faerie) that a year has passed in the world for every day in wonderland. Bravely, he returns to the House, and to Hood, its vampiric spirit. Bravely, he rescues the other children, tricks Hood into spending his magic, and redeems time. The world breathes thanks. The deep dark pond, which appears throughout, is beautifully described, but seems a touch ex machina, especially at the climax. It is there because Barker needed it, and knew how to write it in like a whizz, hey presto. It is *not* there, however, because it *had* to be. An agreeable facility festinates smoothly every page, but no *difficulty* stops us short with savour. It is like reading through cellophane: everything is there, but you can never touch it.

V.

Alasdair Gray's latest novel, *Poor Things: Episodes from the Early Life of Archibald McCandless M.D. Scottish Public Health Officer* (Bloomsbury, 1992), has now won both the Guardian Fiction Prize and the Whitbread Prize for 1992. It was not given a notice here on first publication, because Bloomsbury repeatedly refused to supply a review copy to *Interzone*, perhaps because the book – being very fine, and funny, and literary, and experimentally couched – would simpy have been *damaged* by the thought that it might have sci-fi elements, my dear. And you have to think about the qualities. The merest hint that *Poor Things* might be a genre novel would snuff any chance of a *real* review. So it is on the basis of a private copy that I am able to suggest to any readers who might have missed *Poor Things* that it may be a great book. It is the first for Gray since *Lanark* (1981) which opens his mouth. The story makes plays on *Frankenstein* (1818), invokes echoes of Candide, Pygmalion, James Joyce. There are ironies galore, unreliable narrations, tirades, feminist texts and subtexts, intricate plays with the physical design of the book, wit and ire and sap and a rawness of creative energy it is almost frightening to sup with.

It is sf.

– Interzone 69, March 1993

3. VARIOUS

[The following review, of the novel which won the 1993 Arthur C Clarke Award, is placed here, rather than under 1991, for reasons of convenience. My comments on the giving of the award appear on p. 420 1995.]

NO READER who found Marge Piercy's eleventh novel and third sf text a hard book to open could ever be censured by a just world. *He, She and It* (Knopf, 1991) is, at first glance, an almost supernaturally uninviting object to land upon a desk. Knopf's cover art – so different from the exquisite work that came from this firm only a few years ago – is meretriciously, mercilessly rebarbative, the kind of cover art which hints to the reader that the tale it illustrates is a bomb still-born and deeply resented by the editor who has just now been brought on board to replace the previous editor who managed to jump ship just before his/her chickens came home to roost. In the lower left an execrably executed Chagallesque woman – despite the clear provenance, she is lamingly earthbound – stares away from us towards two bland arches in a wall executed in a style one might designate the School-of-De-Chirico's-Deathbed, and interpenetrated by dim twee stars and a crescent moon. The shadow of a numb humanoid figure is visible inside each arch. In the distance, through the left-hand arch, can be seen a small Eastern European town from a long time ago; through the right-hand arch can be seen a "modernistic" scape which closely resembles any small American city-centre of the 1980s. Holed by art-school symbolisms – by a bombination of "meaningful" images which adds up to a total image which implacably means *nothing at all* – the heart sinks.

For those not sensitive to bad art, the unwelcomingness of the book will have to be conveyed through its seriously – almost dementedly – deficient title, which manages to imply to potential readers that the novel it fronts is one of those nudzhing, 400-page, leaden-hearted prig-proclamations uttered by writers after the inspiration of their earlier years has flagged but PhD theses have been written about them which they can't stop reading though they *know* they must stop *now* and every night they dream paraphrases of the songs they sang in their heat and every morning they transcribe greyly, greyly their dreams; and delivers this dreadful warning through a clutter of awful English monosyllables nearly impossible to recollect in the proper order, and therefore impossible to ask for in the shop, if you were so dumb as to want to. In the mind's eye of this reviewer, it is a title which always turns to *She-He-It*. [In the UK it was released the following year as *Body of Glass*. 1995]

But we do, some of us, eventually, open the book. And we were not dumb to. For we find that *He, She and It* does not, after all, deserve the obsequies it comes cloaked in. Very soon, it comes clear that Marge Piercy has done her homework on current sf versions of the future, and has settled her sf tale into a comfortable recension of that future. Several hundred pages in, the AI-controlled data-net, which dominates the 21st century corporate world she depicts, is even referred to as cyberspace, and a note at the end of the text acknowledges William Gibson; if this seems a routine precaution and courtesy on the part of a mainline author, take a look at the egregious Paul Theroux's slummer's-guide *O-Zone* (1985), whose pig-ignorance of other versions of the thin world it boastingly claims to have created is far more typical of the sort of book non-sf writers create when they think to "redeem" sf by stopping for the night in a clean motel near the airport while making sure they don't drink the water. Though *He, She, and It* starts slow, and starts more than once, and though it closes in a sentimental dying fall which contradicts most of what the author clearly knows about 1991's versions of the nature of next century's AI's in the Net, the body of the book is alert, engaged, contemporary, pro-active in the shticks of genre. It should have come with a real title – those of Piercy's first two sf novels, *Dance the Eagle to Sleep* (1970) and *Woman on the Edge of Time* (1976), are clear proof that she knows what a title is – and it should have been presented like a real book. Because it is one.

After decades of war and plague and nearly terminal pollution of the Mother, the 21st century world has settled into uneasy quiescence. Governments no longer exist. A couple of dozen multi-national corporations, dominated by the Japanese and the Germans, operate through dour arcologies protected against the unshielded sun and the other depredations of an Earth no longer properly habitable by the humans who have inherited our blighting. Non-corporation people live in Gibsonian megalopolises with names like The Glop (at times it is difficult to sort out whether or not Piercy thinks the world is overcrowded or not; her urban imagery derives from novels which assume the world to be choked with humanity, but her story assumes a depopulated Earth), and a few free cities occupy the periphery, surviving through the sale of special skills. The main protagonist of the book, after losing her son in a custody case to a corporation apparatchik, returns to the Jewish free town of Tikva, which is in New England, and where she was born and raised by her grandmother, families being matrilineal – a characteristic of Jewish life in this novel which, one suspects, has more to do with Piercy's approval of the Jews of Tikva than any sustained presentation of a culture which even the novel at hand, by spending dozens of pages in patriarchal Prague, deprecates. Here in Tikva she finds that the genius father of the man she had been madly in love with when they were both adolescents has secretly created a cyborg with the aid of her grandmother, who is also a genius, and that this cyborg has both self-awareness and a risible penis. Alternating chapters – told by her grandmother to this cyborg as part of his training in humanity – tell the story of Rabbi Loew's creation of a golem in the Prague of 1600.

It is a tale which, as we know, and as the grandmother must also know, ends in tears, ends in the death of the golem. So we are warned. Shira, the protagonist, soon becomes sexually involved with Yod the penised cyborg, and the plot begins to thicken, quite satisfactorily. Her old "multi" is after Yod. Shira's revolutionary mother returns to Tikva. Shira's old lover, the flamboyant but significantly unserious Gadi, also shows up. The multi tries to invade Tikva through the Net, but is repulsed by Yod, who is trained to inhabit cyberspace, which he knows like the back of his hand. It is all of it familiar to sf readers, but refreshingly retold. The end (as we were informed at the very beginning) is tears; after fighting unsuccessfully to be recognized as a legal person, Yod is ordered to deliver himself to the multi and to commit suicide by blowing up the bosses, and obeys. But in dealing out this doom, Piercy astonishingly misses Gibson's – and everyone else's – standard cyberspace transcendence routine, seeming not even to be aware that any sf novel written after 1984 would either have Yod download his electronic essence into the density of the Net at the last moment, and so survive; or tell us why in the world not. In doing neither, Piercy reveals a touristic ignorance of local mores, but for the first time, and in any case the essence of He, She and It lies elsewhere.

As usual in a Piercy novel, the ostensible heart of the enterprise is a brawling narrative analysis of the nature of the relations between men and women, though (as usual) her telling of the tale defaults into the awful knowingness of melodrama, for she has a terrible and destructive habit of knowing who's right and who's wrong in her tales. The real heart of the Piercy enterprise lies – quite astonishingly, given the noise of her writing – in the interior monologues of her characters, who seem far more human when they're not dancing out an imposed exemplary plot routine. Small gems of insight infiltrate *He, She and It* throughout, like spies in a fun house; none of the major protagonists turns out (in contrast to the old Piercy model) to have been a monster of sexism all his life and even his wife didn't guess, sort of thing; the parts of the tale set in Prague are warmly and eloquently achieved (though the analogy of golem and cyborg/AI is ultimately unfulfilling); and the flensed world of 2050 is ours soonest.

– New York Review of Science Ficton 43, March 1992

WE BEGIN with the title, and after we finish the book it is the title which remains. *Steel Beach* (Putnam, 1992). It is John Varley's first novel in almost a decade, and probably the most skillful sf epic we're likely to come across in 1992, though it's just about the most frustrating as well. It is a tale which fades in the mind's eye, as most tales do, after the last page shuts. But the title sticks like glue, and may indeed become an sf catchphrase for the end of the millennium. Because *Steel Beach* is where we live now.

Eons ago, there was a fish. It lived in the shallows of the vast tidal ocean, near the very edge of the waters. One day it strayed too far toward the sands, having exhausted its supply of plankton perhaps, or in terror of newly evolved predators, and the tide ebbed, and it found itself stuck on a sand beach, stark naked, trying to breathe the terrible poison air of the new world, which killed it right off. Next day there was a new fish, on another beach. It too perished. Millions more died. But then – maybe a thousand years later – yet another fish strayed too far, and coughed, and choked, and suffered. This time, however, something happened. An impromptu membrane widened slightly in something which still resembled a gill, and a trickle of oxygen filtered into the blood, and the fish stayed alive long enough to flop through drying puddles into the water. Later – because the ocean was unfriendly – it ventured back. Much later – it might have been a thousand years on, or a million – a tribe of lungfish could be found on the beach, breathing and breeding and brawling, preparing to conquer the new continent. Which it did, soon enough.

Today – or in 200 years' time, when Varley sets his tale – we are something like the fish. Having exhausted the bounty of our old habitat, which was the entire planet, we are beginning to feel the need to search, in our billions, for new territories and fresh bounty. Many of us hope that the human race will learn proper husbandry, and will nurture the planet back to health; but others feel that the only solution is to emigrate. Either way, we are beginning, in our swarms, to starve in shallow waters. Have we reached an evolutionary impasse? Is there a solution? Where is the beach?

For Varley, who is writing a novel, the beach was easy to find. In his Future History, we have long been exiled from Earth by Invaders who terminated our lease when they found out what a mess we'd made of things, and 200 years on we are exiles living in habitats carved out of the Moon and Mars and other planets. We survive in corridors of steel, breathing pumped air, trusting that the precarious new ecologies which sustain us will remain stable under the guidance of vast Artificial Intelligences, praying that the vacuum of space will not crack our skins. But the pressure is beginning to mount. As one of the vast AI's explains to the heroine of *Steel Beach*, humans are at an evolutionary cusp.

Think of the human race, it tells her, as fish upon a beach. "Here we are," it continues, "thrown up by the Invasion onto a beach of metal, where nothing natural exists that we don't produce ourselves.... We've had to build our own pool to swim around in while we catch our breath." But "the sun keeps trying to dry up the pool. Our wastes accumulate, threatening to poison us.... And there aren't very many other pools like this one to move to if this one fails, and *no* ocean to return to."

It's only a story, of course, though beautifully told and splendidly arrayed with cunning hooks to keep readers from guessing that Varley has no solution to the problems he presents – for in the end, frustratingly, nothing happens, humanity still gasps and flounders on the steel beach, and the outcome is in doubt.

It's only a story, perhaps, but back here in 1992 its title feels like a metaphor – of warning and of hope – for our time. For we have built our planet of dead trees into a steel beach, and there is no turning back. Here and now we must bring our tools to bear, our hearts, our minds, our will. We must make a new start, for there is no ocean to return to. We must learn to breathe the new air.

– Omni, July 1992

IT IS not easy to think of the Black Death as a good time for stories. A village (say some hamlet near Oxford) might be full of human beings in September 1348, and a graveyard by Christmas: there's only one terrible interest in that. Epidemiologists might wish to sort out who died of what, for there were three kinds of plague – the pneumonic, the septicemic and the bubonic – and they travelled together like Three Horseman looking for the Fourth, whose name is Death, just Death. But non-epidemiologists only need to know that every kind of plague was fatal. A third of the population of Europe died of the disease over a period of maybe twenty years. Over an entire continent the same story was told, again and again, a million times. Words hardly seem necessary, certainly not the battening words of a twentieth-century teller of tales for gain. All the same, Connie Willis has set most of her new novel,

Doomsday Book (Bantam, 1992), in the middle of the horror; and she has managed to tell a story which does not make us sick.

This took some doing, and the primary triumph of this massive, dense, crafty novel resides in the extreme tact of its telling. There are quite a few mistakes in the book, but there is never a cheap moment. Not one death is dwelt on gratuitously; not one person is saved (or killed off) to make the story easier to tell. Of all the characters in the tale, only the protagonist will survive the Black Death with any certainty, and that is because – Doomsday Book being an sf novel – she has travelled through time from the Oxford of 2050 to study the England of 1320; and although a setting error in the university-run time machine has landed her 28 years too late, she has, all the same, been properly inoculated.

Willis's first mistake is Oxford. Her vision of dreaming spires and savants out of Dorothy L Sayers was always more aspiration than reality, and by 1990 it was a vision few still adhered to; sixty years from now, Oxford will be something else again. Unfortunately, it is in this toytown that much of the story is set. The two weeks Kivrin spends in 1348 are interwoven with two weeks in 2050, during which latter period several comically fuddy-duddy professors try to work out what has gone wrong with the project (they take 400 pages to discover what most readers will have guessed in 40: which is Willis's second mistake). So the gussied-up Oxford is too much with us; and it is only Willis's compulsive story-telling gifts which keep us leashed to the book, fixed to its heartbeat.

Willis's third mistake is to modernize the world of 1348. The village Kivrin lands up in is too romantically isolated to seem quite plausible; the people she consorts with are far too individualistic to convince one they have lived their lives, illiterate, in an isolated hamlet surrounded by deep woods (which is not to claim that in 1348 there were no individuals, just that they should not be individualists who have already jumped the gun on Descartes); and finally the landed family she lives with seems somehow too suburban, especially the extremely loud youngest daughter, who would make Shirley Temple seem a model of decorum. But somehow, in the end, these anomalies don't matter. The vision of 1348 may have been discerned through flawed glass, but the tale itself is quite astonishingly gripping, cleverly constructed, cunningly hooked, narrated with such care that its momentum builds irresistibly. It is very hard to put the book down before the final death, the final page, the rescue of Kivrin from holocaust. It is a book which feels fundamentally true; it is a book to live in.

And in the end it does not much matter that no member of the cast is convincingly medieval, because the world of 1348 burns in the mind's eye, and every character alive in that year is a fully realized being. (Even the lollipop girl.) The local priest, in particular, carries the heartbeat of the book as it reaches full spate. Gaunt, dour, devout, illiterate, complex, humble, vision-haunted, he is a figure of clear and evident beauty, and his refusal to succumb to terror, as the Death descends, is genuinely excruciating. As we slowly learn to recognize his nature, it becomes possible to feel, in this one instance, that Connie Willis did, in fact, over the five years *Doomsday Book* took to write, open a window to another world, and that she saw something there.

– The Washington Post Book World SF Column, 28 June 1992

On the Arthur C Clarke Award, 1993

[Several novels are referred to in the polemical piece I'm printing here; most of them I had already reviewed. Those reviews are reprinted here: that of Karen Joy Fowler's *Sarah Canary* on p. 344; of Ian McDonald's *Hearts, Hands and Voices* on p. 367 of Marge Piercy's *Body of Glass* on p. 414; of Kim Stanley Robinson's *Red Mars* on p. 383; of Lisa Tuttle's *Lost Futures* on p.388; of Michael Swanwick's *Stations of the Tide* on p. 350; and of Connie Willis's *Doomsday Book* on p. 418. 1995]

AS I'M GOING to claim that a mistake has been made, and because hindsight is a cheap shot, perhaps I should make it clear right off that I had read and reviewed Marge Piercy's *Body of Glass* (under its original title, *He, She and It*) long before it won the 1993 Arthur C Clarke Award, that I knew what I thought of the book long before finding out what the panel had decided; and that I certainly never dreamed it would be a serious contender for the prize. My immediate reaction when it won – that the decision was so bad my ears must have deceived me – came from the heart. My subsequent reactions – which I expressed aloud after the announcement – welled up from an already-formed matrix of assumptions and convictions about this year's shortlist, about the nature of sf publishing in the UK, about the history and present state and future health of the Arthur C Clarke Award as an institution, and about the nature of sf as a genre.

So. The winner. Marge Piercy's *Body of Glass* – I reviewed it, quite favourably, in the March 1992 issue of *The New York Review of Science Fiction* – is an easy-to-read attempt at crossover sf, though overlong, stylistically a bit overdecorated and – even granting that it's less intrusively melodramatic than the stories this author usually tells in her non-genre works – too damned *knowing* about its various characters.

Karen Joy Fowler's *Sarah Canary* (but see below for the panel's response to that book) is a *genuine* demonstration of contemporary "literary" style at its concise, allusive, complex best. *Body of Glass* in any case fatally gives off that gingerly feel one often detects when a mainstream writer is manipulating sf devices and scenarios to illuminate her own concerns. One can grant willingly that Piercy did a good deal of homework, in contrast to day-trippers like Paul Theroux; and that her near-future USA is described, competently enough, in reasonably up-to-date, cyberpunk-derived terms. But *Body of Glass* still reads like a primer-level guidebook-to-the-future, on the pattern of most mainstream sf; and the very heart of the enterprise – a long narrative tracing of allegorical and literal links between an AI housed in an android body and the golem of Jewish legend – fatally reveals an absence of any genuine new contribution to the complex interwoven record of generic attempts to cope with that issue. Forget that in "The Golem" (1955) Avram Davidson had long ago made a trope out of the AI/golem metaphor, doing so with wit, concision, and a thorough grasp of its various implications; or that "The Golem," having been reprinted at least 12 times, is hardly an obscure text. The real point is that in *Body of Glass* old tropes are presented – as so often happens in this kind of cross-over tale – with an air of portentous, Book-of-the-Month Club Bulletin, Big-Think iconoclasm that in its secondhand staleness is *exactly the opposite* of what sf cognition *should* be: which is threatening, risk-taking, novel, premature. *Body of Glass* is a belated book.

(Sf cognition, as here described, is not common. Nobody will deny this. When we run across it, as we have over the years in some of Arthur C. Clarke's own novels, and as we did in several books on this year's shortlist, we should give praise. It is the sort of thing sf prizes should be awarded for.)

Of the other titles shortlisted for this year's Award, I'd also previously reviewed Ian McDonald's *Hearts, Hands and Voices*, Kim Stanley Robinson's *Red Mars* (since shortlisted for the Hugo [it won 1995]), Michael Swanwick's *Stations of the Tide* (which won last year's Nebula), Lisa Tuttle's *Lost Futures* and Connie Willis's *Doomsday Book* (which has since won this year's Nebula; it's also on the Hugo shortlist). I had furthermore reviewed Karen Joy Fowler's *Sarah Canary*, a brilliant sf meditation on First Contact, whose exclusion from the shortlist on the grounds that it was "ineligible" was a first sign, along with the unwieldy size of the list itself, that all was not well with the panel (the book was shortlisted for this year's Nebula). The remaining novels, Richard Paul Russo's *Destroying Angel* and Sue Thomas's *Correspondence*, I had neither reviewed nor read; and had either won, I'd have had no express response beyond a mild oceanic disappointment that books I did know and love had been passed over.

So it looked to me like a very good year, and I thought there were some exciting books to choose among. I came to The Groucho Club on 25 March 1993 with a pretty clear sense of what I thought about most of these texts, a sense which (for what it's worth) had been amply recorded in print. Several of the shortlisted novels, I thought (and argued, through the tenor of the reviews I wrote and published before the shortlist was announced) were among the most significant examples of the ambitions of 1990s sf during a trying time for the genre. Out of this impressive array, I thought that *Red Mars*, for a number of pretty clear reasons, should win, but I would have been neither surprised nor discontent had the Swanwick, the Tuttle, the Willis or (if it had been "eligible") the Fowler taken the prize; my feelings about the McDonald were exceedingly ambivalent, but if it had won I would not have felt that these feelings constituted reason for complaint. I have already hinted at my sensations when the actual winner was announced.

Let me attempt to be methodical.

1) The book itself (see above) was a good though slightly po-faced read in Piercy's usual style; but *as sf* it reeked of the second-hand in a manner which made it clear its author did not *know* she was reworking old material. It was, in my view, an inherent non-winner of any prize (and as far as I know, the Arthur C Clarke Award is the only recognition the book has received, either within or without the genre).

2) Several of the other books shortlisted (again, see above) are centrally important texts in the sf of the 1990s. This is not the place for me to go on for hours about my own feeling that traditional (or agenda) sf is in a state of crisis, and that books like those by Fowler, Robinson, Swanwick and Willis represent a significant creative response to that state of crisis. What I *can* argue is that – whatever you think about the condition of sf at the moment – it is surely clear that these novels show that *something is happening*. Each of them is full of energy and pertinence, and, like all the best sf novels, each of them is Janus-faced about sf: they gaze backwards knowingly at the web of genre, and they stare outwards, too.

I think the panel of experts should have noticed this.

3) Market and publishing realities. We are in a time of financial constraints. It cost the sf publishers an estimated £3–4000 to supply to the members of the panel of the Arthur C Clarke Awards copies of the large number of books which were read last year. In doing so, these sf publishers assumed they were contributing to a process which would generate an award that was relevant to the sf world, relevant to sf authors, relevant to sf publishing and marketing, and relevant to the audience gathered to hear the announcement. This audience included senior representatives of those publishers seriously involved in sf publishing, but no representative from

Marge Piercy's house, Michael Joseph; her prize was accepted by a representative of Penguin Books, which owns Michael Joseph. What happened on the night was registered by the senior editors of the sf publishing houses of the UK as a slap in their collective faces, and a slap in the face of sf as a mature communal endeavour.

They clearly felt they'd had their money taken, and their time wasted, under false pretences. They felt that good writers had been insulted. They felt that the event was a sham, a public relations flop. They felt – rightly (see below) – that the Award itself would be treated with very moderate respect by Penguin Books, who do not market Marge Piercy as an sf writer. They made it clear their feeling that – *whatever* the motives of the panel might have been – it would look to the world as though the Clarke had been given to Marge Piercy because she seemed upmarket.

Let's look briefly at the Penguin 6 May 1993 re-release of *Body of Glass*, a month and a half after the announcement. It comes with a Press Release which does list the Award; but the book itself – despite consoling rumours that a "Winner of the Arthur C Clarke Award" sticker would be put on the front cover – is entirely blank on the prize. On the back cover we can, on the other hand, read a couple of excerpts from the kind of reviews of the book Penguin wish to emphasize. Martin Mulligan in the *Financial Times* says that it "elevates its author to the pantheon of *haute* sf alongside Doris Lessing and Ursula Le Guin." The *St. Louis Post-Dispatch* says that "*Body of Glass* is much more than sf. It's a touching love story (several, actually) and a gripping adventure tale..." The condescending ineptitude of these quotes gives all the explanation one needs for Penguin's lack of interest in pushing *Body of Glass* as a genre title: because what they *really* want to do is reassure its potential buyers that *Body of Glass* is *not* sf at all, that it's really much more *haute* than that greasy genre stuff.

So the sf publishers' money was wasted, as far as they're concerned; and Arthur C Clarke's own thousand pounds went to a writer whose publishers think that if she wishes to associate with the man she had better sup with a long spoon; and half a dozen genuine sf books of high calibre (each of them better as literature than *Body of Glass*) are set aside. The publishers will probably ante up next year (but there is a strong sense that this may be very much under duress); it would be presumptuous to guess at what Arthur C Clarke thought of the award (but see below); and sf writers continue at their precarious task, regardless.

It's a mess.

4) Everyone who has been involved in any of this knows that Arthur C Clarke himself has made absolutely no attempt to shape the award. He has never said a word in public to suggest that it would please him to have the Clarke given to writers who worked within the extremely broad-church version of sf that he himself

might recognize as home-like. He has never said a word in public to suggest that any of the awards so far granted have given him a moment of disquiet. It is, therefore, entirely to his credit that this year's panel selected the book *least* likely to fit within any definition of sf as Arthur C Clarke has lived and written it for 60 years.

As is well known, Clarke does not normally blurb books; and it is also well known that last year, in the highest possible terms, he *did* blurb one of the novels – not the Piercy – which was eventually to be shortlisted [see above, on p. 381]. It is entirely proper that Clarke's enthusiasm for one particular book had no effect on the panel's decision. This is right, we know that. We do know that. But it is still a temptation to posit an alternate world in which Arthur C. Clarke was innocently given some innocent pleasure, the sf world of England was rewarded for its loyalty, the marketing of sf was made easier, the nature of sf as a genre was affirmed, and a good book was awarded a good prize...

But of course that's an *alternate* world.

In the real world, none of these things happened.

– Vector 173, June/July 1993

III: Individual Writers

1. Karel Capek

UNTIL the dawning of 1990, it had been a long death for Karel Capek. His heart had broken eons ago, at the moment Neville Chamberlain left Munich in 1938, and his body, wracked from adolescence by a spinal disease, had succumbed to pneumonia by the end of that same year of dread for Czechoslovakia, the land of his birth and his career and his deepest loyalty. Within a few months the Germans were in Prague; his writings were banned, and he remained almost unpublishable in his own country for nearly half a century. English translations (mostly awkward) of plays like R.U.R. (1920) and eccentric novels like *War with the Newts* (1936) muddied over the nervous quickness of his best work, turned its sometimes fevered lucidity into gobble. He was dead; he was dust in the mouth. Like Czechoslovakia, Karel Capek seemed irrecoverable.

It has, of course, begun to change. Like Atlantis lifting its long spine from the coils of a dead sea, Czechoslovakia herself, once more, has become visible [until the inevitable split 1995] at the very heart of the Continent, "the spiritual and intellectual crossroads of Europe," as Capek said (not perhaps very memorably) in one of his last pieces, written to introduce a desperate anthology of essays advocating (too late) the preservation of the country. That piece now reappears as the final item in *Toward the Radical Center: A Karel Capek Reader* (Catbird, 1989), published in 1990 to mark the centenary of his birth; edited with very considerable care by Peter Kussi, and including a number of badly-needed new versions of work long familiar in dumbfounding translatorese, this moderately ample volume brings the voice of Capek back to life. The voice of the book is the voice, once again, of a live writer in a live land. One of the varieties of death is undone.

His career was swift and to the point. He was born in Bohemia, in 1890, on the outskirts of an Austro-Hungarian Empire declining spasmodically into rigor mortis. The spectacle must have been educational, and he never failed to show a lithe, almost zany ambivalence about authority, a sense that the governments of the world were inherently phantasmagorical – his compatriot, Franz Kafka (1883–1924), must also have learned much from everyday life in the prison-house grip of Vienna's dying bureaucracies. By the age of eighteen Capek was publishing stories written with his brother Josef (none have been translated); by the end of World War One he had taken a PhD, written several volumes of tales, and stood poised to celebrate in his native tongue the creative exhilaration of a free Czechoslovakia. Within a year he had written R.U.R.

Most authors can be read, and should be read, at a normal walking pace; some, like Walter de la Mare, must be read at half speed to avoid a certain disjointedness; others, like Capek, seem to sizzle on the page, and must be kept up with. Like everything else he ever wrote, R.U.R. reads fast. On an island in the Pacific, Rossum's Universal Robots have been manufacturing what are now called androids – organic creatures in human shape – and exporting them world-wide as slaves. Helena Glory arrives to harangue the "robots" about freedom. At first they do not understand. But every human on the island falls promptly in love with the daft maiden, she marries the boss, ten years pass in the blinking of an eye, the robots of the world rebel, in a fit of inexplicable remorse she destroys the formula which makes them, everyone dies offstage except one human researcher, a few sterile rebels; and two robots, Primus and Helena, fall in love, though neither have any sexual organs. The play ends in a camped Tolstoyan prate about Life. R.U.R. engages moral turpitude and stupidity and despair and sterile decay and death; and played correctly – at vaudeville speed – it is utterly hilarious. Lessons about humanity, and omens of a dark future, dance flickeringly across the stage, and glitter as well through the new translation by Claudia Novack-Jones, which appears in *Toward the Radical Center*; it is the first time sense has been made of this play in English.

The same may be said of the new version of Act Two of *From the Life of the Insects* (1921), Josef and Karel Capek's joint masterpiece of the stage, which has been translated for the *Reader* by Tatiana Firkusny and Robert T Jones. Raw, pell-mell, and now finally available in unexpurgated form, it presents organized human society as a literal vaudeville, with the main roles played by insects not much less horrific than those which haunted Kafka (but rather funnier). The savagery of the play – its sense that the world we live in balances delicately over an abyss – also surfaces in the fiction Capek produced during this period, a time of slowly growing political stress as old realities began to shape the new Europe, and fresh-born Czechoslovakia itself began to seem balanced over an abyss. Nothing from *Krakatit* (1924), perhaps Capek's darkest and most hallucinated novel, appears in the *Reader*; but Kussi has avoided extracts in general, *Krakatit* is not in any case a book which can readily be excerpted, and new versions of some short fiction from 1920–25 amply attest to the mood within the bone.

It is not that Capek often had much time to display hidden depths. *Krakatit* may be open to the darknesses below, but *The Makropolis Case* (1922), a virtuoso scherzo into the arms of Death, skirts the horrors its immortal heroine must inevitably embrace (the new translation, by Yveta Synek Graff and Robert T Jones, finally unveils the manic clarity of Capek's stagecraft in this stunning "comedy"); only in a few stories – "The Footprint" (1917), for instance, or the superbly claustrophobic "Money" (1921) – do moments of terrified repose occur. In 1921, at the age of 31, Capek joined the Prague newspaper, *Lidove noviny*, and for the rest of his life channelled enormous amounts of work through its pages. He was made Director of the Prague Municipal Theater. He met the President of Czechoslovakia, T G Masaryk, became his friend, espoused his virtues and his views of national destiny to the world. He became a public man, one of those who tell the Time but have none.

A decade passed. He had written some short stories of worth, reams of journalistic copy, hagiography addressed to his beloved Masaryk, travel books; but no novel, no play worth serious attention. What happened at the beginning of the 1930s it seems impossible to know, but suddenly Capek produced, in *Hordubal* (1933), *Meteor* (1934) and *An Ordinary Life* (1934), a stunning, mortuary trilogy of novels which are by some accounted his central achievement. Translations by M and R Weatherall were separately published in England before the War, and have now been released in one volume as *Three Novels* (Garrigue, 1990). The book is less an omnibus than one tale in triplicate, three ways of looking the one thing which cannot be seen – the "real" soul of another person (or oneself). The illiterate Hordubal returns from America to his smallholding and his wife and is soon murdered; but forensic knowledge of the method of the crime only murders more deeply the irremediably vacant Hordubal, who could not read, who could not be read. In *Meteor*, three conflicting tales jostle against one another, each claiming to tell the life of a dying pilot; each makes a coherent story according to the laws of narrative (and none can be true). And in *An Ordinary Life*, Old Mr Popel looks back over his own life, seeing it as an arbitrary selection of stories he's told himself, realizing that other stories might have led to another Old Mr Popel. In the end *Three Novels* provides only one message of any security: stories may lie, but we must tell them. There is nothing else.

They are tales of relativity, lessons in the contigency of brute fact, and they tell much of the mental condition of Karel Capek, a Czech patriot in a world of insulting absolutisms. As the 1930s darkened towards catastrophe, a kind of wizening pallor began to show in his work, as though it required all the energy he possessed merely to continue to utter. In this light, the comparative frailness of *War with the Newts* from 1936 seems a sign not of weakness but of solitude. Even refreshed for the English-speaking reader by Ewald Osers's recent translation, and lightened by the *feuilleton* style in which it was written for *Lidove noviny*, the prognosis for humanity suggested by the book haunts its pages with an ashen veracity. A race of large strong docile newts from the South Pacific becomes, like Rossum's robots, a new proletariat in the service of humanity; but they are humorless, devoted, hysterical creatures, a Hitler among them soon organizes the raising of the oceans for Lebens-raum, and humanity dies off. In the new world of the Newt Reich, there can be no room for small amusing fauna.

Soon afterwards, Neville Chamberlain left Munich waving his bit of paper, and the waters began to rise upon Czechoslovakia, and Capek died. For half a century he was frozen; it hurt to read him. There was only one small consolation available from the time of his death, a tiny joke, a quirk of the mouth. In March 1939, when the German tide rose finally over Prague, a newt-like squad of thought police descended upon Capek's home. They had come to arrest him. But the bird had flown.

Today, he has returned.

– The Nation, 7 May 1990

2. M John Harrison

[A rough draft of this piece was published by the 1989 Helicon. That it was not the final version was not the fault of the committee. I was still pretty new with my computer, and copied the wrong document onto my disk. Nowadays, I never make an error, of any sort 1995.]

IT SEEMS simple enough. Here is M John Harrison, who is the author of eight books. Or nine books, if you count the American and British versions of *Viriconium Nights* as separate productions, which you should. Or ten books, if you count *Climbers*, his longest novel to date, and his first for the better part of a decade, which is currently in production at Gollancz [and was published later in 1989 1995]. Or eleven books, if you count the non-fiction *Fawcett on Rock*, written in collaboration with Ron Fawcett, and devoted to the joys of climbing mute prongs of the planet while whistling through your teeth before you come loose and fall and hit the hard Earth with an ooph and maybe live through it. Which may be what all of his books are about. Of which there are only ten, if you ignore *The Machine in Shaft Ten*, which Mike Harrison (he calls himself M John Harrison only because in 1966, when he began to publish, there was already a writer named Michael Harrison, now dead, who had been writing sf and fantasy novels for many years) would like you to, wrongly. Or eleven, if you count *Viriconium*, an omnibus containing two previous volumes.

So it seems simple enough, certainly if everything M John Harrison has written boils down a series of versions of what it means to climb part of the way off the planet and inevitably to fall back again – to have illusions, in other words, and to

430

learn that though they blind they do not hold. Purity of heart – one might say, quoting the theologian S Kierkegaard – is to will one thing, and there may be no better way of understanding Mike Harrison than to work on the assumption that everything he has ever written wills one thing, which is to see the world. When taken in chronological order, his collected stories and novels read like a series of drafts of one final book about True Sight. Sight without signs. At the moment that final book may be *Climbers*, but a decade hence *Climbers* may well seem no more than a harbinger, a transparency staining the white radiance of eternity of the *real* final book, in which sign and signifier finally wed in words that cannot be gainsaid: pure, simple, beyond all paraphrase: the world from which there is no escape, because the signs and symbols we use to pretend that we are escaping will have been stripped in this final book of all the maya and dreck and fantasy we have coated them with, and we will be face to face with the thing itself, which pays no heed. And from this True Sight, whistling rock lullabies through our teeth, we shall, of course, fall.

It is because there are no plots in heaven (because any descripton of Paradise is in truth a description of the Fall, and because novels cannot live on True Sight alone) that there is no story in the world which is not a tale of the Fallen. *Climbers* may culminate Mike Harrison's long campaign to strip his fantasy and sf of all the dreck and maya that clog its origins – of all the garish and risible escapism which makes laughingstocks in the real world of those of us who, long after we've managed to survive puberty or menarche, still read the stuff – but all that means is that his newest novel is his first novel to inhabit our own fallen world without protective clothing, and to tell tales about it. But of course it's not that simple. *Climbers* does not so much turn its back on fantasy as come finally face-to-face with it. From the sclerotic pomp of *The Pastel City* down to the entropy-exuding damp walls of Camden Town in "The Incalling," all of Mike Harrison's previous work glares numbly through the mirrors that appear so frequently throughout the new book. These are mirrors into which we, the Fallen, find ourselves gazing (one is reminded of the character in a recent Arthur Miller play who hates to shave himself, because when he looks into the mirror while doing so, it feels like he's shaving his father) and in which we see the contours of our exile.

Mike Harrison himself sometimes gives the impression that he would like to burn everything he published before 1980, everything stuck on the wrong side of the mirror, but we need not be constrained by his need to keep his mind sharply on the tales of the Fallen he now writes. We can even plunge into the depths of time and take a glance at *The Machine in Shaft Ten and Other Stories* (1975), which collects some of his earliest work (though it also includes the first book publication of

"Running Down"), and when we look at items like "London Melancholy" or the first version of "The Lamia and Lord Cromis" as it appears here and in the American *Viriconium Nights*, we begin to get some sense of where Mike Harrison came from; and why he had to leave.

We are in the middle of the 1960s. Under Michael Moorcock, *New Worlds* was beginning to publish what would come reductively to be known as New Wave fiction, as though Aldiss Ballard Disch Harrison Moorcock Sladek et al could be subsumed under a rubric they would not shred. In this hyperventilated and fragile venue Mike Harrison began his career. From the very first his originality lay not in the exploration of new forms and habitats for speculative fiction, but in his corrosive repossession of the old. In retrospect, for Harrison today, it might seem that this early work owes all too much to the models it infiltrates and subverts; but for his readers in 1966, and for readers even now, there is something deeply exhilarating about the way these early tales, like viruses apeing a victim cell, imitate conventional models (usually sword-and-sorcery or post-holocaust story-types) only to *shut down* the ancient genre machinery, once properly inside the bone of the old, with a smear of entropy and a rasp of asthmatic laughter. This destructive infiltration by mimesis might be called the sarcasm of the virus, and Mike Harrison was a master at it. His short stories were the work of a demolisher who could hold his breath until the dust settled, and live to write and ruin another day. But could he ever create a full-length novel without suffocating inside the models he would need to invade?

It was a near thing. None of his first books, *The Committed Men* (1971), *The Pastel City* (1971) and *The Centauri Device* (1974), feel very wholesome today, in the light of his mature work. Something fiercely truculent and energetic within each of them stalls, like tetanus, at the edge of expression, and each gives off an overwhelming sense of willed refusal of the joy of telling. Mike Harrison has never been an unstubborn writer (or person), and for a few years in the early seventies he gave the impression that the Despite in which he held the kinds of genre fiction he was imitating had very nearly stymied him. The sarcasm of the virus does not, in the end, in itself, lead to new terrain. In the rag-and-bone shop of the heart, sarcasm might be called the lowest form of humus. Something else was needed, some goal he could apply his muscle to achieving, through the slough.

This goal is not descried in *The Committed Men*, which is set in a stagy entropy-ridden post-catastrophe Britain. There may be no rain in the book, but one's memory is of constant polluted rainfall. The narrative may well embody a logic of explanation for the nature of the catastrophe which the men and women of the cast stumble through in a kind of stalled and pinched St Vitus Dance, but one's memory is of a constant tendency for the tale to dissolve into a stained surrealism of dismantling. I rather love the book. *The Centauri Device*, on the other hand, evokes a different response. It gives this reader a kind of metaphorical lockjaw, perhaps out of sympathy for the author, trapped as he is into creating a genuine space opera, writing hardcase (but almost verbless) sentences like: "*Intestinal Revelation* (lately the *Ella Speed*, out of RV Tauri 11 – Stomach – with a cargo of nothing) lay at Egerton's Port, Avernus, that infamous planet at the edge of the Ariadne arm," when all he really wanted to write was sentences like "It was a long journey, and worth nothing in the end," or "Ella groaned and leaned a few degrees more, settling into the mud," or "He coughed miserably." *The Centauri Device* is Mike's only book whose hardcore science-fiction base is undisguised – the only book whose intrinsic structure is therefore a dream of enablement – and demonstrates with utter clarity how unfitted he is to write escapist literature. Which is not to deny that everything he writes is about trying to escape.

At first glance *The Pastel City*, ostensibly a sword-and-sorcery fantasy set in a Dying Earth choked with magic technologies and fun wars at the end of time, seems only a little less rigid than *The Centauri Device*. We meet an Empire older than memory called Viriconium, which is ruled by a young Queen, Good Queen Methvet Vian, whose inherent dignity causes awe in the cast. We meet a a valiant aristocratic soldier out of *Gormenghast* who thinks of himself as "a better poet than swordsman," but who is the reverse, like Gary Cooper, or Salvador Dalí. We run the gauntlet of a traditional Wild Gang recruitment sequence in which the swordsman and the dwarf and the Reborn Man and the bloody axe-wielder all come together to save the kingdom from the other Queen, Bad Queen Moidart. Unsurprisingly, both the British and the American editions of *The Pastel City* duly blurb the book as though it were a companion volume to one of Michael Moorcock's contemporaneous purple fantasies, and it must be said that only slowly does the truth tend to dawn on the reader: that *The Pastel City* is not fantasy at all. There is no saving magic in the book, no wizard, no rune with power, no multiverse to escape into; everyone in the cast is an escapologist of sorts, but no one ever makes good his or her egress from the trammels of Viriconium. If my own distinction between science fantasy and sf is at all workable, then *The Pastel City* is a tale of science fantasy. "Sf," I said in *Foundation 37*, "promulgates a view futurewards in which the plot secret to be deciphered will change the world, and in one bound we are free. Science fantasy opens a view into the deep past in which the plot secret to be deciphered will demonstrate for us how the world became the World we live in, which binds us." In *The Pastel City*, for the first time, and rather falteringly, Mike Harrison found a system of metaphors and dreams worth stripping down, a world worth deciphering, a binding reality to seek through the dreck and maya.

As *The Pastel City* is a work of science fantasy, the axis between fantasy and reality is therefore a temporal one, and reality must lie in the past, in a binding deconstruction of the bathos of the very notion of a Dying Earth. In the Viriconium books that followed – *A Storm of Wings* (1980), *In Viriconium* (1982), and the collection *Viriconium Nights* (US version 1984; radically revised UK version 1985) – the science fantasy element steadily diminishes, having done its job, and the axis becomes a point. Or a mirror. And we are on this side of that mirror. And the rococo turrets of Viriconium are no more than the exudate of our dreams of escape. By the end of the last story in the British version of *Viriconium Nights*, the mere word "Viriconium" is all that remains; "Viriconium!" has become an exclamation, a curse, a sign that the raw world in which the protagonist breathes his every breath is itself the only Viriconium our breaths will ever fog.

The route to that final redaction of the sign is long but exciting. At first glance *A Storm of Wings* may seem to be a perfectly orthodox science fantasy novel about the invasion of a Dying Earth by an alien species; but it is also something rather odder. In the guise of a sequel to *The Pastel City*, it is in fact a profound punning rewrite of the earlier book. Both novels are set in a Viriconium threatened from the north by invaders. In the first version, the life-style of these invaders is subversive of the body politic of Viriconium; in the second, the very Umwelt – the perceptual world – of the invaders intersects and suborns the consensual reality of the sad silly Weltschmerz-und-Weimar-choked city. In the first version, actors strut across the stage of the world to accomplish the tasks of the plot; in the second, fixated and appalled, like flies in molasses, they *spectate* the stage of the world, and the tasks of the plot are accomplished, as it were, by shifts in their perception. The first version is set in Viriconium, a misty boggy land of moors and valleys; the second version, also set in "Viriconium," depicts the land with a richness and precision rarely if ever found in the literature, but this new verisimilitude has the effect of paling out the phantasmagoric contours of the Dying Earth into a kind of gloss laid over the real, like scum over a pond. What is Mike Harrison trying to make us see?

In the final books of the sequence, the city of "Viriconium" begins to tremble at the edge of the eye, like a half-memory of something slept through and deeply desired, but never truly available to the woken escapologist. By the end of *In Viriconium* and the definitive British version of *Viriconium Nights*, it is clear that the empire of Good Queen Methvet Vian lies somewhere west of Sheffield and east of Manchester, and that the rain that falls on "Viriconium" falls also on the real world of the

Pennines, the world that, in his recent books, in prose that mimes with utmost clarity the miracles of the given, Mike Harrison has been inviting us to see.

But it is much easier to dream. True sight is difficult to earn, and never stays. The dream of Viriconium fogs the glasses of every character in the superb stories of the Fallen either collected in *The Ice Monkey* (1983) or published more recently, tales like "Older Women" (1984) or "The Great God Pan" (1987); and it spooks the vision of every climber in *Climbers*. Because every character in Harrison's recent fiction is all too human, every one of them grapples constantly with the temptation to manipulate the signs of the world into a language which will open the door to Viriconium; and every one of them fails. They fail because the world simply *is* in all its muteness, and our fantasies of signification are nothing more than the static we emit in the chaos of our fallen state. Viriconium – Mike Harrison implies in the deepening clarity of his latest work – is a kind of *noise*. It is the sound of humans, signals of the Fallen looking for a Rock.

Viriconium!

– Helicon Programme Book, 1989

3. Aldous Huxley

TOWARD the end of the 1950s, his creative energies thinned out by age and ill-health and loss and too many years in Southern California, Aldous Huxley wrote a series of articles about the future for *Newsday*. In a tone of remote, wearied candour, he outlined for his American audience some of the issues that seemed urgent at the time: overpopulation; the excessive organization of society; propaganda; the chemistry of brainwashing; and so forth. Later, he revised these pieces into a book which he called *Brave New World Revisited* (1958).

This, precisely, it was not. *Brave New World* (1932) was an act of prophecy; its successor was a set of predictions. The one could not be falsified by a failure of world history to march according to its vision, and remains subversively alive at the end of the century to which it gave a dream-shape; its successor, which has been proved wrong in a dozen ways, in accordance with the fate of all books of futurology, is just as dead as any work of predictive non-fiction by H G Wells.

In 1958, Huxley understood *Brave New World* as a work in which he had predicted "the completely organized society, the scientific caste system, the abolition of free will by methodical conditioning, the servitude made acceptable by regular doses of chemically induced happiness, the orthodoxies drummed in by nightly courses of sleep-teaching," and whose only real flaw as a work of futurology, beyond its failure to anticipate the A-bomb, lay in placing several centuries hence the total victory of Technos through chemistry. He then explained – in fatally erring detail – how this victory was in fact upon us.

In 1993, other victories have superseded the Futurama horrors imagined in 1958. Overpopulation has not led to icy fixities of control, but to chaos; chemistry (and electronics) do not marshall our days at the behest of Secret Masters, but do give us chances to opt out into Nirvana, into a seeming infinity of solipsisms. We have become street-wise to dystopia; we inhabit a world of plethora and desecration that neither Huxley – nor any other futurologist half a century back – could have begun to wish upon us. His wisdom lies elsewhere.

It has been estimated that the term "science fiction" appears less than a dozen times in the voluminous published work of Aldous Huxley; but as that term was only first used in a pulp magazine around 1930, and did not spread to the UK for years, it's perhaps surprising he used it as often as he did after the age of 50, and in any case – whatever he called it in 1932 – Brave New World remains a central and representative work of that genre. The dominance of American sf from about 1925 to about 1975, with its technophilia and its booster exuberance and its constant gate-crashing thrust of triumphalist premises into the fragile future, has tended to conceal the true thrust of the sf impulse, which is by no means consolatory. Wells, Huxley, Orwell, Philip K Dick, and a dozen significant figures now writing, have all used the devices of sf to host, and to grapple with, the nightmare of history during a century haunted by what might be called a radical of transformation.

The twentieth century, in other words, is genuinely different. It is a century of nightmares about change and about the end of change, like all centuries; but this time round the nightmares are with us when we wake. The profound impulse of sf is to gain perspectives on the quicksand; the profoundest fear of most serious writers of sf is that somehow the world will suddenly stop shifting at the wrong moment, locking us into a malign stasis. The great dystopias of the twentieth century are nightmares of tetanus. "If you want to imagine the future," said Orwell in Nineteen Eighty-Four (1949), "Imagine a boot stamping on a human face – for ever." "So it goes," says Kurt Vonnegut.

The terror at the heart of Brave New World is not feelies, nor babies in bottles, but fixity. The novel closes with the suicide of Mr Savage, the only character in the book capable of reflecting our humane nostalgia for rounded human beings alive in a supple world. At the end, we can only see his feet:

Slowly, very slowly, like two unhurried compass needles, the feet turned towards the right; north, north-east, east, south-east, south, south-south-west; then paused, and after a few seconds, turned as unhurriedly towards the left. South-south-west, south, south-east, east…

Huxley's second great tale of nightmare, *Ape and Essence* (1948), is in many ways a lesser book than its predecessor, though far more explicitly savage about human nature and history. It is the lesser creation in part because its structure never gels. There is a prologue in 1947, during which two screenwriters find and read a rejected screenplay-of-the-mind; this script is set in the year 2108, a century after nuclear war has destroyed America and bathed the few survivors in hard radiation, and makes up the bulk of the novel. But nothing is made of the wooden complexities of this format. The other problem with the book is hope.

A ship from unscathed New Zealand visits California. A shy biologist, Dr. Poole, is captured by the Californians, who worship Belial (as the Arch-Vicar explains in one of Huxley's best discussion scenes) because He has won. He has managed to persuade Western humanity to believe in Progress:

Progress – the theory that you can get something for nothing; the theory that you can gain in one field without paying for your gain in another;…the theory that you know what's going to happen fifty years from now.

The Vicar goes on to demonstrate his case about the parasitic relationship of humanity to the planet with a scathing diatribe on overpopulation and the ecological devastation that inevitably follows (as indeed it has). He describes Belial's triumph in terms that seem prescient in 1993: the normalization of atrocity; the lust to punish those who have already been punished; the addiction to Nationalism. It all seems definitive enough for one book.

But love comes to Professor Poole, and a sense that Gaia Herself endures beneath the apeish filth; and he and his woman escape in the end, pausing for a moment of mythical circularity at the tomb of the man who wrote the screenplay they are characters in. By 1948, in other words, Huxley was beginning to flinch from the zero horizon that lies at the end of the truest sf texts of the century. It is a view, one supposes, which is difficult to bear. And a decade later, he was talking about the predictive accuracy of *Brave New World* as though details mattered.

In prophecy, they do not matter a whit. In the prophetic literature of the twentieth century, it is not predictions – accuracies or bloopers about the failure of the next technological fix – which hold the attention, focus the vision. It is intimations that we will not get out of this time alive that shape our sense of vision, nowadays. It is a knowing terror that the great wheel will stall.

– New Statesman, 17 December 1993

4. Gustav Meyrink

GUSTAV MEYRINK, it is easy to think, lived a life that more resembled a dream than any of the stories he wrote. He was a bastard, a banker, an inventor, a fin-de-siècle flâneur, a jailbird, a guru who flyted his disciples, a pacifist in love with apocalypse, a magus who contemned the halitosic prattle of occultism. Each stage of his life had the saturated gluey intensity of dream; and the life as a whole seemed spatchcocked out of legend and sleep, a congeries of psychopomp blurbs. He was an Arcimboldo Green Man: rags and patches of life-stuff; granny-knots of circumstance unravelling at a jerk as the century downturned into disaster; a foliate head. The stories he wrote seemed to exfoliate from the life.

He was born Gustav Meyer, in Vienna. His mother was an actress and his father an elderly aristocrat with a position in government. Grotesquely maladroit parent-figures appear and reappear throughout the fiction, most notably perhaps as the crone-courtesan and floundering ectomorph nobleman whose ultimate reconciliation transfigures his third novel, *Walpurgisnacht* (1917; translated by Mike Mitchell for Dedalus in 1993).

He moved to Prague as a young man and became a banker, an athlete, a philanderer, a fencer, and the owner of that city's first automobile. Much of the carnival night life hinted at in *Walpurgisnacht*, and treated in detail throughout his second novel, *Das grüne Gesicht* (1916; translated by Mike Mitchell for Dedalus in 1992 as *The Green Face*), seems to make nineteenth-century Prague visible in a crazy mirror, as topsy-turvy as the new century boded to become.

His first marriage ended badly. He remarried under circumstances which seemed scandalous to the Prague world he mocked, and which occasioned vicious gossip. He challenged one of his new wife's slanderers to a duel, but the challenge was declined on the grounds that, as a bastard, he was inherently incapable of receiving satisfaction. At about the same time, in 1902, he was arrested and imprisoned for three months, on charges of fraud. He was exonerated, but on his release was discovered to have tuberculosis of the spine. He was also destitute. His life as a banker Harlequin had terminated as though he had walked a plank, into a new medium. His first novel, *Der Golem* (1915; translated by Madge Pemberton in 1928 as *The Golem*; a new translation by Mike Mitchell appears from Dedalus in 1995), is structured around visions of unbearable parents, occult amnesia, the false polder of the soon-to-be-demolished ghetto, a supernatural doppelgänger who evokes a lacerating sehnsucht in the blanked protagonist, surreal interrogations and false imprisonment in a Prague like Kafka's, and an invisible new life told through a frame story which opens opaque hints of that new life whose details the novel cannot presume to depict.

But before Gustav Meyer's first life ended, he had begun the life for which he is now remembered. His first story, which was written under the name Meyrink, appeared in the magazine *Simplicissimus* in 1901, and within a few years he had become a central figure in pre-War German literature, a literature whose proleptic convulsiveness and *rightness* about the world to come it is difficult now, nearly a hundred years on, to comprehend. In 1994 it is difficult, and humbling, to realize that long before we were born they had said as much as *we* can about the heartbeat of the century; it is at times almost impossible not to feel that the apocalyptic insights we think to detect are simply, in fact, endogenous fevers of Expressionism: that we are patching 1910 metaphors into our knowledge of subsequent history, shaving them to fit. This indeed must surely happen: it must surely be the case that we do read them selectively, and that the writers and artists and composers and scholars and thinkers and architects of 1910 *could not know* that they were right: that the clock of history (as they intimated) had begun to stutter, setting off all the alarms at once. In the end, however, it may not altogether matter if they knew they were right. In the end, perhaps, it is more important for us to realize that – in their dreams and paranoias and dread – they saw us here.

For English readers, it is not yet possible to know how fully Meyrink's earliest fiction engaged with the first years of turmoil, as he only began publishing his novels after World War One had already started. His initial reputation on the Continent came from the large number of short stories he published before *The Golem* first appeared, and which were collected in several volumes: *Der heisse Soldat und andere Gesichten* ["The Hot Soldier and Other Stories"] (1903); *Orchideen: Sonderbare Geschichten* ["Orchids: Strange Stories"] (1904); *Das Wachsfigurenkabinett: Sonderbare Geschichten* ["The Wax Museum: Strange Stories"] (1907); *Des deutschen Spiessers Wunderhorn* ["The German Philistine's Magic Horn"] (1913), the last being a three-volume omnibus incorporating old and new material; and *Fledermäuse* ["Bats"] (1916). E F Bleiler's *Guide to Supernatural Fiction* (1983) lists only one short story by Meyrink in English. *The Golden Bomb: Phantastic German Expressionist Stories* (1993) ed Malcolm Green includes a different one; and *The Dedalus/Ariadne Book of Austrian Fantasy: The Meyrink Years, 1890–1930* (1992) ed Mike Mitchell includes five: which is a significant start, but one which shows the largeness of the vista to be further unveiled when a projected volume of Meyrink stories from the same translator appears in the Dedalus programme.

On the whole, we are left with a fever of belatedness, through which the past makes the present (and the future) dance to dead tunes. *The Golem* is meant to be taking place around 1890, but scumbles chronology so thoroughly that the reader will find it hard to avoid conflating the destruction of the ghetto with larger devastations, or the mephitic arousals of psyche emblematized by the golem itself with more widespread (and far more vicious) hysterias. *The Green Face*, which was being drafted as World War One began, is ostensibly set in the future, after the end of hostilities, but the outcome and aftermath of the war are viewed, by an act of occultish legerdemain, though the lens of an ashen retrospect: the labyrinth of the trenches, like some rebirthing of Cthulhu; the end-of-the-world perspectives granted by No Man's Land; the taste of a world-order exhausted, of the dithering puniness of secular man sifting the ruins for loot. It is astonishing that the book reached publication in the midst of a total war which was being lost. Like *Walpurgisnacht*, which also appeared before 1918, but far more explicitly, *The Green Face* treats the War to End War as a Saturnalia, a *danse macabre* which ends in Wind: in an apocalyptic harrowing of Europe, obliterating the false face of the material world.

Beneath that face (it is a turn of vision fundamental to occult dualism, and it appears in all Meyrink's work) can be discerned a higher, spiritual world of true effect and cause, which can now be celebrated in a chymical marriage between the scoured protagonist (all his protagonists have been deeply wounded by the harlequinade of appearance) and his dead love (Meyrink females, if they are worthy, are almost certain to be dead).

It may all come down to his actress mother, who abandoned him in early childhood; but it may, as well, have something to do with the fancy-step metamorphosizing almost any European writer of Meyrink's period engaged in whenever the Female Principle was to be distinguished from the Female Body. Whatever the cause, it cannot be denied that throughout his career Meyrink's female characters, with the exception of an occasional nurturing crone from the lower orders, occupy only two categories: either they are avatars of Medusa, whose wormy sexuality turns men into stone, imprisoning them in the maya of existence; or they are Beatrice and – having died well before the end of the novel – await their husband-to-be's union with them in a higher world. Modern readers (of whom half may be presumed to be women) may understandably find this aspect of the male dualist imagination both distasteful and inutile; but it is an inescapable component of Meyrink's world-view from beginning to end.

In each of the first three novels, a transfiguring chymical marriage climaxes the personal story, though in each of these books the jettisoning of the material world is achieved with a panoramic glitter. After the end of World War One, however, Meyrink discarded the contemporary world, and his late work radically disengages from that Europe of aftermath he had so prophetically limned; there are no more prophetic spasms to remind us now, at the end of the millennium, that our visions of doom are epigonic. At the same time, however, he did continue to adhere to the occult dualisms to which (like William Butler Yeats) he seemed to give credence, and which shaped and fortified his work, though at the same time he never lost his marbles: whenever he was confronted with fraudulence or Golden Dawn vaporizings, he proved to be a savage debunker. But dualism in the hands of any male European writer born in the last century is almost invariably fatal to the female of the species, and it does remain the case that the modern reader may have trouble with some of the more didactic passages of his fourth novel, *Der weiße Dominikaner* (1921), now translated for Dedalus as *The White Dominican* by Mike Mitchell, in a style which admirably captures Meyrink's sly swift eloquence. There can be no doubt whatsoever that the ongoing Medusa/Beatrice dualism – even when it is toned down by the fact that the only whorish female in the book is far too old to entrap the protagonist – will be hard for most contemporary readers to swallow. What remains?

In the event, a great deal. What *The White Dominican* loses in being the first fruit of Meyrink's chastened post-catastrophe imagination, it gains in supernal equipoise, in an oneiric serenity which tugs very hard at the roots in dream of our own responses to the allure of Story. We begin with a frame: the author of the tale, who seems to be Meyrink himself, tells the reader that he has never found out for sure whether or not the protagonist of the story "ever actually lived; he certainly did not spring from my imagination, of that I remain convinced." This protagonist, it turns out, has mysteriously caused Meyrink to call him by his proper, heavily symbolic name, Christopher Dovecote, a name Meyrink claims to be unconscious of having used when drafting his novel; and we are cast immediately into a Tale whose material embodiment (the words we read, the paper we touch) is itself a lesson imparted. To understand the Tale we must understand that the words we read are nothing but echoes, caught in the Medusa dust of corporeality. "Being born on earth is nothing other than being buried alive." The true Tale will be what we rise to learn.

We enter the main story, which is told in the first person by Dovecote himself.

He is an orphan, abandoned as an infant on the steps of the local church, but soon is adopted by the dominant figure in the town, Baron Bartholomew von Jöcher, Freeman and Honorary Lamplighter. The town itself is never named. It lies downstream from the capital of the country, which is not named either. Only Paris – which is also the name of the fraudulent impresario who is the real father of the Beatrice figure we are soon to meet – can be recognized as a place inhabiting mortal history. The river comes north from the capital, almost completely encircles the town, and departs southward; on the neck of land separating the river flowing north and the river flowing south is the Baron's house, which has been occupied by his family for something like thirteen generations. Each new generation of von Jöchers abandons the floor occupied by its predecessor, and moves upwards within the house, which must therefore, like so many labyrinth-portals to other worlds, be bigger inside than out. The town itself – empoldered by the river and guarded by the house whose occupants are themselves Guardians of (and Aspirants to) the Threshold to the upper levels – seems utterly secure.

Within this polder, at the top of this ladder of generations of Guardians, Christopher grows up. He finds he is the Baron's true son. He falls in love with the girl who lives in the house next to his. Her name is Ophelia. She too has difficulties in relating her nature to her corporeal parentage: her ostensible father, the town's coffin-maker and a man mentally damaged from the time his own father buried him alive in a coffin as a punishment, is not her father at all. Her true father, the reprehensible impresario Paris with his camp aristocratic mien, and her mother, the failed whorish actress, connive in repression and bad faith. But she transcends her corporeal bondage, she returns Christopher's love, and – as any reader experienced in Meyrink will know from the fact of that love for the protagonist, and from her name – she soon dies, voluntarily. But by then Christopher has undergone night journeys into occult realms; he has been told that he is destined to become transfigured, to rise from the top of the Tree of the Lamplighter family into true reality; and he treats her death as a confirmation of betrothal.

To this point, in *The White Dominican*, we have been gifted with scenes of epiphanic calm which alternate with "real-world" episodes of Dickensian splendour (Meyrink translated Dickens earlier in his career) whenever the lovable, duped coffin-maker comes into view. From this point onwards, in passages that shift levels of import as do dreams, we are invited to follow Christopher into his inheritance. Some of the terms of that invitation are couched with a didactic precision some readers may find distressingly liturgical, because Christopher's ascension is that of a magus, cloaked in arcana; but the flow of the ascent is irresistible.

And the visitations of the Medusa, the corporeal world, in false likenesses of the dead Ophelia, have a power that easily transcends the doctrinaire sexual Manicheanism through which Meyrink articulates his vision of "the impersonal force of all evil, using the mute forces of nature to conjure up miracles which in reality are only hellish phantasms serving the ends of the spirit of negation." But "the head of Medusa, that symbol of the petrifying force that sucks us down," has no final sway, and the chymical marriage will ultimately be consummated, in some realm the pages of the book cannot reach. So be it.

We may baulk at some of the terms in which it is put. But it is his final word. After this novel came only the alchemical tales published as *Goldmachergeschichten* ["Tales of the Alchemists"] (1925) and the intermittently brilliant *Der Engel vom Westlichen Fenster* (1927; translated by Mike Mitchell for Dedalus in 1991 as *The Angel of the West Window*), about Doctor Dee; neither book coins a new metaphor to replace the Medusa. It seems clear that for the Meyrink of the post-War years, the image of the Medusa was definitive. The Medusa, it is possible to think, was nothing less than the entirety of the world which opened its maw to sensitive men and women in 1914. The Medusa, whose image he unforgettably presented to his readers, stares upon us through every newsreel the century has disgorged. It is the tetanus which fixes us upon the wheel of time. It is surely not Gustav Meyrink's fault that, for most of us, there will be no chymical marriage.

– Introduction to *The White Dominican* (Dedalus, 1994)

5. Herbert Rosendorfer

AT LAST. Now we can begin properly. It is true that some of the work of Herbert Rosendorfer, who was born in 1934, and who became a district court judge in Munich in 1967, had already been available in English before 1992; *Deutsche Suite* (1972), translated by Arnold Pomerans as *German Suite*, had appeared in 1979, and *Die Nacht der Amazonen* (1989), translated by Ian Mitchell as *Night of the Amazons*, had appeared in 1991. But these two books, despite the fleering carnival brilliance of their presentation of the lunacies of Nazi Germany, conveyed to readers – surely deliberately – a sense of surreal entrapment, of civilization's endgame interminably prolonged – natural enough, one might think, for an author who spent his childhood in the coils of nightmare. All the same, this gnawing at the poison cud of remembrance seemed obsessive, and conveyed a sense of Rosendorfer as a man caught staring backwards into the black hole of World War Two, unable to escape. But at last we can begin properly, and in Mike Mitchell's joyful translation of Rosendorfer's first novel we can see how partial a view we had of the man. The pleasure is ours.

Der Ruinenbaumeister (1969), which Mitchell has deftly rendered as *The Architect of Ruins*, contains the germ of all of Rosendorfer's work, like a dream. It is a tale of escape into story-land, a discourse about stories, a story about stories within stories within stories: like an onion that makes one smile. Whether or not the book itself represents a long and exceedingly complex dream experienced by the narrator as a series of stories told to him over the course of a few minutes in real time as the train he has boarded carries him and six hundred nuns in the direction of Lourdes, the reader can perhaps decide. But if the reader *does* end up thinking that *The Architect of Ruins* represents a dream, s/he will have also to decide whether or not the narrator – ensconced as he was on a hurtling night-girdled train with a lunatic sneak thief under his seat, and hundreds of females in mysterious all-enveloping habits round about him – is himself caught in the intersections of a larger dream, from which he fails to awaken into a new self only because the last page of the novel intervenes, leaving him with us. For myself, the question can be shelved for the moment. It is perhaps enough at this point to say that *The Architect of Ruins* is like a dream.

The narrator, who is never named and who gives no sign that he himself has any intention of going to Lourdes, has boarded a train full of nuns who are indeed bound there. From under his seat, a criminal on the run grabs his foot and asks for sanctuary, which is granted, and begins to tell his story, after indicating that some of his experiences resemble those described in G K Chesterton's *The Club of Queer Trades* (1904), a collection of stories which may in fact – like most of the fiction he wrote between 1900 and the outbreak of World War One – constitute a set of dreams. Indeed, the tone and pace of *The Architect of Ruins* – pellmell but preternaturally calm, deadpan but hallucinated – very closely resembles at times that of Chesterton's masterpiece, *The Man Who Was Thursday: A Nightmare* (1908), one of the century's secret paradigm texts. In any case, the fugitive under the seat tells the narrator of a previous career as the inventor of an automatic cleaning device which utilizes bugs capable, because of the tiny rubbers attached to their feet, of cleaning rooms very delicately indeed. This venture fails, and he goes into the funeral business, but oversteps the mark when he makes sculptures out of the corpses. The police then invade the compartment, take him away, and the inspector, who remains, describes to the narrator some of the fugitive's further exploits. At the same time the narrator finds himself gazing at a piece of paper which the ex-corpse-sculptor has left behind. On this paper he can see a mysterious pattern of dots. Or holes. *Déjà vu* suddenly afflicts him. He has been here before. Here. He is on a sunlit road, which runs alongside the wall of a vast and infinitely bosky country estate. He goes through the gate. The novel proper – or the dream – now begins; or continues.

He reaches the cool water. An old man, who has been dancing on the green-sward, and whose name is Daphnis, gives him some chilled beer and tells him the story of King Natholocus of Scotland, which is broken off when two mechanical dwarves, who have the secret to each other's wind-up mechanism and who are therefore inseparable though they hate one another, undertake in surly fashion to show the narrator the route to the temple. But before he can reach his destination he boards a steamer, where he finds Dr Jacobi, who will soon tell him of his Alpine experiences hunting a great wyrm or dragon; Don Emanuele Da Ceneda, who will soon tell him of the search for his beloved Stellidaura which has kept him alive for centuries, though this tale is broken off, only to be resumed later, more than once; and Dr Werkenbarth, the architect of ruins, who tells him immediately the story of the dwarves, and describes to him the vast cigar-shaped underground shelter, capable of housing huge numbers, which he has designed in order to preserve the human race. A man known as Alfred arrives to tell a tale. The steamer continues to move noiselessly through the night. Within some of these stories nest inner stories. The cast then disembarks. They see Nankeen and his troupe of half-naked dancers, who disappear – like some White Rabbit and its progeny – down what seems to be a rabbit hole. It is, of course, the entrance to the underground cigar. The cast follows Nankeen inside, because the war has started. We are one-third the way through the novel, and going deeper.

The style more and more reminds the reader of Jules Verne's insanely methodical recounting of his Extraordinary Voyages, many of which convey one through subterranean Crystal Palaces, through tunnels half-choked by the brass veins of immense machineries whose brows thrust through the floors and walls, until we reach the central chambers or Winter Garden where the President resides, close to the levers of power. We also think of Metropolis (1926). The narrator – we are now compressing the tale – inevitably, therefore, meets President Carola deep within the heart of the cigar. He finds he is now a Senator. He is escorted to his bedchamber, where he meets Spring, his attendant, who reads to him the first scenes of a new version of Oedipus the King; these scenes are entirely taken up with a Tristram Shandy dialogue between two guards that serve as a potentially interminable prelude to the tragedy itself, which will never be reached. But the narrator falls asleep. On awaking, he tells Spring that he has had a dream. In this dream he feels as though he had toppled upwards into the infinitely large universe of which our galaxy is but a cell, or perhaps downwards into an infinitely small universe within the atoms that live within the atoms. "Still trembling from the horror," he says, "I found myself in a large and elegant house. It was a Monday." In this house live a retired castrato – music figures through *The Architect of Ruins*, just as it has in Rosendorfer's own life – and his seven nieces, whose names are Do, Re, Mi, etc. Each niece tells the narrator a story. It is the *Decameron-* or *Saragossa*-like heart of the novel. By the end of the sixth story – the seventh is delayed – we are in its closing pages.

At this point, furore and chaos threaten. Ahasuerus the Wandering Jew – whom we have met – now dies, which means the world is ending. Alarums and battles supervene. But the narrator survives, even though a socially conscious dramatist named Uvesohn – it is a jibe on Rosendorfer's part at Uwe Johnson – makes use of his own play to make a ponderous point or two. He rises like a bubble, hearing a few more stories as he rises. Before he reaches the temple, however, he sees Ahasuerus revived, and Dr. Werkenbarth is made Director of Public Ruins for the quality of his work. The puzzle of the sheet of paper covered with dots – or holes – is solved, but the mystery only deepens. The nuns debouch for Lourdes. The novel has ended.

So the outside story, the story told by the narrator himself, the story of his adventures underground, returns full circle. There is no secret about this, and little suspense. Very carefully, whenever the reader might baulk like a horse refusing a blind jump, Rosendorfer calmly and lucidly lays down a cue to notice, a breadcrumb to follow through the forest homewards, for it is none of his intention to construct a labyrinth whose every turning, like a grammar of nightmare, leads the reader deeper and more inextricably into a state of unknowing. His is a labyrinth of return. It is in this that *The Architect of Ruins* differs so markedly from books like Gene Wolfe's *Peace* (1975), which is a posthumous fantasy whose narrator's constantly broken-off stories carry him deeper and deeper into the sphinx chill of a fully realized death; or Robert Irwin's *The Arabian Nightmare* (Dedalus, 1983), whose protagonist sinks deeper and deeper into dreams the ultimate narrator of which – for the protagonist is soon fathoms and aeons adrift from any control over his own story – is almost certainly the Devil. But the narrator of *The Architect of Ruins*, even lying in the arms of President Carola at the bottom of the Jules Verne cigar after the last invasion of the spiders of the enemy from the skies above, never loses his way for more than a moment or two. He does not turn into a nightmare fish in the black waters of unknowing. For he himself is not the creature fish, but a fisher. He is a fisher of stories.

Because there is no exit from *The Arabian Nightmare*, images from Luis Buñuel's *Exterminating Angel* (1962) tend to ghost the mind's eye of readers who've seen the film, and who remember the huge Narrenschiff of a cast which cannot exit the room, cannot escape the story being told about them. Rosendorfer's first novel evokes different Buñuel films, The Milky Way (1969), or The Discreet Charm of the Bourgeoisie (1972), or The Phantom of Liberty (1974). In these films, just as in The Architect of Ruins, the emphasis shifts from souls in Hell who cannot find a storyline which will let them out, to the nature of Story itself. The pilgrims of the first film; the survivor flotsam of the second who cannot finish a meal but who will not perish from the earth; the innocent folk of the third who disappear whenever the story-telling camera leaves them: like the dozens of characters who prance and dream through the stories that make up the bulk of Rosendorfer's album novel, their importance to us – and their blamelessness – lies in the fact that they are being told.

Later, in German Suite, President Carola may turn into an appalling Princess who fucks an ape and refuses to suckle the human child she bears. But now she is innocent of all that, and leaves not a wrack behind when her story turns. She does not, however, seemingly, die. In a novel about the nature of Story, deaths come – as in Wolfe's novel – when the tale is broken. Time and again, in The Architect of Ruins, a story may stop midway through, and we may fear the haemorrhage, the seeping of all the frail concinnities of telling into the stone labyrinth; but then – it may be a hundred pages later – the story will return to us, and be completed, and become whole. Time and again, this does happen. President Carola, and Dr. Werkenbarth, and Ahasuerus reborn, attend upon their tales, and that is the important thing about The Architect of Ruins. We do not know, or care, whether Herbert Rosendorfer's novel is a dream, or not a dream. We do know, and care, that it is whole.

– Introduction to The Architect of Ruins (Dedalus, 1992)

6. James Tiptree Jr

IT MAY NOT be the truth about American writers, but it is the story. So print the story. American writers, let us say, are like meteors. Flashes in the pan. Mayfly angels. Out of the nowhere, into the here they come, hurtling brazenly through their short day to give us joy, strewing largesse and seed about as though there were no tomorrow which indeed there isn't – because the air of the planet soon gets them, seizes shut the wings of song, burns them out. Afterwards, stuck together with mucilage and pulp, they may linger for a few years in the atriums of America, for hire; but it is not a warm world for sharecroppers, and after the mating flight American writers are terribly fragile, like beehives in a frost. They rust. They crumble at the touch. That is the story we are told, the legend we print; half-right but vicious. It may have shaped the lives (it has certainly poisoned our perception of the lives) of writers like Truman Capote, Dashiell Hammett, Jack Kerouac, Theodore Sturgeon. And James Tiptree Jr?

Sometimes the shoe fits. Creative burn-out is not a curse peculiar to writers, nor to Americans; but writers, notoriously vulnerable in the solitude of their craft, can find it terribly difficult in America to discover a middle ground between total obscurity and the fifteen minutes of crowded fame we're all supposed to get and catch our deaths from; and without that middle ground there is no respite. America, it might be said, is a land without a midlist, a land which affords no cushion – no community, no reciprocity, no clerisy, no network of readers – to sustain the writer in her flight. It is, therefore, all the more remarkable that, just a few generations ago, in the flat heart of this continent, a few men and women and boys and girls were able to give birth to the sf community. They did not invent sf itself (though many of them thought they had), but they did manage to invent (or to re-invent) a mutual society in the heart of a cultural maelstrom, a society of readers and writers and workers which still exists, overgrown and market-driven and hype-ridden though it may sometimes seem to have become. From 1926 or so, unlike his peers, the sf writer comes from somewhere and has somewhere to land. From outside the kraal it must seem a warm world indeed.

For the woman who became James Tiptree Jr in 1968, and who nestled within that pseudonym for a decade – like an imago beyond price hiding deep inside the kind of Russian doll we now call a babushka – the world of sf may well have seemed irresistible. Though she remained invisible until her identity was uncovered, the sf community did nourish her, did constitute a middle ground she could (if only vicariously) live inside, as she attested in correspondence. We cannot know for sure why she became James Tiptree Jr, nor why she began almost to confess her true identity through the creation in 1974 of Raccoona Sheldon as a second pseudonym; and it is almost certain that speculations about the motives of Alice B Sheldon (1915–1987), who became Tiptree, would be an impertinence against her memory. All we can know at this stage is that – during the years of secrecy – she burned like a meteor. All we know for sure is that the stories she wrote from 1970 until 1977 – when her health began to fail and her secret identity finally collapsed – comprise the finest and most moving single spate of creative energy the field has ever seen. In the secrecy of the male pseudonym she inhabited during the years of her astonishing prime, and under the cover of the gregarious, life-affirming, gemütlich personality she created in letters and non-fiction for that Tiptree self, Alice B Sheldon wrote free. She wrote young. She wrote to the edge and beyond. And she wrote like a man.

(In 1975, in his introduction to Tiptree's *Warm Worlds and Otherwise*, Robert Silverberg gave voice to a bio-critical speculation about the author which has since become famous. "It has been suggested that Tiptree is female," he wrote, "a theory that I find absurd, for there is to me something ineluctably masculine about Tiptree's writing." Given human nature, it's unlikely many of Silverberg's readers could have failed to enjoy the discomfiture he must have felt in 1977 when Tiptree's identity was uncovered; and there is no denying that what he said was both inapposite in its self-assurance and culture-bound in its assumption that an artifact of language – in this case the phallocentric assembly of themes and tropes and rhythms and rituals and syntaxes greased for power which makes up "masculine discourse" – was in itself inherently sexed, so that only a biological male could utter it. This was surely careless of Silverberg. Artifacts – like jungle gyms, like pseudonyms – are in themselves inherently *learnable*. They can be climbed into. At the same time, of course, Silverberg *did* have a point. To deny that Tiptree did in fact sound "like a man" is to deny one's clear sense that male hegemony utters itself in recognizable terms; it also scants the masterly uses to which Tiptree put that artifactual language which owns the world *and tells it*: tells it what it is, tells it what to do. Having aerated and ennobled that language, having turned the tables on the biological presumptions it rides on, she used the sly potent enablement pheromones of "man talk" as a kind of *speed*. She mainlined on the artifact, from within the babushka of Tiptree, itself snugly hidden inside the larger babushka of the sf community; and in that tongue she said some things which burned. Like ice. Like fire.)

So she wrote like a man, and a meteor, a flash in the pan, a mayfly angel. Three years after beginning to write sf, she was already nearing her astonishing peak, and by 1977 (as we've already noted) she had begun to flame out, though the evidence for this was obscured till later by variable gaps between writing and publication of stories. Before 1977, all we knew of James Tiptree Jr was that he was no longer young, because he had told us that he was middle-aged; he also claimed to be Chicago-born, often abroad in his youth, involved in intelligence work in World War Two; and postal evidence suggested that he lived somewhere near Washington, DC. All the same, many of us found it extremely hard to imagine that James Tiptree Jr was not, in fact, a person perhaps rather younger than he claimed, and certainly in the very peak of condition. I myself thought of him as a wiry sharp man whose colour was the colour of marmalade, like a tiger out of Blake. Whether or not I was ever induced to think of him as a woman I cannot remember; but I know I was not prepared to think of him as a 60-year-old woman whose health was precarious, whose first serious heart attack would quite possibly mark the end of any hope she might have to launch herself again, like a tightrope-walker across the void, like a man who walked home, burning energy like a tiger in the night, giving us the tale still taut from the young muscle of her hands, the touch of her secret breath.

But she was a 60-year-old woman. Her health was indeed precarious. One way or another, the air of the planet did get her. And the work she produced in her last decade – though it would grace the oeuvres of many writers – seemed, in comparison with the work of her prime, churchy and fey, self-pitying and exiguous. Unfortunately, because her publishing career was oddly shaped, most readers by the end of the 1980s knew nothing more of Tiptree than that late work. She had written two novels – Up the Walls of the World (1978) and Brightness Falls from the Air (1985) – but only the latter, weaker volume seemed readily available. The late short stories had been generously hardbacked with the release of Tales of the Quintana Roo (1986), The Starry Rift (1986) and Crown of Stars (1988); and The Color of Neanderthal Eyes (1990), her penultimate tale, and the best work she produced in the final spate that preceded her suicide, finally received book publication as part of a Tor Double. Two stories from her prime had also appeared in doubles – The Girl Who Was Plugged In (1988) and Houston, Houston, Do You Read? (1989) – but the great mass of her best work had become difficult to trace for those who remembered it. Her finest stories had appeared in four paperback volumes – 10,000 Light-Years from Home (1973), Warm Worlds and Otherwise (1975), Star Songs of an Old Primate (1978) and Out of the Everywhere, and Other Extraordinary Visions (1981) – and though each one of them could claim to be among the very few permanently significant collections to appear during that period, not one of them was ever even published in hardback (except for the first, released in England by Methuen in a setting that boasted unjustified right margins and a whole new crop of proofing errors to augment the contemptible slurry of goofs that corrupted the ill-edited original version from Ace). Subsequently, Doubleday did publish, in Byte Beautiful (1986), complete with expurgations to fit its contents to the library market, a collection of old and new work oddly sorted and poorly argued as a conspectus of her distinguished career. James Tiptree Jr had become virtually unknowable.

The publication of Her Smoke Rose Up Forever, as edited by James Turner, comes therefore as an important event. Because almost every story James Tiptree Jr wrote at the apogee of her passage across the heavens is here assembled, Her Smoke Rose Up Forever ranks as one of the two or three most significant collections of short sf ever published. Of the 18 stories in the volume, I would have myself omitted only one, "And I Have Come Upon This Place by Lost Ways" (published in 1972 but written at the end of 1968: all further citations will be of year of composition only), because the cartoon crudity of its telling conforms all too well to the melodramatic epiphanizing of its close. And of those stories Turner has had to omit, I would have argued fervently only for one, "All the Kinds of Yes" (1972), a tale which refines and darkens and speeds up and in the end utterly transforms the comic clatter of Tiptree's earliest work, so that "Yes" closes on a twist of plot (just who isn't an alien in the bloody thing) which is an epiphany which is a world-view which is a shrug which is a benediction, all at once. Of the 17 remaining stories, every single one is a joy, a consolation of achieved form; swift in nuance, extravagant in density, extroverted, athletic; but also (because James Tiptree Jr was possibly the darkest writer ever to publish sf of the first rank) every single one tells some sort of death.

Almost every story collected in *Her Smoke Rose Up Forever* ends in death, literal or metaphorical, experienced or nigh. Our touch upon the planet is death; sex is an intricacy of death; exogamy (our lust for other species and for the stars) is death; the ultimate taste of any human being (as in the 1973 title story) is of an anguish unto death. Death comes as the end; the end is Death's come. The plan is Death. But none of this makes Tiptree a dour writer, though her messages are grim. Because she is an author who talks about the world before turning in, the extroversion of her stories is genuine and exultant. They are crowded with events and folk and things to think about; folding into one breath – one telling – the world and its outcome, they almost seem to *grin*. Like a shaping bone within the babushka of the world, the skull of death may ultimately stare the show shut, but the grin on the mask of James Tiptree Jr is the tender knowing omen-haunted gong-tormented grin of a wise lover with no time to spare, whose time is limited. As so many young writers in America have done, she flashes across the firmament like a meteor, but with one difference. Most American writers burn out because they have ransacked too savagely experiences too slender to grow back after the frost of exposure; James Tiptree Jr burns out from the freight and convergence of the years. The spirit is willing but the body is weak. She burns out *old*. She leaves behind her a body of work no young writer could have conceived, no old writer should have had the energy to shape. And that, in the end, is the secret of her Janus face – her antic glances so deathward-bound, her deathward gaze so full of life.

The stories collected in *Her Smoke Rose Up Forever* have been sorted into several rough thematic categories, and need little further bush. The first two – "The Last Flight of Doctor Ain" (1969; rewritten circa 1974) and "The Screwfly Solution" (1976) – are lessons in what might be called eschatological ecology. Both are told in skewed and variable retrospect, exceedingly complicated to describe but crystalline in the reading. Both are famous. Doctor Ain spreads a virus which will destroy the human race, because the human race has destroyed the Earth its mother (he could be spreading his death seed in anguish and rage this very day). In the second tale, aliens destabilize the fragile equipoise that keeps the two human sexes masked from one another; and men begin to kill the women of the world, because that is the plan of our nature when stripped.

Four tales that further frame our state now follow. "And I Awoke and Found Me Here on the Cold Hill's Side" (1971) argues that any superior alien race will have a Cargo effect on humans, binding them most utterly in the region where they are most explosively at risk – which for Tiptree is always the stress-knot of sex. (But always she is Janus-faced, because clearly she loves sex, finds sex fascinating, writes finely of sexual love.) The Girl Who Was Plugged In (1969), along with "And I Have Come Upon this Place by Lost Ways" (1968), shows a risky aggressiveness of diction and plotting, which the author has not yet fully controlled; the whole flippant time-travel narrative frame of Girl, for instance, while elbowing us ostentatiously away from the sentimental tale it glosses, in truth only underlines the nurse-romance premises that govern that inner tale. (But how brilliantly she almost carries the far-rago off.) And "The Man Who Walked Home" (1971) inscribes the longing for a re-turn to Eden in great flashes across the sky, so vividly that "Man" has become a kind of paradigm of the tale of exile.

Tiptree's most famous single story heads the next three. "The Women Men Don't See" (1972) manages almost miraculously (pace some feminist readings of the tale as a univocal advocacy of radical misandry) to retain a sense of the humanity of the aging alpha male who narrates, who miscomprehends the women with whom he is cast into extremis, who watches them leave the planet altogether rather than remain chinks in his world-machine. "Your Faces, O My Sisters! Your Faces Filled of Light!" (1974) and Houston, Houston, Do You Read? (1974) both carry the an-alysis further – the first in terms of experience traumatized beyond salvation, the second within a science-fiction frame whose orthodoxy makes the arguments it contains about the nature of male humans all the more crushing.

We are barely halfway through. "With Delicate Mad Hands" (1980) and "We Who Stole the Dream" (1977) both show some signs of burn-out, the first through excessive length and sentiment, the second through moral gimmickry; word-perfect over its great length, and almost unbearably dark in the detail and momentum of the revelation of its premise that humans are gametes looking to consummate an exogamous fuck they cannot survive, "A Momentary Taste of Being" (1973) may be the finest densest most driven novella yet published in the field. "Her Smoke Rose Up Forever" (1973) we have mentioned; "Love is the Plan, the Plan is Death" (1971) has a juggernaut drive, a consuming melancholy of iron, a premise the author never backed away from; "On the Last Afternoon" (1971) pits personal transcendence against the cultural/biological survival of the race in a tale of such cumulative dialectical drive that it nearly causes burn-out to *read*; "She Waits for All Men Born" (1974) casts in fable form a lesson about Death, who is the dance and the Dancer and the very flesh of Love; and "Slow Music" (1977), Tiptree's last great story, serves as a requiem for all the gay gorged gangrenous world she loved and gave us the pulse of. At the nub end of our span on earth, two last young people meet, mate, fail to breed, trek a false river to an ambivalent alien transcendence, stop and trip and slide into the beam of transcendence to become an ode by Keats, deathless but thoroughly dead. It is the end. It was very nearly the end for James Tiptree Jr.

Soon she was utterly spent. She died old. She is here.

– Introduction to *Her Smoke Rose Up Forever* (Arkham House, 1990)

Index

John Clute

Learning Resources
Centre